Barbara Sher Tinsley

Reconstructing
Western Civilization

Reconstructing Western Civilization

Irreverent Essays on Antiquity

Barbara Sher Tinsley

Selinsgrove: Susquehanna University Press

Associated University Presses
2010 Eastpark Boulevard
Cranbury, NJ 08512

The paper used in this publication meets the requirements of the American National Standard for Permanence of Paper for Printed Library Materials Z39.48-1984.

Library of Congress Cataloging-in-Publication Data

Tinsley, Barbara Sher, 1938–
  Reconstructing western civilization : irreverent essays on antiquity / Barbara Sher Tinsley.
    p. cm.
  Includes bibliographical references and index.
  ISBN 1-57591-095-0 (alk. paper)
  1. Civilization, Ancient. 2. Civilization Classical. 3. Civilization, Christian. I. Title.

CB311.T57 2006
938—dc22   2005010889

PRINTED IN THE UNITED STATES OF AMERICA

Contents

Introduction

WHAT IS CIVILIZATION, ANYWAY? TECHNOLOGY? Comfort? Culture? Great shopping? Today we shop in malls; once, men mauled to "shop." They enriched themselves by stealing surplus goods. Only when people abandoned nomadic lifestyles which provided no surplus and adopted the settled lifestyles of villagers were there any surpluses to steal. Village life (after 8500 BC) was more productive than that of nomads and more secure. The first security system was a village wall. City life (after 3500 BC) was still a long way off, but when cities sprang up in Mesopotamia (modern Iraq), so did writing, and the beginning of recorded history. Everything before was anthropology. Everything since has been civilization.

But civilization is a word that has not been satisfactorily defined by historians, despite a number of dictionary definitions which suggest refinement and creature comforts. The word was not even used until the eighteenth century. Dr. Samuel Johnson refused to put it into his dictionary in 1772, though his secretary, James Boswell, urged him to. Johnson preferred an older word, "civility," from the Latin *civilis,* city dweller or citizen. Civilization still reflects that prejudice of city folk that culture cannot thrive in the countryside, where fields may grow, but not people.

Villages, made possible by peasant labor, spread across western Asia from the Mediterranean east to Mesopotamia, while cities, also made possible by peasant labor, spread westward from that valley toward the Mediterranean. Cities produced more than villages but for that reason were vulnerable to attack. With city life came those refinements of culture like monumental architecture, big government, drainage and irrigation systems, effective transport—wheeled carts and boats—and institutions of learning. Some literate folk found work in religion, others in government. These professions housed themselves in impressive palaces and temples called ziggurats. The first literate men were Sumerian priests. They built monuments to the gods. The first nonpriestly bureaucrats were kings. They built monuments to themselves. Compared to villagers and peasants, priests and kings were monumentally endowed. Their endowment came from peasants endowed with strong backs.

When historians speak of products, they don't use ordinary words like shopping, but economic terms like "exchange of goods." The story of civilization involved much violence, but violent words such as mauled, mugged, maimed, dismembered, tortured, and raped are largely avoided

7

by the writers of history. The word "booty" is *still* used in textbooks, though it seems to be passing out of ordinary usage. It means stolen property. Booty was a glue that held "civilization" together at the same time that it kept it from bonding. With the onset of cities and civilized living, men were able to organize themselves into armies. War was characteristic of civilization. The priests, politicians, and generals who waged war were often on the defensive, so historians who recorded it did not call it offensive, even if the common people thought it was.

History is peculiarly susceptible to distortion. Words evoke and provoke more readily than they convey objective truths. What history does not say is at least as important as what it does say. It cannot say everything because the historical record is never complete. We complete it by our own inferences, often ignorant of how those affected by the past felt about it. Very few people were able to leave us their thoughts. When facts are available, it is not easy to know whose facts they were, and how they affected people other than the writer, whose purposes were very much his own, or his employer's, not the people's.

Easy or not, history forces us to consider the meaning of human experience, a question many practicing historians avoid. I can remember sitting in a history classroom at a prestigious university in the 1960s, listening to a professor insist that his task was not to make history relevant to us. His attitude stemmed from a notion many historians used to prize and some still do, the idea that history is better when it tells what happened, without bothering to draw any lessons for the present. These essays were written in the belief that the present is a critical key to the future; the past was someone else's future. If we do not understand how the past affected those whose future it was, our own future may be incomprehensible.

The idea that historical behavior is hermetic, sealed off from the possibility that we can profit by learning about it, nullifies its interest for all but the academics who write about it, give papers on it, and more reluctantly, teach it. Philosophizing about history is messy but more rewarding than viewing it as a period piece. Historians should tell what happened. But unless they attempt to answer why this is important now—that is, the relevance to our own lives of past events, most people will not bother to learn history. Because history has changed more than people have, there is every reason to think that we can get out of it things that will reward us in our struggle to satisfy our needs and aspirations. It may also help in reducing the pain attendant on historical changes now in progress.

Reconstructing
Western Civilization

1

Before Civilization

Easing Into It

WHEN WE READ ABOUT HISTORY, WE ARE IN A WAY reading about ourselves, since all of us belong to the same family—the family of man. Families are never easy to understand, but rarely are they impossible. What is history, after all, but the writing of civilized individuals who were raised by families influenced by the community? It always did take a village or a city to help men realize their full potential.[1] Like the writers of history, the subjects of it were people whose past was not just in their bones, but written down on clay, on walls, pottery, monuments, papyrus, and parchment. Our cultural forbears found certain things worthy of recording while other things were left unsaid—for many different reasons. History—at least, the written record of what literate men thought important—had to wait until the invention of writing, somewhere around the end of the fourth millennium. And writing had to wait until the invention of cities. Civilization and history were indissolubly linked, and both have affected the fate of individuals and their families.

History was first made in Mesopotamia, now Iraq, in the fourth millennium. That is where men first learned to write and where they built the world's first cities. Writing continued undaunted by invasion or conquest. Indeed, warfare made it all the more necessary to communicate and to learn, even if it temporarily reduced some men's leisure for learning. Historians think warfare stimulated learning in the long run, since war speeded the pace of invention and technology.[2] It also taught men, and necessarily, their families, how to exist more dangerously, which meant dying at an earlier age, more painfully, or both.

A recent book explains civilization in terms of the tools it produced and continues to produce, and how the tools shaped man as much (or more) than man shaped them, and are thus "double-edged."[3] Its authors associate language with a primitive technology of bone marking (a first step toward writing) and consider all technology "double-edged." This is a point well taken. One might add that the language used to record history is also potentially double-edged, even loaded. Facts do not speak for themselves but are selected and interpreted by those who record them, so grasping what happened in history is inevitably a matter of someone else's interpretation, just as this essay you are reading is an interpretation of historical procedures. As the famous American historian, Carl Becker (1873–1945), once noted, there is no way one could—or should—escape the obligations of interpreting history in order to wrest meaning from it.[4] A recent textbook points to the problem of interpretation on its first page when it states that the very notion of "Western Civilization" is an idea that corresponds to no geographical formation; that has changed location as geographical discoveries were made; and that began in western Asia.[5] Just using the phrase "Western Civilization" represents a composite of many interpretive acts and well as many provable facts.

Interpreting the past is scarcely a modern preoccupation. Long before civilization, primitive men were already manipulating the meaning of experience by speech, gestures, activities, and now, we find, by bone marking, described as a "technology" or applied science.[6] What other technologies did Paleolithic, or Old Stone Age man have at his disposal? He could make hand axes and, much later, spears and bows. He learned how to control fire. He could trap animals. The wonderful pictures of them on cave walls in later Paleolithic times required man to learn paint making and brush making, even lamp making needed for remote areas of caverns. But was his art, like his bone markings, mere compensation for a lack of knowledge about cause and effect relationships?[7]

Anthropologists believe that animal drawings on cave walls were symbolic attempts to manipulate game in order to improve the chances for a better kill, for the food and skins that represented well-being for primitive people. Such paintings are explained in terms of sympathetic magic: what I draw, I hope spiritually and physically to control. Technology and science, on the other hand, deal more directly with physical matter. The spiritual is skipped altogether: what I control I really do control. In other words, the symbolic magician or artist is only indirectly engaged with his environment, while the technician is directly engaged with it. Symbolic cave paintings were regarded as magic, not the way we view science and technology today. But, if cave art was not a substitute for know-how, it does not follow that it was never regarded as aesthetic.[8] Because this art was made between thirty thousand and ten thousand years ago, the artists were already *Homo sapiens* (wise men)—possibly even *Homo sapiens sapiens* (very wise men). Can we exclude the possibility that cave men took aesthetic pleasure from their own productions? Can we be sure that they did not invite their friends in to share a delight in their own creations? Might not they, too, have felt the wonder in these exquisite drawings that we also feel upon viewing them? Paleolithic men had the same capacity for aesthetic appreciation as modern men, without the same opportunities. Can we deny that they took as much satisfaction in their artistic experiences as moderns do in theirs?

As little informed as we are about Paleolithic men, we know considerably more about them than we know about the earliest hominids, their remote predecessors. When we wind time's reel farther back, we reach a point where there was no science or technology and no artistic production either, when hominids (very primitive men) had just gained the ability to walk on two legs (bipedality). This huge slice of time is called prehistory,[9] and it lasted until the rise of cities in Mesopotamia.

PREHISTORY: IT'S ALL IN THE BONES!

Prehistory is the subtext of man's history, the point at which our oldest remote ancestors first split off from the apes and emerged as hominids, animals who walked on two legs but had such small brains that they can only be called transitional beings.[10] Hominids were not yet men, not yet of the genus *Homo* [men] let alone the species Homo sapiens. This last term, only a generation or so ago used to refer to modern man, is now often used with a qualifier, as in *Archaic Homo sapiens* [Neanderthal men] and *Homo sapiens sapiens,* meaning us. For we are the latest of several models. Calling ourselves very wise men is a rather egotistical appellation considering our inability to live peacefully with one another, our pollution of the planet, and cultural myopia. If we persist in using the term *Homo sapiens sapiens,* we ought to translate it to mean real wise guys. Alternatively, we could call ourselves *Homo neglegens* (careless man); *Homo stultus* (foolish man); or even *Homo pravus* (immoral man). The term "man" means human beings of both sexes, since no one sex has a monopoly on carelessness and immorality. The intellectual capacity of early hominids was too small for cultural myopia or sexism. If they were immoral and foolish they at least had an excuse.

Prehistory has only just begun to be unearthed—quite literally—by paleontologists, scientists who study old bones. The first species to stand up on two feet and be counted as hominids did so over four million years ago, about half a million years earlier than scientists suspected as recently as 1995. Man's prehistory is not only the oldest story ever told but is growing older with each new field trip to Africa. Ideally, it would be told by specialists from whole skeletons of single individuals. Because these are almost never found, it must be pieced together like a jigsaw puzzle (this one has no helpful picture on the box) from bones or bone fragments. When Donald Johanson discovered in Hadar, Ethiopia (1974), about 40 percent of a female hominid skeleton 3.18 million years old, he was very happy.[11] He named her "Lucy" after a Beatles song and gave her the formal name *Australopithecus afarensis.* She was only three feet six inches tall and had the brain size of a chimpanzee. Was it patronizing to call her "Lucy" rather than Ms. Afarensis, her family name? Johanson and Lucy rapidly became an "item," as they say in the tabloids. Lucy represented a very early, very primitive hominid. Although she walked on two feet and had straight legs, she was not yet of the genus *Homo*. Lucy was not yet man.

After Lucy came hominids with other names and stories. Most ended unhappily. Then, somewhere around two million years ago, there appeared *Homo habilis* (man with ability) so named because he was the first, though not the last, hominid with the ability to make stone tools, giving rise to the Paleolithic Age.[12] This period lasted over three million years to 10,000 BC. Man made his living for three million years by chipping stone hand axes. Those in the chips today include chocolate chip cookie makers, owners of blue-chip stocks, and manufacturers of computer chips. We are still chipping away at problems of making a living in a hostile environment.

It was thought until very recently that *Homo habilis,* for all his stone chipping ability, was not the species who left his native Africa to settle in Europe and Asia.[13] It was generally agreed that his tools were inadequate, his brain too small for the journey. Some textbooks state that *Homo habilis* merged into *Homo erectus* (erect man) about 1.6 million years ago,[14] and that it was this newer species who went out of Africa armed with superior tool-making skills and a larger brain, "street smarts" for those times. *Homo erectus* in turn is thought by some researchers to have merged into *Archaic Homo sapiens* (old wise man; perhaps merging with Neanderthal man), who in his turn is thought by some, but not by all experts, to have merged into modern man, *Homo sapiens sapiens.*

Consider *Homo erectus.* A "portrait" of him once graced the cover of *Time* magazine.[15] Not long ago paleontologists were comfortable thinking that he was the only species who left Africa one million years ago and eventually filled all known continents with his descendants because of his superior stone tool-making skills. Now they are not so sure. Not only have sophisticated stone tools not been found at all *Homo erectus* sites in Europe and Asia, but more advanced tools have turned up in Africa itself, giving some specialists reason to think that *Homo sapiens sapiens* was producing more sophisticated tools in Africa than any *Homo erectus* could have managed.[16] And some very old bone fossils uncovered in Spain in 1994 and dating three-quarters of a million years seem to indicate that not *all* the people who left Africa were *Homo erectus* types.[17] Homo habilis apparently had enough intelligence to get himself to Europe after all!

Why might *Homo sapiens sapiens* have stayed in Africa while more primitive fellows left, supposing that he did indeed stay in Africa? Did he know something more than *Homo erectus* or *Homo habilis?* Was there a travel advisory? Or did our wise, wise ancestors understand that they could survive without moving out of Africa? Were conditions in places like Zaire better than those of the more archaic *Homo erectus* migrants who helped populate Europe, not without real sacrifice in comfort? It is possible that our Europeans ancestors (migrant Africans!) were multiethnic earlier than we used to think.

Recently, experts have come to think that Homo erectus himself left Africa earlier—perhaps one million years earlier!—than they had thought until just recently. This evidence relates to some skull fragments found at two sites on the island of Java dating back nearly two million years. Did an Asian branch of *Homo erectus* develop into a separate species? Some scientists think it possible that both the *Homo erectus* settlers in Europe and those who went east to Asia evolved separately into *Homo sapiens*.[18]

A British scientist, Chris Stringer, holds that *Homo erectus* did not evolve into Homo sapiens, but that "out of Africa" came the species who replaced him around 100,000 BC.[19] Other scientists, geneticists at the University of California, offer support for Stringer's thesis, claiming (in the "Eve hypothesis") that all humans are traceable to one woman who lived in Africa one hundred thousand years ago.[20] Those scientists who think *Homo erectus* contributed directly to later models of men, including our own species, pooh-pooh this Eve hypothesis. Milford Wolpoff of the University of Michigan thinks that far from becoming extinct, *Homo erectus* mingled with other hominids who followed him out of Africa and thus mixed his own genes with those of his successors, the Neanderthals. At one point, Donald Johanson thought Neanderthals were definitely members of our species,[21] though he has since changed his mind. Another member of the profession believes that *Homo sapiens* evolved in Africa and replaced archaic humans in Asia and Europe without the merging of Neanderthal genes into those of modern men.[22] All these questions concerning man's development in and out of Africa, particularly his biological development and his contribution to our own, are being furiously debated. The history of prehistory cannot yet be written.

Homo habilis and *Homo erectus* have taken a back seat to the interest shown in Neanderthal man,[23] probably because this fellow is much closer to us in point of time. He existed between 130,000 years to 30,000 years ago, and his bones were first dug up on the banks of the Neander River in Germany in 1856. Where does he fit into this story? If he really became extinct it was only after 30,000 BC. Was he of our own species, as Donald Johanson once suggested? Or did he make no contribution to our gene pool as people like Chris Stringer and, lately, Dianne Waddle, suggest? Neanderthals are often portrayed by artists as somewhat stooped, with heavy eyebrow ridges, and chests more barrel-shaped than those of most modern men, in the Alley-oop tradition of comic strip characters. Suppose Neanderthal genes are intermixed with our own, so that they, who were once thought to have become extinct, have instead become us, and we have become sharers of their gene pool? Will we, in order to achieve political correctness, have to stop making jokes about their primitiveness?

Neanderthals existed side by side with more modern-looking men, inhabiting parts of Europe and Asia including Israel.[24] Neanderthal brains were as large as our own, and it has become increasingly common to say of them that these Paleolithic folks were at the very least our close cousins; that if dressed in a good suit and placed on Wall Street, a Neanderthal would fit right in.[25] Neanderthals are quite possibly, as some have long suspected, still holding down jobs in finance, law enforcement, politics, the Church, and football.

POETRY AND PROVOCATION

As if old bones were not dry enough, the words paleontologists use to record their stories are drier still. The account of man's origins in the book of Genesis seems refreshing by comparison. What scientific jargon can compete with its simplicity and poetry? "And the Lord God formed man of the dust of the ground, and breathed into his nostrils the breath of life; and man became a living soul."[26]

Alas, paleontologists are bound by the evidence of their labors (fossils carefully dated by modern technology) to regard these beautiful lines from the Old Testament book of Genesis as symbolic language—poetry—an ancient storyteller's rendering of mankind's intense—even endearing—self absorption. Modern men, still filled with wonder at the human species continue to ask, "Where did we begin?" The question is precisely the same as that asked by the Hebrew author, but the answer has developed with man's intellectual growth. So paleontologists, who must deal with pieces of bone—with tibia (leg bones), maxilla (jaw bones), carpal tunnels (tendon passages of the wrist), and the like—answer the question less poetically. Readers who prefer poetry to bare-bones facts will have no patience with a maxilla (jawbone) found here, and another one there, or a tibia (inner leg bone) with a condyle (joint articulation) at right angles from the shaft (typical of a human knee) as opposed to one whose condyles are concave (apelike). There seems to be no poetry here, and no drama. Wrong. Poetry and drama are still part of the quest for human origins. The poetry and drama of paleoanthropology involves the same sense of awe the biblical author displayed—how did man come to be?

For over a hundred years prehistory has generated intense public interest because of the works of Charles Robert Darwin (1809–82). Though few people actually read the *Origin of Species* (1859), almost everyone has some opinion about it. It was Darwin who invented, if not paleoanthropology itself, then the major concepts upon which it rests. It is inspirational to those who want a scientific pursuit of evidence regarding man's gradual development from apes to modern human beings. It is provocation to biblical literalists who pursue the creationist theme of Genesis 2:7. One could just as easily call this account an inhalation-therapy interpretation of man's beginning because in this account God breathes life and soul into man's nostrils! Lacking modern notions of the origins of life the ancient poet created the wonderful story about dust, God's breath, and man's living soul. He did not get the right answer, but he understood the importance of the question—how did life begin?

Western civilization accommodated scientific inquiry that enabled it to combat its biases. But the accumulation of scientific smarts was painfully slow compared to the persistence of superstition and myth. Not until comparatively modern times did men launch a rational or empirical inquiry into the universe and man's place in it. Today, though few are scientists, the rational majority no longer believe that creationism offers a believable explanation for man's origins.

Our culture has progressed to the point where the naive are in a minority. Still, they are often more vocal than the well-informed and are often used by rich and powerful supporters, who promote their quaint religiosity for nonspiritual reasons. Whether powerful or powerless, the supporters of creationism would like nothing better than to abolish complexity in the social sphere and substitute for it simplistic authoritarianism. The greatest achievements of Western civilization, individual liberty and untrammeled inquiry, lie in the balance. It takes courage to assert that ignorance, posing as religious Truth or Morality, is merely ignorance. Scientists are heroes because they defend knowledge from authoritarianism and superstition, as surely as Copernicus and Galileo did in the Renaissance.

Charles Darwin was such a hero. Here is a passage from his *Descent of Man* (1871) in which the question of bipedality is raised:

> As soon as some ancient member in the great series of the Primates came to be less arboreal, owing to a change in its manner of procuring subsistence, or to some change in the surrounding conditions, its habitual manner of progression would have been modified; and thus it would have been rendered more strictly quadrupedal or bipedal . . . . Man alone has become a bidped, and we can, I think, partly see how he has come to assume his erect attitude, which forms one of his most conspicuous characters.[27]

Darwin sounds bland and inoffensive. But Darwin's readers did not find him bland and many were not only offended but incensed. People read him with astonishment and passion because a phrase like "habitual manner of progression . . . modified" meant that Darwin did not think God made man out of dust and then breathed his soul into him, something first Jews and then Christians believed for more than two thousand years. When Darwin suggested that man had *become* a two-footed or bipedal creature, literalists objected, because in their view man was created all at once, by God.

Might the *Descent of Man* have been better titled *Ascent of Man?* Or was it really all downhill from the apes to man? Darwin objected to creationism, and creationists have never forgiven him. Sadly, some textbook publishers, some state boards of education, and some local school boards and classroom teachers have had to trim their sails in order that the winds of ignorance and prejudice might continue to blow students off course concerning man's origins.

Still, today's paleontologists follow along in Darwin's footprints as much as they follow the tracks of African hominids. The great impact Darwin's writings made on modern thought—equalled only by Marx and Freud—was overwhelming. Yet the modern scientific account of man's origins and the poetic one of *Genesis* have this in common: both concentrate on the shape or form of man.

Gradually, between the emergence five or more million years ago of the first bipedal hominid and the arrival of our own species, man—and the environment—was working on his appearance. It might be truer to say that man's appearance was working on him. Appearances do count! Like Darwin, modern scientists and fashion models who pose on magazine covers know it is all in the bones. When the scientists have collected enough fossilized bones, those bones may not, as the old spiritual would have it, "hear the Word of the Lord," but they will speak through the mouths of paleontologists who will then tell us the secrets that only dry bones can communicate about our human origins.

Prehistory would be less interesting if we were not still affected by it. A difference to be a difference always makes a difference, and those developmental or structural differences in hominid development have made it possible for us not just to have had a prehistory, but to have had history. Between the long millennia of hominid prehistory and the short period of written history, man's larger cranium and more complex brain enabled him to develop consciousness of self, which many other animals also have, and self-consciousness, which only man has. Only people can be occupied, preoccupied, and embarrassed, because their posture permitted physical activity and their brains, mental reflection. Modern people, thanks to prehistoric evolution, can work and think about other things at the same time, like being able to pat one's stomach and rub one's head simultaneously. Man's prehistory was bare-boned, quite literally determined by the shape of his bones, especially those of his legs, head, and hands. Man's culture was bred in the bone. His history, as we are soon to discover, was made of softer fabric—the tissue of his own invention.

Camping Out: Paleolithic Nomads

The several million years of Paleolithic experience were marked by wandering, hunting, and gathering, punctuated by periods of downtime spent in caves. In caveless areas, like the Eurasian plains, people camped out. These were millennia of tribal wandering, the search for sustenance. Our ancestors were migrants, refugees driven by dearth, immigrants lured by lunch. Later, people who moved around would be called a variety of names: barbarians, tribesmen, hordes, vagrants, migrants, gypsies, bums, and recently, the homeless. Although nomads were not stylishly clad, the animals they ate, such as bear, deer, wolves, and mountain goats provided skins for clothing and curtains to hang over cave openings to keep out the weather. Eventually, nomads invented bone needles and learned how to sew. Voilà! The fashion industry was born!

During long millennia, people learned how to communicate and share, as children learn in the lower grades that they must share and cooperate in order to be happy and enjoy the support of their fellows. The Paleolithic period was like the childhood of man, when the performance of tasks needed for survival had first to be determined and next shared. As the song says, "The fundamental things apply as time goes by!"[28]

The division of labor was determined to a large degree by sex, for pregnant women and nursing mothers were less fit to chase and kill animals than for the more sedentary tasks of scraping flesh off hides, sewing skins, minding the kids, and dishing up dinner, long before the invention of dishes.[29] When dinner was not meat—and there must have been many times when the hunters failed to find any or did not return to camp by nightfall—there may have been slim pickings. Then the only food women, children, and old or disabled people may have had was what, in the absence of the hunters, they could dig or pick from plants and trees growing wild near camp.[30]

BEFORE VEGETARIANISM

Were our early ancestors ever vegetarians? Yes, if you consider that our most remote ones, the apes, were exclusively fruit eaters. Later, after the first hominids split off from apes, they ate *anything* they could get their hands on, scavenging at first for meat that other animals had killed, until they developed techniques for killing prey. Long after the Paleolithic era, when man had developed cities, medicine, and philosophy he began to debate the pros and cons of abstaining from meat.[31] Paleolithic men and Neolithic men enjoyed red meat very much. Think of the art that Paleolithic people left on the walls of cave sites, mostly pictures of animals.[32] None whatever of fruit, vegetables, or cereals. Not only did man enjoy meat in Paleolithic times, but there are references in the Hebrew Old Testament to man's enjoyment of meat. The offering Cain made, the one God rejected (Gen. 4:3–5), was vegetables, whereas the one that he accepted was Abel's livestock. The Hebrews thought God (whom they called Yah-weh) preferred meat, like the gods in other cities of the Middle East. The gods were not vegetarians, and neither were most men in early civilization.

FERTILITY GODDESSES—PREHISTORY, HISTORY, SEX

Besides painting and carving animals, Stone Age men also sculpted figures of women, wide hipped and big bellied. These pregnant figures or "Venus" statues represented fertility. The nudes of Rubens, GI pinups, and *Penthouse* magazine are related art forms. Primitive men, however, needed reproduction more than sexual titillation, and prayed for an abundance of plant and animal life and also of human life. Fertility "goddesses" were thought to promote the increase of life in the Paleolithic, Neolithic, and early civilized periods. Such goddesses were rarely vegetarians,[33] no more than the primitive people who worshipped them were. In many areas of Africa and Asia female fertility figures wore cow's horns. They nurtured animals and plants with an equal hand. A high-fiber diet balanced by animal protein was very much on our "primitive" ancestors' menu.

Women, the chief agricultural laborers in the post-Paleolithic and Neolithic ages, got to do the cooking as well the preparing and raising of food. They were the first great chefs of Asia and Europe. We raise the question of women's work and women's place in the earliest stages of civilization because what to do *with* and *to* women troubled men since the dawn of time. The problem of what to do *for* women has only rather recently begun to be seriously considered.

Anyone interested in fertility goddess culture might start by reading a book called *Das Mutterrecht* [Maternal Law] published in 1861 by the Swiss jurist and classical scholar Jacob Bachofen (1815–87). This curious work set the tone for subsequent literature on the topic of matriarchy (now dismissed more as a state of mind than an actual historical or cultural phenomenon) and goddesses. Bachofen was intrigued by Plutarch's treatise on Isis and Osiris, a brother-sister duo who were also man and wife, parents of a kid called Horace (Horus), and one of the many holy families of the ancient Near East. Mary, Joseph, and Jesus were another, but they were latecomers to the region of holy families who busied themselves with the life cycle on earth and in the hereafter.

Unmarried but hardly celibate male fertility gods like Dionysus,[34] and spinster fertility goddesses, like Ishtar of Old Babylonia, worked to promote procreation and propagation. Bachofen described what he believed had been a long period of history in which the maternity of Isis was recognized as the basis of prime authority and cultural supremacy.[35] Bachofen was wrong. Egypt knew very few female rulers, and those few were unpopular, viewed as inadequate defenders of empire. Bachofen led other writers to think that a female-oriented culture in which feminine power superseded male power had really once existed, and thus helped perpetuate your standard male nightmare—a society of sensuous, independent-minded women who circumvented male authority. Fascinating, and to many, repellent, this mythical matriarchy never existed anywhere in the ancient world, which generally kept women subservient. The idea of an ancient culture divinely inspired where female sensuousity, promiscuity, earthy values, instinct, and spirituality all thrived derived from Bachofen. Though he conceded spirituality to women, he denied them the power of logical analysis. When women ceased to rule, Bachofen thought, they resigned themselves to being mothers and wives in a state identified with the Greek fertility goddess, Demeter. What domesticated them was the seductive Dionysus—a Greek god who tamed women by keeping them pregnant and limiting job opportunities to gardening and weaving.[36]

The archaeologist V. Gordon Childe asserted in our own century that woman invented agriculture, not only its methods but the tools used in connection with it.[37] The urban historian Lewis Mumford thought that women were in their very physiology a paradigm for the Neolithic village of enclosed spaces (think womb); thus, villages were walled in (!) protected from penetration by hostile males. Even the symbol for house or town in Egyptian hieroglyphics was identical to that for women, according to Mumford.[38] Home and hearth, but also farm and village—all the old familiar places where women were confined represented produce, propagation, and above all, property. These attributes remained so symbolic of women's position—or plight—down through the centuries, that in the 1990s Hillary Rodham Clinton could still arouse hostility from antifeminists of both sexes when she remarked to a reporter that she would rather practice law than stay home baking cookies!

Some anthropologists assert that the Paleolithic period may have been more egalitarian where relations between the sexes were concerned.[39] But women must always have seemed problematic to men because they were so different. They bled monthly and were not endowed with exterior reproductive organs, and only they gave birth. Although the French are famous for their pronouncement "Vive la différence!" they were also famous for ancient laws that discriminated against the difference, as what culture has not?[40] If "nobody can deny" as that theme from the film *Casablanca* put it, that "Woman needs man and man must have his mate," it is just as true that man traditionally accorded her few privileges, and fewer rights. Although men regarded women in their reproductive and nurturing capacities as "stock," the source of sensual pleasure, perpetual care, manpower, and old-age insurance (offspring cared for elderly parents before Medicare), they also realized that this stock was high risk. Whereas they alone possessed it, the stock itself seemed possessed, that is, responsible to unseen and uncontrollable magic forces.

Goddesses have staged a comeback in contemporary literature.[41] They have awakened in some women a sense of belonging, sisterhood, and power that, although not well reflected by our economic or political structures, or in many patriarchal religious organizations, are attainable in the informal connections that women create for themselves—connections based on labor exchange, information exchange, and friendship.[42]

Some women hope to compensate for the lack of these intangibles by valorizing femininity, reviving feminist imagery. Because myths are supremely affordable, unlike pay equity, childcare, and health benefits, because they offer comfort before harsh reality, their devotees avail themselves of a special moonshine, the reflected glory of the virginal moon goddess and goddess of the hunt, Diana.[43] Diana had received permission from her Father (Jupiter) to maintain her celibate lifestyle after watching her mother in the agonies of childbed. She was one of those virgins who was something of a prick-tease and accorded very intimate favors to the naked shepherd Endymion, as he lay observing the heavenly bodies atop Mount Latmos. Her indiscretions included brief flings with Orion, made from the urine of three gods, and Pan, god of shepherds. Because Pan was ugly, he first disguised himself as a white goat. Diana found him irresistible.

Diana was a knockoff of the Greek goddess Artemis. Both goddesses hung out in forests, with nymphs, shepherds, and wild animals. Their taste in men left a lot to be desired. Aphrodite, the Greek goddess of love and beauty, had higher standards than either of these girls. She consorted with the god of war, Ares, by whom she bore a daughter, Harmonia, and two sons, Eros, god of love, and his brother Anteros, god of unrequited love. By the messenger of the gods, Hermes, she bore Hermaphroditus, who got stuck—quite literally stuck—on a nymph called Salmacis.[44] By Dionysus, god of fertility and wine, she bore Priapus, god of regenerative parts. His own were deformed. It was Zeus who caused her to love the shepherd Anchises, who was blessed with a fine complexion. To him she bore Aeneas. She even had access to childcare, leaving Aeneas with the nymphs of Ida while she carried on her trade of goddess. When her son outgrew their care, she shipped him off to a prep school run by Chiron the centaur. The story of how Aphrodite started the Trojan War is just the sort of dirt men liked to dig up from a woman's past to compromise her talents, which, as you can see, were not inconsiderable.

Through contemporary goddess literature some modern women hope to lessen the burden of gender inequity. They hope that the goddess tradition will somehow empower them to do what cannot easily be done when women and children, the physically and mentally disabled, and the eld-erly do not count for much, and women are left unaided to cope with their problems. Modern readers of goddess literature may believe earth moth-ers and matriarchs will rise from psychological and economic dependency to resist oppression. In the ancient world most of the goddesses appear to have been left-leaning, as were their medieval followers, sometimes asso-ciated with witches, more recently castigated as b——(rhymes with witches) and dykes.[45] They were held to a higher standard of morality, criticized for trying to control their own sexuality, and blamed for the high incidence of rape, out-of-wedlock births, and moral disintegration. The same is true in the postindustrial state. Here women are urged to become computer literate and obtain sixty-hour-per-week jobs irrespec-tive of the availability of childcare. Should the prospective devotees of goddesses find permanent employment in the electronic workplace, they can expect society to blame them for abandoning their ancient rôles as mothers and fertility goddesses.

In the twentieth century, Hollywood, not Homer, shaped our images of women. To the role of fertility goddess were appended the roles of whore, adulteress, and emasculator. In the movies women were less fre-quently cast as pioneer mothers and nurturing housewives than as femmes fatales who tortured good men, or at least, spoiled their domestic tranquility. Who can forget the hilarious scene in the film *Woman of the Year* where Katharine Hepburn, a savvy reporter, tried unsuccessfully to make waffles for breakfast, but managed only to make a mess of her kitchen because she had never bothered to learn how to operate a waffle iron? She had taken the wrong road by indulging herself in a professional life outside the home. In *Adam's Rib,* Kate tried a law career and jeopard-ized her happy marriage. In the post-World War II era, professional women were ridiculed and forced back into the nurturing roles they had been able to abandon in wartime. Hollywood directors, all male, and leading men, all Dionysiac seducers, made us aware that the same foibles anciently attributed to women—betrayal, endangerment of community, the weakening of masculine vitality and virtue—lurked in every woman, except those who were firmly controlled and in the home, or if too homely and fat to get homes of their own, forced to work in dingy offices, schools, and libraries, where their rewards, like their prospects, were restricted. Quite unrestricted was the cellulite prominently displayed by ancient fertility figures. Hollywood, helped by the fashion industry, made bulimia, anorexia, and Twiggy acceptable,[46] but normal women with average figures were not cast. They were outcasts. Hollywood's goddesses were never allowed to be plump, let alone fat.

Whatever the century, whatever the culture, the role played by women in Western civilization has usually been that of supporting actress, rather than star. Whether shaped by Homer or Hollywood, women's history has been *his story* much more than it has been *hers*. If women's history had been a song, it would have been medieval plain chant, repetitious, unisonous (no tonal variety), a plaintive as well as a plain chant, a lament with no harmony and few thematic variations. An elegy. A dirge. In classical Greece, the tragedic chorus must have seemed most convincing when the (male) actors donned female masks.

NOMADS, VILLAGERS, CIVILIZED FOLK

Nomad wanderers eventually learned how to domesticate plants and animals and these in turn domesticated the nomads. No longer could tribes wander freely but were obliged to settle down in walled villages on the theory, reinvented by the poet Robert Frost, that "good fences make good neighbors." After the eighth millennium, in villages like Hacilar and Catal Hüyük (Turkey), Jericho (Palestine), and Jarmo (Iran), men and women gave up some of their individuality. Like villagers everywhere, they ceded nomadic individualism to community custom. Because villagers stored more, ate more, and proliferated; they fulfilled Genesis 1:20 ("Be fruitful and multiply") seven thousand years before the Old Testament was even thought of. This prebiblical inclination to have sex was nonsectarian and proved so popular that it was later incorporated into the Hebrew Bible.

Cooperative village culture meant more than a permanent address. It meant shrunken horizons and the continual scrutiny of nosy neighbors.[47] It meant lost vacation time (crops and animals demand constant tending). It afforded some specialization of tasks, hence the occasional artist-craftsman or natural leader could indulge in alternative lifestyles—alternative to agriculture, that is. First pottery (permanent food storage), then politics, then prophecy resulted. Village leaders were no longer the best hunters but the best property accumulators—and therefore, the best property protectors. When village leaders felt inadequate to the task, it was time for cities.

With cities, village elders gave way to priests, who persuaded the less-propertied classes that the gods did not want or need everyone to be on the same footing. Trickle-down theory was in the making. It was trickling down from the steps of terraced monuments, atop of which were built temples to the gods. The gods and the priest-rulers who serviced them seemed better able to keep an eye on the burgeoning population. No longer did everyone know everyone else in their midst. Strangers walked the streets: immigrants and traders speaking new languages, wearing odd clothing. Protection of private property, not communal prosperity, was the major rationale for social organization. When the city replaced the village, the protection of property became a test of piety, a rationale for stricter laws, and a vindication of the rights of propertied men. Men became property. They sold their children to pay their debts. Men who could write wrote down what they (poor people) owed; wrote down their taxes; sent them a statement. Poor men sold their wives to pay their taxes. With cities came capitalistic enterprises, managed by priests and priest-kings. With cities came labor problems, problems of discipline, litigation. With cities came stratified social classes and class privilege, intercity warfare, regional disruptions, higher taxes. Men.

2

Middlemen: The Civilizations of Mesopotamia

CULTURAL AND LITERARY BORROWING

HISTORY BEGINS AT SUMER. READ THE CHAPTER headings of Samuel Noah Kramer's book of the same title.[1] To Sumerian inventions cited in textbooks—the wheel, lunar calendar, irrigation and drainage, monumental architecture, cuneiform writing—Kramer added schools; juvenile delinquency; wars of nerves; bicameral legislatures; tax reduction; paradise; the stories of Moses, Job, and Noah; legal precedents; pharmacology, farmers' almanacs; moral ideals; proverbs; literary debates; resurrection; love songs; and library catalogs. The idea of an irretrievable Golden Age, which Hebrews later called the Garden of Eden, was one more Sumerian invention.

In Sumerian literature the god of sweet water, Enki, during an argument with other gods, destroyed man's one universal language because he was angry with his fellow gods, not with man. In the Hebrew version of Genesis 11:1–9, written nearly two millennia later, Yahweh created linguistic "confusion" as a means for revenge on mankind, who displeased him by building the world's first skyscraper, a Sumerian temple or ziggurat. Yahweh "confused their speech," sending polyglot speakers out from Shinar (Hebrew for Sumeria) to fill Babylonia, immediately north of Sumer, with babble.[2] That was how Babylon became the Mesopotamian city with a divine handicap: multilingualism. But Yahweh miscalculated, for Babylon became a world-class city. It was especially successful under the rule of Hammurabi, an Amorite (eighteenth century BC) and later, under the New Babylonian (Chaldean) King Nebuchadnezzar (sixth century BC). Babylon prospered because she, and all the other Mesopotamians, adopted the wedge-shaped cuneiform writing of Sumer, five hundred characters pressed with a triangular reed stylus onto a soft clay tablet. This was the original software that enabled these middlemen between the valley of the Tigris and Euphrates Rivers to learn from one another no matter what kinds of sounds they made in their own language. Cuneiform. The e-mail of Mesopotamia.

In Sumer and neighboring Akkad, whose capital was Babylon, the Sumerian tongue and the Semitic Akkadian one not only coexisted, but enlarged the creativity of both cultures. A common source of their languages might appear that will account for a convergence of traditions,[3] but cultural flexibility was a shared attitude. Yahweh may have opposed an easy diffusion of knowledge and a no-growth policy toward cities. But that policy conflicted with: 1) man's own fertility, which the Hebrews thought God had commanded early on,[4] and 2) man's still more fertile brain. Everyone understood that civilization would be multilingual and multicultural.

The French government has made the use of English (*franglais*) in newspapers a punishable offense. American state legislatures sporadically proclaim that they will do business in English only. France and the United States are resisting what has in the past proved culturally feasible and profitable. Mesopotamia, whose cultural horizon by comparison with modern countries was limited, met multilculturalism head-on, using Sumerian script to record Semitic sounds in order to share their technology, governmental know-how, religious inspiration, lore, and literature with the whole valley. They kept the lines of communication open, and those lines were triangular or wedge-shaped. Long after their own tongues were stilled (c. 2100 BC) cuneiform still spoke to Mesopotamia, as the Latin of Rome spoke to polyglot Europeans until modern times. Not until the Mongol invaders of the thirteenth century AD destroyed Mesopotamian irrigation canals did the last but one of Sumer's technologies finally dry up.[5] Their cuneiform still whets our curiosity about their way of life.

One of Kramer's chapters concerned "literary borrowing," something moderns call plagiarism. Kramer recounted *The Epic of Gilgamesh,* once (c. 2700 BC) a real king of Uruk (Erech in the Old Testament) who became legendary. He wished to live forever, but learned to accept mere human status instead, and to be a king, hero, good buddy, husband, and father. When Ishtar, goddess of fertility, propositioned Gilgamesh he spurned her advances. He who was once a king would not stoop to be a male escort. Gillie and Enkidu, his wild-man buddy, challenged Ishtar. She sent a Bull of Heaven to control them. They killed the bull, and Enkidu threw one of its thighs at Ishtar: "In your face, Babe!" Enkidu was the world's first atheist. Ishtar took out a contract on Enkidu and he died. Gilgamesh, like Salman Rushdie, had offended the divine, and was forced into hiding.[6] Seeking immortality, he surfaced long enough to visit a wine shop, where he told his troubles to the barmaid. She discouraged him from seeking eternal life. "Look kid," she told him, "eat well, wash your hair, dance, pay attention to your kid and make love to your wife! That's what life is all about." Gilgamesh thought this over, but dismissed her advice. She was just a barmaid. He then consulted the Sumerian Noah, Utnapishtim, who told him of a plant called buckthorn growing on the seabed. "Get yourself some of that grass, and your troubles are history," said Utnapishtim as he worked to build his boat before the rains came. "Eat the buckthorn and you'll live forever."

Determined not to pass the buck, Gilgamesh had himself rowed to the proper location, dove overboard, and plucked the plant off the ocean floor. While he was bathing, a snake stole the buckthorn. Gilgamesh, who never snacked before dinner, lost his chance for immortality.

Readers may empathize. You do all this work, and someone else, your department chairman, supervisor, foreman, significant other, and so on, steals the credit. But don't feel sorry for Gilgamesh. He was a winner. Remember, his search was for immortality. And that is what he achieved, thanks to the Assyrians, a fierce people living on the upper reaches of the Tigris River. They did a remake of the Gilgamesh epic, recopying it in their own language more than a thousand years after its first publication in Sumer. The Assyrians stored it in their library of over twenty thousand tablets in eighth century BC Nineveh. They did not name their version *Gilgamesh II* or *Return of Gilgamesh.* Nevertheless, by copying and preserving the text, they shared the epic with all humanity. The very first World Wide Web. Will anybody out there tell our story five thousand years hence? Will we achieve immortality? Andy Warhol once said all moderns could hope for was fifteen minutes of it. Gilgamesh has had nearly four thousand years! We should live so long.

Babylonians and Assyrians were literary borrowers. So was Father Abraham, the eponymous Hebrew ancestor who lived in "Ur of the Chaldees" (Gen. 11:31) at a time when the land was still called Sumer, not Chaldea, a name the region was called only after the seventh century BC. Nor was Abram (High Father) answering to Abraham (Father of Multitudes), when he lived in Sumer. He was just Abram. In Sumer the Hebrews mingled with Sumerians. They borrowed from *Gilgamesh* the story of Noah and the Flood, changing the story line for their own spiritual needs. Abram left Sumer at the Lord's request, not because he plagiarized from *Gilgamesh* and had to get out of town. Abram couldn't have been charged with plagiarism. It was not yet a crime. With cultural borrowing there was no recourse to legal action if someone copied a product, story, or weapon. There were no patent offices or copyright laws. One took what came along and attributed it to the gods, one's own or another fellow's. In Mesopotamia, man first attributed *himself* to the gods, a notion he passed along to the Hebrews, who packed their cultural baggage for the slow journey toward the Mediterranean Sea. They followed the Fertile Crescent west. Westward, Oi! Only when they were safely in Canaan (now Lebanon), did the Lord change Abram's name to Abraham, and his wife Sarai's to Sarah. Canaan, the land of milk and honey, may have been washed by Mediterranean waters, but it was fertilized by Mesopotamian culture.

Hebrews were not the first spreaders of that culture. The Sumerians were, for the "black headed people," as they called themselves, had been trading with their neighbors in western Asia and Egypt well over a thousand years before Abraham ever lived—or was invented.[7] For his trust in God Abraham became the epitome of a man of faith. Two thousand years later, St. Paul, another man of faith, complimented Abraham's (Rom. 4) when he urged that Abraham was not great because of outward works (circumcision), but because of his trust in the Lord. Abraham learned a great deal about faith in Sumer, for no subsequent civilization ever had greater. Theirs was the first blind trust.

When the Sumerians arrived in southern Mesopotamia from some undetermined point further east, they had no equipment and only mud, water, and sunshine for resources. But they had the determination to make something of themselves. And they did. They came to the land between the two rivers as immigrants and revolutionaries. Out of necessity they built irrigation systems without which they could not have survived the exceptionally hot (to 120°F) rainless summer months. Agriculture that relied on irrigation was a new concept. Fortunately, when this scruffy lot of migrant workers arrived in Sumer around 5000 BC, there were no immigration officers at the borders to check their documents. Of course not. They had not yet invented writing. They had not yet invented bureaucracy or borders. They had not yet invented civilization.[8]

MESOPOTAMIAN HUMILITY

Sumerians first attributed man's physical creation to gods who made man from mud. They forgot that they had invented the gods and fashioned *them* of mud. This memory lapse produced the most entertaining literature and religious lore, the gist of which was that all man's accomplishments were done by the command of the gods. Sumer's gods were lazy louts who refused to work and lived off welfare, the sacrifices provided by their Sumerian slaves. When Sumerians understood how much their gods depended on them, they concluded quite illogically that they, not the gods, were the dependent ones. Psychological dependence on their gods became their raison d'être for working. Had they ever realized what they were accomplishing on their own, who knows what else they might have made of themselves? Or of us?

The Sumerians excelled in many things, but in none more than guilt. They were masters of guilt and shame, sin and spiritual insecurity—that is, they were religious. What a burden the Sumerians created for mankind when they chose mud to represent man's essence! The Hebrews would use dust, but they had a dry sense of humor. Think what might have been the case had Sumeria been rich in gold. Suppose that children growing up in the Western tradition had been told they were beautiful because they were made of pure gold, not dirt! How many psychiatric wards and prisons could we empty? Sumerians doted on humility. Their downward gaze was directed to dirt. True, from it they built their whole mudbrick civilization, but also their self-image. Their cultural heirs, Hebrews and Christians, preserved this notion, and with it humbled Western civilization forever. A few groups escaped. Minoans, Greeks, Persians, and Romans remained largely outside this humble tradition, choosing humanity over humility. They were later called humanists for thinking man was better than the dirt under his feet. The problem with our Mesopotamian humility is that it is unbearable by anybody but saints. For the majority, humility has instilled guilt, without increasing benevolence. Charity? Maybe, but not benevolence, which makes everyone feel better, not just the giver. How can one love one's fellow man when one is convinced not just of his own guilt but his neighbor's?

Ben Franklin wrote that after overcoming pride, he was proud of himself. So he felt guilty. But he was, after all, an enlightened thinker, a liberal, and a humanist. Most of the men who participated in the writing of our Constitution were enlightened liberal humanists and would no doubt be condemned for it if running for political office today. They were not free of human foibles or sin. An old Sumerian proverb (they invented proverbs, too) proclaimed: "No child was ever born sinless from its mother's womb." Original sin was another Sumerian invention. After the Sumerians, sin was utterly devoid of originality. But never of guilt. We moderns, including Franklin and our Founding Fathers, would have been quite at home in ancient Sumer. Guilty as charged.

Mesopotamian Religion and the Authority of Priests

The Sumerians were very pious, believing the gods kept the rivers' waters from inundating arable land, although it was the Sumerians who first built the dikes. Along with dikes they invented organized religion, and then ziggurats to house it in and promote education, priests to conduct religious rites and to demand from the people burnt sacrifices, the first barbecue. Theirs was an investment in institutional religion, service, self-development, self-abnegation, and awe. The cost, borne mostly by peasants, was awesome, but the return on their investment was great. Not to the peasants necessarily, but to their social superiors, and ultimately, to us. The ziggurats or temple towers attracted free-spending pilgrims who boosted the Sumerian economy and boasted of their more or less voluntary offerings to the religious cult. The priests of the cult directed large-scale agriculture, manufacture, education, trade, and above all, the maintenance of irrigation dikes, for agriculture was the basis of all enterprise in Mesopotamia. The peasants carried all of society on their backs as they went out each day to till the fields. Other means of transportation were sailboats and wheeled carts.

The information pilgrims derived from each other while trekking off to visit the ziggurats became the basis for policy-making, for priests or other officials of temple towns debriefed them at their journey's end. Information gathering became as vital a part of government as tax gathering. For a time there was no distinction between secular authority and religious authority. The first temples were one-room shelters built in Sumerian towns such as Eridu as early as 4900 BC. A millennium later, the one-room temple had become an elaborate ziggurat, a small temple superimposed on a tall base with slanted steps leading up through archways to the shrine above. This structure has been viewed as evidence that institutionalized religion existed in Sumer *before* the advent of literacy, challenging the claim that bureaucratic organization, necessary to build ziggurats, resulted from literacy, and did not precede it.[9] Whether their investment in religion preceded or followed the advent of writing, it paid off so well no other culture ever left home without it.

The temple complex served more needs than spirituality; it also served the life of the mind. Here boys studied to become priests and surveyors, administrators of the priest-king's property, which included individuals as well as other goods. Besides religious lore and mathematical and language skills, Sumerians learned astronomy. Sumerians and Babylonians put a greater emphasis on this science because their gods were not just the makers of the heavenly bodies, they were the heavenly bodies. Astronomy, moreover, gave the priests who excelled at it a predictive edge—knowing precisely when astronomical events would take place enabled them to make lunar calendars and later to pose as prophets, a useful posture but a dangerous imposture. For hundreds of years, the rulers of Sumerian city states were also the chief priests. Only later did Sumerian rulers, called *patesis, ensis,* or *lugals,* free themselves of the priestly establishment, and whenever possible, of the inconvenient restraints that priests, the mouthpieces of the gods, might have imposed on them. We call such restraints ethics.

Of course, rulers always said that they were following the gods' orders, and thus were ethical, but increasingly they followed their own wishes and hoped their subjects would never notice the difference. If there were doubts at all they were resolved by war. War became the ultimate arbiter in all Sumerian disputes, other than those that were of a purely civil nature. For civil disputes, the Sumerians invented arbitration, hoping to minimize lawsuits. Their ultimate trial was war between one Sumerian city-state and another. Until 2100 BC victorious city-states assumed their defeated enemy's store of gods as well as goods, but never their debts.

Every city-state had a patron god or goddess, just as in Europe's Middle Ages every city had its own patron saint. When a Sumerian city-state was conquered, its patron god was assumed, not denied, and hence, the god's devotees were never in denial, and all participated in this assumption. In Mesopotamia, the established gods remained part of the Establishment, though the victorious god became commander-in-chief. Worshippers of demoted gods continued to worship them, and eventually, so did the conquerors. In Sumer and Old Babylon, no matter who won the war or lost it, the gods were not defamed. Mesopotamian gods were founding fathers of civilization's first Anti-Defamation League. They profited by cultural borrowing.

World leaders still invoke the power of God to justify war, no matter how ungodly their cause. Their enemies do the same. For God this must be embarrassing. All belligerents assume that brutal aggression against the enemy is what God himself prescribes. God is coerced into defending not only disparate nations, but disparate types of economies, concepts of justice, methods of leadership, forms of faith, and social behavior. A universal God finds his standards compromised by the winner, at least in the eyes of the God-invoking loser, even though the losing side might have had the better cause. The victorious country and its commander-in-chief make God speak for the collective conscience of their side. When the Godhead was a multiplicity, speaking for many gods was more problematic. The defeated were allowed to keep their old gods whatever the outcome. Now that the gods have been condensed into just one, God's will emerges as the collective will of the victor, and the defeated side must adapt their values and God's to those who defeated them.

Sumerian priest-kings were the first leaders in civilization to promote the abnegation of individuality in the name of the state, and they created a theocracy, the first controlled political environment. Mesopotamian rulers invoked the will of the gods—in defense of privilege and the exaltation of the status quo. Once the rulers got that established, the gods identified with the Establishment and their devotees followed suit.

Pavlov, the Russian psychologist, worked on dogs to learn more about conditioned reflexes in humans.[10] He never was very good in history class. Before him the Austrian educator and later, a monk named Mendel, did it less obtrusively with peas.[11] His research enabled him to predict the kinds of characteristics that in plants are termed dominant and recessive, but in social classes are termed leaders and led. Later American educators talked about "mind-set," tested schoolchildren's personality, aptitude, and intelligence with paper weapons like the Stanford Binet and the Minnesota Multiphasic, hoping individual students could be made to behave like so many predictable peas in pods, responding in predictable ways to applied stimuli, including the singing of the national anthem and the repetition of the Pledge of Allegiance. Mesopotamian rulers had already arrived at the same conclusions but without the peas, tests, dogs, Pledge, and so forth. Samuel Kramer could have told them that civilization began in Sumer.

COMMUNICATION AND THE WORD:
CONVERSATIONS WITH THE GODS

The "Word" became cultural shorthand for God's commands in Hebrew times, but it also reflected the value placed on writing once the Sumerians got the hang of it. Writing, the primary mode of communication for five thousand years, has been grafted onto our computer culture with a new meaning: "Word" for moderns is an electronic process. Words were civilization's first software. They attached meaning to what was formerly a mysterious process, second-guessing the gods or communicating their wishes to the people. Today words on the Internet vie for attention with traditional forms of knowledge and/or spiritual communication. The Internet is spiritual communication for many of its users.

Sumerians worshipped writing as superior knowledge, precisely the way many Internet users do. Overconfidence in the written word immediately expanded credulity, for in Mesopotamia, people tended to believe whatever they read. Lack of critical reasoning about words and images, whatever the medium, is still the major problem for communication. Now as then images can manipulate people, even while we prefer to think of ourselves as the manipulators of images. We still mistake imagery for facts; facts for knowledge; and knowledge for wisdom.

Mesopotamians wanted to learn faster what little information was available. Moderns need to learn slower, because there is so much more information available. Like a reed stylus on a clay tablet, information, whatever its form, makes an impression on the grey matter of our minds. Indelible imprints etch the soft tissues of the indispensable tablet: our brain. When fired, Sumerian clay preserved information in rigid squares. Hastily fired up, our impressions may make us just as inflexible. Rigid squares.

The ziggurat was the religious center, the governmental center, and the entertainment center of Mesopotamia. Temples provided pageants, human sacrifice, live sex acts between priests or gods and humans, speeches, miracles, agricultural jobs, jobs for artisans, trade, education, indoctrination.[12] All these activities enabled men and women to fantasize, escape the drabness of everyday life, view unobtainable treasures, and experience vicariously the triumphs of gods with whom they had absolutely nothing in common, as Gilgamesh discovered. The Sumerian temple was the world's first mass medium.

The priests, kings, and emperors were convinced that they alone answered for the gods because they alone possessed the god's new e-mail address (e for eternal).[13] Nippur was a holy city, like Rome later. Nippur had a direct hookup to Enlil, god of air, creator of the universe. Mesopotamian religion provided an open door through which one could step into the mind of a god.

In the seventh century BC the Chaldeans thought that door was astronomy, and they charted the progress of heavenly bodies so as to be able to predict political events on earth. Astronomy became astrology. The Greeks knew all the right questions to ask of the gods and kept several channels open for answers. One of their channels was the Delphic Oracle, but it broadcast only in riddles. The Romans admired heavenly bodies, too. They thought the planets might influence, not just politics, but their private lives. When in doubt they took to analyzing bird gizzards. It required less math.

Before Congress terminated the program, U.S. astronomers and physicists spent millions of tax dollars listening for signs of extraterrestrial intelligence from outer space. No intelligible message from the universe was ever received, though scientists listened for twenty years. In this way, but at far greater expense, they exactly replicated the efforts of the ancients who were similarly persuaded that answers for mankind would be coming from outer space. Our culture is too forward-looking. If only we were sufficiently backward-looking, sufficiently inner-directed instead of outer-directed, we would seek wisdom from our collective experience.

Mesopotamians were ambivalent about the gods. Should they be feared more than loved or vice versa? And, if feared, how loved? Not to fear them seemed disrespectful of their power. But, if the gods were lovable, could they be altogether respectable? That which is most lovable is often least respectable, though nothing puts a damper on love faster than respectability. The Babylonian gods of love and fertility, Tammuz and Ishtar (in Sumer, Inanna), were not quite respectable, so Mesopotamians could both love *and* fear them. Ambivalence came naturally, for neither love nor fertility was ever wholly respectable. Sex has always been a tantalizing taboo. Tammuz, a shepherd, was either Ishtar's brother, lover, or son, depending on the location. A feminist, Ishtar pursued Tammuz until, weakened by just saying no, he met with an untimely death. A wild boar—everyone meets one some time or another—fatally gored him and sent him to the netherworld. Ishtar, "always chasing rainbows," was in hot pursuit.[14] The rainbow, by the way, was an ancient Sumerian symbol of hope and would fulfill the same function in the Old Testament, too. Ishtar followed Tammuz unto death, taking with her all the forces of life on earth, creating a terrible drought and incalculable agricultural loss, not to mention the cessation of all sexual intercourse: "After the lady had gone down into the land of no return, the bull did not mount the cow, the ass approached not the she ass. To the maid in the street no man drew near. The man slept in his apartment, the maid slept by herself."[15]

Heavy duty. Fortunately, Ishtar was a combination of Wonder Woman and Nancy Drew. She managed to outwit the guardian of the netherworld, Ereshkigal, her own sister, and Namtar, her servant, who made Ishtar strip and deposit her jewels in the netherworld's vault. Only then could Ishtar enter hell, a place called Aralu. There they imprisoned her and afflicted her with sixty separate diseases. These sadly weakened her immune system, but she recovered without the aid of wonder drugs. They had not yet been invented. She and Tammuz fled back to earth. The other gods aided their escape because they were not receiving their usual supply of fresh produce. This ancient tale was popular throughout antiquity. In Egypt the starring roles went to Osiris and Isis. In Greece, Demeter and her daughter Persephone stole the show from Pluto, god of Hades, and in Rome, Ceres played Demeter's part and Proserpine that of the ingenue, whereas Dis, later, god of the Gauls, presided over Tartarus, the Roman hell. The critics dissed the performance as not very original, which, by Roman times, it wasn't. Critics are always stating the obvious. The play was about spring and the return of earth's fertility. For that reason, and because it was staged below ground, a warm, dark place associated with wealth, forgetfulness, and idleness, the play lent itself to sexual interpretations.[16] A more violent but asexual production cast Christ in Osiris's role, and eternal life—Gilgamesh's dream—eclipsed the business about pollination and vegetation. This production brought rave reviews from critics for its entire run—two thousand years. Now that's showbiz!

Everywhere people have looked to religion to provide excitement, glamour, hope, shame, escape, recognition. Consumerism helped some, but in Mesopotamia, where fertility cults and the search for eternal life in the hereafter began, people relied mostly on organized religion and made up stories for the relief of tedium. Religion provided Mesopotamians with the glamor, drama, poetry, and terror of vicarious experience. When it failed, warfare, alcohol, sex, and hallucinogens relieved the boredom attendant on civilized living. If those things didn't work, there was always the abuse of women and children.

STATECRAFT IN SUMER

After 2400 BC kings took control of their states without asking priests for permission. The gods knew who could slay the fatted calf. They ate best when kings were strong. Kings knew how hungry gods could get and fed them a diet of booty (stolen property) washed down with the sweat of peasants. The peasants ate more cereal, dates, and garden produce than barbecued sacrifices, a diet low in fat and high in fiber. If they had lived to middle age this diet would have lowered their cholesterol. As it was, it just lowered their resistance and they died young.

Some kings suspected that they were answerable to the gods for rendering justice to the people, and a few seemed to have tried. Lagash was a city-state of Sumer ruled by King Eannatum sometime in the latter half of the twenty-sixth-century BC. Eannatum defeated the city-state of Umma over a matter of water rights to the Adab Canal which bordered both Lagash and Umma. This incident furnished one of the few basic plots for all subsequent cowboy films. Later, this king captured Iranian Elam, destroyed its capital of Susa, several other Elamite towns, and the Sumerian cities Ur, Uruk, Kish, and Opis. By then Eannatum was king of all Sumer. He ruled briefly, never creating a truly unified state and was soon overthrown by a resurgent Umma.[17] Eventually, a reformer of law named Urukagina threw off the yoke of Kish and made himself king of Lagash and Sumer. Urukagina regarded himself a friend of the poor and forbade officials and priests from taxing them heavily. He rebuilt the sacred shrines of Lagash and reformed the Sumerian law code. That code was destroyed in Urukagina's own lifetime by another king of Umma named Lugal-zaggesi, a madman who claimed the rule of all Sumeria.

The "law" of Mesopotamia was as variable as the opportunities that presented themselves to aggressive neighboring monarchs. The first person ever to invent term limits was a Mesopotamian king who conquered the incumbent of a neighboring state.

THE STATE TURNED EMPIRE—SARGON THE GREAT OF AKKAD

For a rags-to-riches story Horatio Alger could not have improved upon, consider that of Sargon I of Akkad, called the Great.[18] Akkad got its name from its capital city, still unlocated, somewhere near Nippur. Sargon's curriculum vitae listed his mother as a royal priestess; but he was probably an illegitimate kid whose mom had brought shame to her family by thoughtlessly allowing herself to be impregnated. Because of all the embarrassment that Sargon's birth entailed, his mother did not even dare name him. Sargon, meaning Rightful King, was only a title bestowed later. Set adrift on the Euphrates in a basket of bulrushes he was rescued by a gardener who raised him as a humble workman. Clearly, Sargon had to make a name for himself. The little bastard grew up to be the world's first emperor. Maybe. One historian thinks the term was used too loosely in his case, and views Sargon as a "proto-Emperor" whose army, at a mere 5,500 soldiers, hardly passed muster as an imperial force.[19] An opposed view would have it that Sargon accumulated more than the 5,500 troops; that he only dined with this number daily, and that "these thousands of permanent attendants represented an embryonic standing army" numbering in the "hundreds of thousands."[20]

Although documents on Sargon are scanty, they do at least testify to his ambition. He aimed at complete military and political control even if he were obliged to fight revolts against his authority at Ur, Lagash, Zalala, Adab, and Umma.[21] Notwithstanding his unfortunate background, this son of an erring mother made good.[22] Who taught him what hard work, tact, and a lack of scruple can do to improve one's lot? Whoever his mentor, Sargon got his real start as a cupbearer to the ruler of Kish. It was a job that required guts, for cupbearers were tasters of the ruler's drink. They were hired to keep the king from being poisoned. Fortunately for young Sargon, the ruler of Kish had no serious enemies while he was cupbearer. Leaving his employer at Kish no worse for wear than when he had entered his employ, Sargon consolidated his power first over Akkad. He then gained control of areas reaching from the Mediterranean to the Persian Gulf. His putative empire, which he may or may not have effectively controlled, included parts of Syria and what is now Iran.[23]

Akkadian Semites invented the multinational empire establishing new traditions of state, charismatic kingship, and centralized government that marked the state of Akkad.[24] Under Sargon the state protected trade from Syria to Anatolia, now Turkey.[25] When Sargon could not get cooperation from his neighbors, he resorted to more direct methods, namely war. On such an occasion, he defeated the berserk ruler-priest of Umma and Uruk, Lugalzaggesi. The fellow was not the last mad priest in history (one thinks of Savonarola in fifteenth-century Florence, and Rasputin in late czarist Russia), but the first of whom we have any knowledge.

Sargon's government was a commercial enterprise driven by its need to control areas from which came its supplies.[26] "Sargon's empire was not so much a power structure seeking to dominate populations by military force as a means of insuring that international trade should flourish, largely for the benefit of his capital city."[27] So what if he did not control all of Mesopotamia all of the time?[28] This may mean only that he was smart enough to conciliate areas he could not control by military means. We do not know for sure where his power reached or how deeply it was exercised. His authority may have been greatest in a "great ring" around Sumer and Akkad that did not challenge any of the ancient seats of power directly. In Sargon's old age conquered states revolted, leading one authority to suggest that there was no clear indication he even ruled them by then.[29] Most authors place Sargon's reign in the mid part of the twenty-fourth century BC and believe it lasted between fifty-four and fifty-five years. Given that his birthdate and real name are unknown, his fame legendary, and his power disputed, he remains something of a cipher to historians. Even his boundaries were not clearly delineated. Because he allowed some vanquished rulers to direct their own domestic affairs, some experts wonder if Sargon himself understood what he was up to.

Sargon was not the only government leader who failed to understand the nature of his own authority, or its relation to economic and social policy. "Read my lips," said George Bush the elder when he knew he was going to raise taxes despite earlier denials. Given the cowardice and deceit of politicians, what chance has the public or historian of getting the story straight? The revelations made in 1995 by Robert McNamara, Lyndon Johnson's secretary of state, that he and the president knew for several years their Vietnam policy was misguided reminds us that leaders are often neither wise nor frank. It took some courage on McNamara's part to reveal the truth so much later, even if his revelations made the loss of American life in Asia seem pointless. It would have taken much more courage, of course, to reveal the truth when a reassessment of policy was sorely needed.

Even when we think we understand the motives of our leaders, it often turns out that they did not. Sometimes documents that could prove whether they did or did not know what they were doing have been destroyed to prevent us from knowing. Twenty minutes of tape pertaining to the Watergate crisis in the Nixon administration were said to have been accidentally erased by Nixon's secretary. Even when evidence is not destroyed, it is regularly withheld from people by governments because they do not think the people can handle the truth. The Warren Commission sealed the documents to John F. Kennedy's assassination because they did not trust the public's ability to deal with the facts. The administration of George W. Bush does not want to reveal the facts on which terrorist suspects may be condemned and has urged that they be tried in secret by military tribunals.

Even when the facts are there, perspectives on them reflect the cultural attitudes of those who interpret them. As a case in point, consider Sargon's Akkad. Its largely Semitic population is regarded by some experts to have been less Semitic than Sumerian in its culture.[30] A French scholar named Joseph Halévy, born at Adrianople in 1882 and Jewish, became convinced that the Semites were the sole source of all Western Asian cultures and that the Sumerian language was merely a secret form of writing invented by Semitic priests! Halévy erred. The Sumerians created their own language and shared the cuneiform method of writing and other cultural artifacts with Semites who wandered into their territory. Halévy's unrestrained ethnic pride led him astray. In a similar ethnocentric vein, when certain European scholars, including a Czech named Bedrich Hrozny, deciphered the Indo-European language of the Hittites in 1915, they could hardly say enough good things about the Hittites, with whom they overidentified, just as Halévy overidentified with Semites. Thus scholars, who identified emotionally with Indo-Europeans, once attributed a technological and scientific superiority to the Hittites who were not more advanced—but less advanced—than some of their neighbors.

The term Indo-European seems harmless enough today, perhaps because it is so vague. It is used to refer to dozens of languages, supposedly related peoples, and an original homeland now unlocatable (!) but variously described as somewhere between India and eastern Europe! But even innocuous terms like Indo-European are made up of layers of meaning that fluctuate with the political and emotional climate of a given era. The early twentieth century was afflicted by irrational racial interpretations of history. Among the Hittites' supposed triumphs was their purported invention of iron smelting, followed by success in iron manufacture and trade. But in fact this was explainable because the Hittites sat upon rich iron ore deposits, not because they were superior metallurgists! Indeed, the exact effect of iron on Hittite history is still corroding academic discourse, with one authority claiming that the Hittites were "the first to develop a substantial iron industry,[31] whereas another thinks that the Hittite kingdom collapsed because they failed to exploit iron "known for many hundreds of years," leaving the resource to be developed not by the Hittites, but by a conquered tribe that the Hittites failed to control, a race that turned iron into weaponry, unlike the Hittites and others who continued to use bronze weapons![32]

Even when ethnocentric loyalties are not at stake, the reconstruction of Western civilization is complicated by the paucity of evidence and the social and historical prejudices of the people who study and write history. Today few people, and almost no historians, share Ranke's old conviction that history can ever be written "exactly as it occurred."[33] And if it were, would it be as useful?

HAMMURABI, OLD BABYLONIA, AND THE LAW

Around 1750 BC, another Semite, the Amorite Hammurabi, ruled much of Sargon's old territory. The Sumerians of the third dynasty of Ur (2112–2000 BC) had tutored the Amorites of Old Babylonia as earlier Sumerian dynasties had the Akkadians. The dates for Hammurabi's reign vary, but dates were a staple of the Mesopotamian diet. How sweet it was! One textbook says Hammurabi reigned from 1792–1750 BC;[34] another says 1729–1686 BC.[35] In his time—whatever time it was—Hammurabi was a big *macher* [Yiddish, influential guy], surrounded by kings whose supporters were also kings. This was the oldest old-boy system in Western civilization.

Hammurabi's Babylon was still a mediocre state when he ascended the throne as its sixth ruler. The first few years of his rule were insecure. [36] Hammurabi never sought security by claiming to be divine. He never felt obliged, as other god-kings of Mesopotamia did, to take out a divine assurance policy by sending his daughter off to serve as moon goddess at Ur. For thirty years he concentrated on achieving security through bureaucratic efficiency and law reform, rather than relying on a daughter-goddess of Ur. Hammurabi chose statecraft over witchcraft, independent policy over blind tradition. Later, he defeated Assyria, with her chief cities Assur and Nineveh. He captured southern Babylonia, too, taking the the titles "King of Sumer and Akkad" and "King of the Four Quarters of the World." He was no two-bit ruler.

Hammurabi's enduring achievement was his famous law Code. It has been objected that the Code may not even have had the force of law, because only one court document from Old Babylonia refers expressly to it![37] The famous Code was not really a code of laws, but rather, a collection of judicial decisions that made no attempt to provide universal criteria of culpability. These decisions were not intended to be precedents binding subsequent judgments, as in English law.[38] They were not even cited or necessarily followed in the determination of lawsuits.[39] Whatever its legal standing, Hammurabi's Code persisted throughout Mesopotamia as a reference work. Not a few of its principles, including the famous "eye for an eye" found their way into the Hebrew Bible. Hammurabi's concept of law, which he attributed to the god Shamash, patron of law, was handed down from Sumer, where earlier compilations of judicial decisions had been made. The Amorite ruler attributed his Code to divine origins, precisely as Moses is believed to have done, nearly half a millennium later,[40] and as Mohammed did in the seventh century AD, and as the Mormon Joseph Smith (1805–44), would do in western New York in 1827. The enforcers have always doubted that, left to their own devices, people would do the right thing.

A carved picture of Shamash and Hammurabi tops the stone slab or stela on which the Code was carved. If you brave long lines of tourists outside the Louvre Museum in Paris you can see this precious artifact up close. It was once stolen by an Elamite king and not recovered until 1902 at Susa (in Iran). That it was recovered at long last is owing to a French archaeologist who had the decency to steal it again and smuggle it into France, a theft that flaunted the protection given other peoples' property by the Code itself. Still, but for such acts of larceny, the Louvre Museum would not be the "top" as the song says,[41] but a flop, and the same would be true of the rest of the world's great collections. The Elamites, who early appreciated the fine art of collecting, arbitrarily hacked off twenty laws from the stela, leaving 282 intact. Fortunately, the missing twenty turned up elsewhere on a fragmented tablet. It has always been wise to save hard copy. In the ancient world, as in the electronic world, no once could predict a power failure, which occurred after Hammurabi's line petered out around 1530 BC.

Hammurabi's Code provided harsh punishments, including dismemberment and many capital offenses, whereas the Sumerians were more apt to punish by levying fines. The Hebrews, who softened the Code in some instances, were not able to rid themselves of the idea of retribution. Retributive principles are found in Exodus and Deuteronomy, along with a potpourri of Mesopotamian practices that became standards of Christian justice, too: revenge, cruelty, sexism, and class discrimination. Yet intermingled with these harsher traditions were laws urging mercy and protection for the weak. In Hebrew culture, the protections offered by the Deuteronomic Code were not intended for nonbelievers or foreigners. Shortly after the World Trade Towers were struck the Bush administration announced that the protections of the Constitution of the United States were similarly never intended for foreigners. We are still stumbling over the cultural debris of Hammurabi's Code and the Deuteronomic Code. The most notorious of the Babylonian principles persisted as the Mosaic "eye for an eye" retaliatory law (Latin, *lex talionis*).[42] The military has not yet risen to the ethical level of either Code, since generals make preemptive strikes before the enemy damages their side. The Military Code is itself a preemptive strike against any other code, including our Constitution.

Enlightened Westerners no longer expect to injure their attackers in the same way they were injured by them, although the practice of exact retribution still thrives in certain Muslim countries where four fingers of the right hand are amputated to punish thieves and toes are amputated for the second offense. In the U.S. we have found we can do more damage just initiating a lawsuit! No matter how guiltless the party sued, the cost of defending himself will almost certainly be punitive.

We have not progressed much beyond the principle of retaliation, though large-souled folks have urged us to do so. Jesus. Gandhi. Martin Luther King. Punishment and revenge, not rehabilitation or forgiveness, is the foundation of our own criminal justice system. The U.S. is one of the few Western nations to demand the death penalty not only for murder, but for over fifty crimes not resulting in death at all. This was also true of Hammurabi's Code, and of British law in the unreformed late eighteenth century, when the death penalty was prescribed for stealing a linen pocket handkerchief.

The U.S. Crime Bill of 1995 would oblige the death penalty for noncapital crimes even in those states which did not before have the death penalty. When it comes to capital offenses, our own laws are nearly as harsh as Hammurabi's, which were harsher than Sumeria's. The Sumerians already considered theft, the adultery of women (but not men), and bearing false witness as capital cases.[43] In 1995 Americans urged a "Three strikes and you're out" law to punish more harshly defendants with prior convictions, which is not only retaliatory, but bases present punishment on past punishments! Yet the Fifth Amendment to the Constitution states no person shall be "subject for the same offense to be twice put in jeopardy of life or limb."[44] Double jeopardy did not exist in Hammurabi's Code and was never part of ours until 1995.

Hammurabi wrote in his "Prologue" that the gods urged destruction of the wicked and the protection of the weak from their oppressors. What would he have thought of employers who fired workers (euphemism: "downsized") to increase profits, thus impoverishing whole families in order to reward shareholders? He might have approved, because the Code of Hammurabi was by and large protective of the propertied, while claiming before Shamash that the weak were owed protection, too. One authority has written that "militant capitalism of ancient Babylonia is clearly demonstrated by the fact that personal property was regarded as much more sacred than human life."[45] Amorites were already quite amoral in their concern for property rights, which became increasingly sacrosanct in the Western tradition. Nothing succeeds like success is an unprincipled principle we have inherited from our cultural forbears.

A second principle of the Code was "Let the buyer beware" [Latin, *Caveat emptor*]. In Mesopotamia there were only a few consumer protection laws. One of them offered protection against a watered drink in the local wineshop, perhaps because the wineshops were commonly run by female bartenders. If they watered the drink, these ladies were tossed into the Euphrates or the Tigris, whichever was closer. *The Jungle* (1906) by socialist muckraker Upton Sinclair (1878–1968), exposed the filth of Chicago meat-processing plants. That same year Congress passed the first Food and Drug Act. Since the 1960s, Ralph Nader and organizations like the Sierra Club have urged the public to protect the environment and their health by holding big business responsible for the kinds of misbehavior that poison our atmosphere, our environment, our bodies. Some manufacturers agree that responsibility serves the public, that wholesome products benefit everyone in the long run. These enlightened capitalists are a national treasure. The crass among them, on the other hand, argue that protecting consumers lessens productivity and makes American business less competitive. In the 1990s, Congress tried to downplay consumer rights. Industrial irresponsibility threatens now to reach Mesopotamian levels, which were very high for a very flat land. Although Hammurabi affirmed a divine injunction to protect the weak, he largely ignored consumers. Of course, the Mesopotamians did not yet live to consume, like we do. They still consumed to live.

A third principle of Hammurabi's Code was that it was not egalitarian. There was only inequality before the law. One's rights, duties, and punishments depended wholly on one's class. There were several social classes: the first was called men, in other words, gentlemen, who were free property owners. A second group was free men without property, and the last group was slaves with no rights to speak of. [46]

Gender and personal autonomy also defined status or its lack. Women were viewed as weak and received protections based on recognition of that weakness. Many provisions concerned marriage and family. Women caught in adultery could be bound to their lovers and tossed into the river, unless the husband wished to spare his wife. Then the king might spare her partner. The wife of a man who fled the city was free to "enter another man's house" (i.e., cohabit). If her husband returned she was spared going back to him because of his lack of patriotism! Men could divorce childless wives, though they were supposed to return their dowries. Male infertility was undreamed of, and a man was always presumed fertile. If a wife were a gadabout (i.e., walked into the city to chat, waste time), he did not have to return her dowry when he divorced her, but could remarry and the gad-about became the family maidservant! There were no laws concerning gad-about husbands. Running around was a male prerogative. Like all the other prerogatives.

If a concubine took up residence in a man's home she could not be sold, but the wife could consider her a slave. Virtuous women (those certified as such by the city council!) could divorce their husbands if they could prove their men belittled them around town. In that case, they could take their dowries and return blameless to their fathers' house. If their fathers were dead or did not wish to receive them, they were in trouble. But for the fact that they bore children, provided sexual gratification, dowries, and chicken soup they would probably not have been accorded the few privileges they enjoyed in Hammurabi's Old Babylonia.

The selection in 2001 of an Attorney General who spent much of his career trying to prevent a woman's autonomy over her own bodily processes demonstrates how precarious is the defense of women's equal-ity at the dawn of the twenty-first century.[47] Women are still not consid-ered by a very large minority to be equal to men, nor are they adequately protected by our political system. Our representatives may be wishing for a code like Hammurabi's when they contemplate the ero-sion of laws such as affirmative action and *Roe v. Wade*. Mesopotamians never recognized a woman's body as her own, but as some man's prop-erty. The Code put women wholly at the service of the men who acquired and controlled them. A woman's sexuality was denied her, and her reproductive future was written without consulting her in any way. With a bit of luck, the Amorites in Washington may obtain for American women the same kind of protection Hammurabi thought proper for females in Babylonia.

Other kinds of property got considerable protection in Hammurabi's Code. This might have proved a blessing to the victim of robbery, for cities reimbursed the value of stolen property when the thief could not be found. Thieves had to repay thirtyfold the value of an item stolen from a temple or palace, and tenfold the value of any other item.[48] Unwitting buyers of stolen goods were reimbursed out of the estate of the thief, provided witnesses testified to the buyer's own innocence. Lacking witnesses, the buyer was executed.

In Old Babylon, a rich thief could buy enough witnesses to save his skin! Money talked, except when it bought silence. The Code provided for exemption from taxes on homes of on-duty soldiers. It protected borrowers against greedy lenders; farmers from neighbors who forgot to repair their dikes and flooded another man's grain; debtors by letting them sell their wives and children into servitude for three or four years. If debtors sold their slaves into servitude and forgot to reclaim them (or could not afford to) there was no "cause for complaint" (i.e., by the debtor). Slaves' complaints went unheeded.

It has become fashionable of late for Americans to regard harsh law codes as a way to reduce crime. Hammurabi's Code, though surprisingly progressive in a few ways, was, on the whole, harsh. Consider that among their capital offenses was manslaughter, sorcery, theft of property from a god or the palace, receipt of stolen property, kidnapping, helping slaves to escape, housebreaking, robbery or arson, irregularities in performing royal service, and watering drinks in wineshops. The Code provided for maiming criminals by breaking limbs, teeth, cutting off hands, ears, tongues, breasts (but not penises), putting the offender's children to death; torture, impalement, burning, and ordeals.[49] All these harsh punishments, one would think, should have reduced crime. Yet the Code did not seem to have done so. Old Babylonian society was as violent as its law codes. One reason there was so much violence may have been due to the fact that the Code discouraged witnesses from testifying to capital crimes. It executed the witness in a murder trial if the accused could not be convicted! The Old Babylonians badly needed a witness protection program, but the state was less concerned with apprehending murderers than with clearing its court calendar.

Mesopotamian court calendars were clogged anyway. The Old Babylonians had not yet discovered that is was not the harshness of the laws that deters crime, but the creation of a just society. Babylon fell short of justice, a concept that was not much more adequately developed then now, however much the leader claimed to represent justice. Most modern states fall short of being just societies, too, despite good intentions. Good intentions along with harsh criminal codes pave the paths to hell and to city hall, but not to just societies. In Old Babylonia, good intentions without justice may also have paved the road to conquest by the Hittites (1600–1550 BC).

Assyria–The Good-Neighbor Policy That Failed

Assyria was one of the oldest near eastern civilizations, a mixture of Semites and Asiatic nomads, occupying both banks of the Tigris from 3000 BC. Then followed twelve hundred years of peace and quiet, during which historians have little information about her. Gradually, she soaked up so much Mesopotamian culture she appeared wholly assimilated. Assyria was the "Good Neighbor Sam" whose borrowing flattered and who was willing to serve her neighbors' interests, allowing Akkadians and Babylonians to incorporate her territory without fuss.[50] Her northern neighbors also took advantage—she was a constant target for invasion by Indo-Europeans, Hittites, Kassites, Semites, and Hurrians, one group of whom were called Mitanni. One by one and two by two they attacked her until by the end of the thirteenth century BC, Assyria mastered the art of self- defense. She became a military power, the mightiest in Mesopotamia—and the most feared east of the Mediterranean.

Assyrians were artistic, producing some of the best carved bas-reliefs in antiquity. Assyria used her art as an extension of terrorism, controlling enemies by advertising on façades her cruelty toward rebels. Her kings boasted of impaling enemy leaders and feeding bits of sliced victims to the vultures. The technique of terrorizing rebellious client states had not been wholly Assyria's invention, for Egypt and other states were also terroristic. But Assyria's own advertising of these events made her appear different. Her bas reliefs displayed her baseness, though one historian points out that Assyrian retribution was "not meted out indiscriminately," only against "the most flagrant" instances of rebellions in Assyria's "orbit."[51] King Ashurbanipal (669–626 BC) boasted of feeding his victims to vultures and to pigs, dogs, other birds, and fish. When he had fed them the last piece, he sat down to read in the great library he built at Nineveh, filled with precious tablets from all over Mesopotamia. Without Ashurbanipal's cultural interests, we would know much less about Sumerians, Akkadians, and Babylonians. Assyrians produced fine gold jewelry that rivaled the best of Van Cleef.[52] Their bas-reliefs of horse-drawn chariots, warriors on piles of dead enemies, and lions hunted down with arrows sticking out of their hide but still fighting back at the huntsmen, are among the treasures of Mesopotamian creativity. Assyria's ability to combine in the persons of her rulers great refinement and intellectuality with the greatest cruelty— they displayed mutilated victims of revolt in wheeled cages to discourage emulators—taught Persians, Greeks, and Romans how to mix cruelty with culture. Assyria was proficient in diplomacy and psychology. She rewarded cooperation. Even when she chose to deport entire cultural groups to the corners of her empire she provided the deportees with opportunities for job training and resettlement in areas compatible with their former habitat and lifestyle. In her treatment of rebellious Samarians of Israel in the eighth century BC, Assyria encouraged their rapid assimilation with the settled inhabitants of Guzana and the Chabur region.[53] Good governance, not sentimentality, was her motive. If the migrant workers from the Oklahoma and Arkansas dust bowl of the 1930s had received this kind of treatment from our own government, there might never have been a novel called *The Grapes of Wrath* by John Steinbeck (1939).[54] Of course, the "Okies" were never a defeated rebel nation. And they were never fed to vultures and wild animals. Just to creditors and auctioneers.

Assyrian political prominence arrived when a Babylonian named Shamshi-Adad I unified the Assyrian towns of Asshur, Nineveh, and Erbil, creating a nation six hundred miles wide, from Cappodocia to the Zagros Mountains. He collected tribute from neighbors—Amorites, Syrians, Hurrians, Akkadians, Hittites, and others who passed through the territory searching for necessary supplies, especially minerals. The Assyrians, like the Akkadians before, made a living off the trade of others, charging for the use of their roads. Anyone who has paid a toll on a turnpike or bridge is familiar with this principle of highway robbery. The Assyrians developed the technique of selling "protection" long before Mafiosi in our big cities started to "protect" glass storefronts of businessmen in America back in the 1920s. Assyrians were among the first merchants of menace.[55] Proactive Assyrians engaged in trade themselves, providing refined copper to the Old Babylonians as early as 2000 BC. Colonies of private Assyrian merchants settled in Asiatic Turkey (Cappadocia) where many clay tablets reveal extensive trading in copper between Cappadocia and Asshur, the capital Assyrians named after their chief god, Assur.

By the eighth century BC, under kings like Tiglath-Pileser III (774–727 BC) and Sargon II (721–705 BC), the Near East had become the Assyrians' playground. They were an incomparably strong military regime when other powers, Egypt, Syria, the Hittites, the Mitanni, or the Babylonians, once their equal, had weakened or disappeared from the lists of rivals. At last Assyria could terrorize her neighbors and create at Nineveh, Asshur, Kalah (modern Nimrud, the biblical Halah), and Carchemish cities that rivaled Babylon itself. The accommodating neighbor on the upper Tigris had become the neighborhood bully!

The Assyrians took the empire of Sargon I of Akkad as a model—they even named one of their own emperors Sargon II—because they knew how the Akkadians had used the following principles: 1) divide and conquer; 2) unite and rule. Some areas they ruled directly; some they ruled through client rulers (native kings who towed the line and paid tribute), and some they conquered and dispersed, like Israel in 721 BC. Henceforth the Jews of Israel were known as the "Ten Lost Tribes." [56]

The Jews of Judah, paying tribute to the Assyrians, had every reason to distrust their northern kin, the population of Israel, separated from them since after King Solomon's son's reign. Israel, before it was destroyed in 722 BC by the Assyrian kings Shalmaneser V and Sargon II, had been plotting against Judah. The Judeans were proud of their survival and grateful to the Lord for it. The Lord may have saved them from Assyria only to permit their testing by the Chaldeans under Nebuchadnezzar II, who in 586 BC carried the cream of their society—some ten thousand people—off to Babylon in an exile known as the (first) Babylonian Captivity.[57]

The account of Assyria in Palestine found in 2 Kings is very pro-Judah and anti-Israel. The Judeans attributed Israel's fall to the Lord's punishment for following heathen laws, setting up shrines to pagan gods called *baals* and following a corrupt king named Jeroboam, who, it must be pointed out, was a freedom fighter from the point of view of the northern population of Israel. Solomon had overtaxed the northerners and sent them into Phoenicia as indentured slaves to pay off his debts to a Phoenician king. When the Judean King Rehoboam announced that he intended to raise taxes even more than Solomon, Jeroboam took up the cause of Israel.

This second book of Kings does not mention that the Judeans, like most of their neighbors in western Asia (considered tributary or client states by Assyria) were themselves split between a pro-Assyrian and an anti-Assyrian party. The Jews' main concern was saving their necks and homes, not their souls. Whatever the Judeans may have thought about their kin in Israel, that northern kingdom was not destroyed because of pagan worship. During the 730s BC the Israelite King Hoshea kept up his tribute to Assyria *and survived,* despite the fact that Assyria was a polytheistic pagan master.[58] After the Assyrians conquered Syria in 732 BC, Israel, seeing that Assyrian attention was turning to the east, was tempted to rebel against clientage and tribute, and thought that an anti-Assyrian Phoenician alliance would result in her independence.

In Judah, King Ahaz, who died the year Assyria squashed Babylon (727 BC), had been paying tribute to Nineveh, too.[59] Indeed, he had said to Tiglath-Pileser, the Assyrian ruler, "I am your servant and your son," a servile utterance made only to enlist Assyrian help against Israel's planned invasion of Judah.[60] Ahaz kowtowed to Assyria just as Hoshea of Israel had. He even obeyed the Assyrian king in redesigning the altar of the Lord in his temple at Jerusalem, the one used for the sabbath service![61] Only when Hoshea began to foment a rebellion against Assyria with Egypt did Assyria's Shalmaneser V crush Israel. Both Israel and Judah cooperated with Assyria when they thought it to their advantage because they had no chance of survival otherwise. Judah's precarious independence derived from Ahaz's willingness to pay off the Assyrians until 727 BC, a policy that was fiercely debated by different Judean factions, as formerly the same policy was in

Israel. The two kingdoms of Israel and Judah were no different in their desire to survive at any cost. Judah's cooperation with the pagan monarch of Assyria was hardly consistent with fidelity to the Lord, and if the role Judah played vis-à-vis Assyria sounds more principled in the reign of King Hezekiah, son of Ahaz, it is because the historian who wrote up the reports in the book of Kings was ill-disposed to the Ten Lost Tribes of Israel and well disposed to Judah. He conveniently forgot the willingness with which Judah, too, had payed off Assyria, and would again.

King Hezekiah suceeded Ahaz, and the prophet Isaiah discouraged him from cooperating with Assyria. Later on, Judah bought off the Assyrians with thirty talents of gold and other valuables after Sennacherib's attack of 701 BC, thereby reducing the risk of her annihilation.[62] Under Hezekiah, her king, Judah narrowly survived Sennacherib's attack on Jerusalem (690 BC) when illness struck down the Assyrian army. Judah attributed her victory to the Lord, but the plague seems to have been responsible instead. Anyway, Assyria already possessed most of Judah's towns by this time. The Judeans were no longer rich enough for Assyria to care about.

In the early sixth century, Judah was conquered by Chaldea (586 BC) among whose citizens were "New Babylonian" astronomers, mathematicians, imperialists, and aesthetes. Nebuchadnezzar II's hanging gardens and palace at Babylon were renowned. The Chaldeans decided to free themselves from Assyrian control. Their intense study of astronomy, by which they thought they could better understand politics, set them into motion against Nineveh. With the Medes, relative newcomers to Iran, they reduced Nineveh (612 BC) and another Assyrian city, Carchemish (605 BC), to rubble. Assyria was no more. Thus, a shift in Mesopotamian political power determined Judah's fate at this point, not her religious purity or its lack. Now the Medes were convinced that in the absence of Assyria, they should enrich themselves in Asia Minor at the expense of the Lydians. While they were thus occupied the Persians, who had been subject to Mede control, freed themselves.

Realpolitik—practical politics—determined Judah's fate, as it determined that of the Medes, Lydians, Persians, and Assyrians. Jeremiah understood that the Jews were not faithful to the Lord, but it didn't take prophets to see that when a power vacuum was created on the banks of the Tigris, there would be a number of nations who would try to fill it. As it turned out, Persia did just that. In 539 BC, King Cyrus of Persia absorbed both the Medes and the Chaldeans, and sent the Jews home to Jerusalem with funds to rebuild their Temple. Cyrus inaugurated the very first Marshall Plan known to history.

As for the Jews, adversity taught them self-reliance and patience and brought out the best in their religion while they were surrounded by foreign folks not of their own faith. The idea of the brotherhood of all men under the Fatherhood of the same God began in Mesopotamia, during the Babylonian Exile. Jews developed these ideas in the land of those *goyim* [Yiddish, gentiles]. "Gentile," by the way, is a fascinating word. It is Latin in derivation, referring to the *gens* or clan. Jews would use it to distance themselves from non-Jews. Christians, who were non-Jews, would use it to distance themselves from nonbelievers in Christ, especially but not exclusively, the Jews. From *gens* came such words as "gentlefolk," "gentleman," and "gentle," meaning in every case, superior, well born, of good breeding. Who could have thought that a word that sounds so genteel, so considerate, has produced so much discrimination? "Discrimination," by the way, is a fascinating word. It comes from the Latin *discriminare,* to divide up, discern. "Discrimination," like "gentile," has exhibited the most exaggerated swings in meaning, from rejection based on contempt to approval based on refinement.

"Mesopotamia" also gave the world multiple messages. Semantically, it meant a land in the middle (of two rivers), but its many civilizations were never just middling. In this garden between the rivers was cultivated a common Sumerian heritage. Grafted to its stock were Semitic, Indo-European, and Asian slips that blossomed over time to produce diverse, and frequently, though not invariably, wholesome fruits—a harvest called civilization.

3

Forever Egypt

SPLENDID ISOLATION?

EGYPT'S "RED" LANDS, HER DESERTS, LONG PROTECTED her from the invasions that Mesopotamians endured. Egyptologists reject an old theory that Egypt's earliest kings were really Sumerians in disguise who, having invaded Upper Egypt before 3100 BC, taught Egyptians everything they knew, including hieroglyphic writing.[1] Yet foreign influences on Egypt's development cannot be altogether ruled out. B. G. Trigger thinks Sumerian and Semitic experience influenced Egyptian writing, but that influence came from the eastern Mediterranean (the Levant) and the Delta, and not from Upper Egypt.[2]

Although there is no agreement as to why the Egyptians began writing when they did, we marvel at the originality of their efforts. Egyptians, unlike Sumerians, preserved their original pictographs, combining them with alphabetic symbols. It was a system that did not require them to sacrifice the beauty of pictures. With three thousand years of history in which to luxuriate, Egyptians had the ultimate luxury—time.[3] They did not need a more efficient system. The famous Egyptologist Sir Alan Gardiner pointed out that the Narmer Palette, an important archaeological find from the unification era (3100 BC), lacked writing, communicating only by pictures.[4] Once Upper Egypt absorbed Lower (c. 3100 BC) by force, all Egypt got absorbed in writing. Although Egyptians were slower to develop writing than Mesopotamians, their attention span was longer! They were still using hieroglyphics when the Romans took over Egyptian government, long after cuneiform ceased to be a viable mode of communication.

The notion that Sumerian kings ruled Egypt in disguise is a reminder that people have long associated Egypt with mystery and magic, an association that has pyramided into the most irrational fantasies. One of these is the New Age culture's preoccupation with pyramid power, the fantasy that pyramids release energy that defies the laws of physics but relieves stress, that most feared disease of the postindustrial era. With such a shambling gait has this four-sided triangular "wheel"—the pyramid—come full circle, back to its starting point of irrationalism. When moderns turn to antiquity for emotional release from a present that seems too stressful, they should pause to consider how irksome a culture as controlled, superstitious, prescriptive, and exclusionary as ancient Egypt's would seem if they were suddenly obliged to live in it. Not magical release from life's cares, but unremitting toil in the most controlled of cultures was the average Egyptian's lot.

Ancient Egypt, like every other civilization, was afflicted by superstition and romanticism. We no longer attribute its splendid feats of engineering to the supernatural. We understand that Egypt's engineers had to overcome romanticism and superstition, too, or their colossal monuments, the fruit of mathematical and physical knowledge, would never have been built. Superstition is the least mysterious of all man's mental processes. It is the most understandable, given his physical and hence emotional fragility. Moderns who think Egypt was mysterious would never dream of attributing contemporary engineering feats to the occult.

Unfortunately, some textbooks treat Egypt in a way that trivializes her history by romanticizing it, making it appear as exotic as Hollywood movies and Agatha Christie's novel *Death on the Nile* once made it out to be.[5] Exotic is merely a synonym for the unknown, not the unknowable. The unknown *always* seems mysterious until we understand it thoroughly. Egyptians did not regard themselves as exotic, even if they were profoundly immersed in building pyramids to permit pharaohs to live forever. If Egypt had in fact been run by Sumerians, they would have learned from the Sumerian tale of Gilgamesh, once a real ruler, that not even kings can hope to achieve eternal life. Gilgamesh was advised by the Sumerian Noah to make the most of this life and to cherish his family rather than chase after the impossible dream of eternal life. That kind of grown-up wisdom might have saved Egyptian peasants the labor of piling so much stone on stone. The pyramids were pharaonic piles that caused everyone in the Old Kingdom discomfort in the end, until economic necessity and public unrest brought the very wasteful Age of Pyramids, or Old Kingdom, to a halt around 2200 BC.

It takes distance and objectivity for people to see exoticism or absurdity, let alone waste, in a contemporary setting. A missile defense system, as yet less well engineered than the ancient pyramids, may yet prove as unrealizable a means of achieving national security as they were. The Egyptians, like moderns, used symbols and irrational goals to motivate people to make sacrifices. Irrationality in any age is the ultimate exoticism. At least pyramids did not emit any kind of harmful energy, though they still radiate beauty. Will anyone be able to say as much for a missile defense system five thousand years from now?

Though her Red Lands spared Egypt some invasions, she was still vulnerable to penetration on her border with Nubia, the biblical Kush, now mostly the Sudan, and at the Nile delta in Lower Egypt.[6] Nubians attacked

Upper Egypt before unification (3100 BC), when Upper Egypt was a prosperous community of large-scale pottery makers with a capital at Hierakon-
polis. The noble descendants of these manufacturers ultimately took over
and unified Egypt's "Two Lands"—their own Upper Egypt, toward the
equator, and Lower Egypt near the Delta.[7] Thus Egypt, a land long protected from conquest by deserts, was herself the first to penetrate Egypt, a
singular instance of self-absorption and a near approach to political incest
in a country where incestuous unions were common practice.

Upper Egypt once had enough rainfall to sustain woods that fueled its
pottery kilns until rainfall declined around 3500 BC. The woods dried up,
and the pottery magnates moved closer to the river. Only cracked pots
were left behind—fifty million pieces have been found. On the Nile's banks
the former industrialists took up farming, crowding out smaller holdings of
lesser folk, perpetuating the class cleavage they had already made as pot-
ters.[8] First with pots, then with produce, they substituted one kind of earth-
enware for another. Upper Egypt also shipped ideas to Lower Egypt, ideas
that eventually helped unify the Two Lands. From Upper Egypt came 1) a
death cult based on the survival of political leaders, 2) picture writing on a
paperlike product not yet papyrus, and 3) Horus, the hawk-headed sky
god. All these cultural products of Upper Egypt were older than kingship
itself, now demoted to "proto-kingship" (beginner's kingship)[9] as Egyptologists attempt to piece together the story of Egypt's unity.

That story is a whodunit as intriguing as Agatha Christie's novel, with
pictographs carved on Narmer's Palette serving as important clues. The
Palette, a roughly triangular piece of carved slate, was found by an archaeologist digging at Kom el-Ahmer in 1898. On one side was Narmer, nicknamed "Mean Catfish," now thought the victor over the king of Lower
Egypt. Wearing the tall white crown of Upper Egypt, Narmer appears on
one side of the Palette wielding a mace over the head of his kneeling opponent, on which rests Narmer's fist. The downed figure represents King
Wash, whose position clearly indicates that he was all washed up. The
hawk-headed god, Horus, presides over this capitulation. Horus was the
forerunner of other national birds of prey whose privilege it would be to triumph over the weak, the roadkill of history. On the reverse of the Palette,
Narmer also wears the short red crown once associated exclusively with
Lower Egypt. The fact that he wears both crowns indicates that he was
more than a warrior—he was also a semiotician, and a clever politician.

Early in the last century, the name of Egypt's unifier and first dynast was
thought to have been Menes. As late as the mid twentieth century Sir Alan
Gardiner thought Menes's identity was still a "scholarly controversy."[10]
More recently scholars have agreed that Menes was Narmer, the name
Menes ("the enduring") being a title Narmer adopted.[11] Narmer-Menes
may have ruled Upper Egypt before he conquered the north, but he was

apparently preceded by other strong southern men—Skorpion, Ka, and Aha (the "Fighter").[12] Most of these earlier leaders from Upper Egypt have not yet found their way into textbooks, overshadowed by Narmer's greater triumph and by clouds of unknowing. Skorpion may have been the man portrayed on a damaged mace head wearing the short red crown once thought to have originated in Lower Egypt. Since this mace head is older than Narmer's Palette, the "traditional" crown of Lower Egypt is now believed to have started out as headgear of Upper Egypt!

The Sweet Smell of Success

The tall white Crown, the *Kha Hodhit,* of Upper Egypt was soon combined with the short red one, *Kha Dashrit,* to make a dashing bit of haberdash-ery—the double crown of Egypt.[13] The Egyptian word for this crown was *Pi Skhent,* meaning "The Embracer." Greeks later called it *Pschent* and may have pronounced it like our word scent. The double crown had a coiled snake or *uraeus* protruding out the front end. Just how long was the con-queror coiled and ready to spring north towards the Delta? Did Narmer pack his Palette before the conquest? Palettes such as this one were designed to hold cosmetics—eye paint or face cream. We owe our preoccu-pation with skin cream to the Egyptians, who worried about the drying effects of sun on skin. Did they keep a sharp watch out for melanoma? When Narmer made war on Wash, did he pack his cosmetics in this Palette? We know he did not need perfume. He had his own scent. Egyp-tians believed Pharaoh exuded a unique perfume. Who could resist a mus-cular guy like Narmer, fashionably coiffed, ruler of Two Lands, a sweet-smelling hero who went into battle carrying a cosmetic case? If this were the case, he certainly traveled more lightly than King Nebuchadnez-zar, Alexander the Great, Gentleman Johnny Burgoyne, or Napoleon Bonaparte.[14]

The double crown came only slowly to symbolize the despotic power of a pharaoh. Unification meant sacrificing old familiar forms. History is hard work and poses many riddles, and that is no tea party. Speaking of which, remember Alice in Wonderland?[15] She was a drop-in guest at the Mad Hat-ter's tea party, as we are droppers-in on ancient Egypt, with its own mad matter of hats—or crowns! Alice never really felt comfortable at the tea party because she could not solve the riddles asked. Experts in early Egypt, like the Mad Hatter's guests, are expected to solve riddles about Predynas-tic and Early Dynastic Egypt. Like Alice, they must decode the significance of invasions that may or may not have been conquests, of kings who may or not have been real. Some are thought to be "realer" than others, while others hide under aliases or nicknames. The problem of the pharaoh's hats (crowns) is still a riddle, very much like those Alice was asked to solve by the tea party's guests, Dormouse and March Hare, who did not, after all, explain them!

Egyptians irrigated and so kept green for three thousand years the memory of their diverse past. Pharaohs continued to wear two crowns long after the Two Lands were one. Provincial Egyptian noblemen called *nomarchs* (governors) tried periodically for several centuries after 3100 BC to undo the union but were foiled by pharaoh's growing power. The first king of the Second Dynasty, Hotepskhemwy, slaughtered thousands of men who resisted political change. The nomarchs were dwarfed by the superior resources of the pharaohs.

In the Fifth Dynasty, which began in 2470 BC, scribes compiled a list of the kings and data of the first four dynasties. They carved it on a stone that turned up in Palermo, Sicily. This Palermo Stone bears the names of kings, their mothers, and the Nile's annual flood level, plus some of the important events of those reigns. Royal Moms were important because the descent of Egypt's throne was matrilineal, determined through the mother, rather than patriarchal, determined through the father. The Great Royal Queen (kings could have several queens and a harem full of concubines, too) was great indeed. If she produced no son, her eldest daughter helped establish the succession by marrying the son of another wife or even of a concubine. Pharoahs often married their half sisters and, sometimes, their own daughters, in order to secure their claim to the throne.[16] If Egypt's pharaohs owed not only their lives to Mom, but their thrones, too, how could they have escaped being momma's boys? The treatment accorded their mommies' mummies was solicitous. Many royal mothers were buried in elegant pyramids. The pharoahs recognized their debt to their moms, perhaps the last sons who did on so monumental a scale. Yet, while legitimacy passed from one heiress to another, power was generally exercised by the males who married them. Clearly, a woman's "place" was in the tomb.

Cultural diversity, the product of unification, was, as usual, burdensome. To pacify the nobility, some of whom were homesick for familiar bric-a-brac, the First Dynasty gave them land, treasure, and even permission to identify an old god with a new one. The conquered, thus mollified by meaningful symbolism, gradually got over the defeat of Lower by Upper Egypt, though not without some resistance. One way nobles resisted was by having themselves buried in their hometowns rather than near the pharaoh in Memphis, capital of the Old Kingdom. They were dead serious. It was safer to protest when dead rather than alive. For hundreds of years after unification, noblemen were buried in their hometowns in an upright position. Was it a sign of lingering reluctance to take defeat lying down? Only gradually did they forsake hometown burials, and consent to burial in tombs laid out horizontally around pharaoh's pyramid like the rays of the setting sun.

Pharaoh was Re—the Sun God. The nobles were *his* rays, in death as in life, supine symbols of his shining preeminence. If Louis XIV, who built Versailles, thought he was the first Sun King, he was much mistaken.

Egyptian sun king symbolism was more than semiotics. Orthodox religious belief required that a nobleman's survival in life and in death depended on subservience to the king. The pharaoh as sun god (Old Sol) was also Old Sole for he was the sole hope—indeed, the soul's hope—for the nobility to enjoy eternal after life. Pharaoh had become Savior as well as Ruler, for only in proximity to his mummy, buried in his pyramid tomb, could noblemen hope to share in eternity. Royal mummy, pyramid tomb, dead nobleman. The eternal triangle.

THE OLD KINGDOM

If Egypt was long outside the mainstream of civilization, once unified, she entered the stream and did swimmingly, resisting invasion for several hundred years, though not the temptation to invade others. Herodotus, Father of Greek History, wrote 2600 years later that Egypt was the gift of the Nile! The Nile carried mud from Upper Egypt and redistributed it along the banks as it flowed toward the Delta, the Nile's last gift. New mud meant renewed fertility and bigger crops when the waters receded. We're talking wheat here, a yield directly related to the Nile's flood tide, and measured with a *Nilometer*.[17] The very word Egypt comes from an Egyptian word for the Delta's floodlands, *Agubto*. The Greeks mistook the Egyptian word for the whole country, spelling it *Aigubtos*. Naturally the Greeks got it mixed up. It was all Egyptian to them! Their word *Aigubtos* became all Egypt to us.

The Egyptians never knew in advance how much new mud the river would deposit, or how high the waters of each inundation would be. There were good years with good floods, and bad years with bad floods. The latter meant famine, as was noted in Genesis 41. Usually, there was enough rain. The blanket of rich black dirt along the Nile's banks gave Egypt its Black Lands,[18] where wealth was raised in fields irrigated by a *shadoof* and the sweat of peasants. One kind of *shadoof* consisted of a wheel to which buckets were attached. Each bucket was filled when it met the Nile in a downward swoop, and each was then tipped into a canal that led outward to the fields. This technique persists into the twenty-first century. A simpler *shadoof* was simply one bucket on a long pole, a counterpoised sweep which emptied the bucket into a ditch. The vast majority of Egyptians were peasants, serfs who paid taxes on land they did not own. Their taxes were measures of wheat, the number of which was based on calculations made by government assessors of their ripening grain. And that is how the first IRS—Internal River Surveyors—began.

The river beckoned. The current flowed northward, the prevailing winds blew southward. Little effort was needed for a trip in either direction. Merchants sailed into action two thousand years before wheeled vehicles or horses were introduced into Egypt. Living pharaohs made frequent trips up and down the Nile to inspect their kingdom and see to it that their divine presence was familiar everywhere. Dead pharaohs were given one last trip on the Nile—from the eastern shore, where their palaces were located, to the western bank, where, after the Third Dynasty, their pyramids were built. When a pharaoh "went west" it was as a corpse.

More informal—and delightful—was the nobleman's pleasure trip in a skiff made of papyrus reeds, a trip to the Delta marshes, perhaps, where he and his family enjoyed a day hunting wildfowl. Quality time. A wall painting from the Theban tomb of a scribe, Nebamun, shows him standing in the prow of his boat surrounded by lotus blossoms, butterflies, and wild ducks, which he hopes to attract by holding three live, squawking ones in one hand. In the other, poised aloft, is his sharpened throwing stick. His small daughter clutches his leg and the family cat nips a duck who tries to escape. His wife stands in the poop holding a bouquet of wilting lotus blossoms and looks uncomfortable, as many wives would be on a duck shoot.

She would not have to clean or cook the ducks; female slaves did her housework. Servants enabled upper-class ladies to escape the tedium and drudgery of housework their poor sisters accepted as their lot. It is probable that this lady was beginning to wonder when they would dock for dinner. Food was no problem. The Nile's banks were regular health-food delis, where fruit and vegetables grew in abundance, and just out of sight, vineyards provided wine for noblemen. The lower classes drank beer made from fermented bread and thought themselves lucky if there was any bread left over. In the waters beneath the skiff, fish swam in abundance. Poultry and fish were low-calorie staples of the Egyptian diet. Is that why they all looked so thin? Look closely. The figures on temple walls are all slim, eternally young. Good buns, good pecs, good advertisements for healthy living. But before they put up their ads for the very first Club Med, these Egyptians needed advertising space and a reason to advertise. They found both in an Old Kingdom that emphasized eternal life, at first for the pharaoh only, and later, his nobles, too, and provided the necessary space to illustrate it—on pyramid walls and tombs. The sleek Egyptian upper classes forever put their best foot forward, strolling in a paradise of natural abundance and unnatural beauty, in other words, beauty illustrated by the strictest artistic convention.[19]

The Old Kingdom, or Age of the Pyramids

The early dynastic period (3100–2700 BC) had been experimental and tentative. The Old Kingdom (2700–2200 BC) that followed was the least tentative regime that ever existed. One historian put it this way: that the step pyramid of Zoser,[20] whose reign was either the first or second of the Third Dynasty which began the Old Kingdom, lacked any preparatory phase.[21] "Just do it!" could have been Zoser's motto. Not tentative at all. Zoser's was the first stone building on earth, designed by a brilliant architect, Imhotep, a technocrat made "Chancellor of the King of Lower Egypt" and later, god. Zoser's was remembered as an especially glorious reign. He pushed Egypt's southern border to the First Nile cataract, sent an expedition to Sinai for turquoise and copper, and subdued the Arabian tribesmen. In this way he opened up the deserts to the east to exploit their stone and metal. Imhotep was eventually identified with wisdom itself—something to which not all gods, let alone kings or university professors, can aspire. Together Zoser and Imhotep founded the Egyptian Way of Death, one by designing a tomb at Saquara, and the other, by dying and being buried in it.

Egyptologists have spent much of their time studying the pharaonic cult. In contemporary usage the word "cult" has negative connotations. Cult members are extreme in their behavior and never recognize that their cult is only a passing fad. But every cult was once somebody else's spiritual reality, and for them, the truest of the eternal verities. Whether to regard a system of belief as a religion or a cult depends primarily on one's own prejudices, and secondarily on those of other people. The terms themselves, like crooked dice, are loaded.

Egyptians had a concept of divine justice, called *maât,* a principle that clashed with their resignation to the disorder and injustice they thought the basis of the universe.[22] Their pessimism about the nature of the universe is belied by the joyfulness of their wall paintings, the cheery figures so like the Sunday morning comics of our childhood, with everything brightly colored, two dimensional, lined up in tidy rows. The Egyptians were not just pessimists, but cosmic pessimists. They settled for a strong pharaoh to overcome the adversities that a disorderly universe might otherwise produce. Pharaohs more easily calmed their subjects' fears when they were strong and Egypt prospered. But they were not always so lucky. Although the mere assertion of pharaoh's priestly (i.e., magical) powers usually satisfied the people, it also, oddly enough, deflected attention of historians away from him as governor. Unfortunately, pharaoh's mystique hypnotized not just his contemporaries, but modern scholars, too. Only recently have Egyptologists been able to set aside fascination with pharaoh's divinity and pay attention to pharaoh's governance.[23]

Egyptians believed that their pharaoh was a god among gods, and if properly preserved by natron, a natural salt used to preserve his mummy and entrails, would never lead "god's cattle" astray. Then pharaoh could take care of them eternally. Calling men cattle is hardly politically correct nowadays, but the notion persisted that humans were just animals compared to gods and kings. On the other hand, the gods of Egypt were tactful enough not to call people cattle to their faces. Indeed, the gods themselves posed as animals for the people. Artists, who are not easily fooled by politicians or gods, stubbornly depicted people as people. If, as is true, they also represented their human subjects as more beautiful or manly or youthful than they were in fact, they did so because their livelihood required them to make a few happy changes in everyone's appearance. Would an artist depict fat, homely, and insecure folks on temple walls? What kind of advertisement for faith would that have been? What priestly patron wanted his parishioners to march into eternity, where pharaoh was god, looking less than confident and physically fit? Artists worked for priests, courtiers, or royalty who made the intellectual systems that explained and rationalized the excesses of authoritarianism—military, judicial, spiritual, and economic. The ancient Egyptian equivalent of systems analysts were the bureaucrats, especially the priests, who believed that the world was essentially chaotic, with no intelligibility but for the pharaonic despotism that kept out confusion. Smile, please. This advertisement was paid for by His Highness and his bureaucrats for your benefit.

Workers in Egypt did not patronize artists. Workers lived in mud huts with little if any furniture. Their burials were not elaborate. Having few possessions, they could not provision corpses for the afterlife. Not that they were entitled to an afterlife. During the Old Kingdom only the pharaoh and his closest noble associates were. It was the first of many entitlements that only the elite received, and the exclusion of commoners from eternity was enforced until the Middle Kingdom. Excluded from eternity, ordinary folks paid for pyramids, the logo of the Old Kingdom.

Most ancient Egyptians were illiterate serfs. Because we live in a democratic society we have the ability to question our political servants and put them on the spot, as ancient Egyptians could not theirs. If we fail to control our elected officials, who can we blame but ourselves when we see that *maât* has broken down? Do our leaders prefer to protect corporations and global trade rather than workers and the environment? Should we be surprised if we find that we are providing socialism for the rich and capitalism for the poor?

How fragile were the hopes of ancient Egyptians for a better future! They rested in theory on the fate of pharaoh; in fact on wishes and dreams, because, as Gilgamesh learned back in Sumer, no man lives forever, not even kings. Now, when many Americans lack requirements for a secure future—health coverage and a protected income—what can we say about confidence in *our* future? Are the foundations for it laid on something more solid than wishes and dreams?

It is the rare textbook that hints at the exploitative nature of Egyptian society. Authors shy away from words associated with the philosophy of Friedrich Engels and Karl Marx.[24] From the Russian Revolution at the beginning of the twentieth century to the fall of the Soviet Union at its end, textbook authors only hesitantly, if at all, raised questions concerning the exploitation of labor. Textbooks are bought by conservative school boards, people loathe to upset the status quo and alienate vested interests. Where the Old Kingdom was concerned, one textbook states that "Artisans, peasants, and slaves nourished the whole system."[25] Labor is acknowledged briefly, and then dismissed. Few have gone so far as another textbook that absolves the Old Kingdom of *any* exploitation of its population whatsoever. It says only that public works were performed in militias "commanded by civil officials" as if the very fact that peasants served in *militias,* symbols of our own postcolonial independence, absolved the Old Kingdom of their mistreatment of militiamen. This text fails to mention that Egyptian peasants were forced to serve in such militias. Is it helpful to describe the Old Kingdom as "a product of cooperative need" rather than one "grounded in exploitation"?[26] The E-word (exploitation) is used here, but only to deny its applicability. In fact, militias were the prime means for deploying laborers to build pyramids. In the Old Kingdom there was always a need for forced labor on public works. A peasant knew he would benefit directly if the works were irrigation works, for then he might hope for a better crop. But most labor went into pyramids. Indeed, according to one analysis, the Old Kingdom found it necessary to keep villagers employed on several pyramids at once. No pharoah could predict—lacking a pharometer—how long he had still to live. Thus every pharoah had to keep laborers building his own pyramid, and his wife's or mother's as well. His successor, finding those of his predecessor still incomplete, had to finish them, and at once begin construction of his own tomb, his wife's, his mother's, and any children who predeceased him.

To get another perspective on Egyptian exploitation, it is interesting to note that Napoleon Bonaparte, who hoped to defeat England in 1799 by closing off England's Mediterranean route to India, took this opportunity to occupy Egypt. There he calculated, while sitting in the shade of the Great Pyramid, that the three pyramids at Giza contained enough stones to build a wall around France ten feet tall and one foot thick! Napoleon did not lay a permanent hold on Egypt, but he did lay permanent hold on much of her artwork, so much that he was able to supply an Italian museum of Egyptology (at Turin) and France's own great collection of Egyptian artifacts (the

Louvre's) with carloads of stolen artwork. Egypt's conservative and controlled art forms contrasted sharply with her sense of cosmic disorder, unlike their neighbors, the Hebrews, who posited a basic justice in the universe, and Greeks, who perceived order and harmony in it. Bonaparte was neither an artist nor a philosopher nor a judge. But he knew enough to know what he liked. Other peoples' valuables.

Everyone tends to view exploitation differently. Some shrug and say that unless people have expectations for fair treatment and can perceive alternate lifestyles for themselves as realizable goals, they cannot be exploited. Men have argued that women, slaves, and other marginalized groups were not exploited because they never thought of acquiring privileges like education, good housing, the better things of life. Their arguments are misleading. Exploitation is not about the acquiescence of the exploited, made passive through custom and the fear of breaking it. Exploitation is about the determination of the stronger to assure that all custom reinforces the privilege of the elite class. Then the privileged people insist that the underprivileged grumble only because they are lazy or otherwise inferior. In Egypt, the pyramids represented the inferiority of everyone else to pharoah, a god dead or alive.

The purpose of pyramids was political and economic as well as religious. Egypt's villages were kept from fighting one another by obliging their cooperation in pyramid building. This prevented them from consuming their wealth and manpower in warfare, while promoting a growing sense of loyalty to the state. The personal sacrifice of peasants organized in labor gangs (militias) has been compared with modern ideas of sacrifice for the communal good during patriotic wars.[27] Indeed, the Cold War arms race which brought so much prosperity to the U.S. economy in the period after 1945 and before the Soviet collapse in the 1990s was not unlike the pyramid age, also known, until its collapse, as a prosperous era. Nobody questioned government much in either age. But to equate a lack of questioning or protest on the part of common laborers with voluntarism is to ignore conditions of misery and terror under which people have labored. To ignore the necessity that controls the laborer is to wink at his exploitation. By such happy oversight do historians of ancient Egypt not only protect their database, but defend it, justifying the status quo, and even, as in Egypt itself, sanctifying it, perhaps because that was the way the ancient Egyptians rationalized their divine pharaonic system! Just as some dog owners come to resemble their pets, so do some historians appropriate the assumptions of the elite protagonists of a given era and ludicrously come to resemble them.

Eventually the pyramids ceased to be built and the Old Kingdom shut down. It is not generally agreed as to what caused this collapse. Such things as "deep-rooted inner weaknessess" and "general malaise" are said to have "ripped apart the fabric" of Sixth Dynasty rule.[28] Were rulers forced into bankruptcy by such conspicuous and superfluous consumption? Was conspicuous consumption connected to exploiting the masses? Was there no connection between overspending and the civil war and invasion that followed?

Of course there were connections. The direct result of overspending on pyramids was civil war and contention between noblemen for power and income. Pepy II of the twenty-third-century BC, who was reputed to have reigned for ninety-four years, began to experience contempt from his nobility fifty years into his reign. In the last quarter of it, poverty afflicted Memphis, then the capital city, and the social hierarchy began to break down. Redford does not think there was a "diminution" of prosperity at the end of the Old Kingdom—he denies that the pyramids were "white elephants"—and notes that the economy of Egypt suffered because pharaoh was at the end giving away too much of his land to the temples. This scholar thinks "a shrinking tax base" is a possible clue to the collapse of the Old Kingdom. One can imagine that more taxable income might have been available if the labor on pyramids had been diverted to build warehouses for grain, new irrigation and drainage capabilities, and a commercial fleet capable of reaching more customers. Redford, however, does not believe the economy of the Old Kingdom was market-driven, but worked on a different basis: "the proliferation of (priestly) estates seems beneficial, not deleterious."[29] In the Delta region the loss of pharaonic lands (given as endowments to temples) weakened the regime. Such grants, a kind of corporate welfare Egyptian style, became more frequent toward the end of the Old Kingdom, creating a "shrinking tax base" that might have been a "clue" to its collapse. Desiccation in northeastern Egypt at the end of the Sixth Dynasty did not help, and (though Redford does not think Egypt market-driven) neither did decreases in trade with northern and southern neighbors. Diminished trade created shortages, demographic problems, corruption, and arrests.[30] The Egyptians' own analysis of the decay was xenophobic. They felt that invaders from Palestine and Syria were responsible for decline. Redford doubts that this was the case, since recent research indicates that the ultimate causes of collapse were "ecology, sociology, and demography." [31] None of these, however, prevents us from thinking that if the masses of Egyptians had been less exploited, and the classes less privileged, a less troubled adjustment to such problems might have been made. Was it coincidental that the social dissatisfaction that occurred universally during the First Intermediary Period (2200 BC to 2050 BC) followed the insouciance of the Old Kingdom?

INTERMEDIARY REMARKS

The First Intermediary Period was filled with strife and competing authorities. It was not intermediary in the sense that one agency or agent negotiated between extreme positions. It was only in the sense that what happened, happened. There were no mediaries. Egypt waited to see which of its strongmen would bring order out of chaos. The Seventh and Eighth Dynasties (if these were really different and not just one) regarded Memphis as their capital.[32] The poorly documented and still largely unknown Ninth and Tenth Dynasties made theirs the northern town of Heracleopolis. The Eleventh Dynasty set itself up in Thebes, in Upper Egypt. A dilapidated papyrus, the Leyden papyrus, written hundreds of years later during the Nineteeth Dynasty, speaks of the topsy-turvy social relationships, the role of foreigners in Lower Egypt, the restriction of true Egyptian territory to Upper Egypt, and prolonged and aggravated revolution during this First Intermediary Period.[33]

Average people in troubled times seek comfort in religion, since holy truth appears to them to exist in a realm not vulnerable to invaders, of whom there are always too many, or to skeptics, of whom there are always too few. Egypt's native gods, so many that one writer refused even to estimate their number, comforted the perplexed citizenry during these troubled times as household pets comfort those bereft of human company at all times. Indeed, Egyptians seem to have made pets of their gods, to whom they gave the form of cows, bulls, crocodiles, jackals, hawks, falcons, rams, cats, lions, ibises, monkeys, vultures, snakes, even inanimate objects and certain forms of vegetation.[34] Surrounded on all sides by the images of their protective deities, no doubt the horrors of the First Intermediary Period seemed more bearable. The sun god, Re, father of all the other gods, eventually joined up with a local god of Thebes named Amun. The composite Amun-Re, with his wife, Mut, and son Khons, formed one of many near Eastern holy families who achieved maximum dignity during the period of Egypt's great empire (sixteenth to eleventh century BC). Before this merger of Re and Amun, Re, Heliopolis's sun god, seemed a bit standoffish to the average worshipper. During the Middle Kingdom, the power of this sun god set. The merged deity Amun-Re was closely associated with pharaoh, as Re had been, but also with the ram. Like many gods, it was easy to get his goat.

The Egyptians were devoted to another holy family, somewhat dysfunctional, but lovable. The father was a male fertility god named Osiris, whose wife was also a fertility goddess and his sister, Isis. This pair, joined in unholy matrimony, had a son named Horus who liked to masquerade as a falcon. At one point Osiris's brother Set chopped Osiris up like chicken liver. Isis picked up the pieces and put them back together, restoring Osiris to life. Incredibly, it was Osiris who was considered the giver of immortality, rising to become king of the dead and their judge, whereas Isis was restricted, like Rosie the Riveter after the return of the veterans of World War II, to women's work, mere fertility. One historian believes that Set and Horus had agreed to divide Egypt between them, but that Horus's dynastic ambitions, including marriage to his mother, Isis, unsettled Set.[35] He brought a lawsuit against Horus who promptly accused the plaintiff of murdering his father! From all appearances, Horus won, given his triumph in representing Egyptian unity. But his problems were not over. Horus, remember, was older than either his Father or his Mother who was also his aunt, and if Set was right, his wife. Relationships among the gods as in the royal dynasties get very confusing due to incest. Consequently, when Horus grew up, he was called both Horus the Elder and Horus the Child. Despite a traumatic childhood, he seems to have tolerated his multiple-personality syndrome. He had a high threshold for ambiguity. Not only was the child Horus father to the man, but he was also father to the god who was his father, and was a senior god himself! And, if Set were right about his marriage to his mother, he was even his own stepfather. With all this responsibility was it unfortunate that there were no child psychologists in Ancient Egypt? Still, Horus overcame all his hangups, and grew to adulthood, ever mindful of his child within.

Religion in Egypt was a topic kicked around for a long time. No halftime entertainment, her spiritual life was a continuum of play, a grandstand play that kept the Egyptian hierarchy—nobility, priests, pharaohs—quarterbacking until the culture fumbled short of the end zone and the Romans recovered. What they recovered was all of Egypt, but by then the play was over and, as far as Egyptians were concerned, the game was up!

DEMOCRACY IN EGYPT? THE MIDDLE KINGDOM

Long before it was, around 2000 BC or maybe a few decades earlier, the Middle Kingdom was born, founded by a vizier of a former pharaoh. A vizier was not only an adviser appointed by pharaoh to be his right-hand man, but was infinitely more important to pharaoh than an American vice president, since a vizier bore the title "Superintendent of all the works of the King."[36] That made him rather more like our chief justice of the Supreme Court combined with our Secretary of State. By the Middle Kingdom, when viziers were often nomarchs, they were being buried with symbols that referred to them as closely related to gods.[37]

This first vizier turned pharaoh was Amenemhat I, and his name indicates that the power of Amun began to rise in this period, after its eclipse during civil wars of the intervening period. Information about Amenemhet

I is very sketchy, but he seems to have determined to obtain the complete autocracy of the Old Kingdom rulers. He and his descendants ruled with an iron hand for two hundred years, and according to Sir Alan Gardiner, the Twelfth Dynasty kept the nomarchs dependent upon royal favors.[38] Amenemhat left a posthumous testament for his son, Senwosret I, which described his seizure of power as a "tramp" from the southern city of Elephantine, at the Nile's first cataract, north to the Delta where he made the "Asiatics" do the "dogwalk."[39]

The Middle Kingdom came to be known as the one that restored justice after nearly 150 years of civil chaos. Perhaps that is why it produced a number of "instruction texts" written by pharaohs to their sons—they had a lot to learn. There is reason to think that the sons of pharaohs paid no more attention to such advice than anyone else's sons in any age, and it would be foolhardy to credit the success of the Middle Kingdom to such instructions. Herodotus made a hero of the successor of Amenemhat I, crediting him with the consolidation of Egyptian rule over Lower Nubia, perhaps in reality the work of Senwosret III. Rulers of the Middle Kingdom were sculpted with careworn faces, apparently to impress their subjects that they were working hard on their behalf.[40] The sculpture, aided by more public works projects and expanded opportunities for rich merchants to make a bundle in foreign trade (to Syria, Palestine, Crete) convinced writers that the Middle Kingdom was socially responsible. It is believed to have advanced justice and to have democratized religion by permitting the poor to achieve everlasting life through the rites of mummification, once reserved for royalty and nobility. Because that process was prohibitively expensive, the rites remained theoretical for most people. In practice, the poor man, wrapped in a straw mat and thrown into a hole, or tossed into the Nile, could only hope that his soul would be found worthy of eternal life when weighed against the feather of justice. The poor man hoped to be allowed to plow his own little plot of ground in heaven, while the rich man in the Middle Kingdom looked forward to endless days at a fine vacation villa, one stocked with fine wine and roast duck to be consumed by finely dressed revellers. Heaven was another place where the classes did not mix.

The Middle Kingdom is packaged as a golden age in history, perhaps because of its stability.[41] Of course, one man's stability can be another man's depression or chaos. The strong pharaohs of the Middle Kingdom referred to themselves as shepherds of the god's flock, but they were only wolves so far as the conquered Nubians were concerned. They were predators who invaded Palestine and Syria, too, although they did not remain there. The militarism of the New Kingdom that followed really began in this golden age of "peace," stability, sincerity, commercialism, and democratic opportunity—depending on who was writing the history—that came to be associated with the Middle Kingdom, a most "enigmatic" period even for specialists.[42]

As any advertising man will tell you, an effective sales campaign depends on marketing and packaging. The Middle Kingdom was a hot item, attractively packaged as peaceful, just, and democratic, but no one should judge a package by its wrapper. The imperial activities of the Roman Republic (third to first century BC) also antedated by several centuries the formal creation of the Roman Empire. The first age of British mercantile or economic imperialism in the seventeenth and eighteenth centuries prepared the Victorian conscience for a new imperialism, one that claimed a duty to improve the moral fiber of subjugated peoples. Victorian imperialists soft-pedalled less pure motives such as national and economic interests and urged purer motives—self-defense and protection of client peoples. To win public approval for the costs of empire, governors abused native populations, demonstrating little practical concern for their well-being as opposed to their utility in providing goods and labor. In this way the colonized populations of the nineteenth century were forced to pay any overhead costs involved in their own subjugation.

The Middle Kingdom was already experimenting with empire. It thought it was "too hot not to cool down,"[43] but it did just that during the Second Intermediary Period (1786–1636 BC). This brought more chaos, a declining Thirteenth Dynasty, and competing puppet pharaohs ruling from Memphis and Lisht, dominated by their stronger viziers. Centralized control continued for another one hundred years. Egypt was still able to influence her neighbors abroad. Then came the Hyksos, foreigners who spoke the Semitic dialects of Phoenicia and Palestine and penetrated the eastern Delta (eighteenth century BC to 1586 BC). They ruled directly, taxing the Egyptian inhabitants of the Delta and Nile Valley, although without intervening directly to control their native affairs. Native Egyptians called the Hyksos the "Vile Asiatics," a racial slur.[44] Redford notes that these newcomers foreclosed on Egypt's mortgage, bringing about a period of great confusion, civil warfare, and universal insecurity.

Although the Egyptian priest Manetho, writing around 350 BC, believed the newcomers conquered the Delta area, Sir Alan Gardiner thought there had been no "whirlwind invasion," just "an earnest endeavour to conciliate" Egyptian locals and "to ape the weak Pharaohs whom they dislodged."[45] Redford, like Manetho, calls the Hyksos military conquerors.[46] Benson believes the Hyksos period is not yet understood.[47] Most textbooks have reverted to Manetho's early interpretation of the Hyksos as conquerors of the north. What no one disputes is that the Hyksos, Egypt's Fifteenth Dynasty, were strong men who posed as compassionate and pious conservatives by adapting their religious practices to those of Egypt, their Canaanite Baal worship to the worship of Amun-Re.[48] While they made a great effort to affect congeniality, they stole treasure from Egyptian cities like Memphis. They gave this treasure to their supporters in the Delta, unmindful of the fact that these were Egypt's precious resources and might have been better spent on the improvement of her infrastructure. The Hyksos made a great show of their piety and presented themselves at every possible occasion as rulers with kind hearts. Their theft of national resources indicates that flaunted piety may disguise a lack of ethics. People prove they are ethical by deeds that require personal sacrifice, while piety is too often attested by words and rituals. Most Egyptians thought the Hyksos stole the power of state and always regarded them as illegitimate. Whether it was by conquest or just by trickery, the Hyksos exercised power illegitimately. The preference of most Egyptians was for the regular pharaonic successor. When it came down to it, the Egyptians favored insiders over genial outsiders whose piety could not mask flagrant self-interest nor an irregular assumption of office. The Hyksos stole more than Egyptian treasure. They stole the office of pharaoh.

Toward the mid sixteenth century a Hyksos ruler named Apophis was driven from Middle Egypt under circumstances that remain unclear. His ouster may have been the work of Ahmose I, putative hero of the supposed battle of Avaris (c. 1560 BC) and founder of the Eighteenth Dynasty (1575–1308 BC). On the other hand, the hero may have been Ahmose's brother Kamose, credited by some historians with winning some contest over the Hyksos ten years earlier. Manetho never thought Ahmose the victor of Avaris, but only the negotiator of an agreement that left the Hyksos free to depart with 240,000 people and all their household posessions.[49] The problem with the so-called Battle of Avaris is that nothing in the way of records survives. All that does survive are autobiographical sketches of two soldiers who served under Ahmose and were rewarded for killing a few Hyksos in Avaris and in Canaan. These developments occurred without Egypt establishing a sustained presence in Palestine or southern Syria until the reign of Thutmose III (fifteenth century BC).[50] The two Egyptian servicemen did not leave any account of their subsequent reception in Egyptian society for posterity. Were they treated as heroes? Were their families cared for in their absence? Did they get their old jobs back after the war? Did they suffer psychologically from its horrors? When they grew old, did they look up their Hyksos adversaries and swap recollections of battle with them in some charming little Canaanite bistro?

If there was no battle of Avaris, perhaps the Hyksos left Egypt because of the sounds of volcanic activity in the Aegean? For on the volcanic island of Thera, now called Santorini, the earth was preparing for an eruption that would blow the lid off the cone-shaped mountain in the not-too-distant future. The Hyksos may have interpreted the rumblings as a sign of the gods' displeasure that they were still in the Delta.[51] Whatever the reason for their exit, Egyptians rejoiced when the Hyksos took a hike back to Canaan. There they resumed their worship of Canaanite deities, abandoning their feigned allegiance to Egyptian counterparts.[52] Ahmose I, founder of a dynasty that lasted 280 years, pursued the Hyksos into Palestine, ending danger on the northern frontier, initiating the Empire or New Kingdom era (1540–1070 BC) of Egypt's history. During this period Egypt conquered her fear of foreigners by foreign conquest. Payback time.

THE NEW KINGDOM OR EMPIRE

Queen Hatshepsut (1490–1468 BC) wore drag. Her adoption of male clothing included pharaoh's traditional beard, symbol of royal authority, which she tied on the same as any young male pharaoh would have done. Before it occurred to her to call herself pharaoh she let herself be sculpted as the perfect size 6 female she appears to have been when still just the wife of her half brother, Thutmose II. As such, she sits demurely, in rose-colored granite, with one hand resting on each thigh, no beard, prim and proper as you please. She was the daughter of Thutmose I and Queen Ahmose, the Great Royal Wife who bore no sons.

When her father died, Hatshepsut married her half brother, Thutmose II. Widowed early, with one small daughter, she became regent for her nephew, Thutmose III, whom she married. She shared the title of joint pharaoh with him, an unheard of piece of chutzpah, and had herself referred to in official documents with the masculine pronoun. Elsewhere she was styled "the female Horus." Her ability to manipulate language was as marked as her ability to manipulate the symbols of power and the men whom she persuaded to respect them. Her reign was criticized for its lack of military adventurism, though she may have led one expedition in person to Nubia. Had she been blamed for the loss of any military endeavor, she might have found herself dumped in favor of her male consort. Accordingly, she kept a low profile and used the successes of her father, Thutmose I, to represent the dynasty's military luster. She sent scientific expeditions in search of minerals and geological information to Punt, present-day Eritrea or Somaliland. But a punt was not a touchdown, and she was never considered a regular player.

Hatshepsut concerned herself (she would have said himself) with the arts and building up, not with warfare and tearing down. She supervised the construction of her fabulous cliffside tomb at Deir el-Bahri west of Thebes and the decoration of the two largest granite obelisks ever carved. These were placed near that complex, each obelisk a hundred feet long, engraved and polished within the space of seven months from bedrock to erection.[53]

It was not every pharaoh, especially a female one, who could obtain a seven-month's erection.

Yes, we know what Freud would say. But the queen did not need to envy anyone or anything when it came to creativity. She was her own man! She had balls! Not Egypt's first ruling queen,[54] she was the first and only queen to refer to herself as pharaoh.[55] Eventually she reigned as a joint pharoah, with Thutmose, her nephew and second husband. John Ray makes it clear that this was a co-regency "far from equal" and that Hatshepsut assumed its direction.[56] Gardiner wrote that there could be no doubt as to who was the senior Pharaoh, but that, after the twentieth year of her reign, she allowed Thutmose III to appear as her equal on various inscriptions.[57] It had been once been thought that Hatshepsut deprived Thutmose III of all power for over twenty-two years. More scholars now affirm that he actually enjoyed considerable authority in Hatshepsut's lifetime, especially in military matters.[58]

Hatshepsut busied herself making Egypt more beautiful by endowing temples and other monuments with quality art. She raised up a class of male servants of no social status apart from her appointment of them so that they, who owed her everything, would not be among those who privately despised her for playing the king. Of these servants, the favorite was Senenmut, who managed to get not only his own burial monument, but those of his parents, included in the Deir el-Bahri complex.

Ignored by the makers of king lists, Hatshepsut is that rare example of a woman who achieved self-realization despite the incongruousness of her femininity. But, like many women who achieve great things despite cultural prejudice, she was not untouched by self-doubts. She left the following inscription on one of her temples: "Now my heart turns to and fro, in thinking what will the people say, they who shall see my monument in after years, and shall speak of what I have done." The dismay she incurred from the men who feared her temerity is readily understandable. A social order in which all enjoy self- determination without reference to sexual preferences still frightens those of both sexes who wish to impose their own narrow views on those who do not share them. Hatshepsuts are hard to handle no matter what costume they wear, no matter into which society they are born. They challenge the slippery grip so many people, males as well as females, have on their own psychosexual identities.

Thutmose III was no doubt relieved when his aunt-consort was safely dead (1482 BC). He sprang into action, defeating the allied forces of Kadesh in Syria and Megiddo in Palestine. The soft-copy account of his campaign was made on leather and then chiseled on the temple of Karnak, the first hard copy of a battle ever recorded in detail. It is probably not true, though Gardiner thought it was,[59] that in his pique Thutmose III had Hatshepsut's name and image chiseled off as many monuments as possible, a hatchet job apparently done long after Thutmose III.[60]

Thutmose III was one of Egypt's greatest generals. He fought seventeen campaigns in Syria and Palestine and east to the Euphrates. He led armies westward into Libya. It would be a miracle if the opinion of one historian is true, namely, that he treated conquered countries well, never massacring prisoners or civilians, nor executing defeated rulers. He is said to have merely deposed them, taking their sons as hostages back to Egypt. There the same source says they were educated with Egyptian princes and developed an admiration for things Egyptian. In this way these foreign princes became tractable future allies.[61]

Thutmose III brought peace and prosperity to Palestine and Syria, two quintessentially elusive Near Eastern goals, an area that has known little peace since. His goal was to prevent the Hurrians of Mitanni, an empire that spread from the northern Syrian coast east to the Tigris River, from unduly influencing the policy of territories that reached from Asia Minor to the Taurus Mountains and the Euphrates River. To do this he established garrisons everywhere and arranged marriages between Egyptian princes and Mitannian princesses. His methods were defensive and intensive. The close relations between Mitanni and Egypt remained important through most of the imperial period.

Thutmose III's marriage alliances proved he was no racial snob, but some have faulted him for excessive indulgence in cruelty. The "Strongman" mentality developed by Ahmose I was perfected by Thutmose III. The Eighteenth Dynasty boasted of its violent techniques of control and punishment. Thutmose III is faulted for an inordinate reliance on strength, risk taking, and "posturing" to compensate for a variety of flaws, including the mere Theban base that his family commanded, rather than the superior one of Memphis. Unflattering views of the Eighteenth Dynasty are not hard to find in current scholarship.[62]

The admiration of one historian for the most glorious member of the Eighteenth Dynasty, Thutmose III, contrasts sharply with condemnation of the whole Dynasty's efforts as unwise by another. The meaning of history is as various as those who lived it, as those who write about it. Was the Eighteenth Dynasty admirable because it was successful (counting power and wealth as success), or was it successful because it was admirable? The answers to these questions can be asked about every imperial enterprise from Mesopotamia's Sargon I, history's first emperor, to the most modern.

The New Kingdom's exploitation of the conquered, the cost of its success in human and in material terms, are variously assessed. The Egyptians' experience under the Hyksos did not make them more sensitive to the rights of others. If we expect the persecuted in any age to be more sensitive to human suffering when they are in the catbird seat, we set ourselves up for disenchantment. The abused are often most abusive. This seems as true on the individual level, with child abusers or wife beaters, as it does on the imperial level and has turned out to be most aggravated where religion is concerned. New England Puritans proved that true when, having escaped the rigors of persecution in the England of King James I, they arrived in Massachusetts Bay Colony. There they became impatient with the Congregationalists and drove them into the wilds of Rhode Island over a dispute concerning the selection of ministers. It is particularly lamentable when a persecuted minority become the persecuting majority of new minorities once they have achieved power or a measure of independence. Puritan experience repeated that of early Christianity. Shortly after the Roman empire accepted the Church and stopped its sporadic persecution of Christians, Christians began to persecute those they deemed unorthodox. In the modern era, the remnants of European Jewry, having escaped Hitler's Holocaust, began to persecute Muslims whose homeland, Palestine, they both wished to inhabit. Although charity begins at home, historically speaking it often ends there as well.

Historians sometimes point to the benefits of war, viewed as a stimulus of creativity, mother of technological invention.[63] The loss in life, by way of contrast, is rarely mentioned as the cause of reduced creativity of technological and other kinds of discoveries that war casualties might have made had they lived. The arts, medicine, agriculture, and the general well-being do not seem to count as casualties. Only the loved ones of dead warriors deplore war's consequences. Mothers, sisters, daughters, and wives of the maimed, slaughtered, and enslaved do not speak of the benefits of wars, nor rape victims recommend empire as a route to cultural progress. Beauty, they say, is in the eyes of the beholder; in the eyes of those brutalized by war or persecution, tears.

Because he did not tend to his empire or lead troops into battle, pharaoh Amenhotep IV (c. 1364–1347), who later styled himself Akhenaton, after the sun disk and god Aton, was not popular. Although his new name meant "It is well with Aton," it wasn't. Akhenaton was a heretic, deserter of the worship of Egypt's polytheistic pantheon of gods whose chief deity was Amun-Re of Thebes. The new pharaoh honored only one deity, Aton, whom he did not invent but merely recycled, elevating him to a position of monotheistic primacy that excluded all others, if you did not count Akhenaton himself. But Akhenaton still counted himself, and his beautiful wife, Nefertiti, as gods, as the Hymn he wrote to Aton clearly indicates:

> Everything is made to flourish for the king . . .
> Since you did found the earth
> And raise them up for your son,
> Who came forth from your body: the King of
> Upper and Lower Egypt . . . Akhenaton . . . and the
> Chief Wife of the King . . . Nefertiti, living and
> youthful forever and ever.

The Aton or sun's disk was a very old symbol in Egypt, long associated with the most ancient sun god Re and the less ancient compound sun god Amun-Re. This symbol was already popular with Akhenaton's grandfather and father, used to suggest the universal aspects of the sun god. Already in their day the disk was becoming a deity in "its own right."[64]

Around 1374 BC Amenhotep IV was a young king with a misshapen self-image that matched his odd physical appearance—potbelly, long skull, heavy breasts and upper legs. Not only was he not bellicose or religiously orthodox, he was not attractive, which may have been the ultimate offense in Egypt. Unloved and unpopular, the young king abandoned Thebes, the priesthood of Amun, Amun himself, and his old ID. Several years into his reign he adopted a new name consistent with his religious feelings—Akhenaton, Glory of Aton. To everyone else, even his father, who rejected him, he remained inglorious.

Akhenaton's new capital, Akhetaten, Horizon of Aton, was located halfway between Thebes and Memphis, near the modern city of Tell el-Amarna, which is why his reign is sometimes called the Amarna Revolution. Nothing existed on the site but sand and the horizon. In short, like Brasilia in the twentieth century, the new site was a contractor's dream come true, and everybody else's "idea of nothing to do."[65]

Akhenaton's religious revolution started from the top down, which makes it unique in history, since most revolutions start lower on the social ladder. The Glorious English Revolution of 1688 began at the top, it is true, but by default rather than design—the English King, James II, having flown the coop for France. The French Revolution of 1789 began at the bottom, with the storming of Versailles by the *menu peuple* or common people. The Russian Revolution of 1917 started in the middle, led by representatives of the Duma or parliament. No other revolution but Akhenaton's seems to have been begun by the head of state or maintained by the head of state until replaced by his successor. But in this matter as in all others, Akhenaton aimed at pleasing only himself. He seems to have found retreat in religious life his only real interest besides the intimacies of family life. This was unfortunate, since during his reign Egypt was increasingly challenged by the power of Hittites to the north and northeast, by independent-minded military commanders on Egypt's imperial frontiers, and by a top-heavy bureaucracy that included the growing power of the priesthood of Amun at Thebes. No doubt the nobility felt slighted by their pharaoh's removal from the old capital and from the ordinary associations of social and political life that he could not find time for in Akhetaten. His was a profoundly self-serving revolution. Very few of Akhenaton's subjects cared for the self he was serving. Their cares were, understandably, for themselves.

The pharaoh's religious reforms, like his new capital, disappeared shortly after his death, dismantled by the old power elite and blessed by the same gods whose destruction he had ordered. One scholar thinks this Amarna Revolution "robbed Egyptians of a tradition of explaining the phenomena of the universe through an extraordinarily rich imagery which . . . managed to contain the concept that a unity, a oneness, could be found in the multiplicity of divine forms and names."[66] This assumes, of course, that there *is* a unity or oneness about the universe worth preserving, and that it could be explained or understood in a multiplicity of forms and names. It also assumes that ordinary Egyptians, as opposed to the elite classes that profited most by the old order, were aware of being robbed by pharaoh.

Historians often assume that the interests of the rich and powerful represent those of the poor and weak. The same scholar regrets Akhenaton's actions as tantamount to killing the Egyptians' intellectual life by depriving them of imagery.[67] Akhenaton, who was more intellectual than many of his subjects, may have seen himself as clearing away the underbrush of multiple images of the divine, making it easier for men to regulate their troublesome emotions. However Akhenaton rationalized the reasons for his revolution, whether he viewed it as an opportunity to control his own emotions or other peoples,' or as a blow for spiritual truth as opposed to entrenched interests, the passions he released among his opponents he had neither the ability nor the means to control. Given the ambiguity of the human condition and the difficulty man has in understanding nature and himself—let alone divinity—it must be recognized that Akhenaton's rationalizing approach to truth mistook irrational notions for rational truths and even The Truth. His personal vision threatened unimpeded inquiry into the nature of all things, not merely religious things. Perhaps this "heretic" pharaoh traumatized people by forcing them to think about as well as to change their religious conceptions. Thinking and changing are too hard for most people, which is why there have been so few revolutionaries.

Akhenaton has been described by one scholar as an "early rationalizer" and a precocious "glorious dictator,"[68] because he reduced Egyptian worship to the bare monotheistic minimum. Oddly enough, this is almost never the way that historians speak of Moses, the world's second monotheist. Yet Moses ordered three thousand Hebrews killed for worshipping a golden calf! If Akhenaton's monotheism was the equivalent of spiritual dictatorship and fanned the flame of religious intolerance and fanaticism, as this author suggests, why isn't this equally true of Moses? Akhenaton's impatience with diverse images of the divine anticipates the Mosaic prohibition against representing any life forms—animal, human or divine—in sculpture—the "graven images" of the Second Commandment. Muslims in the seventh century AD, Byzantine iconoclastic Christians in the eighth, and Protestant Puritans after the Reformation would all re-create in their own manner the prohibitions of Akhenaton when they legislated against representations of one thing or another. Did they not, by some people's standards, reduce the scope of spirituality? Of Truth?

Sigmund Freud blamed Akhenaton for monotheism rather than Moses in his book *Moses and Monotheism* (1939), but once monotheism was bruited, it was always capable of offering less rather than more spiritual security to worshippers. Monotheism was minimalist. Western culture has been so enthralled with this minimalism—monism or monotheism—that it requires a leap of the imagination for most Judeo-Christians to imagine how alienating such economy appeared in antiquity, with its well-stocked larder of multiple deities, multiple ways of worshipping the divine. Akhenaton's temples were built without a secret chamber where the divine image had always sheltered itself. The pharaoh had an innate prejudice against mystery and mumbo jumbo and wanted to simplify the nature of the divine.

Aton's temple complex in Akhetaten was an architectural clutter of outdoor offertory tables scattered around a roofless temple building. The tables were there for multiple sacrifices of food, seemingly the only religious rite this heretic king valued. Was he potbellied because he was obsessive about food? Akhenaton let it be known that he and his attractive wife, Nefertiti ("the beautiful one is come"), and their six daughters—no *acknowledged* sons—would do the honors of worshipping the one God themselves, while everyone else was directed to worship Akhenaton, further depersonalizing the Egyptians' worship customs.

Thirteen years after moving to his new city of Akhetaten, Akhenaton died, not before Nefertiti rather mysteriously disappeared from public ceremonies, possibly upstaged by her own eldest daughter Meritaten. Akhenaton then married this daughter, who seems to have assumed the role of Great Royal Wife in the beautiful one's place. One author claims Akhenaton married his own mother, Tiy, and their union is the reason why Nefertiti took a back seat to her mother-in-law.[69] Because Akhenaton had no known son for an heir, he chose as his successor Smenkhkare, elder brother of Tutankamen (called Tutankhaton during his childhood), perhaps sons of his father by another wife;[70] or sons of his sister; or even—we do not know for sure—bastard sons of Akhenaton himself.[71] If Akhenaton gave the biggest wedding present a man can give—his daughter and wife, Meritaten—to Smenkhare to wed, it may have been because he was in fact giving his daughter to his son, the standard procedure in Egypt. Alternatively, he may have had a homoerotic relationship with Smenkhare who may or may not have been his son.[72]

Finding himself lonely after such generous gift giving, Akhenaton married his third daughter, Ankhesenpaaten, his second daughter having died in childhood. Akhenaton soon passed to his eternal reward, dying peacefully, if unexpectedly, in his capital city in the summer of 1359 BC. Smenkhare married Ankhesenpaaten, soon widowed for the second time.

Because the title to Egypt's throne passed through the eldest remaining daughter, Ankhesenpaaten was married off a third time to Tutenkhaton, renamed Tutenkamen with the fall from favor of Aton. Tut had succeeded Akhenaton back in Thebes. Ankhesenpaaten, renamed Ankhesenamon, and her new husband could reflect that now nothing remained of Akhenaton's religious revolution. When Tutenkhamen also died at the age of twenty-three, Ankhesenamon was assigned a fourth husband, the elderly councillor Ay, her great-uncle. Ay was the brother of Akhenaton's mother, Tiy. The poor young woman was not anxious to wed a great-uncle and wrote to the Hittite king to be quick and send her a young Hittite prince to wed. Alas. He arrived too late—or maybe too soon, for he was murdered shortly thereafter. A mere pawn on Egypt's great chessboard, Ankhesenamon did indeed wed Ay.[73] In ancient Egypt, men made revolutions. Women made the rounds.

With the reintroduction of the old pantheon headed by Amun-Re, the Aton of Akhenaton slipped back to being a mere disk rather than the sole deity of the land. This was the first slipped disk in all antiquity. There was to be more and more slippage, punctuated by the thirteenth-century appearance of an imperial megalomaniac of note—Rameses II. Shortly after, the glory days were over. Rameses' gigantic self-portraits in stone decorated his temple at Abu Simbel and peered out upon the many centuries of Egypt's long thousand-year decline and eventual occupation by first one then another invader. Nubia, Assyria, Persia, Greece, Rome—she would be bend to them all, the proverbial "weak reed." Her posture in those long one thousand years of cultural deceleration and impotence was one of tenacious, even pathological conservatism, as if the repetition of cultural forms and defense of cultural norms would restore her inert body to eternal life. Egypt, which once mummified the dead to save their souls, finished by embalming herself, without first taking the usual precaution of dying.

4

Our Hebrew Heritage

THE PREMISE OF THE PROMISE

UNLIKE MESOPOTAMIAN AND EGYPTIAN HISTORY, Hebrew history lacks many artistic props. Apart from the occasional stone rampart, a few city gates and stables from the old united Hebrew monarchy of Kings Solomon and Ahab, a water conduit of the eighth-century King of Judah, Hezekiah, and a wall of the Second Temple, rebuilt at the end of the sixth century BC, little architecture remains from ancient Israel or from Judea. A typical textbook reveals a few mementos of the Hebrew past—a Star of David on a stone ewer (undated); a seven-branched menorah (candelabra) from the late sixth century BC; a coin struck by the Roman Senate bearing the slogan *Judaea Capta* [Judea captured] showing a sturdy Roman soldier watching a young woman (Judea) weeping after Pompey defeated the Maccabees in 63 BC. The star illuminates the past back to King David; the candlestick bravely shines out on an uncertain future; a coin commemorates Jewish defeat. Such are the humble artifacts of Hebrew history.

This artistic dearth derives from Deuteronomy (5:7–10) and the second of the Ten Commandments: "Thou shall not make a carved image for yourself nor the likeness of anything in the heavens above, or on the earth below, or in the waters under the earth." Why did God forbid artistic expression? Because artists in Western Asia supplied the idols that fueled a polytheistic faith that He condemned. The first patriarch, Abraham, who hailed from Ur in Sumeria, was himself the son of an idol maker, and Abraham, in rejecting his father's trade, rejected his father's way of life, too, choosing instead monotheism and the Lord. That this may have produced in Abraham a feeling of guilt is understandable—he was Jewish.[1] To honor one's parents was one of Yahweh's Commandments, although it numbered only five on the Rectitude Scale of ten, whereas the prohibition against art was number two, right after "Thou shalt have no other gods before me." The Lord meant to strengthen family values, but it was not first on his list of priorities. For millennia Hebrew youth did not enroll in art schools. They turned instead to poetry and prose, composing an immense literature about philosophy, ethics, theology, cosmogony, history, adventure, lust, incest, genocide, homosexuality, ethnic humor, rapine, and rape. They took nearly all the best research topics, developed plots you wouldn't believe, though many have. All the talent that would elsewhere have gone into graphics and later, graffiti, was absorbed by writing and contributed to that library between two covers that Christians call the Old Testament and Jews, the Torah (Pentateuch).

The Old Testament is the book you would take on your way to a desert island, especially if you were shipwrecked en route and found yourself with no other companion. No matter how long it took for the rescue party to arrive, you would always have something fresh to mull over, something contradictory to resolve, something inspirational to keep up your spirits. This library is so verbally graphic, ethically profound, psychologically complex, and spiritually uplifting that for the Hebrews alone art was superfluous. They drew better with words than anyone has ever been able to do with chisel or colors. The Bible was a collegial effort for which no one subsequently claimed authorship. Patient before the slowness of its production, the unevenness of its story line and the conundrums that no editors or rabbis have ever resolved, the Hebrews attributed the Bible to God, along with everything else under creation, not excluding themselves. When an anonymous committee writes a book, the chairman gets the credit. God was not only Creator and Father but Author. Of everything.

The narrative of Genesis 12–36 revolves upon the Lord's promise, or Covenant, with Abraham. Having rejected his father's faith, the patriarch Abraham founded the Hebrew one. He "put his faith in the Lord and the Lord counted that faith to him as righteousness" (Gen. 15:6–7). The Lord also promised, implicitly and explicitly, to take care of Abraham and his descendants because he preferred them to all other people. The Hebrews became a chosen people because of Abraham's faith in one god.

Some will wonder how a god who played favorites could possibly have grown to become a comprehensive or even comprehensible God for all mankind. Personal growth and expanding insight were not reserved for the children of Israel and Judah alone. God also grew in stature and moral sensitivity. The development of God and of the Hebrew people was a symbiotic relationship. The Hebrews needed God, but he needed the Hebrews, too. Co-dependency is implicit in every contract. Some readers may find the promise made to the children of Israel unfair to other nationalities. It seems the Lord's position was politically incorrect. Fortunately, political correctness had not yet been invented. If it had, the Hebrews would not have been able to invent themselves as a coherent and viable political entity, a process that took some six to eight hundred years after the arrival of Abraham in Canaan to accomplish. The Hebrew triumph was to create for diverse tribes, each with its own stories and customs, cultural viability under a united monarchy in the eleventh and tenth centuries BC. As a nation the Hebrew tribes completed their apprenticeship in the arts needed to ensure political viability, if not in the arts per se. The utility of being the chosen people of God was what was important throughout. The Covenant made with Abraham promised success in the material, political, and biological sense as well as in the spiritual sense, but only on the condition that Hebrew people recognize a spiritual bond with Yahweh and with him alone. They were compelled to stop wandering and to settle down, physically to be sure, but above all spiritually. They were not to stray from the straight and narrow path the Lord had pointed out to them.

Circumcision of the male member became the chief outward and visible sign of this inward invisible promise or spiritual contract. God stated the terms: "everlasting possession of the land of Canaan" and abundant fertility in return for Hebrew faith in Him as signified by adoption of circumcision, the practice of cutting the flesh of the foreskin of every male child on the eighth day of his life (Gen. 17:9–27). It was the sign of the circumcision displayed on this strangest of all billboards—the penis—that would advertise the singular commitment of the (male) children of Israel to the Lord their God and His Covenant with them. As the circumcision was not prescribed for Abraham until he was ninety-nine years old one can only wonder that the poor man did not immediately perish from the shock of the operation. Fortunately, he did not, but lived to father Isaac by Sarah, even though she was ninety at Isaac's birth, and he one hundred. Circumcision not only set the Hebrews apart from their neighbors, it discouraged their neighbors from joining up. It not only set Hebrew males apart from gentile ones, but from Hebrew females as well. Every morning the orthodox Hebrew male gets up and, in a set prayer, thanks God for not having made him a female. No special rite consecrated the Hebrew female child to God, and she could not have helped but notice. Even if she did not spend all her time looking.

All kinds of justifications for this rite have been found—most relating to health and hygiene. Mere rationalizations. Sexual organs produced thoughts of sin more often than of health, and sin had to be paid for—by the substitute sacrifice of blood that was life-cleansing.[2] For the Lord's blessing of fertility and security in the Covenant made with Abraham the Hebrews were willing that their male children should suffer the pain of the only operation they knew how to perform, and their mothers that of subjecting their helpless offspring to such indignity. That much underrated historian, Will Durant, observed that circumcision was a sacrifice and even a "commutation" where God took a part of the whole.[3] And in fact, the whole of the human race—not just the Hebrews in antiquity—were more likely driven by their worries over sexuality than over health, and still are. Otherwise we would have had a national health insurance plan long ago rather than a national abortion debate and homophobia. Our Hebrew ancestors felt that sex was worth a small sacrifice. Judging by the enthusiasm with which they threw themselves into the begetting of children—by their wives, sisters, maidservants—the Hebrews seemed to have found the joy of sex greater than the joy of cooking. They did not stew about it. They just did it. They decided that it was well worth sacrificing a part of the whole in order to preserve what was left and came up with circumcision as a way of showing gratitude.[4] It was a cut above the other ways.

A National Public Radio program recently explored the topic of circumcision. Men called in to complain that the sacrifice of the foreskin is above all a sacrifice in sexual gratification, reducing the sensation of orgasm. Some felt that circumcision cheated them of their rights. They did not realize that the Lord was talking quantity in the Covenant (Gen. 17:4–5), not quality. Multiplification of believers, not better orgasms, was the bargain struck in the Covenant. The Lord promised that Abraham would maximize his progeny and father nations, not that he would enjoy himself, nor even improve health and hygiene. No matter how many wives and concubines patriarchs had, life was not to be all fun and games for them. Less for their wives and concubines.

WAY DOWN IN EGYPT'S LAND

Shortly after their arrival in Canaan famine drove Abraham and his wife, Sarah, south to Egypt. Abraham told pharaoh that Sarah was his sister, an admission that may indicate that Hebrews married their sisters. Incest was not unfamiliar in western Asia through which Abraham had passed en route from his original home in Mesopotamia. Abraham might have been Sarah's half brother as well as her husband, but in failing to mention that he was also her spouse, Abraham sought to avoid a murder—his own, by a jealous and lusty pharaoh. Though pharaoh did marry Sarah, when he subsequently discovered she was already a wife, he gave her back to Abraham and the pair was sent packing. The young couple returned to Canaan and, having founded a nation, were in due time buried at Hebron.[5]

The taboo against sister marriage has not been more powerful than its attraction for scholars. Historians have searched diligently for records that prove the practice existed in Mesopotamian cities near which the Hebrews may have lived, but they come up with information too ambiguous and too inapplicable to Hebrew experience to be of much historical use.[6] We would not be able to understand the patriarch Abraham any better even if we did know for sure how he and his wife were really related because the very existence of the patriarchs themselves has been cast in doubt in scholarly works and in a popular news magazine.[7] The story "revealed" what scholars have known for a long time, that no body of information outside the Bible itself supports the historicity of the patriarchs Abraham, Isaac, Jacob, Joseph, or Moses! At their objective best, historians do not deny that the stories of the patriarchs may "contain a kernel of authentic history," but they point out that because these were only composed after the first millennium, long after the protohistoric era was over, it is impossible in light of the absence of corroborating sources to use them for political or theological purposes.[8] This seems a tactful way of saying that the patriarchs cannot be proved ever to have lived. Scholars do, however, make a variety of uses other than political or historical out of the patriarchs, whether they lived or not. Some view their lives as literature, with varying degrees of historicity thrown in as flavoring particles.[9] Others regard the texts as preserving historical memories of Bronze Age tribes, though not necessarily any information of a precise or particular historical group.[10] The reader not bound by faith to a literal belief in Scripture would probably be well advised to regard Abraham, Isaac, Jacob, Joseph, and Moses as archetypes, composite figures, eponymous ancestors, legendary and literary heroes whom we would sorely miss if we were simply to accept the fact that they had never been born.

The notion of the Covenant prepared the Hebrews to go it alone because it also promised that they would never have to, that God would be with them always. It held out the hope of survival as a nation apart from but spiritually superior to other nations nearby. The issue of a separate existence was predetermined by the nature of the Covenant, but the story began to work itself out in the "lives" of two men, Joseph and Moses. Joseph was a younger son of Jacob sold into slavery by jealous brothers because of his multicolored coat and the preference Jacob showed him above his eleven other boys. Joseph rose to become the chief adviser (vizier) to pharaoh. The only problem with his career is that his success is unattested by any Egyptian records.[11] Documentation aside, one critic analyzes Joseph's life as that of an assimilated Jew living among gentiles,[12] for the chosen were always a minority, always living among gentiles, and always having to choose between assimilation or cultural isolation. It is the same realization that everybody arrives at, Jew or Gentile, male or female, as soon as he or she perceives that even Mom is the mysterious Other, and that with or without the family, he or she is a unique and lonely individual.

The biblical account of the Hebrews in Egypt is so full of conundrums and inconsistencies that it is impossible to say not only how long the Hebrews lived there, but also when they arrived and when they left. Not only is there no documentary mention by Egyptian sources of the Hebrews in Egypt, but the biblical accounts vary wildly. In Genesis 15:13 four hundred years' residence is stated; in Genesis 15:16, four generations; and in Exodus 12:40–41, 430 years. Josephus, historian of the first century, thought they were there 215 years.[13] Some scholars agree that the Joseph story cannot be proved in any of its details to be accurate, but regard it as a domestic and historical novel that connects the patriarchal era of Abraham to the entry of the Children of Israel into Canaan.[14]

If Joseph's story is a historical novel, then Moses's, on whom there is an enormous and conflicted literature, can best be appreciated as a Cecil B. DeMille movie—two in fact.[15] The story of Moses the lawgiver has been characterized as that of the hero who rejected everything that Joseph stood for, namely worldly success and power.[16] Whether or not he was the perfect hero depends on how one chooses to define heroism and the heroic personality.

There is no body of information in Exodus about Moses between his infancy and his arrival into manhood. Babies are rarely heroic, with the possible exception of a Greek kid named Hercules. Little Hercules strangled two serpents that Juno, jealous of his birth, placed in his crib to strangle him. All Moses did in his basket of bulrushes was float and get found by an Egyptian princess, who may have been a single mother but was definitely not on welfare. Although he had an Egyptian upbringing—pharaoh's daughter adopted him—his unmarried Israelite mother suckled him. An untraditional family background did not prevent Moses from achieving great things! Still, Moses grew up predisposed to ambivalence and self-doubt. He was, after all, an Israelite, reared in an Egyptian palace, and no doubt in a cultural quandary. The biblical storytellers did not mean to make Moses's hesitations and self-doubting sympathetic but expected him to be the enthusiastic savior and defender of the Israelites that, with some prodding, he turned out finally to be.

He began very well for a Hebrew leader. He killed an Egyptian (Exod. 2:11–12) who was beating a fellow Israelite. Moses buried the body in the sand when he thought no one was looking. The murder seems not to have troubled him much. Then he realized that others had witnessed his act and that he was in danger of the pharaoh's wrath. Moses fled to Midianite territory the very next day and found favor in the eyes of a local priest whose daughters he had defended. Welcomed into their home, he married one of these daughters, Zipporah, who turned out to be a hearty supporter of the Covenant with Abraham, and later circumcised her own son when Moses seemed reluctant.

Unfortunately, Moses's reluctance popped up in the most awkward places, and it irritated the Lord greatly. For example, when he spoke to Moses out of a burning bush that remained unconsumed by the fire, Moses displayed curiosity, but not, alas, courage. His misgivings show as he converses with the Lord, who may even then have been mulling over a plan to murder Moses to get him to stop the doubting (4:24–25). Out of the inflammable burning bush the Lord finally tells Moses to go chat up the pharaoh concerning the oppression of the children of Israel, whom he wishes Moses to lead out of Egypt. Moses's first reaction was "Why me?" (Exod. 2:11), not exactly the response of a savior! Given proof of the Lord's ability to perform magic—and his assurance that he, Moses, will have a magic staff (a magic wand or cane) to enable him to do similar tricks—Moses agrees to cooperate. But only if his brother Aaron, a good talker, can come along and be his spokesman or *mouthpiece* (Exod. 4:16). This word is a translation for spokesman that turns up in one of the more colloquial editions of the Bible.[17] The Lord was willing.

From this point Moses and Aaron, who became the first of a great line of priests of Israel, confront pharaoh regularly. Pharaoh breaks promise after promise to let the Israelites go despite the brutality of ten plagues loosed serially on his people. Hebrews claimed an exemption so none of them were infected. Pharaoh regarded his Hebrew workers as unskilled laborers and intended to keep them busy making bricks. We might judge pharaoh more harshly but for the fact that the Lord tells Moses that it is not nature that makes pharaoh obstinate, but nurture: the Lord is nurturing pharaoh's obstinacy so that he can demonstrate how powerful a god he really is (Exod. 7:2–5)! The Lord plays an extended game of cat and mouse with pharaoh, suspending the reader between ennui and impatience. One longs to know if ten plagues were really necessary, or if one might not have done the trick? Ten seem excessive, like dropping the atom bomb on Nagasaki only three days after dropping the first on Hiroshima. Did the Lord need to demonstrate his power with ten plagues—bloody Nile, frogs, gnats, boils, plague, maggots, hail, locusts, darkness, the death of Egypt's firstborn—when the Lord himself was hardening pharaoh's heart? Could not the Lord have accomplished his purpose by using appropriate psychology on pharaoh instead? By not hardening his heart? Suppose the Lord had offered the pharaoh an incentive for the release of the Hebrews? Or some domestic advice in return for their freedom? A man with a harem and many wives must have needed counseling.

The plagues set a dangerous precedent for wanton brutality, ethnic cleansing, and violence, no matter how much the Israelites might have equated violence with God's justice.[18] Worse, violence led the Hebrews to believe that any immoral action done in God's name was moral, which made it easy to rationalize any future inhumane act as having been God's will. In the Middle Ages, with its slogan "God wills it," heretic Christians and many Jews and Muslims were set wholly apart as the expendable Other,[19] perhaps because Exodus made mayhem appear acceptable. By then the cost in human suffering that had derived from the habits of associating God with ethnic cleansing on the one hand, and avenging his upholders and followers by violent means on the other, was incalculable. If God blessed only a few and not all, who would protect freethinking Christians, heretics such as the Arians, Albigensians and Anabaptists, Socinians, Greek Orthodox Christians, Muslims, Protestants of every stamp, Roman Catholics? Who would protect Jews, the descendents of the Israelites? Always in the minority, they would have ample opportunity to reflect on the results of war and terrorism done in the name of one true but angry God. Because by then he could be considered somebody else's much more than theirs.

Exodus made the Hebrew God out to be a psychopath and Moses a well-meaning man of faith who, doubtful about his own talents, approached the Hebrews as an authority figure, giving out the Lord's orders with an impatience that one would not have suspected possible from one so self-effacing.[20] This would not be the last time in history that an ordinary mortal and religious reformer would lead and discipline his fellows by assuming the power of the Lord himself.[21] Moses's temper was heroic, even if his self image was not. After Aaron had consented to the manufacture of a golden calf which the Hebrews worshipped as God, Moses avenged the insult to the Lord by compelling the Levites to slay three thousand of the disobedient Israelites (Exod. 32:27–29). The Levites, or priestly caste descended from Aaron, were even then considered a peculiarly religious group and consecrated unto God. Their superior piety is no doubt why they were selected to kill their brethren, that and the fact that Moses was himself a Levite. On whom can one rely when one wishes to take out a contract on three thousand people if not on family? Moses was more than the father of his people; he was also the godfather. Apart from his great faith in the Lord, the rigors of his employment—a choleric Boss, an unreliable workforce, and the absence of a golden handshake—would have earned Moses a hero's place.[22] In literature, if not in history. The reader may hope that the children of Israel appreciated the efforts of those who labored on their behalf to keep the faith pure and holy, and the Israelites uncorrupted.

EXIT RIGHT, THROUGH THE SEA OF REEDS

Before the Israelite families were led from Egypt, they did what most families do before a trip: they prepared a hearty meal to sustain them on the road to Canaan. The children of Israel or rather, their wives, carefully left the leavening out of the bread dough and packed it in kneading troughs to bake along the way. This was the origin of the matzoh, Mother of all Crackers.

Passover is an annual feast of Jews, instituted in Exodus 12–20, to commemorate God's sparing and salvation of the Hebrews when he smote the firstborn of the Egyptians, passing over the firstborn of Hebrews. God told the Hebrews that he would pass over them if they distinguished their households from Egyptian ones by smearing the blood of the paschal lamb on their door posts. He also promised them that on this very first Passover the Hebrew armies would escape from Egypt. Jews celebrate this feast day yearly to commemorate their deliverance from Egypt. Jesus was still celebrating the Passover in Jerusalem with his disciples, and that particular

Passover became a commemorative rite for Christians, who called it the Last Supper, the occasion for remembering and sharing Christ's body and memory during the Communion service. Both Jews and Christians would reinforce the idea of religious obligation by an act of eating, a sacred metaphor that nourishes the sense of the divine, but also perpetuates a legacy of ill will against those not invited to the meal.

The Hebrews' last day in Egypt was hectic. They were packing up, slaughtering lambs and goats, cooking and serving the Passover dinner and eating it, all the while listening to their Egyptian neighbors crying and wailing because the Lord was killing Egypt's firstborn children. Just before leaving, the Israelites went around the neighborhood to their grieving Egyptian neighbors to collect any gold and silver jewelry and other valuables the neighbors might have wanted to give away. Some editions of the Bible say the Israelites "borrowed" these valuables of their neighbors (Exod. 12:35–36), who "lent" their goods in order to get rid of the Israelites before the Lord smote them all.[23] Other editions translate the passage using the word "asked." But the passage concludes in all editions with the words "plundered" and "spoiled" (i.e., despoiled) to describe these transactions. The Lord made the Egyptians render the Hebrews this courtesy, and they were too fearful to refuse. The incident has caused no end of embarrassment. Well-bred people do not steal, not even from their master or the master class. Plundering the Egyptians countermanded two of the Lord's own Commandments, even if they had not yet been issued—one against stealing (the Eighth) and another against coveting (the Tenth). Some have viewed these actions as ignoble, just as the theft by a household servant of his employer's goods today would be frowned on.

A believer might rationalize by saying that God alone defines ethics and if He considered this ethical, it was. God makes the Egyptians give up their goods because all Egyptians owe all Hebrews. Collective guilt was an accepted cultural practice at that time (such an argument might run), so never mind that the neighbors themselves had not enslaved the Hebrews and did not wish to appear guilty of discriminating against them. Neighbors, pharaoh, why make a distinction? What appears to be theft only *appears* to be so. And anyway, it was God's will. This is the story line we are left with. This kind of justification might stretch the belief even of some believers. This plundering was theft all right, they concede, but it was for a good cause. The end justified the means. Besides, stealing from the Egyptians ultimately made Hebrews think about how best to treat their own slaves later on. Israel would reward its own forced laborers with gifts at the end of their period of service, and more importantly, emancipation (Deut. 15:13–14),[24] so why shouldn't they have rewarded themselves with Egyptian plunder when the Egyptians failed to make the offer? This historical theft has produced a rasher of rationalizations.

It is standard knowledge that the Children of Israel crossed the Red Sea on dry land to escape pharaoh's troops, who drowned in their wake. Unfortunately, standards of knowledge change with the vagaries of scholarship, and the Red Sea standard is now substandard. Its translation dates from the era of the Septuagint (AD 270) and Vulgate versions of the Bible, but the Hebrew text used the Hebrew word for reed, not red, and so the conventional "Red Sea" translation appears mistaken. Hebraists know that the original Hebrew expression used in Exodus was "reed sea." Moses and the Children of Israel may have crossed the Gulf of Aquaba, and not the Red Sea proper. Beacause reeds require fresh water to grow in, finding that fresh water is a problem that must be solved before an accurate route of the Hebrews' march can be drawn. The only fresh water lay along the northern Mediterranean coast, but the Bible expressly says that was not the route taken, even if it would have been the shortest. That short coastal route was too heavily garrisoned by the Egyptians. The Lord was afraid they would turn back if they saw the military installations on the road to the Philistines and Canaan. Naturally the Hebrews did not like the detour through the desert or "wilderness," a longer and more difficult journey. They criticized Moses for leading them through it to what they assumed, many rightly, would be their graves. Were there not plenty of graves available in Egypt (Exod. 14:11–12), they asked Moses? This was the beginning of Jewish humor. The Israelites were not happy campers. Their complaints about the route, the lack of water, and unacceptable food gave both Moses and the Lord heartburn.

There are at least three different scenarios in the strata of Exodus concerning the water crossing. One suggests a "natural" parting of water due to wind patterns permitting the Israelites to pass over dry land. The second suggests that Moses caused a miracle by stretching his hand over the sea, causing walls of water to form on either side. In both scenarios, pursuit by pharaoh's troops results in their drowning. These two interpretations are both embedded in Exodus 14:21–22, but they are conflated, because several people wrote them at a great distance in time from the events. A third sequence has nothing to do with seas at all (Exod. 14:24–25) but with wheels. The Lord removes the wheels of pharaoh's pursuit chariots and they retreat. How they could do so without wheels is a mystery.[25] The important point throughout is that the Lord proves he can and does save the Israelites. As exciting as is the pursuit of the Israelites, whom God protects by guiding them during daytime in a pillar of cloud, and by night, in a pillar of fire, that excitement is over in two days. In any adventure movie the chase is short and short of another chase the director has got to come up with something else. The Hebrews may have lacked many things, but plot never was one of them. God knows Exodus was directed by a pro, even if the writers were sometimes confused.

MAKING THE SCENE AT MOUNT SINAI

Exodus is cinema verité (realistic drama) to believers and for skeptics, cinema nonverité. Into the latter category falls the problematic scene where Moses gets the Law. A mountain is one of the required props so that Moses will have a place to climb in order to get the Law, and then come down with it. Thus did the Israelites get a lofty sense of values. Unfortunately, the mountain, which in the Bible is called Mount Sinai at times, but at other times, Horeb (Deut. 4:11) is entirely up in the air, along with the route taken by the Israelites after leaving the Reed Sea. None of the experts agree on the mountain's location. The mountain is more than a mere prop. It is almost one of the cast. A candidate for the part of the mountain exists in both the northern and southern parts of the Sinai Peninsula, but it is not certain at which one the Israelites halted, or even if they halted at any mountain! Some scholars think that after the water crossing they stopped at Kadesh Barnea before moving on to Canaan,[26] but there is no mountain there. Some scholars think that the reception of Torah could have been a scene shot offstage, or at another time, then spliced in later. The place names in the Pentateuch cannot with assurance be tied to any modern place names, even the similar sounding ones, and some folks, like St. Paul (Gal. 4:25), think that the biblical passages would warrant looking for the mountain in Arabia rather than in the Sinai Peninsula! The connection between the present day Jebal Musa or Mount of Moses where a Byzantine emperor named Justinian built a monastery in the sixth century AD is now thought to have been unknown before the fourth century AD, a tradition too late to have much credibility.[27]

At "Mount Sinai," wherever it was, Moses was God's gofer, for Yahweh kept the Israelites at arm's length, behind special traffic control barriers that Moses erected all around the base of the mountain. The mountain was off limits to everybody but Moses and sometimes Aaron. Tight security. The Israelites may have been the Lord's chosen people, but the Lord had no wish to mingle. He made them wash their clothes prior to His appearing before them (Exod. 19:11) which might have proved the adage "Cleanliness is next to godliness" had they ever been allowed to get next to Him. They were not. They could not even get next to their wives for the Lord made them do without sex for a few days because he wanted them *extra* clean. Sex was already considered dirty, and that was before the Ten Commandments had been issued. Predictably, when the Lord came down the mountain in fire and smoke all that laundering was wasted effort. There were no dry cleaners, even in a desert that dry.

Although Moses brought the people out to meet God (Exod. 19:17), this was not a social gathering. Moses alone was summoned to the top for the first summit conference. The Lord threatened to break out against this people from whom he was distancing himself. Moses read the Ten Commandments out loud when he got back down, trying to make himself heard over all the thunder and lightning on the mountain. The Israelites were terrified of the Lord, which Moses explained was the purpose of all that smoke, fire, and thunder. Fear of God might keep them from sin (Exod. 20:21). Immediately, however, fear interrupted any communication that might have been attempted by the Hebrews, who listened to their message taker, Moses, instead of the message Maker, God (Exod. 20:19–20). When God called, the children of Israel were too frightened to pick up. After the beep He left them the Ten Commandments. "Thank you and have a nice day."

There were more than just ten things to do and remember. The Lord left them a dozen or so pages of Exodus—and all of Deuteronomy, collections of ancient Mesopotamian legal practices, many having to do with criminal law, case law about brawling, striking, maiming, kidnapping, and seducing. There were laws pertaining to farm animals, which were always regarded as valuable, as well to lusting after women, whose value was problematic, dependent upon their social status and virginity; in short, the men in their lives. Witchcraft and bestiality were condemned—and guilty persons were to suffer the death penalty for indulging. Did the compromised animals wind up in the stew or in the stews?[28]

In Exodus and Deuteronomy are laws that are sublime—requiring the Israelites to wrong no alien, and to harm no widow or fatherless child, on pain of divine retribution (Exod. 22:21–24). The humanitarianism is marked. On the very next page (Exod. 23: 22–26), the Lord promises to help the Israelites make an end of the Amorites, Hittites, Perizzites, Canaanites, Hivites, and Jebusites who were living in the Promised Land already. The Lord, in an oversight, seems not to have noticed that it would be impossible to succor all the widows and the fatherless children and at the same time eliminate whole foreign populations! The Lord needed an Oversight Committee.

When Moses led the Children of Israel out of Egypt armed with the Law, he led them onto a higher stage of spiritual being than even Hollywood could build. That stage was Canaan, and it was higher ground than could be had in Egypt not only in terms of physical elevation, but of moral elevation. It was the Law that made it possible for the Hebrews to assume the higher ground and not only assume it, but eventually to subdue it and annex it, which is how higher ground has been treated by real estate developers ever since. The higher the ground, the higher the value. If you wanted an assumable mortgage, Canaan was the right place. The Israelites eventually assumed everything.

THE CONQUEST OF CANAAN

The settlement into Canaan was neither tidy nor rapid.[29] Scholars suggest several "models" (conquest, peaceful immigration, and revolt) for this process of settlement but cannot agree on which one was operative.[30] The settlement has not been consistently viewed as a military conquest by united Hebrew tribes, the description given in the book of Joshua, once considered the normative interpretation.[31] The erosion of the conquest of settlement has occurred because archaeological evidence of the Canaanite area has not substantiated physical destruction by warfare of a number of towns reported in Joshua to have been targets for the Israelites.[32] Others think Israelite conquest was never total before King David's time,[33] and at least one archaeologist describes the settlement as peaceful.[34] Some experts believe that any destruction that occurred was more likely the result of egalitarian peasant revolts against Late Bronze Age city-states than of armed Israelite forces.[35] Settlement can be regarded as a variety of situational arrangements, some negotiated, without the benefit of war, others arrived at after war. Peaceful coexistence alternating with violence and accommodation facilitated by cultural exchange between Hebrews and Canaanites probably formed the warp and woof of Hebrew settlement in the Promised Land. At least superficially, Hebrew history sounds like the history not of a chosen people in a unique setting, but of most latecomers to already settled regions.

Among interpretations raised about the "conquest" of Canaan one views it not solely as a Hebrew phenomenon but as a joint enterprise among Hebrews acting together with other, multiethnic folk who had been captive laborers in Egypt and who worked side by side with the Hebrews during the Amarna period. These foreigners, so it is theorized, came to accept the ethics of Yahweh, and, having joined with the Hebrews in their Exodus and in their entry into Canaan, came to resemble their Hebrew and Yahwist brothers.[36] How refreshing to learn that the chosen people were willing to commit to long-term relationships with like-minded neighbors from dissimilar ethnic backgrounds! How reassuring, not to mention politically correct, to entertain the notion of at least one kind of peaceable cooperation and cultural communication in the ancient history of this still-contested space.

The book of Joshua provides the traditional story—minus cooperation, peace, or cultural interchange—of the chosen of God settling into Canaan. This version has the Israelites staging a relatively quick (five-year) military campaign in which the united Hebrew tribes defeat not only Canaanites, but also Hivites, Jebusites, Philistines, Perizzites, Amorites, and Hittites—all more populous groups than they were and well-rooted in Canaanite territory. Then, after eliminating all their opponents, the Israelites are supposed to have divvied up captured land. Historians and archaeologists have labored to explain how the biblical "miracle" of Hebrew conquest might in fact have worked itself out against a broad backdrop of multiple ethnic migrations into Canaan in centuries prior to the thirteenth, when the Hebrews arrived. The Hebrew settlement into Canaan is now thought to be a process that developed over two centuries.

The Bible does not give just one scenario, but in Judges presents a different view than Joshua, one that is probably more accurate. In this account the settlement into Canaan was not a united conquest by one people, but the story of individual tribes (once thought to have been nomadic, but now viewed as agricultural or pastoral) who, not for the first time, reached accommodation with non-Hebrew neighbors living in Canaan.[37] Such agreements were made either by Hebrew tribes acting alone or with their relatives in other tribes. Scholars have studied not only the fate of the chosen Israelites, but of the older settlers as well. Every group was prone, by virtue of limited resources, periodically to suffer the consequences in Canaan of crowding—the pressure exerted by material rather than spiritual forces.[38] Such pressure, rather than the commands of gods or God, resulted not merely in the settling, but also in the unsettling of Canaan, a land more limited in fertility than the slogan about milk and honey indicates. Eventually, factors of territoriality, war, negotiation, trade, and the fatigue of all parties resulted in accommodation of the older to the newer settlers and vice versa! It was not long after the Israelites settled into Canaan than the Canaanite mentality began to settle into the Israelites, who intermarried with them and, sometimes, worshipped their gods or baals. Few cultures living in proximity resist borrowing from each other. The Hebrew settlers were more pragmatic about adopting the customs of their new neighbors than the authors of the book of Joshua thought commendable or inspirational. In any event, when these writers began to write the "history" of the settlement, they made it more glorious by making it more military and also, more uncompromising. Nothing was more uncompromising than the Covenant with Yahweh.

The Joshua authors did not realize that there were impressive paths to glory other than organized violence done in the name of God, and though many Hebrews must have sought to remember Him without murdering their neighbors, one might forget that when reading the bloodthirsty book of Joshua. Just as classical dramatists in seventeenth-century France telescoped the action on stage so that it would not exceed one day, the Joshua writers telescoped the action of the Hebrew "conquest" so that it did not exceed five years, a miraculously short time for a weak and disunited folk to conquer anybody, and thus a kind of "proof" that the settlement into Canaan was God's plan enacted by his chosen people. These writers made the Hebrews appear to have been supernaturally successful because supernaturally led. They mistook success at arms and killing for a sign of divine approval, inventing a cult of violence that more have worshipped for power's sake than for goodness' sake, let alone a good God's. They may very well have turned a deaf ear to Him when recording His instructions. They seem to have misrepresented as God's will the most bloody and unethical acts of their ancestors, and portrayed as military victories what might have been gradual and informal rearrangements of people and property.

The Joshua authors scripted their ancestors' settlement of Canaan to appear heroic and God-inspired. A century earlier (the eighth century BC), in Greece, Homer (probably a plurality, like the writers of Joshua) had made the Greeks out to be heroic when they conquered Troy for commercial reasons—to assure their grain supply. Homer made the Achaeans out to be heroes motivated by the defense of honor rather than portray them as they were, a scrappy lot of independent tribal leaders given in fact to piracy and rapine. Homer's subjects were Mycenaean Greeks who lived four hundred years before him. Homer made them valiant, a united force with a common lofty purpose, characteristics the Greeks had scarcely developed by their classical or golden age (fifth century BC). To these rude Mycenaeans or Hellenes, Homer attributed the highest ideals. The *Iliad* proved to be a masterpiece of world literature. Similarly, the Hebrews emerged in the book of Joshua as a united, not a tribal, people, with a developed sense of political identity and ethnic pride that probably resembled that of the Joshua writers, who followed them by five centuries. These writers, like Homer, also lacked precise information about their ancestors' activities. Although some battles had occurred in Canaan, they were rare.[39] But the Joshua writers needed to convince their contemporaries to observe the fighting spirit of their ancestors at a point in time when Jewish society was far weaker than it had once been. They must have hoped their readers would attain the religious zeal of their ancestors and thus be saved from present political weakness, for they were encircled in the seventh century by Assyrians and Chaldeans, both stronger than the Jews they menaced. The Joshua writers found examples of political heroism and spiritual idealism in the "history" of Israel during the settlement as they imagined it to have been, as they wanted it to be. They were unable to write an accurate history of the settlement into Canaan based on facts long lost, nor did they care to. When present necessity and ignorance of the past afflict writers, the result is not history but poetry, drama, or polemics.[40] The *Illiad* and the book of Joshua make great literature but inaccurate history. Like Pentagon news briefings during one of our covert military actions.

JUDGES

The judges, or elders, of Israel were the natural leaders of every Hebrew tribe. They had their hands full during the two centuries that bridged the settlement into Canaan and the creation of a united monarchy. During these years the Hebrews were divided by tribal identity, geography, and politics, although not to the extent that they utterly forgot their one powerful bond—their ties to God whom they called Yahweh. That their Yahwism was not an all-sufficient bond is scarcely surprising. The tribes, dispersed in hill country with a view of the plains areas that the richer, older inhabitants of Canaan called home, were obliged to cope with a variety of economic and social problems relative to tribal strength and location. The Danites were hindered by Philistines; the Reubenites were "virtually rubbed out" by Moabite aggression, as were the Benjamites. The Galilean tribes were separated from their fellows in Esdraelon;[41] and everywhere the religion of Canaan, with its fertility goddess worship and its potent baals, beckoned to Hebrews who had not quite figured out the riddles of infertility and impotence. The heritage these twelfth- to eleventh-century BC Canaanites and Hebrews left us remains. Do we not fret because we, too, are continually troubled by fertility and infertility, power and impotence?

Biologically, politically, and militarily we are still wrestling with some of the basic dangers and temptations our Hebrew ancestors faced. Our means for coping have changed more than our reactions to threat and danger. The Hebrews, pledged to a rigorous ethic—Yahwism—tried to take advantage of the new "technology" that was making inroads on twelfth-century Palestine, namely, trade by camel caravans and seagoing vessels. These were slowly creating prosperity with all its temptations. Already a few people in the time of Judges were succumbing. Others would remain pastoral and agricultural for centuries and criticize or fear the diversity of lifestyles that a growing economy was making possible for others. With prosperity and urbanity would come changes in law and ethics, changes that would grow more intense with the passage of several centuries and end with a division of the tribes into two separate states.

Not only when the early settlers went to war with their non-Israelite neighbors would they need the wisdom of the judges of Israel, but when they went to bed with those neighbors as well. From proximity came new and troubling insights and temptations, including the temptation to love what is new and yet to condemn the unfamiliar. Intermarriage between Canaanites and Israelites would prove at least as challenging as the camel trade or venturing one's goods upon the sea. Intermarriage and cultural borrowing, not unknown in the days of Exodus, left everyone at sea and began even in the twelfth and eleventh centuries to effect a sea change on these Hebrew hill dwellers.

THE NOT-QUITE-UNITED UNITED MONARCHY

In modern corporate America tall men are more apt to be promoted than short men. Saul, first king of a united Hebrew monarchy, was selected by Israel's last judge, Samuel, for just such a reason—his stature, for he was a head taller than anyone in the neighborhood of Benjamin (1 Sam. 9:2). If Saul rose to great heights, it is also the case that he fell from them, a tragic, wounded man who pleased no one—not God, not Samuel, and most significantly, not himself. His suicide was a mercy killing and by the standards of the cult a great sin, though if it were his last, it was not his first. Tenderhearted, a devoted son, a naive and simple soul though not a simpleton, Saul was a very mediocre candidate for king. But, like many mediocre candidates, he was selected by the judiciary—Samuel and God. The Israelites, hard-pressed by Philistines, were crazy to have a king like all the other nations, hoping that such a leader would be able to rid them of their enemy. Samuel—tired, embittered, as disappointed in his own wayward offspring as God was in his children of Israel—underwrote God's irony, which on this occasion meant giving his children what they had long pestered Him for—a king. One should treat a prayer that is answered like a letter bomb.

Saul, seeking his father's runaway donkeys throughout the territories of Benjamin and Zuph, showed up at precisely the moment God and Samuel were looking for a king for Israel. His inquiries after the donkeys led him to Samuel's parlor. Samuel, with God's connivance and the aid of a stepladder, anointed him, knowing that he was the wrong man for a job neither the Prophet nor the Lord wanted filled anyway. They preferred no king at all.[42] Saul, hoping to lead away his father's donkeys, was himself led off, an anointed leader again encumbered with donkeys. Worse, he suspected that he would make an ass of himself.

Once in office, Saul's finer qualities—compassion and the desire to be loved by his soldiers—contributed to his undoing. He was as much a tragic figure as Oedipus, and like the Greek king of Thebes, Saul, too, was the unwitting protagonist of action planned and directed by unseen forces for purposes he scarcely comprehended. His was an unenviable *Sitz im Leben* (German, situation). Saul was serious about his responsibility to defend Israel and did his best. He was not an unsuccessful warrior, but for Saul, killing was just a job. It gave him no pleasure at all, and he was less successful in it than David, who relished warfare, but, unlike Saul, knew how to lighten up.

The women made merry after David returned from the Philistine front-lines, for his career had blossomed since coming to Saul's court as an ado-lescent musician and slayer of the Philistine giant Goliath. David grew up and won the hand of the king's daughter, Michal, with a bridal gift of two hundred Philistine foreskins, twice the price Saul suggested. He had already won the heart of Saul's son, Jonathan, for the sweetness of his smile. Finally, David won Saul's enmity after the normally docile Hebrew women took to the streets singing: "Saul made havoc among thousands, but David among tens of thousands" (1 Sam. 18:7).

Ever since the time of Deborah, a judge, prophet, and fearless recruiter of troops, the women of Israel displayed an interest in politics despite the repressive patriarchal nature of their culture. True, most Hebrew women were scripted to be fatalities of femininity—"capable wives" and mothers who labored at baking, spinning, sewing, even business (Prov. 31:10–31) from dawn to dusk. Much later (eighth through sixth centuries BC) a few women (Judith, Queen Esther) achieved political prominence as femmes fatales, thanks to designer wardrobes, makeup, and the casting couch. But already in these early centuries Hebrew women were becoming politically aware due to societal upheaval when the norms for prophetesses as well as housewives were changing. A culture that traditionally associated men, but not women, with strength[43] was in a state of flux,[44] and the songs that drove Saul to frenzy were a sign that political crises fostered awareness as proverbs and stability did not. If, in times of crises, women became politi-cally enlightened and chorused their approval of certain leaders like David more than with others like Saul, no wonder men tried frantically to achieve crisis control.

Saul had never been able to conquer his jealousy of his son-in-law, and indeed, tried his best to kill David, just so he would not have to be reminded that the younger man was the better warrior. Why should God, who had him anointed, continually favor David while making Saul's life so difficult and painful? The key to Saul's plight was more than just a midlife crisis; it was his own disobedience. God never forgave Saul for sparing the life of the Amalekite king Agag, a captive, and his determination to gift each Israelite soldier with an Amalekite sheep, actions countermanding God's instructions to kill all the Amalekites and destroy their livestock. Saul was king, but God was the commander-in-chief. Saul was insubordinate, and though tall, he never grew beyond the height of ignorance in Samuel's eyes or in God's. Samuel was so incensed with Saul's obtuse errancy he decapitated Agag before the king's very eyes to show him what obedience meant. Philosophers call this kind of thing an ostensive definition. The story of Agag leaves us all agog.

From then on, Saul endured many physical complaints such as the migraine headaches only David's music had ever soothed and personality

disorders ranging from hypertension and clinical depression to melancho-
lia and a neurotic dependency on Samuel and David with whom he had a
love-hate relationship. Saul suffered from manic depression and panic
attacks. During one of these last he tried to destroy David. The king's
dependency on Samuel has been described as a reflection of his captivity
to "the typology of judgeship,"[45] which means that Saul lacked a strong
sense of self-worth. He was jealous of authority figures. On one occasion
the king killed all the Jewish priests of the town of Nob. He often doubted
his own judgment. At the height of the Philistine campaign, he went to
visit the witch of Endor who put him in touch with Samuel's ghost, a scene
reminiscent of Hamlet's encounter with his father's ghost.[46] This was an
awkward séance. Saul had been killing off the witches in Palestine as proof
of his religiosity, so at first the witch of Endor was worried about her safety
(1 Sam. 28:9). Saul assured her that he had come to consult, not to harm
her. The witch, having produced Samuel's ghost from the other side, pitied
Saul, who looked ghastly from stress. "Stay for dinner," she begged, "It will
do you good." Here was a witch, one of the saved remnant of her profession, showing Saul the compassion of a nurturing mother, a Jewish mother,
which she no doubt was. Saul stayed and ate. The witch slew a fatted calf
for him and baked matzohs (1 Sam. 28:24–25). It was not your standard
nouvelle cuisine, but Saul dined like a king. Kings don't get a lot of home
cooking, you know. He ate in the kitchen without having to dress up for
dinner. It did him good.

The killing of witches became a recurrent theme in the western tradition,
owing in no small measure to Exodus 22:18, which says, "Thou shalt not
suffer a witch to live." Sparing the life of just one, the witch of Endor, was
exactly the sort of error Saul committed in the case of King Agag. He
should have killed her according to God's orders, as he should have killed
Agag, but it is harder to murder one's hostess than one's enemy. And he
did not wish to offend against etiquette. Should he kill her before or after
the first course? Or should he wait until the dessert course? Torah provided
no clue. Situational ethics and his promise to her required him to spare her
life, but not his own. Saul's suicide occurred on the eve of a massive defeat
of Israel by the Philistines at Mount Gilboa (1 Sam. 28:4; 29:1). Saul fell on
his own sword shortly after dining with the witch. He had to kill himself
after the defeat at Gilboa because defeating the Philistines was the raison
d'être of his reign.[47] Full of dinner and remorse Saul convinced himself that
suicide was his just dessert.

Not to conclude that Saul lost his kingdom solely through his own ineptitude. The rivalry between Saul and David had as its basis a cultural fault
zone that underlay the political and even religious ground of Palestine. The
southern tribes of Israel felt isolated from the northern ones. The United
Kingdom of Israel was far from united.[48] Was it a coincidence that David

came from Judah, the southernmost tribe, while Saul was from the smallest northern tribe? Tribal divisions had become unmanageable after Saul drove David into the enemy's camp. David, with six hundred Israelite troops, joined up with King Achish of Gath, who was either a Philistine king or one of their clients. David's betrayal of Israel was public knowledge, yet David never felt abandoned by the Lord nor suicidal. Saul, who never betrayed Israel, felt the Lord's rejection of him most keenly and took his own life. War is hell for sensitive souls.

David, though a poet and musician, was surprisingly insensitive; hence, he succeeded brilliantly at all he undertook to do. A man after the Lord's own heart because he was devout, it cannot be denied that he presided over a cult less than purely Yahwistic. He rather liked many of the Canaanite customs, including that of a fixed localized house of worship, and the incorporation of dancing and leaping to religious music.[49] David was popular with the Israelites, an elected monarch and a military genius. His private life did not inspire confidence, but his peccadilloes were noted only by the prophet Nathan and the Lord, both inclined where David was concerned to remarkable indulgence, though not unwilling to rebuke and punish him. While prophets, political opponents, and media men dramatize the familial failures of national leaders, the Israelites, like most citizens everywhere, failed to get excited about them. They looked to their king for statesmanship, or failing that, peace and security in the body politic. David gave them that.

So, his family was dysfunctional? David was scarcely aware of it. He was too busy cementing treaties of marriage and siring offspring to have much time for the kids. He had wives to look out for them. He would look out for Israel. David was an absentee father. One son, Absalom, killed his half brother, Amnon, because the latter raped Absalom's sister Tamar (2 Sam. 13). Absalom turned against his father in a civil war that proved taxing to all and sundry. Still, David forgave him loudly and repeatedly, furnishing the American novelist William Faulkner (1897–1962) with the title for his novel *Absalom! Absalom!* (1936). David's exact words were "O my son! Absalom, my son, my son Absalom! If only I had died instead of you! O Absalom, my son, my son!" Of course Faulkner could not stuff all that into a title. Kings are edited more often than editors are crowned.

David's family problems were not limited to his children. One of his many wives, Saul's daughter, Michal, started to nag after a while, although in the beginning she was crazy about him. Once, long after the honeymoon was over, when David was moved during a religious procession to dance around the Ark of the Covenant, he stripped off his outer garments and pranced about in whatever kings wore then under their court attire. Michal called out to him from the palace window to stop making a fool of himself. David may have let it all hang out. Was her reaction intensified by her inability to provide her royal consort with a male heir and successor and thus preserve for her father's tribe the prestige of dynastic continuity, while legitimizing the succession from Saul to her husband?[50] Although God cured Abraham and Sarah of infertility when they were past the age of childbearing, Michal remained childless.

This was not true of Uriah the Hittite's wife, Bathsheba, whom God blessed with fertility out of wedlock. One of the most compelling love stories ever written concerned David's seduction of Bathsheba and how he sent her husband, Uriah the Hittite, to his death on the front lines to have a free hand with this lady, already pregnant with the royal seed (2 Sam. 11–12). This incident did not affect David's career as adversely as the Agag affair harmed Saul's, but it did cast an unseemly, not to say, seamy, pall over it. In his seduction of Bathsheba, who became another of his wives and the mother of David's heir, Solomon, David broke three Commandments: the one about adultery, the one about coveting another man's wife, and the one about murder, since he gave instructions to put Uriah in harm's way on the battlefield, in effect murdering him.

David's reign was very bloody, but because he ruled for forty years and brought peace and prosperity to Israel after many campaigns, it was regarded as a harbinger of Yahweh's future Golden Age.[51] One reason this was so was that David lived during a period when Assyria and Egypt were weak enough to allow him to unify Israel and Judah and to lay the foundations for the Temple (2 Sam. 24:18). To this end he purchased the threshing floor of one Araunah on which to build an altar to the Lord. One wonders how much credit David should be given for this, though, since the original idea came from a prophet named Gad, long David's supporter, and under the stimulus of a plague. Egad! How many temples and churches have owed their origins to priests, prophets, and plagues! That David became a role model of ideal kingship and a pattern for the future Messiah testifies to the ability of charismatic leaders to bemuse and confuse the public. Role models for religious folk committed to strong family values and *all* Ten Commandments ought not to seduce other men's wives. Rather they should keep their word and perform their duties according to God's laws—and society's. Still, David remained Yahweh's favorite king.

David's political acumen was demonstrated in many ways, none more triumphantly than in his seizure of Jerusalem for his capital. Until then it had belonged to the Jebusites whom he had defeated in war. Hebron, the old capital, was so closely associated with Judah that it could only have caused jealousy among the tribes of northern Israel, so the change was politically astute.[52] But brilliant political ploys were not always a consolation to David's nearest and dearest. They did not console his fourth son, Adonijah, whom David had never corrected, nor perhaps loved, nor his commander in chief, Joab, who had long served him as a chief supporter, and who on several occasions saved David's life. These two had counted on the succession as Adonijah's by right, the three elder of David's sons having died. David was too busy or too calculating to make a will, or communicate to his family and friends his thoughts on the succession. By inadvertence or design he created a messy succession problem that cost his fourth son, Adonijah, his life.

Charming and popular with his father's subjects, Adonijah, upon David's approaching death, threw himself a celebration party, with many sheep, oxen, and buffalo sacrificed for the occasion. The party was more than a friendly gathering; it was a political party that represented certain factions within the court, including David's commander, Joab, an old priest named Abiathar, and all the king's sons except Solomon. The prophet Nathan and a few of David's most faithful priests were not on the guest list either. Then Bathsheba, urged forward by Nathan to appeal to David on her son Solomon's behalf, approached the king as he lay nearing death. Also on his deathbed—though not at the moment of Bathsheba's visit, lay the virgin Abishag, a lovely young thing procured to keep the old king warm and cozy. David's physical powers were waning, and the pair did not engage in intercourse (1 Kings 3–4). Readers of David's last days may find the baldness of this statement in poor taste, but the Bible, like David, lets it all hang out. This lack of sexual activity may have been a first in David's career and the reason why it got recorded at all. David reaffirmed his promise to Bathsheba that Solomon would succeed him as king, which put the calabash on Adonijah's bash.

His will made at last, David added a codicil: that once king, Solomon should not spare the life of Joab, who had killed Absalom against David's orders during that young man's revolt. Nor should Solomon spare Shimei, son of Gera, an aged relative of King Saul's, whom David had once sworn before the Lord to spare. David did not ask Solomon to spare his brother Adonijah, either, though it would not have cost David anything. With the last breath in his body he urged Solomon to murder Shimei. What we have in Solomon's accession is the story of a successful coup d'état different from countless others only in that the biblical authors took pains to make it clear that King David was, if not the architect of the coup conspiracy (Nathan was), at least, a willing accomplice to murder and to the coup itself. The usurpation of his younger son, Solomon, hinged on fratricide and the assassination, with David's blessing, of the old king's most loyal supporters. But David, as Pierre Bayle, the late seventeenth-century philosopher mused, remained nevertheless a king after the Lord's own heart.

Shortly after David was buried, Solomon (c. 961–922 BC) ordered the murders of his half brother, Adonijah, Joab, and after a time, of Shimei. The biblical authors insist that only then could Solomon rest securely on his throne (1 Kings 2:46), the first and last successor to David that the united Hebrew monarchy would ever know. David's blood coursed through Solomon's veins but so much more blood gurgled around the throne on which Solomon sat it was a mercy he did not wash right out the palace door![53]

Like his father the new king was nothing if not Machiavellian, for as a Renaissance counselor wrote in another season for another prince: "a ruler who is new to power, cannot conform to all those rules that men who are thought good are expected to respect, for he is often obliged, in order to hold on to power, to break his word to be uncharitable, inhumane, and irreligious."[54]

Solomon, whose life and reign are undocumented in any source outside the Old Testament, would act against all these things before his reign was finished. Although his reign was relatively peaceful, it was not secure even after the murders. It was true that he ruled over all the kingdoms from the Euphrates to Egypt's frontier (1 Kings 4:21) and collected tribute from them, but he could not prevent the secession of Edom, the result of one of David's genocidal raids on Israel's southeastern border, or the loss of some of Aramaean Syria. Nor did he retain twenty cities ceded to Hiram for out-standing debts to Tyre. If the first ten chapters of 1 Kings presents a gener-ally prosperous monarchy, the lack of documentation concerning it and the number of centuries that elapsed between David's death and the composi-tion of that book gives us warning that prosperity under Solomon was far less than it was made out to be. Certainly Solomon reorganized his admin-istration using foreign administrative techniques and a professional bureau-cracy designed to minimize the influence of the tribes and increase tax revenues. This kind of activity earned him the title of "wise,"[55] though mod-erns would probably call it politically shrewd if economically hazardous. If his only purpose was to preserve his power and his own security, Solomon would not deserve a reputation for great wisdom, for what politician did not take care to preserve himself? Saul, it is true, did not, but he was no politician. Solomon's reputation for wisdom led the biblical authors twice to assert that he wrote the book of Proverbs, although the general tenor of the book does not suggest that he did, but that some much later author compiled them.[56] He did not write Proverbs, but he did build the Temple. The Temple endured—if not always physically, then spiritually—and kept alive the faith of the Hebrews, which also set the stage for Judaism's heirs, Christianity and Islam.

Unfortunately, in laying the foundations (quite literally) for Judaism, Christianity, and Islam, Solomon condemned his co-religionists to a future of political weakness, the result of his deficit spending. If modern critics of deficit spending had been Solomon's contemporaries, they would have made him stop the building or reduce expenditure in other areas to help pay for it. The authors of 1 Kings wrote up Solomon's reign as the climax of early Israelite history.[57] It was certainly the climax of Israelite solvency and of her united monarchy, after which the northern tribes separated from Judah, and both were left out of pocket and in a weakened condition, prey to stronger neighbors.

Solomon's erections—the Temple, a splendid palace, and additions to cities outside Jerusalem—created a cash-flow problem of catastrophic proportions. Cedar wood, bronze, ivory, gold—raw materials purchased from King Hiram of Tyre—had to be paid for and Solomon's account came up short. So he gave Hiram twenty cities in Galilee (1 Kings 9:11–13) to square his debt. These did not satisfy Hiram because they were poor, and the Phoenician asked Solomon later "what kind of cities have you given me?" If that was all he said, he was a good friend indeed. Had Solomon sought to palm off on Hiram his poorest towns or were these typical of Israel's store? Apparently, they were all too typical, for Israel's cities were small and poor, devoid of the wealth that was attributed to the reign by seventh-century BC writers.[58] One wonders how the inhabitants of these poor towns felt when they discovered their nationality had changed overnight! Were they given something like green cards to keep working in Israel? Perhaps they were unassimilated Canaanites. If so, the transfer may have pleased them. That the biblical authors say nothing about these people may be a tacit admission that they had never had much of a stake in Israel's social order anyway.

Solomon's expansiveness did not include war and conquest, and that seems to speak to the man's wisdom, as did his interest in international trade—with Tyre, principally, but also, in the Red Sea area. Solomon used Phoenician shipbuilders and sailors to help him build a fleet that could trade with Ophir, now Somaliland, and perhaps with India. Although taxes and duties from Arabia flowed into Solomon's treasury from his overland as well as seagoing trade, and although Israel experienced a doubling of population between Saul's reign and the end of Solomon's, his expenses were such that his income was stretched to the max. With debts mounting, he was constrained to trade workers for raw materials, that is, to send forced laborers from the northern reaches of Israel into Hiram's kingdom to work in the forests and stone quarries there.

In the last decades of the twentieth century, the United States, not being able to send cheap labor abroad, sent its industries abroad in search of cheap labor. German automotive companies during the same period sent theirs to the U.S. for the same reason—the cheap labor provided by American workers! Lacking exportable industries, Solomon exported his own subjects instead. In each case, men of wealth and power took advantage of poor workers to further their own agenda. In Solomon's day short-term profits were the prelude to long-term loss and social resentment, for the northerners in his kingdom, those victimized by his policies, separated from the south in the reign of Solomon's son to form a separate kingdom. The loss was nothing less than the united Hebrew monarchy itself.

Biblical authors denied that these forced laborers were Israelites (1 Kings 9:22), insisting that they were Amorites, Hittites, Perizzites, Hivites, and Jebusites. They overlooked evidence (1 Kings 5:13–8, 12:4) in which the workers were said to have included Israelites as well as the conquered and pacified Canaanites added by conquest under Saul and David.[59] But, even if some later authors denied the enslavement of Israelites, the fact that they excused enslaving non-Israelites speaks to the cruelty and discrimination against others not different from those that others practiced against them. If they were chosen, it was not for a set of ethics that was superior to their neighbors.' The practice of sending contract laborers, thirty thousand men at a time, to Phoenicia to quarry stone for Temple blocks or to work in tribal labor gangs closer to home only increased the tensions between the northern tribes and Judah. The northern tribes, closer to Phoenicia and more apt to be conscripted for forced labor there, did not look kindly upon their own exploitation, though in subsequent centuries their sacrifice was rationalized away by seventh-century authors who represented the southern kingdom of Judah, not the northern kingdom of Israel. The writers of 1 Kings did not question the methods employed in the Temple's building. They wished only to persuade their contemporaries that the Lord would never allow Judah's enemies to destroy Solomon's Temple once built. In the sixth century BC Nebuchadnezzar proved them wrong.[60]

Among Solomon's first acts of state was a marriage alliance with the pharaoh (suspiciously left unnamed in 1 Kings) whose daughter (also nameless) he is supposed to have wed (1 Kings 8). This wedding did not make the social register since there is not a single mention of it in any Egyptian document, nor any document anywhere else except in 1 Kings. Solomon's marriage to foreign princesses might be viewed as consistent with his reputation for wisdom. Marriage alliances were supposed to cement better relations with foreign princes. But Solomon lived in a peaceful period, when such alliances were not really necessary. Furthermore, these foreign women brought their pagan gods and retinue along with them and tempted Solomon to worship as they did (1 Kings 11:4–13), something that Yahweh forbade. In other western Asian cultures intermarriage was viewed as breaking down cultural barriers, and had this continued, non-Israelites living in the united Hebrew monarchy would have been more comfortable, although Yahwists would have had to learn the difficult lesson of tolerance. Many centuries later, Alexander the Great attempted to pacify the Persians and Bactrians whom he had conquered by arranging foreign marriages between their daughters and his Greek and Macedonian troops. Solomon, like his father, was probably more ardent in his pursuit of beauty than peace. His huge harem was not stocked with princesses, the wedding of whom could be chalked up to diplomatic necessity, but with babes, the bedding of whom can be attributed to a king-sized lust. The Israelites stressed monotheism, not monogamy, and the biblical writers were no prudes. Solomon was not criticized for having too many women, but too many gods, for lusting after those his wives were allowed to worship in Israel, like Ashtoreth of Sidon, Kemosh of Moab, and Milcom and Molech of Ammon.

No woman at the court expected any better treatment than to serve the lust of the king or his courtiers. In this respect David and Solomon set the tone for the royal courts of Europe for thousands of years, a cultural pattern that prevailed as well during the administrations of several American presidents.

When the queen of Sheba visited Solomon at his court, the harem atmosphere that prevailed in Jerusalem produced very bad press releases. Her country of Saba, or Sheba, on what is now the coast of Somalia, was an important source of frankincense and myrrh, prized for important medicinal properties and essential for Hebrew religious ritual. The queen probably made the arduous journey through desert wastelands to negotiate a trade treaty with Israel,[61] but the Old Testament authors claimed that she was drawn to Jerusalem because of Solomon's great wisdom. Her visit, described in 1 Kings 10:1–12, pictures her as a wide-eyed ingenue meeting a famous motion picture director on a very posh set. She congratulates him for his wisdom, riches, his God, and his good government, gives him between six and seven million dollars in gold (120 talents) and heads back to Saba/Sheba almost at once. Designed to magnify Solomon, the story was used to cut the queen down to size. We learn that Jewish literature "all but ignored this royal encounter."[62] In the third century rabbis in western Asia denied that she ever existed, attributing the "queen" to a mistaken translation of two similar words—woman and kingdom. Her so-called visit, they said, meant only that the whole kingdom of Saba paid court to Solomon![63] The second verse "She came to Solomon" was thought by other critics to mean that she had sex with him.[64] This interpretation is intensified by verse 13: "And King Solomon gave the queen of Sheba all she desired."[65] This sort of reasoning led to the usual conclusion about what every woman needs. The Ethiopians agreed, claiming that all the lady needed or wanted was a baby by Solomon, and that her wish came true. They traced their own royal house to Israel through her son Menelik. Some stories have Solomon entranced with the queen's face and figure but dismayed at the harrowing sight of her hairy legs and goatlike feet. One story even has a depilatory made up for her use before sleeping with the king. In the Middle Ages the queen was identified with Lilith, a demon queen, and her hairiness seemed to reinforce an association with Satan. She was thought to have been a spreader of diptheria in medieval

Jewish literature. Other medieval traditions cast her as a baby killer and a sexual demon or succubus who had intercourse with men against their will while they lay sleeping. In a medieval source called the *Alphabetum* the queen was said to have born to Solomon the sixth-century Chaldean monarch Nebuchadnezzar,[66] thus blaming the queen of Sheba for the Babylonian Captivity that occurred well over three hundred years after her visit to Jerusalem. These queen stories serve as a reminder to women everywhere that glass ceilings were already part of ancient Israel's skyline. They called it God's will. We call it patriarchy.

In the final analysis, Hebrew history and metahistory command our attention because of their miraculous nature. It was a miracle that fewer than a million Hebrew tribesmen could have held their own so long with so few resources, attributing their success to the "fact" that their god had chosen them because they were more worthwhile than any other group of folks. Primitive species generally have survived by the law of natural selection. The Hebrews survived by the law of unnatural selection.

5

Crete and Mycenae

MINOAN PROSOPOGRAPHY

MINOS WAS THE FICTIONAL MINOAN KING WHOSE amazing palace, a maze or labyrinth, Sir Arthur Evans excavated at Knossos after 1900. He named Crete's Bronze Age culture after Minos, whom the Greeks believed was a great grandson of Zeus by Europa. This Phoenician princess was kidnapped by the father of the gods disguised as a bull on whose back she hitchhiked her way west to Crete. Zeus, having plowed the waters, bestowed the same favor on Europa, and the careless girl was eventually delivered of three of his sons. Minos, the eldest, led an exemplary life as Minos I of Crete, but his grandson and namesake had a problematic reign. Minos II foolishly refused to part with the gift of a white bull that Poseidon, God of the Sea, had given him in the expectation of getting it back as a sacrifice. This wily king substituted a lesser bull for the prize steer. In revenge, Poseidon arranged a weird punishment. He made Queen Pasiphae fall in love with this bull, and with the help of the royal architect, Daedalus, who constructed a wooden heifer in which Pasiphae hid herself, the bull inseminated the Queen. She gave birth to the Minotaur—half man and half bull.

The Minoans had a distinct fascination with bulls, a common symbol of fertility in western Asia. Some thought the Cretans worshipped bulls. Large pairs of sculpted bulls' horns called Horns of Consecration decorated the palace grounds on Crete. Sir Arthur Evans decided that the bull was not worshipped, but because he was a favorite animal of an earth god, people sacrificed bulls to him.[1] Frescoes of bull leapers, male and female, once graced a room Evans named the Throne Room. Gold cups displayed amorous bulls and bulls trapped or hunted. All told, Minoans were bullish on bulls. In fact, they went head over heels over them, like the leapers in the frescoes. The story of the Minotaur is not all bull, but like the monster himself, just half.

A mortified King Minos kept the Minotaur imprisoned in his palace in its very own labyrinth, like the teenager's wing of a modern suburban home, a place apart where messy habits—the Minotaur ate young people— could be ignored. The Athenians had slain Minos's other son, Androgeus, in a fit of pique when the lad beat them in their own Panathenaic games. In revenge, Minos demanded that Athens send seven boys and seven maidens to Crete every ninth year where they were fed to the Minotaur. Eventually, the Athenian hero, Theseus, slew the Minotaur barehanded, and was helped to flee by Minos's daughter, Ariadne. She, having fallen in love with Theseus at first sight, (heedless girl—so like her ancestress Europa!) gave this young gallant a strand of yarn which she tied to the labyrinth's entrance, so that Theseus could find his way out. Homer said Daedalus planned his escape. Minos suspected as much and had Daedalus arrested and imprisoned, though he escaped on wax wings and flew to Sicily. His son, Icarus, fled with him. Ignoring his dad's warning to stay far from the sun, the lad flew too close and plunged into the sea, the victim of history's first meltdown. How Minos pursued Daedalus and ran afoul of King Cocalus, who found work for this talented refugee, is another story. Herodotus and Plutarch, Ovid and Virgil all thought the story of Theseus, Ariadne, and the Minotaur—threadbare from centuries of handling—a great yarn.

LITERACY, LEARNING, AND ACCULTURATION

Although Linear A, used on Crete between 1700 and 1450 BC, has yet to be decoded, Linear B, used by the Myceneans on the Mainland, was partially decoded by Michael Ventris and others in the 1950s.[2] This script turned out to be based on an archaic form of the Greek language using many of the same signs of Linear A that the Minoans had used.[3] The Mycenaeans left records in Linear B at Knossos during the late Minoan period (after 1450 BC). Mycenaeans were Greeks present on the mainland of Greece during the Middle Bronze Age, which began around 1600 BC.[4] The fact that they did not speak the language of Minoan Crete did not prevent them from adapting Minoan script to their own Greek speech. The Minoans taught the Mycenaeans how to write and gave them something to think about as well.

The scholarly culture of the German university recognized the importance of a unique kinship with those from whom we learn when they devised the term *Doktor Vatter* to mean dissertation advisor, the intellectual parent of an embryonic PhD. The mentor relationship was viewed as the equivalent of a blood tie, and the significance of it was heightened by choosing fatherhood to express cultural indebtedness. Just as a scholar owes to his *Doktor Vatter* his intellectual formation, so Homer looked back to Minoan Crete as the mentor culture of Mycenaean Greeks, even though linguists know that the Minoans did not speak Greek. Leonard R. Palmer thought Homer was wrong about the role of Crete and suggested that Luvians from Asia Minor, speaking an Indo-European language closely related to that of the Hittites, may have taught both Mycenaean Greeks and

Minoan Cretans alike whatever they knew of architecture, religion, and pottery-making when they crossed the Aegean and settled into mainland Greece around 1900 BC and into Crete two hundred years later. Palmer's belief in Luvian influence on the mainland and in Crete has not found favor in recent decades and is now considered antediluvian.

The second millennium settlers, whoever they were, personified their *minos* or ruler, who took on the personality of "King" Minos. No evidence indicates that a real king by that name ever existed, only an office. These stories have great *dramatis personae* but no verisimilitude. The Mycenaeans cared nothing for such literary refinements, but a great deal for Cretan treasure, and shortly after 1400 BC they either absorbed Minoan culture or displaced it. Both Minoans and Mycenaeans possessed writing, but neither appears to have used it to leave posterity coherent descriptions of their spiritual convictions. All they did leave was cultural inventory: place names, products, and the names of a few gods that the classical Greeks, their cultural heirs, later adopted. Sir Arthur Evans died (1941) before theories of the Luvians had been fully formed. Like Homer, he thought the Minoans had taught the Mycenaean Greeks just about everything they knew, and this became the prevailing modern view.[5]

BLACK ATHENA AND THE ORIGINS OF GREEK CULTURE

In 1987 a controversial book regarding the nature of the origins of Greek culture was published by a scholar named Martin Bernal. In the first of four volumes, entitled *Black Athena,* Bernal accused scholars from various fields of having rejected a body of opinion that prevailed from antiquity until the early nineteenth century, during which time he believed Greek culture was viewed as the product of Egyptian and Phoenician influence.[6] This Bernal called the "Ancient Model" of Greek history. Then, Bernal says, in the first half of the nineteenth century, this view of Greece's past was abandoned for a Romantic and racist one that he calls the "Aryan Model."[7] Gradually, extreme versions of the Aryan Model denied Egyptian and Phoenician influence. Romantic racist writers viewed Greek civilization as the result of northern invasions which overwhelmed the Aegean or Pre-Hellenic culture. These proponents of the Aryan Model denied that "inferior" races from the Near East (Phoenician Semites) and Africa (dark-skinned Egyptians) were important contributors to classical culture and, instead, viewed Greek civilization as a mixture of Indo-European, Hellenic, and indigenous cultures.[8]

The reaction of scholars of Egyptian, Near Eastern, and Greek studies has been mixed and emotional, but scientific and voluminous.[9] Many scholars conceded that racist ideas were prevalent in the nineteenth and twentieth centuries and that some scholars were impelled by prejudice to slight African and Asian culture. All agree that Egypt and the Near East influenced Greece in the ordinary course of events, though most deny that they colonized Greece. Bernal's critics took pains to distinguish between major aspects of Egyptian and Greek culture, and between Egyptian and Nubian, Saharan, Sub-Saharan, Sudanese, Ashanti, and other forms of African culture which they felt Bernal ignored. They saw no concerted plot to suppress evidence of Egyptian or Semitic influence, nor did they accept something Bernal calls the Revised Ancient Model, which retained his thesis that the Egyptians and Phoenicians colonized Greece, although "somewhat earlier" than he had originally maintained,[10] and allows for northern penetration by "Indo-Europeans" in the fourth or third millennium BC while insisting that their language was related to Indo-Hittite language, thus negating any European influence!

Ethnicities damaged historically by white European culture found Bernal's thesis attractive and consoling. European nations once helped themselves to large slices of African and Near Eastern wealth and colonized those regions. Britain, France, Germany, Spain, the Netherlands, Portugal, and Italy wished to own what was valuable. Their politicians and scholars excused their predatory excess by ignoring contributions that Africa and Western Asia made to the world, including Europe. The more they regarded their colonials as culturally inferior the easier it was to assuage their own guilt in the nasty business of taking advantage of them.

In the postcolonial era the temptation for people marginalized by exploitation has been to retaliate symbolically by taking possession not of European countries, because that is impossible, but of European culture, which in any event has taken possession of us all. That is the reason Bernal's *Black Athena* made such an impression. His thesis made sense from the point of view of the culturally dispossessed. To expropriate Greek culture by asserting the ownership of ancient Greece at a point in history when it was still primitive preempts that wonderful culture at its highest point of development, the Golden Age (fifth century BC). This was not merely retaliation for the real insults sustained by Africa and the Near East at the hands of nineteenth- and twentieth-century European imperial powers. It was a recognition by Afro-Asian critics that Greek culture was a magnificent achievement. Hoping to possess it by claiming that Egypt or Phoenicia was its founder was the ultimate in late twentieth-century consumerism and symptomatic of its cultural "values," which put a premium on owning designer merchandise. It was validation by means of preemptive strike—an unfriendly takeover of a European culture often denigrated by those who are critical of Europe's excesses. To own an object is in our credit-card culture the equivalent of meriting it, or having created it. In fact, owning culture is for many moderns considered better than creating it, deserving it, or trying to understand it.

The origins of Greek culture, though complex and heterogeneous, are not, in any event, the most important aspect of the Greek experience. When the flap over *Black Athena* with its ominous racial subtext dies down, everyone, irrespective of skin color and geographical origin, faces the challenge of coping with the ideas and values of antiquity, many of which continue to shape our intellectual and social environment. The development of Greek experience over time, which even the nonexpert can observe was distinct from anything Egypt or Asia had produced, concerns us now, not the color of the various groups who inhabited Africa, Asia, or the European subcontinent.

This way of looking at Greek civilization puts a premium on the value of its artistic, scientific, political, and literary applications for subsequent generations, not on the ethnicity of the group or groups who contributed to its creation. We moderns are equally inheritors of the triumphs of ancient Greece and should be equally prepared to admit that Greek genius was accompanied by certain failures of the imagination as well as its undoubted triumphs. Did the Greeks invent democracy? Yes. Did they learn how to extend its benefits equally to all their citizens? No. Are we moderns in a position to make even more impressive applications of some Greek discoveries? Yes. Should we waste our efforts in useless arguments over giving credit to one or another ancient culture for our inherited opportunities? We are the ones who count now, not our collective predecessors or respective ancestors. Properly to revere the accomplishments of all of them, whoever they were, we must concentrate not on who they were, or what they did, but what we can do now to equal or surpass their efforts, the same attitude that people in the Renaissance adopted when confronting these same classical achievements.

Black, brown, or white, Athena was the goddess of wisdom and had to cope with problems of cultural transmission not unlike our own. How do culturally advantaged groups stimulate underdeveloped ones so that they learn not merely to use borrowed artifacts and cultural constructs, but how to use them wisely for their own and the wider community's advantage? What precisely are the dynamics of acculturation? If we could fully understand why people are motivated to learn from those more learned, or more wise, we might be able to speed the process without wasting so much time groping for effective teaching methods. In the transfer of ideas from haves to have-nots we need people who can defend learning as that which will make people happy, healthy, and wise rather than just rich or trained to enrich others.

The Minoans seem to have been such a people. They used their art and music and dramatic talents—they built the world's first theaters and painted blue monkeys on their walls to enhance their pleasure in things natural—to live more pleasurably. In the intervals between pleasuring themselves and others—even women whom they encouraged to prophesy, engage in athletics, and participate in public as well as private life—they made money. But making money does not seem to have been their only objective. They were certainly adept at selling their olive oil, grain, and lovely pottery to their Mediterranean neighbors. They knew that the good life makes necessary a balance between work and play, and seemed to have discovered the essence of what would later, on the mainland, become a precept of classicism—nothing to excess. They put a premium on industry, discipline, and organized trade, but at the same time, perfected the arts—architectural, graphic, musical, thespian, spiritual—so that the business of business was balanced by the grace of sensitive fine living.

The Minoans may or may not have gone to school to the Luvians, Egyptians, or Phoenicians, but both the Minoans and their protégés, the Mycenaeans, were highly motivated to learn. The Dorians, who destroyed Mycenaen culture in the period after 1200 BC, were Greek-speakers like the Mycenaeans, but impatient of learning. Despite their linguistic affinity with the Mycenaeans, the Dorians were not intellectually curious. They brought the Dark Ages to the mainland which lasted nearly to the time of Homer, the ninth century BC. After Homer Greeks showed the same thirst for knowledge that the Mycenaeans displayed vis-à-vis the Minoans, and all the world, it was said after them, went to school to Hellas; all the world save Sparta, whose immediate ancestors, not surprisingly, were the Dorians! The lust for learning was the inherited bond that united Minoans to Mycenaeans and to Hellenes like the Athenians even if the heritage from Crete was poetic and mythological, not ethnic. They say blood will tell, but it speaks to deaf ears when one chooses not to listen, as in the case of the Dorians.

SEMIOTICS AND ARCHITECTURE

No doubt Minoan legends bear some relationship to facts and ideas that shaped the lives of Crete's inhabitants, just as the physical objects of these cultures served more or less well-defined purposes. But it is hard to establish how symbolic meanings affected the behavior of any people. How did symbolic events affect the Minoans' daily routine? What difference did they make in the behavior as well as the intellectual horizons of Minoans? In our own civilization it is not always clear to what extent cherished symbols affect public and especially private behavior. How can we assume that the hallmarks of Minoan Crete—the double ax, the bull's Horns of Consecration, the labyrinth, dove, snake goddesses, mountain-peak goddesses, poppy goddesses, griffins, dolphins, octopi, earth mothers, and so on, helped to shape Minoan actions as archaeologists, poets, and historians presume? Were

Minoans not capable of saying one thing and doing another? Were there no hypocrites or independent-minded folk? Did everybody on the island pay attention?

Today we have symbols that are supposed to prevent us from inconveniencing the disabled. Yet how many able-bodied people still park in places that the blue and white signs reserve for the disabled only? How many more would park in them if the fines for doing so were not so high? The American flag has become a symbol that can destroy the very national unity it symbolizes, and during the Vietnam war, provoked violence as well, resulting in legislation that made burning it a punishable offense. Conservative politicians seek votes by proposing a constitutional amendment that would protect this symbol. How would archaeologists thousands of years hence explain the use of the American flag? Or the symbol of Christianity—the Cross? In its name just about every kind of action that Jesus disapproved has been performed. Crosses have been burned on the property of minority groups in the United States as signs of contempt and hatred even though love of one's fellow man was central to Jesus's ministry. Under the sign of the cross Muslims were slaughtered and routed from the Holy Land and heretics who were believing Christians were tortured by the Inquisition. A leading historian of the classical period, M. I. Finley, expressed the sentiments of some colleagues in the historical profession, and increasingly, in the archaeological one, too, when he questioned the validity of using the very best archaeological evidence as a substitute for an incontrovertible and provable explanation. He was speaking about the significance of Crete's Neolithic fertility goddesses, but the same question could well be applied to any other religious symbol of Minoan Crete.[11] As Emily Vermeule noted in her book on the Bronze Age, "It is easy to understand what Mycenaeans did at a funeral, but no amount of excavation will tell what they thought."[12]

Despite the problems of interpretation, few scholars of Greek history have resisted the fascination of Crete and Mycenae though aware that they are ill-equipped to evaluate their past in terms that satisfy their own standards for precision and authenticity. Edith Hamilton, who wrote a remarkably fine book on classical Greek culture, was one of the few who could and did. She noted that the real "Greek way" of reason was distinct from that of the "Egyptian way and way of the East," the kind of dismissal of non-Hellenic cultures that has so irritated Bernal. Because she did not mention Crete or Mycenae, it is probable that she lumped them with Egypt and the East, regions she thought gave up on the intellect and emphasized only the anti-intellectual or spiritual.[13] Her pronouncement now sounds unfair. After all, the foundations of algebra, trigonometry, astronomy, clinical medicine, pharmacology, and Kramer's twenty-odd Sumerian "firsts" from Mesopotamia plus the not inconsiderable scientific and mathematical knowledge of ancient Egypt helped shape Minoan, and through Crete, Mycenaean civilization.[14] The way of the East was not devoid of rationality! And, although much of this knowledge was available to the Greeks, they did not always draw upon it, or when they did, did not therefore discard their myths and the irrationality of their most deep-seated social and political prejudices. For that matter, do we not retain our own store of irrational myths and prejudices and ignore evidence that contradicts them?

The Minoans—like all peoples who ever lived—were unique. Their singularity seems to have rested in large measure on their joie de vivre. To express that joy in living, they not only painted blue monkeys on the walls of their apartments, but fat squid and smiling dolphins cavorting in blue water. Their candid camera was fresco art, and they pictured themselves on palace walls—men and women jumping over bulls' backs; cupbearers in processions; a young man strutting in a kilt and wearing little else but a headdress of feathers, the famous Prince of the Lilies; young women garbed as priestesses but looking more like Parisian fashion models with flounced skirts, bare bosoms, and elaborate coiffures.[15] One was in fact called "la Parisienne" by the French workmen who uncovered her portrait on a frescoed wall.

We want to know what relationship these Minoans of Crete had to their more accomplished cultural heirs, the Greeks of the Golden Age (fifth century BC) and the silver century that followed. It would be a mean-spirited historian of antiquity who ignored the eclectic, legendary, and elusive "evidence" that remains. Few readers will be surprised that historians and archaeologists are undecided what Minoans and Mycenaens felt about their public, private, and spiritual lives. Not much more elusive is what these scholars have discovered about the lives of medieval Roman Catholic peasants or shoemakers, late-twentieth-century American blue-collar workers, or indeed, about classical Greeks of the fifth century BC—workmen, slaves, or women. None of these groups wrote about their way of life. One has only to consult the academic history journals to substantiate the fact that even when possessed of a great deal of written documents concerning some individual or group, as often as not historians will disagree over what such evidence means. Sometimes they arrive at quite diverse opinions! The Egyptians, on the other hand, have left abundant information concerning their thoughts on eternity, the role of spirituality in everyday life, their ethical values. Were the Minoans less reflective? Less concerned with spirituality? Too busy with living to think much about dying?

We read in dated accounts that the Cretans at the beginning of the Bronze Age belonged to the "Mediterranean race" associated with slenderness, small but dolichocephalic (long-headed) skulls, and sallow complexions.[16] Few anthropologists today would commit to the proposition that there ever was a "Mediterranean race," and the uniformity of all DNA has outmoded the concept of race anyway. We read that many Minoans had comfortable small houses on a rocky hillside or point overlooking the harbor of an island port called Pseira,[17] but elsewhere that Minoan homes were often very spacious, the rule in towns such as Khamaizi, Mallia, and Vasilike.[18] We may wonder if all Cretans were comfortably housed in small and large houses, and whether or not they, too, had problems with homelessness? We may never know if the Cretans in the seventeenth to the fourteenth centuries BC were more successful in providing suitable shelter for their population than postmodern cities in democratic countries at the start of the twenty-first.

Sir Arthur Evans uncovered King Minos's wonderful palace at Knossos in 1900, exposing it for the first time in 2,300 years.[19] Rodney Castleden pointed out that this labyrinthine building of fifteen hundred or so rooms was actually no palace but a temple complex, a conclusion he and others have arrived at after studying careful measurements of various rooms. Sir Arthur Evans had identified as royal throne rooms, reception halls, and even royal apartments, rooms peculiarly unsuited for their supposed purposes. Some were too small to serve the public and royal functions that Evans ascribed to them. Others were too dark or inconveniently located, and still others unsuitable because adjoining rooms with more pedestrian purposes such as workshops, or sculptors' studios, or scriptoria, and so forth, would have made the purported royal activities of the given areas impossible to perform with any comfort. Castelden felt Evans was so convinced that a Bronze Age palace existed on the site of Knossos that his conclusions were not always consistent with the material evidence.[20] He also objected to an interpretation of Hans Wunderlich, who in the 1970s developed a theory that the labyrinth was not a palace but a "palace of the dead." Castleden thought that idea had been suggested by Oswald Spengler in his *Decline of the West* (1918),[21] but he seems to have misread Spengler, for what Spengler mooted in that work was what Castleden himself maintains, that the palaces of Crete were "cult-buildings" primarily designed to house religious worship services.[22]

Spengler was no expert about Crete, and his comments were based on the early decades of Cretan archaeological research. Modern scholars do not generally condemn Evans but recognize his ability to call a palace a palace without compromising or denying its religious function, too. Nicholas Platon, for example, in charge of the dig that uncovered the palace at the Cretan site of Kato Zakros, describes Sir Arthur Evans always affirming the sacred nature of Cretan palaces and especially noted that the primary function of the palaces was religious. Platon says Evans used the term "priest-king" to refer to Minos in the same fashion that described theocratic rulers in Mesopotamia. He denies that the problem for determining the function of Minoan palaces, with their lack of large audience rooms, problematizes the roles of Minoan kings but not Mycenaean monarchs, who built larger public reception rooms.[23] Olivier Pelon concludes that even if Minoan kings did not have audience halls, they were still kings for all that, well able to perform public office. They might have had to receive fewer people in their throne room,[24] but that would have proved no handicap in giving a royal performance.

Laymen are left to sort all this architectural minutiae out for themselves, which is hard to do when the experts do not agree among themselves. How the Minoans compartmentalized their spiritual from their political concerns is probably an impossible challenge for archaeologists to resolve. The accidental tourist in the field, lost in a labyrinth of research, may well be looking for Ariadne's thread to lead him to the nearest exit.

FEMININITY, FORCE, AND FAME

Anthropologists have speculated on the degree of freedom enjoyed by women in goddess-worshipping societies and the general presumption is that where the goddesses were worshipped there was more respect and liberty for women. So we read that Minoan women had an "unusually high status" because they were allowed to participate in public religious rituals, indeed, played the leading role in them, and were not afraid to bare their breasts in public[25]–literally, since their blouses were cut away in front to expose not merely cleavage, but that to which the cleavage was cleaving. When they participated in bull leaping, a feat even Sir Arthur Evans thought partly "transcended the power and skill of mortal man," mortal women wore athletic garments so masculine in form they were sewn with a codpiece![26] Was this equality before its time, or just a waste of fabric? While there were no "visible traces" in Crete of any "primitive democracy" another source warns, neither were there rigid class distinctions, and perhaps "much greater social freedom between the sexes than in most ancient societies."[27] Sir Arthur Evans, upon viewing two miniature frescoes that showed women attending a spectacle, noted that they were depicted in the highest ranking positions.[28] Nevertheless, he associated only the king with the performance of religious duties, based on finding a lustral or purification pool in the room he identified as the king's throne room. The queen's quarters and other areas of the palace at Knossos, though similarly equipped, did not lead Evans to conclude that the queen might also have performed such duties.[29] Sinclair Hood, a noted archaeologist of Crete, assures us that "The dominance of goddesses in religion meant that women took an important part in religious rites and ceremonies." Hood also thought that "The queens as high priestesses, if not themselves divine, clearly had important ritual functions" suggesting that the throne room at

Knossos may not have been Minos's but Ariadne's, used in ritual by the queen as representative of that goddess. Still, Hood believed that "power was in the hands of kings" not queens, although the succession to the throne was through the female line by marriage to the king's daughter.[30] This kind of matriarchy also prevailed in Egypt. No evidence suggests that the Egyptians were ruled by women except very infrequently, or that women in Egypt were more privileged than men. Hood may well be right about the lack of political power enjoyed or rather, not enjoyed, by Minoan women. Royal women in both Crete and Egypt were given in marriage—an ominous term in the history of women. With them came all the right to power, but if Hood is correct, that power was claimed by their husbands.

Although women may have been treated more civilly in Crete (as in Egypt) than elsewhere, it would be jumping to conclusions to attribute the fact to the worship of fertility goddesses. After all, the Goddess was also worshipped in Babylonia, Phoenicia, and Assyria, where women did not enjoy the freedom of movement or dignity that Minoan women did, though an occasional one of their queens may have exercised political or even military power for a time. One is reminded of the adoration of the Virgin Mary in the High Middle Ages, when women were at least as repressed in their social and civic lives as they had been in classical Greece, in Hellenistic Asia, and in the Roman world, all areas where goddesses had innumerable devotees! Europeans everywhere, even on Crete, understood the difference between goddesses and their own wives and daughters. The Virgin was respected, loved, admired, worshipped, but the achievement of Europe's women to anything approaching equality with men was delayed until the late twentieth century.

Legends and labyrinths, leaping ladies, and a large, if unequal, measure of personal liberty for women. None of these things would have blossomed had the Minoans not made a political and economic success of life on Crete. Poetry and mythology, the art that required palace walls on which to be displayed, and leisured women all cost money to produce or maintain. In what kind of political environment these things were nurtured is disputed. Most scholars point to an absence of abusive force and lack of defensive walls or other fortifications on Crete.[31] Though some evidence of fortification has been found, it was not a prominent feature of Cretan settlements either before or after the appearance of palaces on the island.[32] Minoan artisans, on the other hand, made all kinds of weapons—from daggers, spears, swords, and suits of armor that included greaves, conical helmets, and shields.[33] Were these articles intended only for hunting wild boars, or did the Minoans use them on other types of swine, namely, their two-footed human enemies?

Archaeologists are less concerned with the peaceable nature of Minoan existence than with the shapes of their pots or buildings and the religious symbols associated with fertility gods and goddesses. The political life of preliterate societies is harder to deduce from physical remains than their domestic arrangements or spiritual life, and their politics remains a mystery to the experts who know a great deal more about the goddesses, architecture, and pots than they do about Cretan policy.

Sir Arthur Evans felt Minos to have been a peaceful king. Herodotus and Thucydides believed he was a strong naval ruler and a destroyer. If Sir Arthur was right and those fifth-century-BC historians wrong, Minos was an anomaly among Bronze Age kings. These men were addicted to the use of force in governing. The faith kings placed in their armies was apparently more ardent than their belief in the gods. Perhaps what they really worshipped was their own power. Minos's power according to Homer was naval, and exercised most unjustly not on Crete but on the Athenians. The story of Theseus and the youths he freed reflects that notion. Perhaps Minos made his power felt on the Aegean islanders where his traders put into port, although it is equally possible that Minos had no real navy, only Minoan merchant vessels intent on controlling a sea empire or thalassocracy, from the Greek *thalassas,* sea. Chester Starr long ago (1955) rejected the notion of a real Minoan navy,[34] and Hutchinson, citing him, agrees, finding that Crete's coasts were more likely protected by the sea, not by any naval fleet.[35] If it is true that the Cretans secured the advantages of a monopoly or even controlled trade with their neighbors without resorting to military force, theirs would be an exceptional instance of such commercial success.

The protection of Crete by any force, natural or man-made, was only relative. Most states are subject to catastrophes from which no protection is absolute, and Crete was no exception. Around 1700 BC her palaces at Knossos and at Phaestos burned. Sir Arthur Evans thought their end came as the result of destruction by foreign invaders, perhaps Mycenaeans, but he changed his mind, later attributing them to earthquakes, floods, and fires.[36] Most scholars agree, because the palaces were rebuilt along earlier lines, and no archaeological evidence nor skeletal remains prove foreign invasion between 1700 and 1450 BC.[37]

When and how Cretan civilization ended is still not certainly known. Was the ultimate destruction wholly natural, or partly political? Were the Mycenaeans to blame? Or was the destruction of Crete solely the result of an enormous volcano that blew apart the island of Thera lying north of Knossos in the Aegean? Were the Mycenaeans in control of the island when the destruction occurred, or did they establish themselves at Knossos only afterwards, displaced in their turn around 1200 BC by Greek-speaking invaders from the mainland, the same Dorians who had previously taken control of mainland Mycenae? Centuries after Minoan collapse squatters of the old culture camped out around charred palaces in Knossos, Mallia, and

Phaestos. Did they remember the pretty girls who leaped over bulls? Blue monkeys on ruined walls? Sacred processions in honor of fertility goddesses? The music of zithers in notation systems heard no more?

In classical times, when the Athenians wanted authorities on sacred tradition, they sent to Crete for Minoan wise men, who seemed to have set up a consulting business in prophesy. The Athenians surmised that Cretan wisdom had been in some sense superior to their own. Their error lay in thinking that the knowledge of Minoan Crete was more spiritual than that of classical Greece, when in fact it was more mundane and practical, and if never as rational, not half as tragic. For the Minoans, not unduly restricting the liberty of women or indulging in war (if in fact they did not indulge in it!) showed the Mycenaeans and finally, all Hellas, how much energy and creativity could be released by restraint. It was just a coincidence that they also installed what was perhaps the first indoor plumbing.

This nonliterary, nonrational society demonstrated reverence not merely for fertility, though they worshipped the goddesses, but for life itself. Even before Crete western Asian civilizations, like many modern ones, confused mere fertility with life. It was not a mistake that the Minoans made. They managed to worship the principle of fertility while seeking to enhance the quality of female lives, and by avoiding the pitfalls of militarism they improved the lifestyle of everyone, men and women alike. They viewed life not just quantitatively after the fashion of other fertility worshippers, but qualitatively, affording opportunity to all to develop their goddess-given talents. The classical Greeks, like the Minoans, revered fertility, but unlike the Minoans, they despised the women with whom they procreated, valuing the procreative act mostly for the harvest of male infants who alone could participate in public life and go to war. Long after Minos had gone to his just reward—made king of the underworld or, according to an alternate version of the legend, killed in his bath by the daughters of King Cocalus—Athens remembered Crete. Unfortunately, for all the wrong things.

MYCENAEANS

When the German tycoon and naturalized American citizen Heinrich Schliemann arrived in Mycenae in the Greek Peloponnesus (1875), he was already famous as the discoverer of the site of ancient Troy. An inspired amateur archaeologist, Schliemann soon discovered (1876) a grave circle from the relatively late Mycenaean settlement (1600–1500 BC), whose shaft graves revealed in abundance how luxuriously the Mycenaean nobility had learned to live. The graves yielded gold cups, vases in the shape of a bull's head, artworks in ivory, gold jewelry, bronze swords, and a gold death mask that Schliemann thought was the face of Agamemnon, king of Argos, leader of Achaean forces in the Trojan War. But the mask was three hundred years older than the Trojan War, which may have taken place before the middle of the thirteenth century.[38] It was not Agamemnon's, for he was not yet dead when it was made. He was not yet dead because he was not yet born by 1600–1500 BC! We do not know if Agamemnon ever existed, or if he ever led Achaean Greeks to Troy. Archaeologists who followed Schliemann are pretty sure there was a Trojan War in which Greece may have fought under a Mycenaean king. But the mask of Agamemnon could only have belonged to a much earlier monarch. Schliemann went on to other victories—and defeats. He published his third book, *Mycenae,* in English (1877), married a Greek woman, built two splendid houses in Athens, and in 1878 began an unsuccessful dig in Ithaca, home of Homer's wandering hero, Ulysses. He published two more books (on Troy), did some digging in Orchomenus (Boeotia), and in 1885 uncovered the ground plan of the Mycenaean palace of Tiryns, his last successful dig. Great wealth, great curiosity, and the need to live adventurously and claim other civilizations' treasures for himself enabled Schliemann to prevail over every obstacle, every opponent. In many ways he nearly resembled the Mycenaean heroes he spent so much of his life tracking down.

The Minoans are famous for their palaces, the Mycenaeans for their graves, though neither were particularly grave and both had palace cultures, like the one Schliemann excavated at Tiryns. But neither this palace nor the one uncovered at Pylos captured the popular imagination like the ring of shaft graves at Mycenae. The palaces were empty of treasure when they were excavated, whereas the shaft graves Schliemann uncovered (five) were crammed with consumer goods of the highest quality. Mycenae's aristocracy enjoyed luxury products that they copied from Cretan models when they did not import them or steal them. Minoan and Mycenaean art merged in such subtle ways that only the cognoscenti or the archaeologist can tell them apart. The Mycenaeans must have heard that emulation was the highest form of flattery. It was also the principle of religious conversion, for they borrowed more than opulence and art. They adopted many Minoan gods and goddesses and worshipped them in palace shrines as on Knossos. Besides art, religion, and the Minoan script, they assumed not only all the Minoan virtues that they lacked, but much of Minoan Crete, which they also lacked, until they assumed that, too. Foreclosures were a Mycenaean specialty, for their earliest experiences in the Peloponnesus had been conquest. Shortly after arriving there around 1450 BC they dispossessed and enslaved the older inhabitants, and had been gradually increasing their capacity for fine living at others' expense. They were not called My-cenaeans for nothing.

THE TROJAN WAR

The Mycenaeans' war with Troy could not have been fought against a more simpatico foe, as bold and proud as the Mycenaeans themselves. The enemy was perfect, but the "war" lacks a plausible casus belli and the story, about an assault on a seaside resort, was written long before Mycenaeans attached it to their famous struggle with Troy.[39] This story was first pitched as an antique siege poem about the sack of a walled seaside resort, and the Mycenaeans, called Achaeans in the *Iliad,* found it amusing, and adapted it for their own purposes. They did not write it down, but as was customary in western Asia from which the story sprang, recited it aloud around their halls and campfires. The Trojans, who were preliterate, were still less able to leave us their war memoirs than the Mycenaeans, who could make lists, but not literature. Making lists may be one of the habits of highly effective people, but it is no substitute for reportage. As M. I. Finley tells us in his essay on myth, memory, and history, the reason that the early Greeks left no inquiry into the facts of the Trojan War or any other period of history was due to their lack of interest in the facts of the past, their preference for "Timeless mythology"[40] that resulted from the needs of noble families to establish and enhance their own prestige or to justify their use of power.[41] Like many another power elite, the early Greeks preferred to reconstruct their history rather than simply inherit one not to their liking, one that might embarrass them. Their preference for inventing rather than recording history made them control freaks, for history can be more easily controlled when invented rather than experienced.

The Trojans, like the Mycenaeans, were men of the sea as well as the saddle. Joseph Alsop thought the Trojans and Mycenaeans were like cousins, united by their Indo-European language and horses.[42] Kindred language and the same modes of transportation did not prevent these maritime competitors and trading partners from going to war, as they did in Homer's poetry, nor would this war have been the first—nor the last—fought between illiterate and semiliterate horses' asses. And yet, this is not a tale in which men remain frozen in their idiocy. It is an epic that points to the educability even of military heroes, for these soldiers, the survivors at any rate, came to understand the full scope of war's horrors and what made war happen: blind passion, incapacity to think about the future, one's own family, and the family of man. Not unlike our veterans of foreign wars, some of these Greek soldiers and the folks back home grew in understanding, even if understanding came too late.

Homer's story begins when strife, named Eris, threw down a golden apple as a prize for "the fairest" whom Zeus refused to name.[43] Paris, son of King Priam of Troy, arbitrates, and three goddesses vie for the apple, which in Western civilization is the fruit of choice for wreaking havoc on mankind. All three goddesses bribed the judge, although no one seemed shocked that this was the case, least of all the judge. Athena offered wisdom; Hera, the governance of Asia; and mighty Aphrodite offered Helen of Sparta, the most beautiful of women.[44] Hardly had the love goddess closed her mouth when Paris stuffed the apple into it and made off for Sparta. Menelaeus, Helen's husband, conveniently enough, was away on a business trip to Crete. Helen's complicity in what followed, her seduction and kidnapping, was a matter of debate. A marriage goddess of Sparta by profession, her intimate life was closely, even endlessly reexamined, and many blamed her for the war that followed. The hazards of being a career girl. Before long, Helen turned up in Troy where Paris wed her and housed her in an elegant palace in the same complex where his father, Priam, lived with his other sons, their wives, his daughters and their husbands. It was all in the family. Even after Paris was killed in battle, the Trojans refused to give up Helen. Helen was a descendant of Zeus, who had disguised himself as a swan before impregnating her mother, Leda, who produced her and her brothers, Castor and Pollux, from swan's eggs. To Homer Helen was just a bad egg, the woman guilty of bringing men to their death in the Trojan War. Homer made Helen condemn herself to her brother-in-law, Hector, as "a nasty bitch evil-intriguing," and he strongly hinted that Helen had incestuous hots for Hector. But Hector remained true to his wife, Andromache "of the white arms," while Helen betrayed her second husband, Paris, and Troy to the attacking Achaeans, relatives of her first. It was her way of showing just how homesick she was.

Euripides recast her story in his play *Helen* produced in 412 BC when classical Greece was being torn asunder in the Peloponnesian War. The dramatist exonerated Helen by awarding Paris only the idea or "ghost" of this gal, while sending the real flesh and blood Helen to Egypt for the duration of the war. He wanted his audience to understand that it was possible for a noble woman with a good mind and a great face and body to live the "good" life—i.e., remain a faithful wife. He might have done more with this material, but there were no other roles for good women in those days. Euripides also criticized war, the gods' way of ridding the earth of surplus population. Euripides was a skeptic and friend of the Sophist Protagoras. Euripides' play *Helen* implied that men go to war over phantoms, that is, insubstantial causes, and that the end result is their mutual slaughter and that of their victims, often innocent civilians. Euripides was taken to task for immorality and unorthodox opinions, including his profeminism. He was neither a flag-waver nor a believer. The term playwright is not a good description of Euripides. He played to the left in all his works.

After the Trojan War ended, Helen returned to her home in Sparta and to her first husband, Menelaeus, who welcomed her home. Whether or not her reputation was retrievable, her spouse rejoiced just to retrieve Helen.

Menelaeus was a man of vision, Helen a sight for sore eyes, and Homer a blind man.

Before the war started, Agamemnon, King of Mycenae, sent envoys to Troy demanding Helen's release with compensation. Rebuffed, Menelaeus and his ally, King Nestor of Pylos, went all over Greece enjoining the aid of other Greek kings, many of whom had once been Helen's suitors. Helen's old beaux were crazy about her, so they all contributed to the war. It was a joint rescue effort. Their combined forces met at a bay called Aulis, between Euboea and the mainland. From Aulis they sailed eastward and attacked Teuthrania opposite Lesbos. The attack was a colossal error and the local king promptly defeated them. The Achaeans mistook Teuthrania for Troy (they both began with T and the Mycenaeans couldn't read), not the first time military intelligence fouled up. The Achaeans may have been secretly embarrassed by this defeat, but neither they nor Homer let on. Apparently, Aeolus, god of winds, was miffed, because after they reassembled at Aulis, the Achaeans were becalmed. Officially they blamed Artemis, whom Chalchas, the army chaplain and prophet, claimed was offended because Agamemnon had killed her favorite stag. Anyway, it was easier to blame a goddess whenever something went wrong rather than a male god, even if the god was a windbag like Aeolus. Soon enough, the Achaean troops ate all their provisions, after which their ships began to rot. The troops grew demoralized, and when a plague settled in, they, too, began to rot. Chalchas said they must sacrifice Agamemnon's daughter Iphigenia to Artemis before they could set sail again. While Homer tastefully avoids any mention of this sacrifice, the fact that the ships finally sailed out of the harbor at Aulis led subsequent raconteurs to assume that the girl had been slaughtered. Agamemnon's supposed acquiescence to the sacrifice sealed his own fate by his wife's hand after he returned home from Troy.[45]

That the Greeks could ever imagine a virgin goddess like Artemis insisting on the sacrifice of another virgin for a slaughtered stag may say more about how much more Greeks valued venison than women. That Iphigenia could be portrayed as a patriotic, enthusiastic martyr to the cause of war— one who would willingly consent to her own sacrifice—reminds us that women often support their oppressors. Iphigenia may have escaped death— the myths fuzz up a bit—just as Isaac escaped at the altar of Abraham, and for the same reason: intervention by a god. For as the priest was about to plunge his knife into the victim, Artemis recalled an entry-level job opening that this girl could fill at Tauris. Iphigenia said she did not do windows and was hired on as a priestess. Her task? To murder all strangers loitering in the temple of Artemis!

Euripides wrote up her experiences in his wildly successful romantic comedy, *Iphigenia in Tauris,* in which the only real tragedy is homesickness, and the comedy involves escaping all punishment for refusing to murder two strangers on the island, one of whom is her own brother, Orestes. Euripides whisks all three young people and a statue of Artemis onto a ship and out the harbor. It looks like they are headed home to Greece when an ill wind blows them back to shore and the angry king of Tauris. Euripides, however, springs his deus ex machina on the audience: the goddess Athena makes the king forgive everyone involved, and a sacred rite to Artemis is set up on the mainland to make amends for Iphigenia's poor job performance.

Euripides also wrote *The Trojan Women* and *Andromache*.[46] Prince Hector of Troy seemed fond of his wife and baby son and scheduled a visit before returning to the battle—and death at Achilles' hands. Professor Kitto remarked that this passage illustrates how we misinterpret literature that indicates Greeks did not lack regard for their women folk. Of course, the Trojans were not Greek, though they admired things Greek. Perhaps Kitto ought not to have used this particular example to establish tenderness in Greek families. Especially since Hector refused to do what Andromache begged—provide for her safety and their son's. Hector was moved instead by a different sense of duty, what Kitto called "duty towards himself."[47] This is exactly the point. What the little lady wanted—to be defended from capture—was beyond Hector, because the value of a wife was as nothing compared a man's virtue. Ilios (Greek for Troy) is going up in flames as Hector tells Andromache that his dearest wish is to predecease her. Then he would be spared having to watch as she became a household slave to some other woman. He did not tell her that she was likely to become the concubine of an enemy warrior before she entered domestic service. He was not sadistic. He simply did not wish to see her dishonored. But her safety was not as important as his honor. After kissing his infant son good-bye, he did nothing to try and save him. Hector's priority was to fight on for glory (though he realized it was all up with Troy) rather than feel ashamed at having deserted the Trojans. So much for the feelings of husbands for wives and children among the hellenized Trojans.

One "fact" about the Trojan War (other than Helen's abduction) that most people remember is that during it, the Achaeans resorted to trickery to gain access to Ilios. They constructed a hollow-bellied horse that they ostentatiously dedicated to Athena, taking care to hide some of their best fighters inside, among them Odysseus of Ithaca and King Menelaeus, Helen's aggrieved husband. Then they burned their camp and put to sea, feigning retreat. Instead, they anchored offshore waiting to see if the Trojans were more curious than cautious. At daybreak the Trojans discovered both horse and deserted campsite, and concluded that they were entitled to the wooden horse as well as to a riotous victory celebration that night. It was during this gala event that the Achaeans sailed back to shore, and at midnight, upon receipt of a signal, and with a "full moon rising," they joined the attack that the heroes inside the horse were mounting against the sentries at the citadel's gates. Now, the Trojans were sufficiently hellenized to have reasoned their way around danger. They should never have swiped a sacrificial present left for Athena, goddess not only of wisdom, but of military science, generally depicted with a helmet and spear, who at birth sprung fully armed out of the head of her father, Zeus, father of the gods. It was this goddess, patron of the Athenians, who taught mankind how to manage the horse in the first place! It is not surprising that the Trojans lost the war. You don't tow the vehicle of a goddess, who is a daughter of the commander in chief, Zeus. You especially don't do it when the only "war correspondent" at the front is a blind poet—who files his stories for the other side!

War is what the Achaeans lived for. They only really lived as long as the danger, which they called glory, lasted. War employed the bodies of their heroes, not their minds. Indeed, they seem incapable of disinterested reflection while they quarrel over the dignities due them, mostly which hero will get which woman. Agamemnon, though willing to sacrifice his own daughter, was not willing to give up Chryseis—Apollo's priest's daughter—until his allies shamed him into it. Unmoved by the pleas of her suffering father, the priest Chryses, the king agreed to give the girl up only on the condition that he take Briseis away from Achilles. Achilles, whose temper was as great as his military prowess, calmed himself only when Athena promised him more "prizes"—three or four times more than Agamemnon would get, but only if he mastered his anger. Women were the most visible prizes of war, but their acquisition brought no lasting joy to the men who fought for such prizes. Nor was the greatest war prize the capture of Troy. Rather, it was the gratification of the egotistical impulses of powerful warriors who turned the world upside down in order to experience the raw passions they only felt in war itself. What a pity that they experienced the sweetness of life only when they were about to lose it on the battlefield.

6

Classical Greece

CLASSICAL GREECE! HER ART WAS SO NOBLE, her poetry so dramatic, her drama so poetic, her science so philosophical, her philosophy so scientific, and her politics so impolitic that scholars scarcely know how to account for her accomplishments, or her failure to overcome problems that were no more challenging than those of many other, less brilliant civilizations that endured longer. Classical Greece developed in ways that none of her earliest thinkers could have predicted, nor later ones remedied. She regarded herself as special, superior to the "barbarians" her neighbors, enemies, and trading partners—Persians, Egyptians, Phoenicians, and Babylonians. The Greeks between the sixth and fourth centuries BC were not more artistic than these other people were. And, though they were curious about science, they were less curious about mathematics. They were undoubtedly more verbal. They perfected the Phoenician alphabet, adjusted it to Greek sounds, and wrote more or saved more of what they wrote than any other civilization. Most importantly, they questioned what they wrote. They even began to question their answers, which is not at all common. They were the most critical thinkers who ever lived. Indeed, they seemed to live to criticize, unlike most other folks, who until then lived principally to obey and adore.

We call the Greeks of the sixth through the fourth centuries BC a classical culture because theirs became the standard by which men who were learned judged men who were less so. Classic is something so excellent it can not be easily reproduced, though its imperfections are such that if it were, it probably would not work as well. There would be imitations and approximations of classical Hellenic culture: Hellenistic civilizations followed hard upon the demise of classical Greece. Roman civilization was much in her debt, as was that continuation of Greek and Roman experience, the Byzantine Empire. Muslims preserved much of her scientific legacy, and sporadic neoclassical revivals of this or that affected everything from architecture to fashion. Philosophical and scientific discourses depend on Greek thought; our literature is permeated with their mythology. The way we speak and write, reason and rhapsodize, worship and compete in sports is permeated by our classical heritage. Theater and the movies are influenced by their tragedy and comedy. Finally, democracy. The Athenians conceived of it, though they never achieved it, and we revere it as a last resort.

The Greeks did not start out after the Dark Ages (c. 1200–850 BC) with democratic governors, but with kings. A king or tribal leader was a *basileus,* an official tolerated because he did not exercise absolute, only collegial authority, sharing power with priests, seers, and assemblies of important men that proceeded without rules and were possessed of no particular functions.[1] The Spartans had two kings who ruled in tandem, but could soft-pedal whenever the people threatened to depose them. They were the peoples' first line of defense against barracks officers who might have staged armed revolts against the state.[2] Except for Sparta, which insulated itself from everything trendy, monarchy had disappeared in Greece by 800 BC.

Athens's last king was supposed to have been Codrus, whom the Athenians called the Father of his Country. Sacrificial lamb might be nearer the truth. He reigned for twenty-one years during the eleventh century BC and was a contemporary of Kings Saul and David before sacrificing himself to save Athens during the last Dorian siege. The Oracle, Apollo's priestess (*pythia*) at Delphi, sat cross-legged over a hole in the floor beneath which burned the leaves of a mind-altering substance. The Oracle declared that victory would be granted to that nation whose king was killed in battle. The Dorians accordingly gave strict orders to spare the life of Codrus. But the patriotic king disguised himself and was unwittingly killed by a Spartan who did not realize that Codrus was a king. Moderns may think that there was something fishy about Codrus, and wonder why his death meant Athens had won the war. That isn't how these things usually go. Athenians, on the other hand, had to accept the story in order to preserve the Oracle's credibility. To honor Codrus's memory, the Athenians declared that never again should a king reign over them. It is hard to determine whether this should be taken as an instance of self-sacrifice (Codrus's), civic sacrifice (Athens's), or civil revolution (Athens's). After the Dark Ages, kings were shorn of executive functions that were distributed to public officials who held office for only one year rather than for a lifetime. The concept of monarchy, like the concept of tyranny in the classical fifth century, was generally held by Athenian aristocrats to be unworthy of them, though perfect for all other Greeks and for barbarians. Sometimes it was hard to tell the difference.

A tyrant (Greek, *tyrannos*) was a man who came to power by untraditional means, a usurper, who then proceeded to rule by absolute power, as kings did not. Tyrants were disapproved of as illegitimate rulers and because of that, tyrant was never a title in Greece, only a job description. Although there were words for king and tyrant, most tyrants did not care which of the two he was called since both brought power and prestige.[3] The rose, as Shakespeare knew, would smell just as sweet if called a marigold or a geranium. No matter what Greeks called them, tyrants rarely raised a stink. Some even came close to legitimizing themselves by performing better and more liberally while in office than the aristocratic cliques of oligarchs whom they supplanted and with whom they were never in good odor. Aristocrats insisted that tyrants were destructive of popular freedom. By that, of course, they meant their own.

Among the first tyrants in Greece was Cypselus, who seized power by a coup d'état around 657 BC at Corinth and was succeeded by his son, Periander (d. 585 BC). The policies of the Cypselids alternated between mild and popular, harsh and oppressive, depending on who was doing the reporting. They were consistent in their patronage of the fine arts, genius, and athletics. The tyrants of Corinth managed a system of foreign alliances to secure domestic peace, during which the Greeks made all the preparations necessary to go to war. Under these tyrants there was full employment with high wages, no direct taxation, the protection of transport and trade, and beautification of the urban environment. Prosperity soon led to the maintenance of a Corinthian naval presence in the Aegean and colonies in Macedonia and northwestern Greece. Periander maintained friendly relations with the tyrants of Miletus and Mytilene, the kings of Lydia, Egypt, and perhaps Phrygia, too. Though the playwright Aeschylus (d. 456 BC) thought that tyrants were afflicted with the disease of never trusting their friends, Periander proved them wrong. Supported by firm friends, he felt free to make war against his enemies. What else are friends and enemies for?

According to Herodotus, Periander had a dark side, for the picture he gives of him is "a mixture of intemperance and compassion," a sketch that would fit just about everyone.[4] Historians say things like that because they are so hard to disprove. One tradition claims that Periander had a broad streak of cruelty, committed incest with his mother, put his wife Melissa to death upon false accusation, and banished his son Lycophron because he had wept for his mother. Like Machiavelli nearly two thousand years later, Periander noted that while a man ought solemnly to keep his word, he should not hesitate to break it if it clashed with his own interests. Still, this tradition is very likely from a tainted source, the nobility whom Periander repressed. Herodotus thought Periander had followed the advice of the tyrant of Miletus, who advised Periander's emissary while standing in a field of corn to "cut off those ears which stood taller than the rest"—a metaphor our tyrant was said to have followed by murdering his most eminent citizens.[5] A tradition has it that Periander was considered to have been one of the seven wise men of Greece. Who the other six were is still classified information, apparently, for they are never listed. The demand of the Corinthians for liberty was stronger than anticipated. The good news was that the last of the Cypselids was assassinated around 582 BC,[6] and liberty from tyrants was achieved. The bad news was that as soon as the Corinthians found themselves freed from the progressive and liberal policies of tyranny, they were subjected to the retrograde ones of Dorian oligarchs, who, though never progressive, were regrettably forward.

The Athenians conducted their own experiment with tyranny, but only after they had consented to some social changes. The first were put into effect by a nobleman named Draco (fl. 620 BC) who was not a tyrant, but whose social conservatism made him a champion of the death penalty, which is really all we know about his law code. He "gave" us the adjective "draconic" as a synonym for harshness. Draco's laws were extensively revised by the poet and archon (elected magistrate) Solon, a man of good birth, moderate means, and immoderate political tact. Solon defended the poor against the rich, perhaps the first influential man since the Hebrew prophets to have done so. Early in the sixth century (594 BC) he put out the fires of potential social revolution by appeasing all sides, averting crisis, and ending the grossest kinds of social abuse, serfdom or slavery for debt. He did not side so completely with the poor that he threatened the rich. Most notably, he did not recommend land reform, which would have redistributed wealth. He opened the Assembly to all free men, but created a new Council of Four Hundred to represent property. He eschewed monologue and encouraged dialogue. His own speech was pithy. When asked whether he had given the Athenians the best laws he could give them, he replied pithily, "the best laws they could observe." Not only could he split the opposition, he could split hairs. After one year spent reforming the law, he was out of there.

Solon's moderation reflected the needs of his fellow aristocrats, the business class of Athens, and the poor majority who had the most to gain from immoderation, but also, the most to lose. Solon boasted that he had satisfied neither side, but benefited both. He saved the poor from the wrath of the rich, from slavery, and from a fate he thought worse: having to cope with wealth. Solon thought poor folks incapable of doing this. Of course. They lacked practice. He saved the rich from the wrath of the poor, too: the indignity of banishment and control by a tyrant. Living in an age of tyrants, Solon refused to join their ranks. Two millennia later, during the Renaissance, also known as the Age of Despots, the Medici, Visconti, Sforza, and Gonzaga were blessed with Solon's opportunities, but not his restraint or principles. Solon was the very embodiment of the Greek proverb "Nothing to Excess." Not democracy, certainly. Neither the Athenians nor their posterity ever really believed in democracy, but the influential and educated upper class pretended to. By flattering the ordinary citizen with institutions in which he could participate and express his views, the elite of Athens retained the habit of determining the political fate of everyone in Attica.

Solon and Pisistratus, Athens's first tyrant, stood on opposite sides of a divide when it came to public service. Solon was an elected archon, Pisistratus a usurping tyrant. Curiously enough, both men were accused of the same literary and political crime. It seems both falsified two lines of the *Iliad* in order to have Homeric authority (Homer was the Greek Bible) for seizing Salamis from the Megarians.[7] Solon and Pisistratus agreed that this owed nothing to excess, and everything to success.

Pisistratus was a great orator, defender of the poor, and a superb tactician and patriot. He believed a brilliant society necessitated supporting the arts, and he personally paid for the publication of the first edition of Homer's work in its present form. He built fountains and public works in Athens, including the Temple of Zeus. Of him it might be said that never did a man who wanted power so much, so much deserve to get it. He exercised it so brilliantly, he made tyranny look more attractive to most people than the limited democracy Solon started. Pisistratus took power after a coup in 560 BC. He posed as the victim of the aristocratic parties. His enemies said he even cut himself to make his case convincing. If so, this was the kindest cut of all, for he was given an armed guard of fifty men. With these he seized the Acropolis and installed himself as tyrant.[8]

A radical who defended the interests of the rural poor and of naturalized citizens, Pisistratus did not deprive the rich of their property. After all, he, too, was rich. Instead, he made Athens prosperous by expanding the economy, promoting peace, and attracting alien craftsmen to the city. Like Cypselus and Periander, he gave Athens overseas possessions and planted colonies abroad. So progressive were his methods that he came very close to being a constitutional dictator, oxymoronic though that may be.[9] He and his son, Hippias, succeeded in elevating the role of the state above the role of the clans. Professor Bowra says he looked after the populace "in his own way for his own uses" but concedes that he kept the existing laws.[10] Yet, looking after poor people and keeping the laws is an extraordinary achievement in any age, and one that threatened the affluent and wellborn. Although enemies twice managed to get him expelled from power, Megacles got him back into it.

Megacles was a member of the powerful Alcmeonid clan, but a plutocrat not an aristocrat. A plutocrat gets his power from cash. An aristocrat gets his cash from birth. In return for Megacles' political support, Pisistratus married Megacles' daughter. This union was intended to forge an alliance between the economically disadvantaged who followed Pisistratus and the politically disadvantaged plutocrats who followed Megacles. Unfortunately, Pisistratus neglected to forge a union between himself and his bride. He did not consummate his marriage. So Megacles deserted him and joined with their mutual enemies—the conservative aristocratic landholders.[11] We do not know if Megacles's daughter—or Pisistratus for that matter—ever sought counseling.

Pisistratus was a master of public relations, if not marital ones. He found a tall, imposing woman named Phya, and had her dress up as Athena, patron of Athens, and speak on his behalf. Her speech implied that Pisistratus was the gods' choice. That further soured his critics. Women were not thought fit for political campaigning. Or much of anything except pregnancy. And though goddesses were expected to be heard as well as seen, ordinary women, even tall, articulate ones, were not. Yet Pisistratus's rule was popular. Although his father-in-law betrayed him and sent him into an exile that lasted over ten years, Pisistratus returned at the head of an army of mercenary troops and died, in 527 BC, with his sandals on. He was succeeded by his son, Hippias. Perhaps Pisistratus and Megacles' daughter got counseling after all?

Hippias reigned until 514, the year his brother, Hipparchus, was slain. The murderers were later honored as tyrannicides.[12] Most modern experts think the murder was the result, not of politics, but of a homosexual love affair gone awry.[13] After 510 BC the remaining Pisistratids retired to their private estates outside Greece, hoping to find Persian support for a political comeback. The Greeks refused to take Hippias back. Instead, they sent twenty-five warships to freedom fighters in Ionia trying to overthrow Persian rule in Miletus. Although the Greek masses looked to tyrants for protection and good jobs, aristocrats were jealous of their authority, which they said prejudiced Athenian liberties. Not surprisingly, Athenian "liberties" were defined by aristocrats at the end of the sixth century.

Cleisthenes (570 BC–c. 507 BC), Father of Athenian Democracy, was the grandson of the tyrant of Sicyon and son of Megacles. For a time, Cleisthenes was an important minister in Hippias's government, but after Hippias was exiled, Cleisthenes managed, thanks to Spartan help, to become chief ruler of Athens. The Spartans helped defeat Hippias because their King, Cleomenes I, thought the Oracle at Delphi had ordered him to support the Alcmaeonids, including Cleisthenes.[14] Some say his friends at Delphi manipulated the Oracle in Cleisthenes' favor.[15] Others, that Cleisthenes bribed the Oracle to draw Cleomenes into a political arena from which he could not emerge victorious.

The "arena" turned out to be the Acropolis of Athens, where the Spartan king's men were trapped by the Athenians and forced to capitulate. Cleomenes went home to collect a larger force in order to install his own tyrant (Isagoras) in Athens. Gossips whispered that Cleomenes' support of Isagoras resulted from his love affair with Isagoras's wife. Cleomenes was adept in international affairs, though Herodotus did him no justice. Sparta's allies refused to cooperate in the invasion of Attica, so Cleomenes abandoned Isagoras and his wife as well. Pity. Athens would have been perfect for getaway weekends.

Cleisthenes got a chance to break the nobility's grasp on political power. The ten new tribes he created were determined by residence, not blood. Each new tribe elected its own local council and magistrates and its own military officers. Although Cleisthenes was called the Father of Greek Democracy for his abolition of clan privilege, Sparta, the least democratic of all Greek states, was at least stepfather to Athenian democracy. For without out Cleomenes I's intervention against the tyranny there, Cleisthenes would never have had the chance to reform the constitution.

Sparta soon realized that Cleisthenes was not going about things in the right, that is, the Spartan, way. Like Solon and Pisistratis, Cleisthenes decided, as Herodotus put it, to "take the people into partnership" against the nobles, who then appealed to Sparta for help. According to Aristotle, Cleisthenes invented the system of ostracism in which the Assembly might exile, by majority vote on tiles or shards of pottery (Greek, *ostrakon*), any individual it chose for a ten-year period, providing ten thousand Athenians felt that way. One story has it that Cleisthenes was himself the first to suffer exile, but the allegation (Aelian's) has been termed "weak" and "late," and may be an invention.[16]

Still, Cleisthenes finished his term of office under a cloud. Fearing war against Boeotia, Euboea, and Sparta, he sent ambassadors to Persia (507 BC), seeking aid, but refusing the price—which was the return of Hippias as Athenian tyrant. The next year Cleisthenes managed to defeat Boeotia and Chalcis because Corinth deserted the Peloponnesian coalition. Chester Starr doubted that Cleisthenes "had an idealistic predisposition toward democracy" but rather aimed at breaking the power of the clans over the state.[17] So did Solon. So did Pisistratus. None of the three men were democrats—the term had not yet been invented—but all of them were liberal, and Cleisthenes the most liberal of the three. Cleisthenes finished his career as a de facto champion of democracy because he spoke of creating *isonomia,* equality of rights, even though he did not in fact make all citizens equal. The Pisistratids had provided social welfare in the form of good jobs with high pay. Cleisthenes added more democratic control but not equality, withholding from the poor the right to exercise the most important offices of state. These Cleisthenes reserved to the rich, or "cavalry class" of Athenians. He felt he must console the aristocrats for finding their old clans rendered politically meaningless.

Ordinary Athenians were not, it has been written, jealous of aristocrats, because they could nominate candidates and control them in the Assembly and in the courts.[18] Of course, it is not ordinary citizens who wrote to deny their jealousy of aristocrats, but the aristocrats who wrote to deny that they were the object of such jealousy. Who gets to write history naturally makes a big difference in the way we get to read it. Still, control of public officials by the voting public was one of the most advanced democratic traits of Athenian democracy that, at the end of the sixth century BC, was still not completely formed and was imperfect by modern standards. It could not but be imperfect, given the large numbers of women, aliens, and slaves who were not involved in democratic participation in any way. Fifty years after Cleisthenes disappeared from the scene, the right to serve in the Council was extended to all male Athenian citizens by lot, for a one year term. No people were ever more fond of term limits than the Athenians.

PERSIANS IN, PERSIANS OUT: IMPROBABLE VICTORY

Throughout the last half of the sixth century BC Persia had been closing in on Greece. First Cyrus conquered Lydia, the first nation to invent coinage. Their king was rich as Croesus. That is because he was Croesus. This Lydian monarch did not know how to interpret the Delphic Oracle who told him that if he crossed the river Halys, he would destroy a great nation. He did. He destroyed his own Lydia, not Cyrus's Persia. Ever since, heads of state have relied on intelligence reports but failed to read them intelligently. The Persians had extended westward along the northern Aegean. Macedonia had been reduced to a tributary state. To the southeast Ionian cities of pure Greek culture were controlled by Greek tyrants who were protected, patronized, and patrolled by Persia.

When Aristagoras of Miletus decided to revolt it was because he had failed to carry out a military assignment that Persia had financed in Naxos. Failing to live up to Persian expectations, and worse, his own, Aristagoras tried to live up to Ionian Greek ones by joining forces with Ionians rebelling against Persian control. He applied for aid from Sparta's King Cleomenes I. Aristagoras, armed with a bronze map, something no Greeks had ever before seen, tried to bribe Cleomenes for his support of an invasion of Persia. The king's eight-year-old daughter, Gorgo, nicknamed "Bright Eyes," discouraged her father from helping Aristagoras on the grounds that he would be corrupted by accepting campaign contributions from a foreigner. In fact, it was not Gorgo who persuaded her father to stay at home, but the helots, Sparta's suppressed majority.[19] King Cleomenes was worried that if Sparta became involved in the liberation of Ionians from Persia, the helots might overthrow him! This was the first manifestation in recorded history of the logical fallacy of the slippery slope. In modern times, it has come to be called the domino theory.[20]

Aristagoras appealed to Athens and was promptly awarded twenty ships. Eretrea (on Euboea) pledged five. It was 499 BC. The Ionian Greeks in Asia Minor burned Sardis the next year, but the year after that, the Persians burned Miletus in retaliation. In 490 BC Darius the Great launched an attack on Euboea and Athens, the first of the Persian wars that lasted sporadically until 449 BC.

Of all the battles fought in during the Persian Wars, the frontrunner was the Battle of Marathon. The actual frontrunner, we are asked to believe, was an Athenian messenger named Pheidippides, who ran 140 miles from Marathon to Sparta for help. Then he ran back to Athens to tell them that the Spartans were celebrating a religious festival of Apollo and felt obliged to await a full moon, as religious law dictated. Pheidippides then ran another 22 miles—armed—to fight at Marathon. Having fought, he ran back to Athens to announce "Victory over Persia is ours!" and promptly dropped dead from overexertion. Plutarch said later that piety, not superstition, as Herodotus had written, caused the Spartan delay.[21] Even then men were attempting to distinguish between religion and superstition, never an easy call.

The plain of Marathon was where the octogenarian Hippias led a Persian force that ancients guessed numbered between one hundred thousand and six hundred thousand men with ten thousand horses. Moderns estimate the force at twenty thousand cavalry and infantry combined.[22] Outnumbered two to one, and lacking any cavalry, the Athenians managed to defeat their enemy. Their ablest commander was Miltiades, whose tactics William Butler Yeats would never have approved, for in his poem "The Second Coming" (1921) Yeats lamented, "Things fall apart; the center cannot hold." Miltiades, however, expressly designed the center of the Athenian troops so that it could not hold. He then armed the Athenians in a heavy wing formation with that weakened center. In battle the center gave way, but the more heavily armed wings crushed the unprepared Persians. Their lucky survivors waded out into the water, boarded ships, and escaped. But 6,400 Persians died at Marathon, while the Athenians lost a mere 192, buried in a still visible mound on the plain of battle. The names of most of the dead are not familiar to us, but the name of the battlefield on which they fell, Marathon, has become our word for a foot race. One of the fallen was the dramatist Aeschylus's brother. Fortunately, Aeschylus himself survived to write *The Persians,* the world's first historical drama, a thoughtful study of the moral strengths and flaws of both sides.

When the Spartans finally reached Marathon a day or two later, they admired the grave mound of the heroes, praised the Athenians and went home to eat leftovers from the feast of Apollo. They did not grumble about leftovers. After all, theirs was a Spartan lifestyle which included some of the worst cooking in the Greek archipelago. Standard fare for Spartans was a dish called black soup. It was pork boiled in blood and vinegar. When a Greek king asked a Spartan chef to make him some, he found it inedible. The cook replied, "Sire, the soup is delicious only if you've bathed in Spartan rivers."[23] The Greek king washed his hands of any such cooking and concluded that the cook's response was designed to encourage bathing rather than fine dining. That night he reserved a table for two at a restaurant that featured continental, not Spartan, fare.

Hippias had hoped to establish his grandsons as tyrants in Athens, but the Athenians had already adjusted to their version of democracy. His old friends were opposed to it, but they were outnumbered. It is said that Hippias suffered a coughing fit upon arriving in Attica, a fit so violent he lost a loose tooth in the sand. He had recently dreamed that he had bedded his mother and took it to mean that his mother was Attica, and that he would finally, after twenty years of exile, be laid to rest there. One tradition says he was killed at Marathon,[24] and another that he sailed away with the Persians and died on the island of Lemnos.[25] But whether he left his body in Attica or just his tooth, Athenian tyranny had lost its bite, and the Persians, failing to destroy Athens, were so down in the mouth they sailed home. They only got away by the skin of their teeth.

Ten years after Marathon, in 480 BC, another Persian ruler, Xerxes I, sailed to Greece at the head of a huge army and a sizeable fleet, determined to crush Athens. At the mountain pass of Thermopylae a mounted Persian scout caught sight of the Spartans relaxing before the battle and combing their long hair. Xerxes was flabbergasted that soldiers would spend such time grooming themselves, but Herodotus relates that a deposed Spartan king then in his employ warned that the Spartans were nevertheless "the first kingdom and town in Greece" and "the bravest men."[26] The implication was clear: they might let their hair down, but never their guard.

When the battle began, Xerxes sent in the Medes and Cassians, but they got such rough reception they had to be replaced by a crack Persian unit called the "Immortals." Xerxes learned soon enough how mortal these were, and might have lost more than the twenty thousand men said to have died at the mountain pass of Thermopylae had it not been for a Greek traitor from Malis named Ephialtes. A homeboy, Ephialtes knew there was a trail that ran to Thermopylae along the mountaintop. Soon King Leonidas of Sparta and his one thousand men at Thermopylae heard dry leaves rustling beneath the Persians' feet as they approached from the rear. Leonidas dismissed most of the non-Spartan troops, retaining only the services of some Boeotians and helots to help him defend the pass. The helots, Sparta's *untermenschen* [Ger., downtrodden] were most often used in campaigns to carry burdens, but sometimes, to fight and die. Helots had been slain at Marathon and given honorable burial there by the Athenians. Yet, despite the fact that Boeotians and helots fought at Thermopylae, only the three hundred Spartan "Equals" are remembered in most accounts, ancient or modern. The Boeotians and helots were not only not considered by Leonidas equal to the "Equals," they were not mentioned by most historians at all! Though death is said to be the great equalizer, for Boeotians and helots there was no equality even then. Their heroism remained unsung, their sacrifice unnoticed, unromanticized. In World War II, the services of Japanese American and African American combat troops were similarly underreported and undervalued. In January 1997, the United States Congress awarded the Congressional Medal of Honor to seven black American soldiers, one still living, for their bravery in World War II.

Boeotians were regarded by most Greeks as rude illiterates, strong of body, weak of mind, though a few—like Hesiod, Pindar, and Plutarch—showed what strong-minded civilians Boeotia could on occasion produce. Fortunately, these men of letters were not among those who fought and died at Thermopylae with the Spartan "Equals"! The poet Hesiod was born too soon, perhaps in the eighth century BC; the essayist Plutarch, too late, in the first century AD. Pindar, however, was just under forty in 480 BC and might have lent the Spartans a helping hand at Thermopylae, since Greeks generally remained in active duty until they were nearly fifty years old, after which they were part of the reserves! But the aristocratic poet was too busy writing odes to the victors of scheduled athletic contests—the Olympic, Nemean, Pythian, and Isthmian games—to crease his noble brow over the patriotic battles being fought by the rest of Greece against Persia. He had no time to pay attention to anything as irregular as the battle of Thermopylae. Battles, he might have thought, make poor box office anyway. Suppose they scheduled a battle and nobody came? Alas, nobody schedules battles and, at least initially, every one is well attended.

Although Pindar took no notice of Thermopylae, the noble Lord George Gordon Byron, an avid Grecophile and volunteer "Greek" patriot, speaking for his romantic character, Don Juan, begged the earth to "render back" from its breast a paltry three of the Spartan three hundred "To make a new Thermopylae."[27] Byron had the good fortune, though born lame, to be as handsome as a Greek statue. Had he been born in classical Greece, particularly at Sparta, the chances are good that he would have been exposed to the elements and left to die, just because of his defective foot. It was the Greek way of birth control. Byron may have swum the Hellespont to get a better view of Abydos, about which he was writing.[28] Abydos was the town in Phyrigia, on the Asiatic side of the Hellespont, that had originally been founded as a Milesian (Ionian Greek) colony. Near Abydos, Xerxes built his bridge of boats proceeding on his way north to Greece. But as for a "new Thermopylae," most wars provide them in the shape of battles that are as pointless tactically as the old or first Thermopylae. A large Persian army of 150,000 combatants could not be held off forever by the seven thousand men in the Peloponnesian force, much less by the few hundred Leonidas retained.[29] The stand at the pass has been defended as practical, helping to save the lives of the main body of the Peloponnesian defenses, six thousand men on the coast road below.[30] But the real action was on the plains of Boeotia and at Athens, and the numbers of unarmed civilians who died there must have been greater than three hundred, greater even than twenty thousand. Their deaths, too, are unsung and unremembered.

Of course, one could argue that tactical advantages are not the only kind. The real value of Thermopylae was psychological. The Persians killed off the "Equals" and the unequal civilians. Their navy burned Athens. But they left the Greeks a gift, "Xerxes' legacy," an immense psychological and patriotic satisfaction, a relatively short-lived Pan-Hellenism or sense of Greekness, resulting from the final victory of a host of small independent city-states over a giant empire.[31] For, after the defeat at Thermopylae and the destruction of Athens, the Persians lost the great naval battle at Salamis (479 BC). In that year also they were defeated at Platea by the Spartan Pausanias, nephew of Cleomenes and Leonidas. At the Cape of Mycale, the Persians' shield-wall was penetrated first by Athenians, then by Corinthians, Trojans, and Sicyonians. Finally, the Ionians, seeing their Persian masters faltering, changed sides and fought with Greece—the second revolt of Ionia.[32] If it is really true that "Persia gave the Greeks their identity" then we might call the Persian Wars classical Greece's identity crisis.[33]

Assuming a Virtue: Athens and the League of Delos

What made Greeks identifiable as Greeks was something Herodotus tried to explain. He mentioned the four dialects of Greek language as a key to Greek unity.[34] Mutually intelligible, their practice meant that Greeks could share the same myths, religion, and literature. Greeks also believed blood was thicker than water and organized their political structures in ways they could all appreciate, because family ties were very important. Language, cult, and politics, not to mention sports (a part of their religion), helped Greeks from all city-states recognize themselves in each other.[35] Herodotus, who did so much to "promote the conception of Greece as a unity" as Simon Hornblower reminded his readers, was not himself a Greek but grew up in Asia Minor, in Halikarnassus. When he looked at Greeks he tended to view them as people who were more alike than not—a natural tendency for tourists abroad, missing cultural distinctions that are so important to the natives of every little region but which escape notice by outsiders. The tourist finds similarity everywhere, and Herodotus was a tourist in Greece. "These Greeks!" he may have marvelled. "You cannot tell them apart!" Perhaps because they were so very similar in culture and speech, the Greeks distrusted one another, envied one another, and did everything possible to prevent "aliens" (i.e., other Greeks) from becoming citizens. In so many ways they resemble us.

The Greeks found common ground in defeating Persia. Afterward, Sparta, who had taken the lead in the command of allied armies and navies, permitted Athens, anxious to free Ionia and end Persian domination of the Aegean, to assume leadership in Greece.[36] The Spartans went home to keep a sharp watch on their helots, aware that leaders like Pausanias, the victor of Platea, had been regarded by other Greeks as suspiciously pro-Persian, and thus an unreliable leader of maritime city states.

In the spring of 477 BC, Athens formed a maritime league called the Confederation of Delos (Delian League) with other city-states who pledged to "have the same enemies and the same friends" forever, or at least, until some pieces of iron that they threw into the sea should float. The League anticipated the North Atlantic Treaty Organization (NATO) formed after another terrible war. For in 1949 NATO members also pledged that an attack on any one of the signatories would be regarded as an attack on all and that any action deemed necessary, including the use of armed force, would be taken in response.[37]

Athens and her allies centered their League and its treasury on the sacred island of Delos. They assumed that where their treasure was there would members' hearts be also. And they may have been for a while, but it was not, after all, members' hearts that Athens wanted, but their cooperation and cash—in order to drive Persia out of Aegean trading areas and out of Ionia. Then Athens hoped to gain control of central Greece, expand her trade west to Sicily, east and southeast to Cyprus, Phoenicia, and Egypt. True, expanding Athenian trade to Sicily would provoke Corinth, Athens's chief maritime rival and Sparta's ally. And a third attempt to eliminate competition from "that eyesore," Aegina, lying in the Saronic Gulf in full view of the Acropolis, would certainly provoke Athens's enemies.[38] Although Sparta was a land power, Spartan allies looked to her to restrain the expansion of Athenian power west to Sicily and east to the Black Sea that threatened them all. Two Peloponnesian wars were fought to resolve the tensions that existed between Sparta and her allies and Athens and hers. Until the wars came to warm things up, the two power blocks were frozen in a cold-war posture.

At first, the Delian League members by common consent allowed Athens to assume leadership of League policies and to command its navy. Athens had the most ships, and it was thought only proper that she assess members for ships or a money contribution instead. Individual participants were supposed to remain autonomous, but inevitably they gave up their independence in foreign policy matters which, under Athenian direction, were determined by synods meeting on Delos.[39] The league of equals gradually degenerated, becoming an involuntary association dominated by Athens. Maritime states like Naxos in the Cyclades and Karystos on Euboea were forcibly prevented from leaving the union when the Persian threat diminished. Naxos, an island in the Aegean, was the first Greek city-state and member of the Delian league to be invaded by the members for attempting to secede. She was reduced (470 BC) from League membership to subjugation.[40] If NATO had been run the same way, France's decision to withdraw from all military actions (while still retaining membership) would have meant an invasion of France by all the NATO members!

In 463 BC the island of Thasos, in the Thracian Sea, followed Naxos's example and seceded. She was forced to cede trading posts to Athens, give up claims to silver mines, raze her walls, surrender her ships, and pay tribute.[41] By the 440s, Athens was referring to League members as her empire.[42] An imperial mentality made Athens ever more imperious. She made it more difficult for other Greeks to claim Athenian citizenship. Athens employed many governors and supervisors to keep the members in line, and garrisons were populated by Athenian settlers called *cleruchs,* sent on request to members whose pro-Athenian sympathizers were fearful of falling from power.[43] Garrisons garroted or silenced those whose views contradicted Athenian policy. In their enthusiasm for democracy, the Athenians used their preponderant authority to graft it upon any ally whose loyalty to Athenian interests lagged. Gradually, Athens succeeded in weeding out the oligarchs in her imperial garden, but the native parasites she had nurtured and the transplants she had sent in the form of *cleruchs* proved hothouse flowers, unwilling to sustain her cultivation of empire.

PELOPONNESIAN DAZE

The Peloponnesus was named for Pelops, an eponymous hero whose father, Tantalus, king of Phrygia, lost his kingdom to Tros, king of Troy. Tros claimed Tantalus had kidnapped and raped his teenaged son, Ganymedes, but soon found Phrygia easier to control than his son and so reconciled himself to his heir's absence. The real pederast, however, was not Tantalus. Zeus himself had seduced young Ganymedes and then made him his cupbearer, slaker of more than one thirst. Meanwhile, young Prince Pelops, a grandson of Zeus, had fallen out with his dad. Provoked past bearing, Tantalus finally served him up as a dish to the gods. The gods, aghast at the cruelty of this unnatural father, went on a hunger strike. But the goddess of agriculture, Ceres, distraught over the loss of her daughter, Proserpina, who had been seduced by Dis, god of the underworld, was found absentmindedly snacking on a shoulder cut of Pelops. Zeus restored Pelops to life, minus his shoulder, which he replaced with one of ivory. The story of Pelops was very much a "soap."

Young Pelops went to war and conquered the Peloponnesus. The Spartans, who made their home there, were like their founder militaristic but never one-dimensional. Spartans were famous for their contradictory behavioral traits, combining artistic sensibility and asceticism,[44] provincialism and

Pan-Hellenism[45]; egalitarianism and elitism, lethargy and adventurism, and practicality with the grossest superstition. Prof. J. K. Davies noted that Sparta developed the Pan-Hellenism that defeated Persia in 481 BC, then inexplicably failed to extend her influence and relapsed into "inert sluggishness."[46] Athens may have been the school of Hellas, as Pericles remarked in the Funeral Oration, but it was Sparta who first taught Athens the value of a class action or League to achieve important Pan-Hellenic political ends. Then Sparta panned the Pan-Hellenism she had fostered. After the Persian armies and fleets withdrew from Greece, so did Sparta, to the Peloponnesus. She was fearful of democratic philosophy and Athenian liberals. If liberalism and democracy spread to the Peloponnesus, might it not liberate a helluva lot of helots?

THE FIRST PELOPONNESIAN WAR

Athens began the First Peloponnesian War in 460 BC by agreeing to accept Megara, formerly in Sparta's league, as an ally. This meant war with Corinth, but since Megara was a western Greek port, and Sicily beckoned, Athens risked the addition, soliciting Argos as well. In 458 Sparta defeated Athenian allies at Tanagra in Boeotia, causing heavy losses, while an Athenian victory at Oenophyta, also in this region, resulted in her control of most of the region two months later.[47] This involved Athens in conflicts with Corinth and Epidauros.

Aegina decided to challenge Athens's naval power after Athens sent a League fleet to Egypt to relieve rebels against Persia. Aegina did much trading with Egypt, and war in Egypt was bad for business. Two years later (457 BC) Aegina was conquered and made to pay tribute. The conquest of Egypt, begun in 460 failed by 454. That year, too, the treasury of the Delian League was removed from the island of Delos to Athens. The Egyptian fiasco dismayed Athens's Aegean allies. Athens made a truce with the Peloponnesians in 451 BC. She needed time to subdue her Aegean "empire." Time out.

In the fifth century BC, Athens learned from Thermopylae and Platea how to lead other Greeks in war. In this she surpassed Sparta, but she never rose to the Pan-Hellenism that the Greek Confederacy represented at the height of the Persian War. Pan-Hellenism threatened Athenian imperialism. The brilliant Athenian general Cimon, a political conservative and Pan-Hellenist, was exiled in 461 BC, overshadowed by a democratic imperialist named Pericles.

The Age of Pericles began with the first Peloponnesian War in 461 BC and lasted until his death in 429 BC. During this period, civic participation was the democratic carrot, patriotic sacrifice the stick. "Ask not what your country can do for you, but what you can do for your country." John F.

Kennedy might have taken his cue from the funeral oration that Pericles delivered at the beginning of the second Peloponnesian War (431–404 BC) in which Pericles reckoned that service to one's country is the greatest of all honors, and the only one that is imperishable. The same philosophy served the nationalistic purposes of Napoleon, Mussolini, Hitler, De Gaulle, Churchill, Castro, and every other national leader you can think of. While the liberty of individuals is made possible by the preservation of states, liberty and the state are not coterminous and are often at distinct odds. Long before the modern period, the Athenian polis was already assuming precedence over the individual.

Athenian democracy was not much concerned with individuals. There was no notion of inalienable rights. All questions were determined by a majority vote that provided no insulation against the loss of civil liberties. Democratic Athenians were as capable of repression and injustice as the Greek tyrants and oligarchs. Athenian procedures were as democratic as those of any slave-owning state that also ignores most rights of women and aliens. Athenian objectives were primarily statist.[48] Athens invented democracy, but she had not yet come up with a good reason for having it—the protection and enjoyment of individuality? Singular.

THE SECOND PELOPONNESIAN WAR

According to Thucydides' *History of the Peloponnesian War* the underlying cause of the conflict was her neighbors' fear that Athenian domination of the Aegean was destroying liberty of trade and intercourse. Not that everything went Athens's way. She lost a hundred ships in the Egyptian campaign against Persia and she suffered simultaneous defeat on the Greek mainland. Pericles made the Thirty Years' Peace with Sparta in 446–445 BC. But he was not willing to have peace at any price. He wanted his price. He said questions pertaining to the peace ending the first Peloponnesian War could be arbitrated, but not without a quid pro quo. Thucydides listed the grievances of Sparta and her allies. They included the rights of a neutral state to ally with either League or no league; the discontent of Potidaea, a rebellious dependency of Athens, which became a victim of Athenian blockade; the Athenian decree that deprived Megara, a Peloponnesian ally, of the ability to trade with the Athenian Empire (Megarian Decree); and the discontent of the Aeginetans, who had, like the Potidaeans, rebelled against Athenian control and desired autonomy, contrary to provisions of the Thirty Years Peace.[49] Donald Kagan has observed of these four immediate causes that they were not very immediate, because they went back almost five years before the second war broke out.[50] He suggests that the most expansionist period of Athenian history predated the peace of

446–445 and that the Athenians had no "insatiable" appetite after that, nor did the Spartans appear "unduly afraid" of imperial expansionism.[51]

In Thucydides, one learns that the Spartan king, Archidamus, whose name is given to the first ten-year phase of the second Peloponnesian War, was a friend of Pericles with whom he might have reached some kind of peaceful arrangement—had both men not been caught up in situations where less moderate heads were urging greater commitment. The Greeks were never a people to dither where commitment was concerned. And the one thing they were most likely to commit was war. Pericles never worried that the Athenians would resist war against the Peloponnesians, but only that once they began the war, they might not pursue it.[52] What Athenians most liked to pursue was their own immediate advantage. In this they were like all the other states in the region.

Seeking to unravel the grievances cited by Thucydides, one is reminded of the outbreak of World War I with all the major participants in that contest acting from assumptions, often erroneous, regarding the probable reactions of their counterparts in the Triple Alliance and Triple Entente. Like the tense days following the assassination of the Archduke Ferdinand at Sarajevo after June 28, 1914, the Greeks in their Leagues tried to second guess the responses of all the possible players. In each case during the years preceding the outbreak of hostilities, mounting apprehension was ameliorated by the persistence of optimism that they could be avoided. Some of the same general political problems afflicting the Greek Leagues were also problems affecting participants of World War I. Among them were the protection of trade routes and control of markets; the rights of neutrals or autonomous states; internal dissension and confusion over the direction of future policy; the loss of territories or colonies subsequently aligned with states whose interests conflicted with those of the once dominant power; passive states becoming suddenly aggressive and vice versa; the reduction or exclusion of trade between some areas and others; the influence of grain import and export on foreign affairs; enthusiasm for and fear of imperial expansion; interventionism and isolationism; the acknowledgment of traditional relationships of some states with others; shifting power relationships among all the states and political parties; and, one of the most dangerous circumstances in the pre-Peloponnesian War years as in the period from 1907–14, "the fearful dependence of the powers upon their alliances, their tendency to defer to their more irresponsible partners," the last seeming perfectly to describe Sparta's deference to Corinth.[53]

That is not to say that because one can list some strikingly similar general circumstances prior to the Great Peloponnesian War and World War I, both were inevitable.[54] No. The reasons why these factors can be cited has nothing to do with the inevitability of war, but much with human behavior, which is historically determined, even if in many instances, the protagonists of current events do not accurately read or assess the past. The range of practical political responses of statesmen and governors has been limited by geographical and physical realities not easily changed or avoided. This is not true of their ideals and goals for the future, which are determined mostly by emotion and the distorted memory of the past whose real causes elude the understanding.

In antiquity as in modern times pressing political problems were caused by scarce resources and obdurate environments. Given the precariousness of life in every age and a limited understanding of what might constitute one's true advantage, fifth-century BC Greeks, like early twentieth-century modern Europeans, found themselves threatened by neighbors as confused as they were themselves. No wonder they all just stumbled into unplanned wars.

After Sparta invaded Attica in 432, Athens sheltered behind long walls where, obedient to Pericles, she tried to escape the horrors of war and survive them. Imperial tribute and imported grain enabled her to fight on. Sparta repeatedly burned Athens's farmland; the Athenians repeatedly raided the Peloponnesian coast. A third of all Athenians died of plague, including Pericles in 429 BC. Between 431 and 421 BC, when the Peace of Nicias was declared, the war dragged on. After 424 BC the Athenians adopted a more aggressive policy to alleviate the tedium.

Thucydides (460–c. 400 BC) was given command of seven ships off Thasos, in the Aegean Sea between Macedonia and Thrace. His colleague Eucles was guarding the city of Amphipolis, fifty miles to the west of him, when the Spartans suddenly attacked. Eucles sent word to Thucydides who was unable to reach Amphipolis in time to save it. For this the Athenians exiled him. His misfortune made his reputation. As an Athenian exile, he was welcomed to Spartan battlefields and given research facilities that enabled him to publish without perishing. The rest is history, the *History of the Peloponnesian War* to the year 411 BC. One might conclude from the career of Thucydides that if more historians were exiled from their native land, more history books would be written, and written more objectively. Was it this line of reasoning that led Senator William Fulbright to invent the fellowships that bear his name? Was he thinking of Thucydides off in Sparta?

At Potidaea (432 BC) Socrates the philosopher, then Socrates the hoplite, saved the life of young Alcibiades, who returned the favor in the next engagement. The youth was Pericles' handsome nephew, ward, man about town, and talented future general. He was to become Athens's most amoral and controversial citizen. That he was also a disciple of Socrates, for whom virtue was the quintessence of philosophy, reminds us that even the most talented teacher is not able to efface a perverse nature or overcome inadequate nurture; but that a great teacher like Socrates never gives up trying. Plato hints in the *Symposium* that Alcibiades was Socrates' lover. If he were both disciple and lover to Socrates, it says much for young Alcibiades' good judgment, which diminished with the years. If Socrates was formerly the lover of Alcibiades, it is consoling to think that Socrates' own judgment improved with the passage of time.

Alcibiades was a political opponent of the moderate general Nicias, and a critic of his peace policy. Alcibiades was chief advocate of the Sicilian expedition (415–413 BC) over which he was given joint command with Nicias and Lamachus. The day before the expedition set sail, statues of Hermes, messenger of the gods, were found mutilated in Athens. Alcibiades was suspected of this impiety and of profaning the Eleusinian fertility cult, too. No one suggested that war itself was a profanation, nor held to account politicians on either side for causing the deaths of the fifty thousand Athenians who perished in Sicily. No one viewed the loss of these men or of the civilian casualties as any kind of profanation at all, or connected their deaths to sinning against fertility or humanity. Today we call this wastage collateral damage.

Alcibiades subsequently helped the Spartans plan the Athenian defeat in Sicily, a debacle that ought to have been held as the more serious charge against him, not the profanation of a fertility cult. For it was Alcibiades who first urged the Sicilian expedition and spoke to an enthusiastic Assembly about Athens's need to extend her rule over all Greek states so as to avoid being ruled by them. Thucydides thought the most blameworthy were the Athenian politicians who did not support the men in the field but engaged in intrigues to win leadership of the people.[55] Alcibiades was guilty of devising a rash war policy and then of helping to sabotage it, but he was helped by every level of Athenian society, all of whom shared the blame for imperialism that had run amok; for prior to this disaster, the average Athenian supported imperialist war aims. The rash Sicilian expedition was but an unfortunate part of the greater imperialist policy that was not designed by Alcibiades, but by his uncle Pericles. The irate Athenians who called for Alcibiades' punishment for the fiasco of the Sicilian affair never once cried uncle! Nor did they reexamine their own imperialist policies.

Nothing in the Olympic religion of Greece nor in the mystery cults imported from western Asia discouraged the Athenians from violence attendant on imperialism. Religion did not prohibit violence, it even patronized it. Not only was there an Olympian god of war (Ares), but the gods, one reads in Homer, enjoyed taking sides in wars that men started, or in wars that the gods started but let men fight. Then, too, Greek religion encouraged ritual to the neglect of ethics, and Greek politicians knew how to make political hay out of public piety, an art that some reactionary American politicians have pursued with iliadic fervor.[56] No wonder the Athenians did not take the violence of warfare as seriously as the loss of a few mutilated statues in downtown Athens. Broken religious statuary was desecration of property, art, and religion. Mutilated bodies were neither property, nor art, nor sacred, so they offended neither the state, the muses, or the gods. They never do.

Most accounts of Alcibiades marvel at his flexible morality and sinuous politics. Not only did he betray Athenian military information to the Spartans during the Sicilian war, but he betrayed the Spartans to the Persians after that. With Persian help he betrayed the Athenian empire by instigating rebellion among Athens's Ionian dependents. He proceeded to conspire with the oligarchs at Athens, but not having been asked to participate in their government, fought with the democracy of Samos instead. Yet, when the political climate changed at Athens, he was given command of the Athenian fleet by the democratic party (411 BC). He defeated the Spartan fleet at Abydos in 411 BC and at Cyzicus the next year. He recovered Chalcedon and Byzantium. His efforts were applauded. Back in Athens in 407 BC, he found all proceedings against him canceled and was appointed general with full powers. But not to lose, only to win battles. When he lost an engagement at Notium the same year, they took his command away. He went into voluntary exile (406 BC), having provided himself with a retreat position at Gallipoli. Kagan writes that although the bulk of historical sentiment from Plutarch to the moderns has viewed his dismissal a great loss to Athens, it wasn't. Alcibiades took unnecessary risks as a commander and was "a burden to his native city."[57]

On the whole, Athenians were adept at ridding themselves of burdens. Not only of Alcibiades, but of the still greater burden of moral responsibility. Alcibiades was a product of Athens, the city in which he was reared; that sent him to Sicily; that tried and condemned him in absentia for mutilating statues, but not men; that recalled him to service after he had connived with the Spartans, allied himself with Persia, and helped foment rebellion in the Athenian empire. If Alcibiades were a burden to Athens, she carried it lightly. Like all Greek cities, Athens was rife with the kind of party faction that encouraged the emergence of magnetic leaders like Alcibiades but did not offer them any regular or constitutional means for displacing their opponents or even for effecting compromise.[58] As an Athenian aristocrat, Alcibiades had been exposed to an elitist mentality that, in his exalted social circle, continually undervalued democratic government. He was not the only political leader who contemplated the betrayal of his city to Sparta. At the end of the Persian War, Themistocles found refuge in Persia at the court of Artaxerxes. During the Peloponnesian War, Thucydides was a guest of Sparta. The inventors of democracy were not convinced that it was a good thing and often "betrayed" democracy by supporting elitist parties within and outside Athens. Were they blue dog or yellow dog democrats? Or just not dogged democrats at all?

The policy of ostracism, invented, pace Aristotle, by Cleisthenes to relieve Athens of unpopular citizens, encouraged exiles to seek redress with Athens's enemies. Besides Themistocles and Thucydides, the policy also affected Aristides the Just, honored by all for fairly assessing the taxes due from the Allies in the Delian League, but ostracized nevertheless. He was recalled after an absence of two years to fight the Persians. A similar fate befell Anaxagoras, the philosopher charged with heresy or flirting with Persia. Pericles obtained his aquittal, but he was exiled all the same. Cimon, a general and archon, was exiled for his pro-Sparta policy. The Sophist Protagoras was ostracized for atheism in 411 BC. Even Socrates was given the option of exile in 399 BC, but he chose death as the lesser of two evils, which indicates how seriously Socrates viewed this kind of punishment. He realized that the charges against him (corrupting youth, denying the old gods for new gods, making the worse appear the better cause) were not proved at his trial, but chose to die anyway, in order to protect a system of government that he better than anyone else present realized was subject to the grossest of all abuses—ignorance and demagoguery. Although the relatively small number of men ostracized has often been said to demonstrate how restrained Athenian democracy was, it can just as well illustrate how few were those leaders of men who dared exhibit their individualism![59]

Alcibiades was not ostracized. He was already out of the country. But he was condemned to death on a charge of impiety, which was punishable either by exile or death. No wonder that he sought revenge by aiding the Spartans rather than going home. It is possible to see him and others who betrayed their city, or just departed from its norms, as the products of a flawed social and political environment that encouraged certain types of outrageous behavior from some of its citizens, and outrageously, set about punishing it. Athenians were proud of their city, and there was much to be proud of: Athens experimented with forms of art, reasoning, and government that were entirely untried by other states. The poet Simonides of Ceos, who lived at Athens for a time under the tyrant Hipparchus, said that "The city is the teacher of the man." Thucydides has Pericles say that "Athens (was) the school of Hellas."[60] But in 404 BC Athens lost the war, and was for several years so damaged by a repressive regime forced upon her (the famed Thirty Tyrants) that the rest of Greece was no longer enrolling in her classes, or paying tuition to her school.

ART, INDIVIDUALISM, AND COMMUNITY

Poets and sculptors registered the tension that the rise of powerful and imperialistic city-states generated for citizens in their private and public lives. Between 476 and 431 BC, Athens witnessed the perfecting of tragic drama by Sophocles and Euripides, whose characters challenged ancient taboos, religious traditions, and tribal practices. Oedipus, Agamemnon, Medea, Orestes, Antigone, and so on fascinate because these individuals must decide where to draw the line between the personal imperatives that propel them and the impersonal traditions that compel them. These trage- dians knew that individuals must satisfy the demands of the community and of the gods, and that in the process, the self was in danger of being compromised or crushed by external, uncontrollable forces. If philosophy did not portray the world as comfortably idiosyncratic and personal, but as mechanical and regular (Aristotle), tentative and manipulable (Sophists), or worst of all, accidental and unpredictable (Democritus), theater at least communicated the importance—though not the triumph—of the individual and the dignity of human action. Playwrights were psychological coun- selors, the psychiatrists of the classical age; they put individuals on the spot in the spotlight if not on the couch.

Urban art and architecture spoke less consistently of individualism than drama and more ambiguously. The cityscape of Athens was a product of urban beautification paid for by harbor fees, sales taxes, imperial assess- ments, and the free contributions (liturgies) of aristocrats to improve the place, which advertised their donors' status.[61] Famed sculptors and archi- tects proclaimed not merely polis culture but their own skill. Public monu- ments to dead heroes and private people erected in city squares and over graves commemorated individuals and the state, simultaneously blending private messages with public ones. The sculptor Polykleitos of Argos in the Peloponnesus wished not to concentrate on universal beauty, but on a series of Olympic champions in all their anatomical particularity. Yet, though his subjects were athletes of unusual physical perfection, he thought it necessary to ennoble the human image with supernatural and ideal beauty.[62] Classical art tended to demote the individual in its quest for the universal.

A. R. Burn turned his attention to individualism by considering the meaning of Greek "public" art or architectural sculpture, especially that found on the sculptor Pheidias's frieze of the Parthenon.[63] Pheidias drew his subjects from traditional mythology rather than contemporary culture. Burn said this was not because Greek art was "out of touch" with contemporary life, but because Greeks felt that their everyday experiences had "the same universal significance as the deeds of mythic heroes." Perhaps. But by ideal- izing the heroic, the divine, and the universal, Athenians developed a kind of farsightedness or lofty sightedness that led them by the end of the fifth century BC to disregard the real world with all its inconvenient urgencies.

Frank J. Frost also raised the question of individualism, not with regards to art as the end product, but rather the attitudes and habits of self-definition of aristocrats, the art of being oneself by developing oneself, so to speak.[64]

He posits an early fifth-century individualism in which aristocrats like Sophocles and Pericles engaged in more than one activity, something we associate with "Renaissance Man." He believes such profuse creativity flourished only when Greeks espoused "an amalgam of beliefs about the interaction of humans, gods, and fate" all represented by the polis and "tribal wisdom." Then came rational philosophy that "denied divine intervention in natural processes" and "sophism, which taught that humans could improve their own lives."

The polis neglected individual welfare and failed to reward the wartime sacrifices of its citizens. Not surprisingly, citizens became increasingly selfish, looking to themselves for their security, as the state had looked after its own. The Greeks grew increasingly less interested in government and in the traditional polis culture, which after all, had been the culture of an aristocratic class.[65] In the throes of war and the aftermath of economic disruption, the polis was less able to meet the needs of its citizens. Individualism, never a polis priority, increased due to the weakening of city-state autonomy, the rise of rational and Sophistic philosophy, and the demise of aristocratic idealism.[66] And so, too, did self-reliance and entrepreneurialism increase, all things which have a positive connotation for most of us. Unfortunately, these were ominous results of a breakdown of the city-state system: the abandonment of old gods for new, the spread of oriental mysticism, bourgeois crassness, an increase in violence and warfare, and a decline in public expenditure on art and architecture. Just as individualism came into its own, individuals found themselves reminiscing over the advantages of community! The innovative and classical age in Greece was irretrievable. Downtime.

XENOPHON'S ADVENTURE

In the fifth century BC, the Golden Age of Greece, Greek city-states united only to prevent a common foreign enemy from taking over. In the fourth century BC, they couldn't unite at all because 1) some weren't sure they had a common foreign enemy; 2) those who were couldn't agree on which foreign power the common enemy was; and 3) others were sure the enemy was domestic, a clique of their own compatriots. Between the end of the Peloponnesian War in 404 BC until the Greek city-states were defeated at Chaeronea in 338 BC by Philip of Macedonia, a Greek-speaking "foreigner," the Hellenes were doing what politically volatile, sparsely educated societies that practice art, misogyny, philosophy, imperialism, self-awareness, plunder, profit, proliferation, and patriotism always do in a period of political and economic decline. They were hanging in there for dear life.

Some thought the common foreign enemy was Persia, that immense empire whose decay, some said, set in after Xerxes was defeated at Salamis

(479 BC). They were reassured by a reporter turned historian back from a remarkable assignment in Persia. He was a well-to-do Athenian and former pupil of Socrates who had enlisted in a mercenary army of ten thousand Greeks hired by a Persian prince named Cyrus. The latter was trying to wrest the throne from his brother. When Cyrus was killed in battle in 401 BC, the Greek hoplites were *persona non grata* with the brother. Leaderless (the Persians killed off their generals), and deep inside enemy lines, the troops chose new officers, one of whom was the young reporter. He later filed the story of their triumphant escape from northern Mesopotamia through Kurdistan and Armenia to the Black Sea—a five-month march that took the 8,600 survivors only five months to accomplish, through snowy mountains, across sweltering plains, fighting every mile of the way until they got to Euxine Trapezus (Trebizond), a Greek city on the Black Sea where they were safe. The reporter's name was Xenophon, and his story, the *Anabasis* (Greek, ascent) made headlines.

PERSIA PLAYS HER PART

The *Anabasis* was uplifting because it suggested that Greeks could hold their own against the Persians on Persian soil. But Persia was still stronger—and more clever—than any of the Greek city-states dreamed, and even though she had her own problems, found the perfect weapon for subverting Greek independence: money. In the fourth century, Persia pursued a policy of foreign aid to first one, then another city-state in order to prevent any one of the three leading ones—Sparta, Athens, Thebes—from wielding too much control, from threatening (or supporting) any of her neighbors too much. In the 390s, when Sparta was riding high and Athens not yet recovered from the Peloponnesian War, Sparta posed as the liberator of Ionian Greeks living under Persian rule in Asia Minor. To check Sparta's desire to control all Greece, Persia invested in the rebuilding of Athenian defenses, that is, her Long Walls that Sparta had ordered destroyed after 404 BC. The Persian ruler sent messengers with gold to Thebes and Athens to help them make war on Sparta. When Sparta, alarmed at Athenian recovery, sued for peace, Persia gave her one—the King's Peace of 387 BC, which divested Sparta of patronage over the Asia Minor Greeks, while guaranteeing Sparta's interests on the mainland. Then, for a time, Persia stopped financing Sparta, Thebes, and Athens. Next, Persia compelled all these states to sign the peace in her own capital city of Sardis. The Persian king entrusted execution of the peace to Sparta, and promised to make war against any who did not accept the terms.[67] At that point Persia appeared to mainland Greeks the controller of Greek destiny, and Sparta, a traitor to Hellenic liberty.[68]

Between 379 and 371 BC, war raged between Thebes and Sparta. Athens and Thebes cooperated for a while against the Spartans. Thebes set up a Boeotian League of her own to help her resist Sparta. Athens encouraged the formation of a second Athenian alliance to defeat Sparta. The war against Sparta was fought in the Ionian and Aegean Seas, until Athens, fearing Theban power over central Greece, made a separate peace with Sparta (374 BC). The next year these two fell out over a question of internal politics.

Sparta objected to Athenian support of democratic regimes controlled by pro-Spartan oligarchies,[69] and Athens objected to Sparta objecting. The Athenians ceased to cooperate with Sparta and turned again to Thebes. But by 371 BC, short of money and war-weary, Athens decided on peace once more. The peace was again brokered and guaranteed by Persia. Sparta proposed terms, the Allies, Thebes included, agreed to support disarmament, withdrawal of garrisons, and independence of all Greek states except those in Asia.[70]

In assuming the role of guarantor of mainland Greek independence, the Persians continued to serve their own interests. A general peace offered her king financial as well as diplomatic respite. Patronizing combatants was expensive and distracted from orderly control of Persia's west Asian Greek population. Since the end of the fifth century, Persia enabled first Sparta, then Athens, and finally, all of Athens's allies, including Thebes, to fight, now against one, now against the other major city-states. By weakening them all in turn, but none too much, or too long, Persia reduced Greek ability to damage Persian interests, and maximized their ability to damage themselves and each other. So scripted by Persia, the Greeks rehearsed their parts until they were letter-perfect. In continual warfare among themselves, they shuffled alliances and enemies about like cards in a poker game, with an alacrity and sangfroid suggestive of politics later called Byzantine.

The Greeks were not merely the tutors of Byzantium, but its first settlers, for Byzantium (modern Istanbul) had been founded in the seventh century BC by Megara, a city-state in the Peloponnesus.[71] Wily Odysseus, Homer's hero. He bequeathed to the Hellenes and to their heirs, the Greeks of Byzantium, the rulers of the Byzantine Empire that lasted until AD 1453, a habit—ingrained, inveterate—of complicated and unpredictable political behavior, the kind that made cooperation and trust between the Greek city-states of the fourth century unreliable and, ultimately, unproductive. The Persians preferred it that way and did everything in their power to keep them divided. Because they were all Greeks, there really wasn't much for the Persians to do. They were already divided and had been so since the Persian Wars. Greeks called it autonomy, but it was preparing them for autocracy.

EPAMINONDAS OF THEBES

The fly in the pie of peace was Athenian and Spartan jealousy of Theban power. Neither would agree to recognize the legitimacy of the Boeotian League of which Thebes was leader. When the Spartan king excluded Thebes from the peace, Epaminondas of Thebes (c. 418–362 BC) resolved to fight on. This aristocratic general was a descendant of the kings of Boeotia, a cross between George Washington—he was said never to have told a lie—and Fred Astaire, for Epaminondas was reputed to be an elegant dancer, accomplished musician, and an eloquent orator in a century when oratory was admired as much as athletic ability. He was a skillful military tactician, too, the first Greek general thus to distinguish himself. His development of the phalanx, replete with a striking head, center, and cavalry support, was carefully studied and adapted by Philip of Macedon and his son, Alexander.[72]

Epaminondas's partner in arms as in government and life was his lover and fellow officer, Pelopidas, adept at writing grant proposals which the Persian king, using Thebes as a counterweight to Athens and Sparta, was sometimes willing to fund. Epaminondas and Pelopidas orchestrated the defeat of Sparta at Leuctra in Boeotia during 371 BC. The night before the battle, Pelopidas dreamed that the gods demanded human sacrifice to assure victory. Cooler heads prevailed, and the only victims sacrificed were half of the Spartan army and their leader, Cleombrotus.[73] That was enough to guarantee the two generals and partners in life immense popularity—at least in Thebes, which, from 371 to 362 BC enjoyed a preeminent authority in Greece.

After Leuctra, Epaminondas and Pelopidas invaded the Peloponnesus; for, what good is democracy if it does not impose its superior values on those who resist them? This was to be the first of three separate campaigns. Epaminondas freed the Messenians from centuries of Spartan domination, helped the Eleans of Elis resist the Spartans, and founded the city of Megalopolis in Arcadia. Arcadian real estate values soared, and so did the spirits of everyone in the Peloponnesus formerly under Sparta's thumb. The Spartans were now so reduced in numbers they ceased to be a strong military power. Epaminondas had, however, taken longer than the month alloted for this campaign by the Theban constitution and was seized by his countrymen as a traitor for violating the laws of his country, or else for laxness.[74] At his trial, he begged his judges only to inscribe on his tomb that he had suffered death for saving his country from Sparta! The Thebans then pardoned him, and he fought on. While fighting in Thessaly in 368 BC, he got the tyrant of Pherae to liberate his lover, Pelopidas, from captivity without striking a single blow. Epaminondas was constant in love as in war, and very persuasive. But Sparta was not persuaded. She turned to Athens for help in avenging her honor. Thebes defeated them both at Mantinea in 362 BC, but death defeated Epaminondas, felled in this battle by Gryllus, son of Xenophon.

Some historians believe Epaminondas wished to establish a broader unity among Greek city-states, a new Pan-Hellenism. Will Durant thought he aimed at establishing a Theban Empire to replace the unity that Athenian or Spartan leadership had once given to Greece.[75] Thomas R. Martin agrees that Epaminondas was all about dominance.[76] But Hammond thought him a man of vision who would have promoted self-governing leagues like the Boeotian League to hold Athenian and Spartan leadership in check,[77] and Chester Starr saw him as a far-seeing moderate.[78] Whether Epaminondas dreamed of Hellenic unity, or merely aimed at a practicable balance of power between various city-state leagues is a question for the experts. Epaminondas made it possible for some unaligned or disaffected city-states to realign themselves with Thebes instead of with Sparta or Athens. But to unify all Greece he would have to have had the cooperation of Athens and Sparta in an all-out war against Persia—rather improbable in itself, considering how both these powers had allied with Persia in the past. Besides, Persian aid was instrumental in enabling Epaminondas himself to use the Boeotian League as Thebes's shelter against Sparta and Athens. Would it have made sense to alienate his patron? The German historian Ulrich Wilcken, like Will Durant and Thomas R. Martin, thought Epaminondas aimed at the domination of Greece, not at a Pan-Hellenism compromised by the fact of Theban dependence on Persia.[79] Such assessments are probably correct. Most politicians and generals are not idealists but pragmatists. They do not shoot at stars. They star at shooting. It is left to poets and historians to attribute to them ideals that may seem to justify the blood and treasure spent on less exalted objectives. Today we call it "spin."

TIMOLEON OF CORINTH

When the Corinthian aristocrat Timoleon (411–337 BC) was approached as the likely deliverer of Syracuse on Sicily he was loathe to go. He had already murdered his own brother, Timophanes, when the latter attempted to become tyrant of Corinth. It had been a matter of politics, not sibling rivalry. Although the Corinthians had been grateful to escape tyranny, his own mother rejected Timoleon on the grounds that Timophanes had also been her son. Such is the logic of mothers. Timoleon resolved to stay out of politics after that, because politics had driven him to fratricide and alienated his mother's affections. Although he thought she had always favored his brother and given him more attention, he missed Mom a lot after he had to move out of the house and do his own laundry. He took a place in the country to get away from politics. But politics came to him when the magistrates of Corinth told him that unless he restored liberty to Syracuse, they would consider his brother's death a simple homicide, rather than an act of democratic patriotism, and charge him with murder.

Unable to plea bargain, Timoleon resigned himself to the life of a general and politician. From Greek through Napoleonic times, World Wars I and II, even the Iraq War, there was (Great Scott!) patently no way for a successful general to avoid the political fallout that complicates the lives of great generals.[80] Timoleon delivered Sicily from Carthage and from the tyranny of the cruel Dionysius II, whom he compelled to quit Syracuse, arranging for him passage to Corinth instead. There, to support himself, the ex-tyrant became a schoolmaster! Cicero observed of Dionysius II that as he could not command men, he might still tyrannize over boys. It was noted that Dionysius died from excessive joy upon hearing that a tragedy of his own composition had been awarded a prize for poetry.[81] Dionysius's students thought that if the judges had graded their teacher's work as he graded theirs, his would never have won the prize. They concluded that the judges must have graded on a curve.

As for Timoleon, he finally got a chance to retire from public life. But he was now such a hero, and so beloved, that everywhere he went people asked him for advice. If he went to the theater, they applauded his entrance. When he attended the Assembly, they gave him a standing ovation. He was invited out all the time. Finally, in 337 BC, he died. His grateful compatriots buried him in a public place which they named Timoleonteum so that no one could miss that it was in his honor. Ever afterwards, the Corinthians celebrated festivals and games on the date of his death. Too bad. Timoleon was dying for privacy.

PHILIP II AND THE MACEDONIAN RISE TO POWER

The Greeks could not always decide on who was and who wasn't Greek. A foreigner was, of course, a stranger, and all Greeks tended toward xenophobia, fear of foreigners. Foreigners were *barbaros* (Gr., strange, foreign). Barbarians included anybody who sounded or acted strange—Persians, for example, or Macedonians. Of course, the Macedonians were not really strangers. The Greeks had been trading with them for many years. They were a people of mixed origins, some Greek. They spoke a Greek dialect, though the rest of Greece claimed not to understand it. Macedonians were tribal in government, but they also had a king, and the combination of tribes and kings was something most other Greeks felt they had outgrown, though the Spartans still had not one but two kings, and the Athenians had only been weaned from tribal rule by Cleisthenes in the late sixth century BC.[82] The Macedonians were in some respects (government, law, social relationships, and lack of learning) very much like the Mycenaeans of yore. Athenians especially felt themselves superior to these rude northerners.

Philip of Macedon learned to speak Greek as well as his native dialect, having been sent at fifteen to Thebes, a hostage for Macedonia's good behavior. He boarded at Thebes for three years, apparently with relatives of Epaminondas, whom he greatly admired. His tutor was a Pythagorean, who watched over and protected Philip. At fifteen Philip was probably more capable of protecting his tutor than vice versa. At the court of Macedonia children grew up fast, exposed not only to the rigors of politics and the dangers generated by the envy of power, but witness to the moral and immoral foibles of their privileged elders and to the subservience of their underlings. Philip's happiest and most wholesome experiences may well have been had as a hostage and student away from his family's palace at Pella. As Pythagoreans had been trained to do, his tutor probably urged upon Philip the benefits of vegetarianism, pacifism, and celibacy. "Just say no to it all, Phil, and you'll come out all right in the end!"

Pythagoras (c. 582–507 BC) had himself been not merely a philosospher, but a guru, whose sixth-century BC Greek colony of Crotona, in southern Italy, was a very tony commune devoted to reshaping the mind as well as the body and soul. Pythagoras was a vegan and religious mystic. Bertrand Russell described him as a cross between Einstein and Mary Baker Eddy, the arguably unbalanced if inspired founder of Christian Science.[83] Pythagoras was an idealist because he thought numbers, notably immaterial, were the substratum of the universe, rather than matter. He was one of the pre-Socratic philosophers who kept wondering what the world was made of, which may sound like a silly kind of question to ask, but which philosophers and physicists have always insisted is extremely profound. Pythagoras was also a crank who forbade the eating of beans and insisted that his followers make their beds each morning.[84] He greatly influenced Plato, who also thought that the substratum of reality was non-material, though consisting of ideas rather than numbers. Peter Green says Philip was an unlikely candidate for Pythagorean instruction.[85] He was too full of beans.

When Philip went home to rule Macedonia, he fought many enemies. He could not have been passive and survived. He only resisted the temptation to make love to more boys and women than he had time for. Eventually, he found time for seven or eight wives and a number of concubines! Not only did Philip manage for a long while to keep his throne in a country where the coup d'état had become a fine art, but he managed adroit alliances with neighbors not anxious to see him survive such coups. Much of the political stability he needed on his borders was accomplished by his marriage alliances with neighboring kingdoms, using, for lack of better means, kings' daughters. On their backs—literally—rested the fate of nations. That is how Philip acquired Alexander's mother, Myrtale, better known by her Greek name, Olympias, a princess of Epirus, and by her, his son, Alexander. Others of his wives came from the royalty of Illyria, Molossia, Thessaly, Geta, and Thrace. Philip's enthusiasm for foreign marriages would be reflected by Alexander and enjoined on Alexander's companions at arms. But what Philip elected to do in the interests of policy, Alexander and his men would be obliged to do in the interests of progeny, for Alexander would have to populate an immense empire with a limited number of Greeks.

Demosthenes (383–322 BC), the most famous Athenian orator and political figure in the fourth century, harped continually on the barbarism of Macedonia and its king. He denied that Philip was a Greek, or even related to the Greeks,[86] although Philip's family claimed descent from the Hellenic hero Hercules, whose father, Zeus, had coupled with a princess of Argos. There Hercules was raised to appreciate Greek culture and to practice military arts, preparing himself for heroic deeds performed mostly in Asia. With such an ancestor, how could Philip help but identify himself as a latter-day Hercules, sent to Thebes to imbibe Hellenic culture and study military tactics that would prepare him for the conquest of Persia?

Philip aroused Demosthenes' ire because he succeeded in making the cultural backwater of Macedonia an international force. But the use of force to achieve more force is precisely what had given Athens authority over many of the same regions of Greece and Thrace that Philip looked to control, only Philip was better at force, which is why the Athenians were so resentful. Nothing is more irritating to a great power than being outwitted by a newcomer using similar methods.

Philip was never impatient in deciding when and where to strike, and of course, he did not, like Athens did, have to put up with the vagaries of democratic government when he decided. Democracy is rarely as efficient as autocracy, and Philip, like the Persian emperor he hoped someday to replace, was an autocrat. He let it be known that he was open to proposals when his neighbors had problems, and they came more and more to look to him for solutions. Sometimes he offered his own without being asked, which is quite normal for autocrats as well as democrats. On the Propontis (southern coast of Thrace), for example, he dictated a nonaggression pact to the king of eastern Thrace, and the same with cities further east between the Hellespont and the Bosporus, areas that were of interest to Athens because of her Black Sea grain trade. In 358 BC he captured Amphipolis, a former Athenian colony at his extreme eastern border, garrisoned by Macedonia. He promised to restore it to Athens in return for Pydna, which had been conquered by Athens from Macedonia during his brother's reign. Pydna, with its fine harbor on the Thermaic gulf (Gulf of Salonika), was fifty-some miles northeast of Mount Olympus. Philip conquered it so easily, without Athenian aid, that he refused to keep his word and instead, kept Amphipolis. Next, he captured Potidaea on the Chalcidic Peninsula, taking it from Athens, which had gained it with Macedonian help in the first place. Philip gave it (356 BC) to Olynthus. Not long after, he took the Thracian settlement of Crenides, a valuable center for gold mining, and renamed it Philippi. It became a Macedonian mining town, peopled with engineers and miners who increased Philip's annual income three-hundred-fold.[87] Naming towns after oneself was another habit Philip passed on to Alexander. The long but successful siege of Methone (352 BC) less than thirty miles south of his own capital, Pella, and the key to Thessaly, stirred Demosthenes (first philippic, or speech against Philip) to rouse Athens to the danger of Philip's approach. He hoped they would not be flip about it.

Philip went to the rescue of factions in Thessaly, eventually emerging (352 BC) as a lifelong archon in Thessaly's assembly, for the most part, with the Thessalians' approval.[88] He won recognition by northern Greek city-states (the Amphictyonic Council) of his Greekness, after defeating Athens's ally, Phocis, in the Sacred War, an unholy scuffle prompted by the Phocian domination of Apollo's temple—and treasure—at Delphi. When the war was over (346 BC), Philip had become a fairly creditable Pan-Hellenic champion, president of the Amphictyonic Council. Although he was obliged by Athens, because of her superior navy, to give up the siege of Byzantium and Perinthus (339 BC), he used the time saved to conquer Bulgaria, before again turning southward (338 BC).

The Athenians, who might have repelled Philip by sea, decided to try their fate on land with Thebes, now turned against her Macedonian ally. Although Demosthenes spoke out against a negotiated peace, claiming the Delphic Oracle was working for Philip, Athens's own commander would have been willing to talk the matter out. Instead of talking, they fought the battle of Chaeronea (338 BC) that signaled the end of Greek independence.

Athenian independence was certainly over, though Philip gave Athens terms more generous than those she might have expected in a pact drafted at Corinth (338 BC) at the end of the war. Philip wanted the Greeks to save their strength for the conquest of Persia, and he made the peace provisions palatable for the sake of that great enterprise. Except for Sparta, which insisted on neutrality, all Greece agreed to participate in a league that was committed to respect the liberty, autonomy, and territorial integrity of all, and the obedience of all to the laws of the *hegemon,* that is Philip. Athens and Achaea were allowed to retain their democratic forms of government to prevent them from causing any trouble.[89] The other states were already oligarchies. Both oligarchs and democrats agreed to the most stringent social policies. They allowed property to be freely enjoyed by those already enjoying it, and debtors and slaves were given the right in perpetuity to remain debtors and slaves. No misplaced compassion in that conservativism.

EDUCATION, PUBLICITY, POLICY

The philosopher Isocrates had set up a school (399 BC) for logic and public speaking in Athens with a curriculum that put rhetoric at the service of Pan-Hellenism. He was convinced that if the Greeks did not learn that their salvation was unity against Persia, they would never amount to anything. Beginning with his *Panegyric* of 380 BC, Isocrates, a PR man, college president, and newspaper columnist rolled into one, called for a champion to unite the Greeks. At first he thought it would have to be Athens. But he gave up when Athens proved more interested in controlling her allies, suppressing her lower classes, or opposing now Thebes, now Sparta. Isocrates spied a savior in the strong man of Thessaly who had once captured Pelopidas, one Jason of Pherae. But Jason was murdered (370 BC) before Isocrates could persuade him to unite Greece against Persia. Then he turned to Syracuse's tyrant, Dionysius I, who demurred and died the next year (367 BC). The Spartans were not interested in Isocrates or his proposition. Only in 346 BC did Isocrates in his *Philippus* invite Philip of Macedonia to unite Greece, whether the Greeks were willing or not. After Philip had defeated Greece at Chaeronea, the old man sent the king a congratulatory letter, dying the following year at the age of ninety-eight. His enthusiasm for war against Persia had kept the old professor emeritus sharp until the end. *Emeritus* in Latin means he served out his time, and not, as Demosthenes might have translated it, devoid of merit.

As far as Demosthenes could see, Isocrates had a Persian fixation, when he, Demosthenes, believed Philip was Greece's great common enemy, not her champion. Ultimately, the Macedonian faction in Athens managed to rid themselves of Demosthenes (322 BC) by his own hand. They accused him of absconding with money deposited in the Acropolis by one of Alexander's generals, a charge of treason. Demosthenes took to the road. Philip's agents found him hiding in a temple of Poseidon on a small island off the coast of Argolis. Determined not to give the hated enemy the satisfaction, Demosthenes took his own life by drinking the ink from his pen or some other poison, piously taking care to emerge from the sanctuary first so that it could not be defiled by the shedding of his blood. That was patriotism. That was piety. That was Pan-Hellenism. That was panache.

During the fourth century, Greek minds improved faster than Greek manners. There was that first Utopia, Plato's *Republic,* for example, where they read that Plato (427–347 BC) thought the polis had taken a turn for the worse and might actually be improved upon. By the mid fourth century anyone could see it was definitely not ideal, and since Plato was an idealist, this bothered him, and probably, the board of trustees of his Academy. It also bothered all the city-states who had lost a war recently, and all the politicians who were afraid they would lose the next one. In Greece that was just about everyone. The Greeks were beginning to think Plato was right, because it was growing more and more apparent to those who shared Demosthenes' point of view, or Isocrates,' that warfare between city-states was impoverishing the Greek spirit as well as Greek treasuries. Plato thought that something like divine providence could guide people to virtue provided they learned a lot of mathematics, which was what was mostly taught at his Academy.[90] Perhaps he lost heart, though, because he noted in *The Republic* that he had hardly ever known a mathematician who was capable of reasoning. But by then it was too late for many of his students, because they had already graduated and were back in their own city-states giving advice. Should they have studied the humanities rather than math? If Philip of Macedon's education had been entrusted to a professor of humanities—one of the Sophists, for example, instead of to a Pythagorean mathematician, would Philip have been more virtuous? A better reasoner? Less inclined to insinuate himself into Greek affairs? Had he been taught the famous Pythagorian theorem for no practical good? The correlation between the curriculum studied and life lived was never very great. Most people learn on the job anyway. So perhaps it was not so important if the Greeks could never decide what constituted the perfect education, though Sophists, who tended toward liberal views and idealists, who were usually conservatives, sneered at each other's assumptions and curriculum then and now. They debated these matters until 338 BC, when the Macedonians under Philip conquered them and ended the debate over the relative merits of a mathematical and idealistic education versus a practical humanistic one. In those days the humanities were still considered practical, whereas math was thought idealistic! Fashions in education change, and each side blames the moral and political failures of the state on the inadequacies of the educational system rather than on the political one. Of course. Teachers are always more easily and more cheaply compelled to reform than politicians.

Even those who obtained a formal education in fourth-century Greece treasured a few primitive customs—the love of war, a distaste for political unity, insensitivity to human suffering. Had they thought about this without prejudice, the Greeks could have seen for themselves that the Macedonians were not so foreign as Demosthenes thought, since they shared these customs with all the other Greeks. Greece was proud of its accomplishments, which were impressive. These included sensitivity to art, critical rationalism, and uncritical irrationalism. Like other cultures, Greek civilization in the fourth century was an unstable compound of elements that kept breaking down under pressure.

To keep them more rather than less united, Philip of Macedon applied more pressure, not because he had absorbed the idealism of Pythagoras or Plato, nor much culture at Thebes, but because he understood that the real substratum of the universe was not idealism, but iron. The Greeks learned what they knew about the ultimate substratum of the universe and political unity through Philip, not through philosophy. His was their school of hard knocks from which they graduated by degrees.

7

Alexander the Great

HE HAS BEEN ALL THINGS TO ALL MEN. BESIDES king, hero, god, and con-
queror, Alexander the Great has been viewed as philosopher, scientist,
prophet, statesman, political visionary, proponent of universal brotherhood
and forerunner of Stoicism, a man with charisma, a Greek term meaning
divinely gifted![1] He has also been reviled as a neurotic, sadistic, paranoid,
schizophrenic alcoholic; an unreliable ruler and friend, a treacherous
employer and a megalomaniac of genius who wound up believing that he
was the god he grew increasingly fond of impersonating. His lack of interest
in women appealed to nineteenth-century British writers who admired this
drawing-room affectation, even if with Alexander it wasn't. He preferred
men or eunuchs to women as sex partners, but abstinence to all these. He
never felt more mortal than when having sex or a nap. He was so attached
to his mother. He had an Oedipus complex.[2] That and his admiration of
the poet Pindar were all he preserved from Thebes, home of Oedipus the
King, a city he flattened for rebellion and regretted later.[3] His chivalry
toward older women was marked, and charmed.[4] It especially charmed
older women. He treated them as queens, and queens he treated as his
mother. One middle-aged woman, Queen Ada of Caria, became his
mother when she adopted him, a relationship both found politically advan-
tageous, but also, companionable.

Historians tell us that people interpret Alexander the Great (already so
called in the first century AD) by their own experience and dreams.[5]
Alexander scholars study the experiences and dreams of politicians and
generals, men who experienced much, dreamt of power, and controlled
more than most of us who doubt our ability to control anything whatsoever—careers, daily commute, life partners, children. For us even to imagine—let alone interpret—Alexander's conquests is difficult. How could a
man so in control of others have lost control of himself so often? When he
did, he isolated himself after his excesses, consumed by embarrassment
and sometimes, real remorse, imploring his closest associates for feedback
concerning his behavior that they, knowing his unpredictability, hesitated
to provide.

It may be consoling to reflect that collectively, if not individually, we control more of the obstacles that impede our objectives, including natural disasters, disease, telecommunications, travel, and so forth, than Alexander could, though we create impediments, perhaps on purpose, so that we do not have to shoulder responsibilities that Alexander, at least, never shirked.

Not only was Alexander royal, but a child endowed with unusual athletic ability, a quick mind, and a personality that aroused in others as much affection as later, respect or fear. He was made of much, if not all, the right stuff. His parents were alienated from one another. His mother kept snakes in her bed, while his father kept mistresses in his. Neither could stand the other's bedfellows. Still, they were extremely supportive of Alexander's ambitions, probably because his were not very different from their own—the magnification of authority, the admiration of the neighbors, the favor of the gods. It is easier to support offspring who value parental values. The upshot was that while they treated him as a child when he was yet a child, they treated him as an adult when he was still a teenager.

He studied away from home with friends in a rural retreat. He was given a personal trainer for sports and Aristotle for his tutor. Raised in the expectation of his doing great deeds, he worried only that his father might do them all before he and his friends finished school. At sixteen he was allowed to demonstrate his governmental skills in his father's absence. Two years later he accompanied Philip to Chaeronea where he distinguished himself on the battlefield. Unlike modern adolescents, made insecure by a society that has little trust in or use for them in peacetime and delays their maturation, Alexander from early childhood developed an enormous belief in his own capacity—and confidence in the rightness of his decisions. At Philip's death (336 BC) he had the best trained and the most loyal army in the world when he set out to conquer it.

Plutarch tells us Alexander wept when he heard from the philosopher Anaxarchus that there were an infinite number of worlds.[6] When his friends asked if any accident had befallen him, he answered: "Do you not think it a matter worthy of lamentation that when there is such a vast multitude of them, we have not yet conquered one?" Anaxarchus was a eudaemonist, i.e., a man who lived his life according to reason, not the gratification of the senses. At least, that is what he said. Another court philosopher was Pyrrho (360–270 BC), the first skeptic. Both emphasized the inward happiness that comes from indifference to one's external environment. Although accompanying Alexander to India, they, like Aristotle, succeeded in influencing his behavior only as much as most philosophers influence most men of action, which is very little. Bertrand Russell arrived at the same conclusion in his history of Western philosophy. He thought Aristotle's influence on Alexander "nil" but wondered why Alexander had had so little influence on Aristotle, who seemed not to have realized that the age of city-states had been super-seded by the age of empires.[7]

Alexander spent two years after Philip's death punishing his fathers' mur-derers, shoring up borders in Thrace and Illyria, squelching plots at home, and suppressing a revolt in central Greece. All the Greek states except Sparta reconfirmed in Alexander the honors they had given Philip. After Alexander went north, Athens, having heard a rumor that he had been killed on the Danube, declared independence from Macedonia and sent help to Thebes which had just overturned its Macedonian garrison. Alexan-der rushed back to Greece and leveled Thebes (335 BC), sparing Athens. There was symmetry in the Parthenon, but none in politics. Alexander con-tinued to admire Athens, but not Thebes. To the Parthenon he would send three hundred suits of Asian armor which he liberated after his first victory against Persia in Asia Minor (Granicus, 334 BC). These trophies encouraged the Athenians and others to support their master, who glorified most, if not all, of Greece, and enriched it with Persian treasure. Alexander thought his conquest was world-historical. He would come to regard himself not as the mere leader of a Greek league, nor just king of Macedonia, but king of Asia, king of kings, and colloquially speaking, kingpin.

Alexander respected the supernatural. This reverence was familial, for his father's side claimed descent from the demigod Hercules (var. Hera-cles), son of Zeus, dear to Olympias. She told Philip that on their wedding day Zeus had impregnated her with Alexander! A psychiatrist, therefore, might have said that everything Alexander accomplished reflected a desire to legitimize himself. In classical times there were no psychiatrists, only ora-cles. Croesus learned to his dismay that a consultation cost plenty. Alexan-der consulted only himself. He would go to great lengths—as far as India—to prove that he was a legitimate ruler, though some of his new subjects felt he was a bastard. In any event, he never disavowed his other father, Philip. This kind of paternity case was familiar to all the god-rulers of western Asia and Egypt. How did a man who wished to be the son of a god or the Son of God explain away his human father? At least Alexander did not regard his relationship to Philip and Zeus as a trinity. He had too many natures to compress into just three!

While yet a schoolboy, Alexander identified with Homer's Achilles, the hero of the Trojan War, first of the Greek invaders of Asia, whose lover was Patroclus. When he left Macedonia never to return (334 BC) he stuck a copy of the *Iliad* into his backpack and read passages to his troops as they marched along. He thought that Achilles was lucky to have had an intimate friend, Patroclus, and a poet, Homer, to immortalize them. Alexander never found his poet, so had to make do with mere historians. These folks, normally unemployable, are moved chiefly by their stomachs, while poets must find their souls moved before their pens can be. Still, Alexander needed apologists like the historian Callisthenes, Aristotle's nephew, who had published Alexander's fame as early as 330 BC. From historians he expected supportive accounts. In that respect his "reporters" were no different from those sent to the front in other wars, force-fed information from sources they could neither question nor criticize.

Before fighting his first Asian battle at the river Granicus (near the Sea of Marmara), Alexander paid his respects to Achilles and all the old Mycenaean campaigners—so like his own Macedonians! The Trojans thought he would want to see the relics of Paris, Helen's lover, for Paris, like Alexander, had invaded a foreign land. But Paris loved Helen, while Alexander loved Hephaestion, whom he put in charge of his cavalry. Alexander wasn't big on relics. Hephaestion was said to resemble Alexander so much that he was frequently mistaken for him. It did not matter that someone had saluted Hephaestion as emperor by mistake, because, Alexander said, he and Hephaestion were one. Before Achilles' tomb at Troy Alexander stripped naked, daubed himself with oil, and ran around the tomb. He placed a garland on it and sacrificed to his hero. Hephaestion did the same for Patroclus's tomb. Xerxes, the Persian emperor, had also sacrificed to the tomb of Achilles on his way to Greece in 480 BC, as did the Roman emperor Caracalla nearly 550 years later. Neither stripped, but then, Alexander ate so little, and for most of his life, drank so little, that nudity held no terrors. Greek heroes had the right workout equipment. The naked truth is that those other kings were out of shape.[8]

Alexander liberated the Ionian Greek cities in Asia Minor after winning his first battle against the Persians at the Granicus River, where a supporter named Black Cleitus saved his life in battle. These Ionians prospered in Persia and enjoyed special trading privileges, but they were unhappy because they were not free.[9] So Alexander liberated them. He placed a Macedonian in charge of them as satrap instead of the Persian who had been over them before, telling the Greeks to pay their taxes to this new man, because he was a regular fellow, and freedom meant being taxed by regular fellows rather than tyrants. Later, he used the Persians as governors, and treated them as regular fellows too, but this caused his Macedonians to grumble. The Ionians were happy because they thought they had been freed, but they forgot to ask what it was they were free to do until it was too late to ask questions or do anything but what they were told. Alexander then liberated the rest of Asia Minor. Everyone expected it, and that is what soldiers do when they are victorious. They liberate things.

In the spring of 333 BC, Alexander arrived at Gordium in Phrygia, on the river Sangarius, southwest of Ancyra, modern Ankara. Here he saw a wagon that had brought the peasant Midas to the Phrygian throne by the intervention of an Oracle. The Oracle told the Phrygians to crown the first man they met going to the temple of Jupiter riding in a wagon. A crude peasant named Midas was doing just that, so the Phrygians crowned him king. Midas consecrated his old wagon to Jupiter out of respect.[10] Or perhaps he merely unloaded it, for the wagon was strangely flawed. The knot that tied its yoke to the pole could not be undone. No one could find its ends. The locals fantasized that the man who untied this knot could become king of Asia, judging that unknotting wagons and governing empires were jobs of equivalent difficulty. When Alexander saw the knot, he knew at once that ruling an empire would be the easier job. So he drew his sword and cut the Gordian knot, or according to another authority (Aristobolus) removed a peg that passed through the knot into the pole, holding it in place. Later, he said the gods approved of his solution, because he heard thunder and saw lightning that night. When it came to "untying" the Gordian knot, Alexander untied it not. Conquering heroes prefer pragmatic solutions to complex problems and define their words and actions expediently, sure that they can manage the news after they've made it.

From Gordium, Alexander advanced to Ancyra where the native king submitted. He got through a mountain pass in Cilicia (southern Cappadocia) so narrow that a loaded camel could not pass through. This was just as well. Camels are hard enough to manage when they are not loaded, and the same is true of camel drivers. It would have been easy for the Persians to repel Alexander at these "Cilician Gates," preventing him from reaching Tarsus, repaying Greece for Persian losses at Thermopylae. Instead, the defenders fled. Alexander felt their turn about was fair play. He could not know that from Tarsus, three hundred and sixty-odd years after his arrival there, a hellenized Jewish native of that city named Saul, alias St. Paul, would set out from home on the road to Damascus, determined to persecute converts to a cult called Christianity. Although both men were products of Hellenism and traveled very far to change it, one could scarcely find two more different fellows ever to have walked the streets of Tarsus. Alexander represented himself as the ambassador of high-spirited Hellenism; Paul as the missionary of a higher spiritualism. Alexander was self-promoting; Paul promoted selflessness. Alexander taught Greeks about great things beyond Macedonia's frontiers; Paul taught them about the Great Beyond. Alexander's words translated into power; Paul's bespoke the power of the Word. Yet these two men passed through the streets of Tarsus on their separate journeys to the known, unknown, and unknowable. Who can say which of the two contributed the most to human happiness and which to human misery? Presumptuous to attempt an answer without polling each of thousands, even millions of individuals whose lives would one day be enriched, damaged, or ruined by their success.

When he first crossed into Asia, Alexander emphasized his role as a Pan-Hellenic leader of the Corinthian League. His victories, he said, were for the League in the interest of Greeks everywhere. But, after his second victory, at Issus (332 BC), he wrote to Darius in his capacity of leader (*hegemon*) of the League to say he must address him in the future as the king of all Asia, the possessor of all Darius's possessions, including his family, whom Alexander was holding for ransom.[11] At the time, he did not yet possess all Persia. Alexander bluffed.[12] He would have made a great poker player.

Rather than pursue Darius immediately, he marched down the Mediterranean coast to deprive the Persians of Phoenician harbors at Byblos, Sidon, and Tyre. The first two cities capitulated. But the Tyrians resisted. They provided a casus belli (reason for war) when they refused to allow Alexander to offer a sacrifice to their god, Melkart, in his major temple on their island fortress. The Tyrians pleaded neutrality. Only their king was permitted to sacrifice on the island, though they offered another temple on the mainland for Alexander's use. Separate but equal facilities were, Alexander thought, inherently unequal. Greeks had long equated Melkart with Hercules. Alexander had just had coins struck at Sidon showing him as the youthful Hercules being crowned by Nike (Victory). The message was plain. He needed to control Tyre if he were to secure Greece from a naval invasion by Persia. Without such control, Macedon could not take Egypt. Without Egypt, the Macedonians could not pursue Darius eastward, because their home base (Macedonia, Greece) would be threatened.[13]

At Tyre a great annual festival of the god Melkart was in process.[14] Alexander hoped to use his descent from Melkart-Hercules to induce acceptance as king of Tyre. His posture, if not that of a native son, was at least that of a distant relative. To the Tyrians, however, this posture was imposture. Still proclaiming neutrality, they murdered the heralds he sent to parley and threw their bodies over the wall. It was now impossible for Alexander to accept the Tyrians' claim of neutrality. He imposed on them the direst of penalties. He connected the old port city on land with the offshore island fortress by building a mole or masonry breakwater into the sea and out to the walled island. Historians debate the enduring legacy of Alexander, but the most enduring was surely this mole, since, with the passage of time, sand collected around it and united the island with the shore, forming a peninsula that has ever since endured. Unmolested. The same cannot be said of the Tyrians, seven thousand of whom were killed in battle, compared to four hundred of Alexander's men. Thirty thousand Tyrian inhabitants were enslaved. Fifteen thousand more were smuggled out.[15] The dead and the fled were henceforth ex-urbanites. After Alexander finished his siege, Tyre was flattened.

Before Tyre fell, Alexander received his second embassy from Darius, offering him not just territory west of the Halys River in Asia Minor, as the first embassy proposed, but all the territory Darius controlled west of the

Euphrates, along with an alliance to be strengthened by Alexander's marriage to Darius's daughter! Hearing this, Alexander's general, Parmenio, a trusted friend, formerly his father's commander in Asia, advised him that if he were Alexander, he would accept. The young Macedonian prince answered, "So would I, if I were Parmenio."

From Tyre, Alexander set off for Egypt. At Gaza he subdued a revolt and was wounded in the shoulder. Once again, all the men in town died defending it, the rest, mainly women and children, were enslaved. What happened at Thebes, Tyre, Gaza, and all the other towns from there to India that resisted Alexander's conquest was predictable. Annihilation.

In Egypt, where Persians had taken control as recently as 342 BC,[16] Persian generals had barbecued the Memphites' sacred Apis calf, supposed incarnation of their gods Osiris or Ptah.[17] So the Memphites were pleased to see Alexander sacrificing to Apis. They hailed him a liberator, the son of the sun-god, Amon-Re, and pharaoh of Egypt. Alexander enjoyed his new role. Wherever he went he accommodated local gods and their priestly retinue. Greeks had long since made it a habit to equate other folks' deities with their own. If his treatment of local gods was sometimes better than his treatment of locals, it was not because he was trying hard to be multicultural, but because he never met a god he did not like. The same was not true of humans, whom he disliked whenever they objected to his conquest and rule.

In his treatment of foreign gods Alexander was neither as original as some historians have suggested, nor as diplomatic, though the political advantages of treating local gods well could not have escaped his notice. He was just naturally superstitious, or if you prefer, reverent. Alexander has been called "a churchgoer" by A. R. Burn.[18] There have, one recalls, been many other "churchgoing" generals and warrior monarchs in history, but few have had their religious background, testimony, practices, and inspiration so narrowly scrutinized, so hotly debated as Alexander's. Zealots and warrior-rulers such as King David, Justinian, Charlemagne, Basil the Bulgar Slayer, Saint Louis, Charles V, Phillip II, Oliver Cromwell, Louis XIV, etc., did much more damage in the name of religion than Alexander, who was invariably respectful of foreign deities and their clergy or prophets. He never persecuted anyone simply for conscience's sake. But, some might object, those other kings did not pretend to be gods. They were not megalomaniacs. Alexander knew well enough he was not a god, although in Egypt he allowed himself—it was a very old tradition—to be so identified. It was not his fault that Greeks and Macedonians mistook the Persian habit of prostration (Greek, *proskinesis*), a Persian mark of respect for rulers, for an act Greeks and Macedonians connected only with divine worship. Well, the apologists for zealous potentates might argue, the others did not imagine their ancestors were *engendered* by gods, or especially *favored* by gods.

In point of fact, every monarch who has declared war on his enemies has played God quite as much or more than Alexander, exterminating in their turn Canaanites and Jebusites, Arians and Nestorians, Saxons and Slavs, Muslims and Jews, Lutherans and Anabaptists, papists and Huguenots, etc. These other conquering rulers never tolerated religious diversity as Alexander did. Far from being more tolerant in such matters, Alexander seems simply to have shared the most common and unsophisticated Greek mentality vis-à-vis the gods, accommodating them as a matter of course. Alexander was not just religiously tolerant, he was credulous.

He was more superstitious and retrograde in his beliefs than the most advanced philosophic opinion of his day. His own teacher, Aristotle, might have blanched watching the enthusiasm with which his former pupil threw himself into propitiating foreign gods. For the God of Aristotle was an Unmoved Mover. Not involved with the world, He would not have cared a fig for Alexander's sacrifices or for anybody else's. The God of Aristotle was absorbed in contemplating His own perfection, not anybody else's imperfections. The Unmoved Mover did not equate one god with another. He was His own equation, and therefore, His own solution. For Him it was a zero-sum game. Alexander was no unmoved mover, but a world shaker on the move. Where religion (his, or anybody else's) was concerned, he was easily moved. He had a genetic as well as a cultural predisposition to credulity. First, he was human. Second, he was a descendant of Zeus and Hercules, a man (and in Egypt, a god) of his times. In no need of his child within, he kept in touch with the gods without.

Alexander seems not to have regarded himself a god for the longest part of his career. In the last year of his life, he certainly wished others to regard him as such, possibly as a mark of his superiority and not necessarily of his divinity. Scholars are at odds as to how to interpret the request he made to the Corinthian League in 324 BC in which he required the members publicly to acknowledge him as a god. W. W. Tarn thought that in 327 BC Alexander had no belief in his own divinity but simply allowed others to strike this note.[19] Wilcken thought the whole question was important as an indication that Alexander was thinking of "world sovereignty" and that it was a move quite consistent with an "inner religious experience."[20] More recently, Peter Green has insisted that Alexander took his divine status "very seriously indeed," losing control at the end of his life over "his own latent megalomania."[21] Whatever Alexander in fact felt about his own godhead, it seems less significant than this: that although he was as pious as any Hebrew zealot or Christian fanatic, and no more superstitious than some, he was less bigoted and less arrogant where religion was concerned than most persecuting kings before or since.

After leaving Memphis, and stopping only to found the new city of Alexandria, he set off to visit the temple of Zeus-Ammon at the oasis of

Siwah, near the Libyan border. Did he wish to consult the god about whom Pindar had written a hymn? To share with great men like Cimon and Lysander, and the heroes Perseus and Hercules, the experience of this pilgrimage to an especially reliable Oracle? He may have hoped to inspire his men with zeal for the final conquest of Persia. Would the Persian crown be his? A favorable reply from the Oracle was the equivalent to a winning number in the state lottery. Was he really the son of Zeus-Ammon as the priests in Memphis told him he was?[22] Had he found and punished all his father's murderers?[23] Would he eventually rule the whole world? What did he learn from the old priest who met him privately, keeping his officers cooling their heels in an outer courtyard? Alexander never revealed the questions he put to the priest at Siwah, nor his responses, except to say that he had received the answer that his heart desired.[24] In a letter to his mother he promised to reveal certain secrets when they next met. They never met again, though they corresponded. Alexander trusted his Mom more than anyone, keeping the rest of the world waiting in the outer courtyard of his confidence for some sign of his real intentions. Like Father, like son.

At Gaugamela in September, 331 BC, Alexander defeated but did not kill Darius. He then hired the first of Darius's Persian satraps, Mazeus of Babylon, to carry on his old job of administering Babylon. The pattern of hiring talented servants of defeated rulers, and occasionally, those rulers themselves, provided they professed a new loyalty, defused some of the resentment the Persians might have felt under a foreign ruler. These natives in turn provided him with the expert intelligence only a native staff could provide. From Babylon it was southeast to Susa in the late autumn, where Alexander took possession of an immense treasury. Beyond the Zagros Mountains lay the most famous Persian capital, Persepolis, protected by the impregnable gorge called the Persian Gates. One of the prisoners taken there showed Alexander a route around the pass—Thermopylae in reverse![25]

Persepolis is no more; only pillars, portals, and portraits reveal its former magnificence. It burned on Alexander's watch, while Alexander watched. Historians somewhat apathetically debate whether it was on his orders or because, having thrown a party for his associates, he got too drunk to think straight and allowed an Athenian courtesan named Thaïs to persuade him that the Persians, who burned fifth-century Athens, had it coming. W. W. Tarn says the story about Thaïs is "legend" and that Alexander "deliberately" burned Darius's palace "against Parmenio's advice" because Xerxes had burned a great temple of Babylon.[26] A. R. Burn thinks that it isn't necessary to dismiss the story about Thaïs and points out that if the burning were really, as Arrian suggested, an act of revenge for Xerxes' burning of Athens (not Babylon!) in 480 BC, it clashed with Alexander's new policy of conciliation with Persia.[27] John Snyder says that Alexander deliberately burned Persepolis because the city was economically self-sufficient and a possible center for future resistance to Macedonian rule, making the burning a kind of fire insurance.[28] Peter Green agrees that burning Persepolis was deliberate on Alexander's part, and however inconsistent with Persian reconciliation, it was consistent with Alexander's character when his will was thwarted.[29] Mary Renault notes wryly that like so many things that happen at successful parties, it seemed a good idea at the time.[30] Because it destroyed so much great art, because it revealed Alexander as a maniacal practitioner of power politics, the burning was an inflammation that made the whole world sore.

The symbolism of the burnt capital meant that the conquest as an act of revenge for the Persian War was over. The Persianization of his administration was beginning, a policy that alienated many of his Macedonians. Still ahead was the pursuit of Darius, on the lam and defended only by a handful of Greek mercenaries. Alexander was foiled of his prey by turncoat Persian satraps who left their emperor for dead, chained in an abandoned wagon in a valley south of the Caspian. One of Alexander's soldiers found the emperor inside, barely alive, with javelins protruding from his chest. Darius asked for water, happy to have company in his final moments. Alexander gave him a state burial in Persepolis, where he was laid to rest beside his ancestors. Alexander respected the prerogatives of royalty, granting to his most inveterate royal and noble foes the reverence due their superior rank. His was a class act.

Macedonians found Alexander's employment of Persians and his fondness for wearing Persian robes increasingly hard to handle. A plot of royal pages at Drangiana (Western Turkistan) became known as "Philotas's Conspiracy." Philotas was a general, son of Parmenio. He was first tortured, then executed, for failing to alert Alexander to the pages' plot. Philotas claimed on two successive days that Alexander was too busy to be interrupted by discontented youngsters who, in his view, were pricked on by homosexual jealousies, as if a dagger plunged into Alexander by a young homosexual would not be just as sharp as one wielded by a heterosexual.[31] Philotas lacked judgment, even if he was probably not himself a conspirator.[32] He was a braggadocio known to criticize Alexander's performances while glorifying his own and his father Parmenio's. The talk of a plot coincided with resentment of Persianization, and this made Alexander more than usually sensitive to his own safety. A bodyguard named Demetrius accused of complicity in the pages' plot was dismissed, though not executed. Alexander of Lyncestis, a man imprisoned on suspicion of treason four years earlier, was suddenly tried and executed. Callisthenes, tutor to the plotting pages, had several times objected publicly to the Persianization of Alexander's court. He had opposed prostration before the emperor and had spoken out against deifying Alexander. Arraigned with the pages as an accessory, Callisthenes was found guilty on flimsy charges. The pages were turned over to the troops who stoned them to death, and Callisthenes was either hanged, or dragged around in a prison cage until he died, fat, lousy, and diseased. Alexander sent one of his trusted friends to ride eight hundred miles back to Ecbatana, capital of Media, to arrange the assassination of Parmenio, whose old-fashioned Macedonian sentiments now appeared to Alexander potentially subversive. Though he did not realize it, nothing was more subversive to his rule than his own use of terror and coercion. Sometimes, the worst terrorists are frequently those already in power.

From 329 to 327 BC Alexander's troops attempted to quash revolts of tribal barons north and northeast of the Oxus River in a region called Sogdiana (Samarkand, Uzbekistan). At the borders of the Persian Empire Alexander suffered a painful leg wound while subduing the revolts of a Sogdian baron who had allied with the Scythians beyond the farthest reaches of the old Persian frontier. Despite military setbacks at Maracanda (Alexander's only mistake was the relief of an inadequate force under a divided command), [33] he managed to establish the easternmost Alexandria, nicknamed the Furtherest, modern Khojend. But for Alexander and his men, there was no further rest until the Sogdian unrest was quelled in the spring of 327 BC. One way this was achieved was by marrying a Sogdian baron's daughter. The baron, Oxyartes, then allied with the Macedonians and persuaded his neighbors to do the same. The baron's daughter, Roxane, was an instrument of peace, a beautiful, passive instrument. She bore Alexander a son after his death. She and her infant were eliminated by Alexander's successors. Women were merely instruments of history, seldom instrumental in shaping it.

Alexander made an example of Darius's murderer, a man named Bessus, by having him humiliated, scourged, and mutilated before publicly executing him as a regicide (328 BC). Alexander followed this good old Persian method of dealing with a usurper out of respect for a worthy opponent and a fellow king. Alexander had a sense of honor. But that sense of honor was not to be counted upon. He killed a trusted friend and commander, a man who had earlier saved Alexander's life, Cleitus the Black, after a drunken brawl at a party, very possibly one held to celebrate Cleitus's promotion to the satrapy of Bactria. As the party started to hum, Cleitus objected to comparisons made between Alexander and his father, Philip. He said they were insulting to Philip's memory and to the prowess of the old Macedonian soldiery. He said that Philip's acts were more glorious than his son's and defended Parmenio whom Alexander had just recently had murdered. The conversation grew more heated, revealing splits between the older and younger soldiers, Greek and Macedonian ones, westerners and easterners. When Alexander seemed hugely amused by a skit depicting Macedonians as cowards during an engagement lost to the Sogdian leader Spitamenes, Cleitus attributed the defeat to bad luck, not cowardice. Alexander accused him of special pleading, for Cleitus had fought in that battle. Cleitus reminded Alexander how, at Granicus, this "coward" had saved the son of Ammon's life. He also accused Alexander of preferring barbarian "slaves" to Macedonians, free men who spoke freely. Alexander went for his dagger, but one of his bodyguards had removed it for safekeeping. Cleitus's friends then removed Cleitus—also for safekeeping. Drunken brawlers with a cause are no more responsible than drunken emperors with one, and when Cleitus reappeared at the tent door, reciting democratic verses from Euripides, Alexander grabbed a guard's spear and ran Cleitus clean through!

He was *awfully* sorry when he realized Cleitus was dead and drew out the spear as if to impale himself with it—Peter Green says he did not try very energetically!—whereupon his guards overpowered him and carried him to his own tent.[34] There Alexander remained for thirty-six hours or for three or four days (sources vary), refusing nourishment until, as at the oasis of Siwah, he "heard what his heart desired"—this time from Anaxarchus. The philosopher told him that he was above the law.[35] Still, Alexander suspected that he had done something unethical, something illegal, something to make amends for, a realization many lawless leaders have not had. Water under the gate.

Alexander took the Khyber Pass to northwestern India at the end of summer, 327 BC. Taxiles, king of Taxila, gave Alexander money, sacrificial animals, provisions, seven hundred cavalrymen, twenty-five elephants, troops, and aid—a campaign contribution—with the usual strings attached. He wanted help fighting his enemy, Porus, and other hostile potentates. Alexander was lucky that northwestern India lacked political unity, a need he felt he could satisfy. Against Porus at the Hydaspes (Jhelum) River in Punjab he moved fifteen thousand Macedonian troops and five thousand horses across three swift river channels bridging two islands—during a storm. Porus was counting on his superior numbers and two hundred elephants to win, but Alexander's great sense of timing caused Porus's strategy of putting all his elephants in the center line to backfire. While anything can go wrong on a swirling, congested battlefield, two hundred elephants that backfire is a most lamentable scene. Although the elephants stomped on or impaled on their tusks many Macedonian infantrymen and some who fought for Porus as well, Alexander trumpeted his victory. Afterward, he asked King Porus how he wished to be treated. "Like a king," replied Porus. This seemed to Alexander in keeping with the elegance of his opponent's bearing and his own need for native administrative talent. So he accorded Porus—and his enemy, King Taxiles, too—more territory and more responsibility than either had had before. He made them his allies and friends, and Porus never went to war against him or Taxiles ever again. Alexander understood that one doesn't treat a king of substance as if he were porous, and he also understood the value of trust, royal pride, and, of course, elephants. An Alexander never forgets.

After the battle at the Hydaspes, the horse Bucephalus died. Alexander's horse had been with him since his boyhood, when, by racing Bucephalus into the sun, he alone had been able to ride him. The king was saddened by the loss of this companion. Probably at the site of modern Jalapur, he founded a new town in his horse's honor and named it Bucephala, the original one-horse town.[36] Bucephalus had had the good sense never to let another man ride him, and with Olympias and Hephaestion, was one of the few living things Alexander never suspected of treachery.

When his army reached the Hyphasis River (Beas), Alexander was obliged to end his eastward trek because he could not convince his men to go further. Their polite but firmly conveyed desire to return to Macedonia made an unwelcome impression on Alexander. They had been on the road for eight years and could not see why it was important to Greek, Macedonian, or Persian security to proceed further. Their lack of enthusiasm for a march to the Eastern (Pacific) Ocean, which Alexander believed to be near (it wasn't) sent him to his tent for his regular three-day sulk, after which there was a tearful reconciliation.

Preparations now began (winter 326–325 BC) for leaving India, heading south at the juncture of the Beas and Indus Rivers. A fleet of eight hundred ships under Admiral Nearchus, Alexander's boyhood friend, was readied and many smaller boats besides. The veterans who had seen the heaviest fighting sailed down the Indus with Alexander, while, on either bank, the bulk of troops and elephants plodded on, Hephaestion commanding the forces on one bank, Craterus those on the other.[37] There was such fierce fighting in a town called Malli that Alexander, made fiercer by having to leave India, resolved to punish the town for resisting him. His troops were so demoralized that Alexander, fearing mutiny, mounted a wall first to encourage them. Too exposed, he leapt down inside the wall, where he was hit on the head and face, before an arrow pierced his lung. Friends carried him out on his shield. One of his oldest, Perdiccas, cut the arrow out with his sword, whereupon Alexander fainted. Several days after, he insisted on riding a horse before his men to prove he was alive and well when in fact he was still convalescent.

It took nine months for Alexander to reach the town of Pattala (near Hyderabad) in July 325 BC. There the Indus split into an eastern and western arm and formed a delta bordering the Indian Ocean. Craterus had been sent overland earlier through the Mullah Pass to rejoin Alexander in Carmania. Alexander sailed down the western arm of the Indus to the sea and out on the Indian Ocean. There he sacrificed to Poseidon, praying for the safety of his fellow adventurers before throwing golden wine goblets and other sacred vessels into the brine. It was a speedy way to do the dishes.

Wilcken thought Alexander sacrificed because he believed he had reached the limit of the world.[38] Hamilton disagrees, since the second in command under Nearchus was aware that Taprobane (Ceylon) lay eastward.[39] However much Alexander knew about the limits of the world, he knew nothing about his own and would have denied them altogether had anyone dared suggest he had any. Proving that he had none was more important to him than any political objective or racial harmony principle. The mania of megalomaniacs, who are sick people, is, by definition, unlimited. Those who have tried to plumb Alexander's depths have scraped the barrel. He was more shallow than deep, more selfish than caring, more cruel than kind, more disconnected from his fellow men—and from himself—than connected. He conquered and delegated the responsibilities connected with governance because he was himself ungovernable and could think of nothing better to do with his time than to fill it with ceaseless activity. Did he suffer from attention deficit disorder?

When Alexander finished reconnoitering the coast and both arms of the Indus, he advised Nearchus to wait for October winds before setting sail for the west, while he decided to march westward through the Gedrosian desert (Makran) with a force of seventy to eighty-five thousand men. He intended to create storage bins for grain and wells for water at certain points along the coast where Nearchus's fleet could provision itself. The fleet carried the heaviest food supplies and was to feed the marching troops during occasional rendezvous. Such was the successful strategy used by Xerxes for invading Greece in 480 BC, one Alexander had studied in Herodotus.[40]

Not one rendezvous took place. The coastal mountains were so inhospitable that Alexander's company was driven inland, making the possibility of supply by sea a mirage. They marched through uninhabited desert where the heat in August reaches 127°F in the shade. The hardships experienced were the worst ever. Even when they reached the coast, Nearchus failed to appear. Inland, the satraps to whom he sent requests for provisions (via racing camels) failed him, and all that did not fail him was desert grit and his own. Starvation and thirst, poisonous snakes and plants, flash floods that carried away most of the camp's followers (i.e., women and children), sandstorms, injuries, sickness and exhaustion accounted for the fifty thousand human deaths in his entourage, as well as those of numerous baggage animals, sometimes slain for food. Wagons were left behind; the sick and dying, too. Green warns that while we "cannot return a firm verdict" concerning a conspiracy of his most trusted servants—including several satraps and Admiral Nearchus—one cannot overlook the possibility that Alexander's men had been plotting to bring him down ever since he entered India. [41]

Alexander and his remaining troops reached Pura, capital of Gedrosia. Here he began to search for a scapegoat on whom he could blame the fiasco of the desert march. Like most of us, he wasn't in the habit of blaming himself. He fired the satrap of Gedrosia for failing to forward supplies to him, but the fellow had died in battle before he got the news of his dismissal. He executed the satrap of Susiana and his son—the latter, according to Plutarch, killed by Alexander himself. Alexander discovered that the men he had trusted to govern in his absence—many native princes, but also Macedonian generals—in places like Media (south of the Caspian) and Drangiana (west of the Hindu Kush) had misused their offices to enrich themselves and had injured the locals and the local religious establishments as well. The imperial treasurer, Alexander's boyhood friend, Harpalus, had been living it up in Babylon with two Greek mistresses in succession— Pythonice and Glycera. The former was an Athenian prostitute, named for a primordial snake; the latter, for something sweet. Harpalus absconded to Athens, where he had reason to hope he would find refuge. He was ultimately assassinated on Crete, perhaps by Alexander's agents. Four of the worst generals were accused of crimes against the state or against private parties—and executed forthwith.

At the coastal town of Hormuz, two hundred miles southwest of Pura, Alexander found Nearchus, who told him his fleet was safe and related fascinating stories about Stone Age natives called Ichthyophagi (the Fish-eaters). Later, historians like Strabo, Pliny, and Diodorus Siculus thought they were Indians who dressed in fish skins and housed themselves in shacks built of whalebones. The very sheep they raised tasted fishy according to the Macedonians, who tried eating them. Nearchus told Alexander about a school of whales that nearly capsized the fleet but dove astern into the sea when he commanded the men to blow their bugles. His recitation was a whale of a tale but Alexander bought it. After delivering this fishy story, Nearchus continued his voyage to Susa as planned. He was off the hook.

Upon entering Persis, Alexander was angry to find that the golden sarcophagus of King Cyrus had been damaged during a tomb robbery. Although the satrap in charge had died, the nobleman Orxines had taken up the governance of the province. Alexander had Orxines executed, and Arrian wrote that he had been guilty of tomb robbing, but Curtius thought that Orxines' error was refusing to enrich one of Alexander's favorites, a eunuch named Bagoas, who had then bribed witnesses against Orxines to accomplish his downfall.[42]

At Susa (February 324 BC) Alexander was reunited with Nearchus. The Indian campaign was over. Those who had distinguished themselves, including Hephaestion, were awarded medals or gold crowns. It was then that Alexander staged an opulent multiple wedding in which scores of his officers married the daughters of Persian noblemen. Alexander set an example by marrying two Persian princesses, Darius's daughter, and the daughter of Artaxerxes Ochus. The ceremony culminated in a five-day celebration and took place in Alexander's tent, one-half mile in circumference and large enough to hold a hundred couches. The tent was supported by thirty-foot columns, studded with precious stones. The oriental carpets and curtains were selected by the best interior decorators. The weddings of Macedonian officers, nearly one hundred of them, with royal or noble Persian women were all arranged by Alexander and were intended to produce a race of elite personnel—"a new ruling class of mixed blood" free of the national allegiance that he found so annoying among his Macedonians.[43] When Alexander died the next year, all but one of these Persian ladies, Apama, married to Seleucus I Nicator, were abandoned by their Macedonian husbands. Some of these ladies were expectant mothers. As usual, when authoritarian social experiments fail, those who pay for them are women and children.

In early summer 324 BC, Alexander went to look at the Persian Gulf and then, sailing up the Tigris, stopped off at Opis, where he announced that infirm veterans would be discharged from service and given a generous bonus of one talent each. The speech provoked rather than pleased the troops, many of whom were not ready to retire and did not want to be replaced by younger, Persian recruits. Their anger led them to mock Alexander and his sonship to Ammon. Alexander ordered thirteen ringleaders rounded up and summarily executed that night, without any trial at all. Angrily he said that they could all go back to Macedonia and tell everybody there that they had abandoned their king to barbarians!

Then followed two days when Alexander, enclosed in his palace, refused to eat or talk to anyone. On the third day, he ordered Persians admitted into once purely Macedonian units and declared that only his "Persian kinsmen" could kiss him. This brought his Macedonian troops to plead for forgiveness and brought Alexander out of his palace, weeping, promising to consider them all his kinsmen and no longer to distinguish between them on the basis of nationality. This scene of reconciliation at Opis is bothersome. Men who weep for the right to kiss their leader, a leader who weeps when he learns that his men really love him—these are not the images we have of soldiers and commanders shaped by John Wayne movies and Ernest Hemingway novels. This kind of male bonding seems abnormal and embarrassing, not right for straights or for gays either. Fraternization of superiors and enlisted men defies our military code. These men weeping for their leader's approval, yearning for his embrace, had not wept for the natives they raped or slaughtered. Yet they told Alexander their feelings were hurt. Their *mentalité* was not sexual, but tribal, atavistic. These Macedonians appear to us now not so much as Alexander's troops and countrymen as they do extensions of his persona, symbiotically dependent, psychologically stunted, cleaving to him as if there was neither life nor meaning without his approval, leadership, love. By every kind of circumstance that can bind people to a leader, Alexander had bound his men to him. He represented for them family, fortune, craft, continuity, cult, culture, and class. In Alexander's entourage men wanted more than leadership from the leader—they wanted love. Total commitment. Fidelity. Unfortunately, they also wanted the freedom to be themselves, to be consulted, to be partners in war and government. Moderns would settle for leadership. Greeks had different expectations.

Historians have treated the melodrama and near mutiny at Opis in terms of Alexander's political ideology and practical necessity. They observe that he wanted harmony in an empire run by cooperative Macedonians and Persians who would forget their own cultural differences in order better to help Alexander rule the rest—Asians. Historians also treat the doings at Opis in terms of ethical or religious values, saying Alexander aimed at creating the brotherhood of man under the Fatherhood of God—the same kinds of ideas the second Isaiah was supposed to have come up with after the Babylonian Exile of the Hebrews, but that (after returning to Jerusalem) the Jews, like everybody else then and since, let lapse. Brotherhood, Fatherhood, unity of man, togetherness. Zeno would restate such notions in Stoical philosophical terms for the next generation after Alexander's.

Alexander was neither a Jew nor a Stoic. If, as J. R. Hamilton doubts, he believed in the uplifting notions of universal brotherhood, he did not take that faith with him to the grave.[44] Macedonian resistance had shown how futile was the notion of amiable cooperation, let alone brotherhood. He started to appoint fewer natives to positions of power. In fact, he seems to have cared very little for most people, and the form of political order and social intercourse he thought proper for them were, like his choices of decor, dress, court ceremony, and battle plans, chosen without reference to anything more ideological or philosophical than his own taste and convenience. He was inclined to do as he pleased, and when thwarted was dangerous to himself and others, especially others. That he could be charming and considerate, polite and straightforward, loyal and generous, liberal and loving, even enlightened about policy, ought not to blind us to those less rare qualities he shared with other despots, qualities that made his government abusive of the humanity about which, apart from its usefulness to him, he seems neither to have valued nor identified with.

Naturally, he overreacted to the death of Hephaestion with whom alone he identified. Achilles and Patroclus. Two against the world. At the time of his death, Hephaestion was considered the number two man in the empire, for Alexander had named him *chiliarch,* or vizier. He died at Ecbatana during an orgiastic festival of Dionysus, his drunkenness followed by a high, slow fever. Alexander sent to inquire of Zeus-Ammon at the Oasis of Siwah how his friend should be mourned—as god or hero?

The priests of Ammon said as hero, not god. Alexander compromised. He had Hephaestion's mausoleum constructed of heroic proportions but god-awful taste at Babylon.

He filled the void Hephaestion's death created by pursuing his next project: the conquest of Arabia. His motive, he said, was that the Arabs had not recognized his great achievements, had failed to send a congratulatory embassy to him. The penalty of conquest was so unreasonable for what was at most a diplomatic oversight and at worst a snub, that even Alexander felt it politic to say that the real purpose of the new fleet being prepared at Babylon was scientific exploration of the Arabian coast and offshore islands and, oh yes, establishing a trade route from Babylon to Alexandria, Egypt. W. W. Tarn and Ulrich Wilcken thought these were really his reasons, but the ancient historian Arrian probably came closer to the truth when he wrote that Alexander was not motivated by anything but his desire to control as much territory as possible. Arrian would have called him a megalomaniac except the word did not as yet exist. The ancients had to make do with simpler, pre-psychiatric terms like greed and desire. This was a terrible handicap for politicians because greed and desire were words everybody understood. No one needed to search out underlying causes of this kind of mental instability. They took greed for granted.

Alexander's death (June 10, 323 BC) was so similar to Hephaestion's—it followed a prolonged high fever—that Peter Green thinks both men might have been poisoned and notes that a recent biographer (R. D. Milns) has suggested strychnine as the poison most likely used, placed as Aristotle's friend Theophrastus suggested, in "unmixed wine," to kill the bitter taste of strychnine.[45] Some Greek wines, no doubt, tasted just as bitter without the strychnine, because anciently, resin was used as a wine preservative, as is still the case today with the Greek wine called *retsina*. If he were poisoned, Green feels it quite possible that Antipater, the regent of Macedonia whom Alexander had recently fired and replaced with his friend, Craterus, was a likely suspect. Antipater, summoned to his court in Babylon and fearful over the outcome of a conference between him and his king, had both his sons present at Alexander's court. Were all three involved in this plot? Even Aristotle, irate over the death of his nephew, Callisthenes, might possibly have been implicated. An ancient legend has him concocting the death potion. Undoubtedly there have been more than a few teachers who have thought of murdering their pupils, and the reverse is also true.[46] If, however, Alexander's last illness was not the result of strychnine, which the ancients even before Aristotle had been extracting quite cheaply from several members of the deadly nightshade plant, then he probably died of pleurisy or malaria that took hold following a bout of heavy drinking at a banquet for admiral Nearchus, on the eve of his departure for the Persian Gulf.

Alexander's last twelve days were spent in dicing and in sacrificing. On the one hand he was still eager to gamble; on the other, he tried to propitiate the gods so that he wouldn't have to. In between he slept in the bathhouse (where it was cooler), conferred with Nearchus and others, and then, his illness more intense, lay in delirium, awaiting the end. He took leave of his men silently, since speech finally failed him, after they forced their way through the wall of his room. Just before that, when he was asked to whom the empire should be handed over, he managed to say "to the strongest." He could not have said "to my son," because Roxane was only recently pregnant for the first time. He could not have said "to the wisest" since the wise men in his retinue were botanists and philosophers, specialists in the state of nature, not the nature of the state. The empire he had won by force could only be governed by it. He left no final instructions regarding the brotherhood of man under the fatherhood of God, or, as W. W. Tarn put it, "of a world in which all men should be members one of another," or of "citizens of one State without distinction of race or institutions," "united only . . . by Love."[47] Alexander, unlike Tarn, was a realist.

8

Hellenistic Civilization

Cultural Background

THE HELLENISTIC ERA, IN OTHER WORDS, WHEN Alexander's Greek-speaking generals and their descendants ruled for three hundred years before Christ, is sandwiched between Greek classicism and the Roman Republic. When the latter finally absorbed these Greek-speaking regions of western Asia and North Africa, republican Rome was well on her way toward becoming the empire she would only much later admit to being. Hellenistic civilization was always easy to locate, but hard to place. It was Greek-like (Hellenistic) without being wholly Greek (Hellenic), a hybrid of Greek forms and formulae imposed on Egyptian, Syrian, Persian, and Mesopotamian ones. The mixture was scarcely a real blend, and in the countrysides less apparent. But in cities like Susa and Sardis, Alexandria and Antioch, art, architecture, and religion grew more sensual, personal, passionate, and free than in classical Greece. There were more cultural choices available in everything but government, where there were no choices at all, except conforming to the monarchies, indistinguishable, but for the language of their courts, from the oriental despotisms that the generals displaced.

Hellenistic monarchs meant business—they were in fact businessmen, as well as rulers. They conquered land because they needed markets, and they plowed their profits into infrastructure, like roads and port facilities, urban development, culture, and science. There was more scientific research in Alexandria than there ever had been in classical Athens, and Hellenistic scientists did not need to double as philosophers like Pythagoras and Aristotle had in the past. As for philosophers, they were as evident, if not as prominent, in Hellenistic capitals as in fifth- and fourth-century BC Athens. There were among them Skeptics and Cynics, Stoics and Epicureans, all materialists who concentrated on the physicality of the universe and of society, rather than on its spirituality. For that reason they never got the respect that idealists like Plato achieved. Some paradox was at work, because people devoted to getting and spending should have gravitated toward materialistic philosophies. But idealism was more popular with businessmen and the better sort of urban dwellers, whose crowded schedules left no time to think. They were very grateful to the philosophical idealists,

174

Platonists and Neoplatonists, whose insistence on the invisible and elusive ideal as the most real, spared these people the great inconvenience of having to prove anything.

The lower classes were left to indulge in the mystery and fertility cults that had long captured their imagination. Mysteries were as incapable of proof as idealism, but fertility was readily grasped. Seasonal rhythms held the key. Planting and harvesting was the thing. Sexual intercourse was the thing. The ignorant poor took comfort in worship services intensified by drinking the blood of the gods, especially wine. They made a fetish of fertility. Philosophers said the natives had natural rhythm. If the devotees of fertility cults had any questions, which they did not, they were methodically referred to the cycle of the seasons and the impulses of nature. This was the first rhythm method.

Governments in Hellenistic kingdoms were neither freer nor more personal. Oriental-style bureaucracies replaced the old Greek custom of having nonprofessional citizens administer the laws. That made the new despotisms indistinguishable from the old, only now they were administered by Greek-speaking professionals. These new bureaucrats applied to Greek-speaking minorities as well as to native majorities the benefits of autocracy, such as they were. Greek kings had, like Alexander before them, only to assert their divinity to help paper over any cracks where skepticism (on the part of Greeks) or native resentment (on the part of the conquered) might otherwise have bled through.

Grecophils in every age find Hellenistic culture too emotional and decadent, neither classical enough nor rational enough to satisfy. Alexandria lacked "classical restraint" in art and architecture. Though Greeks in the Golden Age restrained artists and dramatists, they too lacked restraint in war, politics, foreign affairs, and sexual relationships. Fifth-century BC theater was arguably more restrained than Hellenistic theater because everyone was murdered or raped or sacrificed offstage in Athens. Philhellenists[1] admire the restraint of Spartan discipline, forerunner of stick-to-itiveness—or narrow-mindedness. They dote on Platonic idealism, overlooking Plato's ominous tendency to locate everything ideal somewhere other than Greece. Greek xenophobia, which defined all Greeks not of one's own city-state as foreigners, is now politically incorrect. Aristotelian logic is prized by all secular humanists, but his irrational preoccupation with city-states after fourth-century Greeks failed to make them work was neither logical nor restrained, and his insistence that women were men flawed in the uterus was unrestrained emotionalism.

Romanophils, like Grecophils, disdain Hellenistic cultural forms. They proudly point to the ideal of Republicanism, the state as a public thing (Lat., *res publica*). In fact, the Roman Republic never approached the ideal, belonging to no more than three dozen elite families who ran its Senate and everything else worth running. Roman discipline, like Spartan discipline, was re-created by the Brits when they installed cold showers in "public" schools no more public than the Roman "Republic" and encouraged the bullying of underclassmen by upperclassmen and poor boys by rich ones, re-creating in what Americans call private schools the struggle of the Roman social orders, patricians vs. plebians. The same system was installed at West Point, in order to teach future officers how to be beastly to enlisted men. *Pax Brittanica* was a retake of *Pax Romana*. A pox on all your paxes when imposed by conquest!

The Romans brought political stability to western Asia and North Africa, but not emotional stability. The irrational appealed as much to Rome as to Plato, the Hebrews, Babylonians, and Egyptians, many of whose enthusiasms Rome absorbed before she got too absorbed by mere survival. After which she got absorbed by Germans. Roman civil law? Genteel but not gentle. Roman natural law? Purloined from the Stoics and resembling nothing in nature unless it was the Roman Senator Cicero's high-minded but perfervid imagination.[2] Imperial Roman citizenship? It protected one from crucifixion, reserving that punishment for those whose citizenship applications were denied. Rome prided itself on its ability to supply abundant drinking water. Good sanitation. Drains, not brains.

Until two decades ago, Hellenistic civilization, which never brought much reason, restraint, or justice to the ruled, struggled to defend itself from being labeled second-rate. Peter Green, before publishing a history of the era, edited conversations on Hellenistic topics from a symposium of the late 1980s.[3] In his introduction, he notes the reasons for the historiographical recovery of the period since World War II.[4] These include criticism of elitist social planning such as Plato's *Republic;* a multiculturalism that has displaced the Greco-Roman tradition; a modern, popular identification with the erotic and passionate elements in Hellenistic art; the challenge to canons of "good taste" or antielitism in matters of art; and the demise of colonialism and its justification—something that is now affecting even Alexander scholarship.[5]

The Hellenistic age began when Alexander of Macedon tossed his spear into Asia and ended with the battle of Actium in 31 BC. That was the date when Octavian, Julius Caesar's grandnephew, later the Emperor Augustus, defeated Antony and Cleopatra, thus winning control of Egypt. After Actium, Rome controlled the Hellenistic world.

Hellenistic civilization was a mixture of Hellenic with exotic forms— something like a colloidal suspension, an eclectic combination of fact, fiction, and philosophy that presented lumpy solutions to two basic problems all societies must solve: 1) how to distribute scarce goods among populations limited only by their fertility and their fertile invention, and 2) how to make them believe that the gods approve of that distribution scheme.

HELLENISTIC MONARCHIES

When evaluating lifestyles, art, and politics, editing is everything. Scholars are now rethinking what it was that made some cultural artifacts canonical and swept others under the rug, the same process whereby Jewish and Greek theologians in Hellenistic Alexandria sought to determine which sacred writings were canonical and which were just morally unexceptional. The classicists' renewed interest in Hellenistic culture is akin to a newborn's relatives' who, looking for the first time at the blob of unfamiliar protoplasm that is baby's face, suddenly spy a feature—chin, nose, or ears—that suddenly appears like great-grandfather's or Aunt Agatha's. As with babies, so with Hellenistic culture. That which appears at first quite unlike what is more familiar and developed turns out on closer inspection to be a theme one cannot take for granted or ignore. So it was with Hellenistic monarchies. All the monarchs resembled Alexander in one way—their determination to wrest admiration and even reverence from their subjects—but they did not replicate Alexander's desire to rule over immense areas where subordinate native monarchs would reinforce the divine leader's inscrutable purpose. Hellenistic rulers lacked Alexander's grandiosity, preferring to exercise their authority directly without crowned intermediaries beneath them. Alexander's "offspring," originally his leading generals, were more alike in their techniques of governance than they were to their "father" Alexander.

For twenty years after Alexander's death (323 BC), there were four large kingdoms: Persia, Mesopotamia, and Syria formed one under Seleucus; Asia Minor and Thrace made up the second under Lysimachus; Macedonia and Greece a third under Cassander; and the fourth, Egypt, grew to include Phoenicia and Palestine, all united under Ptolemy. Twenty years later, the four kingdoms became three when Seleucus killed Lysimachus in battle and annexed Asia Minor. The Greek cities eventually threw off their Macedonian ruler, forming defensive leagues in a federalist structure preserved until Rome took over in 146 BC.

EGYPT'S PTOLEMIES

Not so long ago Ptolemaic Egypt was judged a highly centralized, efficient bureaucracy,[6] rationally organized and geared for productivity under governmental oversight, a word that, ironically, used to mean neglect but now suggests control. This society is now reemerging as something quite opposite: one whose bureaucratic complexity was fortuitous, the result of inherent ineffectualness which made it susceptible to endless tinkering, an already overburdened system growing ever more dysfunctional and corrupt under Greco-Macedonian management.

The Revenue Laws Papyrus of 259 BC, documents showing corrected royal agricultural regulations and tax laws, formed the basis on which historians judged the Ptolemies to be masters of economic control and bureaucratic centralization. Michael Rostovtzeff helped establish this older view in which Hellenistic kings were seen as rational state planners devoted to the un-Greek notion of the state as private property developed for profit.[7] Currently, these Laws are being studied for evidence of the lack of royal control that usually prevailed.[8] The uncorrected orders may have reflected royal wishful thinking, and the corrected versions concessions made by higher officials appealed to by lower-level bureaucrats doing actual tax collection.[9] In other words, the "order" in Ptolemaic Egypt's system of production and taxation, a supposed discontinuity from a disordered past, may in fact have been ad hoc and disorganized, too. Snafu. Situation normal. All fouled up.

W. W. Tarn thought the Ptolemies less ethical than the Antigonids who ruled Hellenistic Macedonia, or the Seleucids who ruled Syria and Mesopotamia, both dynasties that he felt put the welfare of their subjects at a higher premium than the Ptolemies, whom Tarn wrote were principally interested in their own.[10] Yet both the Ptolemies and the Seleucids ran their empires in selfish fashion. The difference between them was not one of principle, and still less of intent. Both dynasties made the best of the circumstances at hand. The difference was that circumstances enabled the Ptolemies to enjoy more control over their smaller, less populous, and historically more homogeneous territory than the Seleucids could from theirs.

Although the Egyptian bureaucracy was not always fouled, it was often foiled by the circumstances attending a conquest, namely, having to make operative unfamiliar structures until recently administered by natives who neither spoke Greek nor shared the Hellenic lifestyle. The Ptolemies produced intricate governmental structures, bureaucratic overkill. They had neither the time nor the talent to create simpler structures, which take longer to devise but are more efficient in the long haul. Rostovtzeff thought the Ptolemies created a progressive society whose foundation was state protection of private property, an entrepreneurial paradise. Such a country appealed to him all the more for having lived in Russia through the Bolshevik Revolution until 1918, after which he fled to the United States, a land of capitalistic opportunity that allowed him to do his research unmolested.[11]

Although many historians followed his conclusions, some reject Rostovtzeff's view of Egypt as a progressive state, seeing its ultimate objective was war and expansion, which is not progressive, but retrograde. The trade in which the Ptolemies engaged was needed for specie. Egypt was running out of gold. Egypt's grain trade earned the means to make war in southern Syria, Cyprus, and along Aegean shores, where she reminded others that Egypt was now a Greco-Macedonian enterprise. Polybius thought these interests all defensive, aimed against interference from Syria and Macedonia, whose influence in Greece threatened the Ptolemies' own.[12] It is hard to distinguish between defensive and offensive when one's most important priorities are military glory and greed.

Occasionally, the Ptolemies intermarried with the Seleucids, hoping to reduce rivalry around the Mediterranean and in the Aegean by mingling their blood lines in a cozier way than on battlefields. In 252 BC Ptolemy II Philadelphus (285–246 BC) gave his daughter Berenice to Antiochus II Theos, who divorced his wife Laodice and promised to give up all claims to Phoenicia in return for a whopping dowry from his new Egyptian bride. She bore him a son soon afterward. Meanwhile Laodice and her son Seleucus (later, Seleucus II) were not content to play second string to the new Egyptian queen at Antioch. After Antiochus II died in 247 BC, the Seleucid territory divided its loyalties between the old and new queens and their respective sons. The palace guard at Antioch murdered Berenice and her boy but kept the deed hushed up. Ptolemy II died, but his son, Ptolemy III, Berenice's brother, alerted to the murder of his sister and young nephew, went first to Antioch and next to the eastern Seleucid capital, Seleucia on the Tigris, receiving the loyalties of the eastern satraps. He never mentioned that his relatives had been killed. He left Egyptian garrisons behind him to keep order before returning to Egypt. F. E. Peters says that Ptolemy could hardly have thought this "incredible performance" would "hold up" and it did not. But he was not the first monarch to attempt a cover-up that failed. Seleucus II regained control of northern Syria. But he did not regain the satrapies beyond Babylon, nor Phoenicia. And Ptolemy III reestablished sway over the Aegean and eastern Mediterranean. He decided in the future he would wed his dynasty to the sea rather than to a Seleucid. His decision was lucid.

Egypt enjoyed prosperity and security for twenty years while Seleucus II had to cede Anatolia (to a younger brother) in order to fight Ptolemy. Eventually, the fierce Galatian tribes in those parts fell before the rulers of Pergamum, the Attalids, who established their independence from Seleucid rule. Attalus I took the cult name Soter (Savior) for having saved the neighbors from Galatian gang warfare.[13] Each of the Hellenistic dynasts, whether Attalids, Ptolemies, Seleucids, or Antigonids (the dynasty that eventually got control of Macedonia), served as part of a neighborhood crime watch. They watched each other commit crimes or be victimized by criminals in the nearby neighborhoods of the Aegean, Asia Minor, and western Asia. Sometimes they offered help to the victim kings, but only when it was in their own interest. At best, they were volunteer firemen helping a potential neighbor when he was threatened with a roasting at the hands of some rebel leader, client state, or satrap. At worst, they were themselves pyromaniacs, setting some fires on their neighbors' borders or at their court, then turning a blind eye to the spreading conflagration, while the neighbor's house went up in smoke.

Apart from war, the Ptolemies were conservators of the splendid museum that was Egypt. The natives saw their conquest by the Ptolemies as both corollary and cause of their humiliation prepared for by the pharaohs' visible accumulation of art treasures. Of course their new masters, like Hellenistic kings elsewhere, reminded them of their worthlessness. They used their Greek customs and language aggressively, making natives feel that they were the aliens. The natives responded by feeling alienated. They would have liked to feel at home because, after all, they were.

The Ptolemies instituted cults for their own worship, taking cult names or titles suggesting divinity. Ptolemy I (323–283 BC) took the name of Soter (Savior), as Attalus I had. His capture of thousands of Jews from four campaigns in Palestine saved rich Macedonian and Egyptian householders from having to do their own housework. Ptolemy was no savior to Jews, who continued to wait for the Messiah to save them. Ptolemy II married his sister Arsinoë, and before 271 BC had them both canonized as divine. Ptolemy III (246–222 BC) Euergetes [Greek, Benefactor] and his wife, Berenice II, were called Theoi Euergetai, Benefactor Gods. Other Ptolemaic queens were distinguished by the name Thea [Goddess], including the most famous of them all, Cleopatra, last of the Ptolemies, whose proper title was Cleopatra VII, Thea Philopator, (Greek, father-loving goddess). The Ptolemies accepted the perquisites of godhead, inspirational cult names, canonization, and sister marriage because, though lords of the land, they were slaves to etiquette. Unlike the classical gods in Greece, many of whom could not keep their hands off attractive mortals, the Ptolemies kept their distance from the natives. Every hair on their heads was considered sacred or out of this world. The poet Callimachus immortalized a lock of Berenice's hair by referring to it as a constellation. Her husband was generous to the Egyptian temples, maintained peace by his strong defense system and good government, and provided free grain to his subjects during a famine.[14] Berenice was a great horsewoman and raced her chariot to victory at the Nemean games, a kind of Little League Olympics. It is hard to determine how, other than by her title alone, she benefited Egypt, but embedded court reporters, like chariot racers, went along for the ride.

In 200 BC, Ptolemy V Epiphanes [Greek, God made manifest] lost the battle of Panion to Antiochus III and with it, southern Syria (Coele-Syria). He put the best appearance on his loss by obtaining a marriage alliance with his enemy's daughter, Cleopatra I. Antiochus III (the Great) reannexed Coele-Syria, including Palestine, a fact that the Romans regarded with suspicion. Rome was already aware of weakening Ptolemaic governance and beginning to regard Egypt with preproprietary interest.

Early in their rule the Ptolemies made the most of their Hellenic heritage, establishing what amounted to a Greek research university, the Museum, and a library with seven hundred thousand scrolls at Alexandria, from which non-Hellenized natives were excluded. Gradually, Hellenization (the ability of natives to assimilate to Greek culture) opened a few doors to a native elite. But without the importation of Greek merchants and Macedonian troops, Greek culture would not have flourished. It was dependent upon the strength of arms that made empire possible, and it was empire that made trade profitable and trade that sustained the arts. Ultimately brute force enabled Ptolemaic Egypt to indulge in the refinements of art, science, and literature. In this way the relatively high culture of the few was subsidized by the relatively high misery of the many.

Egyptians were at first resigned to their conquest and inferior status. As honey attracted locusts, so their unique treasures attracted the unwanted attentions of yet another invader, whose divinity made itself manifest not by epiphanies, but taxation. This Macedonian god-king remained even more remote from Egyptians than their other gods had. Not Ma'at [Egyptian, justice] but fate [Greek, Tyche] had arranged for the transfer of power from Egyptians to Macedonians. The Egyptians were expected to play a purely supportive role during the Ptolemaic era, and at first, they did. But as the successes of the Ptolemaic economy began to recede in the later third century BC, the natives grew restless. Since there were more of them and ever fewer Greeks and Macedonians, they became a more significant factor in Ptolemaic rule. There were over two hundred different taxes in Egypt. Burdensome monetary policies kept credit dear and coined money in short supply. The Ptolemies did not systematically inculcate racist policies. They did not have to. Royal tax and land distribution methods were themselves racist. In Alexandria the degree of imperial racism was very high throughout the fourth and third centuries BC. Not until the last Ptolemy, Cleopatra VII, had any member of the dynasty bothered to learn the Egyptian tongue.[15]

Galloping inflation and declining trade to the western Mediterranean increased the social tension that not even Ptolemaic paternalism—which always stopped short of encouraging social equality or equity—could repair. After one hundred years of Greek rule, Ptolemy IV Philopator (221–205) tried to compensate the common man for his suffering by giving native troops the chance to bear arms. With their help he defeated Syria, winning a great military victory over Antiochus III at Raphia in 217 BC. However, in defeating the Seleucids, Ptolemy encouraged an Egyptian nationalism that his successors could not deter. Ultimately, Raphia was as much a dynastic failure as it was a transitory success. Civil war and the rise to power of an independent line of Nubian pharaohs in Upper Egypt followed. In Lower Egypt, governmental weakness accelerated nationalist sentiments.

Suddenly the Ptolemies were presented with a bill of payment due for past discriminations and social inequity. Unable to replenish their ranks with immigration from Greece and Macedonia, the kings instituted a desperate policy of affirmative action, not just in the military, as at Raphia, but in the federal bureaucracy, too. They rewarded Greek-speaking natives with benefits—plots of land for military service and government jobs formerly reserved for Greeks and Macedonians. The concessions made to the natives were costly, reducing the government's future revenues and thus weakening it further—"a vicious circle."[16] But was the cause of Egyptian decline the concessions made to resentful natives or the discrimination against a subject people? Circles aside, what was really more vicious?

To argue that the concessions were the cause of weakness in late Ptolemaic Egypt seems wrongheaded. If the Ptolemies had welcomed and rewarded native participation from the beginning, they might not have had to make such risky concessions at the end of their rule. They might have escaped the "vicious circle" of their own making.

The Ptolemies lost Coele-Syria (200 BC) at the battle of Panion to Antiochus III. Imperial decline set in, for Egypt soon lost her possessions on the southern Anatolian coast, too. Only Cyprus and the dependency of Cyrenaica remained. Egypt's empire was almost history. Indeed, for a while it seemed that Egypt herself was almost history, for in 169 BC Antiochus IV (Epiphanes) made an unwelcome appearance in Memphis, imprisoned Ptolemy VI and proclaimed himself pharaoh.

The Alexandrians proclaimed Ptolemy VI's brother, Euergetes II, as the new Ptolemy VIII, Ptolemy VII (son of Ptolemy Philopator) having reigned briefly in between. Antiochus was obliged to vacate Egypt in order to protect other interests, and that left two brothers to share power simultaneously, side by side. They ruled out fratricide. It was a first.[17] But it was a dual monarchy that might have led to dueling had not the Roman Senate intervened between the royal pair, determining that Ptolemy VI Philometer would rule in Egypt and Cyprus (168–145 BC), and Ptolemy VIII, henceforth known as Euergetes II, the younger brother, over Cyrenaica.[18]

When Ptolemy VI was killed in an attempt to regain Syria, Euergetes II (145 BC) promptly married his widow, their mutual sister, Cleopatra II. He also insisted on making his niece, Cleopatra Jr., daughter of his wife and brother, associate queen, with something less than the power of associate dean. Her title was Cleopatra III. Euergetes detested Cleopatra II, whom he regarded as a stubborn donkey. Sibling rivalry. Cleopatra II could not stand her brother-husband either, and as for her daughter, don't ask. The Alexandrians preferred Cleopatra II to her former brother-in-law, brother, and now husband. They made Euergetes II cool his heels in Cyrenaica for five years before letting him enter Alexandria, his capital. And although Cleopatra II fled to Syria at his return, he had to take her back in 124 BC because he could not rule at Alexandria without her. Alexandria, he sighed, was well worth an ass.[19] This trio of alienated family members went on ruling Egypt for eight more years. They were apparently too much for the Roman Senate. Respect for the family, a Roman cultural value, would not have resigned them to this family had it not, like many other supposedly dysfunctional ones, continued to function.

The Romans liked a good performance, and Euergetes II performed very well indeed. He used the Egyptian priesthood to curb the arrogance of Greek bureaucrats, granting to the temples powers that could protect the natives from his own government, an attitude very few government leaders shared. Euergetes softened the ethnic thrust of Hellenism because there had been a considerable mingling of the two cultures by this time. His policy of bringing Egyptians into the government was reminiscent of Alexander's frustrated hopes for his rule in Persia. The Roman Empire in its fears of decline attempted something similar when it employed Germanic barbarians as legionnaires. And even though the Greeks and Macedonians at Alexandria resented Euergetes' policies, as they once resented Alexander's, and applied to Rome for redress, the Romans let their Egyptian client govern as he saw fit. For a Ptolemy, he was quite ptolerable.

In the future, however, Rome would decide the fate of the eastern Mediterranean until Augustus put an end to the Ptolemies once and for all. Even before Rome freed herself from Carthaginian domination in the western Mediterranean (146 BC), she had begun to interest herself in the affairs of its eastern shores, discouraging the Seleucids from expanding into Egypt, for Egypt was a major source of Rome's grain supply. Egypt's peasants thus kept the Roman Republic in power as much as they did the Ptolemies. Theirs was a real vaudeville act. On their shoulders rested not one, but two civilizations, Roman as well as Ptolemaic. In the late second century, Egyptian natives defended their own interests. The priests grew richer with governmental largesse designed to keep them and their followers happy; the natives grew numerous with the usual activities designed to perpetuate the human race.

The magnificent Hellenistic culture continued to absorb Egyptian culture much faster than the Egyptians absorbed Greek customs. Especially with regard to religious attitudes and practices Egypt insinuated itself into the sophisticated and skeptical Greek conscience. They made many Greeks and Macedonians who once prided themselves on rationality believing mystics, devoted to the oracle of Serapis, a combination of Osiris and Apis (the bull) fitted out with a classic Greek male body. This Greco-Egyptian deity, loaded with testosterone and sex appeal, had his own temple or Serapeum at Alexandria where he was portrayed as the god of the underworld (Hades) wearing a basket of grain on his head, sign of fertility. The mania of Serapis worship spread throughout the Hellenistic world from Rome to Mesopotamia and was the ultimate revenge of a superstitious and vanquished Egypt upon her Hellenistic masters, planting in minds that had once opened to philosophical reason a veritable thicket of spiritual rapture. Rapture—unspeakable and irrational—was the price paid by Greeks and Macedonians for the territorial rape of Egypt and western Asia. For them, rapture was rupture.

THE SELEUCID EMPIRE

The Seleucid Empire began when Seleucus I Nicator [Greek, Victor], another of Alexander's generals, captured Babylon in 321 BC. This empire was as undemocratic as Ptolemy's, but less supportive of the arts and sciences. War and trade were its chief concerns, and since war destroyed what trade created, the Seleucids felt they had balanced the economy. Those unfit for the business world or fighting—poets, philosophers, artists, scientists—left Greece, Asia Minor, and the Aegean islands and sailed for Alexandria in Egypt. There they found research facilities and grant money not available at home. In the Hellenistic world there were already drinkers at the public trough.

Seleucus I ceded India (303 BC) to a local ruler named Chandragupta in return for an alliance and Indian elephants, the tank of ancient land warfare. His successor, Antiochus I (280–261 BC), ruled most of Syria, Mesopotamia, and Asia Minor. In the mid third century Bactria and Parthia parted from the Selucid empire. They overran Iran perhaps because, as Professor Walbank remarked, the Seleucids "showed a profound indifference to the Iranians."[20] The Iranians were partial to Parthians because they spoke a related language, a dialect called Pahlavi. Soon the Parthians adopted the Iranian religion, Mazdaism. Their first leader, Arsaces I, established (c. 247 BC) a vast empire southeast of the Caspian Sea reaching to Arabian shores, the only Hellenistic territory to avoid Roman conquest. Although Antiochus the Great won back much of Media, Persis, Susiana, and Babylon in the last decade of the third century, Antiochus VII died fighting the Parthians (129 BC) who controlled everything east of Syria by the end of the second century.

Pergamum's independence began in 283 BC when a eunuch named Philetaerus, guardian of Persian treasure that Lysimachus, another of Alexander's generals, deposited there, changed his political allegiance. After a strange progression of alliances, Philetaerus proclaimed his independence from any overlord whatsoever, in what Peter Green calls "a crabwise" movement, but what we might also term indirection, the essence of deceit. Feigning loyalty to superior powers with whom he courted favor, Philetaerus laid the foundation for his own dynasty. This eunuch proved that one need not have testes to be testy or pass the test of manliness, and that emasculation does not always make for impotence. As the poet Robert

Burns once wrote (of someone else) "he was a man for a' that." His descendents were called Attalids after Attalus I (269–197 BC), the first of Philetaerus's house to claim a crown.[21] Allied with Rome, the Attalids displaced the Seleucids in most of Asia Minor, much of which was lost in 188 BC under Antiochus III (223–187 BC).

Nevertheless, Antiochus III is known to history as "The Great." When he came to the throne (223 BC) the Seleucid Empire was on the point of dissolution. He was not into downsizing and resolved to re-create the empire of Seleucus I Nicator, founder of his dynasty. He played host at Ephesus to Hannibal, the Carthaginian famed for losing most of his elephants (to pneumonia) in one or another of the Alpine passes during the Second Punic War (218–201 BC) with Rome. A refugee from Carthage, Hannibal remained at Antiochus's court seven years. He used Antiochus's financial resources hoping to revenge himself for his own defeat by the Roman general Scipio at Zama in North Africa (202 BC). Hannibal's visit began several years after Antiochus defeated Egypt at Panion (200–199 BC), a victory that gave him Tyre and Palestine, including Judea. Antiochus was glad to host a man whose military abilities were well known. Tradition (traceable to Livy) has it that Hannibal advised Antiochus to invade Italy. Instead, Antiochus III crossed the Hellespont to conquer Thrace. When the Aetolian Greeks appealed to Antiochus for relief from Roman interference, he accepted, posing as liberator of Greeks. It was a pose that Philip II and his son Alexander had frequently assumed in Asia Minor and Greece. But, though the pose was familiar, the job was no snap. Rome allied with Aetolia's Greek enemies against the Seleucids. Antiochus gave westward expansion his best shot, but neither he nor the Aetolians could stand up to the allied forces of Sparta, the Achaean League and Rome, aided by Pergamum and Rhodes. Antiochus lost badly, first at Thermopylae in 191 BC and then at Magnesia-by-Sipylos, in 190 or 189 BC. He had to pay Rome and the allies an enormous fine of fifteen thousand talents, not to mention the talents lost on the battlefield. The treaty with Rome forced Antiochus to keep out of western Asia Minor and Greece, and much of what he lost, more than half his kingdom, was given to Eumenes II Soter of Pergamum who had sided with Rome against him. Antiochus submitted with a jest, saying that he was grateful to the Romans for saving him the trouble of governing too large an empire.[22]

Antiochus was a smooth politician, who patronized the arts and encouraged merit. In Judaea, which he acquired after Panion, he continued the old Persian habit of subsidizing the Jewish Temple, like Cyrus the Great in the sixth century BC. He provided generously for the maintenance of the Temple's sacrificial animals, oil, wine, wheat, flour, salt, and incense.[23] He also decreed that the Jews were to live under Mosaic Law and gave them autonomy within their own land, even enacting legislation to help Jews keep kosher by forbidding the import of "unclean" animals. A gentile, Antiochus knew that the Jews were different, but he valued them for that difference, which was in itself, very different.

Before his showdown with Rome at Magnesia, Antiochus led an expedition as far east as India (212–205 BC) in an effort to recreate Alexander's glory. It was then he decided he should be called Great, an attributive A. E. Household thinks he did not deserve.[24] Peter Green tells us that the result of his efforts in the East was "insubstantial," winning him friends among the eastern satraps, but not "vassals."[25] The point is well taken. What is the point, after all, of being a major power if you cannot make vassals of your friends? Friends have a tendency to pursue their own policies, and to criticize when what you need is flattery. In international relations, major powers need vassals, not friends. Antiochus learned the difference when he earned the admiration of Bactrians and Parthians but not their loyalty. No one wanted to commit themselves. Commitment was expensive. Friendship, merely expansive.

Was Antiochus great? Apparently not, but he had greatness in him.[26] He lost Asia Minor and much of Syria, too, before he recouped his loss at Panion. He did not accomplish what contemporaries or historians thought he should have, though he hung on to reduced power. If he was not great, was he average? Or just mediocre? The fashion currently is to call those who hang in there "survivors," a word that the ancients would never have considered complimentary, since those who merely survived were considered pathetic and without real honor. What had Antiochus III won by surviving? Where was his glory? They must have asked, not of him, but of each other. Antiochus's empire dissolved under him. He hazarded everything to recreate what his ancestors enjoyed, even if they only enjoyed it because they had served Alexander! Antiochus had no Alexander to serve. Yet, he was energetic, courageous, and longed (like Presidents Johnson, Nixon, and Clinton) for a prime place in history. He had a sense of humor apparently, but great humorists hardly rank with the great imperialists, though they make everybody feel better. Antiochus had a sense of honor, too. He wanted to be able to pay his debts—to Rome, not to society. But Eumenes of Pergamum wound up in control of his silver mines in Asia Minor. His credit was maxed out. He decided to steal from the gods.

Although he failed to liberate Greece, he liberated the treasury of an Elamite temple, hoping to pay down the debt with plunder. It was his technique for redistributing wealth while lowering taxes. Unfortunately, the parishioners of the temple of Belus at Susiana accused him of robbing their surplus and murdered him at Elam on the third or fourth of July 187 BC. The followers of Baal had avenged their god by killing their king. Did they put all the treasure back afterwards?

Although Antiochus III may not have been truly great he had great potential. But Antiochus never lived up to it, which is sadder than not having any to begin with. Although he died stealing from a lesser god, he had the tact to support the Mosaic God. He was the failed Robin Hood of antiquity, hoping to give to one God what he stole from another, which is a more serious charge than robbing Peter to pay Paul. Saints are quite often noted for their patience, but gods are notoriously impatient. His son, Antiochus IV, who took the name Epiphany [Greek, Appearance], attempted to eradicate Judaism, a policy that contrasted sharply with his father's desire to placate Jews. The victory (165 BC) of Judas Maccabee (Maccabeus) over Antiochus IV is remembered by the festival of lights, Chanukah. The Seleucid Empire could not hold a candle to the faith of the Jews in their Hasmonean leaders and in the leadership of God.[27] Against such odds, Antiochus IV went down to defeat.

The adjective "Seleucid" is a perfect rhyme for the adjective "pelucid," but the former were not nearly so bright. Sound-wise, "Seleucid" contains words more familiar to us: sell, loose, lucid. The first sound "sel," as in sell people a bill of goods or just sell goods, reminds us that Seleucid kings sold everything they got their hands on and didn't want to keep. This stuff included booty and slaves taken in wars of conquest as well as products bought and traded on the international market. They were not so much venture as vulture capitalists, investing heavily in commodities—those they paid for, and those they stole. Antioch in Syria and Seleucis on the Tigris were major centers for exchange. "Every Seleucid king was a tycoon on an enormous scale," according to Michael Grant.[28] Their government was a conglomerate and they were its CEOs. Naturally, they rewarded themselves handsomely for their business sense. The Seleucids ran a for-profit corporation. Because they were also heads of state, they could really control their "territory," that is, defend their markets and expand them in ways private traders or weaker states could not; for example, commissioning explorers to scout out new caravan routes for Oriental trade.[29] Because the state traded in its own interest, they avoided the expense of middlemen and lobbyists. Model consumers, they spent all the money they saved. Residual overhead was assumed by taxpayers, for the Hellenistic monarchies could not have paid their own way, lacking an industrial base, except by looting subject peoples.[30] All their subjects were subject peoples. In this way, they complimented earlier imperialists, because imitation is the highest form of praise.

A second sound in "Seleucid" is "loos," as in lucid, bright, clear, easily discernible. Their economic goals were easily discernible because they supplemented profits from plunder and trade with taxation, something everybody grasps at once, but the tax collector grasps last. The "loos" sound in "Seleucid" reminds us that politically, the Seleucid Empire was loosely organized. Loose patterns of control over the different satrapies, tribes, dynasts, and military colonies that comprised the empire were patterned after the loose control exercised by Persian mentors who were in charge before Alexander the Great.[31] If the Seleucids kept the reigns loose, they kept them as long as they could, and in this way, too, they copied Persia.

"Sel," sell, sold. The Seleucids sold Greeks and Macedonians on emigrating from the homeland and settling in Greek cities scattered throughout the Hellenistic world, some as far east as Aî Khanum on the Oxus River in Bactria (Afghanistan). In the first half of the third century, Greeks from Magnesia—on the Maeander River (Asia Minor), sent colonists to far-off Antioch-in-Persis in the old Persian heartland. There was a regular flux of Greek settlers from Magnesia to Antioch-in-Persis. The two cities retained a sister-city relationship for several generations. Greek speakers in Asia were as unwilling to learn foreign tongues as those in Egypt. The men who settled into seventy new cities founded by Seleucus I Nicator and Antiochus I, his successor, married foreign women, but their children were considered purely Greek or Macedonian by their fathers, who were in denial. Here is the way it worked. Intermarriage between Greco-Macedonians and "the nations" was the norm, but there was little cultural exchange between West and East. Greek cities were cultural islands adrift in a sea of aliens, many of whom were their wives. F. E. Peters speaks of "an open-ended society in which the Hellenic population permitted, though did not encourage, additions to their ranks by the process of cultural assimilation."[32] Walbank warns that the relationship of Greek-speaking settlers suddenly plunged into Media or Bactria was that of a "governing minority" or "master race" and that, while these settlers were sometimes friendly to the native majority, they were never anxious to understand natives "in their own environment" or on their own terms. Instead, they kept hoping to find some way in which the natives could be proved to be "some sort of Greeks," that is to say, they tried to establish that Asians were really a long lost branch of Hellenic Greeks.[33]

Acceptance of foreigners has been such a difficult problem historically for all peoples (not only Europeans) that those who need encouragement for doing it have sometimes had to invent relationships, where none existed, on the assumption that people will forgive the unpleasant manners and appearance of blood relatives, but not foreigners. A case in point occurred in seventeenth-century England, when the Jews were permitted to settle there for the first time since Edward I outlawed them in 1290. Their readmission occurred during the Interregnum under the Protectorate of Oliver Cromwell. It was then that the Anglo-Israelite theory among Puritans held that the English were really descended from the "ten lost tribes" of Jews transported to Assyria by Tiglath-Pileser in the eighth century BC! This purely imaginary relationship with Jews facilitated their reentry into

England. Not only was Cromwell's tolerant attitude toward Jews ahead of its time (English anti-Semitism was practically a national trust after Edward's reign), but it was also an absurdity, for at no time had the "ten lost tribes of Israel" ever migrated to England! However, the famous Jewish leader of the era, Menasseh Ben Israel (d. 1657), won Cromwell's support for Jewish settlement. Menasseh was personally convinced that the North American Indian tribes, and not Englishmen, were the real descendants of Israel's lost Jews, although, given the delicate nature of his mission to Cromwell (1655), he had the good sense not to mention it. And English colonists in the New World had the good taste not to remark to the Iroquois, Algonquin, and Huron Indian, "Funny, you don't look Jewish!"

Though they failed to prove the link between Asians and Hellenes, Hellenistic settlers imagined there was one, like Oliver Cromwell with the ten lost tribes. One thinks of Adolph Hitler awarding the status "honorary Aryans" to the Japanese. The Nazis, like the Seleucids and Puritans before them, tolerated aliens whom they secretly despised because they needed their support.

The Seleucids produced no fewer than thirteen kings named Antiochus before the arrival of Pompey in Syria. Realizing that the Antiochus XIII was too weak to be useful to Rome, Pompey took over the administration of Syria in 64 BC, ending the dynasty. Ultimately, the basis of all Roman relationships, whether patriotic or just patronizing, resulted from a dominant trait: their unwillingness to share power.

HELLENISTIC PHILOSOPHY

Suddenly, in this most unethical of ages, philosophers turned to the study of ethics. Hellenistic culture prioritized ethics because the universe appeared to behave itself much better than mankind. They asked themselves how best to live in a corrupt age where dynastic interests were pursued as if they were public ones, and consumerism included the reification of civilians and the deification of kings. While financial speculation enriched noblemen and plutocrats and sustained their clients, all were equally adrift on the seas of chance (Greek, *Tyche*). Today we call this state of affairs the stock market.

In our day ethics has shrunk to mean honesty in business, politics, or medicine and expanded to include everything having to do with sex and morals. Some people no longer distinguish between sex and morals, but practically nobody regards ethics as the ancients did, namely, having to do with the good life and, as Aristotle said, "happiness," that is, "living well and faring well."[34] Far from associating ethics with happiness, we moderns assume ethics is something painful, involving renunciation, preventing us from having fun, and or, from doing those immoral things we all enjoy, while enjoining us to do what is boring, unprofitable, or unpleasant.

Some modern philosophers disdain ethics as pointless speculation, because they think its conclusions are unverifiable. These people tell us that since everyone has an opinion about what is ethical, ethics is merely subjective or utilitarian, having nothing of the unalterable, eternal aspect of science and logic, hence, unverifiable. They got most of these relativity-type ideas from the Sophists of fifth-century Athens so Hellenistic people were familiar with them. Priests and pastors, rabbis and mullahs mostly disagree. They know they can verify ethics by looking it up in the Old or New Testament or Koran. Anciently, Aristotle integrated ethics with nature. Ethics for him meant fulfilling the purpose for which individuals and collections of them (states) are designed by their very nature. When these natural purposes were fulfilled, people and states would be their best or happiest. Obviously, the Greeks regarded ethics as part of virtue and well-being. Thomas Jefferson, educated in the classics, incorporated the pursuit of happiness into our Declaration of Independence, because he, like Aristotle, viewed politics as the most likely medium for fostering a love of ethics and welfare. How remote it seems now from American politics, where restraint, welfare, virtue, rationality, everybody's happiness, personal fulfillment, and even nature itself are at best regarded as unaffordable luxuries and at worst, as threats to profit-making and profit-taking. We've come a long way, baby.

In the Hellenistic age the comprehensive meaning of ethics had already begun to deteriorate. Philosophers were increasingly clients or courtiers, no longer participants in political decision-making. They wrote about ethics and happiness because there was a market for political theorizing, but little room for political action. There were then a few important dynasts, none of whom were given to political experimentation. The sage turned his attention from states to individuals, remembering that it was Socrates who first urged man to "Know Thyself," which is much more difficult than the modern concern with finding oneself.

In the Hellenistic age life was surprisingly unsurprising, plagued by an inveterate weariness or ennui that (paradoxically) fed on endless variety: of cults and the occult, consumer art, happy endings at the theater, endowed research, decorative kitsch, sexual titillation too pervasive to seem perversive, spectator sports, and haute cuisine. These pleasant things were spoiled occasionally by mass starvation, militarism, ignorance, plague, superstition, high taxes, a bureaucracy that compromised everyone's freedom of expression, and for millions, slavery, in which there was no freedom left to be compromised. In the Hellenistic kingdoms public rituals of Olympian worship almost entirely displaced genuine religious sentiment. Without meaningful political participation what remained of the old worship seemed merely quaint. Many shopped around for exotic cults that promised conceptual certainty and immortality in exchange for the renunciation of one's critical faculties.

A few sophisticated urbanites turned to philosophers for solutions to life's problems. That was the Greek Way. It kept wise men employed as teachers and off the streets, in gardens (Epicureans) and galleries and private academies (Zeno and the Stoics). Philosophical discussion provided continuity with an important aspect of the classical past—intelligent conversation. Hellenistic philosophy was characterized principally by several centuries of vigorous debate.

The Greeks were always good talkers, even if some twentieth-century critics decry Hellenistic ethics as all talk and little substance. For example, in the early twentieth century W. T. Stace described post-Aristotelian (Hellenistic) philosophy as a symptom of Greek decay, the "essential mark" of which was "intense subjectivism" and the disappearance of "the pure scientific spirit, the desire for knowledge for its own sake . . . gone."[35] In the twentieth century some rather deep thinkers who were very much interested in scientific investigation into the human condition—logical empiricists, pragmatists, activists, Marxists, existentialists, and linguistic analysts—have all pointed the way toward human happiness,[36] but it seems to elude us now as much as it did in the Hellenistic era. We are as unhappy a civilization as any that ever existed but far more scientific. We are at once intensely subjective and scientific and unhappy. One wonders what Stace would have made of that.

Hellenistic philosophers created products designed to satisfy the needs of people who lacked for nothing but happiness and freedom from fear—of the gods, of death. Among them was Epicurus of Samos (341–270 BC), whose Athenian family were poor refugees from Asia Minor. After settling at Athens (307 BC), Epicurus bought a house and a garden. He assembled his three brothers and some good friends, including slaves and women, in the garden. Talking in the garden was Epicurus's method for coping with stress. They talked of what made men happy, happier, happiest. It was a commune, and Epicurus was chief communicator. A prolific scholar, he took time out from his writing to share the truths he felt would make his friends happy. Just like a televangelist, he asked them to contribute to his support. He needed little because he preferred a diet of bread and water, with only a bit of aged cheese for the holidays. His house was paid for. Transportation was cheap and he was uninsured. His needs were minimal.

Epicurus took from the Cyrenaic philosophers, the first being Aristippus (c. 435–c. 360 BC), the idea that pleasure is man's chief good. From Democritus (c. 460–c. 370 BC) he took atomic materialism. The Cynics, an older school of philosophers founded by Antisthenes, Socrates' disciple, utterly rejected the pleasure principle. One of them, Diogenes, who lived in an old tub, a log, or any other low-rent shelter he could find, illustrated the rudeness for which Cynics were famous when he told Alexander the Great, who had dropped by to inquire if he could do anything for the old man, to get out of his sunlight! Cynics (the name came from the word for dogs) shared with other Greeks that dogged Hellenic trait of restricting one's wants. They made positive virtues of unconventionality and poverty and were apparently content to lead a dog's life, snapping at the heels of the well-heeled. Even before Epicurus the Cynics were retreating from an excessive civilization which they utterly despised, but unlike Epicurus, they lacked a congenial garden villa to which to retreat.

Bertrand Russell, no believer in God or gods, though a lord, thought Epicurus did his fellow men a service in freeing them from astrology and other forms of magic but admitted that both Epicureanism and Stoicism suffered from the "taint" of subjectivism, along with Protestantism, with its emphasis on sin and the individual soul.[37] Russell lamented the "natural outcome of a life in which there is much more thought than action," a condition produced by increasing civilization that diminishes the need for vivid action and enhances the opportunities for thought."[38] Russell never fell into the trap of Hellenistic philosophers—inaction. He may have thought that the universities of his own generation were full enough of philosophers who thought too much and acted too little. He addressed himself to all kinds of inquiry, education, public morality, social reform, banning atomic weapons. Active and thoughtful, it would be hard to find a philosopher more civilized or more concerned with human happiness, and Russell was besides a mathematical theorist of the first rank. But, even if it is only rarely the case that civilization produces philosophers with his talents (and opportunities), we ought not to blame Hellenistic philosophers for subjectivity pace Stace. Instead we should applaud their curiosity and humanism. Any study that contributes to human well-being ought to be regarded as the purest of sciences—objective not subjective. What is more subjective than knowledge that satisfies the curiosity of an intellectual elite but ignores the happiness and well-being of ordinary citizens? Are we not able objectively to state the needs of mankind for a productive, healthy life? Why then should we think that the ethics that meets those needs is subjective?

Hellenistic philosophy, including the school of Epicurus (called the Garden School) was "remarkably academic," shaped to a large degree by its response to other schools of philosophy.[39] Epicurus knew that his philosophy was prepared at least in part by many other Hellenistic philosophers whom he had studied, yet he never said a kind word about any from whom he borrowed, including his old teacher, Nausiphanes, whom he called "the Mollusc." Epicurus was fond of saying that he was self-taught, which was not wholly true of Epicurus or anyone else, then or now. This ungrateful posture of his may reflect a certain jealousy of those philosophers whose youth he suspected was more settled and affluent than his own. He seems to have lacked those old school ties that others wore so comfortably. The academic philosophers who were Epicurus's colleagues learned much from each other, and not least, how to define as well as defend their own "territory." Just as their employers and patrons, the Hellenistic monarchs, fought to control the land on their borders, Hellenistic philosophers sought to control the high moral ground at issue among themselves. They hoped to define ethical behavior while their rulers busied themselves with more taxing duties. The number of philosophers in the Hellenistic age who imitated kings exceeded the number of kings who imitated philosophers.

Although Epicurus's ethics stressed maximizing pleasure by avoiding pain, he urged his disciples to avoid any pleasure likely to involve more pain in the end. He did not specify which end. He distinguished between natural and necessary desires, including food, drink, sex, and freedom from anxiety, and natural but unnecessary ones, like desires for specific kinds of food and drink, perhaps for specific kinds of sex as well. Some desires he thought unnatural, like the ambition for fame and political power which he thought traceable ultimately to fear of death. His pedagogy included just saying no to anything unnecessary and unnatural, and he continually urged prudence and restraint. Epicurus discouraged, but did not forbid, sexual intercourse, political involvement, and overeating, anything that threatened a loss of serenity, or *ataraxia*.[40]

Scholars say the concept of *ataraxia* was picked up by Pyrrho of Elis (360–270 BC) when he was with Alexander on the Indian expedition.[41] Pyrrho was much impressed by ascetic Indian holy men whose desire for tranquility was of the same heroic proportions as Alexander's desire for adventure, though he may have noticed that the holy men did not appear to work as hard at achieving serenity as Alexander did at disturbing it. Pyrrho was the first great Skeptic (Greek, *skepticos*). After taking in the sights in India he returned to Elis (in the Peloponnesus) to spend the rest of his life inquiring into the truth of the proposition that travel is broadening. He seems to have concluded that it was not. Nor was staying at home. Nor was anything else. He doubted that men ever learn enough on their journey through life to become wise. He doubted that if they did, their wisdom could make them happy. Pyrrho asked some of the same unsettling questions that would prove basic to Epicureans and Stoics as well as Skeptics in the Hellenistic age: How can we know anything? Can knowledge make us happy? Pyrrho thought one could not learn anything from the phenomenal world because sensory information was contradictory. His advice was to commit oneself to nothing definite (suspension of judgment) and to keep one's mouth shut. Only after giving up all attempts at definite knowledge would men find *ataraxia*. Skepticism was quite popular with those who were fearful of making up their minds.

Once freed from that responsibility, the skeptics presumed they would reach *ataraxia.*

To Epicurus, too, *ataraxia* was the goal. He prized moderate *ataraxia,* for its gentle motions in the body, which he regarded as the physiological explanation of pleasure. Pleasure itself was merely the absence of pain. To Epicurus, pleasure, absence of pain, and *ataraxia* were the same thing. The safest pleasure was friendship; the greatest, absence of pain. To be avoided at all costs was any kind of worry. To avoid worrying was the quintessential goal of every school of Hellenistic thought. Epicurus was especially concerned to eliminate fear of religion and of death. The gods exist, but are totally unconcerned about people, whose souls are material and die with the body, though the atoms persisted and were recyclable. His philosophy was scarcely the vulgar understanding of what Epicureanism is thought to be about in our own age, living it up, something Paul Oskar Kristeller called "vulgar hedonism."[42] The professor was right to distinguish between this and what Epicurus taught, for very few people, hence, not the multitude, have ever been attracted to a philosophy based on moderation in pleasure, a reduction in the number of pleasures, and on mental rather than physical pleasures. It is not, however, useful to regard Epicureanism as having "many aspects of a religious community" as Kristeller and other commentators do, even if Epicurus did write a book entitled *On Holiness.*[43] We know enough about Epicurus from the fragments and reports that exist to suspect that any work he wrote on this subject would fail to satisfy most theologians of the Judeo-Christian sort who followed, and hence would offend most people who proclaim themselves religious. For Epicurus rejected the power of the gods to affect man in any way, shape, or manner; denied their curiosity or concern for man; rejected the notion of Providence, and if Lucretius is right, insisted (because the atoms that fell through the universe had an inherent swerve) that man was a free agent, at once released from the cause-and-effect relationship of the universe and from the whims of any God, gods, or fate(s).[44] Russell says of him that "he had all the fervour of a religious reformer." [45] Sharples agrees that "Epicureanism does seem to have about it something of the closed world of the religious sect,"[46] and Green writes that Epicureanism "is the nearest you get to a body of dogma in the Hellenistic period."[47] Others have noted that Epicurus's philosophy reads like a creed, that he believed the quest for happiness was holy, that he was personally dogmatic, he cloistered himself in the Garden School with his disciples, and so on. Metaphorical speech has made of Epicurus a quasi-religious leader. Metaphorical as well those ancient critics who regarded Epicurus's recognition of the existence of gods as proof that he lacked the courage of his convictions.[48] What convictions? He believed the gods had nothing to do with mankind. Hardly a foundation on which religious belief could be based! It is more useful to view him as A. A. Long did, as one who spent most of his time "doing advanced philosophy" and was "not the leader of a popular sect, like Jim Jones."[49]

Epicurus's philosophy was irreligious by most standards, ancient or modern. His insistence on the reliability of sense perception and observation of the universe would not now pass for scientific, but did then. Fact, based on seemingly verifiable sensory data and reason made Epicurus's system appear eminently sane, safe, and healthy by the standards of the day. But it was suitable only for the leisured class. Little wonder his philosophy was not popular in antiquity, though it influenced a few Roman gentlemen and Enlightenment thinkers of the eighteenth century, too. Reason and restraint. Weak medicine for strong minds. This was the basis of Epicurus's cure for the ills of civilization. For weak people seeking strong medicine there were always cults, religion, and magic. These promised to cure them of unhappiness stemming not from too much civilization, but too little. The customary complaints, the customary remedies.

A contemporary competitor of Epicurus was Zeno of Citium (c. 334–c. 262 BC). A Phoenician from Cyprus, he settled at Athens where (300 BC) he set up a school in a *stoa* or porch on whose walls were displayed the paintings of Polygnotus, foremost painter of the age of Pericles. This was the first school housed in an art gallery and porch. But Zeno did not stoop to answer critics in Plato's Academy who would have framed him for plagiarism. The only thing he had "stolen" from them was Socrates for a role model, no theft, really, for Socrates already belonged to the world. Zeno, noted for his cosmopolitanism, made much of being one with the universe, and no doubt felt that Socrates, already universal, was thus by definition his. He admired Socrates for his indifference to hardship and courage in death. Stoics did not approve of self-indulgence and thought the wise man must accept all that happens to him as providentially ordained.[50]

Like Socrates, Zeno felt that the real nature of a man consists in his rationality.[51] Where Socrates introduced individualism in philosophy with his famous injunction "Know Thyself," Zeno suggested that one inevitably does this when one understands that the self is part of the natural order and conforms to that order with the least possible fuss. Somehow Socrates came to be associated more with Stoicism than with Platonic idealism. Hellenistic philosophers worshipped the memory of Socrates, considered a "saint" long before the Christian era flooded the market with them, and nearly two thousand years before Erasmus of Rotterdam had a character in one of his colloquies confess jokingly that he could hardly help crying out, "Saint Socrates, pray for us!"[52] Socrates endured the extremes of weather, the barbs of playwrights, and the vagaries of Greek temperament in the real world, not the ideal world of Plato, and was "martyred" in the real world, too, the one in which Zeno operated, the material universe of Heraclitus, not the metaphysical world of Plato.

Professor Kristeller says Zeno did not doubt the possibility of trusting some sensory phenomena but not all, because only some were true and valid. In such cases reason and judgment must assent before any perceptions can be considered.[53] On the face of it, Zeno appears to have been skeptical that sensory phenomena always convey true information about the real world, but he had more confidence in the physical world than Socrates, who had not paid much attention to it at all. Cicero claimed that Zeno's method for weighing evidence from the physical world posited four stages through which one passed before a visual appearance could be processed into certain knowledge. Apparently Zeno thought one stage, recognition, was shared by both by the wise and the foolish. The result, assent, was the criterion of truth.

Arcesilaus (c. 315–c. 240 BC), one of the Platonic academics who were still more skeptical than the Stoics and very critical of them, objected that if assent can occur in both the wise and the foolish, then knowledge and opinion must be two different names for one single thing. J. M. Rist thinks Zeno's account was misleading for failing to distinguish verbally between "recognition of perception" and "recognition of knowledge."[54] Arcesilaus was not only a skeptic, but a very astute sociologist. Once a philosopher had established his reputation for wisdom, some people tended to believe that everything he said was true. Even the most errant nonsense of Plato and Aristotle, Galen and Ptolemy, Zeno and Arcesilaus was widely credited by their disciples and admirers until comparatively recent times. The philosophers were no less worshipped than the founders of religions. This is not as incredible as one might think, for any purveyor of information presumed to enhance the life and status of those impressed by it had almost instant guru status. Most people feel inadequate and the thought of being helped or saved by special understanding is flattering. Ordinary nonreflective folks felt irrevocably altered by the revelations made to them by those who claimed to know how the universe operated. Already wise men, usually philosophers, decided that some of these respected ideas, however delightful and inspirational they had seemed over the centuries, were merely erroneous opinions that could be disproved by the real truth. Arcesilaus and skeptics generally said they would be guided by Socrates' remark: "All that I know is that I know nothing." They defended their own opinions by incessant writing and argumentation, which means that they really thought they knew quite a bit. The attitude that truth could save and empower, could lift one's social status from the ignored to the chosen and hold out the prospect that the enlightened would one day be reintegrated into a more permanent universe, lived long after the Hellenistic philosophers themselves had disappeared from the scene.

Bertrand Russell said Zeno was not as discerning as his methods might indicate, that he was impatient with "metaphysical subtleties" and pushed materialism to extremes, at one point allowing a skeptic to drive him to the conclusion that even God was composed of solid matter, as well as virtue, justice, and the Rule of Three. Said Russell, "Zeno, like many others, was hurried by anti-metaphysical zeal into a metaphysic of his own."[55] If Zeno were hurried into metaphysics, the study of the supersensible, he would not only have painted himself into a corner, he would have finished by painting the corner and himself out at the same time! Of course, that's just the kind of thing Zeno would have objected to as metaphysical nonsense. He thought the world was solid and wholly natural, and no philosopher could alter his situation by an appeal to metaphysics, because the only reality was physical. Whatever Russell may have thought, Zeno would have brushed off every kind of metaphysical posture as imposture.

Nature, Zeno felt, was determined by laws set by a benevolent Lawgiver, the soul of the universe, who arranged everything for the best. While under the influence of Crates he wrote a book (*Politeia*), only fragments of which exist, a kind of rebuttal of Plato's *Republic*. There was talk in it of creating a city of wise men, but the critics do not agree if this city included all men, or only wise ones, though Zeno is supposed to have thought in universal terms. What Zeno did seem to indicate was that wise men would aim for virtue, avoid evil, and as for the "indifferent" things in life (*adiaphora*), would select only those that contributed to virtuous behavior. Zeno, like the Cynics, thought everything that was not good or bad was indifferent, although he rather ingenuously thought some indifferent things more indifferent than others. Kristeller thought him self-serving in this respect. Zeno also seems to have counted on virtuous men accepting his definition of things like health, happiness, and possessions as truly indifferent. Stoics generally believed virtue to be a matter of willpower, anyway, so that the virtuous man turns everything unpleasant or bad in his life into the good. The indifferent things just don't count. Stoics were supposed to overcome what they lacked by looking at the bright side of things, even of conditions such as imprisonment, torture, grievous illness, loss of loved ones—all things that that would overwhelm the nonvirtuous but never Stoics. The nonvirtuous are not Stoics. They consistently make immoral, nonnatural choices. Where Stoics exercise their will and find perfect freedom over externals and desires, the nonvirtuous are driven by irrational desires for external objects. The seventeenth-century poet Richard Lovelace (1618–57?), a Cavalier poet imprisoned (1642) by the Commonwealth government for petitioning in King Charles I's favor, perfectly expressed the Stoic philosophy when he wrote "To Althea From Prison." Wrote he: "Stone Walls doe not a Prison make, / Nor I'ron bars a Cage; / Mindes innocent and quiet take / That for an Hermitage." Lovelace contrasted the freedom that exists in the soul with his life in jail and found, as any Stoic would, that even "Inside," he was still free. Zeno would have loved Lovelace.

There was something of Voltaire's simpleton, Candide, in Zeno's optimistic faith that everything would eventually work out for the best. Of Zeno it may be said, if not of Epicurus, that he was as much theologian as philosopher. Inside every human soul Zeno placed a spark of the divine soul he called God sometimes and sometimes, Zeus. The idea (originally Heraclitus's) was for each human soul to get in touch with the rational Divine Soul or *Logos* (Gr.; Rational principle) that gave order to the universe. Meister Eckhart would be saying the same thing in the late Middle Ages.[56] Not only did Zeno think he had the right *Logos,* he thought he had got that *Logos* right! The Hellenistic age was loco (Sp., insane) for Logos, seeing reason everywhere, including places where it was not. This enthusiasm was inherited by Christians who thought it logical to attribute Reason to the incomprehensible will of God and Jesus Christ (John 1:1–18). The reason for this was Beyond them.

It wasn't enough to go along willy-nilly with the universe. One had to go willingly to be virtuous. God, nature, and natural law. Zeno underwrote all three. His ethic was more dogmatic than Epicurus's because he gave his disciples fewer choices. Not only was virtue its own reward, it was the only reward. The only pleasure was virtuous action. Zeno disapproved of all other pleasures, passions and sentiments, and so his ethics may appear to our self-indulgent age premodern, puritanical, intolerant, even fanatical. Not surprisingly, his disavowal of mercy and compassion for suffering humanity seems up-to-the-minute, quite relevant to an era of "downsizing" (wholesale firing), welfare "reform" (communal insensitivity), and "collateral damage" (the accidental slaughter of civilians in war). The end of virtue was not to help the unfortunate, about whom Zeno was blissfully unconcerned, but to help *oneself* live according to nature. For to Zeno, living the natural life and living a virtuous life amounted to the same thing.[57] Whatever Zeno disapproved of he called unnatural. All the things he did approve of were therefore natural and good. The Stoics were well on the way to inventing heresy. All they lacked was political power. When, toward the end of the second century AD one of their number (Marcus Aurelius) became Rome's emperor it was not surprising that he, too, refused to tolerate Christians, Rome's first heretics, nor that after his death Christianity found itself irresistibly drawn to Stoicism, with its sharp-edged distinction between what was virtuous and what unnatural.

Zeno was dark and his neck twisted. He may have resented his more attractive competitor, Epicurus, and having studied with Crates the Cynic, he took on (perhaps he always had) a dogged crudeness of manner that is reminiscent of Cynics, none of whom, starting with Diogenes, were famous for their charm. Not surprisingly, Zeno did not place the same emphasis on friendly intercourse that Epicurus did. Zeno said friendship ought never to be carried to the point where a friend's misfortunes destroy your own tranquility. Both philosophers were materialists, but Epicurus emphasized the randomness of matter, while Zeno stressed the control God (or Zeus) had over it. Although both thought matter mattered, Epicurus thought men free. Zeno thought God, Zeus, or Providence controlled their every move.

Zeno's *Politeia* described the ideal state that Alexander had left uncompleted, a world state that defied provincialism and local laws, in which the only law was natural law. In it there was no crime, no class difference, no ethnic rivalry, no elitism. Nothing but brotherly love (as a principle, not as an emotion!), equality, rationality, and good citizenship. Zeno, unlike Epicurus, believed political participation a positive thing, though he never participated in Athenian politics. Perhaps for that very reason Athenians raised a monument to him after his death.

At the age of seventy-two Zeno, who had put off taking his teachers' retirement, walked out of his classroom. According to the third-century biographer and historian Diogenes Laërtius, he then stubbed his toe so hard it broke and down he went. Striking the ground with his hand he quoted a text from the *Niobe:* "I am coming; why do you call me?" then killed himself, some say by holding his breath. His successor, Cleanthes, also commited suicide, as did the Stoic Antipater of Tarsus (second century BC), a practice other Greeks beside Stoics regarded permissible and even desirable under certain conditions such as incurable pain or a sign from the gods. Epicurus held that if life ceases to give pleasure, the remedy for a free man was to end it. Some Stoics thought only wise men should commit suicide, though Diogenes thought wise men had better things to do with their time. Fools, who did not, were better off dead, and his favorite slogan was "Reason or the Rope." Zeno, ridiculed for centuries for committing suicide over a broken toe, interpreted this accident as "a divine call," similar to the message Socrates inferred as of the gods before drinking hemlock. Rist says Zeno thought he had received his "marching orders," an unhappy choice of words given the broken toe.[58]

There were many disciples of the original Skeptics, Cynics, Epicureans, and Stoics in the Hellenistic world. In our own age we use these same terms to define personality types and the kinds of responses people still make to life's perennial problems, large or small. Although neither Pyrrho nor Diogenes, Epicurus or Zeno, nor their more articulate followers have attracted as much attention or respect as Plato or Aristotle and none have been as revered as Plato's teacher, Socrates, they have probably affected the lives of average people more dramatically than either of their classical predecessors. These four schools of Hellenistic thought—skepticism, cynicism, Epicureanism, and Stoicism—have helped ordinary folks organize their everyday experience in simple, not theological or teleological, terms. Ever since the Hellenistic age these philosophies, minus a few refinements, have been the perennial stock of our ethical ready-to-wear, adaptable for all social occasions, climates and cultural milieux, subject to no higher interpretation or authority than those of the shops, streets, kitchens, and farms of Western civilization.

9

Republican Rome

ORIGINAL MYTHS

TWO HUNDRED YEARS BEFORE PUBLIUS VIRGILIUS Maro, the poet Virgil (70 BC–19 BC) began the *Aeneid,* a work encouraged by Emperor Augustus. Virgil's contemporaries believed that Homer's Trojan War hero, Aeneas, was their cultural ancestor. In Homer's *Iliad* Aeneas, son of Anchises and Aphrodite, Greek goddess of love, was husband to King Priam's daughter Creuse and father of Iulus. They believed Iulus was the "ancestor" of Julius Caesar and Emperor Augustus. In Homer's story Aeneas carried his father and household gods on his shoulders out of burning Troy, holding his son's hand, leaving his wife to follow. Creuse got lost in the confusion, but the rest of the family cruised over to Delos, the sacred island of Apollo and Diana. Now, it might seem odd that a vanquished Trojan hero sailed first to a Greek island. But Romans preferred winners to losers, so Aeneas, though a Trojan loser, was transformed into a Greek winner by Virgil, himself a Cisalpine Gaul, before he was allowed to become a naturalized citizen of Rome.[1]

Greek historians like Strabo and Dionysius of Halicarnassus, both writing in the late first century BC, accused Aeneas of having betrayed Troy to the Greeks to save his own life. Whether Aeneas was a hero or a traitor depended on the sources consulted—Greek or Roman. To this very day, questions of heroism or treachery in human affairs depend on the sources consulted. The *tsouras* (Yiddish, trouble) is in the sources. But for the Romans, Aeneas lent a touch of class to Italy, a founding father with a classical background.

Virgil invented a glorious past to match the glorious present in which he wrote, transforming Rome's defeats into splendid achievements, obscuring the long periods when Rome was not more powerful than her Latin neighbors, and was in fact controlled by her Etruscan ones. Aeneas emerged a pious fellow, who, when tempted by Queen Dido of Carthage to dalliance, resisted and obeyed Jupiter's command to sail at once for Sicily, leaving Dido to commit suicide. She had to commit. Aeneas wouldn't. His decision demonstrated the control he (and by implication all Roman heroes) exercised over emotions, putting politics above passion and pleasure. For Rome, politics was passion and pleasure. There is nothing more noticeable in Roman history than this: the Romans were not romantic.

Virgil took liberties with plot. Dido and Aeneas could never have been lovers because Carthage was founded several hundred years after the Trojan War, long after Aeneas. Of course, Virgil was not wholly free to alter a story concretized (concrete was a Roman invention!) before his own era. In the *Aeneid* the hero is directed by the shades of the dear departed, and by the gods. After a bitter fight against a rival named Turnus, king of the Rutuli, Aeneas won the hand of a Latin princess, Lavinia, daughter of King Latinus. For her he named his capital city Lavinium. His son founded Alba Longa, the capital of Latium situated in the Alban Hills, sixteen miles from Rome. Aeneas was killed in a battle, either by the Latin Rutuli or by the Etruscans and was deified after death. His descendants included Rome's founders, the fabled twins Romulus and Remus.

The twins' grandfather was Numitor, ex-king of Alba, dispossessed by his younger brother Amulius. Their mother, Rhea Sylvia, was compelled by Amulius to become a vestal virgin, a pagan nun. She wanted none of it, but had all of it when Mars, god of war, impregnated her. After the twins arrived, Amulius ordered them placed in a basket or trough on the River Anio (now the Taverone) which empties into the Tiber five miles north of Rome. In the tradition of Sargon I and Moses, the boys were rescued from the reeds. At the foot of the Palatine Hill, now downtown Rome, a she-wolf found them and carried them to her cave to suckle. Her vigilance and industry kept the human from the door—the same techniques that keep the wolf from ours. One day, Faustulus, the king's shepherd, kidnapped the boys. He reasoned that if these kids did not learn Latin soon, it would always remain for them a dead language. Romulus and Remus howled when removed from their lair, but they learned Latin without having to read Caesar's *Gallic Commentaries!* As for the story of Aeneas, it was already in their blood.

The twins became leaders of a band of shepherd warriors on the Palatine, Rome's first settlement. Modern scholars date this event between the tenth century and the year 800 BC.[2] After Romulus restored his grandfather to his throne, the twins resolved to found a city of their own. Remus chose the Aventine for a site; Romulus the Palatine. Similar hill villages lay in Rome's immediate vicinity and in the nearby Alban hills. The practice of augury— prognostication by omens, including bird flight—was already full-fledged. Accordingly, when six vultures flew by Remus's bird-spotting station on the Aventine, but twelve buzzed Romulus on the Palatine, the shepherds flocked to Romulus. Remus was killed by his brother after he jumped over the wall that Romulus was raising around the Palatine. Frenchmen later contended that Remus was not killed, but escaped to Gaul where he founded the city of Reims in the heart of French champagne country. Greece, Italy, France. Such was the westerly route of ancient civilization. As for Romulus, he was not only Rome's founder, but her first fratricide, the Roman Cain.

To make amends, Romulus initiated a festival for dead souls called Lemuria (Latin, *lemures,* ghosts), an early version of Halloween that Romans celebrated in May. The first of Rome's seven kings, Romulus shared his "reign" with a neighboring Sabine king named Titus Tatius. To attract settlers Romulus made Rome a refuge for fugitives from justice. Having secured their lives, he procured them wives, leading his despera-does to the nearby Quirinal hill, where they raped the Sabine women. Once with child, the women negotiated peaceful relations between their former Sabine husbands and their new Roman ones. Eventually the Sabines, like many other Latin tribes, became part of the Roman people. Fratricide and rape. Roman civilization rested on violence. Of course, Romans were not thinking of the role of civilization. They were too busy playing victims and oppressors. Romulus was translated to heaven in a clap of thunder, after which he was worshipped as the god Quirinus, another name for Mars, his father. Whether Romulus was deified because he was guilty of murder and rape or worshipped for those very reasons, is impossi-ble to say. His was the first case of Roman clap.

Virgil's *Aeneid* was approved by Rome's literary lions—Horace, Seneca, Lucan, and Juvenal—and was equally popular with ordinary folks. Its patri-otism assured its adoption as a textbook in Roman schools. Its high-toned morality—the renunciation of dalliance with Dido, for example—captivated St. Augustine four centuries later. He, after all, had had a very difficult time renouncing his own mistress and the mother of his son, when he prayed for chastity, but not yet.[3] Certain scenes like Aeneas's visits to the Greek ora-cles at Cumae, in southern Italy, and a tour of Hades given him by a Sybil, plus his conversation about Rome's future with his father's ghost in the underworld resonated in Dante's *Inferno.* In that late medieval poem, Vir-gil was Dante's prophetic guide. Tasso, Spenser, Shakespeare, Milton, and Bunyan were all influenced by Virgil's divinely inspired prophet, bearer of civilization.

When Virgil was writing, men of letters were making new literary works out of a few Greek originals, and since the days of the Latin poet Naevius (c. 270–199 BC) had referred to this practice as *contaminatio.* When poets and artists used the term it meant "a touch, a connection." When others did it meant "defilement." The name Naevius came from the Latin word *nae-vus,* meaning mole. He was truly a marked man. After participating in the First Punic War against Carthage, which began in 264 BC, he had the audacity to satirize it. He meant only to speak for the public conscience, but forgot to ascertain if the public had one or wanted one. The consul Metellus, offended, forced him into exile. Naevius naively guessed he could ridicule a war effort with impunity. His career was ruined by the Roman assumption that patriotism meant unquestioning support of the war effort, for Rome valued the arts only if they reinforced national policy and very majoritarian points of view. Naevius did more than initiate the artistic tradition of *contaminatio*. His satire revealed the chasm between the power of the imagination and the power of government. Ordinary Romans, yearning for order in their disorderly lives, helped fill that chasm with patriotism and myths that made the monotony of everyday life bearable and helped forestall reality. The Roman patriciate fed them more myths and patriotic nonsense that diverted their attention from their miseries and forestalled revolution. When myths proved inadequate during the social revolution of the second century BC, the senators hit upon bread and circuses. Myth, patriotism, bread, circuses. The Romans were the first to master the art of public control using these four techniques. No state ever needed a fifth.

ETRUSCANS

The Romans crafted their own cultural origins, producing a "history" that still challenges scholars. Little information of a documentary sort ever existed. Its scarcity proved a blessing in disguise. Their patriotism could thrive in the presence of damaging evidence, and fabulous ancestors appeared stronger and nobler than real ones. At the same time, men were spurred to action by shame, the belief that one's ancestors outstripped them in boldness and self-sacrifice. With ideas such as these, how could Rome falter?

The Romans eschewed sloth and complacency. There were dynamic Etruscans to the north. There were clever but less dynamic Greeks to the south, and there were Italic kin living everywhere else on the peninsula, except north of the Po Valley where Gauls and Celts settled. The Etruscans and Greeks were more sophisticated and richer than the Romans; the Gauls fiercer. Although the Romans could ignore or manipulate poor neighbors, it was impossible to ignore richer and stronger ones, nor did they ignore Rome. In the case of the Etruscans, who took over Rome in the late seventh century BC, foreign contact was tutelary. Etruscan engineers taught Romans the arts of drainage and paving. Afterward, Rome never worried about plumbers. No one else could floor her, or plumb her depths.

The Etruscans entered Italy between the tenth and eighth centuries BC. Where they originated remains one of the great mysteries of Western civilization.[4] Specialists cannot read much of their non Indo-European language, used mostly for trade, like the Minoans, whom they resembled. The twentieth-century author D. H. Lawrence read somewhere in the 1920s that Etruscans came from Asia Minor, but should this have proved not to be the case, he noted that in "Homeric days a restlessness seems to have possessed the Mediterranean basin" and everyone was "on the move."[5] Lawrence got it right, because specialists are still debating Etruscan origins. Their so-called "oriental characteristics" refer not to physical traits but to artistic motifs associated with western Asia or Egypt—such things as siren sculptures, sphinxes, canopic jars, and the like.[6] To the Indo-European peoples the Etruscans were exotic or, to be blunt, outlandish. Of course. They came (possibly) from outer space. Asia Minor.

The Romans were Indo-European hill dwellers who entered Italy around 1200 BC, Rome two hundred years later. They preceded the Etruscans, but were less developed.[7] Although Greek poets regarded the Arunci, who spoke a language close to Latin, as the original Italians, the Romans knew that Umbrians, Sabellians, Vestini, Marrucini, Aequi, Paeligni, Frentanians, Peuceti, Praetuttii, Falisci, Oscans, Volsci, Eques, Marsi, Hernici, Samnites, and other Indo-Europeans had already taken up residence in the central peninsula.[8] They concluded that questions relative to arrival time in Italy would henceforth be strictly academic. After the Greeks arrived in southern Italy, (eighth century BC), the Romans left everything academic to them. Greeks invented the academy.

Like other Indo-Europeans, the Latins cremated their dead and buried them in pots, urns shaped like their huts, a common practice in Hungary and Romania, and one that spread by the early Iron Age from Spain to the coasts of Asia Minor.[9] The Etruscans preferred inhumation to cremation, though they settled into Etruria where cremation was common, for the Villanovans with whom they gradually intermingled practiced it. Etruscan newcomers in the seventh century preferred to build whole cities underground to house their dead so that they might "live" in death as pleasantly as in life. Indo-Europeans could do as they pleased, but in death the Etruscans surrounded themselves with the finer things of life. In the end, they refused to go to pot.

With so many different tribes living in prehistoric Italy, all the Latin tribes regarded themselves as one people.[10] Even if "the dates and the reality of events in early Roman history are quite uncertain," the Latin language and worship of common gods at similar festivals gives us a handle on Rome and Latium.[11] Latium was a relatively compact area stretching southeast from the Tiber to the headland of Monte Circeo, and as far east as the Apennines.[12] By 500 BC Latins occupied individual small republics there. Except for Rome, they were city-states without cities, though not without villages and hill forts.[13] Without democracy, but not without government.

Latins shared an ability to make soldiers of shepherds and farmers, like Hebrews. Both Israel and Rome were models for the American colonials, the French revolutionaries, and Napoleon, and for armies of the nineteenth and twentieth centuries. These armies, like those of Saul and David and of Rome, turned farm boys into brave soldiers and brave soldiers into dead men, carrion. Social and spiritual bonds of language and religion helped, too. Men killed to free themselves from having to convert to a new faith or learn a new language. Most Roman historians spent more time writing about antisocial behavior, war and conquest, than about social behavior like religion and speech. It was easier to document violence, and the Romans developed a real taste for it. Thus historians found employment. Violence was easily documented because it only involved the destruction or redistribution of durable goods. Of these the most durable was property, the least durable, people. Speech and spirituality, unlike property, were always harder to grasp.

KINGS AND THINGS

The story of Rome's seven kings is problematic because the first four never existed and there is disagreement about the last three who did exist but whose curricula vitae remain largely undocumented. Nevertheless, the dates of their "reigns" are always provided, though they vary. There is more agreement regarding their accomplishments, many of which can be assumed to have occurred, and some of which can even be proved to have. The best way for the nonspecialist to approach Rome's kings is to recall the Old Testament, with its own book of Kings.[14] Some biblical material reflects historical reality to some degree. All of it was once viewed by Jews and Christians as literally true. Some people still regard the Bible as literally true. They are true believers. The Romans were, for long centuries, true believers of their own cultural myths. Before the modern era, most of what they believed was taken as gospel.

Romulus reigned (753–716 BC) in tandem with the Sabine king, Titus Tatius. Their successor was Numa Pompilius (715–672 BC). Most of Rome's religious institutions were attributed to his invention, including the sacred college of priests (*flamens*); the vestal virgins; priests called *pontifixes, augurs,* or entrail readers; and the sacred calendar. In actuality all these were part of a common Italian culture before Numa. Numa was a student of Pythagoras, the Greek mathematician although Pythagoras was born eighty years after Numa's death. Plutarch, who wrote in the first and second centuries AD, thought Numa's calendar, though inexact, "not without some scientific knowledge." The same might be said of Plutarch's account of Numa. He credited him with expanding an older calendar that accorded but ten months to the year. Plutarch thought Numa added January and February, and an extra "intercalary" month of 22 days to follow February, thus allowing for the difference between the lunar and solar years.[15]

Numa built a temple for the god Janus, who kept open house during war, but closed his gate in peacetime. Numa kept the peace for forty-three years, so Janus's new temple was closed during his entire reign. This king began the worship of the god of landmarks or boundaries, called Terminus. Numa appreciated limits. Ovid said Numa married the nymph Egeria, but others that he merely visited her at night. All agreed he asked her advice on every law. Egeria overlooked Numa's limitations. Four hundred years after his death, fourteen books were discovered in a wooden box. Numa, like President Nixon, had recorded his every utterance. The books described his religious innovations. Livy said (40.29) the Roman Senate feared they might prove subversive and burned them. The senators were true conservatives, professing to respect traditions they did not understand while torching the founder's books that explained them. They prided themselves on strictness but were too ignorant to be strict constructionists.

Tullus Hostilius, third king (672–640 BC), destroyed Alba Longa after winning the battle between the Horatii and Curiatii.[16] He defeated the Etruscan towns of Fidenae and Veii, too, but either his successes attracted the wrath of the gods or of his successor, Ancus Martius. Some say Ancus murdered Tullus while he was performing magical rites in the kitchen. If the gods were involved, Tullus died by lightning; if Ancus was the murderer, he torched the palace to make it seem that his victim had been struck by lightning–divine punishment for impiety. It may yet turn out that Tullus, an inveterate snacker, was merely fixing himself something in the kitchen when the lamp stand fell over, hitting him on the head before setting the kitchen ablaze. If only Tullus had stuck to his diet!

Ancus Martius (640–616 BC), Rome's fourth king, emulated his grandfather Numa by reviving neglected religious observances. He fought against neighboring Latins (the Veintes, Fidenates, Volsci, and Sabines) to defend his territory. All the Latins were very territorial. After defeating them, he settled the conquered on the Aventine hill, the original plebeian class. Ancus fortified the Janiculum hill against Etruria, and connected it to the city by a wooden bridge (Pons Sublicius) across the Tiber. The bridge attracted the homeless and beggars. Romans were not asked to dig into their wallets for spare change as they crossed over, because Rome did not have coins until the third century BC. Still, they urged Ancus to solve the problem of homelessness. His solution was Rome's first prison, built under the Capitol. This was the kind of solution Romans loved. The king also enclosed Mount Martius and the Aventine within city walls and established a saltworks at Ostia that stimulated the Tiber trade.[17] Ancus was a boon to business, harsh on the undeserving poor, a supporter of defense expenditure, and such a credit to Numa's (pious) memory that Romans may have regretted he was merely the figment of late Republican imagination.

The last three kings of Rome ruled from 616 to 509 BC.[18] The first and last of these three were Etruscans, called Tarquins, a Latinized version of the common Etruscan name *tarcna.*[19] The first, Tarquin the Elder (Priscus) (616–579 BC) is attested by frescoes on a tomb at Vulci describing him as "the Roman Tarquin" (Cneve Tarkunies Rumach),[20] and the name of one of his enemies,

Aulus Vibenna, turned up on a vase that dates from the same period,[21] confirmation that real people engaged in real political struggle. Professor Ogilvie believes it possible that this Tarquin was, as reputed, the son of a Corinthian refugee in flight from the tyrant Cypselus. There is evidence of Corinthians living in Etruria, and that, Professor Ogilvie says, together with his name is "almost all that can be said" of the first Tarquin, finding nothing about this reign provable, and all of Livy's comments "romances," "generalized memories of Etruscan achievements at Rome during the Regal period." [22]

Servius Tullius, Rome's sixth king, was of Etruscanized Latin origin. Whichever Latin town he hailed from, Vulci,[23] or Corniculum,[24] he was not handicapped by a nonroyal background, though Servius meant slave or servant. Later, when elitist Romans reflected on his success, they gave him a divine origin. His mother, who sparkled in social situations, conceived him by a flame (a new flame) representing the Greek god Dionysius. Tarquin the Elder reared the lad after he captured Corniculum. Servius worked himself into a position of trust before succeeding his foster father as king. Later, Rome devised very strict rules that governed the steps by which patricians advanced in public service starting with the most junior position first, working up to senior offices without skipping any. Servius came under the old rules, though, and leaped from captive to foster son of the king to the kingship itself. He never forgot his humble origins, for he transformed the formerly elite army into a citizen army. He gave it deliberative status to rival the Curial Assembly.[25] Ogilvie thinks Servius may also be credited with establishing a centralized religious cult of Diana which united all the Latins in common worship with Rome. If true, Servius was the first to make Rome a city of holy practice for much of Italy. Christians thought a centralized cult a capital idea and have been practicing Christianity at Rome since the first century. It is something that requires a lot of practice. They never get it quite right.

Rome's last king was Tarquin the Proud (Superbus) (534–510 BC), who married the daughter of Servius (Tullia) and at her instigation, murdered her father and seized the crown. Under this Tarquin Rome's influence continued to spread throughout Latium, for he forced the Latins to ally with Rome. Defeated cities contributed to Tarquin's Roman building projects. As much as seventy miles of coastline south of Ostia fell under his control.[26] Eventually, he created a united Latium to defend his Etruscan enclave from all contenders. Even before the Renaissance there were *condottieri* (military leaders) who wanted a condo in Rome.

It was this Tarquin who bought the Sibylline books. Neither the Etruscans nor the Latins had begun to publish. Only the Sibyls, women inspired by heaven, had any books in Italy. The ancients never agreed as to the number of these prophetesses. Plato thought there was only one. Pliny mentioned the Sybil at Cumae. She was the one to whom the god

Apollo offered one wish as a token of his affection before propositioning her for sex. The little tease asked for as many years of life as grains of sand held in her palm, and Apollo granted her these. Unfortunately, she forgot to ask for beauty that would last as long. After she refused Apollo's advances, it was too late. The god of beauty was not about to play plastic surgeon to a virgin. As her beauty faded, and her love life languished, the Sibyl took to writing to pass the time away. She wrote prophecies on leaves. Some of these blew away and were lost forever, but the rest filled nine volumes. These she offered Tarquin for a very high sum. Her books were gold-leafed, leather-bound hardback copies, and a matched set. Tarquin would have liked them for his study. But while he spent millions on buildings, he was stingy when it came to books and objected to the high price asked. The Sibyl disappeared, returning soon after with only six volumes, having burned three. However, she did not reduce the price. When Tarquin shrugged at this last offer, she vanished returning with but three volumes. Same price. Tarquin was so astonished that he decided to buy the three remaining volumes and appointed a college of priests to look after them. The prophetic works were thenceforth consulted with great solemnity when the state was in danger. When the books did not help, the Romans grumbled, saying Tarquin should have bought the whole set. Among the burned volumes was the index! Political leaders have to know which questions are relevant to ask when there is terror, or they won't be able to use the answers that turn up. During the sixteenth century, the Catholic Pontifex Maximus provided another *Index,* but it was not the right one for Sybil's works.[27] An offer in time would have saved all nine.

The great temple of Jupiter Optimus Maximus depleted Tarquin's treasury, as Solomon's in Jerusalem reduced his. Unlike the Hebrews, however, Tarquin did not sell his people into slavery to a neighboring king to pay off his debts. Instead, he sold them tickets to the Roman games. He accommodated the fans in impressive new stands built in the Circus Maximus. The games were celebrated annually thereafter on September 13, in honor of the temple's completion. Greeks, Romans, and Etruscans all worshipped sports. Ticket purchases helped the king pay off the bondholders.

In 510 BC the tyrant Hippias, son of Pisistratus, was expelled from Athens and the Athenians launched their independent city-state. Was it just a coincidence that Rome's last Tarquin was also expelled in the same year? Games and new bleachers were not enough to keep Romans rooting for Tarquin whose final regnal year is a matter of debate. Some historians believe the Republic which followed Tarquin's expulsion began as late as 450 BC. They question the *Fasti,* lists of magistrates and events kept with some gaps from the early Republican period to its fall. Because archaeologists are not concerned with written evidence, they disregard the year 510 BC, the traditional starting date for the Republic, discerning a break in architectural style and the importation of Greek vases (an Etruscan but not a Roman practice) between 470 and 450 BC.[28] Using such material evidence they regard this period, not 510, as the point of changeover from Etruscan to Roman culture and political independence. Before the end of Etruscan rule over Rome and neighboring Latin settlements, some Etruscanized Latin officers were bragging about their wives' virtue at Ardea, one of the towns Tarquin had just conquered. They found the topic so intriguing that they all went home to check up on their spouses. Talk is cheap, but so is intrigue. Only one husband, Conlatinus of Rome, was satisfied with what he found. For though the other women were living it up, his wife, the beautiful, virtuous Lucretia, was at home with her servants, spinning. Now Lucretia, as a courtesy, had invited the king's son, Sextus, in to share the hospitality of her house as the prince was returning from camp.[29] One supposes she was merely intent on doing her patriotic duty in extending this invitation to the prince. Somehow, Sextus penetrated her bedroom that night and threatened her with murder if she refused his advances, but silence if she acquiesced.

The Romans never ever believed that Lucretia gave in to his demands for sex out of fear for her life, but because her tormenter promised to slay one of her own slaves and put him in bed with her corpse if she refused, leaving her father, husband, and the whole city to draw their own conclusions. What could the poor woman do? The next morning, the shamed matron entreated her family to avenge her besmirched honor. Whereupon she stabbed herself with a dagger she had concealed in her robe. Why she did not stab Sextus with it is not known. But, upon her death, the Roman patrician, Brutus L. Junius, Father of the Roman Republic, snatched this dagger from her wound and swore upon the reeking blade to avenge Lucretia's honor and Rome's, whereupon the Senate proscribed the Tarquins for all time. Lucretia went down in history.

The story was pure invention, but not pure. It was tainted by hypocrisy, for Rome, we recall, was founded on the gang rape of Sabine women by those felons Romulus employed to increase its population. The Sabine men by admission to Roman citizenship were rewarded for having countenanced this crime. Titus Tatius, the Sabine king, was awarded royal office for not making a fuss about the rapes. What could be more tatty? Everyone else involved, including the Sabine women, was willing to ignore the incident. So why was Lucretia's rape considered so offensive? Lucretia knew her mind was pure, but was nonetheless convinced that her "honor" was down there somewhere, like Australia, and that its discovery made her Sextus's penal colony. Somebody should have reminded her about the Sabine women! Rome blithely colonized women long before Sextus set out to explore Lucretia. Rome was founded on rape, but Lucretia was foundered by it. The tragic result of Sextus's crime was that Lucretia's sacrifice became the standard against which all "good" women would be evaluated down through the centuries. Although the last Tarquin went on to build the first great sewer in Rome, the Cloaca Maxima, it was pretty clear that a healthy relationship between the sexes had already gone down the drain.

It is difficult to deal with imaginary magistrates, but not nearly so bad as dealing with real ones. Moderns accumulate a higher ratio of fact to fiction than ancient Romans but have not yet been able to avoid controversies that information breeds. When one ponders the evidence not presented, misinterpreted by journalists, or suppressed by public agencies or corporations, it is harder to determine whether the Romans enjoyed an intellectual diet richer in fiction than our own.

THE REPUBLIC OPENS FOR BUSINESS

Between 509 and 409 BC the main energies of Rome were spent determining just who would be in charge, first in Rome itself, and then, in Italy. Roman plebeians struggled against their creditors to get a written copy of the laws—the Twelve Tables (451 BC)—and to have a people's assembly (Comitia Tributa) that would pass laws sympathetic to their needs. They struggled to get plebeian tribunes a veto over any of the Senate's laws that damaged their interests (449 BC); to permit intermarriage with the patriciate (445 BC); and to qualify for financial offices (quaestorships) in the state and army (421 BC).[30] The Roman priesthood opposed plebeian candidates on the grounds that poor people offended the gods, unlike the Hebrew God who granted the devoted poor affirmative action. The Roman word "patrician" came from the Latin term *patres* (fathers), the correct form of address for senators in the Republic. The patricians treated each other with the respect due to fathers but stepped on poor peoples' rights, as if they were not fathers as well. To the plebeians they were stepfathers. Because this period was so disorderly, it was known as the struggle of the orders.

Although the social struggle continued throughout the Republic's history, she could not afford to devote all her attention to it. She went to war against the Veii (405–396 BC) and won, and was invaded by the Gauls— and lost (390 BC). By 338 BC, Rome had organized Latium for their mutual defense under her leadership in return for military service. The extralegal arrangement of *clientela* occurred when a rich and powerful aristocrat extended protection to neighboring villagers and peasants in return for their electoral support.[31] Rome rewarded the Latins—a few with full Roman citizenship; others with nonvoting rights and local autonomy.[32] Rome shared with her new clients a common culture. She was flexible. She was building military muscle. Nothing flexes better.

Whenever war raged, the poor Roman farmer found himself poorer when the dust settled. Cincinnatus, victor over Volsci and Aequi and twice dictator, dropped his plough at the age of eighty and went to war a second time (in 439 BC). Famine made the poor desperate. A rich plebeian, Spurius Maelius, was selling grain to the mob at prices so low he angered the patricians, who feared he would make himself tyrant. Cincinnatus ordered Maelius's house pulled down and his corn distributed free to the poor. The senators posed as champions of the people against tyranny, buying plebeian support at Maelius's expense. A campaign contribution. In the welfare reform that followed, the patricians posed as benefactors. What they really posed was the problem of authority. When the *Lex Hortensia* (287 BC) was passed by the dictator, Q. Hortensius, the whole body of the Roman people was obliged to obey all laws enacted by the popular assembly. In fact, the old aristocrats merely accepted some, but not all, plebeian families as capable of holding the consulship. This composite class of notables in turn became exclusive and resistant to the claims of talent and ambition from below.[33] The tribunes, formerly defenders of the plebeians, became members of the Senate, and the popular assembly only rarely passed laws over the Senate's head.[34]

After Rome's victory over the Samnites, Etruscans, and Gauls (Third Samnite War) in 295 BC, she built roads to link all cities in central Italy into a great confederacy. Nominally allies, they were already subjects. The Samnites harbored lasting resentment. When Rome made peace with them she left the Campanians in the lurch, and they turned to the Latins for help. Because Campania bordered Lucania, and the Lucanians and the Samnites had been raiding the Greek city of Tarentum, located on the inside "heel" of Italy, Rome found herself drawn into the affairs of the Greek world.

Tarentum, a Greek city-state in Italy, asked the Greek King Pyrrhus of Epirus for help. Pyrrhus wrote books on military strategy. Cicero considered one of his treatises on warfare a very fine work. At Asculum, in 279 BC, Pyrrhus's elephants frightened the Roman cavalry, and he won the first battle. But it proved a "Pyrrhic" victory, one obtained at too great a cost, because Greek losses were so heavy. When Pyrrhus advanced toward Rome, he found Roman garrisons in all the towns, and his attempts to overawe the Senate by diplomacy met only with Rome's refusal to negotiate with foreigners on Italian soil. Pyrrhus went to Sicily to save the Sicilian Greeks from Carthage, but his despotism alienated them. He returned to Italy and found the Greek cities there less than enthusiastic for his help. Pyrrhus sailed home to Epirus, defeated by the ingratitude of Sicilian and Italian Greeks and Rome's refusal to accept defeat.[35] Weighing anchor from Italy he remarked: "What a battlefield I leave to Rome and Carthage," a statement both insightful and spiteful. Insightful because nineteen years later Rome began the first of three Punic (Carthaginian) Wars, the second fought mostly on Italian soil. Pyrrhus's rhetoric was spiteful. He viewed all Italy, home to Etruscans, Gauls, Latins, and Greeks as a mere battlefield! Clearly, he held the Italians in despite. For a brilliant tactician, it was a tactless remark. It seems he was not as brilliant as Cicero thought. While attacking Argos, Pyrrhus was decapitated by a roof tile hurled at him by his antagonist's mother. His scholarly knowledge of warfare proved as inconsequential in saving his life as his victories over Rome. Pyrrhus's whole life was a Pyrrhic struggle because he lacked insight into the human condition and his own.

CARTHAGE AND ROME

Carthage and Rome had enjoyed good relations since the Republic's foundation. But the two were on a collision course as Carthage expanded into Africa, Sicily, Spain, Sardinia, and the Tyrrhenian islands, and Rome got control of Greek cities in southern Italy. The balance of power was becoming unbalanced, and so was everybody else, including the Mamertine mercenaries at Messana (modern Messina). These Samnite thugs called Mamertines had occupied Messana by force but cowered before the tyrant of Syracuse, Hieron II. Some of the Mamertines appealed to Carthage for help and some to Rome. Rome had scruples. The Mammertines were not nice people. The Senate could not decide whether the advantages of aiding them outweighed the disadvantages, namely, war with Carthage. The popular assembly was baleful. Deciding that the opportunity for looting Carthage outweighed all other considerations, it voted for a Mamertine bail-out.[36]

The First Punic War between Rome and Carthage turned out to be a twenty-two-year-long tennis match. The Carthaginians served first by organizing a Syracusan force at Messana. Rome returned the service by building a fleet and inventing grappling tackle to board enemy ships. They felt they could grapple with anything in their court. But their invasion of Africa under the consul Regulus faulted. A Spartan mercenary showed Carthage how to return the play (invasion) using elephants, where the Carthaginians had the advantage. Rome lost several fleets in storms. The Carthaginian general, Hamilcar Barca, blocked Roman conquest in western Sicily. Rome judged Carthage out of bounds. The set, however, went to Carthage. But in 242 BC Rome equipped a new fleet and cut off the Carthaginian garrisons in western Sicily. Carthage threw down the racquet, sued for peace, paid a huge indemnity to Rome, and lost her claim to Sicily. The match—and western Sicily—went to Rome. Carthage had courted disaster.

For twenty years after the war both Carthage and Rome violated the terms of peace. Rome seized Sardinia, which was Carthaginian, and also Corsica, and raised the indemnity. Hamilcar and his little boy, Hannibal (Grace of Baal) went to Spain in 237 BC. Soon Carthage gained control of southeastern Spain. Rome, allied with Massalia (Marseille) nervously arranged with Hannibal, now commander of troops, a frontier at the Ebro River (220 BC) to separate their spheres of influence. Rome broke the agreement by extending protection to Saguntum, which lay south of the Ebro. Hannibal captured Saguntum. The rest is history.

In the Second Punic or Hannibalic War (218–201 BC), Hannibal and the Roman generals Quintus Fabius (the Delayer) and Scipio (Africanus Major) made names for themselves, but top billing went to the thirty-seven armored elephants that Hannibal marched from Spain to Italy via the Rhône Valley. The crossing of the Rhône River, perhaps at Beaucaire-Tarascon, was made more difficult by the necessity of rafting the elephants to the other side without alarming them.[37] Hannibal, who is said to have "understood" his pachyderms, had the rafts covered with dirt so that they would think themselves on dry land![38] Hannibal understood not only elephants, but the importance of keeping up appearances.

The Carthaginian found the Cisalpine Gauls, recently defeated by Rome (225 BC), sympathetic, but south of a line drawn from Pisa to Ariminum (Rimini) not one community joined up against Rome.[39] At the river Trebia near modern Piacenza (218 BC), and at Lake Trasimene the next year Hannibal was brilliantly successful. Not so the elephants. Polybius wrote that all but one died after the battle of Trebia. Hannibal rode the last beast, a gift from the ruler of Egypt, across the Apennines.[40]

The Roman dictator, Quintus Fabius Maximus, adopted a scorched-earth policy, burning crops to deprive Hannibal of supplies, and avoiding giving battle. Hence his nickname "Cunctator" [Latin, Delayer]. He believed in paying attention to Hannibal from afar. Unfortunately, Rome itself suffered from his attention deficit disorder, and the Senate, finding it reprehensible that a general should refuse to fight, removed Fabius from his command.[41] The word for dilatory tactics like Fabius's is Fabian. The English, with their misplaced admiration for every aspect of Roman militarism, named a socialist group, the Fabian Society (1883), after the unfortunate general. This society was dedicated to spreading social reform, but very slowly. The Romans had a real sense of urgency where Hannibal was concerned. They were too enamored of glory (i.e., bloodshed) to applaud a general who wasted crops, but not men. Even Hannibal was glad to see Fabius go, more fearful of a man who watched him from hilltops and would not engage, than of the overly hasty plebeian consul Varro, whom the Carthaginian handily defeated at Cannae (216 BC).

Cannae was Hannibal's greatest triumph. Roman losses were severe. But though Hannibal's successes won him support in Campania and the far south, it was spotty and unenthusiastic, for Latium, central Italy, and the eastern seaboard (Picenum) remained loyal to Rome. The Italians opted for a familiar master (Rome) of similar culture rather than a self-styled liberator who flattered them in a foreign tongue.[42] When Scipio defeated Hannibal in North Africa (Zama, 201 BC), Hannibal's Italian allies burned their Phoenician grammar books. The age of Italy's Latin literature was just dawning.

The first two Punic Wars were *punishing* (the word derives from the Latin for Phoenicians, Poeni), for Rome as well as Carthage, but also helpful, though only to Rome. The first war helped Rome become a naval power.[43] After the second, Rome helped herself to preeminent authority over the whole Mediterranean basin, including Spain, Sicily, and North Africa in the west and the protectorate of Greece, Macedonia, and Syria in the east. Soon afterward she reduced Cisalpine Gaul to obedience for having sided with Hannibal. The first two Punic Wars helped Rome find herself. By the end of the third war (149–146 BC), she found herself supreme arbiter of Mediterranean destinies, successor to the successors of Alexander the Great.

Historians still argue why Rome became master of the entire Mediterranean basin. What, they ask, caused her insatiable expansionism? The question might not have had to be asked if ancient historians and men of affairs had asked it first, and in public places like the Senate. Most senators wanted traditional Roman institutions to stay intact. They were not consistently interested in expansion outside Italy. But the senators were unwilling to wrestle with temptations to power, profit, glory they did not know how to resist and, in any event, found irresistible. Rome, like most other states, found it less troublesome to go forward, and it was while going forward that they backed into imperialism. They had no sense of direction.

Professor Christ, considering that expansion, dismisses the idea that the Romans felt they were permanently under threat by their neighbors, hence expanded for security reasons.[44] He does not think security was Rome's only foreign and military objective, or that she put her own security above her neighbors.' Christ rejects Theodor Mommsen's view of "defensive imperialism" while admitting that Rome was "primarily interested in the smashing of power centers such as Carthage, Macedonia, and Syria."[45] Was smashing them defensive? Or pre-emptive? Certainly it was not done just for the enjoyment activity brings in the relief (as Cole Porter put it) of that "old ennui." [46]

Of course, the very idea of defensive action put Rome on the defensive. It led her to view as necessary to her defense the elimination of states not really threatening to her security, though perhaps to her pride. The Roman concept of virtue was not by coincidence formed from the Latin word for man (*vir*). *Virtus* meant manliness; manliness, power; power, war; war, expansion; expansion, control. The Republic in the second century was still a long way from the birth of Christianity which would eventually redefine the virtue of men, basing it on faith, hope, charity, chastity, and other angelic qualities. But whether before or after the establishment of Christianity at Rome, whenever empire was at stake, whether republican and pagan, imperial and pagan or imperial and Christian, the old concept of *virtus* was operative. The gods expected humans to defend Rome's borders. The gods had better things to do with their time.

Cicero, looking backward, insisted that Rome got involved in empire because she was such a great friend to her allies, a disingenuous assessment. Professor Christ rightly objects that there was no proportion between defending the Mamertines or Seguntum and annexing Sicily and Spain! One does not oblige one's friends by looting one's neighbors, or robbing Peter to pay Paul, even if you think Peter owes you money, too. No Roman shrank from the consequences of his actions whenever he thought his honor or *virtus* was impugned. Romans took things as they came—literally.

In the early second century, Rome controlled without formally annexing foreign states in whose interest—and her own—she intervened militarily. Thus, she refrained from annexing Philip V's kingdom of Macedonia after defeating him in the Second Macedonian War (200–197 BC). The Roman commander Flamininus declared Greece free in 196 BC. The catch was he did not really mean it. Rome was allergic to the consequences of her own liberality, for, after defeating Macedon in 197, she found herself itching for war with his successor Perseus and defeated him in the Third Macedonian War (171–167 BC). This time, Macedonia and her possessions were dealt out to four republics, a shuffle that ended with Rome picking up all the cards, and declaring (146 BC) that henceforth, Macedonia was a Roman province. For Greece it was a grand slam.

During this Third Macedonian War the Roman consul, L. Aemilius Paulus, so decisively defeated the Macedonians at Pydna (formerly Citron) that he soured them on the use of the phalanx. Polybius, an Arcadian cavalry officer and Romanophil, offered his services to the Romans in their own camp. Wrongly denounced by an Athenian politician as disloyal to the Roman cause, he was one of one thousand Achaean hostages taken to Italy for safekeeping—not theirs, but Rome's of Greece, by now a Roman protectorate. In Rome Polybius became a confidant of the consul Aemilius Paulus, a man so exceptionally honest that the only Greek treasure he reserved for himself was the Macedonian royal library of King Perseus and Polybius, whom he made his sons' tutor and his own. Years later, in 146 BC, Polybius accompanied one of these boys, Scipio Africanus, to Carthage, where he watched while his former pupil burned the civic center

(146 BC) before plowing salt into its wounds. And to think that Scipio had been very carefully educated in the humanities! Polybius was neither surprised nor vexed. He noted in his *Histories* that Romans always understood that expansion was a function of power, not poetry. Polybius admired leaders who kept their feet on the ground. Whose ground didn't matter. Polybius, a typical academic, was passive-aggressive.

GRACCHAN REFORM AND REVOLUTION

Ordinarily in history, revolution precedes reform. In Roman history between the defeat of Hannibal (201 BC) and the last tribunate of the Gracchi brothers (121 BC), reform preceded revolutions that produced more reform and more revolutions. The Gracchan reforms of Tiberius and Gaius Gracchus, though resulting in revolution, were only its superficial cause. The real cause of revolution in the second century BC was desperation. This in turn had many causes—depopulation of Rome's Italian allies during the Hannibalic war; agricultural decline hastened by farmers away on military duty; Rome's failure to extend full citizenship to Italy; governmental plunder of provinces; the impairment of morals that accompanies affluence; and the displacement of Italian labor by slaves. In these years, to the provinces of Sicily, Sardinia, Corsica, and Spain, Rome added Macedonia (148 BC), Africa (146 BC), the legacy of Pergamum, named "Asia" by the Roman Senate (129 BC), and southern Gaul (121BC).[47] These territories offered possibilities for relieving the economic and social desperation of Rome and Italy and even greater possibilities for corrupting the government.

Tiberius Gracchus, a young aristocrat, grandson on his mother's side of Scipio Africanus, offered Romans an exercise in patriotic pragmatism—a chance to do the right thing, but by controversial means. Elected tribune in December 134 BC, he hoped Romans would reduce the profits of the wealthy who, for nearly three hundred years, occupied the bulk of public lands at bargain rates. Wouldn't they like to strengthen the constitution by redistributing such lands on an equitable basis, including remuneration for improvements and perpetual ownership of reduced acreage? Couldn't they persuade themselves to observe neglected laws (the Licinian laws of 367 BC) limiting the amount of public land any one man could occupy to a few hundred acres? Wouldn't it be great, Tiberius asked his countrymen, if the shrinking number of Italy's free farmers might rent public acreage released in this way, feed their families, win voting rights, and serve in the military when needed? If not, there would soon be no Romans or Italians qualified to serve in the legions.

Historians debate whether Tiberius meant to reward just Romans or allies, too.[48] Slave workers on great landed estates had displaced free farmers in the countryside. Without a stake in Rome's prosperity, without ownership of soil, which alone qualified a farmer to bear arms for Rome and exercise his voting rights in his local assemblies, if not in Rome's, wouldn't the Roman constitution suffer? Tiberius's questions were provocative. They provoked many senators who feared a loss of clients, because Tiberius's agrarian law would have caused "a radical shift in voting patterns and thus in the balance of power."[49] When men had land they would cease to be clients and become claimants. Without their landless urban clients, the senators feared loss of electoral support. Worse, they feared their loss would be the land commissioners' gain. And the first commissioners were Tiberius, his brother Gaius, and his father-in-law, Ap. Claudius Pulcher. Tiberius's methods helped make reform suspect. He tried to establish constitutional justice, itself a novelty, by novel means. Patricians detested novelty, especially when it promised to benefit the poor. They viewed the whole program as a zero-sum game.[50]

Tiberius's widowed mother, Cornelia, was exceptional. She had educated him and his siblings progressively, that is, on the literature of democratic Athens. Cornelia was famous for saying that her sons, the light of her life, were her only jewels. These boys, members of Rome's glitterati, saw their light extinguished, victims of senatorial corruption. Romans were lucky. When two talented, rich, and charismatic brothers were assassinated or driven to suicide because of their reform program, the Romans *knew* who was responsible and what the beef was about. They were not cowed by anything like the Warren Commission's report that sealed the results of investigation of the murders until all then living had died. They did not accept the idea that one lone nut was responsible for murder and plots against the constitution because those involved (a number of senators) bragged about it. Romans were not unwilling to murder or martyr their best leaders. They just thought it unworthy of them to lie about it.

The Gracchi were accused of attempting to pervert the constitution, which in plain Latin meant undermining the Senate. Tiberius was accused of tyranny, namely, seeking to achieve extraconstitutional power by alliances with the unemployed of Rome, attempting to substitute people power for the Senate's. He took his land reform bill to the popular assembly first, an unusual, not an illegal act.[51] When a fellow tribune named M. Octavius vetoed his bill, Tiberius had him removed from office and replaced. This, as Professor Scullard points out, though not "formally illegal," changed the relationship of the tribunate to the people, making an office designed to protect the people into one subservient to them.[52] Michael Crawford says the removal of Octavius was reasonable "if one accepted the principle of popular sovereignty," supposedly the basis for the Roman Republic.[53] The problem was that the Senate had paid lip service to popular sovereignty but deferred to its own superiority. It took umbrage at the aggressive assertion of rights it had long since recognized—but only in theory. The civil rights thing. Tiberius surmised that he had better protect himself with the sacrosanct status of a second one-year term as tribune. His re-election (132 BC) was widely viewed in the Senate as illegal. The senators feared reform. The power thing.

When the Senate refused to subsidize the reform commission, Tiberius announced that he would use some of the king of Pergamum's legacy to Rome for the purpose, even though foreign affairs and finance were considered a senatorial, not a popular, prerogative.[54] His enemies called him a tyrant and demagogue. Those who benefited by the system define it as breaches of law and sovereignty, while those who never prospered from either regarded the makers of laws and the definers of sovereignty the real tyrants. Tiberius, without empirical justification, thought the Roman constitution could be transformed into an Athenian democracy. He forgot that Thucydides said that Athenian democracy came very close to being a government by its leading citizen—Pericles.[55] Pericles had been honored at Athens, but at Rome leading citizens like the Gracchi were branded as tyrants and demagogues. Rome's other Leading Citizens were called senators and patriots. In Athens they would have been called oligarchs. The rhetoric thing.

In the end, Tiberius's senatorial enemies, urged on by the Pontifex Maximus, P. Scipio Nasica, murdered him. They determined to save the constitution from subversion by the least constitutional means, clubs and stones. These distinguished critics dumped the bleeding bodies of the tribune and three hundred supporters into the Tiber. Buoyed by their good deeds on behalf of the Roman Republic, the conservative opposition watched as the bodies sank, forgetting that tribunes were supposed to be sacrosanct. Before another century passed, it would be the body of the Republic itself that would be sinking. The entropy thing.

Ten years later, Gaius Gracchus, also a tribune, challenged the Senate's control of finance, provincial administration, and the courts, urging civic equality for all Italians. For the first time (121 BC) the Senate sought refuge in the *senatus consultum ultimum,* a suspension of constitutional procedures enabling them to execute suspects untried in courts of law. The justice system is so often the first victim of legislators already on the defensive. Gaius's supporters were simply massacred. One tradition concerning Gaius's end is that rather than fall by his opponents' blows, he instructed his own slave to kill him. Another tradition has it that the consul Opimius responded to the Senate's order by arranging the murder of Gaius and his supporters. Gaius died before he could run for a third term. The Senate resented any reduction of their power, while the powerless, Rome's plebeians, opposed the admission of Italian allies to citizenship, the one thing that could have made them all more powerful. The Gracchi were martyred by overprivileged politicians and underprivileged plebeians united only by their mutual lack of foresight, insight, and hindsight. The vision thing.

SOCIAL AND CIVIL CHAOS IN THE POST-GRACCHAN AGE

Whenever domestic problems seemed intractable in the last century of the Republic, some foreign struggle, some invasion of an ally's state, some rebellious Roman magistrate or revolutionary freedom fighter, some social war with the Italian allies, some antisocial civil war at home, barbarian tribe, Hellenized monarch, slave or pirate band would antagonize Rome. This gave the Senate an opportunity to intervene, distracting attention from the problems at hand until those at a great distance could be solved by a military hero. After his triumph or victory parade at Rome he would propose an ill-thought out solution to the domestic crisis that, given his achievements, no one dared reject. In this way a succession of generals displaced the indecisive Senate. Men with vastly different political techniques—Sulla, Pompey, Caesar, Cato, Cicero—all thought of themselves as defenders of the homeland. So did the rash tribunate and the ignorant plebeian assembly.[56] It was not so much that the Republic's constitution was coming undone, but rather, that it was unintentionally done in by its defenders.

Occasionally, a foreign potentate blessed with sizeable (unearned) income but no heirs willed his kingdom to Rome. The money flowed in through the tax gatherers (*publicani*) and out to the generals who, by provisioning their troops, created a cash flow to contractors and to the Roman governor. King Attalus of Pergamum set the stage for royal bequests at the end of the second century BC; the ruler of Cyrene followed suit in 96 BC and that of Bithynia willed his kingdom to Rome a generation later. In 80 BC one of the Ptolemies willed all Egypt to Rome. Crassus wanted Julius Caesar to administer Egyptian finances. The annexation-of-Egypt scheme was killed by senators who feared that the wrong people (Equites, plebians) would profit politically at their expense.[57]

Not all kings were as willing as the above, and some, like the king of Cyprus, had to be relieved of his crown against his will. The most unwilling and willful was Mithradates VI Eupator of Pontus (120–63 BC) who began the first of his three wars against Rome (88–85 BC) by massacring Romans in Asia, a gesture toward freeing the Greeks in the area from Roman control. He was following a tradition of his ancestors who had sought to liberate Greeks from Greece. Liberating Greeks was something of a cottage industry in the ancient world. Persia, Macedonia, and Rome all took turns. Pontic potentates vied with Rome to liberate the Greeks, notoriously unable to liberate themselves. Professor Rawson thought it was no wonder that Roman statesmen began to feel themselves the "equals of Hellenistic kings" who were just oriental despots after all.[58] Yet the real object of great men in this declining Hellenistic era was power to the powerful, not empowerment of the powerless. Some of the latter, it is true, took steps to free themselves from dependence, with varying degrees of success. Client-age was the price cities, states, and individuals paid for such privileges as they were able to procure. But now it was Rome, not the Hellenistic monar-chies, that had become chief procurer of privilege and power. In whose interest would she pander?

MARIUS AND SULLA

The last Republican century was an age of generals whose reputations were burnished in Africa (Marius, Sulla), Spain (Pompey, Caesar), Gaul (Marius, Caesar), Asia (Sulla, Lucullus, Pompey), Syria (Crassus), and Palestine (Pom-pey), and tarnished by their enemies when they did not do it themselves. Far from Rome their careers were affected by the political problems they tem-porarily left behind—struggles between conservatives (Optimates), who viewed themselves as defenders of Rome's traditions and pragmatists (Popu-lares), who believed that the public interest could only be served by constitu-tional change. The names of these parties seem to be the most stable thing about them, for their membership and opinions shifted continually as politi-cians changed their tune and their partners.[59] Politicians in the late Republic transformed the misery of others into opportunities for themselves.

Gaius Marius (c. 157–86 BC) was the first general who achieved power independent of the Senate, setting a precedent for Sulla and after him, Pom-pey and J. Caesar.[60] Some think Marius was a plebeian,[61] others an Italian aristocrat.[62] Romans called him a "new man" whose power and prestige derived from his military successes, rather than vice versa. He is variously regarded as a man without a political program and a demagogue whose political program favored the have-nots.[63] His achievements were military. If he was interested in reform at all, it was military reform to strengthen and reward his army. He was a man of action, and that paid off handsomely, for he became one of Rome's richest citizens. The reward for the landless men he recruited was farmland. Critics have regarded this as revolutionary because they thought landless recruits bonded with the commander who paid them rather than the Senate, which expected enlisted men to pay—with their lives mostly, but should they survive, with their livelihood. Most veter-ans returned to farms deeply in debt. Such farms flooded the market, wind-ing up in the hands of Equites and aristocrats.

Professor Brunt questions the degree to which landless men (*capiti censi*) were more dependent upon their military superiors than those who owned a little property (*assidui*). He does not think that Marius's "reform" created a professional army of volunteers or altered "the rural provenance of most soldiers," and he minimizes the degree to which Marius's recruitment was revolutionary.[64] Perhaps the most revolutionary element was that Marius inspired poor boys with hopes for their future, not just Rome's, which they fought to assure. Such hope was deemed revolutionary by oligarchs and plutocrats, a potential threat to their own power and property.

Marius married Julius Caesar's aunt. The Julian connection helped Marius find himself socially. Later, the Marian connection supported Caesar, and Caesar Marian reforms.[65] These proved as popular in Caesar's time as in Gracchan ones. Although none of the Populares' leaders put all the reforms into effect, the whole program—including cheap or even free grain, a more representative jury system, full rights of Roman citizenship for all Italians, and the redistribution of public land—survived the players, and indeed, the play itself. Recent studies of the Roman Empire suggest that large landowners in the interest of political stability sought to curb expropriation of peasant owners. The imperial army continued to distribute land to discharged soldiers.[66] It was the forerunner of our GI Bill.

Marius rose from army ranks to consul (108 BC), an office he held seven times. He got the popular assembly instead of the Senate to award him command of the war against Jugurtha in Africa (109–106 BC). In the Jugurthine War Marius upstaged his former commander, Metellus, but was upstaged in turn by his own cavalry officer, Sulla, when Jugurtha surrendered to the younger man. Jugurtha was dragged in chains at Marius's Roman triumph, but when Sulla became dictator (82–80 BC), he stamped the African leader on his coinage in the act of surrendering, and Marius's role in Africa was ignored. Dictators stamp out what they do not value historically and stamp in what they do. Both Marius and Sulla were men of that stamp.

They had this in common: they allied themselves by marriage to potentially useful great families. Marius married into the Julian clan, Sulla allied himself with the Metelli, and his daughter to a son of his friend and fellow consul, Q. Pompeius Rufus. Sulla's son-in-law came to be known as Pompey the Great. After Marius defeated the Cimbri and Teutones (102–101 BC), he won his sixth consulship using the excellent campaign services that the tribune Saturninus and a praetor named Glaucia rendered him. When these two resorted to violence on behalf of their plebeian supporters, the Senate organized a lynch mob against Marius's campaign managers. Marius tried to protect them when they sought refuge in the Senate building but failed to prevent their murder by the mob that was pelting them with roof tiles torn from the Senate building. Their murder tarnished Marius's image. How could he defend the dispossessed when he could not even defend his own staff? Disgraced, he disappeared into Asia for a decade, hoping to goad Mithradates into invading Asia and then reap the glory that his defeat would bring to Rome.

Marius returned to Italy in time for the Social War (90–88 BC).[67] The celebrated Roman historian Mommsen called this Italy's "most fearful civil war," perhaps because he had not served in any of the others. It was fought largely in central Italy against the still disenfranchised Italian allies. Marius, already in his sixty-fifth year, defeated the rebellious Marsi at Asculum (modern Ascoli), cooperating with Sulla for the last time. Shortly thereafter Sulla besieged Pompeii and Stabiae, defeated the Hirpini and finished off Samnite resistance at Bovianum, victories which made him once again as Keaveney noted, "the People's darling."[68] Shortly afterward, Sulla was unanimously elected consul.

Marius had found momentary acceptance for his service against the Italian allies, who, once defeated, were "rewarded" with Roman citizenship but denied its fruits by a form of gerrymandering that made their votes insignificant. The young and progressive tribune, Sulpicius Rufus, proposed to give them more clout by redistributing their votes evenly throughout the voting districts (tribes). Sulpicius had once hoped to enlist Sulla as a supporter of Italian rights.[69] Now he joined forces with Marius and declared that Sulla, already appointed by the Senate as commander of the war against Mithradates, was relieved of his command. Sulpicius gave it to Marius instead.

The news reached Sulla at Nola, in Campania. What followed was momentous in Roman history. Sulla, supported by nothing more than his army, marched on Rome to lay down the law to tyrants (Marius, Sulpicius) and to the Senate as well! It was an unprecedented event. Sulla, unsolicited by any authority whatsoever, claimed the right to save Rome by force from tyrants, pausing only to consult the entrails of a sacrificed bird (not a chicken presumably) and to catch a good night's sleep. In a dream Sulla received a communiqué from the fierce goddess of war, Ma Bellona, predicting the elimination of all his enemies.[70] The first man to march on Rome was a religious fanatic who consulted priestesses and augurs, with all that entrailed. No baloney.

The Social War over, civil war followed. Sulla won, Rome lost. Marius came in a poor third, for in Rome he had only townsmen and slaves to oppose Sulla's six legions. Marius promised to free any slaves who fought for him, but there were few takers. Sulla justified his illegal putsch by claiming that as a consul, he and his fellow consul, Pompeius Rufus, acted to restore the consulate. Small consolation. Marius fled to Africa, one of ten enemies Sulla proscribed as outlaws. When the tribune Sulpicius was found hiding in a swamp near Rome, his own slave turned him in to Sulla. Sulla freed the slave as a reward, then had him flung from the Tarpeian rock for betraying his master. As he was falling it occurred to the fellow that Sulla, too, had a master whom he had betrayed: the Roman people. It would have made a perfect put-down.

Sulla left Rome for Greece where Mithradates had set up his headquarters in Athens after overunning the Roman province of Asia. He resented Rome encouraging his neighbor, King Nicomedes III of Bithynia, to invade Pontic territory. In 88 BC Mithradates declared war. Mithradates was one of the pin-up boys of ancient historians, another Great. Rejected by his mother, who connived at his assassination, he fled to the mountains at the age of eleven and became a hunter. Returned to his capital (Sinope) in 111 BC, he gained a reputation for military prowess, strength, height, alcoholic consumption, cruelty, and appetite. He was very intelligent. He mastered twenty-two for-eign languages and practiced magic. He assembled a brain trust of Greek scholars (a must after Alexander the Great) giving prizes to the greatest poets and biggest eaters. Distrustful of everyone not a poet or a glutton, he mur-dered his mother, his sons, the sister he married, and at the end (63 BC), his harem, but only to keep the girls from falling into enemy hands.

Sulla was in Greece during the first Mithradatic War (88–84 BC), while Marius seized Rome (87 BC), and together with the consul Cinna, slaugh-tered Sulla's supporters. Though most of the senators fought on Sulla's side after his return from Asia, few had favored his first march on Rome, which they saw as a military coup.[71] Some of those felled by Marius and Cinna had opposed Sulla's candidates for consul in 87 BC and voted for Cinna. Marius died the next year of natural causes. Sulla made a generous peace with Mithradates, leaving him king in Pontus but shorn of his conquests and his fleet. Then Sulla sailed west (83 BC) to Brundisium (modern Brin-disi), determined to settle up with the Marian party in Rome. When mod-ern Italians drink to someone's health their toast is called a *brindisi*. The civil war that followed began with Cinna's murder at Brundisium. For Cinna, the future site of Brindisi proved unhealthful. He was soon toast.

How Sulla won the confidence of the Italians—he promised to recognize the rights the Marian party had guaranteed them—and how he charmed many old enemies into supporting his rise to power proves what a grand old campaigner he really was.[72] Carbo, his opposition consul, thought Sulla combined the attributes of a fox with those of a lion, and Carbo was right on the money. Foxy was Sulla's enlargement of the Roman Senate, sole determiner of Roman justice, legislation, and policy, even if this meant, as it did, that the constitution would have to be largely rewritten. Foxy was his abolition of the old corn dole to reduce the numbers of unruly Romans and thus reduce support for ambitious tribunes, now deprived of the right to run for other offices. Foxy was his creation of the Cornelii, his own per-sonal bodyguard of ten thousand freed slaves formerly the property of rich Marian supporters. Equally sly was settling his veterans in areas of Italy most critical of his old anti-Italian policies. But absolutely leonine was the way Sulla eliminated his political opponents—first by proscribing or posting lists of his enemies, at least seventeen hundred of them—putting a price on their heads to encourage their murders, updating the lists of victims until even his friends began to wonder who might be next?

Sulla had sixteen hundred Equites and seventy senators killed.[73] These acts of Sulla's were not characteristic, for Sulla had often displayed patience and tolerance toward enemies while the outcome of war was doubtful. But Sulla encouraged "scenes of ghoulish savagery." Romans tore the proscribed to pieces and decorated the city with their heads. All this happened because of Sulla's resentment over the treatment his family and friends had received from his political enemies while he was defeating Rome's enemies in Asia and in Athens.[74] Rome's overseas avenger turned vengeful. Nor would the dictator permit even the sons or grandsons of the proscribed to be eligible for public office. Not that they could have afforded a run for office, for a proscribed man's property was auctioned off for a fraction of its value. Sometimes Sulla himself played the auctioneer. Going, going, gone! Sulla banged the gavel down on the proscribed, their property, their posterity. Touchy, touchy.

Sulla was a theater buff whose most intimate friends were actors, an affinity that won him little praise from the senators he wooed but kept from center stage. At best he treated the *patres* (senators) as supporting cast, never leading men. His reforms were scripted for their better performance. Scullard says he may never have been their "fervent champion."[75] He defied the Senate and manipulated its membership by appointing 450 new members whom he, the dictator, preferred to direct. Dictator was Sulla's favorite role (82–80 BC). He played it until he took his last bow, or was forced out of the limelight. Even his son-in-law, young Pompey, withdrew from him toward the end, sensing, no doubt, his father-in-law's growing unpopularity among the Senate body.

Sulla passed the remainder of his life at his country estate in Puteoli, where he amused himself with his trophy wife and his cronies, alternating debauchery with fishing and writing his memoirs. He had always regarded himself as fortunate and beloved by the gods, by Aphrodite especially. Hence his Roman nickname, Felix, happy, and his Greek one, Epaphrodite, beloved of Aphrodite. When he died (78 BC), like Marius of natural causes and in his own bed, they gave him an elaborate funeral. Although Sulla had outlawed such lavish displays of wealth, in death as in life, he ignored the rigorous reforms he forced on others, hoping to restore Rome to a sobriety and restraint that few really wanted or were capable of, least of all, Sulla.[76]

THE FALL OF THE REPUBLIC:
TRIUMPHS, TRIBULATIONS, TRIUMVIRATES

It is harder to explain why governments fail than how they falter. Faltering is a gradual process and so ambiguous that what seems unfortunate to some appears promising to others. In short, faltering is the political process itself, with its triumphs and tribulations for first one party or faction and then for another. When all falter by turns, it is difficult to see that the process as a whole may be failing, for the nonfaltering faction is sure that they have mastered a process that will never master them. By contrast, the collapse of government develops rapidly, is neither ambiguous nor controversial, and devastates all factions so universally that men all despair of mastering anything for very long, and all locate failure either in *post hoc propter hoc,* or in their own pet peeve. *Post hoc propter hoc* [Lat., after this because of this] is a logical fallacy whereby even thoughtful men and well-intentioned people like Cicero failed to locate the real cause of a bad result, the real reasons why the Roman Republic was failing.

After the Social War, people looked to prosperity to alleviate social suffering in Rome and the provinces. The elusory delusory trickle-down. When Sulla's reforms proved unsupportable, Caesar, Pompey, and others eliminated them but continued to enjoy the old entitlements. For the poor, entitlements meant the grain dole and poverty; for the rich, power and privilege. For everyone the bounties of the goddess Fortuna were the Roman equivalent of the lottery. She made gambling godly, and the Romans bet heavily on her rather than make the kind of constitutional adjustments that would have required political unity. The wealthy classes had clients they served and who served them. Every influential man in Rome sought the support of like-minded others. The goddess helped those who helped themselves and others. To whatever.

Stoics like Marcus Tullius Cicero (106–43 BC) thought actions to help the Republic prosper should take precedence over private motivation or party loyalty.[77] In those days political parties did not elect officials or sponsor legislation. Neither major party was organized to discipline anyone.[78] The only discipline Romans regularly accepted was military discipline. Their greatest heroes were men who condemned their own sons to death for breaching it. Politicians shifted their allegiance from issue to issue, and breaches of *amicitia* or political alliance were ordinary. Adept at divorcing themselves from purely political connections, the nobility divorced their wives for the same reasons. No one condemned the politician who breached the marriage contract. They thought him a smart politician. The Romans of the later Republic were into military discipline, not political nor self discipline.

Pompey (106–48 BC), protégé and son-in-law of Sulla, brought his own three legions into the Social War and was awarded a triumph before he held any office at all.[79] He suppressed a Marian revolt in Spain (72 BC) and helped crush that of the slave Spartacus (73–71 BC). Elected consul (71 BC) Pompey's associates began to suspect him of demagoguery. With Crassus as his fellow consul, these two addressed themselves to popular causes,

Crassus by spreading around his vast wealth, Pompey by dismantling Sulla's laws that had reduced the powers of the tribunate. Sent to drive pirates from the Mediterranean in 67 BC, Pompey was given absolute control of the fleet and army in the East and proconsular authority over Asia as far as Armenia. His accomplishments in Asia included the final defeat of Mithridates, Rome's major enemy for thirty years, of the Armenian king, Tigranes, and of the Syrian monarch, Antiochus. A royal flush.

It was Pompey who stormed Jerusalem, rendering the Jewish state a Roman protectorate (63 BC); Pompey who added three new provinces to Rome, and whose triumphal parade gave plebeian admirers visual evidence of the vast wealth his conquests entailed.[80] Breaking with tradition he exhibited his 324 captives or hostages: a pride of princes, including several sons of Mithradates; a quantum of queens; a gaggle of generals; and at least one monarch—Aristobulus, king of the Jews. These dignitaries were unbound and in gorgeous costumes.[81] The pomp of circumstance. Pompey displayed the weapons and war chariots of fallen kings and, for the ladies, piles of looted furniture, jewelry, antiques, and art work. The circumstances of pomp. And of Pompey.

To his surprise, he became an object of suspicion. The Senate refused to assign land to his veterans or ratify his Asian conquests, treating him as a would-be dictator. This was irritating since Pompey had disbanded his troops after his return home, unlike Sulla, who had not. Pompey needed the affection of his fellow aristocrats and their acceptance. He wanted Cato, grandson of the second-century censor, to arrange a marriage for him and his son with two of Cato's nieces. Though the girls were eager, Cato was not. Rejection led Pompey to join forces with Julius Caesar and Crassus in what later was called the First Triumvirate.[82] If Pompey had got the support he deserved from the upper classes, Caesar might never have been in a position to merit the support he got from the masses.

Six years Pompey's junior, Caesar (100–44 BC) was from a respected family but not as rich nor, until he reached the fullness of maturity, as distinguished. His Aunt Julia's marriage made him an early supporter of the popular party, as his own marriage with Cinna's daughter, Cornelia (83 BC), made clear. He refused to divorce her to satisfy Sulla. He could have lost more than his priesthood of Jupiter and his patrimony, which Sulla confiscated, for he had been proscribed. But relatives and the vestal virgins pleaded with Sulla to relent—with positive results.

Caesar's sex life was torrid. Barely out of his teens, he served Rome at the court of King Nicomedes IV of Bithynia, and some Roman businessmen who stopped off to dine there thought he served Nicomedes' lust as well. Gossips like Cicero said Caesar had lost his virginity to a king. No one can be sure whether Caesar's fondness for Nicomedes was exotic, erotic, or both. It was not uncommon for young Roman nobles to go to bed with men as well as women, but the fact that he was taunted about the episode for the rest of his life seems to indicate that the Romans were either less tolerant than the Greeks about gay sex—or more hypocritical.[83]

After Cornelia's death, Caesar married Pompeia, Sulla's granddaughter (67 BC), but divorced her after Publius Clodius Pulcher handed him the perfect excuse.[84] Clodius, an aristocratic radical, was for a time very close to Caesar and hoped to get even closer to his wife. The ladies had gathered at Caesar's house (61 BC) to celebrate the rites of the good goddess, Bona Dea, rites forbidden to men. Disguised as a woman, Clodius entered the house, perhaps to seduce Pompeia. Caesar was then Pontifex Maximus, that is, chief priest of Rome and custodian of religious law. Politically somewhat radical, Caesar's appreciation of the utility of religion was as conservative as that of most aristocrats. He never referred in writing to his religious offices but gave thanks for the credulity of the masses, who accepted from the gods what they would have rejected from the nobility.[85] A reformer of religion, he was not a religious reformer.[86] His *Lex Julia De Sacerdotiis* (47 BC) merely increased the numbers of priestly appointments he could make. Patronage, not piety, was his object. After Clodius was tried for sacrilege and exonerated, Caesar divorced Pompeia. Asked why without first having prosecuted Clodius, Caesar said only that his wife had to be above suspicion. One wonders why? Practically no one else in Rome was.

When Caesar divorced Pompeia he was not yet a great man, but he was an educated one. He had been tutored in Greek literature by a Cisalpine Gaul who may have interested him in the region and its people. Before he was twenty-five, he prosecuted two extortionate governors (77–76 BC) to publicize the corruption of senatorial administration of the provinces and to publicize Caesar. He sailed to Rhodes where he studied rhetoric with Cicero's teacher, Molon (75 BC). He was captured by pirates and held for a ransom that he berated as too low. He vowed to return someday and crucify his captors. Who knows if they even understood him, let alone believed him? When the ransom arrived, the pirates released him as promised. And, as promised, Caesar returned and crucified the lot, but mercifully had their throats cut first so that they should not be unduly inconvenienced by the traditional punishment for men of their profession.[87]

War broke out in the nearby province of Asia. Caesar enlisted as a volunteer. In Rome again, he found he had inherited a place in the pontifical college from a deceased uncle. He was not trained in theology, for the Romans, like the British who imitated them later, believed in a classical education, with on-the-job-training for prospective administrators. By 69 BC Caesar was a quaestor, serving under the governor of hither Spain. Suetonius says he promoted a revolution among the Transpadanes on his way back to Rome, for they had not been given full political rights under Sulla. Caesar was not the first graduate student to involve himself in protest movements.

Once more in Rome, Caesar supported Pompey and Crassus and enjoyed the usual carousals of young aristocrats. Between parties he sought to strengthen his own party, the Populares, discredited since Sulla's death. Speaking at his aunt's funeral, he displayed the bust of uncle Marius (68 BC), banned by Sulla. Plutarch relates that some mourners disapproved—his family included more Optimates than Populares—but the people clapped in favor, glad to see honor done a man (Marius) whose memory had been expunged.[88] He got himself appointed to a commission examining the murders committed by Sulla's henchmen and saw at least one murderer tried by the popular assembly. As a *curule aedile,* Caesar was in charge of public works, games, police, and the grain supply, privileged to sit on a *curulis,* or camp stool. He restored Marius's trophies on the Capitol. The public thought him capital and camp, which helped win him the election for Pontifex Maximus [Chief Priest](63 BC). He had not been idle.

While Pompey was in the East a few aristocrats in Caesar's party plotted to murder the consuls (65 BC) and seize the government. The chief plotter was Catiline, a man with a grudge. He had been unfairly accused of misconduct in office, and although the charges were proved false, Catiline began to make misconduct his only conduct, demagoguery that Cicero and other conservatives feared. Catiline's mistress testified against him, and Cicero used her testimony. Although Catiline fled Rome, some Gallic ambassadors whom he had approached for aid gave written evidence against him. Cicero arraigned the co-conspirators in the Senate, successfully urging their execution. Caesar's unsuccessful appeal for life imprisonment instead has been taken as evidence that he was sympathetic to the defendants and slated for an important office—Master of the Horse—in a government that would have been headed by Crassus as dictator. Caesar may have considered riding Catiline's hobby horse, but if so, changed horses in midstream, condemning the conspiracy with the rest (63 BC). He was too smart to be caught horsing around with traitors.

Caesar, now a praetor (62 BC) or judiciary official just under consul in rank, supported Pompey's requests for land on which to settle his veterans. Pompey was remembered as Sulla's "teenage butcher" from his youthful service in Sicily and Africa. He had offended many aristocrats with more seniority than he in Spain and Italy. He had also put Crassus in the shade during the Spartacus revolt. Cicero's opinion of Pompey was subject to fluctuations, though Cicero viewed himself as a harmonizer of class interests, even a hero of harmony, who could get Optimates and Populares to cooperate, keeping revolution at bay.[89] Cicero felt his defense of the Republic during Catiline's conspiracy on a par with Pompey's conquests in the East. He said as much to Pompey, who resented Cicero's pomposity.

Caesar spent two years in Spain as propraetor displaying great administrative and military talents. Sweeping up the Atlantic coast from Cadiz to Corunna, he added Lusitania (Portugal) to Rome. Enriched by conquests, he enriched his veterans, who hailed him as Imperator (commander). In Rome again (60 BC) he won a consulship and forged a coalition between himself, Crassus, and Pompey, the first Triumvirate. Contemporaries portrayed them as a three-headed monster and as thugs. Cicero, perhaps with Caesar's maritime exploits in mind, said that at last Caesar had the wind behind him. He needed it. He was sailing into history. Showtime.

Caesar refused to let his fellow consul, Bibulus, obstruct his settling of Pompey's veterans on public lands southeast of Rome. Caesar's methods were judicious, even conciliatory, but the conservatives opposed redistributing land even with market value reimbursements to prior owners.[90] Cato filibustered in the Senate. Caesar had him imprisoned.[91] Bibulus refused to convene the Senate and wrote broadsheets describing Caesar as Pompey's "Queen," raking up the old Nicomedes stories. Caesar moved his land bill to the tribunal assembly. Bibulus shut himself up in his own house and watched the skies for streaks of lightning—bad omens—that meant the gods disapproved of the proposed land bill. Lightning struck, but it was Bibulus who was stricken. Caesar's bill passed. Twenty thousand of Pompey's veterans and Caesar's clients were settled on Campanian soil.[92] Veterans' benefits.

The people were happy, but the business community had a grievance. They had overpaid to obtain a state contract for collecting taxes. Crassus wanted a rebate on his Asian contract. In fact, the Senate had taken advantage of them as it had of Pompey. And Caesar, who expected a province for his service as consul (59 BC) had been awarded a paltry directorship of roads and forests. Caesar outfaced Senate opposition and got Crassus a 30 percent discount on the Asia contract. Crassus, whose name in Latin meant gross, dense, grossed huge profits as a result. The Senate was reduced to passing measures as the Triumvirate required.

In the midst of Caesar's consulship he married off his seventeen-year-old daughter Julia to Pompey, thirty years her senior, a happy marriage for all three parties, Caesar, Julia, and Pompey. Pompey took his bride on seaside holidays and cooperated with Caesar as long as she lived. Caesar got Pompey's eastern achievements ratified by the Senate with no opposition.[93] A wedding present. Then Caesar married Calpurnia, L. Calpurnius Piso's daughter, getting Piso elected as one of the two consuls for 58 BC. Caesar gave a niece in marriage to Cato's father-in-law, depriving Cato of some political support. Marriage proved the weapon of choice for intimidating the Senate. It was just one of those things, right behind bribery, physical force, and intimidation.[94]

Caesar, who had a lot of gall, soon got a lot of Gaul, in fact, all of it, receiving command of Cisalpine and Transalpine Gaul as well as Illyricum

(59 BC). He is credited by historians with sensing the importance of the West in Western civilization, but it did not require a whole lot to realize that there was more fame to be got from Gaul than the forestry job he had first been offered. As Caesar aged he worried about his receding hairline and liked to appear at public functions with wreaths of leaves on his head to hide it. His hair-raising military exploits against the long-haired Gauls might been rooted in his inability to raise hair, an obsession that rendered him especially cruel to the hirsute. Historians have not spent much time combing the evidence, but it includes the Freudian slip made when he began his *Gallic Commentaries* with the words "All Gaul is divided into three *parts,*" which some critics regard a hair-brained beginning, but others think hairmeneutically inspired.

In Caesar's absence Cicero had been exiled for having had Catiline's co-conspirators executed without trial. Cato had been sent off on an unpleasant mission to dispossess the king of Cyprus. These affairs were more the concerns of Clodius and Crassus than of Caesar, but he let his colleagues revenge themselves on those who troubled them, while he, Caesar, set out to discipline disobedient Celtic and German tribesmen. Between 59 and 49 BC, Caesar overcame the Helvetii, who gave their name to Roman Switzerland (Helvetia); the German leader of the Suebi, Ariovistus, a false "friend" of Rome in the area now called Swabia; the Belgae, inhabitants of modern Belgium; the Nervii, who got on Caesar's nerves and obliged him to expose himself (militarily); the Aduatuci (near Namur), whom he sold into slavery for treachery and inadequacy; the Parisii; the Treveri (near Trèves); the Eburones, who cut down a Roman legion commanded by Cicero's brother; and the leader of the Senones, a traitor he had flogged to death.

Some say Caesar's greatest achievement was his victory over Vercingetorix, young leader of the Celtic Arverni, whose name lives on in the French province of Auvergne. Professor Scullard thinks Caesar's greatest achievement was strengthening the Rhine as a boundary against Germanic invasion of Gaul, thereby enabling a Latin civilization—France—to withstand the Germanic flood that, centuries later, felled the rest of the Roman Empire.[95] Vercingetorix was hardly thinking about the best way to preserve Latin culture when he rallied other Celtic tribes to resist Roman rule. Like the young Caesar, he was a protester. He would have been a patriot, too, except for the fact that the Celts were still tribal folk and had no nation as yet to defend. Vercingetorix lost to Caesar at Alesia near Dijon. Even young people can't always cut the mustard. Caesar took him back to Rome where he eventually celebrated his triumph (45 BC) after which the prisoner was killed. A Paris Metro stop, Alesia, commemorates the defeat of France's first resistance leader. Few tourists could have pronounced Vercingetorix anyway.

THE CIVIL WAR

Many historians find Caesar and Pompey were on a collision course, that their achievements and pride could brook no equal, let alone a superior. Others say that the Republican constitution was inadequate for governing an empire, as opposed to just milking it. Some say, as Cato the Elder did in the second century BC and Cato the Younger throughout the first Triumvirate, that the Senate had lost its ancestral virtue. Both Catos idealized a past they imagined more virtuous and hung it like a millstone around necks unable to bear the burden of honorable action, however much they coveted its rewards. Professor Gruen rejects the notion that the Republic could not have survived increased violence, selfishness, and loss of community. He finds the late Republic functioned pretty much as always.[96] Its institutions did not fail. Caesar and Pompey did not subvert them.[97] A British classicist, Warde Fowler, wrote in the early twentieth century when the British empire was thriving that Western civilization owed its very existence to Pompey and Caesar[98] and congratulated Caesar, like Oliver Cromwell later, for recognizing that an enfeebled state had "passed into the hands of the army."[99] Such sentiments sound sinister now to democratic ears. Still, they remain popular with many strongmen throughout the world including Africa and the Near East, places where Pompey and Caesar once exercised the same kinds of power. But, where Fowler nearly a century ago saw a bad Republic saved by good men with strong armies, Gruen in 1975 saw a still serviceable Republic done in by the conscientious adherence of all Rome's political and military leaders, including Pompey and Caesar, to law, proprieties, and constitutionalism.[100] He attributes the Republic's collapse to excessive legalism and conservatism on the part of men who regarded themselves its mainstay.

Caesar triggered the civil war that ended the Republic when he crossed the Rubicon against the Senate's will, saying "Alea iacta est" [*The die is cast*]. It was not the last of his good one-liners. Caesar gambled on his ability to win the jackpot—Rome. He counted on aligning the plutocratic Equites with the masses—and on the legions they could field en route. His ideas had once been shared by Pompey, but ultimately Cicero and Cato convinced Pompey to try for a new alignment—the union of the Equites with the Optimates against the masses. The civil war was a social struggle between the classes and the masses.

The Rubicon, a little stream separating Cisalpine Gaul from the rest of Italy, ended in the Adriatic. It proved a stream of consciousness for Roman politicians attached to customs preserved from early Republican times: arrogance, elitism, jealousy, factionalism (networking), and unreflective conservatism. The Republic waited now upon the egotistical impulses of prima donna generals who mistook themselves for the state. Caesar told his troops, who agreed with him, that his rights and dignity were challenged by his enemies including Pompey, with whom he had nurtured a very good relationship. Pompey did not cross his own Rubicon—that is, did not make up his mind to fight Caesar—until shortly before Caesar crossed his. Each felt it impossible to protect the constitution if his own dignity and authority (*dignitas, auctoritas*) was compromised, but they need not have worried.[101] The Republic had ceased to matter. Civil war happened because private interests superseded any thought for public ones.

Two months after Caesar's arrival in Italy he was its master. The Senate fled Rome, and he was made dictator until elections could be held. Pompey fled to Greece, and Caesar went west to defeat Pompey's supporters. He said "I go to Spain to defeat an army without a general, and thence to the East to fight a general without an army." It was epigrammatic, but wrong. Pompey raised a large army in Greece, and Caesar lost the first battle at Dyrrhachium (48 BC). It was Pompey's last hurrah. In Thessaly, at Pharsalus, Caesar turned the tables. Pompey deserted his party, fled to Egypt, and was murdered by the tribune Septimius while Ptolemy looked on. When Caesar arrived shortly afterward, they showed him Pompey's severed head. Caesar ordered the murderer put to death, a law-and-order touch that Pompey would have appreciated.

At the end of their careers Caesar was a de facto monarch,[102] Pompey a cipher whom many suspected would also play the king.[103] Of all things contrary to Roman propriety, none were more so than monarchy, which made a Senate redundant, and subterfuge, for Romans admired candor, though only Caesar and Cato displayed any. Caesar wanted unlimited power for himself to effect societal changes. Cato wanted unlimited power for his faction to prevent them. Their armies clashed in North Africa at Thapsus (46 BC) and Caesar won, after which Cato stabbed himself, hastening death by pulling out his own intestines. Caesar, ever gallant to his foes, lamented that he arrived too late to pardon Cato, but pardoned his son anyway. A tolerant gesture. Cato's gesture was more symbolic: civil wars are naturally intestine. Cato has been revered by aristocrats down through the ages for his defense of an indefensible constitution that favored the few. Caesar has been attacked in the same period for his assault on it. George Washington was held accountable for the same offense—but only by Tories. Unlike Washington, Caesar has not been regarded as the father of his country. It was left to his grandnephew Octavian (Augustus) to claim paternity.

Until his murder on March 15, 44 BC, Caesar had a very full plate. For one thing, he found Cleopatra on it, though his nine-month dalliance in Egypt produced no child, and there is no agreement as to who fathered the boy named Caesarion, born to Cleopatra after Caesar's assassination.[104] Caesar was obliged to eradicate his enemies in Asia Minor (where he came, saw, and conquered), in Spain, and North Africa.[105] In the five years that remained after his entry into Italy, Caesar attempted more reforms than the Republic had ever undertaken, except perhaps during Sulla's dictatorship. He rewarded his own veterans and the poor with land and reduced the number of slaves on great estates to encourage the growth of jobs for free labor. He spent money on construction in Rome to create urban jobs and then reduced the numbers of people eligible for the dole of grain. When the domestic economy could not support all the unemployed, he sent colonists to Carthage, Greece, Spain, and France. He curbed financial profiteering in the provinces, raised port fees to encourage industry, lowered interest rates, and established laws for bankruptcy. He stabilized currency by basing it on the golden *aureus,* which bore his image; had a census taken in Italy; broadened the franchise; restored religious cults; and granted the Jews of Rome special privileges that protected theirs. He hired an Alexandrian Greek to devise the "Julian calendar" of 365 days, replete with three new months, a leap year every fourth year, and a month renamed July in his honor. We still use this calendar with some improvements made during the sixteenth century by Pope Gregory XIII, introduced into Britain only in 1752. Caesar hoped to establish public libraries, drain Rome's malarial swamps, control flooding on the Tiber by building dikes, improve the harbor at Ostia, and build a road across central Italy and a canal at Corinth. He envisioned a rational, progressive, less elitist empire where native populations would enjoy Latin rights and Italians everywhere be granted full Roman ones. His was a very new deal, and like the New Deal of FDR, it dismayed his opponents because so many humble people stood to benefit.

On the Ides of March, 44 BC, Caesar went off to the Senate. Calpurnia, his then current wife, begged him not to, having heard of plots to kill him. En route to the meeting place he chanced upon the same astrologer and mathematician who had once before warned him to beware the Ides of March. Caesar called out cheerily that the Ides had come and the learned fellow dourly remarked that they had not yet passed. At the Senate he offered up the usual pre-session sacrifice to the gods, not knowing that he was himself about to be sacrificed. An unknown person thrust a tablet into his hands warning him not to go inside. He took it, but did not read it. Inside the hall were at least sixty conspirators, many were Caesar's friends, some enemies whom he had pardoned and promoted. The last included the ostensible leader of the plot, M. Junius Brutus, a Pompey supporter whom Caesar made governor of Cisalpine Gaul after Pharsalus, now a praetor. His ancestor was the Brutus who killed the last Tarquin. This Brutus may have been Caesar's own bastard child by Servilia, a longtime mistress. The man was given to Stoical philosophizing about virtue. Cicero dedicated treatises to him intended to give him the courage of his convictions. His wife, Porcia, suspected a plot and stabbed herself in the thigh to demonstrate her own courage. The real chief conspirator was C. Cassius Longinus, lean of mien, and like Brutus, a former Pompey supporter whom Caesar rewarded after Pharsalus by making him his first a legate and then *praetor peregrinus,* with the understanding that he would soon be made governor of Syria. Caesar seated himself, and the conspirators rushed him, daggers drawn. His last words—to Brutus—were "You too, my child?" Then he pulled his toga over his head and submitted to the blows. Whatever Caesar's ultimate ambition—and even now scholars cannot agree on this matter—one thing is undeniable. He was a terrible judge of character, perhaps because in the last decades of the Roman Republic there was so little of it.

10

Princeps and Principate 27 BC–AD 180

AUGUSTUS: WHO DO MEN SAY HE WAS?

CICERO FIRST HAILED CAESAR'S GRANDNEPHEW Octavian[1] as that "divine youth whom Providence had sent to save the State."[2] Thus Cicero unwittingly prepared Rome—and Octavian—for the Hebrew notion of a Messiah or Savior who would bring order, peace, and prosperity to a land torn by civil war and political corruption. Indeed, the parallels between Octavian, later called Augustus, and Jesus, later called Christ, a teenager at Augustus's death (AD 14), abound. Both were hailed by followers as marked from birth for dominion over men, as befit their divine parentage, and were referred to in their own lifetimes as "Father," also, Lord, princes of peace and bestowers of same on grateful, if dissimilar, kingdoms.[3] After Cicero, Augustus had the great fortune to have Virgil (70–19 BC) poeticize about the "birth of the child / Under whom the iron men of war shall disappear / And a golden peace . . . dawn upon the world" because Apollo, that is, Augustus, reigned.[4] Augustus exploited messianic themes about his birth in his autobiography, noting that his parents considered him " the son of Apollo." His father dreamed that the sun rose from his wife's womb. She fell asleep in the temple where she dreamed Apollo visited her in the form of a snake.[5] An astrologer predicted great things of baby Octavian—in Augustus's autobiography! It was a safe "prediction," since, when Augustus wrote it, he had already accomplished great things!

The unknown authors who wrote Matthew's and Luke's account of the birth of Jesus[6] were writing in the latter half of the first century AD after the crucifixion, at a time when Christians had not yet accomplished much. A few hundred had been martyred by Nero. Who could have suspected that Jesus, one of thousands of Rome's crucified felons, would ever amount to anything? The book of Matthew, not attributed to that saint until the second century, has eastern astrologers arriving in Jerusalem to ask "Where is the child who is born to be *king of the Jews?*"[7] But this phrase did not even exist when Jesus was born, an anachronism that did not occur to the author of this Gospel, whoever he was.[8] In Luke the astrologers have vanished, but the angel Gabriel tells Mary that she will bear a child named Jesus, that he will be great, and that his title will be "Son of the Most High," not king of the Jews.[9] Given the timelessness of angels, Gabriel did not worry about anachronism, nor had he ever read the Gospel of Matthew. He had to wing it.

Both Augustus and Jesus aroused devotion, but also suspicion and controversy. Both "saviors" dodged questions they preferred not to answer and referred to themselves as the son of a god or God.[10] Each was very concerned with his public image. Augustus's unfinished autobiography instructed everybody what he wanted them to think about him.[11] Jesus, like Socrates, wrote nothing but was avid for "reviews." He asked his disciples "Who do men say that I, the Son of Man, am?"[12] Did they notice that in asking the question, Jesus provided them with his own answer? Both Augustus and Jesus said that they came not to destroy the law, but to restore it. In his *Res Gestae* Augustus wrote: "By new laws, carried with me as sponsor, many model traditions of our ancestors that were falling out of use in our generation I restored and handed on as models of many things to be imitated by posterity."[13] Yet Augustus abolished many traditions of the senatorial class, and was, as Professor Syme portrayed him, a real revolutionary, even if he felt safer posing as a conservative. Jesus also promoted his conservative image. "Do not imagine that I have come to abolish the Law and the prophets; I did not come to abolish, but to fulfill. I tell you this: so long as heaven and earth endure, not a letter, not a stroke, will disappear from the Law until all that must happen has happened."[14] Law and order is as much the platform of revolutionaries as it is of resisters of change. Conservatives and liberals all rewrite law and reorder society to preserve it from harm. In his reform policy Augustus felt his way, while Jesus, in his, turned the other cheek, a posture more radical than that of Augustus.

The principate was Augustus's own production, a revitalized state that his adoptive father, Julius Caesar, only dreamed of making. Augustus named his successors—his nephew Marcellus, his friend and colleague Agrippa, his grandsons (Agrippa's sons by Augustus's only child, Julia). These young men all predeceased him by AD 2. A third grandson, Agrippa Postumus, the most loutish of Julia's sons, Augustus exiled to a small island. Tacitus said Postumus's murder, crisply supervised by C. Sallustias Crispus, was planned by Augustus two years before his own death.[15]

Although Augustus produced and directed the principate, Jesus did not produce or direct Christianity. He is portrayed in the Gospels as having regarded God as his director. St. Paul, who claimed an acquaintance with Jesus only after his death, has sometimes been regarded as the producer of a faith that Christ intended to preach only to Jews, not Gentiles. Christ and Augustus were superstars, hard acts to follow. Augustus was very concerned about his successor, but circumstances made his stepson, Tiberius, his final choice, because by then there was no other choice left. Jesus was similarly concerned about a successor. He is reported in the New Testament to have named Peter, whose name in Latin (*petra*) meant "the Rock," to carry on his ministry after his death.[16] This designation of Peter as the foundation (rock) on which the church was to rest, recipient of the keys to Heaven, is the justification Catholics eventually gave for papal primacy in the Roman church. After Peter's death, each pope succeeded to this position of authority—at least, that is what each pope maintained.[17] Only princes and prophets ever aspired to successors. Rich folks contented themselves with heirs; poor ones with survivors.

One of Augustus's trials was his family. He had an embarrassment of embarrassing relatives. When possible, he married them off to his followers. His sister Octavia produced five nephews and nieces and Julia produced five grandchildren. He used them all as pawns to further his political fortunes. He had divorced his first wife, Scribonia, Julia's mother, on the grounds of incompatibility. With his second wife, Livia, he got along well. He used her son, Tiberius, whom he at last adopted, as he used his own kinfolk, marrying him to Julia after the death of Agrippa. Julia was anciently regarded by Seneca (d. AD 65), Pliny the Elder (d. AD 79), Tacitus (d. c. AD 117), and Cassius Dio (d. AD 235?) a conspirator against her father's power, though the official charge against her was adultery and excessive immorality.[18] Romans had a high tolerance for immorality but balked when it was excessive. Modern historians think that Julia and her entourage—at least five men—were engaged in an in-house conflict to influence the succession and course of the principate.[19]

Poor Julia. Strictly reared, she was allowed no boyfriends. She was made to marry three of her father's protégés—the last Tiberius, who had dearly loved his first wife and yet had been obliged by Augustus to divorce and marry Julia after Agrippa's death. Augustus divorced the pair (against Tiberius's wishes) after Julia's disgrace, aided by the ironically titled *Lex Julia* or laws regulating marriage, the family, and adultery. Starved for love, Julia engaged in illicit amours, and died—from starvation and still unloved—an exile on a small barren island. Later, Augustus published her affairs before the Senate (2 BC). Still later, he persecuted Julia "the younger," who trod her mother's wayward footsteps. Augustus had executed this Julia's husband for conspiracy. As princeps Augustus converted adultery from a misdemeanor to a serious crime. Adultery, by the way, was all he converted. He could not convert adulterers. Augustus could not persuade Rome's nobility to marry earlier, divorce less, or reproduce at a higher rate. He revived what he believed were ancient Roman family values to restore moral fiber to the principate. These included worship of the gods, fertility, and military expansion. The flip side of these same virtues reads superstition, sex, and war. Thus translated, they look a lot like everybody's vices in every age.

Jesus never married, but his disciples did, a fact the Western church conveniently forgot when they decided, several centuries later, to forbid clergy to marry. Jesus attended wedding feasts, though, and even turned water to wine for a wedding at Cana.[20] Unlike Augustus, he did not make marriage and the family a big issue. Jesus felt that families get in the way of fulfilling one's religious mission. He never exiled any of his family members, but he kept them at a distance. Once, while addressing a crowd, he was interrupted by a messenger who told him that his mother and brothers wished to speak to him. Jesus asked, "Who is my mother? Who are my brothers?" and pointing to the disciples said, "Here are my mother and my brothers. Whoever does the will of my heavenly Father is my brother."[21] Both Jesus and Augustus considered family those relations who did His/his will. It was all relative.

Unlike Jesus, whom some said planned a Second Coming or manifestation when he would judge mankind, Augustus came only once since he had but one life. Thus he had to judge everything as he went along. He was extremely judgmental. Yet, he also manifested himself twice, the first time as Octavian, later as Augustus. As Octavian he was a Roman teenager out for blood, like Pompey before him. Later, he was the wiliest of the triumvirs, allied with two lesser talents (Lepidus, Antony) until he could defeat both, Lepidus in 36 BC and Antony at Actium (31 BC).[22] Then Octavian closed the chapter on his old self. He melted down eighty silver statues of Octavian the soldier, before emerging as princeps (first citizen) then "Augustus," a cognomen awarded him by the Senate.

As Augustus he was associated with augury or divination (a word related semantically to Augustus) and thus to Romulus the augur, god-founder of Rome. This was as significant to the credulous Romans as Jesus's cognomen *Christos* was to credulous Christians. The word "Christ" was a translation into Greek from the Hebrew Messiah, meaning anointed by God. Shakespeare thought a rose by any other name would smell as sweet, but Shakespeare did not, unlike Augustus and Jesus, hold a leadership position.[23]

Augustus reinvented the Roman Empire, giving it discipline and order, thus preparing it later for Christian discipline and a new order that would preserve, if fragmentarily, some of the empire's most precious legacies for the West. It became a commonplace among Rome's Christian population that like the Fall of man and the fall of Rome, the rise of Christianity was a chapter of man's history that God had written so that his Son might triumph over Caesar. While most Romans rejected Christianity until the end of the fourth century, Christians were so impressed with things Roman they imitated them in matters of law, rhetoric, and administration, preserving, to some degree, a civilization that had once rejected them as incapable even of understanding it! Rome, like Judea and Greece, was to become part of the Christian canon.

After Caesar's death (44 BC), Octavian, with Cicero's and the Senate's encouragement, raised an army among his great-uncle's veterans to stop

Antony, then consul, from becoming dictator. Antony thought the "boy" owed everything to his name (Caesar), but Octavian owed more to ready cash. He won over the Macedonian legions by offering each man five hundred drachmas. Antony offered only one hundred.[24]

Syme wrote of Cicero and Octavian that neither was the dupe of the other, though Syme did not say how Cicero felt at the end of his days when his pursuers, Antony's henchmen, were about to decapitate him.[25] Perhaps he called out to them "Unhand me"? They did—and nailed his severed hands along with his head to the rostrum in the Forum. He was duped indeed, because Octavian joined forces with Antony and did not lift his hand to prevent Cicero's proscription, though Cicero had made him a consul. Augustus wrote in his autobiography twenty years later that "Cicero had been swept this way and that by the tides of fear and greed" and did not understand the forces threatening to destroy the Republic. Augustus claimed he felt sorry for Cicero in his old age and did not share Antony's bitterness.[26] Later he praised Cicero to his grandchildren, leaving out the dreadful particulars of the senator's death. Every generation rewrites history for the children. What they leave out is called the generation gap. Augustus made history his story. Two or three generations later, the four writers of the Gospels of Matthew, Mark, Luke, and John made their story His story. If Jesus could have read their versions, would he have recognized their stories as history? As His story?

Octavian arrived in Rome with eight legions. Cicero thought he would soon dispose of this "boy," who proved to be nondisposable, enjoying power first as triumvir, then as princeps or emperor and finally as "Father of his Country," *pater patriae,* as the Senate pronounced him in 2 BC. He was arbiter of Rome's destiny and most of the civilized world's for fifty-six years! A legend in his own time and a subject for historical debate, Augustus was at home in the world of sports and public shows, but also in the company of poets and scholars.[27] While yet a brash youth he observed the disdain of his elders give way to respect; respect to gratitude; gratitude to love; love to adulation; and adulation to reverence. He was not only the son of the deified Caesar, but the savior of the Republic and empire, god among men, God's gift to the civilized world. The fact that he wound up in the good graces of the vast majority some thought a miracle, and it was. A miracle of political know-how.

Augustus had cooperated with Antony for over a decade. In the end, he did not pursue him because Antony was screwing Cleopatra, but because the couple was screwing Rome, for Antony diverted Egypt's prestige and property for his own use, not Rome's. After Actium Antony joined Cleopatra in Alexandria. There they made their last stand against Octavian. In the end, Antony fell on his sword, thinking that Cleopatra had already died, and she, bereft of every aspiration of further power, clasped snakes (asps in

Shakespeare's *Antony and Cleopatra*) to her breast to escape Octavian's greater venom. He would have paraded her in chains through Rome. Cleopatra eluded his grasp, but Egypt did not. It became his own peculiar province, off-limits even to senators. Egyptian treasure enabled Augustus to buy off any opposition to his power.

The principate brought peace to Rome after a century and more of civil wars. Augustus's state looked like a Republic but was really a monarchy. "Princeps" was a "general form of address" once used in Republican times to describe Pompey.[28] In the Republic it meant any prestigious leader. In Latin the word for prestige, *praestigium,* meant delusion as well as illusion. Yet, Augustus's authority was never delusional. He was one of those rare rulers really adored by the masses. They wanted him to exercise still more authority and would have conferred upon him the powers of dictator and censor. He thought that politically unwise. Julius Caesar perished on the floor of the Senate because he threatened its traditional liberties. Augustus claimed to have preserved them and died in bed of old age.

Augustus extended clemency to all who submitted to his will. Colin Wells says that Virgil, Augustus's friend, had Jupiter advise Aeneas "to rule the nations by your empire . . . and impose the way of peace," sparing the submissive and defeating the proud.[29] The economic historian M. Rostovtzeff writing in the 1920s said that Augustus followed the "longing Roman citizens had for Peace," but that Rome under Augustus was "not a time of rest" but "unflagging and strenuous military efforts."[30] Syme wrote that "Pax et Princeps" meant peace was paid for domestically by submission and the loss of a liberty only a few had ever enjoyed. Like Tacitus, Syme was no flatterer of Augustus.[31] Foreigners were compelled to observe peace or were pacified by force of arms.[32] Jesus, later nicknamed the Prince of Peace, said he came not to bring peace, but a sword to earth.[33] Perhaps the important thing for world-class leaders is not that they deliver on peace but that they are believed to have delivered.

Since Virgil, historians have acknowledged that Roman military power was the reverse side of Roman peace and power, but it was also the underside of Rome's "moral superiority." Moral superiority is always assumed to rest with the strongest, for might makes right as far as most people can tell. Only when a still mightier power objects is a new right established. Historians cite the blessings brought by Augustus to the empire. To the Senate, enhanced dignity, if not power. The old senatorial class was obliged to share its reduced membership with Equites and Italians. Poor Romans under Augustus's direction enjoyed a surer grain supply. They probably did not enjoy a stricter supervision of public morals, which he also directed. New territories like Armenia provided more opportunities for military service and trade. Everyone in the capital applauded new public services, including a fire department, a water commission, and the repair of eighty-two old temples–plus many new ones, visible reminders of the ruler's resolve to restore the early Republic's old-time religion. Eventually, Augustus took up the duties of pontifex maximus and other religious enterprises. He boasted that he found Rome a city of brick and left it a city of marble. True, the marble was merely applied over clay bricks or unsightly concrete structures. But the princeps had a talent for making everything look better than it actually was, or sound better. Thus he preferred the term principate to empire.

Some historians think Augustus could be viewed positively only if one divided his rule into a before and after. Before 27 BC when he claimed to have restored the Republic to the Senate and Roman people he was just another revolutionary leader, to whom legality and benevolence were unknown. After that date, what Gabba calls "the standard motifs of imperial ideology–*clementia, pax res publica restituta*" seemed "useful fictions" masking suppressed liberty.[34]

Augustus made do with the powers of consul until 23 BC, and when he was not a consul as well as princeps, with compensatory powers. To these were added the powers of a proconsul, greater than those of any other magistrate; tribunician powers and privileges (without having to be a tribune first); imperator (commander of troops); pontifex maximus (after Lepidus died, 12 BC) and the title *pater patria,* Father of his country. He set the standard for the enjoyment of constitutionally sanctioned powers that the Senate only wished they could refuse him. Too late. The restored Republic had become, not a dyarchy as the historian Mommsen once argued, nor even a constitutional monarchy, as textbooks would have it, but a benevolent dictatorship. Augustus had the capacity correctly to assess the public's will and mood. A consummate politician, he understood the public because he held so many of their prejudices himself. [35] Those he did not share, he carefully concealed.

The Julio-Claudians

For more than a half century after Augustus, the four Julio-Claudians (Tiberius, Gaius [Caligula], Claudius, Nero) commanded the Roman Empire, if not the affections of all their subjects. Yet some of Rome's citizens found even the most outrageous of these emperors, the deranged Caligula and the matricide Nero, acceptable, though the most despised, Tiberius and Claudius, were more learned and more talented rulers. All were hated by some factions before the end of their reigns, and two (Caligula, Nero) died violent deaths. The Claudians, Tiberius and Claudius, were more handicapped than the Julians, Caligula and Nero, because the legions believed only Julians sensitive to the military. Yet, all four emperors bribed their troops, rather than risk military plots. The legions' pro-Julian prejudice stemmed from the victories of the first Caesar and his great nephew, Octavian. That it was prejudice and not fact was demonstrated when both Julians proved less capable of military triumphs than either Claudian. The legions learned how to make emperors, but not how to predict their military success, let alone evaluate their other qualities. The mistakes they made were legion. Despite the bribes, none of the Julio-Claudians was secure from revolts. Predictably, they found this revolting.

Tiberius's reign began with threats of mutiny in lower Germany, Pannonia, and Gaul. In Caligula's reign one of the Rhine commanders, his former brother-in-law, revolted (AD 39), a revolt whose suppression burnished the reputations of two future emperors, Galba and Vespasian. A possible mutiny in Gaul may have delayed Rome's conquest of Britain the next year, when Caligula's Gallic legions refused to embark for the invasion of Britain, leaving Suetonius to write that the madman, Caligula, then commanded them to pick up seashells on the beach, long supposed a humiliating punishment.

Claudius took pains to win over the legions by bribery, to keep the troops happy.[36] Scarcely was Caligula dead when Galba's friends offered to make him emperor instead of Claudius. In the second year of his reign (AD 42) Claudius's Dalmatian commander, Scribonianus, attempted a revolt. His first name was in fact, Furius! Nero (AD 54–68) was unpopular with the legions he studiedly neglected. He made them furious, too. Consequently, Nero was threatened first by a revolt of a Gallic governor named Vindex (pronounced Win-dex'), which meant vengeance. Vindex's unsuccessful revolt ended in his suicide. Wiped out, he left his prospective ally, Galba, governor of northern Spain, a clean slate. Elected emperor by his troops, Galba waited prudently until Nero committed suicide before marching on Rome to claim the empire (68–69 BC).

With few exceptions the Julio-Claudians got bad press in ancient times. No one was more critical than Tacitus (c. AD 56–c. 120) whose *Annals* began with the reign of Augustus, and whose *Histories* with that of Nero. Tacitus identified with an idealized republican past, siding with the Senate against emperors he thought had subverted his idealized Republic. He presented the Julio-Claudians as conspirators against republican virtues, and the historians from Augustus through Nero as sycophants who lied under the constraints of terror. When the Julio-Claudians disappeared, said Tacitus, the histories of their reigns were the products of irritation and hatred.[37] He regarded his own books far removed from bitterness and partiality, though they were not. Tacitus was still too close to his subject and political connections to be impartial.[38] It might seem that the more remote people are from the past the more likely they are to view it objectively. Still, reasonable historians often interpret the same facts differently. Nothing is more common after all these centuries than for historians to reject their colleagues' conclusions as tainted, often by their presentist political opinions.

Edward Gibbon (1737–1794), who wrote *The Decline and Fall of the Roman Empire,* thought Tiberius "unrelenting," Caligula "furious," Claudius "feeble," and Nero "cruel" and along with two of their immediate successors (Vitellius, Domitian) condemned them all to "everlasting infamy."[39] Gibbon lived in the Age of Reason and was a voracious reader of classical historians whose prejudices against the principate he inherited. Like Tacitus, Gibbon regarded himself an impartial observer of Roman history and a defender of republican liberty and freedom. He frequently wrote in an ironic vein but would have been surprised could he have known that modern historians view his admiration of republican liberty as an irony of time and place. Even the great Gibbon fell into the trap of presentism.

TIBERIUS (AD 14–37)

The first of our four emperors, the Claudian Tiberius, was fifty-five when he assumed office. He seems always to have sought an early retirement that steadily eluded him. Suetonius records that he complained that being princeps was like having "a wolf by the ears"—he couldn't let go.[40] During his reign John the Baptist preached and was imprisoned and Christ preached and was crucified.[41] Tiberius trained first his nephew, Germanicus, then his son Drusus, then Germanicus's two elder sons to succeed him. They predeceased him instead. After the death of his nephew Drusus (AD 20) he had but two possible heirs left: an infant grandson (Tiberius Gemellus) of the Claudian line, and his eight-year-old great-nephew, Gaius, Germanicus's last son, nicknamed Caligula (little boots) for the military boots he wore as a child. Caligula was a Julian, a descendant of Augustus, but Tiberius's preference rested on his prefect of the Praetorian Guard, Sejanus. Sejanus overstepped himself, and at last (AD 31), Tiberius had him executed.

Suetonius, who had nothing good to say of Tiberius, claimed that in eliminating Sejanus, the princeps acted with his usual cruelty and craft. Modern historians no longer view Tiberius a monster of iniquity and lust, but as insecure and embittered, suffering from paranoia and depression, lusting mostly after intelligent conversation and security from plotters.[42] Today we would diagnose him as clinically depressed and prescribe antidepressants. His greatest sin was his inability to inspire the Senate with his own sense of honor and responsibility. His second greatest was designating Caligula his heir.[43]

Tiberius resigned himself to his desk job until Caligula could grow up and relieve him of his cares. He made the boy live with him at his villa on Capri. They brought each other little cheer. Tiberius could control mutinies on the Rhine, Panonnia,[44] and Thrace,[45] but he could not control his adolescent great-nephew on the frontiers of manhood. Not even emperors escape the defeats of parenting, nor the temptation to ignore the emotional and intellectual needs of their adolescent wards while deploring the results of such neglect.

A moderate ruler until late in his career, Tiberius endured the unpopularity his social reforms and economies earned him.[46] He eliminated public shows and kept provincial governors from stealing the store. He was damned for his virtues as well as his vices, the chief of the latter being suspicion of critics as disloyal plotters. He initiated treason trials to pursue suspects. Tiberius grew unable to endure those he disappointed—the senators, his mother, Rome. He would not let anyone get to know him well, his family least of all. His powerful intelligence impressed Tacitus, but his skepticism and irony alienated others. His associates were professors of classical philology, a peculiarity suspect in every age except Renaissance Italy when those trained in the classics were getting the respect that eluded them forever after.

Distrusted by his peers, Tiberius was never able to sell himself to the masses, either, though he reduced taxes and administered the laws justly.[47] As he aged he grew insensitive to the opinions of others, and more sensitive to his own, a state of affairs in which the old and powerful most nearly resemble the young and insecure. It is hard to say whether he was more hated for his long moderation or his brief abandonment of it when he began to prosecute critics as traitors. Tiberius remained loyal to Augustan programs despite the fact that he disliked the principate. The Senate's refusal to deify him after his death would have pleased him. He had discouraged his worship when alive. He had not found it necessary to be a god in order to keep his distance.

CALIGULA (AD 37–41)

In the beginning, Caligula made everyone happy. He ended Tiberius's treason trials, abolished sales taxes, recalled political exiles, and staged public shows.[48] He adopted Tiberius's grandson, Gemellus, as co-heir, and gave him a royal title, prince of youth. He carried out the terms of Tiberius's will. He treated senators respectfully. After an illness, he changed. He started his own treason trials and raised taxes. He obliged his father-in-law to commit suicide on a spurious charge of attempting to usurp his throne. He forced Macro, a friend and adviser, to commit suicide (AD 38), for giving unwanted advice. In May of that year Gemellus had taken cough medicine that Caligula said was an antidote for poison! He implied that Gemellus had hoped to see him poisoned, while Gemellus was planning to replace him.

When, as seems plausible, he had Gemellus murdered, no one objected.[49] Tiberius, after all, was thought to have murdered Agrippa Postumus, Tiberius's co-heir. Nero would subsequently rid himself of Britannicus, Claudius's son and heir. It was a Julio-Claudian tradition, a family value. Getting rid of possible successors provided for public tranquility. The emperor shrugged it off. Gemellus was prince of youth, not maturity. He simply eliminated that entitlement.

The young emperor became predictable only in his cruelty. He enjoyed seeing people tortured and even beheaded during mealtimes! His, not theirs. He tested new poisons on people of high rank at mealtimes. Theirs, not his. He reminded his mistresses that he could have their pretty little heads removed from their pretty little necks. Freud would have asked about his childhood. It was traumatic. His father may have been poisoned with Tiberius's connivance. His two brothers died on charges of treason against the same emperor, who exiled his mother. In addition, Caligula suffered from epilepsy, anciently thought a kind of madness, though sometimes, divine inspiration. Was he acting up, or merely acting out?

Caligula was so busy suppressing plots among his Rhine commanders that was not ready for a scheduled invasion of Britain in AD 40. Neither were his troops, whom Suetonius claimed would not embark for Britain, but whom a recent biographer thinks were not allowed to invade Britain because Caligula aborted the invasion out of fear for his own situation and realization of his growing insanity.[50] That insanity was problematic. Suetonius wrote that Caligula ordered his legions to pick up seashells on the Gallic coast by way of humiliating them for insubordination and mutiny![51] Professor Balsdon wrote that the term "seashells" (*musculi*) may have represented a kind of Roman siege works which the men were ordered to pack up, and that the nature of the command may have been misinterpreted.[52] Caligula never invaded Britain, but annexed it anyway, hoping to muscle in on the glory that later fell to his Uncle Claudius. Fate nipped his vain hope in the bud. A case of nipotism, not nepotism.

Caligula liked things oriental and despotic. The Oriental despotism of the East cast its shadow over Julius Caesar, Tiberius, and now, over Caligula. There was something shady about all the Julio-Claudians. Under each the threat of despotism increased. Antony had dreamed of ruling the East like an oriental potentate. Caligula, his grandson, was into potency and soon into his three sisters, just like the pharaohs. But the family that slept together could not be kept together. Caligula exiled two sisters for plotting against him. Suetonius accused him of prostituting two of them to friends.[53] He seems to have been genuinely in love with the third, Drusilla. He made her his heir and after her death arranged her consecration by the Senate. Renamed Panthea (every goddess), she was given a temple, a shrine, and a priesthood of twenty members. Not every goddess was as lucky. Madness? Megalomania? Maudlin grief? Incest clashed with Roman propriety and disapproval of incest was the last proper notion Romans clung to in what was Rome's most immoral age. Crane Brinton called the reign "one of the moral troughs of Western history."[54] He meant a depression, not a basin. Make no mistake. It was not a place where one drank in morals. It was rather a sinkhole of iniquity.

Was Caligula insane or just eccentric? His uncle Claudius represented this assassinated ruler as a bona fide madman, perhaps to sanitize himself.[55] Caligula's madness is often cited in connection with the rumor that he made his horse a consul. He did not. But he did for two months make a consul of Claudius, a man the senators wrongly believed lacked horse sense. Caligula made Claudius the butt of jokes. He liked to horse around.

He announced himself a god-ruler. He was rumored to have built a bridge to the Capitol from the Palatine so that he could communicate with his brother Jupiter![56] He built another bridge made of ships at Baiae (AD 39) and rode over it wearing Alexander the Great's breastplate. To be regarded as a god was no reflection on his sanity. Though he was certainly a madcap, he may or may not have been a madman. Roman emperors reenacted the role of Hellenistic rulers whose claims to divinity were but one more royal "perk." Alexander the Great encouraged the practice. Augustus and Tiberius discouraged it, with little success. Caligula aped Alexander. When it came to godhead, he did not monkey around.

He insisted that his statue be displayed in the synagogues of Alexandria and Jerusalem! When the Jews sent an embassy in AD 40 to dissuade him, it was led by Philo Judaeus, an Alexandrian Jew whose life's work was reconciling scripture to Greek philosophy. Philo thought he saw many of the doctrines of the philosophers in the Pentateuch and suggested that God communicated with His Creation via the *Logos,* God's thought and Word, which he found analogous to Platonic ideas. The Jews ignored this theory, but Christians later rescued it from oblivion, associated the Word with Christ. Caligula led the old mystic on a foot race through his villa near Rome, observing that "men who thought him no god were more unfortunate than criminal."[57] This view spared Philo a criminal record, but not the obligation of making his philosophy clearer. The visit did not clear the emperor's statues from Jewish temples, either. But what could one expect from the meeting of such an elusive old thinker with such an elusive young stinker?

Was Caligula's cruelty proof of his insanity? One need not equate madness with cruelty, for cruelty has its uses, and rational if unsympathetic rulers have always availed themselves of it. Machiavelli regarded cruelty useful to leaders who instill terror in their subjects to spare them from foreign conquest. Caligula's cruelty was gratuitous, willful, motivated by a young man's need for amusement. Professor Balsdon was not amused by tales of Caligula's madness but thought them distortions or inventions based on the young emperor's impetuosity, frank tongue, cruelty, and fear of assassination.[58] Caligula was assassinated by a tribune of the Praetorian Guard. He was not so mad when attacked as to be unaware of the ultimate penalty for self-indulgence.

Madness, like beauty, must in any case be judged by the beholder. Nero, the last Julio-Claudian, was at least as cruel as Caligula in his treatment of Rome's Christians, whom he used as torches to light his gardens or had dressed in animal skins to be torn apart by dogs—or crucified. Nero's cruelties were not regarded as evidence of madness, however excessive they were viewed by finer-souled contemporaries. Suetonius, critical of Christian superstition, thought they ranked among Nero's good deeds![59] In our own era, the madness or sanity of a political leader is often determined by talk-show hosts and opinion polls that reflect the prejudices of those who pay the pollsters' salaries. History provides a more balanced diagnosis, but only in the long run, not the short one. The ultimate madness for all politicians is throwing away the opportunities power brings to do good.

The Jewish historian Flavius Josephus (AD 37–95?) believed that abuse of power was Caligula's overriding flaw, noting that not even his superior education preserved him from "the disastrous effect of power," or gave him the advantage of self-control.[60] Josephus was hardly the one to talk about the abuse of power, however. Most historians regard him a scamp or scoundrel. He himself abused power by kowtowing to it for personal advantage and by exchanging the losing side (Jews) for the favor of the winning side (Romans). He even took the name Flavius because his patron, Emperor Vespasian, was a Flavian. Lord Acton (1834–1902), often quoted on power, wrote in his letter to Bishop Creighton that "power corrupts and absolute power corrupts absolutely."[61] Acton advised people about to write history not to do it! Did he think writing history corrupts absolutely, too? No, Acton, himself a historian, was only having a bit of fun.[62] And that was what Caligula was having. Historians and emperors must have their fun. Who does more damage must be left to the judgment of posterity.

There was a broad streak of exhibitionism in Caligula and his nephew, Nero, son of his sister Agrippina the younger.[63] The senators were disdainful of them in part because they performed in public as charioteers, artists, musicians, athletes, even though in AD 19 Augustus had a law passed prohibiting senators from appearing in public spectacles. They expected their emperor to be a role model. The Roman elite were devotees of health spas and consumers of art. They were not professional athletes and artists. They patronized art. They did not especially like it. Worse, they detested being patronized, treated as an abject audience obliged to cheer on the performances of a Caligula, a Nero. These were years when a number of senators began to dream of ending the principate and reinstating the old Republic. They regarded their emperors as bad actors—on stage or off.

A few plotting senators lent support to the assassination of Caligula by a disgruntled Praetorian guardsman named Chaerea whom Caligula had often ridiculed as a womanizer.[64] Suetonius says that Caligula had an upset stomach and was debating whether or not to get up for lunch, but was at last persuaded by friends to do so.[65] En route to the dining room, he stopped in a corridor beneath the Palace to talk with some Asian boys who were rehearsing a play. Chaerea and two accomplices fell on him there with swords. The twenty-nine-year-old emperor died of thirty wounds, one for each year of his life, and one to grow on. But he grew lifeless instead. Had he been in charge he would have scheduled this violence during, not before, lunch, because he so enjoyed watching people die during the lunch hour. Caligula never got to lunch, but at least he got his just desserts.

Claudius (AD 41–54)

Claudius was the first emperor deified since Augustus. The gods, a handsome lot, with the exception of the lame Vulcan, must have been embarrassed by his presence.[66] As a lad, Claudius had had infantile paralysis. His head and hands shook; he slobbered at the mouth; his legs were spindly; his gait shambling; and he was potbellied.[67] Neither Augustus nor Tiberius nor his mother could stand him. Upon maturing, he became an historian. Naturally, no one took him seriously. After Caligula's assassination Claudius hid behind curtains until some Praetorians found him and set him on the throne. He thought they had kidnapped him to kill him. When he saw they had not, he offered them fifteen or twenty thousand sesterces apiece as a reward for making him princeps. Once promoted, he confessed that he had always lusted after power, something most academics never admit or achieve, unless they become deans.

Claudius began his reign like Caligula had—denouncing his predecessor's treason trials and taxes, inviting political exiles to return home, staging new games. Romans took sports (and the grain dole) seriously. Bread and circuses. Again like Caligula, the new emperor was soon conducting his own treason trials. Still, he gave the Senate real privileges, sharing new provinces with them (Britain, Lycia) and reserving for them the best seats in the Circus. This was shrewd because senators had become mere benchwarmers, "yesmen" who no longer stood up to debate Rome's business or the empire's.[68]

History was Claudius's first love and refuge from politics. He wrote twenty books of Etruscan history and eight of Carthaginian, all in Greek, the language of learning. He also produced a forty-three volume Latin history of Rome from the death of Julius Caesar. He skipped the years of the Second Triumvirate (at Livia's request) so as not to embarrass Augustus, for Claudius was Antony's grandson. One of his comedies was performed at Naples and won a prize. He translated a work by the poet Aratus of Cilicia (third century BC) and wrote a treatise on the alphabet to advocate the use of several new letters to rationalize Latin spelling.[69] Forget his detractors. Claudius was a spellbinder.

This pedant, antiquarian, glutton, who never dined in style before his accession, but with a few old cronies, all drinkers and gamblers, rejuvenated government. First, he revived the office of censor. This rid him of some inefficient senators, whom he replaced with new patricians, provincials from Gaul, galling others considerably. Second, he centralized administration by employing learned Greeks, ex-slaves, or freedmen. He put them in charge of ports, the treasury, grain distribution, highway construction, and other social services. Claudius and his advisers began to try cases formerly tried before the Senate, trials the Senate believed were more open to bias and corruption,[70] but which actually showcased Claudius's humanity and efficiency.[71] In provincial matters, imperial officials replaced senatorial ones.[72] The Senate took umbrage, but they had earlier been cast into the shade by Tiberius and left in the dark by Caligula. None of the emperor's innovations were unconstitutional. An emperor with the legions on his side was the constitution during the principate.

Claudius was not merely emperor of Rome, but a believer in the benefits of Roman empire. Under him Rome gained five provinces, including Britain, his most popular acquisition. Although he was only in Britain for two weeks, he was given a Roman triumph (AD 44). Perhaps the Senate figured that any Roman, even Claudius, who could endure two weeks of English weather before the invention of the umbrella and raincoat, deserved one. He named his son and heir Britannicus. He annexed Thrace and Lycia, expanded Roman citizenship in Gaul, set up colonies at Cologne and Trier. Like Augustus, he refused to expand eastward into Germany. Perhaps he did not think he could improve upon his brother's action there.[73] It had been very affirmative.

Claudius installed Herod Agrippa, that debonair and stalwart friend of Rome's princeps, as ruler of Judaea. The region had been a Roman province since AD 6. After Herod's death (AD 44), Judaea was again reduced to a province. Herod was a client ruler. Rome's clients defended their own territories so that Rome could economically defend hers.[74] Though client states were often located on imperial frontiers, the benefits to Rome were not marginal. Their victories were Rome's. Their defeats, often leading to Roman annexation, were likewise Rome's victories. When Rome took stock of a weak client state, it was well on its way to becoming a province. A margin call.

A hostile tradition (Suetonius, Tacitus) had it that Claudius was dominated by his wives and freedmen. Such charges were exaggerated.[75] There is reason to think that Claudius, far from being manipulated by his wife and courtiers was in fact manipulating them to rid himself of his enemies. Fifty-one when he entered upon his office, Claudius was then married to Valeria Messallina, a cousin once removed, whom he may not have removed soon enough.[76] She gave him a daughter (Octavia) and a son (Britannicus) and more headaches than anticipated. Messallina married him when she was fifteen and he nearly fifty, and that may partly explain her nymphomania. But how to account for the murders she arranged? She may have hoped by murder and sex to secure the succession for her son from cliques and clans with viable claims to the throne. On the other hand, she could have just liked sex. Was Messallina a heroine, a whore or both? A bigamous marriage to a handsome lover named C. Silius was her most unforgivable act. She forgot to tell Claudius, who was at Ostia on business, and worse, she forgot to divorce him. It was her silliest affair, but also her most serious. The marriage was solemnized during the vintage of AD 48. Some say it was less an idyll than a plot to overthrow Claudius. New wine, new bottle. Others think Messallina was shopping for political support against the influence of the freedmen and was hoping to bring Claudius around.[77] Narcissus, fearing that Claudius might forgive her, had Messallina killed. She died in the arms of her mother who reproached herself, as mothers usually do, for Messallina messing up. Everyone agreed the marriage to Silius was a fatal *mésalliance*.

Claudius's political posture was fairly progressive, always excepting the underhanded methods used to eliminate political rivals. His reign recalls F.D.R. and the New Deal Democrats. Were public facilities needed? Claudius built a new harbor at Ostia, near Rome; drained the Fucine Lake to expand farmland; and built two new aqueducts for Rome. After Augustus no one built more roads than he to unite the west with its center, Rome. Claudius was a pragmatist who thought government could promote the interests of humanity by creating opportunities both physical and political where they had never existed. He promoted the productive use of power and used learned freedmen as a "braintrust" to advise him. Despite new techniques and respectable goals—security, prosperity—he was subject to scorn by his critics and defamed by his senatorial opponents. Nothing loses like success.

Soon after Messallina's death, Claudius took his brother's daughter, Agrippina the Younger, Caligula's last living sister, for his fourth wife. She was a Julian, and Claudius was eager for the marriage, not because of her charms, but because she was a great-grandaughter of Augustus. This niece-wife was not a nice wife. Her affair with Seneca, the Stoic philosopher whom Claudius, at Messallina's urging, exiled in AD 41, was only one of a number of indiscretions. Claudius adopted her son, by her first husband, Cornelius Domitius Ahenobarbus. Claudius preferred young Lucius Domitius Ahenobarbus, later called Nero, as heir over his own son, Britannicus.

Agrippina, eager to promote Nero while he was young enough to defer to her in matters of governance, had Claudius assassinated (AD 54). Tacitus said he died of a plate of poisoned mushrooms that Agrippina had ordered for him, and Nero, speaking after Claudius's deification, observed that mushrooms were the food of the gods!

NERO (AD 54–69)

Nero Claudius Caesar, "son of the deified Claudius," like most seventeen-year-olds, was at his accession only moderately interested in current events. Until AD 62 he devoted most of his attention to sculpture, painting, music, and sex. The years AD 56–61 were the most prosperous of his reign, or of any reign to date. There was even the appearance of a return to a senatorial principate. Nero served as consul three times, but spent most of his time sowing wild oats, and let his tutor, Seneca, and Burrus, Prefect of the Guard, run the store.[78] Under their direction, the empire secured its frontiers, cleared the seas of pirates, restored Armenia to Roman control, and brought about peace with Parthia. Corruption of justice declined, and Roman finances were prudently managed. Roman peace (*pax romana*) prevailed. The maintenance of law and order and the collection of taxes remained the chief governmental interests. If the empire was "undergoverned," it was because Nero was overruled.[79]

For the first year, Agrippina was the power behind the throne. Her picture was engraved on the principal (obverse) side of Roman coins facing Nero, in such a way as to outface him. The very grammar which described the Queen Mum's attributes indicated her precedence over Nero. Her attributes were in the nominative case, indicating royalty. This meant that the coins were hers. Nero's attributes were in the dedicatory dative, meaning that Agrippina merely dedicated her coins to him.[80] A year later, however, her image was partially obscured by Nero's own, and mother and son were no longer looking at each other—or listening to each other. Nero longed to cut not merely the purse strings, but the apron strings. In the new issue, he assumed the nominative case, and Romans assumed Mom was nearing the past tense. As for the genitive case, that is, who owned the empire, Agrippina or Nero, and the accusative case, that is, who would be accused of what, the problems were more than verbal—they were substantive.

Nero's handlers wanted Agrippina out of politics. Seneca and Burrus removed her influence, rumored incestuous—over her son. When Nero, disregarding Agrippina's advice, took as mistress a freedwoman named Claudia Acte, he felt himself a freed man. Yet Nero, like Augustus and Caligula, was not yet free. Technically he was but co-heir with Britannicus to Claudius's estate. When Agrippina, out of spite, began to show the lad favor, Nero had him poisoned at court during the feast of the Saturnalia, celebrated December sixteenth or seventeenth to the twenty-third. Ostensibly an occasion when Romans gave lip service to the equality of all humans, this feast was marked with revels, gift-giving, banquets, and sex. This occasion, not gifts given the infant Jesus in a manger, is more likely the origin of Christmas gift giving. It was a pagan solstice celebration.

Nero insisted that Britannicus sing for the guests. Tacitus said his song was about loss of home and throne, though it may have referred as well to a Greek play, the *Andromache* of Ennius.[81] It won sympathy for Britannicus, a brave boy to allude to his delicate situation. Nero, fearing for his own safety, ordered his stepbrother poisoned while at table. He passed off the boy's seizure as an epileptic attack. Britannicus died before dessert arrived. For Nero, this was the sweetest part of the meal.

The murder of Agrippina, "the distinguishing mark of Nero's principate," still fascinates.[82] Though hatred of mothers may be more common in modern than in ancient societies, where most mothers had little legal power over children, the number of matricides then as now was rare. No doubt more mothers perished from childbirth, wifebeating, and broken hearts than from matricide. The Hebrews made it obligatory to *honor* one's mother and father, though they said nothing about not breaking their hearts. The Romans gave the male head of household the power of life and death over children and wife (*patria potestas*). A son had no power at all while his dad lived, unless he became emperor. Then he could do anything he pleased to anyone, including his mom. Absolute, despotic power was the chief reason there were so many applicants for every imperial position. Was the Roman Empire a great government or what?

Michael Grant believes that "the timid Nero" only had Agrippina killed after he heard she was listening to plotters.[83] Anicetus, Nero's former tutor, now commander of the fleet near the Bay of Naples, concocted a plan to get Agrippina aboard a ship rigged to founder. Mother and son met at the home of Otho, a charming scoundrel (briefly emperor after Nero's suicide) who had helped Nero procure as mistress Claudia Acte, and who ultimately furnished him with his own wife, Poppaea. After a cordial evening, Agrippina boarded the ship to return home, unaware that lead weights in its roof were to crush the people below. The roof collapsed, killing some of the voyagers. Agrippina, thrown overboard, swam to some nearby boats and reached safety. When Nero heard she was safe, he dispatched Anicetus and two assassins to her villa. Perceiving their intentions, she pointed to her navel saying "Strike the belly that gave birth to such a monster." Dio Cassius wrote that Nero, viewing her corpse, said that he had not known until then what a beautiful mother he had. Perhaps he said this so that people would not think his relationship with his mother was incestuous, as rumored. Though power over his family members was undisputed, Nero's cruelty to them made a bad impression. Agrippina's remains were cremated on one of her dining room couches right after the murder, and Nero, not sure of how the news of her death would be received, worried about this (the murder, not the upholstery). Although Agrippina had founded the city of Cologne (Colonia Agrippinensis), in modern times notable for its perfume (*Kölnwasser* or *eau de Cologne*), her murder has gone down in history as exceptionally malodorous.[84]

Nero took heart when the Senate thanked the gods for providing a happy ending to Agrippina's foiled plot against him. Nero fostered his popularity with the Roman mob by lavishing on them two monetary gifts in which every Roman collected eight hundred sesterces. New games (the Juvenalia) kept Romans entertained and enabled the emperor to perform in public as a charioteer and musician. Special ushers equipped with poles prodded the audience to applaud him. When the future emperor, General Vespasian, dozed off, he narrowly escaped with his life! In AD 60, Nero introduced the Neronia, a festival modeled after Greek exercises in poetry, oratory, sporting events, and music. To accommodate these he built an amphitheater, a circus (where the Vatican now stands), and a gymnasium-swimming pool complex open to the public. Romans loved health spas.

In the last half of the first century, rules of etiquette were changed so that Romans might view their lawmakers as entertainers. In the last half of the twentieth century, political traditions changed in the U.S.A., too, enabling Americans to view their entertainers as lawmakers.[85]

Nero had star quality and craved the limelight. Following Burrus's death, he appointed his own administrators, real thugs, and rejoiced when Seneca retired. Seneca did not get a golden handshake. He was already one of the richest men in the empire. This scholar, orator, and lawyer was one teacher who did not need his teacher's retirement. And once Seneca was gone, Nero revived the treason laws; had his divorced wife Octavia murdered; married his current mistress, Poppaea; and had murdered or forced to commit suicide several men whose political connections worried him. He was an actor with an attitude, director of the greatest show on earth—the Roman Empire.

Everybody knows that Nero fiddled while Rome burned on July 18, 64 AD. Many Romans believed he started the fire himself. Like much of what everyone "knows," this is not so. First, there were no instruments of the viol family prior to the fifteenth century. Nero played the lyre. Second, Nero was out of town when the fire broke out. Professor Salmon said no responsible student believes that Nero was an incendiary and adds that after hurrying back to Rome, he worked hard to bring the fire under control and provide for the homeless, accommodating them in public gardens and emergency shelters.[86] He may well have plucked his lyre and recited his tragic poem on the Sack of Troy while watching the fires burn, a self-indulgence that led

Romans to think he had set the fires for this purpose. When he used the cleared space for new buildings—including his sumptuous Golden House—they concluded that the fire had been essential to his desire for urban renewal. *Post hoc, ergo propter hoc.* They forgot that the fire also destroyed his own newly redecorated palace on the Palatine.[87] Nero's reconstruction helped Rome better resist similar conflagrations, and that was good. Unfortunately, the fire so blackened his reputation that he needed a scapegoat. Because Poppaea would not let him persecute the Jews, of whom she was fond, he lit upon the Christians.

To the fire of 64 may be attributed the persecution of the poor and of the rich. Unlike the Christians, neither of these groups were smeared with pitch and burned to light Nero's garden paths, and neither was crucified. Instead, the poor were made to bear the burden of reconstruction and conspicuous consumption by inflating money, namely, currency depreciation. The rich were systematically murdered and their estates declared forfeit to the princeps. This kind of "fundraiser" created an atmosphere of suspicion and elitist revolution. The way money is supplied to the state or its politicians is a barometer of corruption in modern as it was in the classical age.

The Conspiracy of Piso (AD 65) is recounted by Tacitus and other historians who disagree on its meaning. One of the Praetorian prefects may have been involved, as well as the philosopher Seneca and his nephew, the poet Lucan, who implicated his own mother. Many senators were co-conspirators. G. Calpurnius Piso, who was supposed to replace Nero as princeps, was a handsome aristocrat, known for his skill at board games like backgammon and, like Nero, an actor and lyre player. These were not leadership skills, but so dissatisfied with Nero was the search committee of plotters that they ended the search before most candidates' applications could be reviewed.[88] Or even received. The practice became strictly academic.

The plot was betrayed to Nero by one of the senators' freedmen. The plotters' grievances included insults endured at court. They hated Nero's crimes and misdemeanors, because his crimes were not only high, but also low, and as for his misdemeanors, they could not have been any meaner. The conspirators thought he had dishonored the imperial office. They disapproved of his lifestyle because it was more flagrant than theirs. They criticized Nero's public exhibition of himself and resented his popularity with the Roman mob.[89] The mob continued to love him. There was some talk among the plotters of making Seneca the next princeps, but it came to naught. Their attempts to oust Nero from the principate resulted in their own disappearance from the political scene. Nero presided as judge. Among the victims of the conspiracy was Seneca, who, like Socrates, stoically took his own life. He urged his wife not to spend much time mourning him. If she were anything like the majority of Roman wives, she wouldn't. After Seneca's death Rome had to wait another ninety-five years before she got an emperor who was also a Stoic philosopher.[90]

After the conspiracy, Nero avoided visiting his legions, most of which despised him. He devoted himself to the sporting life. His pregnant wife Poppaea died (AD 65), probably from a kick he gave her, perhaps, as Suetonius wrote, because she reproved him for staying too long at the races. He made amends with a sumptuous funeral, delivering her funeral oration himself, declaring Poppaea and their baby daughter goddesses. He remembered Poppaea all the rest of his years—but he only had three left. In AD 66 he married his long-time mistress, Statilia Messalina, widow of a consul named Vestinus, who had married Statilia during her prior affair with Nero. Vestinus made crude jokes about his rival before his execution as a plotter in the Piso affair. Nero could not believe anybody could be so careless.

To disguise the lack of Nero's military activity, a visit from the compromise candidate for the Armenian throne, Tiridates, was hailed in Rome as a military triumph, though in fact it was a diplomatic feat for which General Corbulo was responsible. He had brought peace between Rome and Parthia.[91] Nero boasted that he alone could bestow Armenia on his guest, or take it away. It was almost the same line that Nero's own generals were rehearsing in Gaul, Spain, on the Rhine, and in Judaea about the same time Nero was delivering it to Tiridates in Puteoli (modern Pozzuoli on the Bay of Naples).

There were other plots against Nero. Two were discovered and squashed during his trip to Greece in late AD 66 and 67, a trip he made to participate in the Greek games, rescheduled for his visit. The leader of one plot, Annius Vinicianus, apparently aimed to make General Corbulo princeps. The plot ended in the general's suicide. The other involved the Scribonius brothers, each commander of a Rhenish province. Like Corbulo, they died by their own hand. Suicides reduced court costs. Plots in Gaul, Spain, Germany were not unknown to Nero, though Suetonius insists that he did little about those in Gaul, except to replenish himself by pillaging.[92] In Judaea, Jewish Zealots in Jerusalem massacred the Roman population. Concurrently, Greeks in the Levant and in Egypt massacred Jews. So what else was new? Ethnic struggles are not peculiar to our own times. General Vespasian, whose mediocre social background was nonthreatening to Nero, was sent to Judaea to quell the Zealots before they could damage Roman civilization.[93] Most international crimes have been committed to save civilization, at least, somebody's conception of it.

Thanks to fellows like Vespasian, Nero was free to enjoy his yearlong visit to Achaea (Greece) without much thought for anything but art and sports, especially charioteering, poetry, music, drama, dance. These were the only cultural struggles that got his attention. Nero struggled to excel in such pursuits. His efforts paid off handsomely, for the Greeks awarded him a total of 1,808 wreaths and gold crowns for contests in which they proclaimed him the winner. Back in Rome he decorated his bedroom with some of his prizes. Because he won contests in all four sets of the Greek games, they hailed him as Periodonices, from the Greek word *periodos,* meaning all the way 'round. Nero thought that was something he could sink his teeth into.[94]

Magnanimously, Nero granted all Greece tax exemptions and declared the province "free," that is, nearly autonomous. He posed as liberator of Greece. *He* was not perturbed when he observed that some of the contests he won he had not even entered! He did not think to beware Greeks bearing gifts.[95] He took everything they offered, and lots they didn't–especially works of art. What a decorator Rome had in Nero! At home in Rome, he would surround himself with Greece. He found out shortly that as far as his career was concerned, the fat was already in the fire.

In spring of 68 the aged aristocrat Galba joined Vindex's Gallic revolt. Alarmed by fits and starts, Nero dithered. He thought he might go to Gaul and win the hearts of the rebels by weeping. Then again, he thought it best to stay home composing victory hymns and poems ridiculing the rebels in Spain and Gaul. Perhaps he would execute all the Gauls in Rome. Then again, why not poison the whole Senate? Or turn the wild animals loose on the mob? Or go rule from Egypt, or Parthia? They owed him big time in Parthia! One new legion, the Phalanx of Alexander the Great, created for the purpose, was dispatched to Lugdunum (Lyons), which remained loyal, as did three Rhenish legions under Verginius Rufus who defeated Vindex at Vesontio (Besançon). It was a wipeout.

Ultimately, the support Nero could have counted on had he chosen military action earlier, collapsed. His legate in Africa defected. One of the two prefects of the Guard won over the troops. In June (AD 68) when Nero left Rome by sea, this man (Nymphidius Sabinus), along with some senators, told the Praetorians that Nero had deserted them, and in return for a large donative, they named Galba Nero's successor. Nero's downfall was due to frivolous ineptitude rather than cruelty, which as one scholar implies, was not as objectionable then as it is to moderns.[96] His admirers–the Roman mob, the Greeks, several military units–lacked the power to save him, and his critics–overtaxed provincials, senators, Praetorian guardsmen and troops whose pay was in arrears–lacked the will. Perhaps Nero could have saved himself had he not flaunted his artistic nature while neglecting more manly virtues. The Romans confused virtue with physical strength–a mindset that has produced much mischief ever since.

Deserted one night by his body guards (the Praetorians), Nero panicked. Suetonius says that he sent around to friends in the palace to help him but could not rouse a soul. When he got back to his own bedroom, even the sheets had been stripped off his bed, a sure sign that he had outstayed his welcome. "Have I neither friend nor foe?" he cried, accepting his freedman Phaon's offer to take refuge in his house in Rome's suburbs.

On horseback, Nero and several others made their way through thorns and twigs to Phaon's villa. He had to crawl through a narrow passageway dug into the cellar at the back of the house in order to enter unnoticed. Tired, thirsty, and muddy, the princeps threw himself on an old mattress in the basement and covered himself with a discarded cloak. His friends urged him to make a run for it, but Nero ordered them to dig his grave while he watched, all the while weeping, "What a swell artist the world loses in me!" He reproached himself for cowardice. Suicide was not in his playbook! Still, the Senate had pronounced him a public enemy, to be killed in the ancient tradition—stripped naked and beaten to death with rods. Rewriting his own last act, Nero, helped by his secretary, finally managed to drive a dagger into his neck. He exited center stage. Without applause. As he expired, he was thinking, "Ye gods! Who booked my last performance in the 'burbs?"

THE YEAR OF THE FOUR EMPERORS

The year AD 69 was the year of the Four Emperors, and Tacitus observed that "a well-hidden secret of the Principate had been revealed: it was possible for an emperor to be chosen outside Rome." No emperor after Nero and before Vespasian (AD 69–79) had time for anything but survival techniques. All failed. Two months after his arrival in Rome Galba was murdered by Otho, whose initial support for the old man was supposed to have been the price for Otho's succession. When Galba adopted the brother of the conspirator Piso as his successor, Otho appealed to the Praetorians to murder the old man, who was slain in the Roman Forum. Otho was proclaimed emperor at Rome in early January of AD 69, just a scant two weeks after the profligate glutton, Aulus Vitellius, commander of German legions, had been named emperor by soldiers who despised the Galba-Vindex rebels and naturally, their supporter, Otho. Otho was popular with Roman troops, whom he restrained from massacring the Senate en masse. He was acceptable to the troops on the Danube and Euphrates, seventeen legions in all. However, the West as a whole preferred Vitellius, and in April, in a town near Mantua, Otho did the most practical thing he could think of—he committed suicide, just after Vitellian troops fought his to a standstill near Cremona. In July those troops were at Rome. Vespasian, whose Egyptian and Judaean legions had proclaimed him emperor on July 1, was preparing for destiny. Buttressed by Balkan troops, he overcame Vitellius at Cremona again! They say that what goes around comes around, but this time Vitellius went around and, coming back to Rome, was killed in the Roman Forum. Rome didn't need him. Vitellius wasn't vital.

VESPASIAN (AD 70–79)

Vespasian, conqueror of the Isle of Wight and Britain (to Somersetshire), governor of Africa, and pacifier of Palestine entered Rome in AD 70.[97] There he quickly restored discipline to Vitellius's demoralized army, put the empire on a sound financial footing, increased taxes, and set an example for those who had never tried living the simple life. Vespasian was no sybarite. He regularly vacationed in the old farmhouse where he grew up. Never changed the furniture. Made himself the arbiter of senatorial membership by assuming the office of censor. Like Harry Truman he broadened the basis on which military men could serve the state, and like no U.S. president he put veterans to work—in the provinces where they were valued for their Roman know-how. Vespasian's advice to both his sons was to look after the military and never mind about the rest. But he didn't coddle the army. Suetonius cites two examples. Once, when a young officer came to thank him for a recent commission, Vespasian observed that he reeked of perfume. Drawing back his head in disgust he told the officer: "I would rather you had smelt of garlic" and revoked the appointment forthwith. On another occasion, when some marines marching from Ostia and Puteoli to Rome asked for an allowance for shoes, he ordered that in future they should be made to run the distance barefooted.[98] Vespasian may have been the first to mutter that old saw, "spare the rod, spoil the army."

In his first year as emperor he suppressed a serious Gaulish revolt and made the German frontier secure, while his elder son Titus captured and destroyed Jerusalem. The rest of the empire looked forward to peace under Vespasian, but the Jews after the Jewish War could only look forward to 1,878 years of homelessness. Diaspora. Vespasian and Titus, who was virtual co-ruler with his father, celebrated Jewish discomfiture with a great triumph, later (AD 82) recorded on the Arch of Titus. A tourist attraction it always was. Is it arch to point out that to Jews it was no mitzvah?[99]

Titus fell madly in love with a Jewish princess named Berenice. She had already been married several times, once to her uncle, and may have lived incestuously with her brother, King Herod Agrippa II. She is mentioned in the New Testament (Acts 25) as having witnessed an interview between St. Paul and her brother. She was already forty, thirteen years Titus's senior, when their relationship began. Titus, who had a reputation for generosity, did not care about the difference in their ages. She had been very beautiful, and he was one of those rare men who understood that older women can teach a young man a thing or two despite a sagging chin or a thickened waist. Later, after his father died (AD 79), he gave up on such education. The Romans had become impatient with the Jews, and Titus, not yet as popular with the Romans as he became at his death, and fearful of angering them, sent Berenice home without marrying her, but not without regretting her absence. Romans of both sexes were expected to sacrifice private pleasure to political duty. Romans were not yet romantic.

Before he died, Vespasian sent General Agricola to Britain (AD 78) and there, as governor, Agricola pacified most of the island, conquered North Wales and advanced far into Scotland. Agricola was humane and enlightened. The historian Tacitus, his son-in-law, regarded him a model of the older Roman virtues. Vespasian beautified Rome. He built a new forum, a temple of peace, public baths, and started the Colosseum. He reorganized the eastern provinces, raising Judea to the status of a province. He enlarged Syria by adding the client state Commagene to it, absorbing Cappadocia and lesser Armenia into Galatia.

A gruff old soldier, Vespasian recognized the necessity of tolerating critics, and once remarked that he would not kill every dog that barked at him. He did kill one, the Stoic philosopher Helvidius Priscus, who returned from the exile to which he was condemned by Nero demanding the restoration of the Republic! He was one of those academics who lose touch with reality. Priscus was merciless in his treatment of Vespasian, who asked him not to attend the Senate if he meant to abuse him so. When Helvidius refused, Vespasian banished him and later sent men to kill him. Suetonius says he recalled the men but was falsely informed that Priscus was already dead, so cancelled the order for their recall. Later, he regretted the murder and was extremely patient when his friends spoke to him frankly, or other philosophers proved impudent.[100] If a gruff old soldier-emperor could learn patience, one would think a philosopher liked Priscus might have learned manners.

Many a soldier has died with his boots on, whether by choice or not, is hard to say. But few have wanted to die standing up, which is how Vespasian, having contracted a bowel disorder, thought he should go. His effort to get off his bed and stand up was all the more remarkable since at the moment of death he was having an extremely strong attack of diarrhea. Suetonius did not record how that all came out.

Titus (AD 79–81)

Titus succeeded as expected (AD 79). He became very popular for ending treason trials, banishing informers, forgiving his brother, Domitian, for plotting against him and for seeking as pontifex maxiumus to avoid shedding blood. Under Titus, the Colosseum was completed, more baths were built in Rome, and when Pompeii was destroyed by Mt. Vesuvius (AD 79), he visited the ravaged city and contributed to its relief. He did the same in 81 when Rome was suffering from a fire and plague. The empire was mostly at peace, except for some fighting in Britain. Titus had plenty of experience governing, having held the consulship for seven years in succession under his father. At the end of that reign, he was given sole command of the Praetorian Guard. Charming, handsome, intelligent, and generous to a fault, Suetonius called him "the darling of the human race" and noted that his death from fever in the same farmhouse in Reate where his father died caused universal grief. Like Vespasian, he was deified soon after his death. Although one encyclopedia account of Titus claims the verdict of contemporaries upon him was "universally favorable," it is probably the case that they forgot to poll Berenice and the Jews.

DOMITIAN (AD 81–96)

Of the three Flavians, Domitian was the least flavorful. He left many contemporaries with a bad taste in the mouth because he destroyed the illusion, carefully fostered by Augustus and Tiberius, that the Senate had an essential part to play in imperial government. Domitian denuded the Senate of members and respect, so that they, not the emperor, appeared unclothed. He was well educated, though there is a tradition that he had been neglected due to a reversal of his father's fortune.[101] He excelled in poetry, writing, and oratory, though Suetonius claimed he only simulated an interest in it, and later gave it up.[102] Between his unfortunate introduction at the age of eighteen to Roman politics as Italy's ostensible caretaker and his last decade of tyranny, his early reign (AD 81–85) proved equitable.[103] In this respect he resembled Tiberius, whom he apparently idolized, and Caligula, both of whom finished their office as tyrants, but began by taking seriously their role as administrative reformers.[104] They found that reform on a daily basis gets tougher and tougher. When the going got tough, Tiberius, Caligula, and Domitian got going.

If one believes Suetonius, Domitian spent hours at the beginning of his reign in seclusion catching flies and stabbing them with a sharpened pen.[105] One wonders how, if this tyro were in seclusion, Suetonius learned of this habit? The record shows that early on he enacted useful laws, reformed religion and morals (the public's if not his own), inaugurated public works, increased military pay, and improved the economic lot of the proletariat. He censored scurrilous lampoons; enforced the Julian laws against adultery, tried to end child prostitution and sodomy, and abolished the practice of castration. He forbade the performance of lewd pantomimes and ordered the execution of vestal virgins who de-vested themselves. Of virginity.[106] He issued sumptuary laws to curb spending on luxuries and an edict to prevent big growers from producing more wine than grain. Naturally, he alienated big growers and big drinkers. The rich did not live by bread alone, and the rich, that is, the big growers, won.[107]

There were sound economic reasons for reducing conspicuous consumption, and if Rome had not been such a firetrap, Domitian might have made a bonfire of other peoples' vanities, like Savonarola in Renaissance Florence. But Savonarola's puritanism attracted respectable intellectuals and aristocrats to his cause because that monk was wrapped in the odor of sainthood; Domitian's reforms stank in the nostrils of Rome's opinion makers. When Domitian declared himself Master and god (Lat., *Dominus et deus*), the opinion makers thought he was only rapt in himself.

Rome's great rulers were great military heroes. Titus won an arch for demolishing Jerusalem. Where would Domitian win his? He led an expedition against the Chatti in southern Germany (AD 83)—but the Chatti were scarcely worth talking about. They simply retreated into the forest, and Domitian spent more time building military roads through their territory than he did in fighting them.[108] In 85 the emperor hurried to the lower Danube to confront King Decebal of Dacia (Romania), who wreaked great damage on Rome's Balkan provinces and stirred up other tribes in southern Germany against her. Until 89 the war with Dacia sputtered fitfully, punctuated by a second Chattan scuffle. Domitian raced between the Rhine and Danube.[109] Despite a Roman victory at Tapae, two days' march from the Dacian capital, and a triumph over the Chatti and the Dacians (end of AD 89), Decebal was able to force Rome to pay an annual tribute to assure continued peace.[110] Decebal's racket did not bode well for the empire.

Although Domitian checked (for a time) the activities of the loathed informers (Latin, *delatores*), which would normally have made members of the aristocracy happy, his supervision of provincial governors angered them. Domitian was courageous to attempt to heal social ills, but not politic enough to sweeten the pill. Where Titus had been ingratiating, Domitian was merely grating. Consequently, his reputation, despite many fine accomplishments, was soon shredded.

Domitian was a good administrator, but he was regarded as an autocrat. His preferred style of ruling was oriental despotism. Michael Grant says absolute monarchy had always been his intent. Absolutism is frequently the objective of successful heads of state. There was a connection between his building up of Rome and his tearing down of the aristocracy. He was an ambitious raiser of monuments but paid for them with other peoples' money. Thus, the capitoline temple, the completion of the Colosseum,[111] a stadium, a circus,[112] a temple to his father and brother, his brother's arch,[113] his own mansion on the Palatine, a shopping center in the Saepta, granaries, a waterworks, splendid libraries, the music theater called the Odeum, all earned him odium. True, he never paid out more than he took in. He balanced his checkbook by rigorous tax collection, including the Jewish poll tax, and by confiscating properties of murdered or exiled enemies. His income matched his outgo. Taxes and confiscations were income; exiled enemies outgo.

He employed talented servants, among whom were J. Agricola, Tacitus's father-in-law; J. Frontinus, militarist and technical writer whose defeat of the Silures in southeast Wales and pacification of Britain made possible Agricola's later success there; L. J. Priscus, a well-known jurist; M. U. Trajanus, later the Emperor Trajan;[114] and Julius Quadratus, who served fairly and squarely in several provincial governorships. Did these good men really believe that when serving their master they were also serving God? Matthew 6:24 says you cannot serve two masters, God and money, but Domitian's employees might have argued that they served only one, their *dominus et deus,* Domitian. The Master of worldly things was the Deity of the empyrean realm as well. On this, he insisted. So where was the conflict of interest?

Domitian thought his wife, Domitia Longina, daughter of General Corbulo, had betrayed him, first with his brother Titus, and again with an actor named Paris. Accordingly, he divorced her in AD 83, but then, pretending that the populace demanded her return, re-wed her. That is one encyclopedia account, based on sources that belittle Domitian (Dio Cassius, Suetonius).[115] There is no proof that he divorced her. In light of her role in his demise, he undoubtedly should have.

Suetonius emphasized his insatiable sexual needs. Domitian called making love "bed wrestling." It was a whole lot more fun than wrestling with his conscience. Suetonius claimed the emperor depilated his concubines with his own hand, which may be of psychological interest, in light of the fact that he once wrote a treatise on baldness and rued, like the first Caesar, nature's vagaries.[116] He persistently refused to marry his niece Julia, daughter of Titus, although the rumors that he seduced her shortly after her marriage, loved her openly, and caused her death by compelling her to have his child aborted, have been labeled "a farrago of nonsense" by his recent biographer.[117]

His interest in the provinces was keen and laudable. A letter of his to a procurator in Syria, one Claudius Athenodorus, insists that the privileges of the city of Epiphaneia (Syria) be preserved, and that these included freedom from arbitrary requisitions of beasts of burden without a permit from the emperor himself. To enable the poor farmers of the hinterland to make ends meet the emperor advised Claudius, "use your own beasts of burden (or else) rent them."[118] Domitian was a stickler for detail. He was also good at pinning responsibility for wrongdoing on the appropriate donkey. That may have been done as much to preserve provincial loyalty as to relieve the plight of the provincial poor. Neither in imperial Rome nor the empire at large nor in our own country has central government made its prime concern the relief of poverty and suffering. Domitian may have dimly conceived of such reforms, but he had neither the information nor the means to bring it about. In the U.S. at the beginning of the second millennium we do. And we haven't.

There is a tradition that Domitian persecuted Jews and Christians. The tradition regarding Christians stemmed from Eusebius (d. AD 330?), who cited only one case, that of Flavius Clemens's wife, Domitilla, and more especially, from the sixteenth-century historian Caesar Baronius. No contemporary author mentioned Domitian as a persecutor of Christians, and most modern historians now regard the old saw about Domitian being the second persecutor (after Nero) untrue. Vespasian taxed Jews harshly in order to recoup the money lost in the Jewish wars, and Domitian continued to collect that tax. But the object was to get money from the Jewish community in Rome and elsewhere. The practice of Judaism was allowed to continue. Though Jews and Christians were regarded as atheists because they did not worship the Roman gods or the emperor, both were grudgingly tolerated, provided they did not try to convert others. Under Domitian, they were safe enough unless wealthy enough to attract the attention of informers.[119] Neither Jews nor Christians had defenders at court. They were not part of Domitian's crowd.

Actually, Domitian had no crowd. Like Tiberius he grew increasingly isolated and preoccupied with the dangers of plots. In 88 the commander of two legions in Moguntiacum (Mainz), L. Antonius Saturninus, revolted and proclaimed himself emperor. Six other German legions remained loyal, and together with help from the Spanish legion (Trajan's), the revolt was squashed before Domitian could arrive. He put his cousin, Flavius Clemens, to death in 95, exiling his wife, Domitilla, who was a Christian.[120] Domitian's last decade was a reign of terror in which informants, freedmen, and favorites were said to have managed everything. He executed at least eleven senators and exiled many others during the ensuing treason trials.[121] Domitian, entering into paranoia, suspected anyone who appeared (as Agricola in Britain) to have outshone him on the battlefield.[122] He was supposed to have kept an enemies list just like Richard M. Nixon. Domitian included Pliny the Younger, who served Domitian as quaestor, tribune of the plebs, praetor, and once Trajan's commissioner of the treasury. Like the journalist Daniel Shore, who was proud that he had been on Nixon's list, Pliny bragged of being on Domitian's. Domitian was unapologetic. He lamented that people would never believe how many plotters were out to get him until he fell their victim. One or two courtiers murmured, "We believe you, Domitian." Soon, everybody would.

The emperor continued to perform his military duties. Another war on the Danube took him to Pannonia (Bosnia, Croatia, parts of Hungary) in spring of AD 92, until the quarrelling tribesmen there were pacified. Home by January 93, Domitian celebrated his second imperial salutation, followed by an ensuing four years' peace and prosperity excluding, perhaps, Africa.[123] One reason Domitian got some peace after 93 was that he outlawed philosophers and astrologers. Stoics and stargazers not only studied politics but seemed to the emperor critics of the status quo. Though a reformer, he had conservative instincts, and it was his power that he wished above all to conserve. Not a bit starry-eyed, he feared the scientific *accuracy* of astrology, and that others might use such knowledge to plot against him. Knowledge was already a world wide web. Domitian was the spider at its center. He intended to limit access. After banishing philosophers and astrologers from Rome or maybe the empire (historians are uncertain), he stoically resigned himself to their absence. Epictetus (c. AD 50–c. 138), the Phyrigian Stoic and Domitian's contemporary, taught that the only good is within oneself. Domitian thought to himself, "How true!"

The plotters who helped slay Domitian are variously listed by the sources (Suetonius, Dio Cassius, Eutropius) to include Domitilla, widow of the executed Flavius Clemens; Domitian's wife; her steward, Stephanus, who, Suetonius says, was under indictment for embezzlement;[124] two of Domitian's valets (Satur, Parthenius); his aid, Clodianus; an unnamed gladiator; a secretary; a notary, and, but without general agreement, both Praetorian prefects, Petronius Secundas and Norbanus.[125] Had the latter concluded that because Domitian had eliminated their predecessors their lives, too, were threatened?[126] All but the prefects and his wife were members of Domitian's staff—none was a senator! His domestics were frightened because Domitian had just executed one of his freedmen, Epaphroditus, for helping Nero commit suicide twenty-seven years earlier. The staff decided to rid themselves of this unreasonable employer before he could read their old employment records.

Some said that Stephanus killed him while he slept, before he could reach for his dagger under his pillow.[127] Or else, Parthenius's servants helped Stephanus slay the emperor, killing Stephanus in the fray.[128] Or else Stephanus, ushered into Domitian's mirror-lined bedroom on the pretext of handing him an important document, struck him in the groin as he read it. When the emperor called for a slave (a young boy, witness to the murder) to hand him the dagger he kept under his pillow, only the handle could be found.[129] It is clear from these divergent accounts that Domitian failed not only to grasp the dagger but also the plot. The historians barely got a handle on it either. They hoped their readers, like Domitian, would get the point.

Nerva (AD 96–98)

The day Domitian died (September 18, 96 AD), the Senate named Marcus Cocceius Nerva emperor. Some might think that Nerva was in on the plot, but this former counsel to Vespasian and Domitian had not thrust himself into power. Instead, power was thrust upon him by the plotters. He was a gentle, respectable, and childless old man, sixty-one, sixty-two, or sixty-six when he took office, and in poor health.[130] He overindulged in wine drinking and had a tendency to vomit up his food. Nerva had a nervous stomach. It must have seemed to the Senate that he would be a docile interim emperor, a "temp" whose service could be taken for granted. They were confident he would demand—and receive—no fringe benefits. Not only did he share the Senate's sympathies, he couldn't easily say no to anyone. His consul, Fronto, said that "to have an Emperor under whom no one may do anything is bad, but to have one under whom everyone may do everything is worse."

This was too harsh. Nerva could be firm, but his chief aim was conciliation.[131] Accordingly, he recalled the exiles and attempted to see that their property—what was left of it—was returned. Many of the informers were executed and Rome basked in restored justice. He assured the senators that he would never put any of them to death—an old privilege. His chief counselors were senators, and all claims against the state treasury would be heard by a magistrate (praetor) and witnesses. Still, Nerva was as much in charge as Domitian had been, and the tasks still performed by the Senate were hardly indispensable. Nerva was not a constitutional monarch, but a polite, benevolent autocrat. The Senate understood their situation and Nerva his.

Nerva's contributions to Italians were unusually generous. Exemptions from inheritance taxes increased, and new lands were given to the landless. Nerva sold off his own property to provide funds for redistributing land. His was the last Agrarian Law passed by the popular assembly (*comitia*), an old Republican body composed of citizens who could vote yes or no to any proposal made by a magistrate. Loans to formerly indigent farmers were creatively financed, with half the funds coming from government and half from private sources such as Nerva's. The farmers were to repay interest on loans to their municipality, and the latter to maintain poor children. Under Trajan, Hadrian, and the Antonines, this practice, a kind of children's food bank (*alimentationes*), was to become the most famous charitable enterprise in the Roman world, the brainchild of a childless old man whose stomach was weak, but whose heart was strong.

Childlessness made Nerva vulnerable to the whims of the army and Guard, the only groups disappointed with him. The soldiers loved Domitian because he was the first in many years to raise their base pay. The military resented the fact that the Senate damned Domitian's memory and tore down all his monuments, something that would not have happened had Domitian had a son to succeed him. Nerva, like Domitian, had no son, but unlike his predecessor, Nerva learned from experience that he needed a successor. He had two unpleasant surprises. One was the abortive plot of a rich descendant of the old triumvir Crassus, but it came to nothing. The other occurred when the prefect of the Praetorians, Casperius Aelianus, demanded that Domitian's murderers, Parthenius (*partheno* meant unfertilized in Greek) and Petronius Secundus, be handed over for execution. His men had surrounded Nerva in his own palace on the Palatine hill and insisted that he hand over the two prisoners. Mutiny on the mounty! Nerva owed his position to those murderers. Considering the danger of his situation, it was brave, but futile, to bare his own neck to Aelianus's soldiers. They seized the prisoners despite Nerva's disapproval. Petronius was lucky. They dispatched him with one stroke of the sword. Parthenius was not as fortunate. They cut off his genitals and thrust them into his mouth before cutting his throat.[132] Those muddled murderers. They thought they were committing parthenogenesis!

The murder of Domitian's assassins taught Nerva that he could no longer go it alone. In October AD 97, he adopted the commander of the Rhine legions, M. Ulpius Trajanus, to be his son, colleague, and successor, informing the general of his adoption by mail.[133] For three months the two men ruled jointly. In late January of the next year, Nerva died after a high fever and was promptly deified. His sixteen-month reign had left him enervated.

TRAJAN (AD 98–117)

We moderns may soon decide for ourselves the sex, genetic traits, even the intelligence of our offspring. The Romans were even more advanced. They selected all these plus their child's curriculum vitae completed to middle age. They adopted grown men with successful careers to inherit their name and fortune. Gone was the bother of raising a son, while the money saved on nurses and tutors was freed up for other things. In the case of Nerva and Trajan, it was spent on a nice little adoption ceremony at the capitoline temple of Jupiter, attended by priests, vestal virgins, senators. Refreshments were catered and served on the terrace after the ceremony. The best people in Rome attended. The adoptee, Trajan, was in Cologne and could not attend. Unlike most new additions to the family, he immediately recognized how much he owed the new father.

Trajan's biological father, a common legionary, had worked his way up to legionary commander in the Jewish War and was made consul and governor of Syria and Asia. Of Umbrian origin, the family had settled at Italica near Seville, Spain, where Trajan was born on September 18, 53 AD. He skipped the classics, was raised a soldier, served in Syria under his father, became commander of the Seventh Legion in northern Spain in the 80s. He was a praetor by 85, a consul by 91. Nerva appointed him governor of Upper Germany, where he was popular with the legions on the Rhine and Danube. He stayed out of Rome to inspect her frontiers on these rivers and did not return until more than a year after Nerva's death. When he entered the city, it was already in his corner, where it remained. It was his good fortune to be tall, well built, handsome, and only forty-six at his accession. He came to the throne straight from central casting, with the approval of Senate, army, Praetorian Guard and a host of flattering reporters whose accounts have almost all disappeared.

Trajan was Rome's most beloved emperor, designated early in his reign *Pater Patriae,* and for the remainder of his nineteen-year reign he conciliated and charmed everyone with the possible exceptions of Dacians and Parthians, whom he defeated.[134] The subject of legend and poetry in the middle ages, Dante did not hesitate to place him alone of all Roman emperors in Paradise. Less flattering views were not unavailable in the early modern period. "Trajan was ambitious of fame; and as long as mankind shall continue to bestow more liberal applause on their destroyers than on their benefactors, the thirst of military glory will ever be the vice of the most exalted characters."[135] The last was the opinion of Edward Gibbon, who sized up even the kindest of autocrats without confusing kindness and autocracy. Pliny the younger (AD 113) who claimed that "the Emperor bade us to be free, so we were free" would have been appalled by Gibbon's cynicism and would have rejected as a useless ad hominem Professor Syme's dictum on Trajan: "he looked stupid and was believed honest."[136] Trajan was Alexander with a tad less megalomania, but without Alexander's interest in things intellectual; Pompey minus the arrogance and guile.[137] Trajan was Rome's Superman—performing wondrous victories over Rome's enemies—Dacia and Decebal (AD 101 and 105–6), Parthia and Parthamasiris—adding Arabia, Dacia, and Armenia (AD 115) to the empire while moving eastward.[138] Between wars he assumed the genial nature of Clark Kent, schmoozing with senators to whom he had no intention of paying attention. He set the stamp of autocratic government permanently on a principate that was never intended by its designer (Augustus) to be anything else but autocratic.

His wife, Pompeia Plotina (d. AD 123) seemed very much like Lois Lane, Clark's loyal secretary. Dio Cassius applauded her for her modesty, and she, upon entering the palace, said that she hoped she would leave it as humble as she entered it—or words to that effect. Most secretaries are humble. A few feign humility, hiding their independence until the last minute. Plotina was one of these last. She thwarted a disapproving Trajan over the marriage of his niece to Hadrian. Rumors existed that Plotina herself loved Hadrian, seven years her junior. They both denied the rumor, which persisted until her death. She may have forged documents after Trajan's death to "prove" he had adopted Hadrian when he had not![139] This Lois Lane did not make coffee. She seems to have preferred making emperors.

Trajan was a good provider. He provided Romans with more columns and markets, forums and basilicae, circus seats, temples, arches, baths, and fountains; Italians with more rural improvements, forts and barracks, harbors, child maintenance allowances, aqueducts, and highways; and everyone with a sense of peace and prosperity. He provided Rome with new provinces, Armenia, Arabia Parthia, and Dacia, audaciously taking as part of his title the name "Dacicus." Construction companies and poor parents loved him. Poor children did too, for they were henceforth better fed, though boys were fed better than girls. Certainly Trajan provided well for the boys whom he made love to, for Trajan was a pederast. Child abuse was scarcely in its infancy, so Rome did not object to men making love to boys as long as the men played the aggressor, not the passive role.[140]

The only contemporary writers on whom we have to rely for personal information on Trajan are the accounts of Tacitus (d. AD 117) and his friend Pliny. Pliny's *Panegyric* to Trajan was written in AD 100–101, a six-hour-long thank-you speech for a two-month appointment as consul. Every senator who heard it was thankful the appointment had not been for four months! There is a bit of irony in Pliny's relationship with Trajan, always deferential, for Pliny himself might have had a shot at being emperor. His guardian, L. Verginius Rufus, had three times declined the honor, after the deaths of Nero, Galba, and Otho.[141] Pliny's career was exceedingly honorable anyway, for he served in a number of public posts under three emperors.

Henderson long ago described the interest that Trajan, "a plain practical man," had in governing Rome's provinces. He wanted them orderly—not surprising for a general. He had four provincial governors tried for extortion. They were not orderly. Pliny was appointed to defend the one from Bithynia, a man named Bassus who stooped to break the law by accepting gifts from the provincials he governed. Bassus got off lightly, but he had been caught off-base and brought low, his chances for further imperial employment ruined. Pliny made such a good defense for a man he knew was guilty that Trajan rewarded him by giving him the governorship of Bithynia. Was it a promotion or a punishment?

An acclaimed letter writer, Pliny's tenth book was his published correspondence with Trajan. Many of these missives dealt with Pliny's concerns as governor of Bithynia, (AD 111–13) situated on the southern coast of the Black Sea from Nicomedia opposite Byzantium almost to Trapezus (Trebizond) in the east. The most famous of the letters involved Pliny's quandary as to how to deal with Christians in the courts of justice. Was membership alone a crime? It was, and Pliny had been ordering their execution in cases where they would not abjure. Yet, so many Christians were there in his province, and so vigorous was the sect (after a period of quiescence) that he needed Trajan's advice. Trajan answered that "no formula" could apply to every case. Christians were not to be "sought out," but if reported and convicted, were to be punished.[142] Anyone who abjured and worshipped Roman gods was to be forgiven. No anonymous accusations were to be investigated or considered. Trajan adopted a law-and-order position without evincing the slightest sign of outrage. That the law against the sect was itself outrageous seems not to have occurred to him.

The letters tell us much about Pliny and give invaluable glimpses of Trajan's views of governance, though no understanding whatsoever of religious belief. Pliny wrote long letters, uncertain how to proceed on practical matters and the emperor wrote short ones, pragmatic and self-assured. If Pliny had been emperor, and Trajan governor of Bithynia, we would probably know just as much about Pliny as we do now, but a lot less about Bithynia and Trajan. Still, if Trajan had been governor of Bithynia, it wouldn't matter. Our interest in people is determined by their authority and power, not by their insight and capacity.

Trajan's last three years (114–17) were spent on the eastern frontier. He conquered all of Mesopotamia including the Persian capital of Ctesiphon near modern Baghdad. When he reached the Persian Gulf he looked eastward toward India and said, "If only I were younger." At that very moment, Trajan had to fight off a Mesopotamian rebellion. Forced to abandon a siege at a desert stronghold called Hatra, the emperor appointed a young Persian prince to rule over Ctesiphon before setting off for Rome.

While his conquest of Parthia was a hands-on experience, Trajan failed to keep in touch with the rest of the empire. Rebellions also occurred in Africa, Libya, Palestine, Sarmatia (Ukrainia), and Britain. The most pressing was the Jewish rebellion. Jews massacred hundreds of thousands of non-Jews in Egypt, Cyprus, and Cyrenaica. The absurdity of it overwhelmed the emperor. The Jews were actually hitting back at the Romans! Would they never get over that David and Goliath thing?

Suddenly Trajan died, at Selinus in Cilicia, on August 9, 117. He suffered from a circulatory condition that he himself thought the result of poison and a stroke that left him partially paralyzed. A modern biographer thinks he suffered from aggravated hypertension, complicated by atherosclerosis, a form of arteriosclerosis, and the kidney disease called nephritis (Bright's disease).[143] It is impressive how, using purely literary sources of the classical age, a modern historian so neatly diagnoses the diseases of a man who died nearly two thousand years ago. Were he alive today, Trajan would be lucky to get so clear a diagnosis from his doctor. Of course, he would receive a much larger bill. Practicing historians may be cheaper than practicing physicians, but they are not always more reasonable.

Trajan's reign was the apex of benevolent despotism posing as constitutional empire. In sixth century BC, Greece tyrants like Cypselus of Corinth and Pisistratus of Athens exercised power and benevolence not unlike Trajan, though on a minute rather than a massive scale. The Greeks of Corinth and Athens lamented how unfortunate they were to be deprived of liberty, while their cities grew lovelier from their tyrants' generosity and rational use of men, space, and other natural resources. It was Trajan's good fortune to have lived in an era when such liberty as the Greeks had clamored for, the Roman Senate fantasized about, and Gibbon later admired was discredited. Like Cypselus and Pisistratus, Trajan provided the peace and prosperity that philosophical critics rarely bothered to conceive let alone deliver. For this Romans forgave him any loss of liberty—and overlooked picayune foibles like his fondness for young boys and his dipsomania. To them he was the best. A Prince. *Optimus principis.*

HADRIAN (AD 117–38)

Publius Aelius Hadrianus, the Emperor Hadrian, joked about death as he lay dying and wrote a poem twitting his soul about its pale stiffness, pathetic indecisiveness, and diminished sense of humor! Gifted intellectually, Hadrian was an amateur painter and sculptor, an urban planner and architect, designing, among other things, his own tomb, Rome's Castel San Angelo, and the Pantheon.[144] He left Agrippa's name (Agrippa had built the former pantheon on the same site) prominently displayed on the new pediment. Hadrian did not need official graffiti to advertise himself. He knew who he was.

Hadrian was no cynic, content to live in a barrel. Though he cheerfully endured the rigors of travel and war, he built a luxurious spread near Tivoli, thirty kilometers from Rome. Hadrian's villa, or palace complex, occupied 165 manicured acres overlooking the Sabine hills, with easy access to the city. Its porticoes and pools, sculptures and colonnades imitated those he saw abroad, for Hadrian visited every region of his vast empire, spending more than half his twenty-one-year reign traveling. At his villa the emperor could sit and chat with friends in gardens—as Epicurus, much admired by him, had recommended doing in the Hellenistic age. There, surrounded by luxury, Hadrian regretted that he was not again on the road, cheerfully enduring physical discomfort to understand and to improve the civilization Rome had inherited from Greece, Persia, and Egypt. Hadrian was happiest traveling, but he was nearly as happy in his palace complex. Apart from his palace, he had no other complex.

Despite his considerable (but selective) geniality, boundless confidence, and ability to master any subject, Hadrian was, from the beginning of his reign, unpopular with the Roman elite. For them he was too gifted. It is difficult for ordinary politicians to appreciate a statesman, especially when he is their boss. Hadrian's unpopularity owed partly to the fact that Trajan never got around to adopting him, and Plotina, his friend and supporter, may have lent herself to a court conspiracy in which she insisted, but did not satisfactorily prove, that such was Trajan's deathbed wish.[145] Hadrian, governor of Syria at the time, had already been proclaimed emperor by the army rank and file, a piece of "evidence" more to the point, but one the Senate found rankled.

It did not help matters that Hadrian decided upon his accession to give up the territories won by Trajan east of the Euphrates and Tigris rivers. Although this was consistent with Augustus's preference for natural boundaries, it seemed to many a repudiation of Trajan's glory, for the Parthian wars, which brought Rome three new provinces, were a source of pride and potential profit. Even more disturbing for the Senate was the fact that four important senators, ex-consuls, had been assassinated before Hadrian reached Rome—perhaps eliminated by his remaining guardian, Attianus, who had already warned him about three other enemies.[146] Neither those three nor, according to Birley, the four consulars had been harmed by Hadrian, but the Senate, which had itself given the order to execute the four ex-consuls for treason, later blamed Hadrian for their deaths. Perhaps they were suffering from a collective guilty conscience. They finished by blaming Hadrian for breaking the usual promise new rulers always made, not to seek any senator's death, however richly he deserved to die.

No wonder Hadrian, sensing the ill will that he could not dissipate and had not caused, took comfort in extended absences from the capital. Traveling, he wrested pleasure from duty, domestic or public, combining Epicurean propensities with Stoic service. He scrutinized and improved every imperial province, endowing each with great monuments, both useful and decorative. Most provincials felt for him a genuine sympathy and gratitude, and styled him A Man for all Greeks (*Panhellenios*); a new sun-god (*Helios*); Restorer of Gaul (*Restitutor Galliae*); and Divine Savior of the World.[147] To Christians these titles were worthless. Their Savior restored their sense of self-worth. Their Savior could save souls. What was Gaul to them? Rome found Christians galling.

Nothing Hadrian ever accomplished is more widely remembered than the seventy-mile long wall (Latin, *vallum*) that he had built across northern Britain from the Tyne to Solway beginning in AD 122. His barrier was begun at the Tyne with a bridge not only named for him (Pons Aelius), but designed by him. Hadrian, whose crossing of the North Sea was commemorated by the title "Oceanus" on imperial coinage, was determined to demarcate the limits of Roman authority, as he had already done on the Rhine and Danube. His expansionist critics thought that regarding expansionism, Oceanus was all wet.

Hadrian was more inquisitive than acquisitive, and a believer in firm discipline. He inspected bridges and laws, recruits and officers. He made common soldiers more comfortable and officers give up their luxuries. His tolerance of cultural differences was only exceeded by his enthusiasm for most of them. He abolished distinctions between the provinces and Italy, provincials and Romans. The Greeks with whom he identified since adolescence (he was nicknamed "the little Greek" [*Graeculos*] while still a schoolboy) loved paradox. Hadrian was nothing if not paradoxical. He was sociable though remote; humane though not overly so; honored, but feared; affectionate, though not regarded with affection; a patient and tolerant (if not a loving) husband. He had married his wife, Sabina, Trajan's grandniece, at Plotina's urging. He took her on some of his journeys and demanded that due reverence be paid her as empress. When her courtiers did not seem reverential enough, Hadrian sacked them. One such was the historian Suetonius. When Sabina died, he gave her divine honors. Even the best historians could not claim the worship that mediocre monarchs and their wives regularly achieved. Some said Hadrian and Plotina were lovers, but their bond was their mutual love of Greek culture. When Plotina died, Hadrian was in Provence. He built her a splendid temple at Nîmes. He wrote hymns in her honor. He wore mourning for nine days. He owed her big time for his accession, for her friendship.

He was a great lover of children and made it a point to feed more poor children under the public feeding program than had been fed under Trajan. Hadrian was a real compassionate conservative who left no child behind in his effort to maintain them at public expense. Hadrian, like many of his predecessors, not only saw to it that children were fed, but fed upon. The love of boys was one of those Hellenic traits dear to his heart. The beautiful Bithynian Greek boy Antinous, whom he attached to his retinue on one of his trips to Asia minor, "a youth of quite exceptional beauty," was, if it is not too catty to say so, his catamite, a word derived from the name of the Phrygian Ganymedes, Jupiter's child paramour.[148] Hadrian lost Antinous in what may have been an accident, or perhaps, a suicide, for the young man drowned in the Nile while the royal party was sightseeing on a barge.[149]

Birley notes Hadrian baffled contemporaries, had "several competing personalities" and was fond of playing roles, chief of which was that of Hellene.[150] Baffling or not, he gave his underlings and subjects clear orders. He would not tolerate extortion. He appointed officers of consular rank to replace local magistrates, continuing the centralizing tendencies that characterized the principate after Vespasian. He improved the quality of Roman law, getting jurists to advise him on it and setting high standards for justice that later influenced the code of the Byzantine emperor Justinian who ignored all laws prior to Hadrian's.[151] Hadrian abolished tax farming and gave professional procurators the direction of the treasury. He made the postal service an imperial, not a municipal responsibility, and saw to it that mailmen followed his instructions to the letter!

He was straightforward about spending on infrastructure. He constructed libraries, gymnasiums, and baths, taking care that women were given a greater number of hours for bathing in towns where there was only one bathing facility! On only one of his buildings (the temple of Venus and Rome) did he have his own name inscribed. He brought (most of) his subjects a golden age of peace and prosperity and was naive enough to think that his service, generosity, and concern for his empire were sufficient to procure him an honored place in history.

A self-conscious humanitarian, Hadrian ameliorated the conditions of Rome's slaves. Not himself religious, he supported Greek and Roman traditions of piety and restored old and built new temples, especially in Rome and Athens. Early Christian scholars of Christianity were divided over whether Hadrian persecuted Christians. Eusebius, Jerome, Augustine, and Orosius thought he did. Lactantius and Tertullian thought not.[152] Birley suggests that Justin Martyr (Flavius Justinus) and Eusebius may have tried to make Hadrian's practice toward Christians appear milder than that of Trajan, who made the practice of that religion illegal.[153] Perowne notes that Hadrian did not understand Christians and was not interested in them,[154] whereas his behavior toward the Jews was unmistakably hostile.[155] Syme suggested that Hadrian's cosmopolitanism was offended by Jewish rejection of Hellenism.[156] In fact, Jews, Hellenists, Christians, and Romans all worshipped authority and authoritarianism, abstract thought, and legalistic discrimination. They just differed on how to define and apply their different programs. They needed better programmers. They needed better programs.

The Christians were too dispersed throughout the Roman world to persecute easily, but Jews, more concentrated in their holy land, made a lovely target. Hadrian forbade circumcision throughout the empire, a practice the Jews thought guaranteed their male members' validity. The validation of womenfolk was another thing Jews, Romans, and Greeks agreed on. No one thought them worth validating. Hadrian's impatience with Jews stemmed from their practice of circumcising their male members. Hadrian did not think anyone could improve on this universal coupling joint. His thinking reflected the Hellenic appreciation of unimpaired, ideal male beauty. He, who had carefully surveyed his whole empire, could not see why they insisted on the sanctity of but one spot in it—Jerusalem. Further, their lack of attachment to the rituals and symbols of imperial government (emperor cults) seemed to him a willful rejection of mankind's dearest values—Roman ones, of course. In short, though he was reputed to be a most tolerant fellow, Hadrian wrote off the Jews as antisocial, superstitious bigots, a threat to empire. They were particularly intolerable because they were particular and intolerant. Was Hadrian?

He detested war and would have preferred to avoid it. When he could not, as was the case of the Jewish insurrection in Palestine, Hadrian sent his best general (Julius Severus) to Judea to defeat the Jewish leader, Simon bar

Kochba. When Rome won, the ruins that had been Jerusalem became the site of Hadrian's own new city, Aelia Capitolina (after his patronymic Aelius).[157] He forbade Jews the right of entry, except on one day of the year, a concession that only made them more bitter, like the bitter herbs of the Seder that recalled another inhospitable land, Egypt. A nineteenth-century biographer remarked that Hadrian lost his reputation for humanity after the cruelties of the Jewish War (AD 132–35) and also the happiness he once had peacefully traveling through his empire.[158] Hadrian, like every other tourist, learned to his dismay that although travel broadens, it also sullies. The Jews, who would travel even further than Hadrian, never developed his carefree regard for it. Suffering would be the distinguishing mark of the diaspora. For Jews, the best journeys were those into the interior—spiritual explorations of their relationship with God.

Marguerite Yourcenar's compelling novel *Memoirs of Hadrian* (1951) won her the plaudits of European *littérateurs* and catapulted her into the all-male Académie Française. It did not appeal to the British historian of Rome, Ronald Syme.[159] Hadrian anticipated the existential implications of life in an ethically ambiguous, decadent, obscurantist social order. His *pro forma* concern for preserving traditional religious rites, enjoyment of tourism, faith in his ability to improve his empire culturally and materially, recognition of the need for proper boundaries to all but his own behavior, love of peace but willingness to disturb it in order to compel pious Jews to act like everybody else, unwillingness for decorum's sake to divorce an unloved wife, eagerness for sexual gratification with (among others) the boy Antinous, passion for hunting, reliance on astrology for policy decisions—all were implicated in Hadrian's existential plight.

A progressive, sensual, talented, educated fellow with a desire to know and improve everything, some arrogance, more humanity, and an enormous appreciation for the things of this world made Hadrian Western civilization's first fully evolved political liberal.[160] *Homo politicus liberalis.* The trouble was that while Hadrian was fully evolved, his empire and subjects were not. *Impero populusque illiberales.*

ANTONINUS PIUS (AD 138–61)

His successor and adopted son, Antoninus Pius, insisted, against strong opposition, on the Senate granting Hadrian divine honors.[161] He threatened to resign until they did. Antoninus may have earned his nickname Pious by insisting that the Senate honor his "father," even though he had been his "son" for less than half a year![162] But for the fact that Antoninus was a man of fifty-two, such politicking would have made him a child prodigy. Instead, it made his "father" a god and him an emperor.

Because the reign of Antoninus Pius is not well documented, historians have had time to mull over its significance, harder to do when facts press in on all sides than when they remain fuzzy, the record scanty. The significance of his reign is hard to pin down. Edward Gibbon noted that despite Hadrian's restlessness and Antoninus's tranquility—the latter rarely traveled farther than from his palace ten miles west of Rome to his favorite villa, twenty miles south of it—both men adopted Augustus's rejection of imperial expansion. The result of this policy, said Gibbon, who excepted "a few slight hostilities, that served to exercise the legions of the frontier," was that for forty-three years Hadrian and Antoninus Pius offered "the fair prospect of universal peace."[163] But even so, the much touted "Pax Romana" was a Roman pox or plague to discontented provincials in Britain, northwestern Africa (Mauritania), Egypt, Germany, and Judea, where two rebellions occurred. Scarre notes that the reign was scarcely untroubled, but instead, there was "near continuous fighting and unrest."[164]

Michel de Montaigne remarked two centuries earlier than Gibbon that "by diverse means we arrive at the same end" (*Essays* 1.1).[165] Under Hadrian and his adopted son, two different personalities certainly, Rome did arrive at the same end, but it was not really peaceful. Rome's safety was not threatened, but that of many of her subject peoples' was. The Roman peace was as relative as the "peace" that has prevailed since the end of World War II. It was piecemeal.

Born in Italy in AD 86 to a family originally of Nemausus (Nîmes), young Titus Aurelius Fulvus Boionus Arrius Antoninus had an ordinary career for a man who was both extraordinarily handsome and extraordinarily rich. His service as quaestor, praetor, consul, and governor of the province of Asia (135–36) was accomplished without much military or administrative experience or skill. The extraordinary aspect of his career was that he became emperor. He owed that to the unanticipated death of Hadrian's first choice for his successor, Lucius Ceionius Commodus. Antoninus Pius was Hadrian's second choice. But Hadrian had also a short list of backup candidates for office for whenever Antoninus expired and insisted that Antoninus adopt two boys—Lucius Ceionius Commodus, orphaned son of his first choice, and Marcus Annius Verus, nephew of Antoninus's wife, Faustina the elder. Obediently, Antoninus adopted both boys, and both succeeded him on his own death, though the elder, Marcus, received the most attention.

Though Antoninus came to the job without the proper qualifications, an emperor could operate quite efficiently by means of those who had them— his generals and governors. His was a personality that threatened no one whose loyalty and services were necessary to run the empire. Except for his refusal to serve as emperor at all without the Senate's deification of Hadrian, Antoninus had no opposition, ran no risk, took no hostages, and was, therefore, never any one else's hostage, and certainly not fortune's. Everyone agreed that he was exceptional—not for his talents, as Hadrian had been, nor for his military experience, as Trajan was, nor for any literary or artistic skills—he had none—but for his moderation in all things, his justice, compassion, and reserve. He had character. Which goes to show that really nice people without any particular skill, providing they are well born and rich, have a good presence, outstanding posture, and never offend anyone—including the gods—are more appreciated than quirky geniuses like Hadrian, Claudius, or Tiberius.[166]

Antoninus may or may not have loved his wife, Annia Galeria Faustina the elder, but to dispel any doubts, he had a temple dedicated to her on her death in 140, so that if he did not really love her in life, at least when she was dead he let it be known that he worshipped her memory! Shortly after her death, he took one of her slaves as a concubine. He was thought so good a man, that this was regarded not as a sin but a symptom. Of his virility? Of his loneliness? In any event, it was not held against him as a *peccatum* [Latin, fault, sin] but written off as a peccadillo. A really good man can often get away with things that a worse one would be held accountable for. Certainly this paragon of piety had human weaknesses, but his popularity and paganism spared him the moralizing with which theologians (and later journalists) in the Christian era would surely have reproached him. It is not true that before she died Antoninus wrote of his wife Faustina: "I would rather live with her on Gyara [Rome's Devil's Island in the Aegean] than in the palace without her."[167] Although Antoninus wrote those very words, he wrote them not of his wife, but of their daughter, also named Annia Galeria Faustina, called the younger, future bride of his adopted son, Marcus, later the Emperor Marcus Aurelius.[168] So obviously, it could not be the case, as another work claims, that these were words attributed by Marcus to his own Faustina![169] In every civilization, needless confusion has been caused by a multiplicity of identical names. The confusion caused by identical superstitions, human foibles, and social injustices has been even worse, but is less likely to be eliminated. Under Antoninus, Rome was not yet experiencing much confusion, just ordinary delusion. It has therefore been described as an age of peace and prosperity.

MARCUS AURELIUS (AD 161–80)

If the reign of the pious Antoninus, who studied no philosophy, was happy and peaceful, that of his adopted son Marcus, who studied diligently and would have preferred the philosophical life, was a period of bitter warfare, turmoil, revolt, invasion, and plague. There is no rule of proportionality governing man's fate. Just because Marcus Aurelius prepared for trials by studying Stoicism was no reason to think he would not be called upon to be stoical. He was. He admired his adoptive father and for many years co-ruler Antoninus for his legendary piety—which in Roman terms meant more than mere reverence for the gods, but also for everything sanctified by time—a combination of provincialism and patriotism blended with pity, justice, compassion, and family feeling. Marcus might have guided his own life by such pieties, the habitual and anticipated repetitions of old rituals, familiar symbols, and respected values. For there are times when the pieties work really well—the easy and peaceful times that do not try men's souls. But Marcus chose to pay his debts to society with a standard he valued even more than Roman piety—the Stoic standard of understanding oneself in relation to the universe. He wrote, "In conformity to the nature of the universe every single thing is accomplished" (*Meditations* 6.9).[170]

To the Stoic, ignorance about the universe brought misery in its wake, and ignorance, Marcus had to believe, was curable through the study of philosophy. If one could not convert the world to rational thinking, one could serve as a role model for rational behavior. While sitting in camp at Carnuntum up on the middle Danube, Marcus tried in his *Meditations,* or private journal, to define rationality. He decided that it was paying attention to everything important, neglecting nothing, especially not the good, the modest, the true, the rational, the magnanimous. He admonished himself: "Therefore fix thyself in the possession of these." Otherwise, he concluded, "depart at once from life . . . not in passion, but with simplicity and freedom and modesty" (*Meditations* 10.8).

Marcus did not, despite a frail constitution and continual stomach problems, hasten his own end. Instead, he pushed himself to the limits of his fragile endurance by devoting himself to war and governance. Few men were as strong-minded, as determined to live according to reason and nature. He was already earnest as an eight-year-old, when Hadrian nicknamed him "Verissimus" for his attachment to truth. Now, strong principles and an attachment to the truth are the stuff of which martyrs (and prigs) are made. Hadrian thought Marcus something of a prig. The intellectual historian Crane Brinton thought him something of a martyr. To be precise, Brinton thought that Marcus took upon himself the role of martyr.[171] But martyrs died hoping for a better future; Aurelius counseled himself to enjoy what right reason enabled him to do and perceive in this life, and was oblivious to any future, apart from a transformation of the matter of which his body was made. The only similarity between Christian martyrs and Aurelius was that they all put relatively little value on that which this world had to offer. They all denigrated flesh and matter. Unlike the Christian martyrs, whom he actively persecuted, Marcus did not anticipate a better world anywhere else, or rewards for patient suffering. He noted that the rational soul derives its satisfaction from seeing itself, analyzing itself, and "making itself as it chooses." One of its greatest rewards was comprehending "the periodical renovation of all things" and realizing that no one who came after would ever see anything more or better than he himself had seen in forty years of contemplating "the uniformity" in all things (*Meditations* 11.1).

Christian martyrs did not waste time contemplating uniformity. They wanted to escape from it. They did not study philosophy to understand their own nature or that of the universe. They already had the answers to the essential questions revealed to them from a higher source. Marcus thought they were programmed by their religion to martyr themselves.[172] In that way he justified his persecution of them.

Marcus was himself programmed—from early childhood, first by Hadrian and then by Antoninus Pius for the career of Roman emperor. Born of Roman stock settled in Spain, Marcus Annius Verus was orphaned at the age of three and adopted by his grandfather Verus. Although Hadrian took an interest in the boy, Birley points out that he could not have spent much time around him, because Hadrian was seldom in Rome when Marcus was growing up.[173] Still, the emperor saw to it that the six-year-old child was enrolled in the order of Equites, and a year later, made a priest of the Salii, an order devoted to the worship of Mars, god of war. Marcus's priestly crown, tossed with those of his colleagues at a banqueting couch accidentally fell on the brow of Mars's statue. Later this was called an omen that Marcus was destined to rule. Romans were hooked on omens, like all superstitious people. It was easy for them to detect omens after the fact, when witnesses had either disappeared or felt free to embellish them. Had the crown accidentally caught on the sleeve of Mars's statue, it would have been interpreted to mean that the tosser would fall short of the mark, or else that his was a physical, not a mental prowess. Or that his wartime activities would be determined by the accidents of war itself, or if, by the gods, then without reference to Marcus. Marcus would have subscribed to this last. He wrote:

> If the gods have determined about me and about the things which must happen to me, they have determined well, for it is not easy even to imagine a deity without forethought; and as to doing me harm, why should they have any desire towards that? For what advantage would result to them from this or to the whole, which is the special object of their providence? But if they have not determined about me individually, they have certainly determined about the whole at least, and the things which happen by way of sequence in this general arrangement I ought to accept with pleasure and to be content with them. (Meditations 6.44)

Marcus, renamed Marcus Aurelius Antoninus when Antoninus Pius adopted him (AD 138), was groomed for the succession by bestowing on him the title Caesar and the quaestorship the next year, admitting him to the Senate. In AD 145 he became consul and two years later, acquired the power of tribune, at which point Antoninus indicated that Marcus would be his successor. His marriage the same year to his cousin Annia Galeria Faustina, daughter to Antoninus, was expected, as he had been affianced to her for six years. He was twenty-four and she but fifteen when they married. According to Marcus, he had postponed the proof of his virility until the marriage could be consummated. Faustina would later become the subject of scandal, but no modern scholar knows whether she was unfaithful to Marcus, or merely a flirt. It was rumored that this woman, who produced fourteen children, sometimes took her pleasure with sailors and gladiators at seaside resorts in Italy or on other occasions, with ballet dancers![174] Birley felt that most of the stories about her must be discounted, inventions that later sought to explain the behavior of their terrible son Commodus, disastrous successor to Marcus. All Marcus wrote about her when he was among the Quadi at the Granua was this encomium: "I have such a wife, so obedient, and so affectionate, and so simple."[175] Although few wives today will wish to be remembered for obedience and simplicity (artlessness? naiveté?), it is hard to imagine that many husbands would be anything but delighted if they were.

Michael Grant draws our attention to the only thing Marcus ever wrote about sex in his *Meditations,* that "copulation was but friction of the members and an ejaculatory discharge."[176] Grant noted also that Marcus disapproved of passion though not of sex.[177] Nobody bothered to record what Faustina thought of either! Fourteen children! Was she as philosophic as her philosopher husband? Have her own thoughts on lovemaking and childbearing vanished? Did she ever give voice to them? What wouldn't it be worth to be able to read the empress's *Meditations* on maternity and matrimony during the reign of Marcus Aurelius? Marcus's thoughts on her conjugal functions survive. While she was in residence at a military outpost in Cilicia in southeastern Asia Minor, he had coins issued in her honor depicting her as Mother of the Camps (*Mater castrorum*), and on the other side associated the empress with the Roman goddess of love, Venus. When Faustina died in 175, he had her deified with all required pomp. Would he have honored her thus if she had written her *Meditations?* Would we honor him if he had not left us his? Shortly after she died, he took one of Faustina's servants to be his concubine. Like father, like son.

Marcus spent most of his reign defending the empire. His first efforts took him to Syria, where he fought against the Parthians, giving his brother and co-emperor Lucius Verus the credit, but seeing that the conduct of battle was entrusted to a seasoned warrior, Avidius Cassius. In 167–168 Marcus and Verus were in Pannonia (Hungary) and Noricum to the south and southeast of Vindobona (Vienna), where peace was cemented with the

Marcomanni. The next year Verus, who had become his son-in-law, died. Marcus became sole emperor. Later that year (169) war broke out on the Rhine-Danube frontier and Marcus settled down for three years at Carnuntum, two days' march east of Vindobona (Vienna). Eventually, for his efforts in Germany Marcus took the title Germanicus. Between 169 and 174 the Marcommani were driven out of Pannonia, and the Quadi were beaten by the "thundering legion" not far from Cracow, where the thirsting troops of Rome's legions were saved by a most propitious thunderstorm.[178] Afterwards, Marcus exiled the leader of the Quadi to Alexandria. Perhaps he felt that this barbarian would profit by exposure to the most enlightened and philosophic of second-century Roman cities. If so, he was the first victorious general to extend the benefits of higher education to a conquered general. Historians of education debate whether or not this was the first example of a course in general studies.

On his return to Italy, Marcus, passing through Athens, was initiated into the Eleusinian mysteries. These had eluded the uninitiated for centuries. He took this occasion to endow schools of rhetoric and philosophy, lest they, too, become mysteries to the uninitiated. Back in Rome in 176 Marcus, with Commodus, his only surviving son and heir, celebrated the German triumph commemorated by the Aurelian Column now in Rome's Piazza Colonna, formerly in Marcus's own temple. On it, the events of his northern victories file upward a hundred feet into the air. Few columnists today will ever file so lofty a story, however inflated their prose.

The next year, 177, began the persecution of the Christians, the only real blot on Marcus's unblemished record. Perhaps he had imbibed his tutor Fronto's prejudice against them. Christians were widely regarded as superstitious, immoral zealots who stubbornly refused to perform elementary civic obligations, including that of emperor worship and the piety Rome showed her founders and ancestral heroes. The worst persecutions took place in Gaul, Lyons, and at Vienna in 177, where many Christians were cruelly tortured for their lack of civic loyalty. Perhaps Marcus derived his contempt for them from his reading of Epictetus, who condemned them as fanatics. It is hard to square his indifference with his *Meditiations,* which contained sentiments like this: "Love mankind. Follow God" (7.31); or this: "If thou art able, correct by teaching those who do wrong; but if thou canst not, remember that indulgence is given to thee for this purpose" (9.11); or "He who acts unjustly acts impiously. For since the universal nature has made rational animals for the sake of one another to help one another according to their deserts, but in no way to injure one another, he who transgresses her will, is clearly guilty of impiety towards the highest divinity" (9.1). And certainly his persecutions were inconsistent with this: "Men exist for the sake of one another. Teach them then or bear with them" (8.59). Marcus, like the Christians he persecuted, found it easier to write noble sentiments than always to act upon them. *Populus in omnibus inconstantissimus.* [Everybody changes their mind].

Aurelius spent the last years of his life (177–180) on the Danube, fighting off Germans. Although he had done many good works for the empire—founded schools, orphanages, and hospitals; reduced cruelty in criminal laws; suppressed the use of informers; reduced excessive power of fathers over children and masters over slaves; increased wives' inheritance rights; ameliorated provincial government; and expanded the principle of merit in government employment; Marcus allowed his bureaucrats further to sap the energies of municipalities. On his watch the currency was depreciated to pay for wars and gifts (really bribes) to soldiers and civilians alike. Given that his philosophy taught him the impermanence of all things and promoted in him a sense of "indifference towards the things which (lay) between virtue and vice," it is creditworthy that he took as instrumental and reformist a position on as many problems as he did.[179] Marcus proved by so many of his actions that a Stoic could be indifferent but also compassionate. Toward the Christians and toward his heir, Commodus, however, he was not indifferent, but passionate, and his passion blinded him to his more usual ethical sensitivity. Indeed, Stoicism could not make this philosopher-king dispassionate, as later, Christianity could not make Catholic emperors compassionate.

Marcus Aurelius suffered many years from pains in his stomach, and from time to time, Galen, his court physician, was on hand to prescribe for him prescriptions that often contained barbiturates. When death came Marcus was near Sirmium on the Danube in what is now Hungary, not too far south of modern Budapest. Plague had broken out among the legions and Marcus may have succumbed. Alternatively, he may have died of stomach cancer. Shortly after his death, the Roman Senate made him a god. Nothing Marcus wrote indicates that he would have been gratified by this honor. As he remarked in his journal, "Have I done something for the general interest? Well then, I have had my reward" (*Meditations* 11.4) He had never tried to be a god, only a man. A harder task.

Although Commodus (180–92) was the last of the Antonines, he disgraced his forbears by devoting himself to luxury and lubricity, and left no hostages to posterity, that is, he died childless. In the end, his favorite mistress, Marcia, engineered his death by poisoning, and when it appeared likely that he would recover, he was strangled. Commodus was remembered for his handsome appearance and yellow hair, and for his devotion to the slaughter of wild beasts in the arena and senators and servants outside it. In short, the last of the Antonines was as far removed from the restraint, virtues, and public service of his forbears as could be. To attempt a biographical sketch of this nonentity and megalomaniac would be incommodius.

11

Four Fathers and the Primitive Church

INTRODUCTION

FOR ROUGHLY FIVE HUNDRED YEARS (AD 100–600), the Fathers of the Church were cementing the doctrine and traditions that supported the edifice of Christianity for another fourteen hundred. The structure still stands after additions and corrections, church councils, papal bulls, strained communications, excommunications, schisms, persecutions, forged documents, anathemas, witch hunts, reforms, Reformations, Inquisitions, censorship, ecumenical rapprochements, and apologies by the Pope John Paul II to all except heretics and atheists for the Church's sins.

Historians call the first few centuries of Christianity the Primitive Church, namely, the first (Latin, *primus*). Primitive Christianity was not primitive in the sense of being undeveloped. It was in fact on the cutting edge where social services were concerned, providing even health care to converts. Besides material comforts, the early church provided the faithful with hope for a better world to come. It also promised eternal punishment for those with flawed faith. Of course the idea of faithfulness could hardly be defined before the faith itself was. But the Church promised an eternity of punishment for heretics who disagreed with it. That also comforted the faithful.

It took tremendous courage for Christians to withstand the sporadic persecutions conducted by Nero, Marcus Aurelius, Decius, and Diocletian. One of our four Fathers, Tertullian, sensed that persecution served a purpose—he would have said God's—when he averred that the blood of the martyrs was the seed of the Church.[1] More systematic persecution by Rome might have drowned the seedlings and doomed the crop.

When Rome fell in the West (AD 476) the Church, strengthened by the protection and patronage of a declining empire that had adopted its faith, was free to persecute pagans as it pleased or was able.[2] The Eastern church was better equipped for this because it was stronger. The church was stronger in the East because the Roman emperor, domiciled after 330 at Constantinople, could better protect it there. From Constantinople the Church quelled heretics and persecuted pagans occupying lands from the Balkans to Egypt. It was only in the sixth century that the Emperor Justinian

I (527–565) reestablished his authority over western Ostrogoths, converts to Christianity but Arian heretics who denied the Trinity.

East and West, the Church preserved the texts of classical paganism, even as it sought to convert the Slavic, Germanic, Asian, and African pagans on its borders. As keeper of the flame (tradition), the Church monopolized access to the past because increasingly, only clergymen were literate. As keeper of God's keys (divine authority), the bishops of Rome claimed to control access to the life hereafter. Always, Christianity provoked admiration, resentment, wonder. Those it provokes today wonder how an institution armed largely with anecdotal material, harsh polemics, distorted Platonism and recycled pagan mythology could have lasted into the modern era when the scientific method might have destroyed it, but did not.

The Fathers are revered for their services to Christianity and Western civilization, though some of their writings are no longer considered orthodox;[3] and some were downright uncivil. Defining faith was not a business for the politically correct, the overly refined. Orthodox faith, however, was only beginning to be identified in the first few hundred years of the Church, and the only people capable of identifying it were the Fathers. Christianity went by their rules, not those of the numerous groups the Fathers deemed heretical. The Fathers called their rules The Rule of Faith, and insisted that it was a faithful reflection of God's meaning, Christ's words, and apostolic teaching. Everyone else had to take this on faith! There was hardly any other way it could be taken. Most people weren't readers of the Bible, which, before our first Father, Irenaeus, meant simply the Old Testament or Hebrew canon. This could only be less than explicit where Christianity was concerned, and being pre-Christian, inexplicit. But interpretation was the key, and the Hebrew Bible or Old Testament was interpreted to appear consistent with the New Testament. Christianity thus assumed a seamlessness with many of the main tenets of the old Hebrew faith, as seamless as Christ's own robe was said to be. Things might have been easier for everyone after St. Jerome, the third Father, translated the Bible from the Hebrew and Greek into a more reliable text called the Vulgate. But for several hundred years many people, even St. Augustine, the fourth Father, preferred reading more familiar editions.

Interpretation inevitably meant translation. Nonscholars thought that interpretations of scripture owed their validity to the inspiration God gave interpreters. Scholars like Jerome were aware that interpretation depended on the linguistic proficiency of interpreters. Irenaeus, the first Father in this chapter, thought the Bible must include the New, as well as the Old or Hebrew Testament.[4] But scholars now question his proficiency in Hebrew. Robert M. Grant, for example, notes that Irenaeus considered the Old

Testament to be a Christian book because he read that Moses spoke of the preexistent Son of God in Hebrew at the beginning of Genesis: "Bereshith bara Elohim basan benuam samenthares." But Grant points out that Irenaeus mistook the word *bara* for Son, when it really meant "created." His point is that Irenaeus's confidence that the Hebrew Bible bore out the Christian concept of Jesus as the Son of God stemmed from his ignorance of the meaning of *bara,* which he mistook for the real Hebrew word for son, *bar.*[5] Nobody corrected Irenaeus. Thus, there was no bar to his erroneous interpretation, and no bar to Jesus being termed Son of God. St. Jerome was convinced that Christ was at work in the Hebrew Bible, whose authors had never heard of him, since he had not yet been born. So convincing to their followers were these gifted, but not infallible, laborers in the vineyard of interpretation, that the sonship of Christ never em-bar-rased the Church, which in any event, did not raise the bar of proof higher than that set by the Fathers, who were often mediocre linguists. The Church reserved to itself the interpretation of Holy Writ, whether or not it was writ right. Those who attempted to question or break its Rule of Faith were beaten about the ears with it. It was less a matter of linguistic skill than of who was in charge.

At best even the Fathers could only interpret the past, they could not predict the future. They would have been appalled to think those who came after them, including later Fathers, would add to the Rule of Faith ideas which to some of them would have seemed suspect. To moderns it seems obvious that institutions, even those professing to be of divine origin, change over time. To Irenaeus change was suspect. He did not perceive that he was himself an agent of change who transformed the very sources on which faith rested, and he would have been miserable if he had. A recent biographer notes that Irenaeus was "naive" in his view of the uniformity of church tradition because he insisted that uniformity set the orthodox apart from Gnostic heretics.[6] From the first century to the seventh, the Fathers struggled with Christianity's identity crisis, a complicated task that made it necessary continually to protect what had not yet been wholly created, to rescue what they valued from three traditions: Jewish, Greek, and Roman, while defining and preserving their own changing traditions which they invariably regarded as impervious to change.

PATRIARCHY AND ANTIFEMINISM

Christianity owes a great debt to the F-word—Fathers. But what about that owed to another F-word—Feminism? Feminist historians have shed much light on the contributions made by women in the life of the primitive or early Church. But one searches in vain for a group called Church Mothers.

There are only Church Fathers. Patristics is the study of the Church Fathers; there is no study called Matristics. As a rule, women did not write, or were at best barely literate. The Fathers were educated men, acquainted with Greek philosophy. The Church grew out of Greek and to a lesser extent Roman classical traditions with their philosophical, but also legal and administrative, experience as much as from Jewish and apostolic roots. If the Fathers tolerated the spiritual insights of untutored women in their midst, they did not transcribe or teach them, and that devalued them and prevented their dissemination.

In her popular book on the Gnostic gospels, Elaine Pagels studied early traditions of Gnostic Christians whose ideas about God and things divine were not wholly male, as in Judaism, orthodox Christianity, and Islam. Pagels found great receptivity among Gnostics[7] to ideas that the female principle included both the natural and the divine.[8] She thought Irenaeus and Tertullian disapproved of women exercising too much authority in Gnostic Christian churches. Although some historians agree with her, others protest against what they consider an oversimplified or distorted feminist view. Daniel L. Hoffman, for example, asserts that Pagels overlooked the degree to which feminist "images" in Gnosticism were negative; and he found Irenaeus and Tertullian not more but less antifeminist than the Gnostics, and "relatively positive" in their views of women.[9] Hoffman cites orthodox apologists such as Justin Martyr (d. AD 165) as receptive to female prophets and insists that both Irenaeus and Tertullian were not opposed to orthodox widows, martyrs, virgins, deaconesses, and evangelists acting as teachers and prophetesses while disallowing unorthodox women acting in the same capacities.[10] They did not, however, permit women to baptize or serve as bishops.[11]

We do not know if the Fathers were more misogynistic than Jesus. We read that he rebuked Mary's sister Martha when she asked him to make Mary help out in the kitchen. Jesus said Mary had chosen the better part, which was to listen to him in the living room.[12] Jesus did not ask Mary for her opinions, however. Would he have hushed her up if she had hazarded any? Or would he have engaged her in spiritual discourse? Because Jesus wrote nothing himself, we can only wonder. Paul (1 Cor. 34–35) observed that women should be silent in church because their speaking there would be "shocking." Yet even Paul allowed women to prophesy (1 Cor. 7–11), providing they wore a veil, although whether they were to do this over long or short hair seemed to him a matter for clarification. Perhaps he did not want them to forget their head covering (veil) if their heads were shaved bald! He did not suggest a remedy for bald-headed men, however, though one may suppose bald female heads would not have reflected less well on women than bald male heads do on men! Both reflect equally, but the light they shed scarcely illuminates the quality of spiritual insight! Paul seemed, as Pagels observes, ambivalent about women; but was he more ambivalent than the average Greek, Jew, or Roman of his era? Many Christian churches are still ambivalent about women in leadership positions. Not all Christians, Jews, let alone Muslims, have permitted women to guide their flocks. Patriarchal prejudice against women has only just begun to erode in organized religion. Only the disorganized are prepared to let bygones (like patriarchy) be bygones.

The Church never lacked mothers who helped out. Mary was especially helpful. She helped God out at the Annunciation. She gave birth to Jesus, nursed him herself, and devoted herself to raising him without the help of nannies. She had no other career. In her day there were few respectable career choices save wife and mother. The Roman Catholic Church regards her as the New Eve, cooperating in the Redemption, even though her cooperation was subordinate and not deemed necessary.[13] As far as Rome is concerned, Mary is Queen of Heaven and Mediatrix, that is, she cooperates in transmitting spiritual life to all as a mediator.[14] She is the mother of all men—but not a Church Mother in the same way as our four Fathers were Church Fathers. Still, no Mary, no Jesus. No Jesus, no Apostles. No Apostles, no disciples. No disciples, no Church Fathers. No Church Fathers, no Church.

Consider St. Helena (d. c. AD 327), mother of Rome's first Christian emperor, Constantine the Great (d. AD 337). She founded several churches. She would have shocked her son had she tried to preside over the Council of Nicaea in 325, though. Instead, Constantine called the council to decide on key theological propositions. He was not even baptized at that point, something he put off until on his deathbed, whereas Helena had converted as early as AD 313. And though Constantine was purported by the Church historian Eusebius to have adopted the sign of the cross as early as 312, he merely extended (Edict of Milan, 313) his predecessor's policy of tolerating Christianity, while also tolerating the pagan cult![15] Although Constantine may not have been a complete spiritual sluggard, for it was quite common in the period to delay baptism until one's end was near, he was nevertheless still only a catechumen or neophyte in the faith compared to his mom.[16] Yet it was he who presided at Nicaea. All Helena could do was serve the Church as a patroness. For her generosity the Church credited her with finding the true cross and made her a saint. Poor church mothers cleaned the church and embroidered altar cloths. On feast days guess who was in the kitchen cooking? Not Church Fathers.

Then there was Monica, St. Augustine's mom. Monica set her son's foot on the right or Christian path when he was of a tender age, even though he got off it for a couple of decades. She refused to have him under her roof when she found out he was involved with Manichaeans. Tough love. But for Monica, the Church would have been cheated of its most influential theologian. Augustine might forever have remained a Manichaean dualist, caught up by the notion of a powerful evil instead of preaching the absolute nonexistence of it? Good child-rearing on the part of the mothers of Church Fathers was never enough to qualify them as Church Mothers, though. Their contributions were not considered necessary, however helpful. Thanks for your help, dear lady, but we could have done just as well without it? One thinks not!

What women in Jewish, Christian, and pagan antiquity lacked, besides civic equality, was any recognition of their intellect. Thus denied they had little chance to make intellectual contributions. They were rendered incapable of interacting as equals in Church and society, this in the fourth and fifth centuries when the Church became the most useful society of all. Though Hoffman makes a good if limited case for early Christian recognition of feminine spiritual capabilities, women remained vessels of convenience. This was no accident. Their handicap was handed down from mother to daughter in the form of wombs, vaginas, and fatty breast tissue. Men called them the inferior sex and lectured them on their Christian duty to accept inferiority as God-given. Is there any wonder that male-female relationships have worked out poorly in Judeo-Christian culture?

The Fathers did not credit heretics in helping to shape Christian doctrine, though they were instrumental. While much is owed the Fathers, much is also owed the Nestorians, Montanists, Arians, Pelagians, Donatists, Gnostics, Valentinians, Monophysites, Monothelites, Marcionites, Docetists, and other heretics for their contributions to orthodoxy. While the Church identified with Christ, it did not always embrace his ethics or his charity, nor did it embrace all those who were seeking him.[17] The Fathers wrote polemical sermons that belittled their heretic neighbors' spiritual self-esteem. Eventually the Church succeeded in forcing heretics to differentiate themselves from what only gradually became the Church. It seems harsh that just because heretics were on the losing side of the sifting and winnowing process that produced orthodoxy they should be denigrated. Many of them published, but were allowed to perish without so much as a sign of remorse, let alone gratitude, from their orthodox critics for having helped them consolidate orthodoxy.[18] The Church could light candles to heretics in the interest of ecumenism, for many whom they called heretics were good Christians and might have been productive members had they been treated with respect.

Of course, many of the heretics were as intolerant of the orthodox as the orthodox were of them. Scarcely anyone (other than Jesus) thought seriously of turning the other cheek, and the Fathers never thought of it. Yet sometimes the principle points of certified heretics were incorporated into churches that are today recognized as Christian, at least by their own membership.[19] Are heretics not entitled to a permanent feast day, a movable feast day, or at the very least a toast at the annual church picnic? In our present ecumenical age when the very ground for Luther's Reformation seems about to crumble beneath the feet of Catholics, Episcopalians, and Lutherans, could not the Church say a prayer for its ancient heretics? Instead, Irenaeus's polemic *Against the Heretics* launched it on a road that stretched two thousand years into the future, none of those twenty centuries without heretic martyrs. The only other work of his that survived (*Epideixiz*) is a concise exposition of Christian doctrine, making St. Irenaeus the first systematic theologian of the Church. Without the spirit that infused primitive Christianity's fight against heretics, Western culture might have proved more tolerant, more disposed to alternative lifestyles, to discussion rather than persecution. That it was not to be, we owe in part to Irenaeus, the first of our four Fathers.

IRENAEUS (C. AD 130–D. C. 200–203)

No one knows much about Irenaeus, priest or bishop of Lyons at the end of the second century. Born in Asia Minor, c. AD 130, probably near Smyrna, directly across the Aegean Sea from Athens, Irenaeus said that as a child he heard the preaching of Polycarp, bishop of Smyrna, saint, and martyr (d. c. AD 155). Polycarp was long considered one of the Apostolic Fathers of the Church, one whose career spanned the period between the age of the Apostles and early Catholicism. Irenaeus, who came after the age of the Apostolic Fathers, was considered a link through Polycarp to St. John the Apostle. As it turns out, this link was claimed by the great nineteenth-century German scholar Harnack to have been bogus, for Polycarp, he thought, was only influenced by a presbyter named John, not by St. John the Apostle.[20] The confusion was Irenaeus's, not Polycarp's. Harnack felt that Irenaeus's writings betrayed no signs of Polycarp's ideas, and so the notion of Irenaeus as the conveyor of apostolic ideas through Polycarp was rejected by this scholar.[21] And yet, one finds encyclopedia articles relating that through Polycarp, Irenaeus bridged the gap between the Apostolic Fathers and the later, but still early, Catholic Church tradition.[22] Writing history is a tricky business, and one cannot take all one reads for the gospel, which was also true of the Gospel.

Irenaeus is nevertheless considered a distinguished Father of the early Church, neither because of Polycarp nor despite him. As it turned out, Irenaeus *did* transmit the apostolic tradition of St. John the Apostle to Christian posterity! He was the earliest of the Fathers to include the Gospel of John along with those of Matthew, Mark, and Luke as part of the canon, a list of books that Christians were to regard as scriptural. This goes to show that it's not who you know, but what you think should be known that counts. Irenaeus thought that John was the real thing, even if he did not know who John was. After Irenaeus, every Christian could tell a book by its cover, because the cover told them what was canonical. If it wasn't canonical, it was shot down!

Irenaeus was a priest, perhaps a bishop, at Lyons between AD 177 and 178 during the time of Marcus Aurelius's persecutions. He was sent to Rome around this time to appeal to its bishop, Eleutherius, for more toleration for Montanist Christians. Irenaeus's polemic *Against Heretics* was written several years later.[23] By that time he had given up on folks like Montanists, whose story is best left for a discussion of Tertullian. Irenaeus spent more time wrestling with the Valentinians. His era was a critical period for Christianity. Coinciding with the Church's growing intolerance, it could not escape being critical.

Valentinians were Gnostic dualists who posited two rather than one great spiritual Power. Hebrews were monists, and Christians, who inherited Judaism's monotheism, were as well. But some Christians were quite fascinated by dualism, with its two Powers. They posed a problem for orthodox ones, who, as monists, were restricted to one. Dualism emanated from the doctrine of the Persian prophet Zarathustra, whom the Greeks called Zoroaster. His exact dates are unknown, but in modern times he is thought to have lived until the mid sixth century before Christ. Whether or not Zoroaster's name meant "old camel" as the *Columbia Encyclopedia* suggests—he was born in Bactria, where camels were common, or because he lived to be seventy-seven, a reasonably old age for the times, or because he went a long time between drinks—is not known. Irenaeus wrote slyly that "not all understand" the Gnostic writings because not all have lost their brains![24] Certainly the Valentinian *Pleroma* (Heaven or Fullness) with its thirty *Aeons,* or quasi-personal aspects of Bythos, the Primal Father, was not user-friendly.

Valentinians posited a Primal Father named Bythos [lit., *abyss*] or First-Beginning, whose companion, Silence, was his thought.[25] The product or fruit of this Power-Pack was Mind or Only Begotten, who was called Beginning of all things but also Father. The abysmal difficulty for noninitiates is trying to understand the Gnostic *oikonomia* [Greek, plan, economy]. Valentinus himself had once been an orthodox Christian, but who knows how long he had been entertaining unorthodox notions? Who, for that matter, knew what was and was not orthodox? "Don't ask, don't tell" had much to recommend it before the Fathers worked out the essentials of Catholic theology.[26]

Tertullian called Valentinus the Platonist among Gnostics, and St. Jerome ranked him with Marcion as the most learned heretic. St. Jerome was rarely this effusive. Hippolytus (d. c. AD 236), probably one of Irenaeus's theology students, thought Valentinus something of a Pythagorean as well as a Platonist.[27] Plato recognized the value of higher mathematics. It kept incompetent undergrads out of his Academy. Later Christians admired mathematics because the Platonists and Neoplatonists believed mathematicians were explorers of eternal realms of being.[28] Valentinus was by turns Rome's first antipope, theologian, heretic, martyr, and finally, after reconciling with the orthodox Church, saint. His earlier alienation from the Church was perhaps the result of Montanist leanings, for Montanists were convinced that sinners, even if forgiven, could not be members of the Church. Later, the Donatists, who so irritated St. Augustine, had the same rigid standards for church membership, and certain sects in the Protestant Reformation upheld similarly rigorous qualifications for church membership. In the primitive church such views were called rigorist.[29] Tertullian would earn the appellation rigorist for his rigidity on forgiveness, penance, sin, and church membership. Hippolytus criticized Pope Zephyrinus for too much leniency toward sinners and lapsed Christians. During the reign of Pope Pontian, Hippolytus was the heretic bishop of a separate church. His book refuting all heresies was entitled *Philosophumena.* The persecuting Emperor Maximinus of Thrace (AD 236–38) with great objectivity banished both Pontian and Hippolytus to the mines of Sardinia where they died, but not before Pontian had, with great leniency, received Hippolytus back into the Church. The Church was right to forgive Hippolytus for being excessively strict toward sinners. The fact that Rome sainted him must be regarded, not as having rewarded his position, but as having shamed him for holding it. In effect, the Church demonstrated God's mercy toward grave sinners and lapsed Christians by sainting one who returned to God, the very position Hippolytus once rejected. Fortunately the Church canonizes its saints after they die, not before. Had Hippolytus been sainted in his own lifetime, would he not have appeared hippo critical?

Valentinus (fl. c. AD 150) said that the *Aeons* were abstractions of the thought of the Primal Father. The last *Aeon,* a wayward feminine principle named Sophia, fell from grace. Before she had been reinstated in the *Pleroma* [paradise], she gave birth to an aborted monster called Achamoth [ugly desire], who was ultimately the origin of everything in the created universe.[30] Achamoth's ugliness was really symbolic of the widespread prejudice against reality or materialism. Those who held such a prejudice imbued all created or material things with a negative quality. This negativity was shared by Platonists, Gnostics, and Christians who resented their obligation to live out their lives on earth, now considered a tainted environment. Could it be that in our own era, the polluters of earth really believe in the futility of trying to keep pure that which Gnostics, Neoplatonists, and early Christians habitually viewed as irrevocably impure, namely, earth? Is disrespect for our environment a result of traditions which depreciated the material world as opposed to the spiritual? Are industrial polluters really closer to God than those who put Earth First?

For Valentinians the immediate cause of material things was the Demiurge, created in the image of the Primal Father. The Demiurge was clearly the creator God of the Old Testament, but not the equivalent in dignity of the Primal Father, and hence, an inferior god. Some Gnostics felt that Demiurge had emitted Christ as his son, who belonged to one of the three classes of men. Highest in dignity was the class of spiritual (*pneumatic*) men, destined by their very nature to salvation, for they alone were "true Gnostics," perfected by the right information or *gnosis*. Next came the *psychic* class, capable of salvation, but also apt to make wrong choices and miss salvation altogether. They would be saved by faith and good works, but not by *gnosis,* reserved only for pneumatics. The third class of men was merely earthy (*hylic*) whose members were doomed to perish with the material world. Irenaeus resented the fact that Gnostics supposed that members of his Church were merely "psychic" rather than pneumatic. In these terms Irenaeus struggled to establish definitely the condition of what neither side had ever seen and could hardly have understood—the essence of a human being's soul or spirit. But the aim was still more ambitious, for these primitive churchmen were attempting to answer the most important questions ever asked: what is the nature of the universe? What power was responsible for its creation? Who am I and how do I fit in? Are others better than me or inferior? What chance do I have to live well, die well, or live again? Where can I get reliable information on these matters? Whom do I trust? How can I know? The Church was attempting to answer questions that in our day physicists, priests and pastors, rabbis and gurus, psychologists, psychiatrists, and talk-show hosts try to answer every day.[31] What is the Truth? Whom can we trust?

The Fathers—like the Gnostics—were teachers. They all tried to answer such questions in a way that would save men's souls without insulting their intellect—but without encouraging them to question the answers provided, either. Neither the Gnostics or Irenaeus brooked opposition. His refutation of the heretics, written about 180, was the first systematic attempt to explain Christianity as a monistic, rather than a dualistic faith, one assumed to be true because assumed identical (so far as Irenaeus knew) to that which the Apostles had received from Christ and passed on to a succession of bishops, Irenaeus's predecessors. Irenaeus, like all the Fathers after him, was reconciled to the questions that came from Greek philosophy. After all, philosophers asked questions because they were ignorant and did not have access to the Truth, which was to be found only in scripture, the apostolic tradition, and the Rule of Faith. Believers alone had the right answers to all questions, secure in the knowledge that only the Church could provide them and interpret scripture, the sole source, and the soul's source, of Truth.

TERTULLIAN (C. AD 155–222)

Quintus Septimius Florens Tertullianus gave birth to the Latin literature of the Church in the West, works gestated after his conversion to Catholicism (AD 190–95) and even after his separation from the Church (AD 207–208) when he became leader of a small and heretical Montanist congregation at Carthage. Before him, Latin-speaking Christians had only a translation of the Hebrew Bible. Little else was written in Latin, and thus for non-Greek-speaking Western Christians, the Bible was their only text. In this ideal marketplace, where bookshelves were nearly bare, Tertullian became not only an author of Christian reading material, but their retailer, wholesaler, distributor, publicity agent, and literary critic. To the zeal of Christianity he added the legalistic and Stoical zeal of his other profession, that of a Roman lawyer. His caustic style was ironic and humorous in a way that was not good-humored but overwhelming. Although he knew a good deal of Plato and had an affinity for certain aspects of Stoicism, Tertullian was not a philosopher. Gerald Bray has pointed to the futility of the debate over the extent to which Tertullian was or was not interested in or an adept of spec-ulative philosophy.[32] In his work *On the Soul* Tertullian remarked that "philosophers are the patriarchs of the heretics" and spoke of philosophy as an abomination, nonsense. He berated the useless hollowness of it all.[33] He gave philosophy such a drubbing that the Church, even when it thought Tertullian had deserted them for the Montanists, continued to use his works, on the theory that a man who hated logical thinking couldn't be all bad. In fact, after he left the Church around AD 207 or 208, he was still writing about the need to preserve orthodox faith. It was the structure of the Catholic Church he now castigated. Not surprisingly, some churchmen regarded Tertullian as an embarrassment. St. Cyprian (d. 258), bishop of Carthage and Tertullian's disciple, called him his master and asked daily for Tertullian's works to be brought to him. But he never asked for him by name![34] Not until the sixteenth century, during the Catholic Counter-Refor-mation, when Catholicism needed plenty of ammunition to use against its Protestant critics, did Tertullian come into his own.

The discipline of martyrs was more to Tertullian's taste than philosophi-cal speculation. In *To the Martyrs,* he described them as not only admirable, but serviceable.[35] Their blood was seed, and it was the blood they shed, not the books they read, which won his applause. He thought that anyone who committed one of the sins for which neither the Church nor its priests could offer forgiveness could yet be saved if he died a martyr for the faith. In this he borrowed from the pagan convert (Saint) Justin Martyr of Samaria (d. c. AD 160), who had tried to convert men to Christianity through philosophical argument. Justin thought a seed of *logos* or divine order existed in everyone, and that Christians are themselves seed, a cause in the nature of things.[36] Tertullian, like Justin, remembered that Jesus had spoken of himself metaphorically as a wheat seed (John 12:24) who must return to earth before he could produce a rich harvest. Tertullian's world was, if not altogether seedy, at least earthy, appropriately enough for Christian believers whose God was related to numerous Asian fertility gods. Fertility. Blood sacrifice. More fertility. Blood was no mere metaphor in the ancient world. It really was considered seed. The devout had been drinking the blood of the gods' victims for thousands of years in order to grow spiritually. In the Dionysian rites Dionysus, god of wine, art, and drama, himself an import from Asia Minor into Greece, relished human sacrifice. The consumption of victims' blood and flesh by his faithful represented a primordial drive to celebrate and even propagate the divine first by bloodletting, then by blood drinking, believed necessary for the survival of communicants and cult. Eventually, wine was substituted for blood, but the notion remained that faith was propagated by means of blood, not wine. Tertullian, then, struck an old and, for the times, reasonable chord in Western civilization when he insisted that Christian martyrs propagate the faith by enduring the torments of martyrdom, a bloody business, and in the process, obtain their own salvation.

Almost as celebrated as Tertullian's statement on blood being seed was his attitude toward philosophical truth versus scriptural truth. Tertullian asked, "What has Athens to do with Jerusalem?" He answered this to his own satisfaction in *On the Prescription of Heretics* in which he sought to disassociate philosophy from faith:

> What has Athens to do with Jerusalem; what concord is there between the Academy and the Church? The Christian's instruction comes from the porch of Solomon who taught that the Lord should be sought in simplicity of heart. Away with all efforts to produce a mottled Stoic-Platonic-dialectic Christianity! Where is there any likeness between the Christian and the philosopher; between the disciple of Greece   and the disciple of heaven; between the talker and the doer; between him who builds up and him who pulls down; between the friend and the foe of error; between one who corrupts the truth and one who restores and teaches it?[37]

Tertullian did not say that philosophers were outlaws, though elsewhere he did make that comment about them having been the patriarchs of heretics! Lewis W. Spitz, Stanford's distinguished scholar of Renaissance humanism, once referred to Tertullian's query concerning the two kinds of information systems as a question that had become "terribly shop-worn" in modern times.[38] He was right, because by the twentieth century, men had been attempting to explain the difference between rational thought and religious belief for nearly two thousand years. As always, there were 1) pietists who believed that revealed religion was righter than logic and empirical experience; 2) philosophers who believed just the opposite; 3) the apathetic masses of humanity who hoped to avoid the effort of understanding by affirming that both were right; and 4) skeptics who affirmed that all parties were delusional since nothing could be known with certainty.

Eric Osborn concluded that for Tertullian Athens had everything to do with Jerusalem "provided you travel (economy class) by way of Ephesus and disembark at Jerusalem."[39] Well, this answer, with its pun on Tertullian's use of the word *oeconomia,* is one Christians could approve, for it suggests that the wise man may be instructed by Greek philosophy, but must seek ultimate wisdom in Christ. The position of believers was that revealed, scriptural truth is the only reliable kind. Jews and Christians, even those who were scholars, were largely oblivious to the historical process by which men have created and questioned, invented and recorded, borrowed and distorted, preserved and lost, translated and edited, the bits of history, fantasy, and fiction which, over thousands of years, became embedded in that library each group called the Bible.

Edgar Allan Poe, while reading Tertullian's *On Christ's Flesh* came upon the paradoxical statement that the poet and mystery writer, not in a happy state, found all the more distressing:[40] "The Son of God has died. This is believable because it is absurd; buried he has risen again. This is certain because it is impossible."[41] Paradoxes were stylish in Tertullian's day. Philosophers as well as holy men used them. Would such men speak nonsense to elucidate their most sincere messages? Hundreds, perhaps thousands of gods like Tammuz of Sumer, Osiris of Egypt, Dionysus of Thrace, and Jesus of Nazareth had been dying and returning to life each spring for a long time. All, having died, rose to live again, bringing with their return the promise of renewed life and joy to their faithful. Poe, suffering from a "disordered state" induced by poverty, domestic woes, drugs, and alcohol, was pushed to the far side by Tertullian's paradox.[42] He thought it partook of his own mental disorder. Poe's mental disorders contributed to the success of his tales of mystery and suspense. Tertullian's disorder, a penchant for paradox, was a common rhetorical technique in antiquity, one this Church Father used to elucidate the chief mystery of Christianity, the sacrifice of Christ that Christians required for their eternal salvation.[43] By creating paradoxes, unbelievable or absurd statements that were also self-contradictory, Tertullian attempted to convey the essence of God's *transcendence.* The last is a theological term that means God's ability to dispense with all those limitations human beings must put up with—those of time and place, thought and order, facts and evidence.

Poe was a pedophile (or would be so classified today) who married his thirteen-year-old cousin. His curriculum vitae lurched back and forth between episodes of alcoholic excess and opium-eating. Tertullian was a rigorist whose Puritan intolerance of human weakness—whether for luxury products, mind-altering substances, amusements like theater and gaming, or the joys of sex—many would now find either quaint or neurotic. Tertullian reproved Christians for trying to find biblical support for theater, prizefighting, and chariot-racing. He deplored those who cited David's dancing before the Ark as a permit to indulge in physical display, or Elijah's drive to heaven in a fiery chariot to justify excess in motion. Tertullian approved of only one "play," the biblical Last Judgment. He said he would rejoice to see mighty kings "groaning in the depths of darkness" and provincial governors who persecuted Christians melt in fierce flames. He would laugh to see philosophers blush as they and their students burned up together for having taught that the world was no concern of God's. Hans von Campenhausen was appalled at Tertullian's capacity for describing sadistic, dreadful, and grandiose punishments.[44] This scholar found Tertullian's attitude singularly lacking in compassion and found Tertullian the only Church Father who took such pleasure anticipating God's revenge on sinners. Poe seems to have been less shocked than von Campenhausen, but then, Poe lived a hard life. He recognized in Tertullian certain of his own gifts. Tertullian and Poe were both rhetoricians, admirers of Greek and Latin literature, obsessed with the mysterious elements of life and death and the soul's spiritual trajectory through them. The Father of Christian Latinity and the father of the mystery story kept their audiences enthralled by audacious rhetoric, taut narrative, and keen insight into the hearts and souls of men. But Poe preserved the Greek as well as the Christian notion of pity, while Tertullian seemed a stranger to pleasures unconnected to divine retribution.

Tertullian's intellect trod an evolutionary path between the pit of heresy and the pendulum of religious zeal. He began to swing soon after his conversion to Christianity around AD 190, and swung in widening arcs from Catholic conformity, if not from Catholic orthodoxy, through contemporary prophecy, criticism of Catholic episcopal and papal laxity, through Docetist strictures against church membership for sinners, until he reached Montanism, whose spokesman and leader some, but not all, scholars think he remained until death relieved him of his duties.[45] Tertullian's restlessness was a reflection of his rigorist moral views. Osborn says of him: "He is forever on the move, seeking more of what he has found," and adds that his works reveal his awareness of contradiction, conflicts, and paradox.[46]

Tertullian had written a tract (c. AD 212) against an Asian Monarchian called Praxeas, a nickname meaning busybody. The real person behind that name has not been certainly identified.[47] Praxeas had persuaded the bishop of Rome to reject the Montanists, whose leader (Montanus) had preached an early end of the world, Christ's second coming and the establishment of a perfect society in a New Jerusalem. Tertullian was early attracted to Montanist prophets. He liked their reproof of laxity among the Church hierarchy.[48] Tertullian criticized Praxeas for turning the Church away from Montanism's higher moral standards and holier religious practices. As far as Tertullian was concerned, Montanists were the Moral Minority, the superior and saved remnant. Although Praxeas had himself reverted to orthodoxy, Tertullian felt that his followers, called Modalistic Monarchians had left "tares" (weeds) behind which were threatening the Church in North Africa and elsewhere.[49] Praxeas believed Godhead was in Christ, and that he could never be subordinate to the Father. Praxeas said the names Father and Son were but different modes of the one God, who was the Father before the Incarnation, but later called the Son. Modalistic Monarchians taught that the Father, as well as the Son, had suffered on the cross. Tertullian said that was blasphemy and heresy because orthodoxy did not permit the Father to be crucified, but only the Son.

In *Against Praxeas* Tertullian established, though he did not invent, the clever formula of the Trinity, belief in which allowed Christians to profess faith in one God—the monotheistic God of the Jews—but to maintain that his unity or substance was tripartite, consisting of three persons, the Father, Son, and Holy Spirit.[50] This tripartite scheme had the advantage of permitting Christ to suffer on the cross all alone rather than with his Father. The disadvantage was that it was necessary to persuade folks that one could be three and three one. Fortunately, most people had no problem with this new math. Arithmetically challenged Christians, such as the Arians, and later, during the Protestant Reformation of the sixteenth century, Socinians and Unitarians, never got the hang of it. They were called Antitrinitarians and Judaizers for their obstinacy and considered unfit for citizenship in Protestant as well as in Catholic societies.

According to Kenneth Scott Latourette, Tertullian, "like an advocate" was not always fair to his opponents. Lawyers have been the object of criticism since antiquity. Tertullian used the Latin word *substantia* [substance] to represent God's oneness, and the word *personae* [persons] in the legal sense of parties in a legal action to represent Father, Son, and Holy Spirit.[51] For God's administrative activity Tertullian used the Greek word *oeconomia* [household management], from whence comes the word economy. He used the Greek *Logos* [thought] to represent the scriptural word Wisdom, also the Son of God, which the Gospel of John (John 1:1–18) identifies with Jesus Christ. Many of the ingredients common to primitive Christianity and many common to other forms of western Asian spiritualism were on the table by Tertullian's day. Although they went by a variety of names, depending on who was in the kitchen, when measured out and stirred up with others ingredients according to each cook's taste, they produced a number of different kinds of spiritual dough. When all the loaves were divided, not all those on the receiving line felt they were being nourished in the same way.

Irenaeus had already identified *Logos* with the Son of God, the Mind of God, and the Father Himself, but there were those who, like some Gnostics, were tempted to regard *Logos* as a separate God. In antiquity, there was nothing to prevent people from regarding the parts of Trinity as three separate gods. Indeed, there seemed much to recommend it, namely, the prevalence of polytheistic religions in and around the Mediterranean basin and western Asia. In his deployment of these signs and symbols, Tertullian did not merely refute the Modalistic Monarchians, with whom he was, as a believer in God's unity, substantially in agreement, but the Gnostics, Christians for whom there was not only a creator God, but a God superior to the Creator God. Tertullian felt that Praxeas "crucified the Father," and he developed the first full-length doctrine of the Trinity to refute him.[52] Von Campenhausen thinks that Praxeas was mistaken to have interpreted the Gospel of John in a way that denied any difference between God the Father and the Son. He thinks Tertullian turned out useful formulae, with legal and logically precise definitions and distinctions, but regards him nonetheless as having dealt only with the unity in the Trinity, neglecting problems that eventually arose over the equality of rank between the divine persons.[53]

The business of unifying, but keeping distinct, three persons of God was something that would tax the energies and talents of more theologians than just Tertullian, whose best efforts left some feeling that the Son and the Spirit were still playing second fiddle to the part played by the Father.[54] Warfield says that Tertullian stressed the unity of the Father, Son, and Spirit because he was in fact arguing against Monarchians, but not conscious of an indebtedness to them. He was thus "prepared for a certain pluralism in his conception of God," and the resolution of these twin desires for unity on the one hand, but distinction on the other, produced a Trinity in which terms like division, diversity, distinction, condition, power, separation, undivided substance, and so forth, abounded.[55] Of course, "ill-disposed and perverse" people could insist that Tertullian's allowance of distinctions in the substance, condition, and power of the three persons might seem to be separations. Tertullian's unity of the three was less than a tight fit. Warfield did not see it that way, nor did Tertullian nor the Church which adopted his exposition. Osborn wrote that Tertullian argued against Praxeas that simple people must recognize that the one God could only be understood in terms of his economy, by which he meant his multiplicity.[56] The three-in-one, one-in-three formula was a clever appeal to the early third-century consumers of Christianity at a time when they were tempted by the wares of Monarchians stressing God's unity, and by Gnostics stressing his diversity. In such a marketplace, Tertullian's One God the Father who could only be understood through the Son and the Holy Spirit meant that for Christians, the Trinity was not just a good deal, it was a packaged deal. Tertullian was not merely the indispensable theologian of the Catholic Church—though he had in fact already left it—but the best marketing strategist against both Dynamistic and Modalistic Monarchians who could never decide how much unity or how much independence to include with their different notions of the godhead.

It was left for Tertullian's posterity and for Poe to ponder weak and weary over the paradoxes that lay at the heart of Tertullian's Christology, but still more, at the rigidity of this Church Father who was so quick to condemn human weakness and so slow to realize—he seems not ever to have realized fully—that humanity is too frail, too insecure, too human to achieve the moral and ethical purity of a Jesus Christ. Will the controversy this Church Father still provokes ever be resolved? Poe's raven, properly cued, would probably screech "Nevermore." Tertullian, doughty polemicist for orthodox Truth as he saw it, remained a rigorist—and a rigid personality—until his death. Upon which his mortal remains were claimed by rigor mortis. His authorial remains were acclaimed by the Church of Rome.

St. Jerome (AD 331? 345? 347?–420)

St. Jerome published a scholarly translation of the Bible, the Vulgate [Latin, *vulgatus,* ordinary, common].[57] His Latin usage was ordinary. Like Martin Luther who translated the Bible into colloquial German, Jerome knew he had to touch the hearts of common folks. He wrote commentaries on all the biblical prophets, letters to friends, and acerbic polemics against his own and orthodoxy's enemies. Artists have portrayed him in the desert as an old man (he wasn't yet) wearing tattered clothes, dreaming of beautiful dancing girls; almost nude with angels helping him translate (Guido Reni and Van Dyck); in his study contemplating a skull (Van Aelst and Van Cleve); in his Bethlehem study as an old man, cozily ensconced with the lion whose paw he delivered of a nasty thorn (Dürer), his cardinal's hat on the wall, his halo shedding a strong reading light;[58] taking communion; hearing the last trumpet; and having his bad dream.[59] In this nightmare Christ the Judge asks him who or what he is. Jerome answers "I'm a Christian." The Judge says he is lying because he is really a Ciceronian, that is, an affected literary snob.[60] Whereupon an angel beats him about the head and back. The next morning, Jerome reported bruised shoulders. Later, he swore off reading "Gentile authors" saying, "O Lord, if ever again I possess worldly books or read them, I have denied thee."[61] Later still, he rediscovered the classics, teaching them to boys at his Bethlehem monastery, initiating a pedagogical pattern revived in the Renaissance and continued in the Reformation.[62] When he had the dream, Jerome was suffering from a guilty conscience. He was trying to practice asceticism while a guest in his friend Evagrius's villa at Antioch. Jerome struggled with asceticism while surrounded by luxury.

Born at Stridon in Dalmatia, then eastern Italy, perhaps as early as 331, but maybe as late as AD 347, Jerome was sent at twelve to Rome for his education.[63] He studied rhetoric at the school of Donatus.[64] He studied Latin literature and heard cases in the law courts. His pals included Rufinus, with whom in later life he quarreled so dreadfully over Origen. With them he enjoyed the perquisites of affluent Latin boyhood—classical authors, good wine, better food, worse women. On Sundays the boys explored Christian burial places. Coxcombs in the catacombs. As for the Christian mysteries, they had the rest of their lives to comb them out.

At nineteen Jerome was baptized, a sign that he was not only Christian, but an ascetic, for baptism was then more often received in old age, when sinning was less likely. Baptism was thought to wash away past, but not future sins. A youthful baptism meant separating oneself from ordinary Christian society. It meant the repudiation of marriage, public service, and ordinary Roman entertainments. Early baptism was symbolic, shorthand for holier-than-thou. It was declaring war on one's relatives, one's past, one's culture. In Jerome's youth Christians were just beginning to feel that assimilation into Roman society was now possible. They were sure that postbaptismal asceticism would once again render them social outcasts. By Jerome's maturity Christians longed for social acceptance.

In Jerome's youth the persecutions were just bad memories. Constantine the Great (d. AD 337) had legalized Christianity and preferred it over the Roman cult. The ranks of pagan Romans thinned as the fourth century drew to a close. Emperor Theodosius I (d. AD 395) practically extinguished the old religion and proclaimed belief in the Trinity the test of orthodoxy. The orthodox continued to hammer out doctrine they thought might unify the empire against barbarian incursions. It didn't. Jerome lived into the age when the hammering would be performed, not by Christians, but by barbarians who smashed Rome in AD 410. Ten years later Jerome died in his bed at Bethlehem not knowing how the struggle for civilization would end, fearing it already had.

His schooling over, Jerome and a buddy went to Triers, now the imperial capital, perhaps to find employment. There Jerome became interested in literature, both classical and Christian. For many years his preference for good Latinity strained his conscience and made scripture and pious works seem barbarous. He resolved to dedicate himself to Christ, not sex, but, upon returning home for a visit, dedicated his sister to Him instead. The price of his guilty conscience was *her* renunciation of worldly pleasures. But how long would the world endure? Christians believed that Christ would soon return to earth to begin a thousand-year reign. Having sex in his presence might be too embarrassing. The scrupulous would wait for Christ to come first. His reappearance they called the Second Coming.

Such apocalypticism was popular in the fourth century. Some Christians, contemplating residence in heaven sooner, rather than later, did not marry. Jerome at the urging of a group of celibates in Rome, wrote a polemic (AD 383), on Mary's perpetual virginity (*Against Helvidius*), a graphic description of family life, with prattling infants, budgeting, and last-minute house-cleaning before the arrival of guests.[65] Jerome described dining to the blare of kettle drums, shrill flutes, and shrieking lyres, and the wife, wearing see-through clothing, exposing herself to the leering of her husband's dinner guests.[66] Domesticity and piety did not mix, according to Jerome's view. Though family values get good press now, the Fathers disparaged family life, even if Jerome did remark grudgingly that virginity was the fruit of marriage.[67]

By 373–374 Jerome had traveled to the East in search of role models for purity. He found them in ascetic monks. In AD 378 his town and his family's estate were obliterated by rampaging Goths. He could not go home again. But, worried that his "poor body" was not up to the rigors of a monastic lifestyle, he went to stay with a rich friend, Evagrius, who had a nice villa at Antioch. There he learned Greek, attended lectures, and thought about becoming a monk. He hung around for over a year. He wished to achieve sainthood through self-denial like the desert hermits but dreaded the thought of leaving his library behind. This he never did. He took it everywhere he went. A gentleman deserved Cicero, Virgil, and Ovid for company. One cannot help wonder: did Evagrius deserve Jerome?

Although psychoanalysis was not yet available, it seems that Jerome was as neurotic and obsessive a saint as they come. Conflicted, anxious, hypochondriacal, hyperaggressive, manic, preoccupied with sex, self-centered, paranoid, controlling. Where his store of books was concerned, he was a regular Squirrel Nutkin. But Jerome was also a gifted rhetorician and aesthetically discriminating. His lack of theological imagination was never held against him. After all, he was a contemporary of St. Augustine. How much more doctrinal innovation could the Church absorb?

Eugene Rice says that Jerome was viewed in the best possible light by the fourth century, though some contemporaries regarded him a desecrator of sacred text because his revisions of the Old Latin Bible changed the wording.[68] Jerome remarked that his services were criticized by "two legged asses," folks verbally challenged. Fiercely orthodox, he corrected any errors he found in sacred text. Simple souls assumed that God had inspired the writers of his Word and prevented them from making errors. The Septuagint Bible (in Greek) was believed to have been translated from the Hebrew by seventy-two individually inspired monks working in separate cells—all of whom miraculously produced the same text under divine inspiration! Jerome, who studied Hebrew in his desert cave and Greek in the lecture halls of Antioch, knew better. Nothing trains the mind like learning irregular verbs and criticizing irregular ideas. An honest scholar will admit that he attends conventions to prove to the "two legged asses" of this world that they really are donkeys. In choosing scholarship, Jerome chose the right career. You bet your sweet donkey.

Rice says that by the seventh century Jerome was venerated as a saint; by the twelfth as an angel.[69] This was perverse, for Jerome had condemned Origen's followers who denied that the resurrected body would be identical to the fleshly one we inhabit on earth! In Jerome's opinion, the body was where it was at. And where it was at was, Jerome knew, in the loins and under the navel, the location of desire. Lust. Sex. To protect the world from it, Jerome dedicated himself to chastity. It was too late for virginity. He would find others for whom it was not. He would be the Apostle of Sublimation.

In the summer of AD 374 or 375, Jerome set off from Antioch to see if he could make it out on the desert! He felt that if he could make it there, he could make it anywhere. Though later he referred to himself as a young man during his desert sojourn, he may have been around forty. Luckily, he continued to receive money from home, but clearly it was not too soon to find his life's work. Somewhere eighty-eight kilometers south-southeast of Antioch, near Chalchis, in northern Syria, he sublet a roomy cave which housed his library, but no lion. He hired assistants to copy manuscripts. He had made arrangements for Evagrius to bring him his mail regularly. To Jerome's Thoreau, Evagrius played Emerson. Jerome's wilderness was high maintenance.

He began to study Greek and Hebrew, the latter with a converted Jew. Jerome says he studied it to divert his mind from sex. Monks had to mortify the senses because their senses mortified them. Jerome wrote to friends and to Pope Damusus, a friend of Evagrius, for news, forgiveness, sympathy, company, theological insight. His friends answered. The pope did not. In one letter addressed to three friends he asks: "Why is it that with such stretches of sea and land between us you sent me so short a letter?"[70] He wrote (AD 374) to his friend Heliodorus to join him in the desert: "Come, and come quickly. Do not think of old ties—the desert loves the naked." He urged Heliodorus to resist his family's tears and join him in Christ's work. "In these matters to be cruel is a son's duty."[71] Heliodorus did not come.

Jerome was finicky when judging who among his friends deserved his loyalty. Ferdinand Cavallera noted that he could be very kind to his friends—

indeed who cannot?—but that he also indulged in jealousy, suspicion, brooding, anger, and was self-centered.[72] Jerome admitted that "Polemics have nothing to do with truth . . . their only objective is to conquer, to crush one's adversary."[73] Von Campenhausen thought Jerome "lacked all round the decisive requirement for lasting greatness: character."[74] At least Jerome did not keep his feelings to himself. Maybe he should have.

In the semiarid desert near Chalcis colonies of scruffy hermits maintained varying degrees of contact with one another.[75] These Syriac monks wanted Jerome to accept their definitions of the Trinity, to subscribe to "three *hypostases*" of the Trinity. Jerome called these three "persons." He did not want to subscribe to *hypostases*. He said he did not understand the differences between the Greek term *hypostasis* and the Latin term for person. He said he believed what the Council of Nicaea (AD 325) and later the Council of Constantinople (AD 381) had prescribed. The monks thought Jerome a Monarchian heretic. He soon tired of their visits and arguments, also of their dirty clothes and uncouth speech. He wrote again to Pope Damasus to tell him exactly what to believe about the Trinity. More than one author has remarked that controversy did not interest Jerome much.[76] A brilliant scholar, exegete, and translator, Jerome was not a creative theologian. He would believe whatever he was told to believe.[77] Like Tertullian's, Jerome's intelligence was catechetical, limited by the opinion of a Church that discouraged catechumens from independent analysis. Jerome's adherence to orthodoxy endeared him to the Catholic Church, but his unwillingness to grapple with theological difficulties may not have been in the best interest of Christian culture. It was certainly not in the best interest of culture per se, of which the Church was already serving as final arbiter. On the other hand, the anti-intellectualism of Christian culture did not prevent the Church from succeeding in converting Europe, western Asia, and North Africa! Irrationality would prove to have many advantages. But intellectual rigor also has advantages—of liberty, justice, humanity, and reality. Those who seek, as Jerome did, only the approval of orthodox opinion make it less likely that their posterity will reap these rewards. Jerome was a first-rate scholar. He was not a first-rate intellectual. He took too much on faith.

In his *Life of Paul of Thebes* Jerome said of himself that out on the desert he worked up a sweat by manual labor, ate barely enough to stay alive, wept copiously—for his sins or from frustration?—and felt he was mingling with angels. In his letter to Eustochium on virginity he wrote that on the desert he was "surrounded by bands of dancing girls." But though his "limbs were cold as ice, [my] mind was burning with desire, and the fires of lust kept bubbling up before me when [my] flesh was as good as dead."[78] In this struggle with his sexual needs he differed from Erasmus, who felt himself old by his early forties, and noted that sex was no longer a problem. Jerome at the same age could not repel impure thoughts. After two or three years, Jerome fled the desert where his "limbs were cold as ice." It was probably just as well for his circulation.

He visited Antioch again, where he wrote the *Life of Paul of Thebes,* the only one ever written. It includes an account of Paul's torture by a harlot who fondled him until, unable to control his desire, he bit off the end of his tongue and spat it at the face of his tormentress.[79] In Antioch Jerome enjoyed long soaks in his friend's bathtub. Despite his long desert sojourn he cleaned up well. He became a candidate for holy ordination, which he accepted on his own terms. These included his refusal to supervise a parish or diocese where he would be distracted by the problems of ordinary Christian life. Although many of his best friends were Christians, he did not want them hanging around on a regular basis, where they would have demanded spiritual counseling and detracted from his scholarly pursuits.

In AD 379 Jerome was off to Constantinople, where he studied with Gregory of Nazianzus, as dazzling a stylist of Greek as Jerome was of Latin. They discussed Origen, for both men were great admirers of the preceding century's most famous Father, synthesizer of Stoicism, Neoplatonism, and Christianity. In homage, Jerome translated several of Origen's homilies. Critics think this translation was his most Original.

When refuting the layman Helvidius, Jerome pointed out all the man's "errors," including the one stating that Jesus was not an only child.[80] Although most theologians now believe Helvidius was right, Jerome insisted that "brethren" meant cousins, not siblings, a view inconsistent with his linguistic expertise. His conviction that Mary had preserved her virginity even after Jesus's birth compromised his translation. He bestowed virginity on Joseph and Jesus, too. Whatever was lost in the translation, he vowed that it would not be the Holy Family's virginity.

As a translator, Jerome mixed classical techniques with biblical exegesis.[81] He translated the *Chronicle* of Eusebius of Caesarea (d. AD 339?) and brought it up to date. But he was not gifted as a historian because he could not distinguish the important from the trivial. His treatment of Christian themes was "entirely uncritical," and "colored by his violent prejudices."[82] Jerome lacked a feel for history writing because the historic mind set did not yet exist.[83] Yet not every piece of classical historical writing was vitiated by strong prejudices.[84] In short, his attempt to write history never rose above the polemical. Good pietists and polemicists are seldom good historians. They lack objectivity. Opinionated writers should write essays. Jerome expressed his opinions abundantly and forcefully in letters and polemical tracts. If he had had a computer, he would have flamed everyone who did not agree with him. St. Augustine, who wrote Jerome at least eight letters between AD 394 and 419, receiving at least nine in return, knew that Jerome was touchy.

Between the summer of 382 and autumn of 385, Jerome was in Rome. There Pope Damasus I (d. AD 384) became his patron, employer, and close friend. As papal secretary, Jerome learned about church administration, and as archivist, where all the best documents were hidden. It was a scholar's dream come true. After work, he mingled. His boss, Damasus, was also a good mingler. Jerome was introduced to Rome's important prelates and beautiful Christian women, once socialites, now ascetics. Damasus, nearly eighty, charmed the ladies and was sainted for pressing papal claims to supremacy, asserting his authority over schismatics, adorning martyrs' tombs with precious marbles and inscriptions, and writing Virgilian verse about the glories of virginity.[85] Virgil, virginity, and verse bound the aged pope to his more virile secretary. Jerome earned his saint's crown by accepting Damasus's invitation to revise the Bible from the Old Latin text, which had been based on the Greek Septuagint. After twenty-two years, Jerome produced the Vulgate. Its Old Testament was based largely on the Masoretic Hebrew text, while its New Testament grew from correcting Latin passages that seemed too much at variance with the least corrupted, and oldest available, Greek manuscripts. The work earned him his title "Doctor of the Church." Jerome would not have objected to being a doctor of the church. No doctor of the church has ever been charged with malpractice.

The Old Latin version of the Septuagint had been prepared in the third century BC at Alexandria for Greek-speaking Jews who could no longer read Hebrew. Latin speakers in the West required their own translations, and by Jerome's era, many were flawed. Damasus asked Jerome to produce a reliable one. At first, Jerome tried to retain the wording of the Old Latin version wherever possible, using the Septuagint as the ultimate authority. But the longer he worked, the more radical his treatment became. Occasionally, his translation reflected not a particular text, but his own doctrinal taste.[86] Although he claimed later that he had "restored" the New Testament to its Greek original, scholars now believe that Jerome is responsible for only the Four Gospels, because when referring to any other parts of the New Testament, he did not quote the Vulgate but other texts.[87] Would Jerome, so self-assertive and confident of his scholarship, have refrained from citing his own edition out of modesty? Not likely.

By Damusus's death (December 11, 384 AD) Jerome had acquired a coterie of admirers—widows and virgins, aristocratic converts who invited him to dinner, dressed plainly, fasted incessantly, and did without men.[88] They could not do without Jerome, though. He helped them to study scripture. They flattered and funded him, and he gave them spiritual guidance and arguments for asceticism. The most intellectual of these ladies was Marcella, a beautiful older widow with an insatiable appetite for Jerome's religious instruction. The most devoted was Paula, widowed young with several children while still in her twenties, extremely rich, and only in her mid thirties when Jerome met her. She had several daughters and a little boy. Blesilla, the eldest daughter, widowed at twenty, experienced a remarkable inner conversion to Christ, learned Hebrew in short order, gave up the life of a Junior Leaguer, and died of a fever—all before her twenty-first birthday. Jerome eulogized Blesilla in a letter to Marcella (AD 384).[89] He reproved her mother for showing excessive grief over a daughter now feasting with Christ.[90] At the end of his life Jerome relied on Paula's younger daughter, Eustochium, for nursing care and domestic comforts. In his mid-life, he wrote an embarrassingly long poetic letter to the teenaged Eustochium urging on her the virtues of virginity, an outrageous piece urging her to give up good food, wine, the liberty to leave her room and walk about freely; the company of married women and most other women, too; men whose hair was long and who wore gold chains; men whose feet were bare and whose beards were black; and perfumed clergymen who sought office merely to visit women freely. They were the ones who walked on tiptoe around puddles.[91] In his relationships with virtuous women Jerome hoped to prepare the Roman world for those changes that would result in their conversion to Christ. He would make these women role models for a new Christian nobility.[92] Some might object that Jerome deprived them of intellectual and spiritual independence. But, in so far as he trusted them to exemplify the new asceticism, he might be viewed as a more forward-thinking Father than most, even a feminist.[93] To view him as profeminist, however, requires us to recognize that obedience to male leadership was the price women paid for respect in the world of Christian Rome. The price was the same in pagan Rome. Marcella, Paula, Eustochium, and their friends thought any kind of toleration a bargain. They did not conceive of themselves as independent and equal. It was enough for Jerome that they did not conceive.

Jerome's lady friends were not the world's first nuns. Pagan Rome had its vestal virgins, though it left them free to marry if they pleased after years of chastity. Pre-Christian Rome was already into the idolization of the hymen. Although Christians wrote no hymns to the hymen, they nevertheless revered it and sang its praises. This mucous membrane, named for the Greek god of marriage, hangs like fringe on the lower edge of the vaginal opening in some women. In others, it circles it, and some women are not born with one at all. Some hymens have several openings, others have but one, and in a few instances, the hymen entirely blocks the vaginal opening, preventing the flow of menstrual blood, in which case surgery is indicated.[94] The membrane can be stretched by exercise, masturbation, a tampon, or intercourse, but the notion that the worth of a woman is entirely governed by the nature of this slimy tissue is as preposterous an idea as any ever invented by men to control female behavior and deny them their humanity. The mischief created by making a fetish of virginity has been incalculable. The fact is that not all females have hymens. Why, if God was so careless in their distribution, would He care about their maintenance? Jerome, hung up on virginity, did incalculable harm to women in propagandizing for it. As a result, Christianity made an intact hymen a kind of cross on which all women, married or not, were hung up and crucified. There was never an eleventh Commandment concerning virginity. The second one prohibits the worship of idols.

In a letter to Eustochium (AD 384) Jerome read and commented on the Song of Songs. He urged this young teenager to preserve her virginity forever. Eustochium, he wrote, was to remain in the privacy of her own room, where Christ, "her Lover," would come and sport with her, for though a virgin nun, she was wed to Jesus. "When sleep overcomes you, he will come behind the wall, will thrust his hand through the aperture, and will caress your belly, and you will start up, all trembling and cry, 'I am wounded with love.'"[95] She was to wait until Christ knocked and to open when she heard him say, "Open to me, my sister, my love, my dove, my undefiled."[96] Jerome seems to have been visualizing the girl's defloration by Christ. His letter is not so different from the kind of pornographic messages that parents fear circulate on the Internet. Most parents would be suspicious if a middle-aged man sent such an e-mail to their young daughters. Paula did not suggest that Jerome's letter was improper. Perhaps Eustochium did not show it to her. If she did, Jerome might have said that he was thinking only that virginity was spiritual wheat, that is, the "bread" of eternal life. He might have said that everything else—chastity, even marriage—had a lower caloric value for nourishing the soul, and he, Jerome, was, uh, feeding Eustochium the Bread of Life. Far better for her than the empty calories of marriage. Jerome made no effort in his letter to downplay the frankness of the biblical Song of Songs. Whenever Augustine and Ambrose referred to the Song, they, at least, "transposed" the lines[97] so that their sexual references were diverted to more spiritual channels.[98]

Before these ascetic women met Jerome they had voluntarily given up a life of pleasure, men, second husbands (or, if virgins, first husbands), fine cuisine, and the theater. Paula even gave up bathing, except on doctor's orders, for there were already clergymen preaching that the sight of a woman's own body would be enough to distract her from thoughts of God. They did not think body lice would be as distracting. Eustochium had since childhood opted to preserve her virginity. The rejection of life's pleasures would cause many a Christian conscience to convulse, many a breast to be beaten because the heart hungered for beauty, comfort, cleanliness, physical joy, and intellectual stimulation. But ascetics vibrantly disapproved of stimulation.

Then Jerome had to leave Rome. Blesilla's death alarmed some of her kin, who blamed her excessive fasting and penance on Jerome's counsel. A cry was raised: "Monks to the Tiber," and Jerome, feared as a rival by the new Pope Siricius, packed his library for a second journey to the East.[99] The rest of his equipment—Paula, Eustochium, and a few of their lady friends—were re-united with him, either on Cyprus, at Antioch, or in the Holy land itself. The joy of the expatriates once in the Holy Land was palpable. They were pilgrims and set off to visit all the sites sacred to Jesus and the Apostles. They were not so unlike those pilgrims in Chaucer's *Canterbury Tales,* except they had no bawdy Wife of Bath for counsel on matters of the heart. They were more reminiscent of Mark Twain's *Innocents Abroad.* Paula, who had abandoned an elder daughter and a small son sobbing on the quay at Rome, seems never to have been reunited with those particular children. She and Eustochium quickly forgot them and Italy. Mommy didn't live there anymore. Nothing in her old life as a mom compared to her transports of joy before the tombs of Sarah and Isaac in Hebron, the place where Lot had been seduced by his daughters, the spot in Bethany where Jesus raised Lazarus, and Mount Tabor, scene of His Transfiguration. Paula was transfigured from Roman matron to Christian nun. Unlike later nuns, she had her own male escort—Jerome. Overcome with tears before the manger where the baby Jesus laid, she wept harder at the cave believed to have been his tomb, place of his Resurrection. She was in ecstasy, Jerome wrote, prostrating herself before a cross at Calvary. She covered the slab on which the Lord was presumed to have lain after the crucifixion with innumerable kisses. Had she covered her little boy with kisses before running off to the Holy Land to meet Jerome?

Next, the little group made an excursion to Alexandria where Jerome found Didymus the Blind, a biblical scholar and monk. For a month Jerome attended lectures in Didymus's school, while his entourage did what women do when their man is in graduate school—they made the best of it, until school was over and they could return to Palestine.

At Bethlehem, Paula built two monastic establishments in which they would spend the rest of their lives. Her fortune was spent maintaining Jerome and his monks and herself and nuns in their attempt to win salvation by physical work, prayer, and abstinence. Jerome and Paula were the heads of their respective monasteries. They were not the first two Catholics to set their religious establishments side by side, nor the last. They were well aware that at Jerusalem, another such "couple," Jerome's old school friend Rufinus, and Rufinus's significant other, a Roman matron named Melania, had also founded dual religious establishments on the Mount of Olives. In the twelfth century, Abelard and Heloise were eventually ensconced in their own nearby digs, and a century later, St. Francis and St. Clare followed suit, giving us a suite of unconventional conventuals.

Paula and Jerome, like Rufinus and Melania, created a beachhead in Palestine for Christian monasticism. Paula's ladies were divided into three groups according to their social status. None of these contemplatives ever contemplated equality. But all devoted themselves to prayer and hospitality for itinerant Christians. Besides praying several times daily and in the middle of the night, the ladies did a great deal of manual labor—keeping gardens, paring vegetables, making cabbage soup, and sewing clothes—tasks women have always been told justify the expense of their maintenance. After AD 410 they were receiving refugees, people whose lives had fallen apart after the barbarians destroyed Rome and other places in the empire. Jerome, sensibly, did not engage in any manual labor, though he thought it an excellent idea for everyone else in his monastery. He spared himself for scholarly work and it made his reputation, though it ruined a number of other peoples.' Wars of words. Through it all he continued to translate scripture. His was an age of transcription; ours of encryption.

In AD 393 he wrote *Against Jovinian,* another apology for virginity and celibacy, a polemic against a former monk named Jovinian. It was at Marcella's request that Jerome undertook this work. Jovinian claimed all sins were equal, that one could not sin after baptism, and that virginity is no more holy than marriage. He also denied that Mary had kept her virginity in the process of delivering Jesus, an error for which Jerome had rebuked him. Jovinian preached justification by God's grace alone, a position taken up by Luther in the Protestant Reformation. In his letters, Jerome decried Jovinian's approval of remarriage for widows, something that Marcella, Paula, and other friends also denounced.[100] Jerome said marriage was the typical lifestyle of men in the Old Testament under the Law: be fruitful and multiply was their watchword.[101] But in the New Testament, Jerome insisted, it had been replaced by something better, namely, virginity. Jerome went to great lengths to emphasize that in both the Old and New Testament truly good, pious, and holy men were far more apt to have been virgins or eunuchs than married men. Jerome felt that holy men were holier when not wholly men.

One of their number was the revered biblical exegete of Alexandria, Origen, who had himself castrated in order to bring the Word to women without succumbing to temptation. Origen beckoned to Jerome his whole life long.[102] But Jerome's admiration for him was as an exegete, not as a theologian. When Origen's theology was criticized at Rome, Jerome repudiated it, too. In AD 393 Jerome and his old friend Rufinus were reexamining their views on Origen because Bishop John of Jerusalem seemed to accept some of Origen's statements concerning the resurrected body. Origen never wrote about the resurrection of the body as flesh, and the Church generally believed that souls would have bodies in Heaven. Would the resurrected bodies have vaginas and penises?

Breasts with nipples? A digestive tract? An anal sphincter? The Church did not go into details.

Jerome, defender of the fleshly reality of the resurrection body, had begun by the mid 390s to distance himself from his published admiration for Origen, whose theological writings Jerome once claimed were belittled only by the envious.[103] He continued to admire Origen's literary achievements but would henceforth condemn his doctrine.[104] The first skirmish in the Origenist wars was fought between Jerome, siding with the conservative Bishop Epiphanius of Salamis, and Rufinus, siding with Bishop John of Jerusalem. The war ended with apologies all 'round, the lifting of bans, and the nervous assurance of all concerned that they were equally steadfast in their orthodoxy, even if each man secretly thought the others less so than himself.

Eventually, Rufinus left Jerusalem for Rome. There he translated Origen's *First Principles* into Latin, introducing his work with indiscreet references to Jerome's past praise for Origen. Now some of Origen's ideas were distinctly raffish. He maintained there were more worlds than one and that souls had preexisted before entering bodies. Christ was just as old as his Father, whom he equaled, and he had existed before all worlds. All souls would be saved and reunited with God, and God continued to create the universe. These notions of Origen's now embarrassed Jerome. He was enraged that Rufinus had used his name to support views he now repudiated. For twelve years Jerome argued with Rufinus over Origen. Historians refer to this struggle as "the tribulations of St. Jerome" though they tried Rufinus as well. Still, Rufinus has gone down to defeat, and only saints like Jerome experience tribulations. Jerome thought Rufinus's defense of Origen omitted passages Jerome now viewed as insupportable. Rufinus claimed they had never been written by Origen in the first place, that others had inserted them into Origen's text. Jerome made his own literal translation of Origen's *First Principles,* including all the unorthodox elements left out by Rufinus. Each argued that the other's method was harmful to Christian conscience. Their pain was felt by their friends in Jerusalem, North Africa, and Italy. Not only was Jerome alienated from Rufinus, but the Church was nearly alienated from Origen. Double detestinarianism.[105]

Just when Jerome ought to have been thinking about retirement, a Briton named Pelagius left his monastery and arrived in Rome. He published his first theological work in AD 405. He felt the morals of Romans scandalously lax. Muttering "No sex please—I'm British" he set about to raise the bar for Latins who doubted they could do the right thing. Pelagius's slogan was "If I ought, I can." He thought the body need not be broken, merely restrained, for men to behave well.[106] He stopped his ears to Augustine's suggestion that the human will was in bondage because of man's total depravity after the Fall. Pelagius defended man's free will.

He argued that Adam died not because he sinned, but because he was mortal; that sin results from a flaw of one's will, not of one's nature; that every baby is born sinless and all babies, even the *unbaptized,* should they die as babies, would have eternal life; that Adam's sin was not passed on to all men; that men—even non-Christians—can live without sinning. Grace (divine aid) is not necessary to avoid sinning, because God provided it at birth to all men, along with a nature and a free will that enabled man to avoid sin and do good. Pelagius viewed man positively, as empowered by God, created in perfect shape, with no taint of original sin. If one believed Pelagius, man emerged a capable being who was up for anything he put his mind to. This was clearly a threat to the Church. If man were in such good shape, the Church, its sacramental system, and its hierarchy were redundant. The next thing you knew people would demand it be downsized, and thousands of bishops and abbots would be pink-slipped.

St. Augustine, the sixteenth-century reformer John Calvin, and a century later, American Calvinists called Puritans rejected the Pelagian notion that man could still help save himself if God were willing. They embroidered the slogan "In Adam's Fall we sinned All" on their samplers. Romans had no samplers. They might have embroidered it on their sleeves, but togas were sleeveless.

Pelagius thought the Romans were spoiled. Their slaves waited on them hand and foot. Pelagius blamed their low expectations on the servant problem. Romans were very self-serving. In any event, he urged that all men could stop sinning, irrespective of the Fall of Adam. If the lazy Italians would only buck up and stop whining about being incapacitated by original sin they would be better off. Having survived British winters, thick fog, and thin oatmeal, Pelagius had that British trait of taking oneself in hand—not to commit mortal sin, but to avoid committing it.

Pelagius acquired a disciple, an Italian lawyer with the heavenly name of Celestius. The year before the Goths conquered Rome, Pelagius and Celestius sailed to Sicily (AD 409), and then to Africa. At Carthage in 411, Celestius was condemned by a church council and with him the Pelagian principles that both espoused. Celestius stayed in Africa where he provoked Augustine to write fifteen treatises against him.[107] Pelagius went to Palestine, and had been preaching there for several years before Jerome took notice. In AD 415 the Council of Diospolis declared to the dismay of Augustine, that Pelagius was orthodox. Jerome later referred to this council as a "wretched synod" and at once, though he was now past seventy, began writing his *Dialogue Against the Pelagians.*[108] Jerome used scripture to disprove the basic tenets of Pelagianism.

Jerome denied that anyone but Christ had ever managed to avoid sin, because Adam's tainted everybody else. Jerome created a character named

Critobolus whom he used to destroy Pelagian confidence (Jerome called it arrogance) in self. Every thing Critobolus found in scripture to support a liberal view of man was something Critobolus misinterpreted. Unfortunately, Jerome's point of view carried the day. His views became the views of Church and State. Humans could do nothing good by themselves because they were thoroughly corrupted by Adam's sin. Behavior modification was not in man's power, but in God's. If anyone in either Testament had accomplished anything that pleased God, Jerome suggested that he could not do it twice, or for a longer time, or claimed that the achievement was inadequate to warrant his salvation. At one point Jerome ridiculed Critobolus as having "worn out the same question" like a "sort of stage device" that failed to convince.[109] Critobolus was the worst sort of Pharisee whom the *Dialogue* reduced to quivering jelly.[110] Jerome left his "opponent" with this thought: that he "killed" him if he did not convince him; and that otherwise the character killed himself. For the Pelagian, it was a lose-lose situation. Unfair. But Jerome never said that polemics was fair. Indeed, he said it wasn't.

In Jerome's *Dialogue* he did not play fair. He said neither the Old nor New Testament mentioned "free will." This was a specious argument because he knew that the phrase was less important than the thing itself. Jerome offered dozens of biblical examples that disproved man's free will with this kind of logic:

> Every word uttered by the saints is a prayer to God; every prayer and supplication elicits the mercy of the Creator, so that we, who cannot be saved through our own strength and endeavors, may be saved by His mercy. But where mercy and grace exist, there the will ceases to be free to a certain degree, because it is free only insofar as we wish, and desire, and assent to what is pleasing.[111]

Jerome's rhetoric was strong, but his logic was chopped. Not every word saints uttered was prayer. Jerome was a saint, but many of his words were rude, not prayerful. God must have known the difference if Jerome did not. What Jerome uttered when he discovered after publishing his *Dialogue Against Pelagians* that some Pelagians had torched his monastery was probably not prayerful either. Nor is it the case that every prayer elicits God's mercy. Many have prayed to no avail. Jesus prayed to God to remove the cup (of crucifixion) from his lips if it were His will. It was not, and look what happened. Trying to figure out when God will and will not be merciful is no easy task, as Jerome surely knew. He was, for example, tortured for years by sexual desire, prayed to overcome it, and was frustrated when he could not. Freedom is not assenting to what an external force decides is right or wrong for you; freedom is making up your mind to abide by your own decisions whatever the outcome. Jerome, who was a Roman patriot, should have known better than to equate freedom of the will to a desire for what is pleasing. The Christian martyrs could have set him straight. Freedom of the will was a question not of God's mercy, but of who was in charge. Once it had been the Roman Empire in the West. Next it would be the Roman Empire in the East. Now it was the barbarians. Eventually it would be the Roman Catholic Church, then kings, then nations. Jerome was a superb linguistic scholar, but an irrationalist of the first water. He makes an embarrassing saint.

St. Augustine (AD 354–430)

With St. Augustine we stand at the place where pagan antiquity ends, where a once persecuted minority, Christians, assume the mantle and burden not only of religious orthodoxy, but of secular orthodoxy, blurring philosophy, religion, and politics in ways the Romans had not dreamed of, and that medieval, Renaissance, and modern men have not yet sorted out. In Augustine's lifetime the Roman Empire ceased to define its objectives in terms of a cult of pagan nationalism and redefined them in conjunction with a new cult, the Apostles.' Christianity endorsed the values of a dead Jew whose humanity, spiritualism, and political apathy made Rome's conversion one of the most awkward U-turns on the historical highway, a supremely ironic about-face. Augustine launched the Church on a new road to faith because he ceased to concern himself with the adaptation of classical philosophy to Christianity. With the advent of this Father the early medieval world waved goodbye to philosophy, hello to theology.

He did not start out as a critic of antiquity. For nine years a student of Manichaeanism, Augustine only turned to Platonic philosophy in order to clarify what the Manichaeans left obscure. Finally, he forced Platonism and Christianity into an embrace that would have made Plato shudder and Christ blush. Augustine left his mark on theology, affecting the way men and women viewed themselves then and now. Thanks to him Christians would regard themselves as diminished beings permanently flawed by Adam's sin, unable to do good by themselves without the Grace of God, who alone could save them from the enjoyment of his own Creation and redeem them from original sin. Moderns are still embarrassed by what is natural, still burdened by a sense of guilt for the sin they never committed, the original one, though not as much by those they commit regularly. These are not original enough to worry about.

Augustine refined the nature of Trinity, defined the nature of soul, designed the nature of Grace, and consigned man to a predestined fate. For those uninterested in Christian theology Augustine's most memorable legacies are psychological. Admired for his relentless pursuit of spiritual knowledge, Augustine is loved for his disarming frankness about his inner life. Supremely aware of his own needs, vices, and passions, but not how ordinary it was to have them, he informs us in his *Confessions* that these things corrupted him throughout a protracted adolescence. Unfortunately, they had a similar effect on the Western tradition, which has only just begun to recover from his preoccupation with the second-rate nature of Nature, the inherent decadence of civil society, and the nastiness of sex. That his theology caused much misery for the West should not prevent us from trying to understand Augustine, even as we convalesce from the debilitating effects of his legacy. We are struck by his psychological hangups and heroism as he undertook to save himself and posterity from the afflictions and joys of our common humanity.

He was born in the small North African town of Tagaste, November 13, 354. His mother Monica was a Christian who sought in religious zeal refuge from the ordinary disappointments of married life. His father, Patricius, was a pagan whom Monica converted to Christ shortly before his death. Schooled in classics at the nearby town of Madaura, their son returned home for a year at the age of sixteen because his father could no longer afford the tuition. Enforced idleness was punctuated by escapades with friends. The most famous was the theft of a neighbor's pears. Although this prank might "appear trivial to many readers" to others it may seem much like the gang activity of adolescents today.[112] Augustine and his gang got away with their crime, but the recollection of it affected Augustine always.

Describing the incident in his *Confessions,* written when he was bishop of Hippo, he referred to "a gang of youthful good-for-nothings" who had sneaked up to the tree "in the dead of night" and carried off "huge loads" of fruit, eating a few pears, hurling the rest to pigs. Augustine confessed that he enjoyed "the sin itself" hugely.[113] He would not have done it but for the sociability involved, the company of friends being "an inscrutable seduction of the mind." "Someone just says: 'Let's go; let's do it!' and the result is one does in the name of friendship what one never would have done acting all alone."[114] Elsewhere in the *Confessions* he notes that he was in the habit of rewarding his playmates with snacks filched from the family larder. He wanted to be popular, and treating his friends from the family larder seemed as good a way as any to win their loyalty. Garry Wills tells us that the pear incident parallels Augustine's separate explanation of the story in Genesis where Adam, "to maintain his 'bond of company' with Eve," deliberately commits sin.[115] The rest of Augustine's life is partly an extended brooding on this boyish prank—giving him occasion to reflect on the nature of human depravity, the desire for love and acceptance by one's fellows, rather than love of God. The theft set him to pondering the nature of evil and the desire to placate God by disassociating himself from it. Augustine's assumption that criminality is a reflection of human depravity rather than of social circumstances that could be remedied still impairs our ability to reduce juvenile delinquency. This is the first and best documented example in Western civilization of the consequences of peer pressure—and pear pressure.

In the autumn of AD 370, Augustine went to Carthage for further instruction at the expense of a rich patron. There he studied rhetoric and opened his own grammar school. He taught in Carthage or Tagaste until 383. Perhaps it was in his patron's villa that he met the anonymous woman whom he impregnated, and with whom he lived faithfully for fifteen years. It was normal for a young Roman citizen to cohabit with a woman he could not marry legally. Their association was a kind of second-class "marriage" even the Church did not condemn. Their son was named Adeodatus [God-given], born before Augustine was twenty, perhaps when he was only sixteen or seventeen. This made Augustine an unwed teenaged father and Adeodatus an illegitimate child. Later Augustine wrote that children "compel us to love them," another kind of learning experience.[116] The Church never referred to Augustine as an unwed father, only as a Church Father.

Even if the Church had not recognized him as a Father, he would have made it as a writer. His *Confessions,* written somewhere around 397, six years after he had become a bishop, illustrate the significance he attached to ordinary actions of life in this mundane world because, insignificant in themselves, they threaten our relation with God. Every action, enjoyment, and challenge man experiences is a test of his spiritual status which Augustine felt he had passed, but only after three decades (until his conversion at age thirty-two) of continual failure! He said a great deal is gained by the man who weeps for the things of this life—sticky relationships that slake lust, temptations, pride, joy in doing what we know is wrong, if at the end, he emerges into the light of God's presence. Choosing God over everything in His creation earns God's Grace, forgiveness of misguided choices.[117] Thus for Augustine, life is genuinely significant only when one gives it the cold shoulder.

The title of Augustine's other bestseller, *The City of God,* might suggest that Augustine was the first urban planner, but he was not. Augustine did not think the advantages of urban life or earthly life outweighed the disadvantages. In his preface he wrote that he was defending God's city against "those who prefer their own gods to its Creator." If anything, he was the first exurbanite wannabe. Real cities meant adjusting to foreigners who hoped to profit from Roman culture, people whose priorities were not God and Christ. When Augustine was young, Carthage was full of misguided Manichaeans. Rome attracted philosophical critics and radical heretics. When he was fifty-six, Rome was conquered by the Visigoths (AD 410), Arian Christians who rejected the Trinity. When Augustine lay dying, Hippo was under attack by Vandals. Nevertheless, the real barbarians had already penetrated the city gates. They were the boys in the pear orchard, their children, their grandchildren. Degenerate mankind. Us.

In AD 384 Augustine moved to Rome with his small family, where he hoped to obtain serious-minded pupils, unlike the rowdy Carthaginian boys who acted up in class. He lied to Monica, telling her that he was merely seeing a friend off at the port, then, loading up his family, gave her the slip. In Rome, his students were polite but dropped his class before paying their fees. Augustine later described his resentment to God:

> I hated them in my heart, though the hatred I felt was not a perfect hatred. I think that I hated them more because of what I was likely to suffer from them personally than because of the wrong they did to everyone concerned. . . . I was more anxious not to have to put up with their evil ways for my own sake than that they should learn good for your sake.[118]

Peter Brown tells us that Augustine's Manichaeanism consoled him by offering him the hope that he could preserve the purity of his soul apart from the impurity of physical lust, and deflect the "wanderings" of that soul on its way toward the truth.[119] The dualist solution made it possible to posit a separate good and a separate evil, the dual gods of Manichaeanism. This, together with discipline, gave Augustine hope that he could retain a purity apart from his sinful side. We smile at the famous prayer he made to God while not yet a Christian: "Make me chaste and continent, but not yet."[120] This ejaculation reveals the ambivalence the young man of parts felt toward his most sinful part.

Augustine wrestled with the dilemma posed by a strong desire to enjoy life and an equally strong desire to be holy. After his conversion to Christianity he capitulated to the prevailing view of the Fathers, who made renunciation of most enjoyments a requirement for the salvation of one's soul. Christian churches still wrestle with enjoyment and sin. How much, and what kinds of pleasures can believers experience before their immortal souls are tempted, damaged, lost? Marriage, divorce, education, birth control, fashion, abortion, getting, interest charges, spending, indebtedness, dancing, drinking, military service, medical treatment, food, and labor-saving devices have all been condemned by Christians influenced by Augustine's thoughts on enjoyment. His is the classic portrait of a good person convinced that only a puritanical renunciation of one's human nature and of Nature, seducer of the soul, can bring man to God. Augustine believed the main purpose of a Christian's life was preparation for the afterlife by loving obedience to God and love of our neighbor. Such convictions open up a chasm between us and Augustine. Most of us do not love God better than ourselves, much less our neighbors, whom we barely tolerate, if indeed we know them at all. When Augustine was not busy preaching to the townsfolk in his large bishopric or participating with other church leaders at conferences, he displayed that reclusive habit of Catholic clergymen, withdrawal from real neighborhood life behind garden walls.

Though he holds prime place in the late classical canon, the Catholic canon, the Christian canon, and the canon of Western civilization, Augustine did not explode the conflicts between their divergent ideals, even though he is the biggest gun in Christianity's arsenal. One critic thinks his significance is due to his universality, transcending time, place, thought, piety, and style.[121] Perhaps, but even the great classics are not so universal that they do not open up chasms between our values and theirs. We bridge the chasm that divides us from Augustine by our sympathy for his insecurity and his ambivalence toward contemporary life that attracted him but also frightened him. Who cannot relate to his despair at the pointlessness of the quotidian round? Who cannot feel his joy in discovering a meaningful substitute for life's pleasures and boring relationships? Augustine was, like most good people, extremely sensitive. He searched for meaning and understanding about the universe and his place in it. He lacked confidence in his native powers and needed to believe that the corrupt material world in which he was stuck was not all there was. No more than Augustine could are we able to control all the factors—economic, political, aesthetic, interpersonal, and impersonal—that affect us. Everyone's life is a work in progress, and sometimes, we see very little progress. Are we so different from Augustine in this respect? Reading his *Confessions* we rejoice that he found satisfaction in religion, shelter from the seductive world. Epicurus also took comfort behind garden walls with a few like-minded friends. Monasticism began to grow from Hellenistic seed, even if it blossomed in late antiquity and reached full growth during the Middle Ages. The cloistered life offered its adherents what we moderns consider the greatest of luxuries—time for reflection. Though it is frequently referred to as a communal lifestyle, it probably offered more privacy than any other lifestyle then available.

The literary power of the *Confessions* and *The City of God* are bridges over the chasm that divides us from this saint. He wrote many more books of interest mostly to theologians, who have made an industry of Augustinian research. These two belong to everyone and give us Augustine the human being, the only one from antiquity who presents himself to us inside out. Caesar lets us share his strategic triumphs. Cicero lets us admire his rhetoric and skill at philosophical imitation. Marcus Aurelius shares some sense of the burdens of power, but only Augustine details the progress of his heart, mind, body, and soul. He is so sincere, so human, we feel we know him personally. As T. S. Eliot once wrote in *The Waste Land* (1922) in a different context about a different chap, he is our "semblable," our "frère" because his vulnerability lets us imagine a similar vindication and relief, knowledge and hope, an end to all fear and yearning. Aren't we as vulnerable? Don't we worry about goals more worthwhile than the mere mundane? Don't we, too, seek for solutions approved by our intimate friends? Our revered teachers? Our Mom?

Technically a Manichaean at Rome, Augustine's associations with the sect no longer met his needs. He broke ties with them, though he would never be free of their preoccupation with the power of evil over the good. His theology would reflect their hold on him, as we in the West reflect his on us.[122]

Augustine found a new job late in AD 384, at Milan, as a court orator. Because the city was the center of imperial administration, he soon found interesting acquaintances, pupils, and opportunities for advancement. Monica joined him with two of his cousins, his older brother, and some staff (scribes, servants), for whom Augustine would now have to provide. His responsibilities ballooned. Monica made arrangements for his worldly success, including his engagement to a girl of social standing to advance his career, a trophy wife. Augustine let his companion, mother of Adeodatus, be shipped to Africa like so much surplus baggage. He registered some pain at his own loss, none for hers: "Meanwhile my sins were being multiplied. The woman with whom I was in the habit of sleeping was torn from my side on the grounds of being an impediment to my marriage, and my heart, which clung to her, was broken and wounded and dropping blood."[123] His passivity at the separation is scarcely more reassuring than his haste at replacing his companion at once with a new concubine. "I found another woman for myself."[124] This was a temporary convenience, for his fiancée was probably twelve and had to wait two more years before she reached the legal age for marriage. But, by that time, he was in pursuit of something other than brides, because he had grown disenchanted with his job and with his attempt to live a worldly lifestyle.

It was fortunate that he had friends, Alypius and Nebridius, to share his intellectual and spiritual quest, as well as two churchmen, Simplicianus and the latter's old pupil, Ambrose, now bishop of Milan. The two clergymen were steeped in Christian interpretations of Platonic thought. His mother revered Ambrose, one of the West's greatest Church Fathers, but the bishop was too busy to be accessible to parishioners and refused to be interrupted while he was reading. Augustine did not like Ambrose's sermons very much anyway. He found other role models to guide his steps to God and Christianity. People were always helping Augustine.

The novelist and journalist Rebecca West startled her public in 1933 when she described Augustine's young manhood in terms of an alarming immaturity that made him overly concerned with being taken care of, rather than caring for others. Augustine does seem self-centered. In fact, he seems much like some of our own young people who have delayed assuming some of the tasks of maturity. West never gave Augustine credit for getting beyond the egocentrism associated with prolonged adolescence. She remarked: "He retained the curious quality which made him lovable in spite of his complete egotism."[125] Peter Brown alludes to this disquieting desire for praise and affection.[126] Faith made Augustine secure where once he had been insecure, content where once he had been ashamed of his attraction to idleness, worldliness, and friends who were sometimes as foolish as he felt himself to be in their company. Christian readers have been inspired by the *Confessions* and grateful to Augustine for witnessing to the spiritual change for which a heart faithful to God may hope. Some of the credit for his conversion should go to his long-suffering friends and counselors and much to Monica. Most saints made enormous demands on their supporters, but for the latter there were as yet no support groups.

Augustine's conversion must be understood against the background of fourth-century cultural change. In Milan stories of dramatic conversions to Christianity were stimulating others to emulation. Just a month before his conversion, Augustine learned about three friends of an official who had converted after reading a biography of the Egyptian monk Anthony. Augustine wondered why he should be left out of this new and wonderful source of communication called religious conversion? The desire to hook up to a greater source of information burst upon the early twentieth century when Americans got their first telephones and in the mid twentieth century when they got television sets. More recently, cell phones and the Internet have abolished isolation and sensory deprivation, even for those not suffering from it. Converting to these technologies puts the powerless in touch with the world beyond. According to Webster's Dictionary, "a *communicant* is one who *communicates.*" Augustine heard these conversion stories while he was studying academic skepticism, a philosophical position which denied the possibility of reaching definitive answers to life's pressing questions. If only he could communicate! Would conversion to Christ provide a better hook-up?

Meanwhile, Augustine was consulting learned friends about Platonism and concluded that there was no conflict between Plato's Ideas and the notion of Christ as the Ideal made flesh. Warren Thomas Smith asks whether the Christian philosophers of Milan were really true to Plato? He says they were not, at least in the classical sense.[127] But Platonism was so prestigious in the fourth century that it did not matter to men like Simplicianus, Ambrose, and Augustine whether their edited versions of Plato's work were accurate. Classical Greek philosophers had been dead for hundreds of years. Why should Christians let dead white pagans limit their own interpretations of divine cosmology? They were crafting a totally new ethos for a Christian public, one where faith and traditions took precedence over pagan Greek explanations of the universe that had never been quite rational—let alone accurate—in the first place? As the Hebrews carried off Egyptian treasures on their flight with Moses out of Egypt, so Christians carried off Greek philosophy to create a classical-sounding version of cosmology that would be compatible with their preferred search engines—Genesis and St. Paul. At last they had access to DSL!

The drama of Augustine's conversion is related in his *Confessions*. He had been talking with Alypius when suddenly he was overwhelmed with tears. Fleeing to the garden, he flung himself under a fig tree thinking, "How long, Lord; wilt Thou be angry forever?"[128] Just then he heard a child's voice saying "Pick up and read," or, says James O'Donnell, "Pick up and sort," a work song sung by Italian agriculturalists.[129] Augustine was puzzled. He could not place the words as part of any children's game, nor, says Garry Wills, being African, was he familiar with Italian work chants. What he did do was immediately pick up his New Testament. The book fell open to Romans 13:13, verses that discourage drunkenness and sexual intercourse. He seems never to have had a problem with strong drink, but Augustine enjoyed sex and the memory of it haunted him all his life long. He wrote: "I had no wish to read further; there was no need to. For immediately I had reached the end of this sentence it was as though my heart was filled with a light of confidence and all the shadows of my doubt were swept away." [130] That this puritanical passage from Romans swept his doubts away is not a convincing explanation of a conversion. Years of questioning, self-doubt, study, dissatisfaction, Monica's anxiety for his soul, the rhetoric of Ambrose, the Platonism of Simplicianus, and the knowledge that there were happy converts while he remained miserable drove Augustine to a point where he was ripe for conversion. He let a childish ditty and a fortuitous reading of scripture sway him. Relieved of an immense burden, his own bad conscience, he felt possessed of sufficient energy to lay the basis for the biggest burden after Jewish guilt that Christians were ever to bear, Augustinianism. That his conversion happened in a garden was emblematic of Augustine's life and of his theology. Believing himself damned in two gardens, he was saved in another, and determined to vegetate no more.[131] His career in the Church would bear strange and wonderful fruit.

At a villa in Cassiciacum near Lake Como, Augustine, Monica, Adeodatus, and several friends took a break from their day jobs to help Augustine read, write, and relax. His actual baptism by Ambrose and that of Adeodatus, too, performed during Easter week of AD 387, in an octagonal pool still visible beneath the cathedral square of Milan, proved anticlimactic to what had happened under the fig tree at Cassiciacum.

Garry Wills objects to the translation of Augustine's title as *Confessions,* preferring that it be called *Testimony.* Wills believes that the word confession evokes an invidious sexual connotation that most people think hints at preconversionary sexual excess, which Wills believes far from excessive. Indeed, Augustine may have been more continent than most young men of the time, or even any time, but what sexual activity he did indulge in gave him a profound feeling of sinfulness. In modern times Romanticism, naturalism, and Freud found ways to deal with self-loathing. Before Freud the contempt of humans for their bodily functions was profoundly Christian. After Freud there was anorexia and Weight Watchers.

The ancient Egyptians seem to have escaped this contempt for sexuality, as did the pre-Socratic Greeks, Minoans, and pagan Rome. From the Church's point of view, self-loathing or revulsion from sex was the very foundation of sanctity. St. Ambrose, who baptized Augustine in Milan, considered virginity the key to a pure life quite as much as the Gnostics, Manichaens, Neoplatonists, and Pelagians. We know how Irenaeus, Tertullian, Origen, and Jerome felt about sex. Christians, Jews, heretics, and post-Socratic philosophers all looked askance at the corruptibility and impermanence of the human body and its functions. Manichaeans regarded all flesh as under the domain of the Devil.[132] Neoplatonists assumed that the body was once united with the One, and had been dispersed in the universe (where it fell) into the "impoverishing plurality of time"–which was not a good thing.[133] All these truth seekers revered unity over plurality, preferring the simple to the complex, and hence, the unit one to the unit two, without any rational understanding of either simplicity or complexity, the real nature of the universe, or the potential beauty of human love. Bodies embarrassed the four Fathers almost as much as they sustained them. Augustine suffered immensely from his own sexual desire, whereas Jerome just made everyone else suffer. Origen became a eunuch for God, widows renounced remarriage, virgins renounced men, and it was a toss-up whether self-loathing, prudery, misanthropy, misogyny, or self-mutilation would prove the best antidote to physical desire.

Peter Brown says Augustine's humiliation by his body was based on the view that sexual feeling was a punishment. The fig leaves that Adam and Eve pasted over their genitals proved to Augustine that those were the parts where sin originated. "Ecce unde." That's the place![134] With such views on sex and marriage, is it any wonder that Augustine lost interest in marriage? If only he could have lost his interest in sex as well we might all have felt better about ourselves! In that we do not, we are all Augustinians.

Augustine returned to Africa after his baptism, a trajectory interrupted by the death of Monica at Rome's port of Ostia. Having seen her son safely converted, she died a happy woman. Later she was canonized so Augustine and his mom both wear crowns in heaven. At Tagaste once again Augustine gave himself over to study and scholarly chats with celibate friends in private gardens–a kind of Christian Epicureanism that James J. O'Donnell describes as anchronistic monasticism.[135] Adeodatus died the next year. Augustine completed a study on music. In AD 391, while visiting the church at Hippo Regius, he was set upon by the parishioners there and forcibly ordained a priest–a position he had not sought and had hoped to avoid.

As a priest he found himself involved in the Donatist controversy that had raged for generations. The Donatists were African Christians who had, early in the fourth century, taken as their role model Bishop Donatus. This man, they believed, had maintained Catholic purity by refusing to cooperate with imperial persecution under Galerius and Diocletian. Donatists achieved unity—and moral superiority—by refusing to accept any clergymen whom they judged to have cooperated with the persecutors. The orthodox condemned their rigorism, because they had not been rigorous with themselves during the persecution and some of them, no doubt, retained a sense of their own guilt. Nothing makes people loathe their erstwhile fellows more than being secretly in agreement with them. Both groups shared an identical liturgy and ritual, but each regarded the other as heretical. Augustine started a tactful debate. Christ, he may have remembered, urged turning the other cheek. But Donatists were too cheeky.

So Augustine determined to destroy the movement. At one point he composed a popular anti-Donatist song. Each letter of the alphabet began a couplet which ended with a refrain about choosing the better faith. Augustine combined the skills of a PR man with those of a copywriter to promote orthodoxy. R. A. Markus observed that "Augustine's prophetic interpretation of the Theodosian Age equipped him with a powerful theological justification for religious coercion" and thinks he may have been the "chief theorist" of persecuting bishops as early as 401.[136] Peter Brown writes that Augustine lost patience with Donatism because it reproduced the static thought of Judaism, with its concern for the maintenance of the Law and the purity of ritual. Augustine, steeped in Platonism, regarded the world as a "hierarchy of imperfectly-realized forms," of which one was the visible or earthly Church.[137] It was not necessary, nor possible, to be pure on this earth. Being orthodox was more than enough.

In 411 Augustine participated in the Council at Carthage that resulted in imperial enforcement of an orthodox peace. Although he protested against government use of capital punishment, he grew convinced that compulsion could bring about results where persuasion failed. Teachers used force to get children to work; parents to get them to obey. God himself, Augustine wrote, uses force on occasion because he loves us. Tough love. Christ, he remembered, thought it correct to "compel" everyone to come in to participate in a feast (Luke 14:23). Augustine did not see that a closer reading of Luke shows us that the story was not about force at all, but about charity. It is hard to see why Augustine thought Christ had compelled people to convert, when the point of the story was that one should offer food to the hungry—not force them to eat! The Church chose a metaphorical rather than a literal reading of the incident and on this foundation built a superstructure of persecution of conscience!

Augustine's reconciliation to forcing conscience did much to damage the reputation of the Roman Church. It set up a program that would repeat itself until early modern times. The Dominican Order of monks, formed in the early thirteenth century and following the Augustinian rule, was early devoted to teaching and preaching with an added goal of converting heretics, pagans, and Jews. Dominicans were soon made directors of the medieval Inquisition and not long after their founder's death were administering torture to obtain confessions of guilt, that is, heretical belief. The reliance by Dominicans and other orders on force to compel conscience ultimately resulted in the Crusades, the Spanish Inquisition, the Roman Inquisition, and wars of religion to exterminate heresy. In the late seventeenth century, a Protestant philosopher named Pierre Bayle wrote a lengthy rebuke to the forcing of conscience by Louis XIV and the Catholic Church.[138] Forcing people to accept a particular religious orthodoxy gave kings and emperors and later, modern secular governments, too, a pattern for depriving people of liberty not only in matters religious, but also in matters political, economic, and sexual.

Augustine's attitude toward Donatists, Pelagians, and other heretics greatly contributed to the church's penchant for persecution. Because he finally had had it with Donatists, he persuaded Rome's African military commander that the empire could not tolerate Donatists. Augustine presided over the restoration of orthodoxy, the redistribution of Donatist property and, ultimately, of Donatists who joined the orthodox Church.[139] As a young man Augustine believed people could be led to virtue by reason alone, but in maturity he followed the path that persecuting Roman emperors had once taken against Christians, using force to make men docile if persuasion could not make them wise. It was not the path of righteousness, but the path of expediency. Augustine surely knew the difference between them.

It was not Augustine but the ancient Sumerians who first stated that no child was born sinless from its mother's womb. The Hebrews contributed the story of Adam and Eve, who, if they did not corrupt all their descendents, at least made it difficult for them to live and worship without a lot of emotional stress. Finally, under Augustine's tutelage, Adam's sin of disobedience passed to everyone except Jesus Christ who, with his Father and the sacraments of the Church, could secure men's salvation. All men? No, just a favored few. Pelagius rejected hereditary guilt for Adam's sin, emphasizing the healing nature of baptism instead. He enraged Augustine, who stressed not man's natural capacity, once baptized, for doing good, as Pelagius did, but rather his incapacity to do good without God's grace and belief in Jesus Christ as Lord even after baptism. Augustine wrote to Jerome to warn him of Pelagianism, a major threat to the authority of God, Christ, scripture, and Church Fathers like Jerome and Augustine.

But Augustine was uncertain how to explain the way in which individual souls came to be corrupted, and without clarification was unable to defend original (hereditary) sin while still preserving the benevolence of God. In AD 415 Augustine pleaded with Jerome by mail to answer some questions about the origin of the soul. He could hardly teach the students Jerome was sending him if he could not himself understand how guilt was incurred through Adam. He listed what he believed about the soul. He was sure that man's sinful soul was not God's fault, but that of Adam's faulty will.[140] But he still did not understand how Adam's guilt had passed to the rest of mankind. He thought the question of inherited guilt very difficult. No one should contradict the Apostle (Paul), who taught that "every soul, even that of a tiny baby, needs to be delivered from the bond of sin."[141] But Augustine confessed that he was puzzled as to how the soul had "contracted that guilt by which it is condemned, even if it is the soul of an infant who died without baptism"?[142] He was aware of no less than five different theories about the origin of souls. He had already rejected the Manichaeans' theory that every soul was a part of the divine soul. Of the remaining four theories, he wrote that he was anxious to accept the one favored by Jerome (he wasn't really), that God created every soul individually before sending it forth in a new body. That notion would have handicapped Augustine from attributing Adam's sin—and penalties for it—to all men as descendants of Adam. Augustine was hardly the first to maintain original sin, but he distinguished with more insistence than anyone else the punishment and guilt that accrued therefrom.[143] The immediate result of the Fall, according to Augustine, was that all mankind became unduly subject to the sin of desire (Latin *concupiscentia*), which in its English form, concupiscence, is almost invariably taken to mean carnal lust. Henceforth, in order to do anything good at all, man needed God's Grace. One could even say he lusted after it.

Do we need a psychoanalyst or theologian to deduce that Augustine, like Tertullian and Jerome, was really hung up on the nastiness of Adam's sin? Like St. Paul, the Apostle to whom Augustine was much indebted, Augustine felt that man, without God's help, could do nothing good.[144] For in disobeying God, Augustine would have us know, man lost control over his will; and what is more symbolic of the lack of control than that most impertinent organ, the male member? Even antismoking ads on TV have made fun of the inadequacy of human will in that regard by showing men smoking bent cigarettes while a beautiful woman walks disdainfully past. In the history of literature only Michel de Montaigne, the sixteenth-century French essayist, was as impressed as Augustine with the gravity of the uncontrollable will in that respect.[145] Montaigne's was problematic; he could not always rise to the occasion; whereas Augustine resented the likelihood that he would rise to every occasion that presented itself, because he could not but be aroused by concupiscence. Thus, when arguing against the Pelagian sentiments of his long-time antagonist and fellow bishop, Julian of Eclanum, Augustine observed that control over sexual desire was ineffective, or as Elaine Pagels put it "hideously out of control," in marriage as outside it, and that, but for the restraints imposed by Christian marriage, "people would have intercourse indiscriminately, like dogs."[146] That, and the fact that Christian marriage produced more Christians, were the only advantages Augustine saw in marriage, a worm's eye view, but also his own. Montaigne concentrated on mental tricks to free a fellow from impotence and from cutting a graceless figure in the bedroom. Augustine recommended celibacy and concentrating on God to free men from damnation and cutting a Graceless figure in Hell.

Garry Wills spotlights Augustine's treatment of sex and will, noting that for him impotence was "the extreme example of inner dividedness, where desire is rebellious not only against reason but against itself."[147] Wills thinks that Augustine, widely thought to have despised the body, was in fact attempting to break away from the tradition (seen in Manichaeans, Gnostics, and other Fathers) of contempt for the human body. Wills thinks Augustine's meditations on the meaning of God become flesh in Jesus "turned that whole world upside-down"[148] and made of Christ's flesh "a paste put on blind eyes to heal them."[149]

It may be that in Augustine's day preaching on the Incarnation would have helped to heal those who denigrated a fleshly humanity. But in the modern era, a message of the sinfulness of sex produces those aberrations of human behavior we associate with ignorance and patriarchy, namely, the denigration of women, and the abuses of sexuality, including rape, child molestation, spousal abuse, and the denial of a woman's right to choose; also in antifeminism, pornography, pederasty, and as many neurotic and psychotic illnesses as can be described on a police docket, or in a textbook of abnormal psychology. Our society needs more than a healing plaster compounded from some dogmatic religious idea. It could not heal antiquity, and it cannot heal our modern age, which is even more heterogeneous with regard to belief systems. Moderns need radical rehabilitation of basic social, economic and educational institutions. We need to heal the holistic human being, body and mind, and the whole social community, state, and nation as well. We need to apply more humane laws, not spiritual plasters, to irruptions in the body politic. It is doubtful if religious institutions, which perpetuated sexism from the get-go, will heal the wounds they were the first to inflict. We do not need faith-based charity but people-based social reform. We need faith in ourselves and our government. After all, we created it to do for us collectively what we cannot do as individuals, working within church groups or any other kind of small community. Our social order must be our new community. It must have more options than Augustine's. It must put those new options to work for the whole community, not just the portion that we agree with.

Augustine was a most determined Father. He was also a determinist, because he was not a Pelagian. Yet it pained him to think that man, even after the Fall, had no freedom of the will left at all. He suggested that even sinful men, Adam's seed, still retained the ability to choose between good and evil. The problem was not that men lacked will, but that their will was paralyzed by concupiscence. The upshot was that Augustine took back with one breath what he conceded in the other, leaving man free to do bad, but not good. This peculiar freedom reflected perfectly the pessimism of St. Paul, who observed that he could not do what he willed, but only the very thing he hated; nothing good dwelt in him as a fleshly being.

Augustine's world was falling apart. The barbarians threatened the weakened empire. His reaction was to make God's will—not man's—the final arbiter of man's fate. His was a comprehensible if not a sensible attempt to allay his great foreboding for the future of mankind. His profoundest insight, some would say, was predestination, which others find incredibly irrational. In an essay on perseverance, he made it plain that God would not allow even faithful Christians to persevere until the end, but predestined most to falter, making them forfeit eternal salvation. The numbers of the elect whom God intended to save, were, Augustine convinced himself, very small. Peter Brown has pointed out that this minimalism was quite consistent with the heritage of African Christianity, and perhaps it is not unreasonable to infer that a continent with as much desert as arable land would produce belief in scarce resources, the scarcest being salvation.[150] But the lack of fertility in Africa was nothing compared to Augustine's preoccupation with the infertility of souls. In his study of Augustine, Edwin Lee points out four stages of Augustine's concept of predestination, each marked by a gradual decrease of man's initiative in responding to God's selection of him as salvable.[151] Peter Brown makes the plea that predestination was for Augustine "a doctrine of survival" and intimates that it was received by the panic-stricken faithful wondering if they would survive the takeover of their society by Vandals and other barbarians.[152] Nevertheless, for most people, predestination was not a doctrine of survival, but a denial that most would survive.

When Augustine lay dying (AD 430), the town of Hippo was surrounded by Vandals. Neither the Vandals nor Augustinian theology was heavily invested in the survival of the masses, deemed by Augustine the "massa damnata," or nonelect of God, and by the Vandals, a cheap labor pool. Was it more than a coincidence that by the end of the seventh century Christians and Christianity had disappeared from North Africa, though not from Ethiopia nor the Holy Land? Elsewhere in the East election would reside not in God's hands, but in Allah's.

If Augustine's theology failed to grow in his native land, it flourished in western Europe as in a garden. Those who tended it weeded out barbarians and Arians, Celts and Vikings, Saracens, Magyars, Huns, Saxons, herbalists, Druids, homosexuals, vegans, witches, heretics, nudists, Jews, and God only knows how many other blooming idiots seeking a place in the sun. The fertile ideas planted by our Four Fathers grew at the expense of their enemies, whose descendants Christianity first harrowed, then mowed down, next acculturated, and finally, cultivated. Brought to the New World by conquistadors, Jesuits, trappers, traders, and Puritans even more attracted to Augustinian predestinarianism and the sinfulness of mankind than Catholics, primitive Christian ideas flourished in America as in a hothouse. God knows America has done those Four Fathers proud.

Notes

CHAPTER 1. BEFORE CIVILIZATION

1. Or, as Hillary Rodham Clinton put it in a book about the well-being of children, *It Takes a Village* (i.e., a community) to support families in rearing children.

2. The textbook by Robert E. Lerner, Standish Meacham, and Edward McNall Burns, *Western Civilizations: Their History and Culture,* 13th ed. (New York: W.W. Norton, 1993), makes this point. Here the "arms race" results in "the advance of metallurgy," or bronze manufacture. To obtain copper and tin for bronze, villagers had to produce a surplus of tradeable goods (1:20).

3. James Burke and Robert Ornstein, *The Axemaker's Gift: A Double-Edged History of Human Culture* (New York: Putnam, 1995).

4. "Everyman His Own Historian" (1935), in which he denied the possibility of anyone being wholly objective about an "intangible" (vanished) past.

5. Mark Kishlansky, Patrick Geary, and Patricia O'Brien, *Civilization in the West* (New York: Harper Collins, 1991), A:2–3.

6. See n. 4 above. The bone markings on tools may have been attempts to record lunar intervals, a kind of calendar to record seasonal changes and their own activities.

7. In December 1994, new caves filled with paintings pictures were found in a gorge near the town of Vallon-Pont d'Arc in the Ardèche region of France (northwest of Avignon). These caves of Paleolithic art are more extensive and more informative, including for the first time pictures of the rhinoceros, absent from caves at Lascaux in southern France and Altamira in northern Spain. The site has remained undisturbed by man and has already yielded evidence that those who lived there had developed a fairly complex culture replete with primitive altars, flint knives, and the remains of fireplaces. It has been said to be the "only totally intact cave network from the Paleolithic era." Archaeologists expect it to reveal more information concerning the development of symbolism in human culture. (From a report by Marlise Simons in the *New York Times,* reprinted in the *San Francisco Chronicle* as "Stunning Discovery of Stone Age Art," January 19, 1995.)

8. Lerner, Meacham, and Burns, *Western Civilizations,* rules out "aesthetic delight" as an explanation of cave art because the art rooms were not, the authors point out, the rooms where people normally lived, but the darkest interior areas of caves (11).

9. Dates in prehistory are obtained from techniques based on measuring the decay of carbon or of radioactive minerals in rock bearing strata with the bones found between them. The dates change frequently because of new finds by paleontologists, especially in Kenya, around Lake Turkana, where, for several decades, an area of intense investigation into man's origins has been in progress. See for example, Meave Leakey, "The Farthest Horizon," *National Geographic,* September 1995, 38–51. Ms. Leakey, wife of Richard, the successor to his father Louis Leakey, has discovered what she thinks is a new species of hominid, between 3.9 and 4.1 million years old. She has named it *Australopithecus amanensis,* and thinks it is a direct ancestor of Lucy.

10. Donald C. Johanson and Maitland Edey, *Lucy: The Beginnings of Humankind* (New York: Simon and Schuster, 1981; New York: Warner Books, 1987), observe that to the question "Just exactly what is a hominid?" there is no "simple answer" but "it is safe to say that a hominid

is an erect-walking primate. That is, it is either an extinct ancestor to man, a collateral relative to man, or a true man. All human beings are hominids, but not all hominids are human beings" (18–19).

11. William H. Kimbel, Donald C. Johanson, and Yoel Rak, "The First Skull and Other New Discoveries of Australopithecus Afarensis at Hadar, Ethiopia," *Nature* 368 (March 31, 1994): 449.

12. It should be remembered, however, that the dating of any hominid depends entirely upon the most recent testing of that hominid's oldest bone fragments.

13. Louis Leakey did consider for a time that *Homo habilis* had left Africa and gone out to populate the world, but he changed his mind. (He speculated on this problem in a movie produced in 1966 entitled *Dr. Leakey and the Dawn of Man*) Lately, new evidence has emerged that makes some scientists think Dr. Leakey's first instinct was right. See n. 18 below.

14. Lerner, Meacham, and Burns, *Western Civilizations,* 8. However, recent fossil finds in Asia seem to indicate an earlier emergence for *Homo erectus.*

15. March 11, 1994.

16. In 1995 archaeologists digging in Zaire uncovered ninety-thousand-year-old tools which seem to indicate that the level of sophisticated tools there had to have been the work of *Homo sapiens sapiens.* Had he stayed in Africa all the time? Or, is it possible that *Homo erectus,* having left earlier, doubled back to Africa and developed into modern man? These are some of the conundrums that paleoanthropologists have of late begun to pose. The story does not yet seem crystal clear.

17. John Noble Wilford, "European Fossils Provide Clues to Prehuman History," *San Francisco Chronicle,* August 11, 1995. Wilford reports on the basis of two articles published the same day (August 11) in the journal *Science,* by Dr. Eudald Carbonell and the University of Taragonae concerning a discovery at Gran Dolina, a cave site in the Atapuerca Mountains near Burgos, Spain. In it were found crude stone tools and the fragmented remains of at least four individual hominids. See Josep M. Parés and Alfredo Pérez-Gonzalez, "Paleomagnetic Age for Hominid Fossils at Atapuerca Archaeological Site, Spain," *Science* 269 (August 11, 1995): 830. Dr. F. Clark Howell, an anthropologist at the University of California at Berkeley thinks that the Spanish fossils (mostly skull fragments and teeth and jaw fragments) are undoubtedly older than any hominids ever found in Europe.

18. See *Time* magazine, cover story, "How Man Began," March 14, 1994, 80–87. The article refers the reader to two others in the March issue of *Nature* and in *Science.* The *Time* article points to competition during certain periods between two different types of hominids with the ultimate victory—survival—going to *Homo sapiens sapiens* (called *Modern Homo sapiens* here).

19. See the conclusion of Dianne M. Waddle, n.22 below, which supports this view.

20. Brenda Fowler, "Where Did He Go? The Neanderthal's Trail May Be Cold, But the Debate about Him Is Incandescent," review of *The Neanderthal Enigma: Solving the Mystery of Modern Human Origins,* by James Shreve, *New York Times Book Review,* December 17, 1995, 21.

21. Johanson and Edey, *Lucy:* "I consider Neanderthal conspecific with sapiens, with myself" (20).

22. Diane M. Waddle, "Matrix Correlation Tests Support a Single Origin for Modern Humans," *Nature* 368 (March 31, 1994), upholds the notion that *Homo sapiens sapiens* evolved in Africa 100,000 to 200,000 years ago "replacing archaic human groups through Asia and Europe" and concludes by asserting that Neanderthal man did not contribute to the gene pool of modern *Homo sapiens sapiens* (452).

23. See James Shreve, *The Neanderthal Enigma: Solving the Mystery of Modern Human Origins* (New York: William Morrow, 1995).

24. See, for example, the British science journal *Nature* (April 27, 1989), wherein lies a report by two Israeli archaeologists, Yoel Rak and Baruch Arensburg, teamed up with colleagues from the University of Bordeaux, France, and State University in Moorhead, Minnesota,

which contends that Neanderthals could speak any modern tongue, having been equipped with bones for speech anatomically identical to our own.

25. This is the statement made in Lerner, Meacham, and Burns, *Western Civilizations,* 9. It is in agreement with the views of Johanson and Edey. Kishlansky, Geary, and O'Brien, *Civilization in the West,* 4, calls Neanderthals a subspecies of *Homo sapiens sapiens* while referring to Neanderthals as "the earliest *homo sapiens* in Europe." Some paleoanthropologists call the Neanderthals *Archaic Homo sapiens.*

26. Gen. 2:7.

27. Darwin, *The Descent of Man,* 2nd ed. (New York: A.L. Burt, 1874), 57.

28. "As Time Goes By," words and music by Herman Hupfeld, premiered in the 1931 musical *Everybody's Welcome.* The song, featured in the classic film *Casablanca* (1942) was the theme song for Woody Allen's 1972 comedy *Play It Again, Sam.*

29. Pottery was used only after men settled into villages during the Neolithic village period.

30. The numbers of Paleolithic people who lived much beyond their thirties was almost certainly very small given the hardship of the nomadic lifestyle.

31. One source attributes its beginnings to the growth of Hinduism, which began in the third millennium in India. Among the ancients in the west were Pythagoras, Plato, and Plutarch, and in modern times Jean-Jacques Rousseau, Count Tolstoy, and George Bernard Shaw were some famous vegans. Concern for global ecology and the high cost of living plus the undoubted problem of too much animal fat in our diet all promote the growth of this trend in the early twenty-first century.

32. See above, n. 8.

33. The Roman fertility goddess, Ceres, like her Greek predecessor, Demeter, was a grain goddess. Both were associated with marriage, and birth as well. However, Demeter's rites included the sacrifice of rams, and her favorite animal was the pig. It seems unlikely that she was vegan. To avoid rape by Poseidon, god of the sea, Demeter changed herself into a horse. The ploy failed, and she gave birth to a horse named Arion and a daughter (goddess of harvests) Persephone. Like her mother, Persephone was raped (by the god of the underworld, Hades), an occupational hazard for fertility goddesses.

34. The union of virginity and celibacy with fertility and procreation was anciently asserted, rational or not. In Sumer, Ishtar assumed the role of an older Sumerian virgin mother-goddess. In Arabia Athtar, in Phoenicia Astarte, and the Hebrew Ashtoroth and the Greek Aphrodite continued these traditions. The Greek goddess Artemis and her Roman look-alike, Diana, were both virgins, and both were patronesses of childbirth. The Virgin Mary is not unrelated to these other virgin goddesses. The Roman Catholic Church insists that her virginity was preserved even after the birth of Jesus, which preferred to identify the "brothers of the Lord" and his "sisters" as cousins, rather than siblings, and is still resisting its more outspoken theologians on this matter.

35. Bachofen's work is described by Stella Georgoudi, "Creating a Myth of Matriarchy," in *A History of Women in the West,* ed. Pauline Schmitt Pantel, vol. 1, *From Ancient Goddesses to Christian Saints* (Cambridge, MA: Belknap Press of Harvard University Press, 1992), 449–63.

36. Dionysus was a Thracian or Phyrigian god. *Dio* may suggest son or child, perhaps "son of God." He later became identified with wine and Hesiod called him the giver of the gift of wine. Not unsurprisingly, he was often drunk. Homer mentions him in the *Iliad* as "raging." He was fond of orgies and wild dancing, and the Greeks were rather anxious to civilize his cult. Accordingly, they had him born at Thebes (in Greece) and, like most vegetative gods, had him rise again after death. Regeneration was, quite simply, the lot of fertility gods.

37. V. Gordon Childe, *What Happened in History* (1942; repr., Baltimore: Penguin, 1967), 65.

38. *The City in History* (New York: Harcourt Brace Jovanovich, 1961), 12–13.

39. See Kathleen Gough, "The Origin of the Family," in *Toward an Anthropology of Women,* ed. Rayna R. Reiter (New York: Monthly Review Press, 1975), 69–70.

40. The French (and Spanish) preserved their Salic law, a compilation of Germanic tribal customs that discriminated against female inheritance from the early Middle Ages through modern times. Women were not allowed to succeed to the crown in their own right.

41. See Monich Sjöö and Barbara Mor, *The Great Cosmic Mother: Rediscovering the Religion of the Earth* (San Francisco: Harper, 1987); Patricia Reis, *Through the Goddess: A Woman's Way of Healing* (New York: Continuum, 1995); Martha Ann and Dorothy Myers Imel, *Goddesses in World Mythology: A Biographical Dictionary* (New York: Oxford University Press, 1993); Jennifer Barker Woolger and Roger J. Woolger, *The Goddess Within: A Guide to the Eternal Myths That Shape Women's Lives* (New York: Fawcett Columbine, 1987); Gabriel (no last name), *Goddess Meditations from Isis to Sophia: 365 Wisdom Poems to Invoke, Visualize and Embody the Goddess* (n.p.: Trinosophia Press, 1994); Cynthia Eller, *Living in the Lap of the Goddess: The Feminist Spirituality Movement in America* (Boston: Beacon Press, 1993); Carol P. Christ, *Odyssey With the Goddess: A Spiritual Quest in Crete* (New York: Continuum, 1995); and Judith Gleason Oya, *In Praise of an African Goddess* (San Francisco: HarperCollins, 1992).

42. See for example Diane Stein, ed., *The Goddess Celebrates: An Anthology of Women's Rituals* (Freedom, CA: Crossing Press, 1991), where Stein discusses the creation of religious rituals by women seeking validation in a male-dominated world: "Rituals in Women's Spirituality create a microcosm, a 'little universe' within which women try out what they want the macrocosm, the 'big universe' or the real world to be" (2).

43. Also, somewhat surprisingly, patroness of childbearing. In Africa she was associated with the Great Mother, goddess of fertility, and was thought to be identical as well to Isis and Proserpina, daughter of Ceres, Roman goddess of agriculture.

44. Hermaphroditus left home at fifteen to see the world. When he reached Caria, he bathed in a fountain over which the nymph, Salmacis, presided. She attempted to seduce him, and when he resisted, forced herself upon him, begging the gods to make them two, but with only one body. The gods obliged. Hermaphroditus then begged the gods to make all who bathed in that fountain effeminate.

45. For example, Zsuzsanna Budapest, a Hungarian-born self-styled "witch," is considered the mother of the Women's Spirituality movement. She traveled (in the 1980s and 1990s) around the country empowering women with her insightful wisdom and witchcraft.

46. Twiggy was an exceptionally emaciated young woman, a fashion model in the 1960s.

47. Especially for women. Villages did trade with others for items (precious metals especially) not obtainable in their area—but women were undoubtedly not expected to participate in these forays and must have missed the change of scenery that nomadic life had provided.

CHAPTER 2. MIDDLEMEN

1. Kramer's classic *History Begins at Sumer: Twenty-Seven Firsts in Man's Recorded History* (1956; repr., Garden City, NY: Doubleday, 1959).

2. Ibid., 222–23.

3. A. Leo Oppenheim, *Letters from Mesopotamia* (Chicago: University of Chicago Press, 1967), 26.

4. Gen. 9:1: "And God blessed Noah and his sons, and said unto them, Be fruitful, and multiply, and replenish the earth."

5. Henry Bamford Parkes, "The Theocratic Basis of Civilization," in *The Advent of Civilization,* ed. Wayne M. Bledsoe (Lexington, MA: D.C. Heath, 1975), 153.

6. Indian novelist whose life has been threatened by an Islamic fatwa for having had the audacity to challenge the divine messages in the Koran with his novel *The Satanic Verses.* He has since become a great celebrity. Like Gilgamesh.

7. See chapter 4, "Our Hebrew Heritage," for current views on the historicity or lack of historicity of Abraham.

8. Tom B. Jones, *From the Tigris to the Tiber* (Homewood, IL: Dorsey Press, 1969), 26.

9. Charles Keith Maisels, *The Emergence of Civilization: From Hunting and Gathering to Agriculture, Cities and the State in the Near East* (New York: Routledge, 1990), 138.

10. Ivan Petrovich Pavlov (1849–1936), Russian physiologist and experimental psychologist, received the 1904 Nobel Prize in physiology and medicine. His work on conditioned reflexes and the cerebral cortex pointed to a mechanistic theory of human behavior that was much valued by the Soviet government.

11. Gregor Johann Mendel (1822–84) was interested in problems related to heredity. From his experiments on gametes he determined such things as the law of segregation and the law of independent assortment, as well as the nature of dominant and recessive genes.

12. Demonstrative of fertility.

13. His old e-mail address was changed to protect the god from increasing junk mail—too many requests from peasants who could not make adequate sacrifices to cover the cost of satisfying their requests. Sumer invented cost analysis and the bottom line.

14. Words from "I'm Always Chasing Rainbows," lyrics by Joseph McCarthy, music by Harry Carroll. The song was the only hit of the 1918 musical *Oh, Look*. Its original form was Chopin's "Fantaisie Impromptu." Hence, we have here a clear-cut case of cultural borrowing. The song was revived by Perry Como in 1946.

15. Will Durant, *Our Oriental Heritage* (New York: Simon and Schuster, 1954), 239.

16. The underground, of course, was the source of gemstones and precious metals.

17. Maisels, *Emergence of Civilization,* 175.

18. Horatio Alger (1834–99) of Revere, Massachusetts, wrote over one hundred stories about boys who were born poor, but who gained wealth through hard work. One of his most popular was entitled *Ragged Dick* (1867).

19. Maisels, *Emergence of Civilization,* 177–78.

20. H. W. F. Saggs, *Babylonians* (Norman: University of Oklahoma Press, 1995), 71.

21. J. N. Postgate, *Early Mesopotamia: Society and Economy at the Dawn of History* (London: Routledge, 1992), 40–42.

22. It is important to note that it was even in Sargon's day an erring mother, not an erring father, who was blamed for an unwanted child.

23. Hallo-Simpson, 55–56.

24. Piotr Michalowski, *Letters From Early Mesopotamia,* ed. Erica Reiner (Atlanta, GA: Scholars Press, 1993), 19.

25. Saggs, *Babylonians,* 68–70.

26. C. Leonard Wooley, *The Sumerians* (New York: W.W. Norton, 1965). Wooley anticipated Saggs's view.

27. Saggs, *Babylonians,* 71.

28. Maisels, *Emergence of Civilization,* 176.

29. Hallo-Simpson, 56.

30. A somewhat different view is suggested by Oppenheim.

31. Martin Perry et al., *Western Civilization* (New York, 1989), 20.

32. Mortimer Chambers, Raymond Grew, et al., *The Western Experience,* 5th ed. (New York: McGraw Hill, 1991), 1:28.

33. "Wie es eigentlich war."

34. Spielvogel, 8.

35. Cottrell, 149.

36. Oates, 61.

37. Ibid., 75. Oates indicates that experts are not in agreement as to the "legislative purpose of the Code," adding that the true purpose may have been justification rather than justice.

38. William H. McNeill and Jean W. Sedlar, eds., *The Ancient Near East* (New York: Oxford University Press, n.d.), 2:138.

39. Hallo-Simpson, 176.

40. No independent proof of Moses's existence exists outside the Old Testament.

41. From Cole Porter's "You're the Top" (1934) which contains the line: "You're the top/ you're the Louvre Museum."

42. Exod. 21:23–25: "Wherever hurt is done, you shall give life for life, eye for eye, tooth for tooth, hand for hand, foot for foot, burn for burn, bruise for bruise, wound for wound."

43. Cottrell, 149.

44. Added in 1791 as part of the Bill of Rights.

45. Tom B. Jones, in his article "Hammurabi," *Collier's Encyclopedia*, vol. 11 (Crowell Collier and Macmillan, 1966).

46. Oates, 68.

47. John Ashcroft, former Senator and Governor of Missouri.

48. The Code is not without ambiguity. Another provision says that all apprehended robbers were to be put to death, and still another provided for the death of all housebreakers, regardless of property loss.

49. Saggs, *Babylonians* (London: British Museum Press, 1995), 104.

50. A 1964 movie starring Jack Lemmon, with Romy Schneider and Edward G. Robinson. Lemon portrayed a married advertising designer who was obliged to pretend marriage to his foreign neighbor next door so that she could secure an inheritance. He had to continue the charade for a long time to avoid offending a puritanical client who chanced to see them together.

51. H. W. F. Saggs, *The Might That Was Assyria* (London: Sidgwick and Jackson, 1984), 262.

52. See article with illustrations by Philip Elmer-De Witt, "The Golden Treasures of Nimrud: An Assyrian Fortress City Yields Archaeological Prizes of Rare Delight," *Time* (October 3, 1989): 80–81. Van Cleef is a designer of modern jewelry, mentioned in this article.

53. Saggs, *Assyria,* 263.

54. The movie of the same name (1940) starred Henry Fonda, John Carradine, Jane Darwell, Russell Simpson, Charley Grapewin, and John Qualen. Director: John Ford.

55. From E. J. Allen's book about the Mafia, *Merchants of Menace: The Mafia* (1962).

56. The attack on eighth-century BC Israel was begun by the Assyrian King Shalmaneser V, who destroyed Samaria, Israel's capital, in 722 BC. The fate of Israel was settled by Sargon II, who completed the devastation and put an end to this northern Jewish state (See 2 Kings 17:6).

57. The second so-called Babylonian Captivity was of the papacy, lodged in the town of Avignon (now part of France) between 1305 and 1378 AD.

58. Hallo-Simpson, 137.

59. Ibid., 2:8–9.

60. Ibid., 16:7–8.

61. Ibid., 16:16–18.

62. J. B. Pritchard, ed., *Ancient Near Eastern Texts,* 3d ed. (Princeton: Princeton University Press, 1969), 288.

CHAPTER 3: FOREVER EGYPT

1. L. A. Waddell, *Egyptian Civilization, Its Sumerian Origin and Real Chronology; and Sumerian Origin of Egyptian Hieroglyphs* (London: Luzac, 1930), viii–ix.

2. B. G. Trigger, "The Rise of Egyptian Civilization," in *Ancient Egypt: A Social History,* ed. B. G. Trigger, B. J. Kemp, et al. 36–37 (London: Cambridge University Press, 1983).

3. Paul Johnson, *The Civilization of Ancient Egypt* (London: Weidenfeld & Nicolson, 1978), 24.

4. Sir Alan Gardiner, *Egypt of the Pharaohs: An Introduction* (1961; repr., Oxford: Oxford University Press, 1978), 405.

5. The movie of the same title (1978) starred Peter Ustinov, Bette Davis, David Niven, Mia Farrow, Angela Lansbury, George Kennedy, and Jack Warden. It was the second in her Hercule Poirot mysteries and was directed by John Guillermin.

6. Lower Nubia lay south of the First Cataract of the Nile, south of the Aswan Dam.

7. "Two Lands" referred to Lower Egypt (near the Nile Delta) and Upper Egypt (toward the equator).

8. Michael Allen Hoffman, "Where Nations Began," *Science* 4 (October 1983): 42–51.

9. John Baines, "Origins of Egyptian Kingship," in *Ancient Egyptian Kingship,* ed. David O'Connor and David P. Silverman (Leiden: E. J. Brill, 1995), 99.

10. Gardiner, *Egypt of the Pharaohs,* 404.

11. K. A. Kitchen, *Pharaoh Triumphant: The Life and Times of Rameses II, King of Egypt* (Westminster, England: Aris & Phillips Ltd., 1982), 7.

12. Trigger, "Rise of Egyptian Civilization," 50.

13. The sound "dash" meant red in Egyptian, not dashing! The word *Dasherto,* for example, meant Redland, and the Greeks probably borrowed it, calling it "desertos," whence our English word "desert." From Douglas S. Benson, *Ancient Egypt's Warfare* (Ashland, OH: BookMasters, 1994), 13.

14. Nebuchadnezzar traveled from Jerusalem to Babylon with ten thousand Judeans; Alexander packed scholars and scientists on his campaign trail; Burgoyne, captor of Ft. Ticonderoga, traveled with thirty wagons of private baggage; Bonaparte ransacked Egypt for antiques and packed enough of them to outfit the Egyptian museum of Torino and the collection in the Louvre.

15. *Alice in Wonderland* (1865) was written by Charles Lutwidge Dodgson (1832–98), who, like Narmer, did have an alias—Lewis Carroll!

16. Trigger, Kemp, et al., *Ancient Egypt,* 44. See also Kurt Mendelssohn, *The Riddle of the Pyramids* (New York: Praeger Publishers, 1974), 32–33.

17. Benson, *Ancient Egypt's Warfare,* 13.

18. Ibid. In Egyptian, *Kimto.*

19. The left foot was conventionally shown extended and was presumably their best. Even animals walk with the left foot forward.

20. Also rendered Djoser.

21. Mendelssohn, *Riddle of the Pyramids,* 35.

22. See Jan Assmann, *Maât, l'Egypte pharaonique et l'idée de justice sociale,* Conférences essais et leçons du Collège de France (Paris: Julliard, 1989), 47.

23. O'Connor and Silverman, *Ancient Egyptian Kingship,* xxiiff.

24. Engels (1820–95) edited volumes 2 and 3 of Karl Marx's (1818–83) *Das Kapital* and shared with the author socialist views on the role of capital in the formation of the state (Engels himself wrote *The Condition of the Working Class in England*).

25. Chambers, Grew, et al., *Western Experience,* 1:15.

26. Lerner, Meacham, and Burns, *Western Civilizations,* 1:53.

27. Mendelssohn, *Riddle of the Pyramids,* 142ff.

28. Jaromir Malek, *In the Shadow of the Pyramids: Egypt during the Old Kingdom* (Norman: University of Oklahoma Press, 1986), 117. Malek, as many other authors, expressly denies the element of exploitation (119).

29. Donald B. Redford, *Egypt, Canaan, and Israel in Ancient Times* (Princeton: Princeton University Press, 1992), 60.

30. Ibid., 62.

31. Ibid., 64.

32. Barry J. Kemp, "Old Kingdom, Middle Kingdom and Second Intermediate Period c. 2686–1552 BC," in Trigger, Kemp, et al., *Ancient Egypt,* 112.

33. Gardiner, *Egypt of the Pharaohs,* 110.

34. A. Rosalie David, *The Egyptian Kingdoms* (New York: Elsevier Phaidon, 1975), 78.

35. Margaret A. Murray, *The Splendour That Was Egypt: A General Survey of Egyptian Culture and Civilisation* (1949; repr., New York: Philosophical Library, 1957), 171.

36. Gardiner, *Egypt of the Pharaohs,* 104–5.

37. David P. Silverman, "The Nature of Egyptian Kingship," in O'Connor and Silverman, *Ancient Egyptian Kingship,* 83.

38. Gardiner, *Egypt of the Pharaohs,* 128.

39. Redford, *Egypt, Canaan, and Israel,* 74. Redford does not describe what must have been a humiliating act, possibly akin to groveling, or maybe just a retreat. He gives as reference W. Helk, *Der Text der "Lehre Amenemhets I für seiner Sohn"* (Wiesbaden: n.p., 1969), 79a.

40. John Baines, "Kingship, Definition of Culture, and Legitimation" in O'Connor and Silverman, *Ancient Egyptian Kingship,* 22.

41. Spielvogel, 20.

42. Redford, *Egypt, Canaan, and Israel,* 71.

43. Words by Cole Porter (1893–1964) from one of his four hundred hit songs, "Just One of Those Things."

44. Redford, *Egypt, Canaan, and Israel,* 57ff.

45. Gardiner, *Egypt of the Pharaohs,* 170.

46. Redford, *Egypt, Canaan, and Israel,* 115.

47. Benson, *Ancient Egypt's Warfare,* 33.

48. Donald Redford, "The Concept of Kingship during the Eighteenth Dynasty," in O'Connor and Silverman, *Ancient Egyptian Kingship,* 170.

49. Hans Goedicke, "The End of the Hyksos in Egypt," in *Egyptological Studies in Honor of Richard A. Parker,* ed. Leonard H. Lesko (Hanover, NH: Brown University Press and University Press of New England, 1986), 39–40, agrees with Manetho.

50. Redford, *Egypt, Canaan, and Israel,* 138–39.

51. Ibid., 41.

52. Ibid., 117.

53. Murray, *Splendour,* 50.

54. Queen Sobekneferu, daughter of Amennemmes III, became Queen regnant and the last ruler of Twelfth Dynasty, probably due to the lack of a male heir.

55. Ian Portman, *Luxor: A Guide to the Temples & Tombs of Ancient Thebes* (Cairo: American University in Cairo Press, 1989), 45.

56. John Ray, "Hatshepsut: The Female Pharaoh," in *Western Civilization* (Guilford, CT: McGraw-Hill/Dushkin), 1:10. Originally published in *History Today,* 44 (May 1994): 23–29.

57. Gardiner, *Egypt of the Pharaohs,* 184.

58. David O'Connor, "New Kingdom and Third Intermediate Period 1552–664 B.C.," in Trigger, Kemp, et al., *Ancient Egypt,* 218–19.

59. Gardiner, *Egypt of the Pharaohs,* says that it was not long after her death that Thutmose began to "expunge her name wherever it could be found" (187). But see n. 62 below.

60. See C. F. Nims, *Zeitschrift für ägyptische Sprache und Altertumskunde* 63 (1966): 97–100 and P. F. Dorman, *Abstracts of Papers,* Fourth International Congress of Egyptology (Munich, 1985), 55–57.

61. Murray, *Splendour,* 51–52.

62. Redford, "Concept of Kingship."

63. Lerner, Meacham, and Burns, *Western Civilization,* note that war "stimulated the progress of technology," and also economic life, with the need for obtaining metal for better weapons the driving force of a village "arms race" (1:20).

64. Donald B. Redford, *Akhenaten: The Heretic King* (Princeton: Princeton University Press, 1984), 171.

65. Words from Cole Porter's "I Get A Kick Out of You," 1934.

66. Barry J. Kemp, *Ancient Egypt: Anatomy of a Civilization* (New York: Routledge, 1989), 264.

67. Ibid.

68. Ibid., 265–66. O'Connor views Akhenaton as a kind of "early rationalizer" or precocious "glorious dictator."

69. Immanuel Velikovsky, *Oedipus and Akhnaton: Myth and History* (Garden City, NY: Doubleday, 1938).

70. David, *Egyptian Kingdoms*, 25.

71. Redford, *Akhenaten,* does not rule out the possibility that the brothers were bastards of Akhenaton though he thinks it less than likely (192–93). Kemp, *Ancient Egypt,* thinks "Good evidence exists for making Tutankhamun a son of Akhenaten, though not necessarily by Nefertiti" but another wife (266).

72. Redford, Akhenaten, 193. Redford thinks it less likely that the boys were Akhenaton's sons, but does not rule it out.

73. David, *Egyptian Kingdoms,* 25.

Chapter 4: Our Hebrew Heritage

1. Dorothy F. Zeligs, *Psychoanalysis and the Bible: A Study in Depth of Seven Leaders* (New York: Bloch Publishing Company, 1974), 4.

2. Suggested by Aaron Wildavsky, *The Nursing Father: Moses as Political Leader* (Tuscalosa: University of Alabama Press, 1984), 43. Wildavsky ruminates on the hesitation of Moses to have his son circumcised and on the sign of blood as atonement for sin (Lev. 17:11).

3. Durant, *Our Oriental Heritage,* 313.

4. Zeligs, *Psychoanalysis,* thinks that circumcision is "Partial castration" "offered" to God in return for the "privilege of adult sexuality" (148).

5. Abraham was the patriarch of the Hebrews. He is also regarded as such by Christians and, through his son, Ishmael, by the Egyptian slave girl Hagar, who was his concubine, of Muslims, too.

6. P. Kyle McCarter, Jr., "The Patriarchal Age: Abraham, Isaac and Jacob," in *Ancient Israel: A Short History from Abraham to the Roman Destruction of the Temple,* ed. Hershel Shanks, 11 (Washington, DC: Biblical Archaeology Society, 1988).

7. *Time,* December 18, 1995.

8. McCarter, "Patriarchal Age," 16–17. See also J. Alberto Soggin, *A History of Ancient Israel* (Philadelphia: Westminster Press, 1984), 96–99.

9. Thomas L. Thompson, *The Historicity of the Patriarchal Narratives: The Quest for the Historical Abraham* (New York: De Gruyter, 1974).

10. William F. Albright, *From the Stone Age to Christianity: Monotheism and the Historical Process* (Garden City, NY: Doubleday, 1957); John Bright, *A History of Israel* (Philadelphia: Westminster Press, 1959); Roland de Vaux, *The Early History of Israel,* trans. David Smith (Philadelphia: Westminster Press, 1978).

11. McCarter, "Patriarchal Age," notes that "The biblical Joseph story has more in common with a historical romance than a work of history" (26). Similarly, see Soggin, *History of Ancient Israel,* who confirms that the Egyptians do not record a vizier named Joseph (112).

12. Aaron Wildavsky, *Assimilation Versus Separation: Joseph the Administrator and the Politics of Religion in Biblical Israel* (New Brunswick, NJ: Transaction Publishers, 1993).

13. Nahum M. Sarna, "Israel in Egypt: The Egyptian Sojourn and the Exodus" in Shanks, *Ancient Israel,* 33.

14. Soggin, *History of Ancient Israel,* citing the work and conclusions of Martin Noth and Gerhard von Rad, skeptics about the historicity of the Joseph story (113-14).

15. The first version of *The Ten Commandments* was a 1923 production, the first part in early color, the second in black and white. The second, by the same name (1956), starred Charlton Heston as Moses, with Yul Brynner, Edward G. Robinson, Sir Cedric Hardwicke, John Derek, and Anne Baxter. A television miniseries (trimmed down to a video release) of 1975 entitled *Moses* also exists. Directed by Gianfranco De Bosio, it starred Burt Lancaster in the role of Moses, with Anthony Quayle, Irene Papas, Ingrid Thulin, and William Lancaster.

16. Wildavsky, *Assimilation Versus Separation.*

17. *The New English Bible With Apocrypha* (New York: Oxford and Cambridge University Presses, 1970).

18. Harry M. Orlinsky, "The Situational Ethics of Violence in the Biblical Period," in *Violence and Defense in the Jewish Experience,* ed. Salo W. Baron and George S. Wise, 45 (Philadelphia: Jewish Publication Society of America, 1977).

19. Norman F. Cantor, *Inventing the Middle Ages* (New York: William Morrow, 1991), 136.

20. Adin Steinsaltz, *Biblical Images: Men and Women of the Book,* trans. Yehuda Hanegbi (New York: Basic Books, 1984), 76.

21. See by the author *Pierre Bayle's Reformation: Conscience and Criticism on the Eve of the Enlightenment* (Selinsgrove, PA: Susquehanna University Press, 2001) for examples of Mosaic temper, authority, and violence on the part of religious reformers of the sixteenth century.

22. Yahweh did not permit Moses to reach the Promised Land, but gave him a look at it from afar, a kind of sneak preview.

23. *The Holy Bible: Self-Pronouncing King James Version* (Cleveland: World Publishing Company, n.d.).

24. Wildavsky, *Assimilation Versus Separation,* 81-83.

25. Soggin, *History of Ancient Israel,* 124-25.

26. Sarna, "Israel in Egypt," 44. Soggin, *History of Ancient Israel,* 129.

27. Sarna, "Israel in Egypt," 44.

28. Stews, a neighborhood occupied chiefly by brothels.

29. A brief bibliographical treatment of the settlement of Palestine is to be found in Thomas L. Thompson, *The Origin Tradition of Ancient Israel; I. The Literary Formation of Genesis and Exodus 1-23* (Sheffield, U.K.: Sheffield Academic Press, 1987), 15ff.

30. Norman K. Gottwald, *The Tribes of Yahweh: A Sociology of the Religion of Liberated Israel 1250-1050 B.C.E.* (Maryknoll, NY: Orbis Books, 1979). Gottwald defends a peasant revolt interpretation of settlement that is critical of both the united conquest and peaceful immigration theories of A. Alt and Martin Noth (see n. 34 below).

31. See John Bright, *A History of Israel,* 3rd ed. (Philadelphia: Westminster Press, 1981), 129-33. Bright, whose first edition (1959) supported the notion of the united Hebrew tribes military conquest, the "normative conquest tradition," has had to revise his view for lack of precise archaeological (as well as chronological) evidence to support the book of Joshua interpretation.

32. Manfred Weippert, *Die Landnahme der israelitischen Stämme in Palästina,* 2nd series, vol. 21 (London: SCM Press, 1971).

33. Gottwald, *Tribes of Yahweh,* 141.

34. See A. Alt, "The Settlement of the Israelites in Palestine," in *Essays on Old Testament History and Religion* (Oxford: Blackwell, 1966), 133-49, and Martin Noth, *The Old Testament World,* trans. Victor I. Gruhn (Philadelphia: Fortress Press, 1966), a translation of the 4th edition of *Die Welt des Alten Testaments: Einführung in die Grenzgebiete der alttestamentlichen Wissenschaft* (Berlin: A. Töpelmann, 1964).

35. George E. Mendenhall, *The Tenth Generation: The Origins of the Biblical Tradition* (Baltimore: Johns Hopkins University Press, 1973), 23.

36. Ibid., 21.

37. Thomas L. Thompson, "The Background of the Patriarchs: A Reply to William Dever and Malcolm Clark," *Journal for the Study of the Old Testament* 9 (1978): 1–43.

38. For a materialistic interpretation of the conquest see George E. Mendenhall, "The Hebrew Conquest of Palestine," *Biblical Archaeologist* 25 (1961): 66–87.

39. Michael Grant, *The History of Ancient Israel* (London: Weidenfeld and Nicolson, 1984), 54.

40. See (on a different historical topic) the author's *History and Polemics in the French Reformation: Florimond de Raemond, Defender of the Church* (Selinsgrove, PA: Susquehanna University Press, 1992). Here history is treated as propaganda, i.e., polemically, to serve the spiritual needs of religious sects.

41. Bright, *History of Israel,* 177–79.

42. Elie Wiesel, *Five Biblical Portraits* (Notre Dame, IN: University of Notre Dame Press, 1981), 77.

43. David J. A. Clines, *Interested Parties: The Ideology of Writers and Readers of the Hebrew Bible* (Sheffield, UK: Sheffield Academic Press, 1995), chap. 10, "David the Man: The Construction of Masculinity in the Hebrew Bible."

44. For an interpretation of Hebrew women's lives in a period of change see Jo Ann Hackett, "Women's Studies and the Hebrew Bible" in *The Future of Biblical Studies: The Hebrew Scriptures,* ed. Richard E. Friedman and H. G. M. Williamson, 141–64 (Atlanta: Scholars Press, 1987).

45. Joel Rosenberg, *King and Kin: Political Allegory in the Hebrew Bible* (Bloomington: Indiana University Press, 1986), 127.

46. Located south of Mt. Tabor, in Israel; in modern times, the Arab village of Indur, destroyed in the Arab-Israeli War in 1948.

47. André Lemaire, "The United Monarchy: Saul, David and Solomon," in Shanks, *Ancient Israel,* 92.

48. Bright, *History of Israel,* 198.

49. Grant, *History of Ancient Israel,* 85.

50. Rosenberg, *King and Kin,* suggests that David exposed his genitals in the dance around the Ark, and that this dance was not unrelated to the inability of Michal to provide a child that would fuse the house of Saul with that of David, proving that not all leaps of faith were David's (118). Some are made by historians.

51. Grant, *History of Ancient Israel,* 85.

52. Isaac Asimov, *Asimov's Guide to the Bible* (New York: Wings Books, 1981), 301.

53. See n. below with this reference (1 Kings 2:11–13).

54. Niccolò Machiavelli, *The Prince,* edited and translated by David Wootton. (Indianapolis: Hackett Publishing Company, Inc., 1995), p. 55.

55. Lemaire, "United Monarchy," notes that it was for the reorganization of the administration of his kingdom that the biblical tradition accords him the title "wise" (99).

56. Asimov, *Guide,* 509. Lemaire, "United Monarchy," calls the tradition of the wise Solomon who authored three thousand proverbs and one thousand songs an "exaggeration" (106).

57. Asimov, *Guide,* 324–25.

58. James B. Pritchard, "The Age of Solomon," in *Solomon & Sheba,* ed. James B. Pritchard (London: Phaidon Press, 1974), 35.

59. Lemaire, "United Monarchy," 101.

60. See chapter 2.

61. Gus W. van Beek, "The Land of Sheba," in Pritchard, *Solomon & Sheba,* 48.

62. Lou H. Silberman, "The Queen of Sheba in Judaic Tradition," in Pritchard, *Solomon & Sheba,* 65.

63. Ibid., 69–70.

64. Pritchard, "Age of Solomon," 9.

65. Ibid.

66. Silberman, "Queen of Sheba," 77.

CHAPTER FIVE: CRETE AND MYCENAE

1. Leonard Cottrell, *The Bull of Minos* no v.1.(1953; repr., New York: Holt, Rinehart, Winston, 1958), 248.

2. Ibid., 214.

3. R. F. Willetts, *The Civilization of Ancient Crete* (Berkeley and Los Angeles: University of California Press, 1977), notes that the Linear B script had "many" signs different from Linear A, including the numerals and the system used for expressing fractions, which changed from one corresponding with an Egyptian to one based on a Mesopotamian system (101).

4. Ibid., xiv.

5. This view of Minoan civilization has been dubbed "Knossocentric" by Leonard R. Palmer, who joins with such scholars as James Mellaart and D. L. Page in rejecting it. It makes Anatolia (modern Turkey) rather than central Europe the original home of the Greeks, raising the possibility that both Mycenaeans and Minoans owed much to Asia Minor. See Leonard R. Palmer, *Mycenaeans and Minoans: Aegean Prehistory in the Light of the Linear B Tablets* (New York: Alfred A. Knopf, 1962), chap. 7. Palmer's views are criticized by G. E. Mylonas, "The Luvian Invasions of Greece," *Hesperia* 3 (1962): 284–309, and by F. Schachermeyr, *Kadmos* 1 (1962): 27–39.

6. *The Fabrication of Ancient Greece 1785–1985,* vol. 1 of *Black Athena: The Afroasiatic Roots of Classical Civilization* (New Brunswick, NJ: Rutgers University Press, 1987).

7. Ibid., 1.

8. Ibid., 2.

9. Mary R. Lefkowitz and Guy MacLean Rogers, eds., *Black Athena Revisited* (Chapel Hill: University of North Carolina Press, 1996), and Josine H. Blok, "Proof and Persuasion in Black Athena: The Case of K. O. Müller," *Journal of the History of Ideas* (October 1996): 705–15, is an attempt to demonstrate that Bernal's thesis rests on a serious misinterpretation of the man he thought chiefly responsible for perverting the Ancient Model (Müller). Mary R. Lefkowitz's extended rejection of Bernal and the Afrocentic interpretation of Greek history is *Not Out of Africa: How Afrocentrism Became an Excuse to Teach Myth as History* (New York: Basic Books, 1996). In it the author maintains that the assumption that Egypt was the source of all Greek culture was a reflection of ancient and inadequate research into Egyptian history, and that the perpetuation of such ignorance is politically motivated as well as scientifically indefensible. See also *Black Athena Writes Back: Martin Bernal Responds to His Critics* (Durham, NC: Duke University Press, 2001).

10. That is, in the first half of the second millennium BC, rather than in the second half.

11. M. I. Finley, "Archaeology and History," chap. 5 in *The Use and Abuse of History* (1971; repr., New York: Elisabeth Sifton Books/Penguin Books, 1987).

12. Emily Vermeule, *Greece in the Bronze Age* (Chicago: University of Chicago Press, 1964), 282.

13. Edith Hamilton, *The Greek Way to Western Civilization* (1930; repr., New York: Mentor Books, 1958), 30.

14. For a description of Samuel Noah Kramer's work, refer to chapter 2 herein.

15. The so-called "Prince of the Lilies" fresco, found at the south entrance to the Central Court of the palace at Knossos.

16. R. W. Hutchinson, *Prehistoric Crete* (London: Penguin Books, 1962), 59.

17. Ibid., 286.

18. Peter Warren, *The Aegean Civilizations* (New York: E. P. Dutton, 1975), 93.

19. Ibid., 85.

20. Rodney Castleden, *The Knossos Labyrinth: A New View of the "Palace of Minos" at Knossos* (London: Routledge, 1990), chap. 5.

21. Ibid., 60: "Wunderlich's alternative interpretation—a palace of the dead—was not entirely original. It had been foreshadowed by Oswald Spengler in his *Decline of the West.*"

22. Oswald Spengler, *The Decline of the West* (1918; repr., New York: Alfred A. Knopf, 1939): "The palaces of Crete—which are not kings' castles, but huge cult-buildings for a crowd of priests and priestesses—are equipped with megalopolitan—nay, Late-Roman—luxury" (88).

23. Nicholas Platon, *Zakros: The Discovery of a Lost Palace of Ancient Crete* (New York: Charles Scribner's Sons, 1971), 257.

24. Olivier Pelon, "Reflexions sur la fonction politique dans un palais Cretois," in *Minoan Society Proceedings of the Cambridge Colloquium 1981,* ed. O. Krzyszkowska and L. Nixon, 251(Bristol: Bristol Classical Press, 1983).

25. Kishlansky, Geary, and O'Brien, *Civilization in the West,* A:39.

26. Quoted from his book *The Palace of Minos,* vol. 3 (1930) by C. W. Ceram, ed., *Hands on the Past: Pioneer Archaeologists Tell Their Own Story* (New York: Alfred A. Knopf, 1966), 98. Evans believed it would have been impossible to seize the horns of an onrushing bull, and modern bull handlers have testified to this effect.

27. Hutchinson, *Prehistoric Crete,* 257.

28. Castleden, *Knossos Labyrinth,* 55.

29. Ibid., 56.

30. Sinclair Hood, *The Minoans: The Story of Bronze Age Crete* (New York: Praeger Publishers, 1971), 117. However, Ariadne is usually cited as Minos's daughter. Perhaps the author meant to speak of Pasiphae, who was Minos's wife, not their daughter, Ariadne!

31. Willetts, *Civilization of Ancient Crete,* 63.

32. Crete was dotted with palaces found at places like Gournia, Hagia Triada, Kato Zakros, Mallia, Phaistos, Knossos—the last three having been the major palace sites.

33. Hood, *Minoans,* 116ff.

34. Chester G. Starr, "The Myth of the Minoan Thalassocracy," *Historia* (1955): 282–91.

35. Hutchinson, *Prehistoric Crete,* 98–99. He thinks that if Crete had any naval force it would have devoted itself to protecting Cretan merchant vessels from piracy, or to have executed piratical raids on the ships and ports of enemies.

36. Ibid., 301, and Hood, *Minoans,* 51.

37. Hood, *Minoans,* 52.

38. Carl W. Blegen, *Troy and the Trojans* (New York: Frederick A. Praeger, 1963), 164.

39. According to T. B. L. Webster, *From Mycenae to Homer* (New York: Frederick A. Praeger, 1959), 117.

40. M. I. Finley, *Use and Abuse of History,* 25.

41. Ibid., 28.

42. Joseph Alsop, *From the Silent Earth: A Report on the Greek Bronze Age* (New York: Harper & Row, 1962), 42.

43. The account of the Trojan War below follows, very roughly, a recapitulation found in Michael Wood, *In Search of the Trojan War* (New York: Facts On File Publications, 1985), 21–25.

44. From the title of Woody Allen's 1995 film of the same name.

45. Clytemnestra and Agamemnon's cousin had been living in sin during the absence of the king at Troy. When he returned to Mycenae, the guilty pair murdered Agamemnon.

46. Andromache was the wife of Prince Hector of Troy, Priam's oldest son. When Hector was killed by Achilles at Troy, Andromache was claimed by Neoptolemus of Epirus, who first married her, then divorced her. Her last husband was another son of Priam named Helenus.

47. H. D. F. Kitto, *The Greeks* (1951; repr., Baltimore: Penguin Books, 1968), 58.

CHAPTER SIX: CLASSICAL GREECE

1. Chester G. Starr, *The Economic and Social Growth of Early Greece 800–500 B.C.* (New York: Oxford University Press, 1977), 30.

2. N. G. L. Hammond, *The Classical Age of Greece* (London: Weidenfeld and Nicolson, 1975), 16. Hammond uses the term "colonels" instead of barracks officers.

3. A. Andrewes, *The Greek Tyrants* (London: Hutchinson's University Library, 1956), 25.

4. Stephen Usher, *The Historians of Greece and Rome* (New York: Taplinger, 1970), 17.

5. Ibid., 6.

6. Hammond, *Classical Age,* 20.

7. Finley, *Use and Abuse of History,* 14.

8. Andrewes, *Greek Tyrants,* 100.

9. Hammond, *Classical Age,* 56.

10. C. M. Bowra, *Periclean Athens* (New York: Dial Press, 1971), 9.

11. Hammond, *Classical Age,* 55.

12. Andrewes, *Greek Tyrants,* 101.

13. Hammond, *Classical Age,* 57; A. R. Burn with J. M. B. Edwards, *Greece and Rome 750 B.C.–A.D. 565* (Glenview, IL: Scott Foresman, 1970), call the assasination "the result of a private quarrel" (30).

14. A tribe of Athenian nobles.

15. G. L. Huxley, *Early Sparta* (London: Faber and Faber, 1962), 77.

16. A. R. Burn, *Persia and the Greeks* (1962; repr., Stanford, CA: Stanford University Press, 1984), 191.

17. Chester A. Starr, *A History of the Ancient World* (New York: Oxford University Press, 1965), 255.

18. Burn, *Persia and the Greeks,* 183–84.

19. Helots were once free peoples of Laconia whom Spartans had defeated and on whom they depended for food and domestic labor. Some were Laconians, defeated in the ninth century BC; some were Messenians, defeated by the end of the eighth century BC. By formally declaring war on helots annually, the Spartans were able to beat, slay, and brutalize their helot dependents. They humiliated them in other ways, and consequently, lived in fear of helot uprisings.

20. The so-called domino theory was a Cold War notion held by U.S. strategists stating that if one country fell to communism, its neighbors would soon fall, too. It was a major reason for U.S. involvement in the Vietnam War. Dwight D. Eisenhower first used the term in a press conference on April 7, 1954. He was referring to the strategic importance of Indochina and said, "You have a row of dominoes set up. You knock over the first one, and what will happen to the last one is a certainty that it will go over very quickly."

21. Burn, *Persia and the Greeks,* 239–41 and n. 10.

22. Starr, *History of the Ancient World,* 283.

23. Related in Lerner, Meacham, and Burns, *Western Civilizations,* 1:107.

24. J. Lemprière, *A Classical Dictionary, Containing a Copious Account of All the Proper Names Mentioned in Ancient Authors, etc.* (London: George Routledge and Sons, Ltd., n.d.), 276.

25. Burn, *Persia and the Greeks,* 252.

26. Herodotus, *The Persian Wars,* book 7.

27. *Don Juan,* canto 3, stanza 7. George B. Woods, Homer A. Watt, and George K. Anderson, *The Literature of England,* II (Chicago: Scott, Foresman and Co., 3rd edition, 1948) 235.

28. Byron wrote a verse tale entitled "The Bride of Abydos" in 1813.

29. Burn, *Persia and the Greeks,* 328 and n. 41. Another fifty thousand souls went along to service the army's needs.

30. "[I]t was necessary that a strong rearguard should stay. For otherwise the enemy, strong in cavalry, would have rounded up the whole army in the open within the day" (Ibid., 418).

31. Simon Hornblower, *The Greek World 479–323 B.C.* (London: Methuen, 1983), title of chap. 1.

32. Burn, *Persia and the Greeks,* 549–50.

33. Hornblower, *Greek World,* 11.

34. Herodotus, *Persian Wars. The History,* trans. David Greene (Chicago: The Univerisity of Chicago Press, 1987), 99.

35. J. K. Davies, *Democracy and Classical Greece* (1978; repr., Cambridge, Harvard University Press, 1993), 11–13.

36. Kitto, *Greeks,* 118.

37. This was the Guarantee that formed Article V of the North Atlantic Treaty of April 4, 1949, to which there were (initially) twelve signatories: The United States, Canada, Great Britain, France, Belgium, Luxembourg, the Netherlands, Italy, Portugal, Iceland, Norway, and Denmark. Greece and Turkey joined in 1952; the Federal Republic of Germany in 1955; Spain in 1982. France opted out of the military organization in the 1960s on the grounds that it subordinated her interests to Anglo-Saxons.

38. A descriptive term used by Pericles. Athens had failed to conquer it in the seventh century BC and as recently as 487 BC.

39. Malcolm F. McGregor, *The Athenians and Their Empire* (Vancouver: University of British Columbia Press, 1987), 34.

40. Ibid., 39.

41. Davies, *Democracy,* 44–45.

42. Hornblower, *Greek World,* 28.

43. Ibid, 29.

44. Aristotle marveled that they had had no musical training but nevertheless were able to judge good music from bad. Plutarch quoted Pindor to the effect that the Spartans were "no less musical than war-like." (Plutarch, *The Lines of the Noble Grecians and Romans,* trans. John Dryden and rev. Arthur Hugh Clough [New York: Random House Inc., 1932], 67.) Poets flourished in Sparta, the Dorians were possessed of a four-string lyre, and Pelops was supposed to have introduced the old Phrygian scale into Sparta. Spartans excelled at dancing and choral singing. (H. Michell, *Sparta* [Cambridge: Cambridge University Press, 1964].) The adjective "Spartan" became synonymous with asceticism.

45. For provincial pride, review the Spartan chef's comment regarding black soup (see above, n. 24). Spartan Pan-Hellenism was established in 550 along with the (Spartan-led) Peloponnesian Confederacy.

46. Davies, *Democracy,* 40.

47. Bowra, *Periclean Athens,* 55.

48. A similar view of Athenian democracy is mooted by Peter Berkowitz, "The Debating Society" in *The New Republic,* November 25, 1996, who observes that Athenian democracy lacked the "fundamental premise" of American democracy: the belief that all human beings possess a natural freedom and equality (36).

49. McGregor, *Athenians,* lists these as four grievances that were "immediate causes" of the Great Peloponnesian War (128–30).

50. Donald Kagan, *The Outbreak of the Peloponnesian War* (Ithaca: Cornell University Press, 1969), 345.

51. Ibid., 345–46.

52. Thucydides, *The Peloponnesian War,* trans. John H. Finley, Jr. (New York: Modern Library, 1951), 71.

53. Gordon A. Craig, *Europe Since 1815* (1961; repr., New York: Holt, Rinehart, and Winston, 1966), 486. The author is describing these conditions with reference only to World War I, not to the Peloponnesian War.

54. An interesting treatment of the relationship between both these wars and their inevitably is to be found in Kagan, *Outbreak of the Peloponnesian War,* chap. 19, "The Causes of the War."

55. Hammond, *Classical Age,* 147.

56. Var. of idiotic; derived from the *Iliad,* whose Homeric war heroes attribute to the gods what they themselves engaged in.

57. Kagan, *The Fall of the Athenian Empire,* 323–24.

58. Herbert Muller, *Freedom in the Ancient World* (New York: Harper & Brothers, 1961), 202.

59. Thomas R. Martin, *Ancient Greece from Prehistoric to Hellenistic Times* (New Haven: Yale University Press, 1996), 111–13, claims that no more than several men were ever ostracized before the practice was abandoned after c. 416 BC, and that there was no evidence it was used "frivolously" (112).

60. Thucydides, *History of the Peloponnesian War,* parag. 41. John L. Beatty/ Oliver A. Johnson, *Heritage of Western Civilization,* 7th edition , vol. I, (Englewood Cliffs, N.J.: Prentice Hall,1991), p. 91.

61. For example, Thomas R. Martin, *Ancient Greece,* notes that Cimon paid for the massive defensive walls that eventually connect the city core with its harbor several miles away, and for shade trees and running tracks (108, 117).

62. Giovanni Becatti, *The Art of Ancient Greece and Rome* (New York: Harry N. Abrams, n.d.), 162–64.

63. A. R. Burn, *Pericles and Athens* (1948; repr., London: English Universities Press, 1956), 146–47.

64. Frank J. Frost, *Greek Society* (1971; repr., Lexington, KY: D. C. Heath, 1992), 113.

65. Ibid., 116–17.

66. For a similar treatment with a more defined social thrust, see Arnold Hauser, *The Social History of Art,* trans. Stanley Godman (New York: Vintage Books, 1957), 1:90ff.

67. Starr, *History of the Ancient World,* 363.

68. Will Durant, *The Life of Greece* (New York: Simon and Schuster, 1939), 461.

69. Hammond, *Classical Age,* 209.

70. Ibid.

71. Starr, *History of the Ancient World,* 219.

72. Peter Green, *Alexander of Macedon, 356–323 B.C.: A Historical Biography* (1970; repr., Berkeley and Los Angeles: University of California Press, 1991), 24–25. Green mentions Epaminondas's "oblique echelon" and "principle of economy of force coupled with overwhelming strength at the decisive point" as tactics used by the Macedonians.

73. Ibid., 210.

74. The accounts by Plutarch and Diodorus vary. The former says that after the 370 BC campaign he was accused of exceeding his term of one month and acquitted. Diodorus says it was after the 369 BC campaign and that the charge was laxness.

75. Will Durant, *Life of Greece,* 463.

76. Martin, *Ancient Greece,* 177.

77. Hammond, *Classical Age,* 226.

78. Starr, *History of the Ancient World,* 364.

79. Ulrich Wilcken, *Alexander the Great,* trans. G. C. Richards (1931; repr., New York: W. W. Norton, 1967), 9–10.

80. The film *Patton* starred George C. Scott as General George S. Patton and Karl Malden as Omar Bradley. Directed by Franklin J. Schaffner, 1970.

81. Lemprière, *Classical Dictionary,* 208.

82. Cleisthenes had broken up the old clans or blood-related tribes of Athens, replacing them with modern ones without any reference to blood relationships. These new tribes were given their own courts, thereby eliminating ancient familial vengeance.

83. Bertrand Russell, *A History of Western Philosophy* (1945; repr., New York: Simon and Schuster, 1966), 31.

84. Ibid., 311–12.

85. Green, *Alexander of Macedon,* 19.

86. Martin, *Ancient Greece,* 188.

87. Green, *Alexander of Macedon,* 31.

88. George Cawkwell, "Philip and the Amphictyonic League," in *Philip of Macedon,* ed. Miltiades B. Hatzopoulos and Luoisa D. Loukopoulos (Athens, Greece: Ekdotike Athenon S.A., 1980), 80.

89. M. B. Sakellariou, "Panhellenism: From Concept to Policy," in Hatzopoulos and Loukopoulos, *Philip of Macedon,* 142.

90. *The Republic* 7, p. 204 in *The Republic of Plato,* Translated with notes and interpreted essay by Allan Bloom, (New York: Basic Books Inc., 1968) 204. See also Gilbert Ryle, "Plato," in *The Encyclodpedia of Philosophy* (New York: MacMillan, 1967), who notes that mathematics, astronomy, and eventually thanks to Aristotle, rhetoric were courses taught at Plato's Academy. Ryle says Socrates objected to teaching young men logic (dialectic) and that it is not clear that Plato taught in the Academy of which he was the head (6:318).

CHAPTER SEVEN: ALEXANDER THE GREAT

1. Eugene N. Borza, "Introduction to Alexander Studies," in Wilcken, *Alexander the Great,* ix.

2. Ibid., 487. A. R. Burn, *Alexander the Great and the Hellenistic World* (1947; repr., New York: Collier Books, 1961), thought Alexander had a "mother fixation" that also came out "not unpleasantly" in his dealings with "other middle aged queens" (17).

3. Oedipus was king of Thebes (located in Boeotia in central Greece), which was the home of the poet Pindar. Thebes was anathema to Alexander having sided with Persia in the Persian Wars and because it had joined with Spartans during the Great Peloponnesian War against Athens, much admired by Alexander. Most of all, Thebes had joined with Athens against Philip at Chaeronea and in 336 BC revolted against Alexander's authority in Greece.

4. Peter Green, *Alexander of Macedon,* 483.

5. Ibid., xii, quoted from E. Badian, *Studies in Greek and Roman History* (New York: Barnes and Noble, 1964).

6. In his treatise, *On the Tranquility of the Mind.*

7. Russell, *History of Western Philosophy,* 160–61.

8. Robin Lane Fox, *Alexander the Great* (London: Dial Press, 1974).

9. Wilcken, *Alexander the Great,* 91.

10. J. R. Hamilton, *Alexander the Great* (1971; repr., Pittsburgh, PA: University of Pittsburgh Press, 1992), 64.

11. Based on Arrian's relation (2.4) in M. M. Austin, *The Hellenistic World from Alexander to the Roman Conquest* (Cambridge: Cambridge University Press, 1981), 15–16.

12. W. W. Tarn, *Alexander the Great* (1948; repr., Boston: Beacon Press, 1962) suggests that Alexander really wished "to induce Darius to fight" and that he did not "really claim" to be king until Darius died.

13. John W. Snyder, *Alexander the Great* (New York: Twayne, 1966), 84.

14. Green, *Alexander of Macedon,* 247–63, offers a detailed and very clear account of the siege of Tyre.

15. Ibid., 262.

16. The Greeks had helped the Egyptians throw off their Persian masters in the fifth century and Egypt had been ruled by Egyptians from 404 until 342 BC.

17. J. R. Hamilton, *Alexander the Great,* 74.

18. Burn, *Alexander the Great,* 105.

19. Tarn, *Alexander the Great,* 78.

20. Wilcken, *Alexander the Great,* 212.

21. Green, *Alexander of Macedon,* 452.

22. Ibid., 273.

23. Ibid. Green hints that if Alexander had been a party to the murder of Philip, but could be certain Zeus was his real father, then he would not have been guilty of parricide, but only of mere murder—a venial offense.

24. Arrian, 3.3–4, in Austin, *Hellenistic World,* 20. On this visit to Siwah see Wilcken, *Alexander the Great,* 124–29.

25. Mary Renault, *The Nature of Alexander* (New York: Pantheon Books, 1975), 128.

26. Tarn, *Alexander the Great,* 54.

27. Burn, *Alexander the Great,* 122.

28. Snyder, *Alexander the Great,* 130–31.

29. Green, *Alexander of Macedon,* 320.

30. Renault, *Nature of Alexander,* 133.

31. Green, *Alexander of Macedon,* 343–345.

32. Green, *Alexander of Macedon,* considers Philotas not to have been a conspirator, although willing enough to tolerate a plot against Alexander that might eventually be useful to his own ambitions (p.345).

33. C. Bradford Welles, *Alexander and the Hellenistic World* (Toronto: A. M. Hakkert, 1970), 39.

34. Green, *Alexander of Macedon,* 364.

35. Ibid., 365.

36. Snyder, *Alexander the Great,* 158.

37. J. R. Hamilton, *Alexander the Great,* 118–19.

38. Wilcken, *Alexander the Great,* 196.

39. J. R. Hamilton, *Alexander the Great,* 123.

40. Green, *Alexander of Macedon,* 430.

41. Ibid., 437.

42. Hamilton, *Alexander the Great,* 132.

43. Green, *Alexander of Macedon,* 448.

44. Hamilton, *Alexander the Great,* 143. He says W. W. Tarn "misinterpreted Alexander's prayer at the Opis Feast of Reconciliation; Alexander prayed only for harmony and partnership in rule between Macedonians and Persians."

45. Green, *Alexander of Macedon,* 476–77.

46. Alexander of course had made threatening statements concerning his former tutor. See Green, *Alexander of Macedon,* 379, 459.

47. Tarn, *Alexander the Great,* 147–48.

CHAPTER EIGHT: HELLENISTIC CIVILIZATION

1. Var. of Grecophiles. People who admire classical Greek culture.

2. Cicero (Marcus Tullius Cicero, 106–43 BC). Politician, philosopher, and Rome's greatest orator, Cicero was also a student of law who derived much from Stoical philosophy. In his *De Legibus* [On the Laws] he denied the validity of any law or tradition that was not just. He thought only those laws that conformed to the law of nature genuine law. Unfortunately, no one, not Cicero nor later, Aquinas, ever stated to the satisfaction of all men just what nature has to do with man-made laws.

3. Peter Green, *Alexander to Actium: The Historical Evolution of the Hellenistic Age* (Berkeley and Los Angeles: University of California Press, 1990).

4. Peter Green, "Introduction: New Approaches to the Hellenistic World," in *Hellenistic History and Culture,* ed. Peter Green (Berkeley and Los Angeles: University of California Press, 1993), 1–11.

5. Peter Green, "Introduction: New Approaches."

6. Starr, *History of the Ancient World,* notes that "No ancient structure ever surpassed the skill and complexity of this machinery" (409).

7. Born in Kiev, Russia, October 28 1870. d. New Haven, CT, October 20 1952. Among his works: *The Social and Economic History of the Hellenistic World* (Oxford: Clarendon, 1941).

8. See for example Eric Turner, *Cambridge Ancient History,* 2nd ed.

9. A. E. Samuel, "The Ptolemies and Ideology of Kingship" in Green, *Hellenistic History and Culture,* 171.

10. W. W. Tarn, *Hellenistic Civilisation* (1927; repr., Cleveland, OH: World Publishing Company, 1965), 209.

11. Rostovtzeff, *Social and Economic History,* 1:269ff.

12. F. W. Walbank, *The Hellenistic World* (1981; repr., Cambridge: Harvard University Press, 1993), 102.

13. F. E. Peters, *The Harvest of Hellenism* (New York: Simon and Schuster, 1970), 161ff.

14. Green, *Alexander to Actium,* 262.

15. Ibid., 313.

16. Walbank, *Hellenistic World,* 119.

17. Peters, *Harvest of Hellenism,* notes that the Egyptians had already had ample experience of father-son and brother-sister, but that the rule of two brothers was unusual (180).

18. Ibid., 180.

19. Readers may recall that when Henry of Navarre converted (again) to Roman Catholicism and turned his back on Protestantism, he was said to have remarked: "Paris is well worth a Mass," and only then (AD 1594) was he able to enter his capital, Paris.

20. Walbank, *Hellenistic World,* 125.

21. Nominally, Philetaerus and his successor, Eumenes I, were under the overlordship of the Seleucids, from which Attalus I Soter (241–197 BC) freed Pergamum.

22. H. W. Household, *Rome, Republic and Empire* (London: J.M. Dent & Sons, 1936), 1:173–74.

23. Green, *Alexander to Actium,* 82.

24. Ibid., 171. Household says Antiochus was "misnamed."

25. Ibid., 295–96.

26. Green, *Alexander to Actium,* 422–23. Green thinks that while "he never quite achieved the greatness of his public title" obtained through skillful propaganda, "He was a man of energy and mercurial brilliance rather than solidity" who "undoubtedly left his mark on the dynasty."

27. Hasmonean or Asmonean, from an ancestor of the Maccabees called Hashmon. In the reign of Antiochus IV (175–163 BC) they were first led by Mattathias, who began the uprising

against Antiochus IV. When Mattathias died, his eldest son, Judas, took over the leadership of the guerrilla warfare that was continued after Judas's death (?161 BC) by his brothers Jonathan and Simon, and by his grandson, John Hyrcanus I. The family remained in power until removed from power by Pompey, who claimed a Roman protectorate called Palestine.

28. Michael Grant, *From Alexander to Cleopatra: The Hellenistic World* (New York: Charles Scribner's Sons, 1982), 56.

29. Green, *Alexander to Actium,* 329.

30. Finley, *Use and Abuse of History,* 131.

31. Peters, *Harvest of Hellenism,* 227.

32. Ibid., 226.

33. Walbank, *Hellenistic World,* 63.

34. Aristotle, *The Ethics of Aristotle* (The Nichomachean Ethics Translated), trans. J. A. K. Thomson (London: Penguin Books, 1956), book 1, chap, 4, p. 29.

35. W. T. Stace, *A Critical History of Greek Philosophy* (1920; repr., New York: St. Martin's Press, 1965), 340.

36. Not to mention experts in many other fields (psychiatry, economics, religion, medicine, education, sociology, education, etc.) all of whom have tried their best to make men happier in one way or another!

37. Russell, *History of Western Philosophy,* 247–48.

38. Bertrand Russell, *Principles of Social Reconstruction* (1916; repr., London: George Allen & Unwin, 1954), 166.

39. Paul Woodruff, in his "Response" to A. A. Long, in Green, *Hellenistic History and Culture,* 160.

40. Russell, *History of Western Philosophy,* thought that Epicurus discouraged sexual intercourse because it was too "dynamic" a pleasure that had never "done a man good and he is lucky if it has not harmed him." In addition, he considered marriage and children (of whom he was fond) distractions from more serious pursuits (245). But R.W. Sharples, *Stoics, Epicureans and Sceptics: An Introduction to Hellenistic Philosophy* (New York: Routledge, 1996), believes that Epicurus permitted sex as a necessary desire that frees the body from disturbance (86–87).

41. Reported by Diogenes Laertius, *Lives of Eminent Philosophers,* tr. R.D. Hicks, vol. 2, "Pyrrho" (New York: G. P. Putnam's Sons, 1925), 475. See also Everard Flintoff, "Pyrrho and India," *Phronesis* 25 (1980): 88–108; David Sedley, "The Motivation of Greek Skepticism," in *The Skeptical Tradition,* ed. Myles Burnyeat (Berkeley and Los Angeles: University of California Press, 1983), 15.

42. Paul Oskar Kristellar, *Greek Philosophers of the Hellenistic Age,* trans. Gregory Woods (New York: Columbia University Press, 1993), 5.

43. Ibid.

44. A. A. Long, addressing the notion of free will, often attributed to Epicurus because of the swerving atom theory (that modified Democritus's physics) avers that it is only found in Lucretius's references to Epicurean thought Green, *Hellenistic History and Culture,* 163–64).

45. Russell, *History of Western Philosophy,* 245.

46. Sharples, *Stoics, Epicureans and Sceptics,* 7.

47. Green, *Hellentic History and Culture,* 163.

48. Sharples, *Stoics, Epicureans and Sceptics,* 56–57.

49. Long, "Hellenistic Ethics," 163.

50. F. H. Sandbach, *The Stoics* (1975; repr., Bristol: Bristol Press, 1989), 67.

51. A. A. Long, *Hellenistic Philosophy* (London: Gerald Duckworth, 1974), 110.

52. Erasmus, *The Godly Feast [Convivium religiosum],* in *The Colloquies of Erasmus,* ed. and trans. Craig R. Thompson (Chicago: University of Chicago Press, 1965), 68.

53. Kristellar, *Greek Philosophers*, 27. But Bertrand Russell, *History of Western Philosophy*, believes Zeno went to extremes when, to combat the skepticism of the metaphysicians toward materialism, he asserted that immaterial ideas such as justice, virtue and even number were also solid matter (253).

54. J. M. Rist, *Stoic Philosophy* (Cambridge: Cambridge University Press, 1969), 140.

55. Russell, *History of Western Philosophy*, 253.

56. Eckhart (1260–1328) was a German Dominican and professor of theology whose *Book of Divine Comfort* contained much the same message, that a spark of divinity was in every man's soul. Many of his notions were condemned in 1327 by Pope John XXII, but his followers continued to promote his mystical teachings

57. Sharples, *Stoics, Epicureans and Sceptics*, 101.

58. Rist, *Stoic Philosophy*, 243.

CHAPTER NINE: REPUBLICAN ROME

1. Erich S. Gruen, *Studies in Greek Culture and Roman Policy* (Leiden: E. J. Brill, 1990), maintains that the traditions of Greek as well as Trojan origins of Rome were products of Hellenic culture, but the Romans preferred to identify with Troy, rather than Greece (11–12).

2. Cf. Jacques Heurgon, *The Rise of Rome*, trans. James Willis (Berkeley and Los Angeles: University of California Press, 1973), 22. The Romans believed Rome was founded in 753 BC.

3. An old edition of the *Encyclopedia Britannica* quaintly refers to the saint's prayer as "ejaculatory" (!). For more on Augustine, see chapter 11.

4. E. T. Salmon, *The Making of Roman History* (London: Thames & Hudson, 1982), 26.

5. D. H. Lawrence, *Etruscan Places* (1932; repr., New York: Viking Press, 1961), 36–37.

6. Raymond Bloch, *The Etruscans* (New York: Frederick A. Praeger, 1958), 90.

7. That is, the Asiatic wave of Etruscans, not the Villanovans who were already in Etruria and whom most scholars believe blended with the newcomers.

8. Jean-Michel David, *The Roman Conquest of Italy*, trans. Antonia Nevill (Oxford: Blackwell, 1994), 26.

9. Emiline Richardson, *The Etruscans: Their Art and Civilization* (Chicago: University of Chicago Press, 1964), 141.

10. E. T. Salmon, *The Making of Roman Italy* (London: Pitman Press, 1982), 4–5. Salmon's first chapter provides a very clear description of the peoples of Italy to 350 BC.

11. John Boardman et al., eds., *The Oxford History of the Roman World* (1986; repr., Oxford: Oxford University Press, 1991), 480.

12. Salmon, *Making of Roman Italy*, 1.

13. Michael Crawford, "Early Rome and Italy," in Boardman et al., *Oxford History*, 18. Crawford says that central Italy lacked cities until the time of Cicero (first century BC)

14. The analogy will not work for biblical literalists.

15. Plutarch, *Lives of the Noble Romans*, ed. Edmund Fuller (1959; repr., New York: Dell, 1964), 59.

16. These were two sets of triplets—born to two sisters. The Horatii were Romans, the Curiatii Albans. Two of the Romans were killed. The third, Horatio Cocles, killed the Curiatii, much to the dismay of Horatio's sister, who was in love with one of the Curiatii. The story may have been intended to commemorate the rights of Romans to appeal judicial sentences, for Horatio was condemned to death but freed on an appeal to the Roman people.

17. Karl Christ, *The Romans: An Introduction to Their History and Civilisation*, trans. Christopher Holme (1984; repr., Berkeley and Los Angeles: University of California Press, 1985), 6.

18. It is important to note that these traditional dates have been rejected by some authorities. The noted archaeologist A. H. McDonald, *Republican Rome* (New York: Frederick A. Praeger, 1966), follows the scholarship of E. Gjerstad (*Legends and Facts of Early Roman History* [1962]; *Etruscan Culture*, etc. in thinking that the Etruscan Kings, beginning with Tarquin the Elder, had political control of Rome between 525 and 450 BC, when the Republic, according to these scholars, was first established (36). More recently, the *Oxford History of the Roman World* (1986) provides a warning as to the uncertainty of dating early Roman history but dates the foundation of the Republic as 509, immediately following the fall of the last Tarquin in 510 BC (480). This traditional date is commonly cited for the end of Etruscan rule over Rome.

19. Robert Maxwell Ogilvie, *Early Rome and the Etruscans* (Atlantic Highlands, NJ: Humanities Press, 1976), 64.

20. Ibid., 62.

21. Bloch, *Etruscans,* 102.

22. Ogilvie, *Early Rome,* 62.

23. Bloch, *Etruscans,* 102.

24. Ogilvie, *Early Rome,* 63.

25. Ibid., 64.

26. Ibid., 76.

27. The original term "Pontifex Maximus" was the head of the college of pontiffs, the highest priestly organization of Republican Rome. The *Index* of prohibited books (*Index librorum prohibitorum*) was a list of books the Roman Catholic Church considered dangerous to its faithful. Modeled after a slightly earlier Louvain catalog of such books, and issued by Pope Paul IV in AD 1559, the *Index* was intended to discourage Catholics from reading the writings of certain Catholic reformers (including Erasmus of Rotterdam) and most Protestant ones. The Old Roman Republic did not need to discourage reading, even though they had lost their own index. The truth was, Romans hated reading until they conquered Greece in the second century BC. After that, they went to school to Hellas, that is, they hired learned Greeks to tutor their children.

28. Ogilvie, *Early Rome,* 80.

29. The name Sextus did not refer to sex but to the sixth. It was a common Roman first name, as were Quintus [Fifth], Septimus [Seventh], Octavian [Eighth], and Decius [Tenth].

30. Household, *Rome, Republic and Empire,* observed that not until 409 BC did any plebian obtain the quaestorship, lowest of the five great offices of State (36).

31. McDonald, *Republican Rome,* 46.

32. A. H. McDonald, "Pre-Revolutionary Rome," in *The Romans: The People and Their Civilization,* ed. J. P. V. D. Balsdon (New York: Basic Books, 1965), 7.

33. McDonald, *Republican Rome,* 47.

34. Burn with Edwards, *Greece and Rome,* 98–99.

35. W. Warde Fowler, *Rome,* revised by M. P. Charlesworth (1912; repr., London: Oxford University Press, 1960), 35.

36. Michael Crawford, *The Roman Republic* (Cambridge: Harvard University Press, 1993), 49.

37. Dennis Proctor, *Hannibal's March in History* (Oxford: Clarendon Press, 1971), 102.

38. Gavin De Beer, *Alps and Elephants: Hannibal's March* (London: Geoffrey Bles, 1955), 87.

39. Salmon, *Making of Roman Italy,* 78.

40. De Beer, *Alps and Elephants,* 96.

41. Serge Lancel, *Hannibal* (Paris: Librairie Arthème Fayard, 1995), notes that his posture was not understood at Rome ("À Rome, tous ne comprenaient pas son attitude"). Lancel says it took the Romans two generations before they could appreciate Fabius's contributions to Rome's ultimate victory over Carthage (164).

42. Tony Bath, *Hannibal's Campaigns* (Cambridge, UK: Patrick Stephens, 1981), thinks Hannibal "over-estimated the spirit of rebellion" in the southern parts of Italy, which regarded Hannibal's troops as the aliens, not Rome (143).

43. Elizabeth Rawson, "The Expansion of Rome," in Boardman et al., *Oxford History,* 50.

44. Christ, *Romans,* 36ff.

45. Mommsen (1817–1903) was a noted German historian and archaeologist whose historical works included his classic three-volume *Roman History* (1854–56), a history of Roman coinage, and a history of Roman law. He received the Nobel Prize for literature in 1902.

46. In his introduction to the tune "I Get a Kick Out of You," 1934.

47. Bequeathed to Rome by Attalus III of Pergamum.

48. According to Arthur Lintott, there is no clear evidence that poor Italians were beneficiaries of Tiberius's agrarian reform. See "Political History, 146–95 B.C.," in *The Last Age of the Roman Republic, 146–43 B.C.,* vol. 9 of *The Cambridge Ancient History,* 2nd ed. (Cambridge: Cambridge University Press, 1994), part 1, 64. Michael Crawford, "Early Rome and Italy," says that although we do not know if the Italians as well as the Romans were included in the land reform legislation, the Italian elite class was as adversely affected as the Roman elite (42).

49. Berstein, 201.

50. Robert Wright, *Nonzero: The Logic of Human Destiny* (New York: Random House, 2000), 5. Wright says the term means that "the fortunes of the players are inversely related" in a zero-sum game, with one player's gain representing another player's loss. He argues that what could unify man's cultural struggles would be the common provision for human needs.

51. Luciano Perelli, *I Gracchi* (Rome: Salerno Editrice, 1993), points out that there were a number of bills introduced during the second century that were first introduced into the popular assembly rather than in the Senate and that their numbers increased as the age of the Gracchi drew nearer. The difference with Tiberius's bill was that it was one that directly affected the personal interests of many senators (97).

52. H. H. Scullard, *From the Gracchi to Nero: A History of Rome from 133 B.C. to A.D. 68* (1959; repr., London: Methuen, 1970), 28.

53. Crawford, *Roman Republic,* 108.

54. Scullard, *Gracchi to Nero,* 27.

55. Household, *Rome, Republic and Empire,* 199.

56. The point is made by Gruen, *Studies,* conclusion.

57. Scullard, *Gracchi to Nero,* 106.

58. Rawson, "Expansion of Rome," 67.

59. Erich S. Gruen, *The Last Generation of the Roman Republic* (Berkeley and Los Angeles: University of California Press, 1974), 48.

60. Sulla's name can be a tricky one to look up in the library. The Italians spell it Silla, which seems silly; an older English rendition is Sylla, which is also the French spelling. The computerized library poses a special threat. Punch in Sulla for Subject, and you are likely to get hundreds of listings which contain the Italian words *sulla* meaning "on the" from any title containing those words. The German spelling, like the English, is quite sensibly Sulla.

61. Phillip A. Kildahl, *Caius Marius* (New York: Twayne, 1968) says in the preface he had the "handicap of lowly birth."

62. Crawford, "Early Rome and Italy," 44. Andrew Lintott, "Political History, 146–95 B.C.," notes that Marius was a member of the Equite class from Arpinum (86).

63. *The Columbia Encyclopedia,* 3rd ed., s.v. "Marius, Caius." Kildahl, *Caius Marius,* says that Marius, after establishing his power did nothing to put into effect a policy because "he possessed no consistent policy or philosophy." He thinks Caesar "intentionally ascribed" his own policy to Marius but his policy was "nebulous" (129).

64. P. A. Brunt, *The Fall of the Roman Republic and Related Essays* (Oxford: Clarendon Press, 1988), 253.

65. Michael Grant, *Julius Caesar* (New York: McGraw-Hill, 1969), 149–59.

66. Peter Garnsey and Richard Saller, *The Roman Empire: Economy, Society and Culture* (Berkeley and Los Angeles: University of California Press, 1987), 77.

67. So called because the Latin word for allies was *socii.*

68. Arthur Keaveney, *Sulla, The Last Republican* (London: Croom Helm, 1982), 52.

69. Ibid., 58.

70. Ma Bellona, formerly Duelliona, was often confounded with the Roman goddess of wisdom, Minerva, and Ma may stand for Minerva. It might, on the other hand, stand for Mars, god of war, since Bellona was Mars's sister, daughter, or wife. Her temple at Rome was near the Porta Carmentalis.

71. Brunt, *Fall,* 461.

72. Keaveney, *Sulla,* 136.

73. Ibid., 155.

74. Ibid., 158–59.

75. Scullard, *Gracchi to Nero,* 80.

76. There is a controversy concerning Sulla's reforms. Some regard him as a real reformer in the sense of having restored senatorial powers to a more pristine state. Others regard him as an opponent of real reform (Perelli, *Gracchi,* 140).

77. Brunt, *Fall,* notes that the Roman was expected to place "duty to the fatherland higher than duty to family and friends" (40).

78. Ibid., 35ff.

79. Robin Seager, *Pompey, a Political Biography* (Oxford: Basil Blackwell, 1979), notes that the sources gave his age at his first triumph as anything from twenty-three to twenty-six, but believes it took place in AD 81, when Pompey was twenty-five (12).

80. Pontus with Bithnia; Cilicia and Syria from the coast of Cilicia to Egypt. Between these and the Euphrates were two major kingdoms (Cappadocia and Galatia) plus smaller ones that were henceforth in Rome's sphere of influence.

81. Peter Greenhalgh, *Pompey, the Roman Alexander* (London: Weidenfeld and Nicolson, 1980), 170.

82. The word meant "three men" in Latin.

83. Grant, *Julius Caesar,* 24.

84. Gruen, *Last Generation,* 78.

85. Zvi Yavetz, *Julius Caesar and His Public Image* (1979; repr., Ithaca: Cornell University Press, 1983), 110.

86. Brunt, *Fall,* refers to Suetonius and says that Caesar was "never deflected from any plan by religious scruples" and that while acknowledging the unpredictable aspect of fortune, allowed no role to the gods (59).

87. J. F. C. Fuller, *Julius Caesar: Man, Soldier, and Tyrant* (New Brunswick, NJ: Rutgers University Press, 1965), 55.

88. Plutarch, *Lives of the Noble Romans,* edited by Edmund Fuller (N.Y.: Dell Publishing Co., Inc. 1964), 184.

89. Miriam Griffin, "Cicero and Rome," in Boardman et al., *Oxford History,* 105.

90. Michael Grant, *Julius Caesar,* 75.

91. But the order for his imprisonment was rescinded. J. P. V. D. Balsdon, *Julius Caesar* (New York: Atheneum, 1967), calls Cato's imprisonment "an evident mistake in [Caesar's] tactics." (59).

92. Ibid., 83.

93. Fuller, *Julius Caesar,* 70, citing Dio 38.7.5.

94. From "Just One of Those Things," title of a Cole Porter song, 1935.

95. Scullard, *Gracchi to Nero,* 134.

96. Gruen, *Last Generation,* 500.

97. Ibid., 504.

98. Fowler, *Rome,* 112.

99. Ibid.

100. Gruen, *Last Generation,* 507.

101. Brunt, *Fall,* says that Caesar offered the Senate a "compromise peace" that "would have made him the first man in the state but not its master" (491).

102. Crawford, *Roman Republic,* 185.

103. Seager, *Pompey,* 189.

104. Balsdon, *Julius Caesar,* is almost certain that Caesarion was not Caesar's child (57, 159), but Prof. Scullard refers to the boy as Caesar's son (150).

105. Caesar's most famous line: "Veni, vidi, vinci" [I came, I saw, I conquered]. It is not true, as some suggest, that he pronounced upon first seeing Cleopatra, "I came, I saw, I concurred."

CHAPTER TEN: PRINCEPS AND PRINCIPATE

1. In his *Philippics* against the consul Marcus Antonius (Marc Antony).

2. Quoted in Ronald Syme, *The Roman Revolution* (1939; repr., Oxford: Oxford University Press, 1967), 181.

3. On the predicted role of the Hebrew Messiah, characteristics later asserted of Jesus, see Isaiah 9 and Micah 5:4–5.

4. Virgil, *Fourth Eclogue.*

5. Olive Kuntz Gilliam, *The Memoirs of Augustus* (New York: Vantage Press, 1965), 17.

6. "Matthew's" account was not considered to belong to St. Matthew until the second century, and the same was true of St. Luke's.

7. Matt. 2:2.

8. According to the Gospel of John (19:19) Pontius Pilate put a sign on the cross that read "Jesus of Nazareth, King of the Jews." In other Gospel accounts it is clear that Pilate was not the first to describe Jesus by the phrase first used by ordinary folk in Judea.

9. Luke 1:26–32.

10. Augustus's title after 27 BC was Imperator Caesar divi filius Augustus—proclaiming him son of a (new) god (i.e., Julius Caesar, his adoptive father) and as such "holy and venerable in his own right." See H. Galsterer, "Syme's *Roman Revolution* after Fifty Years," in *Between Republic and Empire,* ed. Kurt A. Raaflaub and Mark Toher (Berkeley and Los Angeles: University of California Press, 1990), 19. Jesus was later said to have told the disciples: "Everything is entrusted to me by my Father; and no one knows who the Son is but the Father, or who the Father is but the Son, and those to whom the Son may choose to reveal him" (Luke 10:22).

11. Ibid, 11. The autobiography has survived only in fragments from quotations by other ancient authors or from what Zvi Yavetz, "The *Res Gestae* and Augustus' Public Image," in *Caesar Augustus: Seven Aspects,* ed. Fergus Millar and Erich Segal (Oxford: Clarendon Press, 1984), calls "some obscure intermediate source" (1). The work, in thirteen books, reveals Augustus's concern to project a public image different from that projected by his enemies.

12. Matt 16:13–14.

13. Robert K. Sherk, ed. and trans., *The Roman Empire: Augustus to Hadrian* (Cambridge, Cambridge University Press, 1988), 43.

14. Matt. 5:17–18. Some scholars believe that this passage reflects a controversy of early Christians over the old Hebrew Law, whether it was still binding on them. They believe the lines nullify Jesus's more relaxed attitude toward the Law (Robert W. Funk and the Jesus Seminar, *The Five Gospels: The Search for the Authentic Words of Jesus* [New York: Macmillan, 1993], 140).

15. Syme, *Roman Revolution,* 409–410, 439. Others attributed the murder of Postumus to Tiberius.

16. Matt.16:17–19.

17. Protestants, following an antipapal medieval tradition, reject the idea that Jesus appointed Peter as his successor. They base their conclusion on an interpretation of Jesus's words to Peter that make his confession that Jesus was the "the Son of the living God" the foundation of the church, rather than the pun on Peter's name, namely, rock = foundation.

18. Called "the Elder" to distinguish her from her daughter, Julia "the Younger."

19. K. A. Raaflaub and L. J. Samons II, "Opposition to Augustus," in Raaflaub and Toher, *Between Republic and Empire,* 428–29.

20. John 2:1–11.

21. Matt. 12:46–50.

22. Lepidus was allowed to keep the office of high priest (pontifex maximus) after his dismissal from the triumvirate, which became in effect, a dyarchy of Antony and Octavian.

23. *Romeo and Juliet* 2.2.67.

24. Zvi Yavetz, *Plebs and Princeps* (New Brunswick, NJ: Transaction Books, 1988), 78. Such payments were called donatives.

25. Syme, *Roman Revolution,* 143.

26. Gilliam, *Memoirs,* 63.

27. For the variations in opinions of Augustus and his reign, see Raaflaub and Toher, *Between Republic and Empire,* a collection of nineteen scholarly essays on his career and its significance.

28. Scullard, *Gracchi to Nero,* 219.

29. Colin Wells, *The Roman Empire,* 2nd ed. (Cambridge: Harvard University Press, 1992), 76.

30. Rostovtzeff, *Social and Economic History,* 51–52.

31. Ibid., 2.

32. Ibid., 304.

33. Matt. 10:34–36. The scholars of the Jesus Seminar believe that these words were the work of Christian community, not stated by Jesus, a reformulation of the prophet Micah (7:5–6). See Funk, *Five Gospels,* 173–74.

34. Emilio Gabba, "The Historians and Augustus," in Millar and Segal, *Caesar Augustus,* 78.

35. Some of our most popular presidents—Harry Truman, Dwight Eisenhower, and Bill Clinton—resembled Augustus in that respect.

36. E. T. Salmon, *A History of the Roman World from 30 B.C. to A.D. 138* (New York: Macmillan, 1944), 158.

37. Donald R. Kelley, ed., *Versions of History from Antiquity to the Enlightenment* (New Haven: Yale University Press, 1991), 92.

38. Tacitus was a substitute consul under Nerva and later, proconsul of Asia. His father-in-law was Cn. Julius Agricola, the conqueror and later, governor, of Britain.

39. Edward Gibbon, *The Decline and Fall of the Roman Empire,* ed. H. H. Milman (New York: Thomas Y. Crowell, n.d.), 1:131.

40. Cited by T. P. Wiseman, trans. and commentator, *Death of an Emperor,* by Flavius Josephus (Exeter: University of Exeter Press, 1991), viii.

41. Luke, chapters 3–23, v. 48.

42. Robin Seager, *Tiberius* (Berkeley and Los Angeles: University of California Press, 1972), 249.

43. David Stockton, "The Founding of the Empire," in Boardman et al., *Oxford History,* 170.

44. Roman province south and west of the Danube, including parts of modern Austria, Hungary, Yugoslavia. They were subjugated by Rome in AD 9.

45. Thrace occupied the southeastern tip of the Balkan Peninsula and included in the first century AD the cities of Adrianople and Byzantium.

46. Seager, *Tiberius,* 142.

47. Yavetz, *Plebs and Princeps,* 108–9.

48. Scullard, *Gracchi to Nero,* 293.

49. But Balsdon, *Julius Caesar,* thinks Gemellus was driven to commit suicide—that he was not murdered (37). Yet he does admit that two other murders, of Agrippa Postumus at the beginning of Tiberius's reign and of Britannicus, son of Claudius, were "parallels." The elimination of contenders for the succession was viewed as necessary to public peace.

50. Arther Ferrill, *Caligula: Emperor of Rome* (London: Thames and Hudson, 1991), 128.

51. Suetonius, *The Lives of the Twelve Caesars,* ed. Joseph Gavorse (1931; repr., New York: Modern Library, 1959), 194.

52. J. P. V. D. Balsdon, *The Emperor Gaius (Caligula)* (1934; repr., Westport, CT: Greenwood Press, 1977), 91.

53. Suetonius, *Lives,* 181.

54. Crane Brinton, *A History of Western Morals* (New York: Harcourt, Brace and Company, 1959), 131.

55. Salmon, *Roman World,* 148.

56. Ibid., 150.

57. Ibid., 155.

58. Balsdon, *Emperor Gaius,* 214–15.

59. Michael Grant, *Nero: Emperor in Revolt* (New York: American Heritage Press, 1970), 161.

60. Flavius Josephus, *Death of an Emperor,* trans. and with commentary by T. P. Wiseman (Exeter: University of Exeter Press, 1991), 31.

61. Ferrill, *Caligula,* notes that a variation or "twisted version" of this quotation runs: "Power corrupts, and absolute power is even nicer," which he says applies "especially well to Caligula" (10)!

62. John Emerich Edward Dalberg Acton, 1st baron, was a Liberal MP and editor of a monthly magazine, *The Rambler.* He became professor of modern history at Cambridge (1895) and his collected lectures and essays appeared in print after his death.

63. Agrippina was the daughter of Germanicus and Agrippina the Elder. She bore the future emperor Nero to her first husband, Cn. Domitius Ahenobarbus. She married the Emperor Claudius in 49 BC.

64. One Cassius Chaerea, a tribune of the Praetorian Guard.

65. Suetonius, *Lives,* 201. But Balsdon, *Emperor Gaius,* says that Caligula had been to the theater on the morning of the deed (24 January AD 41) and had already attended the theater before leaving belatedly to go to lunch.

66. Vulcan, god of fire and metalwork, was the son of Juno. She conceived him without her husband Jupiter's help, an act of revenge because Jupiter had earlier procreated Minerva, born from Jupiter's head, without her help. Vulcan was either born lame, or else suffered a broken leg after Jupiter kicked him off Mt. Olympus for having attempted to free Juno, whom Jupiter had fastened with a golden chain.

67. Salmon, *Roman World,* 157.

68. Scullard, *Gracchi to Nero,* 301.

69. Barbara Levick, *Claudius* (London: B. T. Batsford, 1990), 18–19.

70. Wells, *Roman Empire,* 116.

71. Ibid., 116.

72. Scullard, *Gracchi to Nero,* thinks that Claudius "unwittingly began the centralization which centuries later choked the Roman world in bureaucracy" (302).

73. Germanicus had defeated the Germans at the Weser in AD 16 and was considered a hero by the legions there.

74. Wells, *Roman Empire*, 130.

75. Salmon, *Roman World*, 170. But Scullard, *Gracchi to Nero*, thinks that even if he was not dominated by his court, the court influenced his policy (313).

76. Levick, *Claudius*, 55.

77. Ibid., 65.

78. Salmon, *Roman World*, notes that the period was referred to later by Emperor Trajan the *quinquennium Neronis* (176–77). Trajan spoke of Nero's architectural contributions, which came at the end of his reign, but scholars believe this period after Agrippina's death was a period of general happiness.

79. Garnsey and Saller, *Roman Empire*, 20.

80. Grant, *Nero*, 36.

81. *Annals* 13.15.2–4.

82. B. H. Warmington, *Nero: Reality and Legend* (New York: W. W. Norton, 1969), 46.

83. Grant, *Nero*, 74. Nero was timid in the sense that he did not enjoy blood sports or viewing others in agony, as Caligula had. He was not too timid to endorse bloodletting when his safety was at stake.

84. The inventor of this perfume at the end of the seventeenth century was an Italian named Farina, but the product is never referred to as *acqua di Colognia. Peccato.*

85. Among sports figures, musicians, dancers, and actors who became lawmakers in the U.S. during the last half of the twentieth century were George Murphy, senator from California; Sonny Bono, congressman from California; Bill Bradley, senator from New Jersey; Jack Kemp, congressman from New York State; Jesse Ventura, governor of Minnesota; and President Ronald Reagan.

86. Salmon, *Roman World*, 181.

87. Grant, *Nero*, 154. In the summer of 1999 the Romans were preparing to put on exhibit this "golden house" of Nero, some of which survived the flames.

88. Ibid., 213–15.

89. Warmington, *Nero*, 167. The situation has some of the same elements as that leading up to the impeachment and trial of President Clinton in the fall of 1998 and winter of 1999.

90. Marcus Aurelius, like Seneca, was a Stoic philosopher. He became emperor in AD 161. See below.

91. Grant, *Nero*, 226.

92. Suetonius, *Lives*, 270.

93. The Zealots were a Jewish faction which venerated the Torah and despised heathens and Jews who conformed to Roman culture. They had been organized since 37 BC and had rebelled under Augustus over the census, which they regarded as a plot for their subjugation. They disappeared after the destruction of Jerusalem (AD 70). The apostle St. Simon was a Zealot.

94. Was he thinking of periodontal, meaning all the way around a tooth?

95. Virgil, *Aeneid* 2.49.

96. Warmington, *Nero*, 163. Warmington, who may be flattering moderns here, says that Nero's persecution of his own family members and potential rivals counted more against him than his persecution of slaves and Christians.

97. A work he left to his son Titus to complete, so that he could assume the imperial dignity.

98. Suetonius, *Lives*, 328.

99. A *mitzvah* (Yiddish), a good work.

100. Suetonius, *Lives*, 330.

101. Brian W. Jones, *The Emperor Domitian* (New York: Routledge, 1992), says the family's poverty was a myth, an invention of Flavian propaganda during the reigns of Gaius (Caligula) and Nero (1–2).

102. Suetonius, *Lives,* 345. But according to Jones, *Emperor Domitian,* there was much testimony to his adeptness at poetry. Jones believes Domitian had a sound education (12–13).

103. Real power (AD 69–70) was exercised by a mature supporter and confidant of the emperor named Mucianus while Vespasian was absent in Palestine.

104. Salmon, *Roman World,* says that Domitian studied Tiberius's *Acta* during his semiretirement, before his succession to Titus (225).

105. Suetonius, *Lives,* 346.

106. Will Durant, *Caesar and Christ* (New York: Simon and Schuster, 1944), 290.

107. Pat Southern, *Domitian: Tragic Tyrant* (New York: Routledge, 1997), 58. The object of the law, to increase cereal production, failed, as did compliance. The law was repealed in Asia and not in force in Africa in the third century.

108. Jones, *Emperor Domitian,* 128. Jones thinks that although Domitian claimed a triumph in this war, it was undeserved.

109. Derek Williams, *Romans and Barbarians: Four Views From the Empire's Edge, First Century AD* (London: Constable, 1998), 160–61.

110. Southern, *Domitian,* notes that the peace with Decebalus was, as Syme pointed out elsewhere, face-saving for both sides, even if it outraged some critics as shameful. Southern says that was mostly Trajanic propaganda (108).

111. On the ground formerly covered by an artificial lake, part of the three hundred acres Nero took as his yard for the Golden House.

112. This circus is visible in the outline of the Piazza Navona in downtown Rome.

113. Julian Bennett, *Trajan, Optimus Princeps: A Life and Times* (London: Routledge, 1997), thinks there is some evidence that the arch was really a work completed under Trajan, that Domitian may have conceived of the arch, but out of envy for his brother and spite over the fact that he did not share in the power, had failed to execute the monument (148).

114. Salmon, *Roman World,* 232. Trajan served Domitian as military tribune all over the empire.

115. *Encyclopedia Americana,* s.v. "Domitia Longina."

116. Suetonius, *Lives,* 360.

117. Jones, *Emperor Domitian,* 38.

118. Sherk, *Roman Empire,* 136. The letter was found on a stone stele damaged along the right side and bottom, in Ephiphanea. The language was Greek. Pat Southern, *Domitian,* says that this incident shows that Domitian was anxious to protect centralized control of provincial affairs, and to defend his imperial prerogative (57).

119. Jones, *Emperor Domitian,* 114–19.

120. Flavius Clemens's children had been named heirs to Domitian, who had no sons. Their father's execution ended their chance for that.

121. Jones, *Emperor Domitian,* 180.

122. Derek Williams, *The Reach of Rome: A History of the Roman Imperial Frontier First–Fifth Centuries AD* (London: Constable, 1996), who uses the word "paranoia" to identify the "demonic" transformation of Domitian from a quiet younger brother into an imperial monster (40).

123. Southern, *Domitian,* 111.

124. Suetonius, *Lives,* 359.

125. Jones, *Emperor Domitian,* 193–95.

126. Michael Grant, *The Twelve Caesars* (London: Weidenfeld and Nicolson, 1975), 253.

127. Williams, *Romans and Barbarians,* 165.

128. Salmon, *Roman World,* 235–36.

129. Southern, *Domitian,* 118.

130. The disparity is a feature of his biography, not unlike the "bio" of Erasmus of Rotterdam and many other historical figures. Historians make shift with incomplete and inaccurate records.

131. J. Wells and R. H. Barro, *A Short History of the Roman Empire to the Death of Marcus Aurelius* (London: Methuen, 1931), 208.

132. Chris Scarre, *Chronicle of the Roman Emperors* (London: Thames and Hudson, 1995), 87–88.

133. Ibid., 90–91, says it is not known whether or not Trajan was forewarned by friends and there is a tradition that he covertly seized power through their assistance.

134. Bennett, *Trajan, Optimus Princeps,* 145. Bennett thinks the title was bestowed on him partly for his help in enabling Rome to combat flooding. The fosse Traiana, for example, was a channel that reduced the danger of inundations at Rome.

135. Gibbon, *Decline and Fall,* 1:48. Gibbon added that Trajan could not get the eastern exploits of Alexander out of his mind.

136. Quoted in Royston Lambert, *Beloved and God: The Story of Hadrian and Antinous* (London: Weidenfeld and Nicolson, 1984), opposite figure 17.

137. Bernard W. Henderson, *Five Roman Emperors* (Cambridge: Cambridge University Press, 1927), says that modern criticism "fastened upon the one chapter in Trajan's career which alone affords a griphold," his eastern wars. He thinks the term "megalomania" as applied in textbooks of his day to Trajan's expansion beyond the Euphrates a tiresome expression. But he also recognized that Trajan's empire had neither the men nor the money to defend the empire's frontiers beyond that river boundary (339).

138. Parthamasiris was king of Armenia. He was deposed and killed by Trajan (AD 114).

139. Scarre, *Chronicle,* 95.

140. Lambert, *Beloved and God,* 862–87.

141. It is noteworthy that Hadrian, who was a ward of Trajan, succeeded him as emperor.

142. The death penalty was enacted for any who persisted in maintaining the "Name," that is, for unrepentant Christians.

143. Eugene Cizek, *L'Epoque de Trajan* (Paris: Société d'Édition "Les Belles Lettres," 1983), 468 and n. 1.

144. Williams, *Reach of Rome,* says Hadrian was "perhaps the most intelligent of all Rome's rulers" (85).

145. Anthony R. Birley, *Hadrian: The Restless Emperor* (London: Routledge, 1997), says that Plotina had "at best . . . stage-managed" the adoption (77).

146. His cousin Trajan and Acillus Attianus were his two guardians after his father died in Hadrian's tenth year. Most of the time he was looked after by Attianus, since Trajan left Spain, Hadrian's native country, for service on the Rhine soon after the elder Hadrian's death.

147. Salmon, *Roman World,* 305–6.

148. Bernard W. Henderson, *The Life and Principate of the Emperor Hadrian* (London: Methuen, 1923), 131.

149. Lambert, *Beloved and God.*

150. Birley, *Hadrian,* xiv.

151. The Byzantine (i.e., eastern Roman) Emperor Justinian (d. AD 565) is famous for his law code, the *Corpis juris civilis,* which drew upon the best principles of Roman law and influenced western European jurisprudence and legal education for over a thousand years.

152. Ferdinand Gregorovius, *The Emperor Hadrian: A Picture of the Graeco-Roman World in His Time,* trans. Mary E. Robinson (London: Macmillan, 1898), 324.

153. Birley, *Hadrian,* 127.

154. Stewart Perowne, *Hadrian* (London: Hodder and Stoughton, 1960), 66.

155. Ibid., 182. Perowne blames Hadrian's behavior during and after the Jewish wars.

156. Ronald Syme, "Fictional History Old and New: Hadrian" in *Roman Papers,* ed. Anthony R. Birley (Oxford: Clarendon Press, 1991), 6:175. (First delivered as a James Bryce Memorial Lecture, May 10, 1984, Somerville College, Oxford, 1986).

157. Destroyed by Titus in AD 70.

158. Gregorovius, *Emperor Hadrian,* 155.

159. See Syme, "Fictional History," 157–81. Syme distinguished between history itself and the fictional history that follows, an effort which he calls "legitimate and harmless" but seldom (done without) dissembling the author's own milieu and opinions" (157–58). He faulted Yourcenar for lack of insight into her sources (the *Vita Hadriani* and *Historia Augusta*), on which she based her *Mémoires,* a work which contained mistakes and fabrications about Hadrian, including one Syme labels "peculiar and repellent" (162).

160. Syme, "Fictional History" points to the essential qualities of Hadrian not by using the term "modern" but noting his distrust of dogma; hostility to distinctions of class, nation, race; cosmopolitanism; inquiry into foreign religions and occult science; fascination with the exotic (161). These things are, it seems to me, quintessentially liberal preoccupations.

161. Born Titus Aurelius Fulvus Boionus Arrius Antoninus in AD 86, Antoninus came from southern Gaul (Nemausus or Nimes) originally but had achieved wealth and status in Rome. Hadrian, who adopted him just five months before his own death, made him adopt two young men as his own heirs, one of whom was his brother-in-law's son, Marcus Annius Verus, later known as the emperor Marcus Aurelius.

162. Scarre, *Chronicle,* notes that the *Historia Augusta* gives four other explanations of how Antoninus earned his nickname (108)!

163. Gibbon, *Decline and Fall,* 1:50–51.

164. Scarre, *Chronicle,* 110.

165. Michel de Montaigne, *The Complete Essays of Montaigne,* ed. and trans. Donald M. Frame (1957; repr., Stanford: Stanford University Press, 1965).

166. In old age Antoninus had splints bound to his chest to help him stand erect. Splints were all that antiquity offered for problems relating to erection. Now, there's Viagra.

167. Scarre, *Chronicle,* 110. The quoted lines are mistakenly taken as proof of Antoninus Pius's affection for his wife, Anna Galeria Faustina (the elder).

168. Anthony Birley, *Marcus Aurelius* (Boston: Little, Brown, 1966), correctly distinguished between the two when noting that in a letter to Fronto, a learned counsel, famed orator and Marcus's tutor (108).

169. As is claimed by Michael Grant in *The Antonines: The Roman Empire in Transition* (London: Routledge, 1994), 54.

170. Marcus Aurelius, *The Meditations of Marcus Aurelius,* ed. Charles W. Eliot, trans. George Land, vol. 2, The Harvard Chronicles (Cambridge: Harvard University Press).

171. Brinton, *Western Morals,* wrote that there was "a touch in someone like Marcus Aurelius of the pride of the martyr, the man who deliberately does what is difficult and unpleasant because clearly he wants to do it, gains stature with himself by doing it" (119).

172. Anthony Birley, *Marcus Aurelius: A Biography,* rev. ed. (London: B.T. Batsford, 1987), observes that the only reference in the *Meditations* to Christians was in connection with martyrdom, where Marcus thought that willingness of the soul to depart from the body was wonderful when it came from a "specific decision, and not out of sheer *parataxis like the Christians.*" Birley tells us that this word was used elsewhere to describe the drawing up of troops in battle and the marshalling of a political party and reveals that Marcus felt Christians were not expressing individual choice but rather had been *trained* to die (154).

173. Ibid., 38.

174. Birley, *Marcus Aurelius* (1966), 306.

175. Marcus Aurelius, *Meditations* 1.10.

176. Grant, *Antonines,* 53.

177. Ibid., 182.

178. F. H. Hayward, *Marcus Aurelius: A Saviour of Men* (London: George Allen & Unwin, 1935), 157.

179. Marcus Aurelius, *Meditations* 7.31.

CHAPTER ELEVEN: FOUR FATHERS AND THE PRIMITIVE CHURCH

1. Tertullian stated in his *Apology:* "The oftener we are mown down by you, the more in number we grow; the blood of Christians is seed." Quoted in John Lawson, *A Theological and Historical Introduction to the Apostolic Fathers* (New York: Macmillan, 1961), 288.

2. The date of the "fall" of Rome has always been a matter of debate. Some date its fall from the Visigoths' destruction of Rome in 410; others, from the Vandals' sack of Rome in 455; still others from the removal of the boy emperor of the West, Romulus Augustulus, by the German chieftan Odoacer in 476, the date used here. Edward Gibbon delayed Rome's fall until the Byzantine empire was overthrown by Ottoman Turks in 1453!

3. Denis Minns, *Irenaeus* (London: Geoffrey Chapman, 1994), says Irenaeus "would have been appalled at the thought that God would offer grace to some and withhold it from others," as St. Augustine later insisted (136).

4. Mary Ann Donovan, *One Right Reading?: A Guide to Irenaeus* (Collegeville, MN: Liturgical Press, 1997), 14.

5. Robert M. Grant, *Irenaeus of Lyons* (London: Routledge, 1997), 29.

6. Minns, *Irenaeus,* 133.

7. Gnostics refers to a diverse array of religious sects promising salvation on the basis of secret or divine knowledge. Gnostics included Manichaean dualists, as well as Jewish, Hellenistic, Iranian, and early Christian cults.

8. Elaine Pagels, *The Gnostic Gospels* (New York: Random House, 1979), chap. 3, "God the Father/God the Mother."

9. Daniel Hoffman, *The Status of Women and Gnosticism in Irenaeus and Tertullian* (Lewiston, NY: Edwin Mellen Press, 1995), 3.

10. Ibid., 88–89.

11. Hoffman finds Tertullian critical of women with heretical views, but he accepted women teachers in church communities when they were modest and orthodox. He did not believe they should be bishops (Ibid., 175–80).

12. Luke 10:38–42.

13. Protestants reject the role of Mary as co-Redemptor and as yet there is no Catholic definition of the co-redemption, although authoritative papal teaching does exist.

14. Only for Catholics. Pope Pius XII established the feast of the queenship in 1954.

15. Eusebius (c. AD 263–339?) of Caesarea, also called Eusebius Pamphili, was a Greek apologist and bishop. His views on the Trinity were less than orthodox, best described as semi-Arian.

16. Latourette notes that Constantine "continued to support both paganism and Christianity, and that when the first coins appeared in 314 with a cross, it was accompanied by the figures of two pagan deities, Sol Invictus and Mars Conservator. The same source notes that until his death Constantine bore the title of *pontifex maximus* (chief priest; now the pope's title) and the Roman Senate classed the emperor among the gods" (92).

17. Minns, *Irenaeus,* makes the same point , though more gently, when he notes that "it was only at the time of Irenaeus, and in consequence of the crisis of Marcion and the gnostics, that the orthodox consensus, the majority view, or, as it is often called, the Great Church, came into existence" (10–11).

18. The apology issued by Pope John Paul XXIII in a special Mass of contrition, given at the start of the Lenten season in the jubilee year 2000, contained expressions of Catholic remorse to those it had injured in the whole of its near 2000 years' history. Absent from any mention at all wesre the heretics it had demonized and persecuted.

19. A good example is the Unitarian church which still rejects the Trinity, as the heretic sects of Monarchians and Arians once did.

20. A. von Harnack, *Chronologie der altchristlichen Litteratur* (1897). Grant, *Irenaeus of Lyon,* notes that it is not clear how the John mentioned by Polycarp is related to extant Johannine literature, even if Irenaeus assumed that the Gospel of John, the Epistle (1–2), and the apocalypse (Revelation) came from him (37).

21. Von Harnack, *Chronologie,* 1:325–29.

22. As in the *Collier's Encyclopedia* article "Papacy," where one reads that "Polycarp was in turn a disciple of St. John."

23. *Adversus Haereses.*

24. Grant, *Irenaeus of Lyons,* 58.

25. The terms used to explain Valentinus's system vary depending on the author and translation. In Dominic J. Unger, trans. and ann., *St. Irenaeus of Lyons Against the Heresies,* with further revisions by John J. Dillon (New York: Paulist Press, 1992), the terms for the Primal Father as stated by Irenaeus are not *Bythos* but "First-Being, First-Beginning, First-Father, and Profundity" while the Silence is termed Grace as well and also Thought (1:23).

26. This was the phrase that described the policy adopted by President Clinton to facilitate military service by homosexuals in the armed services.

27. R. McL. Wilson, "Valentinus and Valentinianism," in *The Encyclopedia of Philosophy* (New York: Macmillan), 8:227.

28. Stephen F. Barker, "Number," in *The Encyclopedia of Philosophy,* (5: 526–30).

29. Rigorism during the Protestant Reformation was found among certain Anabaptist groups who used the term "gathered church" rather than the term "rigorist." In the gathered church only those who were willing to practice all the rules and lead pure lives were admitted to membership.

30. Later, St. Augustine would make of desire or concupiscence a similar bugbear.

31. This refers to a popular newspaper columnist who answers questions concerning manners and morals sent her by anguished readers. The nature of anguish has not changed much over the course of Western civilization.

32. Gerald Lewis Bray, *Holiness and the Will of God: Perspectives on the Theology of Tertullian* (Atlanta: John Knox Press, 1979), 35–36.

33. *De anima.*

34. R. A. Markus, *Saeculum: History and Society in the Theology of St. Augustine* (Cambridge: Cambridge University Press, 1970), observes that "Cyprian's ecclesiology differed from Tertullian's only in that it identified the Church of the bishops with the Church of the pure" whereas for Tertullian, the pure Church was one removed from the contaminations of the world as it really existed. He indicates that Thomists usually assume polemicists are not into philosophy, except as it serves to rally their followers against the discipline required for rational thought (107).

35. *Ad Martyras.*

36. Eric Osborn, *Tertullian, First Theologian of the West* (Cambridge: Cambridge University Press, 1997), 76.

37. Quoted from *De praescriptione de haereticorum* in H. B. Timothy, *The Early Christian Apologists and Greek Philosophy* (Assen, Netherlands: Van Gorcum, 1973), 58.

38. Lewis W. Spitz, "Luther and Humanism," in *Luther and German Humanism,* ed. Lewis W. Spitz (Aldershot, Hampshire: Ashgate, 1995), 70.

39. Osborn, *Tertullian,* p. 47.

40. *De Carne Christi.*

41. The word absurd is sometimes translated "inept," sometimes "impossible," and sometimes "foolish."

42. Edgar Allan Poe, "Berenice—A Tale," in *The Unabridged Edgar Allan Poe,* ed. T. Mossman (Philadelphia: n.p., 1983), 158.

43. Jean-Claude Fredouille, *Tertullien et la conversion de la culture antique* (Paris: Études Augustiniennes, 1972), 226 ff.

44. Hans von Campenhausen, *The Fathers of the Latin Church,* trans. Manfred Hoffman (Stanford, CA: Stanford University Press, 1960), 27–28.

45. Osborn, *Tertullian,* denies that Tertullian was a schismatic despite his attachment to Montanist theology of the spirit (176–77). He thinks Tertullian was always influenced by a strong transcendent spiritualism that was strengthened, not instigated, by the Montanist prophets (212–13). Bray, *Holiness,* believes Tertullian merely defended the Montanists because they shared his views on holiness and discipline, but was not otherwise interested in them. He thinks that the fact that Tertullian's writings survived intact and that he was later regarded as a Father of the Latin Church adds to the weight of the evidence that he was not himself a Montanist (62). This is not the view of Cahal B. Daly, *Tertullian, the Puritan and His Influence: An Essay in Historical Theology* (Dublin: Four Courts Press, 1993), who portrays him as having defected from the Catholic Church, repudiating its hierarchy and questioning the hierarchical constitution of the Church (10–11). Von Campenhausen, *Fathers,* thinks that Tertullian, having abandoned the Montanists, wound up as the leader of his own sect, but one that was theologically very close to Judaism (35).

46. Osborn, *Tertullian,* 256.

47. See Osborn, who cites several texts that propose solutions to this mystery (Ibid., 120 n. 10).

48. Benjamin Breckinridge Warfield, *Studies in Tertullian and Augustine* (1930; repr., Westport, CT: Greenwood Press, 1970), 8.

49. They were also called "patripassianists." Patripassionism taught that God the Father had suffered with Christ on the cross, a position the orthodox, and Tertullian with them, felt blasphemed the Father. The term "modal" refers to their explanation of the Father, Son, and Holy Spirit as three modes of the one (Father's) substance.

50. Warfield, *Studies,* observes that "If it is very easy to exaggerate the originality of Tertullian's doctrine as set forth in this tract [*Against Praxeas*] . . . it is equally easy to underestimate it." He maintains that Trinitarianism was inherent in the elements of the Gospel, but that Tertullian was the first one to make "a scientific adjustment" of it, as Augustine adjusted original sin, Anselm the doctrine of satisfaction, and Luther justification by faith (18–19).

51. Latourette, 145.

52. Bray, *Holiness,* 7.

53. Von Campenhausen, *Fathers,* 31.

54. Bray, *Holiness,* 7.

55. Warfield, *Studies,* 62–63.

56. Osborne, *Tertullian,* 59.

57. Eusebius Hieronymus in Latin.

58. The symbolism is as follows: the lion represented bestial behavior; the thorn, removed by Jerome, sin. Hence, Jerome had the ability to remove sin from people who otherwise would remain quite beastly. The story of cooperative, even loving lions and their human benefactors was recycled from the first-century tale of Androcles (a Roman slave) and his lion.

59. Letter 22, in *Select Letters of St. Jerome,* trans. F. A. Wright (Cambridge: Harvard University Press, 1963), 127. According to Eugene F. Rice, *Saint Jerome in the Renaissance* (Baltimore: Johns Hopkins University Press, 1985), who recounts this dream, it took place probably during Lent in AD 374 (3).

60. One who by training and preference was devoted to literary works including those of Cicero, rather than to Scripture and works of Christian piety. Jerome did have a struggle about this and shortly after his dream, decided to give up reading secular works. Eventually, he was able to read and even to teach them again in a school he ran in Bethlehem without feeling so guilty.

61. Letter 22, in *Select Letters,* 127.

62. See Lewis W. Spitz and Barbara Sher Tinsley, *Johann Sturm on Education: The Reformation and Humanist Learning* (St. Louis, MO: Concordia, 1995).

63. In the controversy over the year of his birth, Jerome resembled Erasmus of Rotterdam, his admirer and editor.

64. Aelius Donatus, who flourished during the first half of the fourth century, wrote the *Ars grammatica* [Elements of Grammar] that was used as the standard Latin grammar throughout the Middle Ages.

65. *De perpetua virginitate beatae Mariae adversus Helvidium liber unus.*

66. *Against Helvidius,* in *Saint Jerome: Dogmatic and Polemical Works,* trans. John N. Hritzu (Washington, DC: Catholic University of America Press, 1965), 40–41.

67. Ibid., 38.

68. Rice, *Saint Jerome,* 24.

69. Ibid., 32.

70. Letter 7, in *Select Letters,* 21.

71. Ibid., Letter 14.

72. Ferdinand Cavallera, S.J., "The Personality of St. Jerome," in *A Monument to Saint Jerome: Essays on Some Aspects of His Life, Works and Influence,* ed. Francis X. Murphy (New York: Sheed & Ward, 1952), 17–18.

73. Ibid., 19.

74. Von Campenhausen, *Fathers,* 181.

75. J. N. D. Kelly, *Jerome: His Life, Writings, and Controversies* (London: Gerald Duckworth, 1975), 47.

76. Gustav Bardy, "St. Jerome and Greek Thought," in Murphy, *Monument,* 89. Von Campenhausen, *Fathers,* finds that "one seeks in vain to find in him solid methodological and theological principles" (181).

77. Letter 15, in *Select Letters.* See Kelly, *Jerome,* who notes that in objecting to the "three hypostases" formula of the East, Jerome admitted he was ready to be guided by the pope on this matter (53).

78. Letter 22, in *Select Letters.*

79. Kelly, *Jerome,* 61.

80. *Adversus Helvidium.*

81. Ilona Opelt, *Hieronymus' Schreitschriften* (Heidelberg: C. Winter, 1973), 36.

82. Kelly, *Jerome,* 75.

83. Henri Crouzel, "Jérôme traducteur du Peri Archôn d'Origène" in *Jérôme Entre L'Occident et L'Orient* (Paris: Etudes augustiniennes, 1988), 156.

84. To stick just with the Latin historians, examples of objectivity can be found in the work of Aulus Gellius (d. 123 BC); Pliny the Younger (d. AD 113); Sallust (d. 34 BC) Tacitus (d. AD 120); Marcellinus (d. AD 400).

85. Kelly, *Jerome*, 82. Kelly notes that Damasus was called "the matrons' ear-tickler."

86. Ibid., 87.

87. Ibid., 88.

88. See Christa Krumeich, *Hieronymus und die Christlichen Feminae Clarissimae* (Bonn: Dr. Rudolf Habelt GMBH, 1993). Krumeich credits Jerome with envisioning the conversion of pagans facilitated by changing the basis of Roman culture to accord in every respect with Christian idealism. To do this, he began by transforming small communities (largely made up of women) into exemplary models after which larger segments of society could be patterned.

89. Letter 38, in *Select Letters*.

90. Letter 39, in *Select Letters*.

91. Letter 22, in *Select Letters,* passim.

92. Krumeich, *Hieronymus:* "So wird der Christ das Schöne, Wahre und Gute der Heiden aufnehmen als überlieferte Güter der Kultur und sie seinem Gott darbringen; so stellt ein Hieronymus den christlichen clarissimae heidnische exempla vor Augen, um sie dazu zu ermuntern, selbst christliche exempla einer neuen Nobilität zu werden" (6–7).

93. Ibid., 380.

94. *The Columbia University College of Physicians and Surgeons Complete Home Medical Guide* (New York: Crown Publishers, 1989), 779.

95. Quoted from Kelly, *Jerome,* 102.

96. Song of Songs 5:2.

97. Kelly, *Jerome,* 103.

98. The Church maintained that Christ was the Lover, the Church his bride, so that there was never any *real* sex intended by the poem's authors.

99. *Select Letters,* viii–ix.

100. Letter 54, in *Select Letters,* 265.

101. Opelt, *Hieronymus' Schreitschriften,* 45.

102. *Dogmatic and Polemical Works,* xii.

103. Von Campenhausen, *Fathers,* 170–71. The distancing of himself from Origen was set in motion when Vigilantius, an Italian priest and friend of Paulinus of Nola, a good friend of Jerome, visited Jerome in Bethlehem. When Vigilantius returned to the West, he reported to Paulinus that Jerome was a confirmed Origenist. Jerome replied with a letter to Vigilantius in which he roundly denied the charge of Origenism on his part. Five years later (AD 407) he wrote a treatise entitled *Contra Vigilantium,* written in the space of one night in AD 407. It was one of his most violent polemical writings and was critical of Vigilantius for denying the veneration of relics of saintly martyrs and the keeping of night vigils.

104. Kelly, *Jerome,* chap. 18.

105. Not to be confused with the Calvinist notion of double predestinarianism, also double predestination, the peculiar notion that some are preordained by God to salvation, whereas others, the majority, are preordained to damnation.

106. "Corpus non frangendum, sed regendum est."

107. *Dogmatic and Polemical Works,* 223, n. 1.

108. *Dialogus contra Pelagianos.*

109. "Dialogue Against the Pelagians," in *Dogmatic and Polemical Works,* 365–66.

110. Ibid., 373.

111. Ibid., 362.

112. Vernon J. Bourke, Introduction to *Confessions,* by St. Augustine, trans. Rex Warner (New York: Signet), 40 n. 29.

113. Augustine, *Confessions* 2.4, p. 40–41.

114. Ibid., 2.9, p. 47.

115. Garry Wills, *Saint Augustine* (New York: Viking Penguin, 1999), 14.

116. *Confessions* 4, p. 70.

117. *Confessions* 10.

118. *Confessions* 5.12, p. 107.

119. Peter Brown, *Augustine of Hippo: A Biography* (Berkeley and Los Angeles: University of California Press, 1967), 51ff.

120. *Confessions* 7.7, p. 174.

121. Vernon J. Bourke, Introduction: "It (*Confessions*) has that universality which is the special mark of a great classic" (xiv).

122. Kam-lun Edwin Lee, *Augustine, Manichaeism, and the Good* (New York: Peter Lang, 1999), compares his own view, that there is a "Direct Link from the Manichaean Idea of Evil" to Augustine's concept of the "uncontrollable impulse" in human behavior (54) to that of the scholar Johannes Van Oort, who has written extensively on the Manichaean influence in this Father's theology. Van Oort concludes only that Manichaean views might have shared a "common root" with Augustine's view of evil desires [*concupiscentia*], Lee finds that Augustine's sexual view of desire (evil) owed much to Manichaean thought. See also N. Joseph Torchia, O.P., *Creatio ex nihilo and the Theology of St. Augustine: The Anti-Manichaean Polemic and Beyond* (New York: Peter Lang, 1999). Torchia locates Augustine's views on good and evil in his understanding of the Creation out of nothingness (*nihil*) (117). Augustine differed from the Manichaeans for whom "evil existed in its own right, whereas for Augustine, it was wholly dependent on God, and had no existence in its own right."

123. St. Augustine, *Confessions* 6.15, pp. 132–33.

124. Ibid.

125. Rebecca West, *St. Augustine* (New York: D. Appleton, 1933), 130.

126. Brown, *Augustine of Hippo,* 205–6.

127. Warren Thomas Smith, *Augustine: His Life and Thought* (Atlanta: John Knox Press, 1980), 52.

128. *Confessions* 8.12, p. 182.

129. See Wills, *Saint Augustine,* 47, who cites this in O'Donnell.

130. Ibid., 183.

131. Eden and his neighbor's pear orchard.

132. Wills, *Saint Augustine,* 23.

133. Robert J. O'Connell, *St. Augustine's Confessions: The Odyssey of Soul* (Cambridge: Belknap Press of Harvard University Press, 1969), 144.

134. Brown, *Augustine of Hippo,* 388.

135. James J. O'Donnell, *Augustine* (Boston: Twayne, 1985), 7.

136. Markus, *Saeculum,* 36, 136.

137. Brown, *Augustine of Hippo,* 221.

138. Pierre Bayle (1647–1706), *Commentaire philosophique sur ces paroles de Jesus-Christ, Contrains-les d'entrer* (1686–87). See as well his essay "Augustin" in his *Dictionnaire Historique et Critique.* See my *Pierre Bayle's Reformation,* chap. 9.

139. See Von Campenhausen, *Fathers,* 239–40.

140. Ibid., 184–85.

141. Ibid., 187.

142. St. Augustine, Epistle 166, in *The Correspondence (394–419) Between Jerome and Augustine of Hippo,* by Saint Jerome, ed. Caroline White (Lewiston, NY: Edwin Mellen, 1990).

143. Eugène Portalié, S.J., *A Guide to the Thought of Saint Augustine* (Chicago: Henry Regnery, 1960), 207.

144. Rom. 7:14–20.

145. Michel de Montaigne, "Of the Power of the Imagination," in *The Complete Essays of Montaigne,* trans. Donald M. Frame (Stanford, CA: Stanford University Press, 1965). In the essay Montaigne refers to a certain acquaintance (himself, most likely) who was so fearful of nonperformance, having been told by a friend of his own problem, that he had to talk himself through the problem before he could cope with it, and was even then subject to relapse if he remembered his friend's story or his own unfortunate experience.

146. Elaine Pagels, "Augustine on Nature and Human Nature," in *Saint Augustine the Bishop,* ed. Fannie LeMoine and Christopher Kleinhenz (New York: Garland, 1994), 92. Quote from St. Augustine's *Unfinished Work Against Julian.*

147. Wills, *Saint Augustine,* 134.

148. Ibid., 139.

149. Ibid., 140.

150. Brown, *Augustine of Hippo,* 406. Brown may have mixed his metaphors when he spoke of "the arctic current of specifically African views of the church"—perhaps something like gritty determinism might be more effective, but Brown referred to the views of St. Cyprian, that is, that the Church was a community of "saints" in a hostile world.

151. Lee, *Augustine, Manichaeism,* speaks of what Augustine considered "God's secret administration of salvation" (85).

152. Brown, *Augustine of Hippo,* 407.

Bibliography

SELECTED BIBLIOGRAPHY

Albright, William F. *From the Stone Age to Christianity: Monotheism and the Historical Process.* Garden City, NY: Doubleday, 1957.

Alsop, Joseph. *From the Silent Earth: A Report on the Greek Bronze Age.* New York: Harper & Row, 1962.

Alt, Albrecht. "The Settlement of the Israelites in Palestine." In *Essays on Old Testament History and Religion,* edited by Albrecht Alt, 133–49. Oxford: Blackwell, 1966.

Andrewes, A. *The Greek Tyrants.* London: Hutchinson's University Library, 1956.

Ann, Martha, and Dorothy Myers Imel. *Goddesses in World Mythology: A Biographical Dictionary.* New York: Oxford University Press, 1993.

Aristotle. *The Ethics of Aristotle* (The Nichomachean Ethics Translated). Translated by J. A. K. Thomson. London: Penguin Books, 1956.

Asimov, Isaac. *Asimov's Guide to the Bible.* New York: Wings Books, 1981.

Assmann, Jan. *Maât, l'Egypte pharaonique et l'idée de justice sociale.* Conférences essais et leçons du Collège de France. Paris: Julliard, 1989.

Augustine of Hippo. *Confessions.* Translated by Rex Warner and with an introduction by Vernon J. Bourke. New York: Signet.

Austin, M. M. *The Hellenistic World from Alexander to the Roman Conquest.* Cambridge: Cambridge University Press, 1981.

Badian, E. *Studies in Greek and Roman History.* New York: Barnes and Noble, 1964.

Baines, John. "Kingship, Definition of Culture, and Legitimation." In O'Connor and Silverman, *Ancient Egyptian Kingship.*

——. "Origins of Egyptian Kingship." In O'Connor and Silverman, *Ancient Egyptian Kingship.*

Balsdon, J. P. V. D. *The Emperor Gaius (Caligula).* 1934. Reprint, Westport, CT: Greenwood Press, 1977.

——. *Julius Caesar.* New York: Atheneum, 1967.

Bardy, Gustav. "St. Jerome and Greek Thought." In Murphy, *Monument.*

Bath, Tony. *Hannibal's Campaigns.* Cambridge, UK: Patrick Stephens, 1981.

Becatti, Giovanni. *The Art of Ancient Greece and Rome.* New York: Harry N. Abrams, n.d.

Bennett, Julian. *Trajan, Optimus Princeps: A Life and Times.* London: Routledge, 1997.

Benson, Douglas S. *Ancient Egypt's Warfare.* Ashland, OH: BookMasters, 1994.

Bernal, Martin. *The Fabrication of Ancient Greece 1785–1985.* Vol. 1 of *Black Athena: The Afroasiatic Roots of Classical Civilization.* New Brunswick, NJ: Rutgers University Press, 1987.

——. *Black Athena Writes Back: Martin Bernal Responds to His Critics,* Durham, NC: Duke University Press, 2001.

Birley, Anthony R. *Hadrian: The Restless Emperor.* London: Routledge, 1997.

——. *Marcus Aurelius.* Boston: Little, Brown, 1966

——. *Marcus Aurelius: A Biography.* Revised edition. London: B.T. Batsford, 1987.

Blegen, Carl W. *Troy and the Trojans.* New York: Frederick A. Praeger, 1963.

Bloch, Raymond. *The Etruscans.* New York: Frederick A. Praeger, 1958.

Blok, Josine H. "Proof and Persuasion in Black Athena: The Case of K.O. Müller." *Journal of the History of Ideas* (October 1996): 705–15.

John Boardman et al., eds., *The Oxford History of the Roman World.* 1986. Reprint, Oxford: Oxford University Press, 1991.

Borza, Eugene N. "Introduction to Alexander Studies." In Wilcken, *Alexander the Great.*

Bowra, C. M. *Periclean Athens.* New York: Dial Press, 1971.

Bray, Gerald Lewis. *Holiness and the Will of God: Perspectives on the Theology of Tertullian.* Atlanta: John Knox Press, 1979.

Bright, John. *A History of Israel.* 3rd ed. Philadelphia: Westminster Press, 1981.

Brinton, Crane. *A History of Western Morals.* New York: Harcourt, Brace and Company, 1959.

Brown, Peter. *Augustine of Hippo: A Biography.* Berkeley and Los Angeles: University of California Press, 1967.

Brunt, P. A. *The Fall of the Roman Republic and Related Essays.* Oxford: Clarendon Press, 1988.

Burke, James, and Robert Ornstein, *The Axemaker's Gift: A Double-Edged History of Human Culture.* New York: Putnam, 1995.

Burn, A. R. *Alexander the Great and the Hellenistic World.* 1947. Reprint, New York: Collier Books, 1961.

——. *Pericles and Athens.* 1948. Reprint, London: English Universities Press, 1956.

——. *Persia and the Greeks.* 1962. Reprint, Stanford, CA: Stanford University Press, 1984.

Burn, A. R., with J. M. B. Edwards, *Greece and Rome 750 B.C.–A.D. 565.* Glenview, IL: Scott Foresman, 1970.

Cantor, Norman F. *Inventing the Middle Ages.* New York: William Morrow, 1991.

Castleden, Rodney. *The Knossos Labyrinth: A New View of the "Palace of Minos" at Knossos.* London: Routledge, 1990.

Cavallera, Ferdinand, S.J. "The Personality of St. Jerome." In Murphy, *Monument.*

Cawkwell, George. "Philip and the Amphictyonic League." In Hatzopoulos and Loukopoulos, *Philip of Macedon.*

Ceram, C. W., ed. *Hands on the Past: Pioneer Archaeologists Tell Their Own Story.* New York: Alfred A. Knopf, 1966.

Chambers, Mortimer, Raymond Grew, et al. *The Western Experience.* 5th ed. Vol. 1. New York: McGraw Hill, 1991.

Childe, V. Gordon. *What Happened in History.* 1942. Reprint, Baltimore: Penguin, 1967.

Christ, Carol P. *Odyssey With the Goddess: A Spiritual Quest in Crete.* New York: Continuum, 1995.

Christ, Karl. *The Romans: An Introduction to Their History and Civilisation.* Translated by Christopher Holme. 1984. Reprint, Berkeley and Los Angeles: University of California Press, 1985.

Cizek, Eugene. *L'Epoque de Trajan.* Paris: Société d'Édition "Les Belles Lettres," 1983.

Clines, David J. A. *Interested Parties: The Ideology of Writers and Readers of the Hebrew Bible.* Sheffield, UK: Sheffield Academic Press, 1995.

Cottrell, Leonard. *The Bull of Minos.* 1953. Reprint, New York: Holt, Rinehart, Winston, 1958.

Craig, Gordon A. *Europe Since 1815.* 1961. Reprint, New York: Holt, Rinehart, and Winston, 1966.

Crawford, Michael. "Early Rome and Italy." In Boardman et al., *Oxford History.*

———. *The Roman Republic.* Cambridge: Harvard University Press, 1993.

Crouzel, Henri. "Jérôme traducteur du Peri Archôn d'Origène." In *Jérome Entre L'Occident et L'Orient,* edited by Y. M. Duval. Paris: Études Augustiniennes, 1988.

Daly, Cahal B. *Tertullian, the Puritan and His Influence: An Essay in Historical Theology.* Dublin: Four Courts Press, 1993.

Darwin, Charles. *The Descent of Man.* 2nd ed. New York: A.L. Burt, 1874.

David, A. Rosalie. *The Egyptian Kingdoms.* New York: Elsevier Phaidon, 1975.

David, Jean-Michel. *The Roman Conquest of Italy.* Translated by Antonia Nevill. Oxford: Blackwell, 1994.

Davies, J. K. *Democracy and Classical Greece.* 1978. Reprint, Cambridge: Harvard University Press, 1993

De Beer, Gavin. *Alps and Elephants: Hannibal's March.* London: Geoffrey Bles, 1955.

de Vaux, Roland. *The Early History of Israel.* Translated by David Smith. Philadelphia: Westminster Press, 1978.

Donovan, Mary Ann. *One Right Reading?: A Guide to Irenaeus.* Collegeville, MN: Liturgical Press, 1997.

Dorman, P. F. *Abstracts of Papers.* Fourth International Congress of Egyptology. Munich, 1985.

Durant, Will. *Caesar and Christ.* New York: Simon and Schuster, 1944.

———. *The Life of Greece.* New York: Simon and Schuster, 1939.

———. *Our Oriental Heritage.* New York: Simon and Schuster, 1954.

Eller, Cynthia. *Living in the Lap of the Goddess: The Feminist Spirituality Movement in America.* Boston: Beacon Press, 1993.

Erasmus. *The Godly Feast (Convivium religiosum).* In *The Colloquies of Erasmus,* edited and translated by Craig R. Thompson. Chicago: University of Chicago Press, 1965.

Ferrill, Arther. *Caligula: Emperor of Rome.* London: Thames and Hudson, 1991.

Finley, M. I. *The Use and Abuse of History.* 1971. Reprint, New York: Elisabeth Sifton Books/Penguin Books 1987.

Flintoff, Everard. "Pyrrho and India." *Phronesis* 25 (1980): 88–108.

Fowler, W. Warde. *Rome.* Revised by M. P. Charlesworth. 1912. Reprint, London: Oxford University Press, 1960.

Fox, Robin Lane. *Alexander the Great.* London: Dial Press, 1974.

Fredouille, Jean-Claude. *Tertullien et la conversion de la culture antique.* Paris: Études Augustiniennes, 1972.

Frost, Frank J. *Greek Society.* 1971. Reprint, Lexington, KY: D. C. Heath, 1992.

Fuller, J. F. C. *Julius Caesar: Man, Soldier, and Tyrant.* New Brunswick, NJ: Rutgers University Press, 1965.

Funk, Robert W., and the Jesus Seminar. *The Five Gospels: The Search for the Authentic Words of Jesus.* New York: Macmillan, 1993.

Gabba, Emilio. "The Historians and Augustus." In Millar and Segal, *Caesar Augustus.*

Gabriel. *Goddess Meditations from Isis to Sophia: 365 Wisdom Poems to Invoke, Visualize and Embody the Goddess.* N.p.: Trinosophia Press, 1994.

Galsterer, H. "Syme's *Roman Revolution* after Fifty Years." In Raaflaub and Toher, *Between Republic and Empire.*

Gardiner, Sir Alan. *Egypt of the Pharaohs: An Introduction.* 1961. Reprint, Oxford: Oxford University Press, 1978.

Garnsey, Peter, and Richard Saller. *The Roman Empire: Economy, Society and Culture.* Berkeley and Los Angeles: University of California Press, 1987.

Georgoudi, Stella. "Creating a Myth of Matriarchy." In *A History of Women in the West,* edited by Pauline Schmitt Pantel. Vol. 1 of *From Ancient Goddesses to Christian Saints.* Cambridge: Belknap Press of Harvard University Press, 1992.

Gibbon, Edward. *The Decline and Fall of the Roman Empire.* Vol. 1. Edited by H. H. Milman. New York: Thomas Y. Crowell, n.d.

Gilliam, Olive Kuntz. *The Memoirs of Augustus.* New York: Vantage Press, 1965.

Goedicke, Hans. "The End of the Hyksos in Egypt." In *Egyptological Studies in Honor of Richard A. Parker,* edited by Leonard H. Lesko. Hanover, NH: Brown University Press and University Press of New England, 1986.

Gottwald, Norman K. *The Tribes of Yahweh: A Sociology of the Religion of Liberated Israel 1250–1050 B.C.E.* Maryknoll, NY: Orbis Books, 1979.

Gough, Kathleen. "The Origin of the Family." In *Toward an Anthropology of Women,* edited by Rayna R. Reiter. New York: Monthly Review Press, 1975.

Grant, Michael. *The Antonines: The Roman Empire in Transition.* London: Routledge, 1994.

——. *From Alexander to Cleopatra: The Hellenistic World.* New York: Charles Scribner's Sons, 1982.

——. *The History of Ancient Israel.* London: Weidenfeld and Nicolson, 1984.

——. *Julius Caesar.* New York: McGraw-Hill, 1969.

——. *Nero: Emperor in Revolt.* New York: American Heritage Press, 1970.

——. *The Twelve Caesars.* London: Weidenfeld and Nicolson, 1975.

Grant, Robert M. *Irenaeus of Lyons.* London: Routledge, 1997.

Gregorovius, Ferdinand. *The Emperor Hadrian: A Picture of the Graeco-Roman World in His Time.* Translated by Mary E. Robinson. London: Macmillan, 1898.

Green, Peter. *Alexander of Macedon, 356–323 B.C.: A Historical Biography.* 1970. Reprint, Berkeley and Los Angeles: University of California Press, 1991.

——. *Alexander to Actium: The Historical Evolution of the Hellenistic Age.* Berkeley and Los Angeles: University of California Press, 1990.

——, ed. *Hellenistic History and Culture.* Berkeley and Los Angeles: University of California Press, 1993.

——. "Introduction: New Approaches to the Hellenistic World." In Green, *Hellenistic History and Culture.*

Greenhalgh, Peter. *Pompey, the Roman Alexander.* London: Weidenfeld and Nicolson, 1980.

Griffin, Miriam. "Cicero and Rome." In Boardman et al., *Oxford History.*

Gruen, Erich S. *The Last Generation of the Roman Republic.* Berkeley and Los Angeles: University of California Press, 1974.

——. *Studies in Greek Culture and Roman Policy.* Leiden: E. J. Brill, 1990.

Hackett, Jo Ann. "Women's Studies and the Hebrew Bible." In *The Future of Biblical Studies: The Hebrew Scriptures,* edited Richard E. Friedman and H. G. M. Williamson. Atlanta: Scholars Press, 1987.

Hamilton, Edith. *The Greek Way to Western Civilization.* 1930. Reprint, New York: Mentor Books, 1958.

Hamilton, J. R. *Alexander the Great.* 1971. Reprint, Pittsburgh, PA: University of Pittsburgh Press, 1992.

Hammond, N. G. L. *The Classical Age of Greece.* London: Weidenfeld and Nicolson, 1975.

Hatzopoulos, Miltiades B., and Luoisa D. Loukopoulos, eds. *Philip of Macedon.* Athens, Greece: Ekdotike Athenon S.A., 1980.

Hauser, Arnold. *The Social History of Art.* Translated by Stanley Godman. New York: Vintage Books, 1957.

Hayward, F. H. *Marcus Aurelius: A Saviour of Men.* London: George Allen & Unwin, 1935.

Helk, W. *Der Text der "Lehre Amenemhets I für seiner Sohn."* Wiesbaden: n.p., 1969.

Henderson, Bernard W. *Five Roman Emperors.* Cambridge: Cambridge University Press, 1927.

——. *The Life and Principate of the Emperor Hadrian.* London: Methuen, 1923.

Heurgon, Jacques. *The Rise of Rome.* Translated by James Willis. Berkeley and Los Angeles: University of California Press, 1973.

Hoffman, Daniel. *The Status of Women and Gnosticism in Irenaeus and Tertullian.* Lewiston, NY: Edwin Mellen Press, 1995.

Hoffman, Michael Allen. "Where Nations Began." *Science* (October 1983): 42–51.

The Holy Bible: Self-Pronouncing King James Version. Cleveland, OH: World Publishing Company, n.d.

Hood, Sinclair. *The Minoans: The Story of Bronze Age Crete.* New York: Praeger Publishers, 1971.

Hornblower, Simon. *The Greek World 479–323 B.C.* London: Methuen, 1983.

Household, H. W. *Rome, Republic and Empire.* London: J.M. Dent & Sons, 1936.

Hutchinson, R. W. *Prehistoric Crete.* London: Penguin Books, 1962.

Huxley, G. L. *Early Sparta.* London: Faber and Faber, 1962.

Jerome. *The Correspondence (394–419) Between Jerome and Augustine of Hippo.* Edited by Caroline White. Lewiston, NY: Edwin Mellen, 1990.

——. *Saint Jerome: Dogmatic and Polemical Works.* Translated by John N. Hritzu. Washington, DC: Catholic University of America Press, 1965.

——. *Select Letters of St. Jerome.* Translated by F. A. Wright. Cambridge: Harvard University Press, 1963.

Johanson, Donald C., and Maitland Edey. *Lucy: The Beginnings of Humankind.* New York: Warner Books, 1987. First published in 1981 by Simon and Schuster.

Johnson, Paul. *The Civilization of Ancient Egypt.* London: Weidenfeld & Nicolson, 1978.

Jones, Brian W. *The Emperor Domitian.* New York: Routledge, 1992.

Jones, Tom B. *From the Tigris to the Tiber.* Homewood, IL: Dorsey Press, 1969.

Josephus, Flavius. *Death of an Emperor.* Translated and with commentary by T. P. Wiseman. Exeter: University of Exeter Press, 1991.

Kagan, Donald. *The Outbreak of the Peloponnesian War.* Ithaca: Cornell University Press, 1969.

Keaveney, Arthur. *Sulla, The Last Republican.* London: Croom Helm, 1982.

Kelley, Donald R. . ed. *Versions of History from Antiquity to the Enlightenment.* New Haven: Yale University Press, 1991.

Kelly, J. N. D. *Jerome: His Life, Writings, and Controversies.* London: Gerald Duckworth, 1975.

Kemp, Barry J. *Ancient Egypt: Anatomy of a Civilization.* New York: Routledge, 1989.

———. "Old Kingdom, Middle Kingdom and Second Intermediate Period c. 2686–1552 B.C." In Trigger, Kemp, et al., *Ancient Egypt.*

Kildahl, Phillip A. *Caius Marius.* New York: Twayne, 1968.

Kimbel, William H., Donald C. Johanson, and Yoel Rak. "The First Skull and Other New Discoveries of Australopithecus Afarensis at Hadar, Ethiopia." *Nature* 368 (March 31, 1994), 449–52.

Kishlansky, Mark, Patrick Geary, and Patricia O'Brien. *Civilization in the West.* Volume A. New York: Harper Collins, 1991.

Kitchen, K. A. *Pharaoh Triumphant: The Life and Times of Rameses II, King of Egypt.* Westminster, UK: Aris & Phillips Ltd., 1982.

Kitto, H. D. F. *The Greeks.* 1951. Reprint, Baltimore: Penguin Books, 1968.

Kramer, Samuel Noah. *History Begins at Sumer: Twenty-Seven Firsts in Man's Recorded History.* 1956. Reprint, Garden City, NY: Doubleday, 1959.

Kristellar, Paul Oskar. *Greek Philosophers of the Hellenistic Age.* Translated by Gregory Woods. New York: Columbia University Press, 1993.

Krumeich, Christa. *Hieronymus und die Christlichen Feminae Clarissimae.* Bonn: Dr. Rudolf Habelt GMBH, 1993.

Lambert, Royston. *Beloved and God: The Story of Hadrian and Antinous.* London: Weidenfeld and Nicolson, 1984.

Lancel, Serge. *Hannibal.* Paris: Librairie Arthème Fayard, 1995.

Lawrence, D. H. *Etruscan Places.* 1932. Reprint, New York: Viking Press, 1961.

Lawson, John. *A Theological and Historical Introduction to the Apostolic Fathers.* New York: Macmillan, 1961.

Leakey, Meave. "The Farthest Horizon." *National Geographic* (September 1995): 38–51.

Lee, Kam-lun Edwin. *Augustine, Manichaeism, and the Good.* New York: Peter Lang, 1999.

Lefkowitz, Mary R. *Not Out of Africa: How Afrocentrism Became an Excuse to Teach Myth as History.* New York: Basic Books, 1996.

Lefkowitz, Mary R., and Guy MacLean Rogers, eds., *Black Athena Revisited.* Chapel Hill: University of North Carolina Press, 1996.

Lemaire, André. "The United Monarchy: Saul, David and Solomon." In Shanks, *Ancient Israel.*

Lemprière, J. *A Classical Dictionary, Containing a Copious Account of All the Proper Names Mentioned in Ancient Authors, etc.* London: George Routledge and Sons, Ltd., n.d.

Lerner, Robert E., Standish Meacham, and Edward McNall Burns. *Western Civilizations: Their History and Culture.* 13th ed. New York: W.W. Norton, 1993.

Levick, Barbara. *Claudius.* London: B. T. Batsford, 1990.

Lintott, Arthur. *The Last Age of the Roman Republic, 146–43 B.C.* Vol. 9 of *The Cambridge Ancient History.* 2nd ed. Cambridge: Cambridge University Press, 1994.

Long, A. A. "Hellenistic Ethics and Philosophical Power." In Green, *Hellenistic History and Culture.*

———. *Hellenistic Philosophy.* London: Gerald Duckworth, 1974.

Maisels, Charles Keith. *The Emergence of Civilization: From Hunting and Gathering to Agriculture, Cities and the State in the Near East.* New York: Routledge, 1990.

Malek, Jaromir. *In the Shadow of the Pyramids: Egypt during the Old Kingdom.* Norman: University of Oklahoma Press, 1986.

Markus, R. A. *Saeculum: History and Society in the Theology of St. Augustine.* Cambridge: Cambridge University Press, 1970.

Martin, Thomas R. *Ancient Greece from Prehistoric to Hellenistic Times.* New Haven: Yale University Press, 1996.

McCarter, Jr., P. Kyle. "The Patriarchal Age: Abraham, Isaac and Jacob." In Shanks, *Ancient Israel.*

McDonald, A. H. "Pre-Revolutionary Rome." In *The Romans: The People and Their Civilization,* edited by J. P. V. D. Balsdon. New York: Basic Books, 1965.

——. *Republican Rome.* New York: Frederick A. Praeger, 1966.

McGregor, Malcolm F. *The Athenians and Their Empire.* Vancouver: University of British Columbia Press, 1987.

McNeill, William H., and Jean W. Sedlar, eds., *The Ancient Near East.* Vol. 2. New York: Oxford University Press, n.d.

Mendelssohn, Kurt. *The Riddle of the Pyramids.* New York: Praeger Publishers, 1974.

Mendenhall, George E. "The Hebrew Conquest of Palestine." *Biblical Archaeologist* 25 (1961): 66–87.

——. *The Tenth Generation: The Origins of the Biblical Tradition.* Baltimore: Johns Hopkins University Press, 1973.

Michalowski, Piotr. *Letters From Early Mesopotamia.* Edited by Erica Reiner. Atlanta: Scholars Press, 1993.

Michell, H. *Sparta.* Cambridge: Cambridge University Press, 1964.

Millar, Fergus, and Erich Segal, eds. *Caesar Augustus: Seven Aspects.* Oxford: Clarendon Press, 1984.

Minns, Denis. *Irenaeus.* London: Geoffrey Chapman, 1994.

Montaigne, Michel de. "Of the Power of the Imagination." In *The Complete Essays of Montaigne,* translated by Donald M. Frame. Stanford, CA: Stanford University Press, 1965.

Muller, Herbert. *Freedom in the Ancient World.* New York: Harper & Brothers, 1961.

Mumford, Lewis. *The City in History.* New York: Harcourt Brace Jovanovich, 1961.

Murphy, Francis X., ed. *A Monument to Saint Jerome: Essays on Some Aspects of His Life, Works and Influence.* New York: Sheed & Ward, 1952.

Murray, Margaret A. *The Splendour That Was Egypt: A General Survey of Egyptian Culture and Civilisation.* 1949. Reprint, New York: Philosophical Library, 1957.

Mylonas, G. E. "The Luvian Invasions of Greece." *Hesperia* 3 (1962): 284–309.

The New English Bible With Apocrypha. Great Britain: Oxford and Cambridge University Presses, 1970.

Nims, C. F. "The Date of the Dishonoring of Hatshepsut." *Zeitschrift für ägyptische Sprache und Altertumskunde* 63 (1966): 97–100.

Noth, Martin. *The Old Testament World.* Translated by Victor I. Gruhn. Philadelphia: Fortress Press, 1966. A translation of the 4th ed. of *Die Welt des Alten Testaments: Einführung in die Grenzgebiete der alttestamentlichen Wissenschaft.* Berlin, 1964.

O'Connell, Robert J. *St. Augustine's Confessions: The Odyssey of Soul.* Cambridge: Belknap Press of Harvard University Press, 1969.

O'Connor, David. "New Kingdom and Third Intermediate Period 1552–664 B.C." In Trigger, Kemp, et al., *Ancient Egypt.*

O'Connor, David, and David P. Silverman, eds. *Ancient Egyptian Kingship.* Leiden: E. J. Brill, 1995.

O'Donnell, James J. *Augustine.* Boston: Twayne, 1985.

Ogilvie, Robert Maxwell. *Early Rome and the Etruscans.* Atlantic Highlands, NJ: Humanities Press, 1976.

Opelt, Ilona. *Hieronymus' Schreitschriften.* Heidelberg: C. Winter, 1973.

Oppenheim, A. Leo. *Letters from Mesopotamia.* Chicago: University of Chicago Press, 1967.

Orlinsky, Harry M. "The Situational Ethics of Violence in the Biblical Period." In *Violence and Defense in the Jewish Experience,* edited by Salo W. Baron and George S. Wise. Philadelphia: Jewish Publication Society of America, 1977.

Osborn, Eric. *Tertullian, First Theologian of the West.* Cambridge: Cambridge University Press, 1997.

Oya, Judith Gleason. *In Praise of an African Goddess.* San Francisco: HarperCollins, 1992.

Pagels, Elaine. "Augustine on Nature and Human Nature." In *Saint Augustine the Bishop,* edited by Fannie LeMoine and Christopher Kleinhenz. New York: Garland, 1994.

———. *The Gnostic Gospels.* New York: Random House, 1979.

Palmer, Leonard R. *Mycenaeans and Minoans: Aegean Prehistory in the Light of the Linear B Tablets.* New York: Alfred A. Knopf, 1962.

Parés, Josep M., and Alfredo Pérez-Gonzalez. "Paleomagnetic Age for Hominid Fossils at Atapuerca Archaeological Site, Spain." *Science* 269 (August 11, 1995): 830.

Parkes, Henry Bamford. "The Theocratic Basis of Civilization." In *The Advent of Civilization,* edited by Wayne M. Bledsoe. Lexington, MA: D.C. Heath, 1975.

Pelon, Olivier. "Reflexions sur la fonction politique dans un palais Cretois." In *Minoan Society Proceedings of the Cambridge Colloquium 1981,* edited by O. Krzyszkowska and L. Nixon. Bristol: Bristol Classical Press, 1983.

Perelli, Luciano. *I Gracchi.* Rome: Salerno Editrice, 1993.

Perowne, Stewart. *Hadrian.* London: Hodder and Stoughton, 1960.

Perry, Martin, et al. *Western Civilization.* New York, 1989.

Peters, F. E. *The Harvest of Hellenism.* New York: Simon and Schuster, 1970.

Platon, Nicholas. *Zakros: The Discovery of a Lost Palace of Ancient Crete.* New York: Charles Scribner's Sons, 1971.

Plutarch. *Lives of the Noble Romans.* Edited by Edmund Fuller. 1959. Reprint, New York: Dell, 1964.

Portalié, Eugène, S.J., *A Guide to the Thought of Saint Augustine.* Chicago: Henry Regnery, 1960.

Portman, Ian. *Luxor: A Guide to the Temples & Tombs of Ancient Thebes.* Cairo: American University in Cairo Press, 1989.

Postgate, J. N. *Early Mesopotamia: Society and Economy at the Dawn of History.* London: Routledge, 1992.

Proctor, Dennis. *Hannibal's March in History.* Oxford: Clarendon Press, 1971.

Pritchard, James B. "The Age of Solomon." In Pritchard, *Solomon & Sheba,* 1974.

———, ed. *Ancient Near Eastern Texts.* 3rd ed. Princeton: Princeton University Press, 1969.

———, ed. *Solomon & Sheba.* London: Phaidon Press, 1974.

Raaflaub, K. A., and L. J. Samons II. "Opposition to Augustus." In Raaflaub and Toher, *Between Republic and Empire*.

Raaflaub, Kurt A., and Mark Toher, eds. *Between Republic and Empire: Interpretations of Augustus and His Principate*. Berkeley and Los Angeles: University of California Press, 1990.

Rawson, Elizabeth. "The Expansion of Rome." In Boardman et al., *Oxford History*.

Ray, John. "Hatshepsut: The Female Pharaoh." In *Western Civilization*. Vol 1. Guilford, CT: McGraw-Hill/Dushkin.

Redford, Donald B. *Akhenaten: The Heretic King*. Princeton: Princeton University Press, 1984.

——. "The Concept of Kingship during the Eighteenth Dynasty." In O'Connor and Silverman, *Ancient Egyptian Kingship*.

——. *Egypt, Canaan, and Israel in Ancient Times*. Princeton: Princeton University Press.

Reis, Patricia. *Through the Goddess: A Woman's Way of Healing*. New York: Continuum, 1995.

Renault, Mary. *The Nature of Alexander*. New York: Pantheon Books, 1975.

Rice, Eugene F. *Saint Jerome in the Renaissance*. Baltimore: Johns Hopkins University Press, 1985.

Richardson, Emiline. *The Etruscans: Their Art and Civilization*. Chicago: University of Chicago Press, 1964.

Rist, J. M. *Stoic Philosophy*. Cambridge: Cambridge University Press, 1969.

Rosenberg, Joel. *King and Kin: Political Allegory in the Hebrew Bible*. Bloomington: Indiana University Press, 1986.

Rostovtzeff, Michael. *The Social and Economic History of the Hellenistic World*. Oxford: Clarendon, 1941.

Russell, Bertrand. *A History of Western Philosophy*. 1945. Reprint, New York: Simon and Schuster, 1966.

——. *Principles of Social Reconstruction*. 1916. Reprint, London: George Allen & Unwin, 1954.

Sakellariou, M. B. "Panhellenism: From Concept to Policy." In Hatzopoulos and Loukopoulos, *Philip of Macedon*.

Salmon, E. T. *A History of the Roman World from 30 B.C. to A.D. 138*. New York: Macmillan, 1944.

——. *The Making of Roman History*. London: Thames & Hudson, 1982.

——. *The Making of Roman Italy*. London: Pitman Press, 1982.

Sandbach, F. H. *The Stoics*. 1975. Reprint, Bristol: Bristol Press, 1989

Saggs, H. W. F. *Babylonians*. Norman: University of Oklahoma Press, 1995.

——. *The Might That Was Assyria*. London: Sidgwick and Jackson, 1984.

Samuel, A. E. "The Ptolemies and Ideology of Kingship." In Green, *Hellenistic History and Culture*.

Sarna, Nahum M. "Israel in Egypt: The Egyptian Sojourn and the Exodus." In Shanks, *Ancient Israel*.

Scarre, Chris. *Chronicle of the Roman Emperors*. London: Thames and Hudson, 1995.

Schachermeyr, F. "Luwier auf Kreta?" *Kadmos* 1 (1962): 27–39.

Scullard, H. H. *From the Gracchi to Nero: A History of Rome from 133 B.C. to A.D. 68*. 1959. Reprint, London: Methuen, 1970.

Seager, Robin. *Pompey, a Political Biography.* Oxford: Basil Blackwell, 1979.

——. *Tiberius.* Berkeley and Los Angeles: University of California Press, 1972.

Sedley, David. "The Motivation of Greek Skepticism." In *The Skeptical Tradition,* edited by Myles Burnyeat. Berkeley and Los Angeles: University of California Press, 1983.

Shanks, Hershel, ed. *Ancient Israel: A Short History from Abraham to the Roman Destruction of the Temple.* Washington, DC: Biblical Archaeology Society, 1988.

Sherk, Robert K., ed. and trans. *The Roman Empire: Augustus to Hadrian.* Cambridge, Cambridge University Press, 1988.

Shreve, James. *The Neanderthal Enigma: Solving the Mystery of Modern Human Origins* New York: William Morrow, 1995.

Sharples, R. W. *Stoics, Epicureans and Sceptics: An Introduction to Hellenistic Philosophy.* New York: Routledge, 1996.

Silberman, Lou H. "The Queen of Sheba in Judaic Tradition." In Pritchard, *Solomon & Sheba.*

Silverman, David P. "The Nature of Egyptian Kingship." In O'Connor and Silverman, *Ancient Egyptian Kingship.*

Sjöö, Monich, and Barbara Mor. *The Great Cosmic Mother: Rediscovering the Religion of the Earth.* San Francisco: Harper, 1987.

Smith, Warren Thomas. *Augustine: His Life and Thought.* Atlanta: John Knox Press, 1980.

Snyder, John W. *Alexander the Great.* New York: Twayne, 1966.

Soggin, J. Alberto. *A History of Ancient Israel.* Philadelphia: Westminster Press, 1984.

Southern, Pat. *Domitian: Tragic Tyrant.* New York: Routledge, 1997.

Spengler, Oswald. *The Decline of the West.* 1918. Reprint, New York: Alfred A. Knopf, 1939.

Spitz, Lewis W. "Luther and Humanism." In *Luther and German Humanism,* edited by Lewis W. Spitz. Aldershot, Hampshire, UK: Ashgate, 1995.

Spitz, Lewis W., and Barbara Sher Tinsley. *Johann Sturm on Education: The Reformation and Humanist Learning.* St. Louis, MO: Concordia, 1995.

Stace, W. T. *A Critical History of Greek Philosophy.* 1920. Reprint, New York: St. Martin's Press, 1965.

Starr, Chester G. *The Economic and Social Growth of Early Greece 800–500 B.C.* New York: Oxford University Press, 1977.

——. *A History of the Ancient World.* New York: Oxford University Press, 1965.

——. "The Myth of the Minoan Thalassocracy." *Historia* (1955): 282–91.

Stein, Diane, ed., *The Goddess Celebrates: An Anthology of Women's Rituals.* Freedom, CA: Crossing Press, 1991.

Steinsaltz, Adin. *Biblical Images: Men and Women of the Book.* Translated by Yehuda Hanegbi. New York: Basic Books, 1984.

Stockton, David. "The Founding of the Empire." In Boardman et al., *Oxford History.*

Suetonius. *The Lives of the Twelve Caesars.* Edited by Joseph Gavorse. 1931. Reprint, New York: Modern Library, 1959.

Syme, Ronald. "Fictional History Old and New: Hadrian." In *Roman Papers,* Vol. 6., edited by Anthony R. Birley. Oxford: Clarendon Press, 1991.

——. *The Roman Revolution.* 1939. Reprint, Oxford: Oxford University Press, 1967.

Tarn, W. W. *Alexander the Great.* 1948. Reprint, Boston: Beacon Press, 1962.

——. *Hellenistic Civilisation.* 1927. Reprint, Cleveland, OH: World Publishing Company, 1965.

Thompson, Thomas L. "The Background of the Patriarchs: A Reply to William Dever and Malcolm Clark." *Journal for the Study of the Old Testament* 9 (1978): 1–43.

——. *The Historicity of the Patriarchal Narratives: The Quest for the Historical Abraham.* New York: De Gruyter, 1974.

——. *The Origin Tradition of Ancient Israel; I. The Literary Formation of Genesis and Exodus 1–23.* Sheffield, Eng.: Sheffield Academic Press, 1987.

Thucydides. *The Peloponnesian War.* Translated by John H. Finley, Jr. New York: Modern Library, 1951.

Timothy, H. B. *The Early Christian Apologists and Greek Philosophy.* Assen, Netherlands: Van Gorcum, 1973.

Tinsley, Barbara Sher. *History and Polemics in the French Reformation: Florimond de Raemond, Defender of the Church.* Selinsgrove, PA: Susquehanna University Press, 1992.

——. *Pierre Bayle's Reformation: Conscience and Criticism on the Eve of the Enlightenment.* Selinsgrove, PA: Susquehanna University Press, 2001.

Torchia, N. Joseph, O.P. *Creatio ex nihilo and the Theology of St. Augustine: The Anti-Manichaean Polemic and Beyond.* New York: Peter Lang, 1999.

Trigger, B. G. "The Rise of Egyptian Civilization." In Trigger, Kemp, et al., *Ancient Egypt.*

Trigger, B. G., B. J. Kemp, et al., eds. *Ancient Egypt: A Social History.* London: Cambridge University Press, 1983.

Unger, Dominic J., trans. and ann. *St. Irenaeus of Lyons Against the Heresies.* With further revisions by John J. Dillon. Vol. 1. New York: Paulist Press, 1992.

Usher, Stephen. *The Historians of Greece and Rome.* New York: Taplinger, 1970.

van Beek, Gus W. "The Land of Sheba." In Pritchard, *Solomon & Sheba.*

Velikovsky, Immanuel. *Oedipus and Akhnaton: Myth and History.* Garden City, NY: Doubleday, 1938.

Vermeule, Emily. *Greece in the Bronze Age.* Chicago: University of Chicago Press, 1964.

von Campenhausen, Hans. *The Fathers of the Latin Church.* Translated by Manfred Hoffman. Stanford, CA: Stanford University Press, 1960.

von Harnack, A. *Chronologie der altchristlichen Litteratur.* 1897.

Waddell, L. A. *Egyptian Civilization, Its Sumerian Origin and Real Chronology; and Sumerian Origin of Egyptian Hieroglyphs.* London: Luzac, 1930.

Waddle, Diane M. "Matrix Correlation Tests Support a Single Origin for Modern Humans." *Nature* 368 (March 31, 1994).

Walbank, F. W. *The Hellenistic World.* 1981. Reprint, Cambridge: Harvard University Press, 1993.

Warfield, Benjamin Breckinridge. *Studies in Tertullian and Augustine.* 1930. Reprint, Westport, CT: Greenwood Press, 1970.

Warmington, B. H. *Nero: Reality and Legend.* New York: W. W. Norton, 1969.

Warren, Peter. *The Aegean Civilizations.* New York: E.P. Dutton, 1975.

Webster, T. B. L. *From Mycenae to Homer.* New York: Frederick A. Praeger, 1959.

Weippert, Manfred. *Die Landnahme der israelitischen Stämme in Palästina.* Göttingen, 1967.

Welles, C. Bradford. *Alexander and the Hellenistic World.* Toronto: A. M. Hakkert, 1970.

Wells, Colin. *The Roman Empire.* 2nd ed. Cambridge: Harvard University Press, 1992.

Wells, J., and R. H. Barro. *A Short History of the Roman Empire to the Death of Marcus Aurelius.* London: Methuen, 1931.

West, Rebecca. *St. Augustine.* New York: D. Appleton, 1933.

Wiesel, Elie. *Five Biblical Portraits.* Notre Dame, IN: University of Notre Dame Press, 1981.

Wilcken, Ulrich. *Alexander the Great.* Translated by G. C. Richards. 1931. Reprint, New York: W. W. Norton, 1967

Wildavsky, Aaron. *Assimilation Versus Separation: Joseph the Administrator and the Politics of Religion in Biblical Israel.* New Brunswick, NJ: Transaction Publishers, 1993.

——. *The Nursing Father: Moses as Political Leader.* Tuscalosa: University of Alabama Press, 1984.

Willetts, R. F. *The Civilization of Ancient Crete.* Berkeley and Los Angeles: University of California Press, 1977.

Williams, Derek. *The Reach of Rome: A History of the Roman Imperial Frontier First–Fifth Centuries AD.* London: Constable, 1996.

——. *Romans and Barbarians: Four Views From the Empire's Edge, First Century AD.* London: Constable, 1998.

Wills, Garry. *Saint Augustine.* New York: Viking Penguin, 1999.

Wood, Michael. *In Search of the Trojan War.* New York: Facts On File Publications, 1985.

Woodruff, Paul. "Response." In Green, *Hellenistic History and Culture.*

Wooley, C. Leonard. *The Sumerians.* New York: W.W. Norton, 1965.

Woolger, Jennifer Barker, and Roger J. Woolger. *The Goddess Within: A Guide to the Eternal Myths That Shape Women's Lives.* New York: Fawcett Columbine, 1987.

Wright, Robert. *Nonzero: The Logic of Human Destiny.* New York: Random House, 2000.

Yavetz, Zvi. *Julius Caesar and His Public Image.* 1979. Reprint, Ithaca: Cornell University Press, 1983.

——. *Plebs and Princeps.* New Brunswick, NJ: Transaction Books, 1988.

——. "The *Res Gestae* and Augustus' Public Image." In Millar and Segal, *Caesar Augustus.*

Zeligs, Dorothy F. *Psychoanalysis and the Bible: A Study in Depth of Seven Leaders.* New York: Bloch Publishing Company, 1974.

Index

377